SOUTH-WESTERN

KEYBOARDING AND COMPUTER APPLICATIONS

Includes commands and directions for
WordPerfect® 5.1, Lotus® 1-2-3, 2.3
MS-DOS® Microsoft® Works 2.0 and 3.0
MS-DOS® Microsoft® Works 2.0, Macintosh®

Jerry W. Robinson, Ed.D.
Keyboarding Instructor
Moeller High School
Cincinnati

Jack P. Hoggatt, Ed.D.
Professor of Business Education
and Administrative Management
University of Wisconsin
Eau Claire

Jon A. Shank, Ed.D.
Professor of Administrative Management
and Business Education
Robert Morris College
Coraopolis (PA)

Betty L. Boyce, M.A.
Business Education Center, Retired
California State Polytechnic
University, Pomona

Copyright © 1995
by SOUTH-WESTERN PUBLISHING CO.
Cincinnati, Ohio

ISBN 0-538-62193-1

1 2 3 4 5 6 7 8 9 10 H 01 00 99 98 97 96 95 94

Printed in the United States of America

I(T)P
International Thomson Publishing

South-Western Publishing Co. is an ITP Company. The ITP trademark is used under license.

Library of Congress Cataloging-in-Publication Data

Keyboarding and computer applications : includes commands and
  directions for WordPerfect 5.1 MS-DOS, Microsoft Works 2.0 and 3.0
  MS-DOS, Microsoft Works 2.0 Macintosh, Lotus 1-2-3 / Jerry W.
  Robinson ... [et al.].
      p.   cm.
  Includes Index.
  ISBN 0-538-62193-1
  1. Electronic data processing—Keyboarding. 2. Application
software. I. Robinson, Jerry W.
  QA76.9.K48K52   1995   93-32416
  005.36—dc20   CIP

SOUTH-WESTERN PUBLISHING CO.

Keyboarding and Computer Applications brings you into the computer age in a hurry by giving you an opportunity to develop a wide range of skills. In *Keyboarding and Computer Applications*, you first develop keyboarding skills on a computer key-board. Then you apply those skills as you complete word processing, spreadsheet, database, and integrated software applications that include importing spread-sheet data, bar and pie charts, and clip-art graphics. You learn some basic desk-top publishing concepts, too.

Computer Skills

Why are computer skills im-portant? Modern computer hardware and software have a significant effect on the way we work, live, and learn. Many tasks that we per-formed manually in the past can now be completed more effectively and efficiently using com-puters. Software application improvements expand the need for keyboard-ing skills for everyday use of computers. Today, typical uses of computers involve the wide range of applications performed in this full-color textbook.

Commands and Concepts

Lessons give software-specific commands for Word-Perfect 5.1 and Lotus 1-2-3, Microsoft Works for IBM PCs and compatibles, and Micro-soft Works for the Apple Macintosh. Occasionally, after completing an assign-ment for your software, take a few moments to review information relating to the other software; and notice similarities and differences in the programs. This compari-son will help you see *the big picture*—the *concepts*— involved in the applications. Knowing concepts will help you transfer learning to various software packages in the future. Because software changes rapidly, the student who understands concepts will have an advantage over one who knows only *how to*.

Acknowledgments

The authors, who are widely recognized for their many educational publications and experience, bring a wealth of expertise to each facet of *Keyboarding and Computer Applications*. The support of technical reviewers, school personnel, and software companies was ongoing during the writing of this publication. The authors express appreciation to the following individuals—current or recent teachers of com-puter applications and/or keyboarding—for their critiques of the original drafts:

Elizabeth Beisel, North Allegheny High School, Wexford, PA

Susan Boleware, Mississippi State University

Julianna Delafave, Richard-son High School, Dallas

Jeanette Kosiorek, Youngs-town (OH) State University

Lynn Matthews, Moores-town (NJ) High School

Jennifer McDonald, Oak Hills High School, Cincinnati

Connie Morrison, Computer Education Consultant, Lexington, OH

Patricia Wathen, Formerly Princeton High School, Cincinnati

Laurence Zibell, West High School, Green Bay, WI

Thanks go to keyboarding/ computer applications teach-ers and students at Moeller High School (Cincinnati) for "road-testing" selected manu-scripts and giving feedback. Special thanks are due **James Bauer**, Business Department Chairman, and **Daniel Ledford**, Principal, for their generous cooperation in this effort.

Special thanks are extended to **Glenda M. Hoggatt** (Altoona, WI) for her technical review of a large portion of the manuscript.

Appreciation is expressed to the Administrative Manage-ment and Business Education faculty at Robert Morris College (Coraopolis, PA). Thanks also go to the cus-tomer support staff at Word-Perfect Corporation, Microsoft Corporation, and especially to **Michael Pearse**, Lotus Development Corporation.

Organization and Outcomes

Keyboarding and Computer Applications is organized into five carefully designed parts, each part opening with a glossary. Within each part, lessons are grouped into units. (The list of contents appears on pp. iv-vii.) In addition, a hardware and software overview (pp. 1-8) and appendices covering telecommunications terms, language skills, document formats, DOS commands, Macintosh OS commands, database print formats, and application software com-mands are included (pp. 426-452).

Keyboarding. The ability to operate a keyboard has never been more important than it is now, in a time that our society has labeled the *Computer Age* and the *Information Age*. At one time a select group of office employees used keyboards; today, everybody does! Besides using computers in all areas and levels of work, people also use computers—and the keyboards attached to them—for personal and family tasks, even entertain-ment. Whatever their purpose, *skilled* keyboard operators get better results than unskilled users.

Basic keyboarding skill consists of the fluent manipu-lation by "touch" (without looking) of the letter keys, figure/symbol keys, and service keys. By presenting just two keys in a lesson and by providing frequent review and intensive and extensive practice, this textbook assures mastery of keyboard operation. Scientifically designed drills allow you to develop maximum skill in minimum time. After complet-ing Part 1 of *Keyboarding and Computer Applications*, you will be able to (partial list):

1. Operate the letter, punctuation, and service keys by touch and with correct technique.
2. Use basic word process-ing features when you key and when modifying existing copy.
3. Key copy containing figures and symbols as

well as words at acceptable speed.
4. Key from handwritten (script) and rough-draft input.
5. Operate the numeric keypad by touch with proper technique (teacher's option).

Word Processing Applications. Once you master the computer keyboard, you will want to apply your skills—immediately and often—to your everyday activities. Perhaps you will be required to write a report in one of your courses. Maybe you will want to write a letter to a friend who moves far away, or to someone who offers part-time jobs for high school students. Reports and letters are examples of word processing; and among computer users, word processing is the No. 1 application.

Word processing includes *formatting* (arrangement, placement, and spacing) of commonly used documents, such as letters, reports, and tables. It also involves *document production* (turning out quality documents in quantity). The features of word processing software make formatting and document production seem easy—but only after you have learned what features are available and how and when to use each one.

Word processing mastery is built into *Keyboarding and Computer Applications*. Simple features and formats gradually give way to more complex document production tasks. After completing Part 2, you will be able to:

1. Format reports (two styles) with reference lists and title pages.
2. Use more than twenty *new* word processing features.
3. Format business and personal-business letters, envelopes, and simplified memos.

4. Format and key two- and three-column tables.

Part 2 also gives you opportunities to use what you learn as a part-time "employee" of a real-estate firm and, then, a manufacturer of educational software. In addition, ample practice is provided for building your basic keyboarding skills.

Spreadsheet Applications. The second most popular computer application: the spreadsheet. At first, spreadsheets (also called worksheets) were used mostly for financial analysis. Today, though, any project that requires a large volume of numbers—from medical research to automotive engineering to candy sales—is likely to be done with spreadsheet software.

A worksheet appears as a simple grid of rows and columns. With it an operator can create formulas to calculate simple numbers, such as a total or average. Not all worksheet manipulations are so simple, however! (Its ability to handle more numbers in more complex ways than is possible otherwise helps explain the popularity of the spreadsheet.)

For example, a worksheet allows entry of a set of values (numbers) to calculate a *What If* condition (IF the wages paid to part-time employees is increased by $.25 an hour, WHAT will be the effect on profit?). Thus, a spreadsheet enables a user to forecast results and make decisions.

This textbook provides for mastery of essential spreadsheet tools. After completing Part 3, you will be able to:

1. Access and exit spreadsheet software, read a worksheet screen, manage files, and enter data.
2. Edit and format data, write and copy formulas,

and print a worksheet.
3. Use IF functions to make comparisons and answer *What If* questions.
4. Create, view, save, and print bar charts and pie charts.

Database Applications. A continuous, endless growth of knowledge has earned these final decades of the twentieth century the name *Information Age*. Database software is one means of dealing with the facts-and-figures explosion—that keeps on happening.

Databases—collections of related information stored in computer memory—replace paper-stuffed multidrawer file cabinets in many organizations, including schools and homes. You may have used a database, or seen one used, even if it wasn't called by that name. For example, the *card catalog* of library materials in your school may be in the form of electronic records (a database), not cards. Instead of looking up information in a large reference book, perhaps you *dial up* an information service (a database). At the grocery store, perhaps you have seen a cashier pass items over a scanner, causing prices (in a database) to appear on the sales register screen.

In the future, you can expect database usage to increase—in frequency, in complexity, and in effects on our lives. Therefore, you will need more knowledge of database concepts—more than using the card catalog or watching a cashier ring up a sale. In *Keyboarding and Computer Applications* you will become familiar with these concepts in hands-on database activities. After completing Part 4, you will be able to:

1. Create simple databases.
2. Print reports of complete or selected information; print mailing labels.
3. Sort database files for a variety of useful reports.

4. Calculate values on numerical data.
5. Do *wildcard* searches for data.

Integrated Software Applications. Once computer users had several types of application software, combining those applications was the next logical step for software vendors and users. Integrated software, such as Microsoft Works, allows spreadsheet data to be combined with word processing text, for example, and the resulting document to be combined with a database mailing list. Combining the applications already learned will become your next logical step as well.

Desktop publishing (DTP) involves computer-designing pages for, say, a newsletter, to look like typeset pages, such as those in some textbooks. DTP includes text in various styles and sizes; line drawing, called clip art; and other graphics. The process also involves a knowledge of basic design principles. After completing Part 5 of this textbook, you will be able to:

1. Combine word processing files.
2. Import database files into word processing documents.
3. Import spreadsheet data and charts into word processing text.
4. Prepare text in columns in newspaper style.
5. Design page layouts from thumbnail sketches.

Keyboarding and Computer Applications was designed to help you enter the computer age. You, not the textbook, will determine the level to which you develop your skills. You can improve your performance by taking an active part in your learning process and by following your teacher's directions as you proceed.

—The Authors

CONTENTS

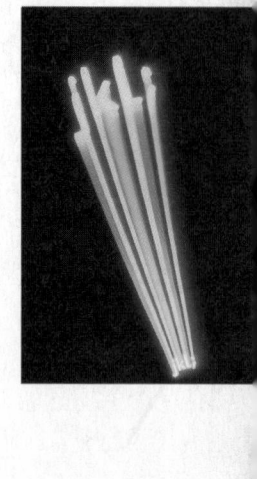
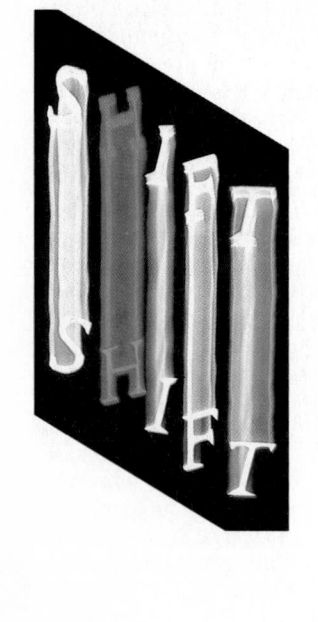

CONTENTS

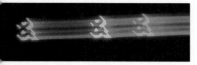

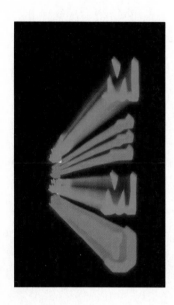

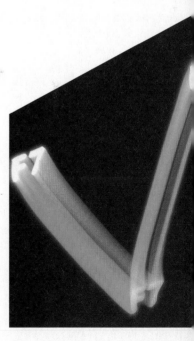

CONTENTS

CONTENTS

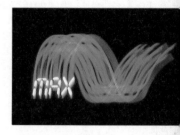
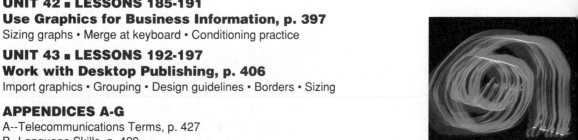

You are about to leave on a fantastic journey to a place called *Keyboarding and Computer Applications* (KCA for short). Before you depart, take time to read this travel brochure (pp. 1-8) to gain information about the trip. These pages describe the climate and terrain of KCA and the major sites (and sights) that you will visit en route. Of more immediate concern, the next few pages detail

- items to be packed for the journey (textbook, template, etc.),
- role of the tour guide (teacher)
- maps and other travel helps (learning outcomes, guides, assessments, etc.),
- itinerary (contents), and
- transportation options (computer hardware and software).

Get an overview now of your travels! You may not have time to do so once you set out on the year-long journey. When you reach p. 4, browse through the information about transportation modes (hardware/software options). Travelers may

choose from two types of computers and three software packages. Once you know which system (hardware and software combination) you will use, study those pages in detail.

PACK YOUR BAGS

Plan to travel light. Almost everything you'll need for the year is packed neatly in the pages of this textbook!

Textbook

Inside you'll find five Parts, each containing just what you'll need for the regions you'll visit. Part 1—Keyboarding through Part 5—Integrated Software Applications. In each Part, things are sorted into Units. For example, in Part 3—Spreadsheet Applications, graphics (bar charts and pie charts) make up a separate unit. Every Unit breaks into Lessons. In Part 2—Word Processing Applications, for example, a Unit about preparing reports divides into six Lessons, each one about right for a day in transit. For travelers' added convenience, Lessons divide into even smaller segments.

Student's Template

The tour guide (teacher) will distribute a computer disk titled *Student's Template for Keyboarding and Computer Applications*. If you do not receive *Student's Template* at the time of departure, you can expect to get it before you have to use it in Part 2—Word Processing Applications. In addition to several word processing files, this disk contains files you can use for spreadsheet, database, and desktop publishing applications.

Naming files. Besides the prestored files, enough space has been reserved on the disk for you to store files that you will create as you go. At first, file names will be provided, often including the Lesson number. Beginning in Part 4—Database Applications, following the guidelines, will assign descriptive names to some of the files he or she creates.

Maintaining files. Regularly during the year you will delete files that are no longer needed. You will be told when and which and how.

Thus, space on the template will be opened for more new files; and you are likely to require only one disk for the entire trip. (Additional copies of *Student's Template* will be available, though, should you need a replacement for any reason.)

A number of files that you will create must be kept for later use—a good reason NOT to delete files unless directed. Occasionally, files you create will be used again in the same Unit; others will be held for some time (and distance) before being reused. The table on page 2 shows the schedule for reusing files.

ASK FOR ASSISTANCE

Your teacher will lead the group's tour of *Keyboarding and Computer Applications*. Tour guides give reliable information about each area, adding meaning and interest to your travel experience. In addition, every tour guide is prepared to help with specific problems, such as hardware or software difficulties. Ask your teacher for assistance any time your software

INTRODUCTION

I

File Name	Created in	Reused in
146B	Lesson 146	Lessons 185-186
148B	Lesson 148	Lessons 187-189
148D1	Lesson 148	Lessons 187-189
148D2	Lesson 148	Lessons 190-191
148D3	Lesson 148	Lessons 190-191
152B3	Lesson 152	Assessment Activity after Lesson 191
HOTELS	Lessons 161-163	Lessons 175-178, 181-184
NEWS	Lessons 173-174	Lesson 192
POSTAL	Lesson 181-184	Lesson 193
STATES	Lesson 158	Lessons 181-184
SUPPLIER	Lesson 154	Assessment Activity after Lesson 184

fails to function as indicated in the textbook. Additionally, ask for help if the printer you are using fails to provide appropriate printouts.

Software manufacturers update their software products often. By the time you make the journey to *Keyboarding and Computer Applications*, you may be using a newer version of a program described in this textbook. In that case, your teacher will modify the textbook directions to work with your updated software.

MAPS INCLUDED
As any seasoned traveler will attest, enjoyment comes from anticipating what's around the next turn in the road—and reflecting on how *far* I've come. Features of this textbook serve as maps. The maps not only enable you to reach your destination; they allow you, in effect, to see around turns in the road and to see how you've progressed.

Glossaries and Learning Outcomes
Each Part opens with a Glossary of technical terms common to that area. All 43 Units begin with a list of Learning Outcomes— specific things that you will be able to do as a result of working your way through the Unit.

Unit Overviews
In many Units a one- or two-page summary appears before the Lessons. You can refer to these handy information capsules as needed while in that area, or even after you've moved on.

Learn and Apply
Daily excursions always advance a traveler ahead of where he or she started that morning. You can be sure, though, that each day's experience will stick with you. All trips follow the time-honored learn-and-apply plan, a reliable way to help travelers remember where they've been.

Read-and-do is another name for how your textbook is organized. You learn a topic by *reading* a short passage about it. Then you *do* what you've learned by following step-by-step directions. (Three sets of directions are given; you choose the one for the hardware/software you're using.)

Assessment
After *reading-and-doing* through several related topics, you will be ready to apply your knowledge and skill with only general directions to guide you. By the time you reach your destination—the end of a Unit—you likely will feel capable and confident— ready to show what you can do. Sometimes a day or two will be spent reviewing, before your abilities are assessed.

ITINERARY
Take a few minutes right now to look at the travel plan outlined on pp. iv-vii. See the five Parts of *Keyboarding and Computer Applications* as it has been described. (Try to remember the names for all five Parts.)

Read the titles of some of the Units. Note the Lesson numbers—197 in all.

Glance at the topics indicated for each Unit. (Can you find one or more familiar topics?)

Don't miss the Appendix list. Most of the appendices you'll use often, once under way. A few, such as Appendix A— Telecommunications Terms, make fascinating side trips for anyone interested. Note that an index is provided.

TRANSPORTATION
Little time remains before departure. Determine which of the following systems you will use.

- Macintosh computer with Microsoft Works software (pp. 4 and 5),
- IBM PC or Compatible computer with Microsoft Works software (pp. 6-8), or
- IBM PC or Compatible computer with Word-Perfect 5.1 software (pp. 6-8). WordPerfect users will use Lotus 1-2-3, Version 2.3, for spreadsheet applications. Basic information for using Lotus appears in that part of the textbook.

Skim the information about caring for disks (come back to it from time to time as you work with disks).

Hurry on to pp. 4-8. Tomorrow morning—we're OFF!

Spreadsheet Feature	LOTUS	WORKS DOS	WORKS MAC
Draw Lines (p. 268)	\= (then copy as needed)	Fill first cell of line with =; then copy as needed	Click on Edit Menu, Draw On; on Tools palette, click on Line Tool; draw line; click on Edit Menu, Draw Off
Edit Cell (p. 255)	F2; make changes; Enter	F2; make changes; Enter	Click on Entry bar; make changes; Return
Erase Cells (p. 248)	/, R, E; highlight cells; Enter	Alt, S; E; highlight cells; Alt, E; E	Click on first cell in range, drag to last cell in range; click on Edit; select Clear
Footer (p. 283)	/, P, P, O, F, key footer, Enter	Alt, P, H, key footer, Enter	see Header
Format Changes (p. 249)	Highlight first cell in range; /, R, F; select format; Enter; highlight last cell in range; Enter	Highlight first cell in range; Alt, S; select option; Alt, T; select format; Enter	Highlight range; click on Format; select Set Cell Attributes; select options; Return
Format Worksheet (p. 270)	/, W, G; select options	Alt, S, A; Alt, T; select options	Click on Select, All Cells; select options from Format Menu
Formulas (p. 253)	+, key formula	=, key formula	=, key formula
Graphing (see Charting)			
Header (p. 283)	/, P, P, O; H, Entrer; key header, Enter	Alt, P, H; key header, Enter	Click on File Menu, Page Setup; click on choices; key header/footer; Return
Help (p. 233)	F1	Alt, H; H; follow prompts	From Window Menu, Help; follow prompts
IF Function (p. 275-276)	@IF(comparison,value-if-true, value-if-false)	=IF(comparison,value-if-true, value-if-false)	=IF(comparison,value-if-true, value-if-false)
Insert Column(s) (p. 267)	/, W; I, C, specify column(s), Enter	Alt, E; I, C, Enter	Click on Column letter in border; click on Edit; Insert
Move (p. 282)	/, M; specify range; Enter; specify upper-left cell of receiving range; Enter	Alt, S, E; specify range; Alt,E, M; highlight upper-left cell in receiving range, Enter	Highlight range; click on Edit Menu, Move; key address of receiving cell, Return
Name Worksheet (see Save)			
Print (p. 258)	/, P, P, P, R; specify range; Enter, A; G; P, Q	Alt, P, P, Enter	Click on File Menu; select Print; select options; click on OK
Retrieve File (p. 235)	/, F, R; select drive, select file name, Enter	Alt, F; highlight file name, Enter	From File Menu, Open; select drive; highlight file name; click on Open
Right-Align Cell Label (p. 238)	" (before label)	Alt, T, S, R	From Format Menu, select Cell Attributes; click on Right button; click on OK
Save (p. 240)	/, F, S; Esc as needed to specify drive; key file name; Enter	Alt, F, S; key file name; Enter	From File Menu, Save; select drive; key file name; click on Save
Set Margins (p. 283)	/, P, P, O; M; select margin(s) to be set; key setting(s); Enter	Alt, P, M; key settings, Enter	Click on File Menu, Page Setup; click on choices; key settings; Return
Statistical Formulas (p. 264)	@function (cell address.cell address)	=function (cell address:cell address)	=function (cell address:cell address)

Keep disks away from magnets.

Keep disks dry.

Do not touch the exposed part of the disk.

Avoid exposing disks to direct sunlight.

Store disks at temperatures between 50°F and 125°F.

Do not use an eraser on a disk label.

Follow these guidelines when working with your computer to ensure your safety and to protect the computer from harm:

Computer Equipment

- Place all computer components on a sturdy, flat surface in a dust-free area that is not in direct sunlight.
- Do not remove or insert computer cables without proper supervision or without turning off the equipment.
- Take care not to spill any food or liquid on or in any computer component. If you do, turn off the computer immediately, unplug it, and notify your teacher before cleaning up the spill or turning on the equipment.
- Do not attempt to open or service the computer's high-voltage power supply—call an authorized service provider.
- Make sure the ventilation openings on the computer and monitor are not obstructed so the equipment does not overheat.
- Don't use aerosol sprays, solvents, or abrasives near your computer equipment.
- Before moving an IBM PC or compatible, determine if the hard drive needs to be "parked." If so, consult your teacher for the "parking" procedure.
- Avoid jolting or jostling your computer if it becomes necessary to move it.
- Do not drop books or other objects on or near computer equipment.

Floppy Disks and Drives

- Avoid exposing disks to extremely hot or cold temperatures.
- Do not use an eraser on a disk label; use a felt-tip pen when writing on disk labels.
- Keep disks dry and free of dust.
- Do not touch the exposed part of a disk.
- Keep disks away from magnets, x-ray devices, and direct sunlight.
- Do not bend or fold a disk or attach a paper clip to it.
- Carefully insert disks into and remove them from the disk drive and replace each disk in its envelope when it is not being used.
- Use a disk only on the computer system for which it is formatted.

Spreadsheet Feature	LOTUS	WORKS DOS	WORKS MAC
Cell Pointer Move (see p. 236)			
Center Labels (p. 238)	^ (before label)	Alt, T, S; C, Enter	From Format Menu, Select Cell Attributes; click on Center button; click on OK
Charting (pp. 287-288)			
Create	p. 287	p. 287	p. 287
Explode (pie chart wedges)	p. 288	p. 288	NA
Legend	p. 287	p. 287	p. 287 (bar charts), p. 288 (pie charts)
Patterns (pie chart wedges)	p. 288	p. 288	NA
Printing	p. 288	p. 288	p. 288
Save	p. 287	p. 287	p. 287 (bar charts), p. 288 (pie charts)
Title	p. 287	p. 287	p. 287 (bar charts), p. 289 (pie charts)
View	p. 287	p. 287	p. 287 (bar charts), p. 288 (pie charts)
Clear Screen (p. 238)	/, W, E, Y, Y (if changes not saved)	Alt, F; C; select Y or N	From File Menu, Close; click on Y or N; click on ss icon
Column Width (p. 251)	Move cursor to column; /, W, C, S; key # spaces desired; Enter	Move cursor to column; Alt, T, W; key # spaces desired; Enter	Click on cell in column; click on Format; select Column Width; key # spaces desired; click on OK
Copy (p. 282)	/, C; specify range, Enter; specify upper left cell of receiving range; Enter	Alt, S, E; specify range; Alt, E, C; highlight upper-left cell in receiving range, Enter	Highlight range; click on Edit Menu, copy; highlight upper-left cell in receiving range; click on Edit Menu; Paste
Copy One Cell (p. 246)	/, C; specify copy cell, Enter; specify receiving cell; Enter	*Adjacent:* Alt, S, E; move cursor to receiving cell; Alt, E; select Fill Down or Fill Right *Nonadjacent:* highlight copy cell; Alt, E, C; highlight receiving cell; Enter	*Adjacent:* Click on copy cell; drag to receiving cell; click on Edit; select Fill Down or Fill Right *Nonadjacent:* Click on copy cell; click on Edit; select Copy; click on receiving cell; click on Edit; select Paste
Copy to Range of Cells (p. 247)	/, C; specify copy cell, Enter; specify receiving range; Enter	*Adjacent:* Highlight copy cell; Alt, S, E; highlight receiving cells; Alt, E; select Fill Down or Fill Right *Nonadjacent:* Highlight copy cell; Alt, E, C; highlight upper-left cell in receiving range; Alt, E, C; then copy as needed to adjacent cells	*Adjacent:* Click on copy cell; drag to receiving cells; click on Edit; select Fill Down or Fill Right *Nonadjacent:* Click on copy cell; click on Edit; select Copy; upper-left cell in receiving range; click on Edit; select Paste; Fill Down or Fill Right
Delete Column(s) (p. 267)	/, W; D, C; specify column(s), Enter	Alt, E; D	Click on Column letter in border; click on Edit; Cut
Display Formulas (p. 279)	*all formulas displayed:* /, W, G, F, T *one formula displayed:* /, R, F, T	Alt, S, A; Alt, O, F	Click on Option Menu, Show Formulas

KNOW YOUR MACINTOSH

The illustrations below show the major parts of a Macintosh. The following copy identifies each numbered part. These parts are found on almost all computers, but their location may vary. If you are using a Macintosh computer other than the model illustrated, see the manufacturer's booklet for the exact location of each part.

1. **Keyboard:** an arrangement of letter, figure, symbol, and other keys used to input characters, commands, and functions to the computer.

2. **CPU (Central Processing Unit):** the internal operating unit or "brain" of a computer.

3. **Disk drive:** a unit, connected to or situated inside the computer, that reads and writes onto disks.

4. **Monitor:** TV-like device used to display text and graphic images on a screen.

5. **Printer:** a unit attached to a computer that produces text on paper (hard copy).

6. **Numeric keypad:** a calculator-type keyboard used when large amounts of numeric data are to be keyed (not available on all keyboards).

7. **Function (F) keys:** special keys used alone or in combination with other keys to perform special functions.

8. **Space Bar:** a long bar at the bottom of the keyboard used to insert a space between words or characters.

9. **Caps lock:** a key that when locked down causes all letters to be capitalized without affecting any other keys.

10. **Shift keys:** keys used to make capital letters and certain symbols.

11. **Control (Ctrl):** a key depressed as another key is struck to perform a special function.

12. **Tab:** a key that when struck causes the cursor (enter point) to move to a preset position, as in indenting paragraphs.

13. **Escape (Esc):** a general purpose key that is often used to transfer to another section of the application software and to "back out" of commands.

14. **Delete:** a key that when struck moves the cursor one position to the left, deleting any character occupying that space.

15. **Return:** a key that when struck causes the cursor to move to the left margin and down to the next line.

16. **Arrow keys:** keys that move the cursor in the direction indicated by the arrow on the key; serve as an alternative to using a mouse to move the cursor.

17. ⌘ **(Command):** a key that when depressed at the same time another key is struck causes that key to serve as an alternative to choosing a menu command.

18. **Num Lock:** a key used to switch the numeric keypad back and forth between numeric entry and editing.

19. **Mouse:** a device that is rolled across desk surface to control movements of an indicator on screen.

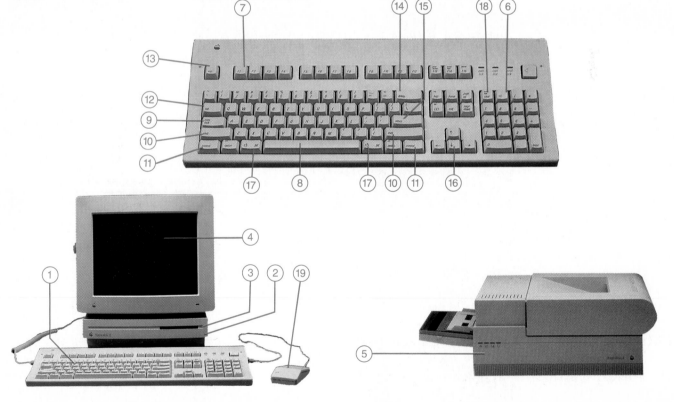

Word Processing Feature	WORDPERFECT	WORKS DOS	WORKS MAC
Macro (p. 182) ✶ indicates any letter used to store a macro	Ctrl F10; Alt ✶; key description or strike Enter; key text; Ctrl F10	Alt /; highlight Record Macro; Enter; Alt ✶; Enter; key text; Alt /; highlight End Recording; Enter	From Macro Menu, Macros On; Start Recording; ✶; Tab; key description; Return; key text; from Macro Menu, Stop Recording; click on Stop or Enter
Margins (p. 54)	Shift F8; L; M; #" (LM); Enter; #" (RM); Enter; F7	Alt, P; M; Alt E; #" (LM); Alt R; #" (RM); Enter, Enter	Click and drag triangles (◁, ▷)
Move (p. 75)	Block text to be moved; Ctrl F4; B; M; move cursor to desired position; Enter	Block text to be moved; Alt, E, M; move cursor to desired position; Enter	Block text to be moved; click on Edit; drag to Cut; move cursor to desired position; click on Edit; drag to Paste
Page Break (p. 120)	Ctrl Enter	Ctrl Return	Click on Format; drag to Insert Page Break
Page Numbering (p. 187)	Shift F8; 2, 6, 4, 3, Enter; 8, 4, Y(es), F7	Alt, P, H; Alt U; Alt N; Enter; delete footer line; move cursor to header line; Tab, Tab; Alt, E, P; P; Enter; ↓, ↓	Click on File; drag to Page Setup; in Header box, key &,R; key &,P; click on OK; click on Format; drag to Title Page
Print Preview (see Document View)			
Print Size (see Font Size)			
Reveal Codes (p. 74)	Alt F3 OR F11	None	None
Search to Find (p. 180)	F2; key text; F2	Alt, S, S; key text; Enter	⌘F; key text; Return
Search to Replace (p. 180)	Alt F2; Y; key search text; F2; key replace text; F2	Alt, S, R; key search text; Tab; key replace text; Enter	⌘R; key search text; click on Replace With box; key replace text
Spell Check (p. 122)	Ctrl F2	Alt, O; S	Click on Spell; drag to correct spelling
Tabs (p. 147)	Shift F8; L; T; Home, Home, ←; Ctrl End; key #" (from LM); Enter; D; R; F7; F7	(Clear all tabs:) Alt, T; T; Alt A (Set:) # (tab position); Enter; Alt L, Alt R, or Alt E; Enter; Alt D	(Clear:) drag tab into text (Set:) click under ruler—once, left; twice, right; three times, decimal
Typeover Mode (p. 50)	Ins (Insert)	Block text to be replaced; key replacement text (on *3.0*, Ins [Insert])	Block text to be replaced; key replacement text
Undelete (p. 72)	F1; R	Alt Backspace	⌘Z
Underline (p. 52)	F8	Ctrl U (Ctrl Space Bar)	⌘U
Underline Existing Text (p. 74)	Block text to be underlined; F8	Block text to be underlined; Ctrl U	Block text to be underlined; ⌘U

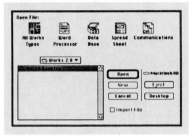

Open

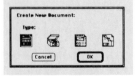

New

Close

Powering Up a Macintosh

Power up (turn on) your Macintosh computer as follows:

1. Turn on any external devices connected to your Macintosh.
2. **Macintosh Classic or LC models:** Press the on/off switch on the back of the computer. If the Macintosh LC monitor does not turn on, make sure that the monitor's on/off switch is on. **Macintosh II models:** Press the Power On key (upper-right corner on extended keyboards; above the 4, 5, and 6 number keys on standard keyboards).
3. When your computer is powered up, a "desktop" will appear on the screen. The desktop is a field with a bar of menu names and icons across the top. Once the desktop is displayed, the computer is ready to accept instructions from you.
4. If your Macintosh doesn't power up, it will display an icon representing a 3.5" disk with a ? (question mark). If this mark is displayed, ask your teacher for assistance.

Powering Down a Macintosh

Power down (turn off) your Macintosh computer as follows:

1. Use the mouse to point to the Special Menu in the menu bar.
2. Press and hold down the mouse button.
3. Drag through the items in the Special Menu until the Shut Down command is highlighted, then release the mouse button.
4. **Macintosh LC and Classic models:** Press the on/off switch on the back of the computer when a message on the screen indicates that it is safe to do so. If you have a Macintosh LC, switch off the monitor. **Macintosh II models:** The computer and monitor turn off by themselves when the Shut Down command is selected.

Retrieving a File on Your Macintosh with Microsoft Works Software

To retrieve (or open) an existing file (document) stored on your hard disk or internal or external disk drives:

1. Choose Open from the File Menu.
2. Select (highlight) the name of the file you want to retrieve.
3. Click the Open button.

Creating a New File on Your Macintosh with Microsoft Works Software

To create (open) a new file (document), you can use the New command or the Open command. To use the New command:

1. Choose New from the File Menu (displays the Create New Document dialog box).
2. Click the icon for the type of document you want to create.
3. Click the OK button (a new window is opened for you to create the document).

To create a new document from the Open dialog box, which is displayed when you start Works or when you choose the Open command from the File Menu:

1. With the Open dialog box displayed, click the icon for the type of document you want to create.
2. Click the New button.

Closing a Document on Your Macintosh with Microsoft Works Software

When you want to remove a document from the desktop, you close the file. During the close process, Works will save or delete this copy of the document, or cancel the command. If you want to save this copy of the document on a disk, you should elect to save the changes. To use the Close command and save the copy:

1. Choose Close from the File Menu.
2. Click the Yes button to save the changes.

Printing a Document on Your Macintosh with Microsoft Works Software

To print a document using the default page setups:

1. Make certain the printer is turned on and ready for printing.
2. Choose Print from the File Menu.
3. Click the OK button.

WORD PROCESSING FEATURES

Word Processing Feature	WORDPERFECT	WORKS DOS	WORKS MAC
Block (p. 72)	Alt F4, arrows	Shift, arrows	Click and drag
Bold (p. 52)	F6	Ctrl B (Ctrl Space Bar)	⌘ B
Bold Existing Text (p. 74)	Block text to be bolded; F6	Block text to be bolded; Ctrl B	Block text to be bolded; ⌘ B
Center (p. 52)	Shift F6	Ctrl C (Ctrl L)	Format, Justification, Center (Format, Justification, Left)
Center Existing Text (p. 74)	Place cursor at beginning of text to be centered; Shift F6	Move cursor to any place on line to be centered; Ctrl C	Move cursor to any place on line to be centered; click on Format; drag to Justification; drag to Center
Center Page (p. 178)	Shift F8; P; C; Y; Enter, Enter		
Clear Screen (pp. 10, 117)	F7; N; N	Alt, F; C; N; N; W (on 3.0, Enter)	File; Close; No; double-click on WP
Copy (p. 75)	Block text to be copied; Ctrl F4; B; C; position cursor for placing text; Enter	Block text to be copied; Alt, E; C; position cursor for placing text; Enter	Block text to be copied; click on Edit; drag to Copy; position cursor for placing text; click on Edit; drag to Paste
Cursor Move (p. 50)			
Beginning of Line	Home, ←	Home	Drag I-beam pointer to desired location; click; release mouse
End of Line	Home, →	End	
Top of Screen	Home, ↑	Ctrl PgUp	
Bottom of Screen	Home, ↓	Ctrl PgDn	
Right One Word	Ctrl, →	Ctrl →	
Left One Word	Ctrl, ←	Ctrl ←	
Delete (p. 72)			
Word	Ctrl Backspace	Shift Ctrl →, Del	Block text to be deleted; depress Delete key
End of Line	Ctrl End	Shift End, Del	
End of Page	Ctrl PgDn	Shift Ctrl End, Del	
Delete File (p. 129)	F5; Enter; highlight file name; D; Y; F7	Alt, F; F; D; Enter; highlight file name; Enter; Enter; Esc	Select File; select Delete; click on file name; click on Delete; click on OK
Document Retrieval (p. 120)	Shift F10 or F5; Enter; highlight file name; R	Alt, F; O; key or highlight file name; Enter	⌘ O; double click on file name
Document View (p. 117)	Shift F7; 6	Alt, P; V; Alt P	⌘ P; click on Print Preview; click on Print
Font Size (p. 198)	Ctrl F8; 1—Size; select size	Alt, T; Alt S; select size; Enter	Click on Format, select size
Indent From LM (p. 143)	F4	Alt, T; A; set indent; Enter	Drag LM (and PI)
Hanging Indent (p. 178)	F4; Shift Tab; key text; Enter, Enter	Ctrl H; key text; Enter, Enter; Ctrl G	Reset LM 0.5" to the right
Line Spacing (p. 54)	Shift F8; L; S; 1 (SS) or 2 (DS); Enter; F7	Ctrl 1 (SS); Ctrl 2 (DS)	Format; Spacing; Double (or Single)

KNOW YOUR IBM PC OR COMPATIBLE COMPUTER

The illustrations below show the major parts of an IBM PC. The following copy identifies each numbered part. These parts are found on almost all computers, but their location may vary. If you are using an IBM PC or compatible computer other than the model illustrated, see the manufacturer's booklet for the exact location of each part.

1. **Keyboard:** an arrangement of letter, figure, symbol, and other keys used to input characters, commands, and functions to the computer.

2. **CPU (Central Processing Unit):** the internal operating unit or "brain" of a computer.

3. **Disk drive:** a unit, connected to or situated inside the computer, that reads and writes onto disks.

4. **Monitor:** TV-like device used to display text and graphic images on a screen.

5. **Printer:** a unit attached to a computer that produces text on paper (hard copy).

6. **Numeric keypad:** a calculator-type keyboard used when large amounts of numeric data are to be keyed (not available on all keyboards).

7. **Function (F) keys:** special keys used alone or in combination with other keys to perform special functions, such as setting margins and centering copy.

8. **Space bar:** a long bar at the bottom of the keyboard used to insert a space between words.

9. **Caps lock:** a key that when locked down causes all letters to be capitalized.

10. **Shift keys:** keys used to make capital letters and certain symbols.

11. **Control (Ctrl):** a key depressed as another key is struck, causing that key to perform a special function.

12. **Tab:** a key that when struck causes the cursor (enter point) to move to a preset position, as in indenting paragraphs.

13. **Escape (Esc):** a key used to transfer to another section of the software and to "back out" of commands.

14. **Delete:** a key that when struck moves the cursor one position to the left, deleting any character occupying that space.

15. **Return (Enter):** a key that when struck causes the cursor to move to the left margin and down to the next line.

16. **Arrow keys:** keys that move the cursor in the direction indicated by the arrow on the key.

17. **Alternate (Alt):** a key that when depressed immediately before or as another key is struck causes that key to perform a special function.

18. **Num lock:** a key used to switch the numeric keypad between numeric entry and editing.

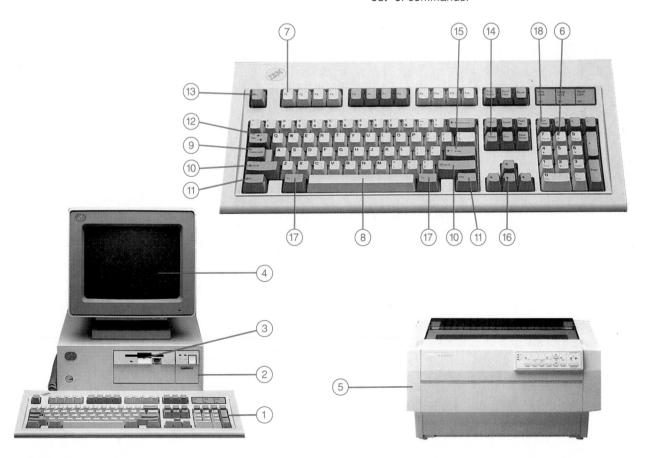

WORDPERFECT

Adapt the steps for designing a print format for form letters.

WORKS DOS

Adapt the steps for designing a print format for form letters without keying the form letter. **Note:** The database document must be open.

WORKS MAC

Label format. Adapt the steps for designing a print format for form letters without keying the form letter. **Note:** The database document must be open when you create the print format.

Report format. Report formats are designed using the Report Menu with the database document open.

PRINTING MERGED DOCUMENTS

Once the print format is designed the next step is to print. Follow the steps below for the software you are using to print merged files.

WORDPERFECT

1. Clear the screen.
2. Depress **Ctrl F9**; select **1—** Merge.
3. At the prompt for the primary file, key the primary file name or depress **F5** to list the directory, and then retrieve the correct file.
4. At the prompt for the secondary file, key the secondary file name or depress **F5** to list the directory, and then retrieve the correct file.
5. If the PRINT command is not coded in the primary file, the two files merge on the screen and can be saved as a new file; to print screen merged files, depress **Shift F7** and select print document.

WORKS DOS

1. Open the database and word processing files to be merged.
2. From the Window Menu, select the word processing file, if necessary, to display it on the screen (activate it).
3. From the Print Menu, select Print Form Letters or Print Labels.
4. In the Databases box, select the file you want to use (more than one file will show if more than one is open).
5. Enter or select OK.
6. At the Print Dialog box, select the appropriate options. **Note:** You can also print a single copy to review by selecting Print from the Print Menu.

WORKS MAC

1. Open the database and word processing files to be merged.
2. From the Window Menu, select Print Merge.
3. From the File Menu, select Print Merge.
4. At the Print Dialog box, select appropriate options.
5. Return or click on OK. **Note:** You can also print a single copy with the placeholders displayed by selecting Show Field Names from the Edit Menu and then selecting Print from the Print Menu.

Open:
Works DOS

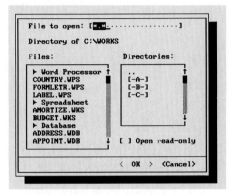

Create:
Works DOS

The following information applies to IBM PCs and most compatibles that have a hard disk drive (named the C drive) with one or two other disk drives (one named A and one named B). If your computer has a different configuration, your teacher will give you the information you need; or you should refer to the user's manual for your equipment.

Powering Up an IBM PC or Compatible Computer

Power up (turn on) your IBM PC or compatible computer as follows:

1. If there is a disk inserted into either drive A or B, remove it by turning the lever on the drive door so the disk can be removed from the disk drive (5.25" disks) or by pressing the button to eject the disk from the drive (3.5" disks).
2. Turn the computer's power switch or button on.
3. If the monitor still is not on, turn the monitor's power switch or button on.
4. If a printer will be used, turn on the printer's power switch or button.
5. The computer will display C> to tell you that it is turned on (powered up) and ready to accept instructions from you.

Powering Down an IBM PC or Compatible Computer

Power down (turn off) your IBM PC or compatible computer as follows: (Some systems require the hard drive to be "parked" before powering down; see booklet from manufacturer.)

1. Prepare to remove each disk from its drive by turning the lever (5.25" disks) or by pressing the button to eject the disk (3.5" disks).
2. Gently remove each disk from the disk drive and store it safely.
3. Turn off the power switch or button for each piece of equipment that you are using.

Retrieving a File on Your IBM PC or Compatible Computer

Microsoft Works Software

Microsoft Works lets you retrieve (or open) existing files (documents) stored

on your hard disk (C) or in internal or external disk drives (A, B):

1. Depress the **Alt** key; hold it down as you strike **F**. Release the keys; strike **O** (chooses Open Existing File from the File Menu and displays the Files dialog box, listing all files and folders on the current disk).
2. Select (highlight) the name of the file you want to retrieve.
3. Strike Enter (Works displays a copy of the file you selected).

WordPerfect 5.1 Software

To retrieve an existing file (document) stored in the current directory (disk):

1. Strike **F5**; strike Enter (displays a listing of files in the current directory).
2. Select (highlight) the name of the file you want to retrieve.
3. Strike **1** or **R** (displays a copy of the file you selected).

Creating a New File on Your IBM PC or Compatible Computer

Microsoft Works Software

When you create a new file (document), Works displays an empty window in the tool you choose. To create a new file:

1. Depress **Alt** and hold it as you strike **F**; release; then strike **N** (chooses the Create New File option from the File Menu).
2. Key the underlined letter of the tool you want to use (a new window is opened for you to create the document).

WordPerfect 5.1 Software

To create a new file (document) from a directory listing, strike **F7** to display a clear screen and then begin keying the document.

To create a new file when there is a document on the screen, strike **F7**, then key **Y** (to save the document) or **N** (to not save the document).

1. If N is keyed, strike Enter at the *Exit WP* prompt (displays a clear screen) and begin keying the new document.
2. If Y is keyed, key the file name at the *Document to be saved* prompt; strike Enter; and key **Y** at the *Replace*

WORDPERFECT

1. Clear screen and key the form letter; then locate the cursor at the first line of the letter address.
2. To code FIRST and LAST name fields on the same line with one space between fields, do the following:
   a. Press **Shift F9**; select **1—Field**. **Note:** Repeat this step for each field you select.
   b. Key **FIRST** at *Enter Field:* prompt, Enter; strike Space Bar one time.
   c. Press **Shift F9**; select **1—Field**.
   d. Key **LAST** at Enter Field prompt; strike Enter twice.
3. To print ADDRESS field, press **Shift F9**; select **1—Field**; key **ADDRESS** at *Enter Field:* prompt; strike Enter to select. Strike Enter again to move cursor to next line.
4. To print CITY, STATE, and ZIP fields on the same line, adapt the procedure in Step 2 used to code the FIRST and LAST name fields on the same line.
5. Your field should look like this: {FIELD}FIRST~ {FIELD}LAST~ {FIELD}ADDRESS~ {FIELD}CITY~ {FIELD}STATE~ {FIELD}ZIP~
6. Save as a primary file by including the .PF extension.

WORKS DOS

1. With the database file open, create a new word processing document from the File Menu; then key the form letter and locate the cursor at the first line of the letter address.
   a. From the Edit Menu, select Insert Field/Insert Database Field (**Alt, E, F**). **Note:** Repeat this step for each field you select.
   b. Select (highlight) the correct database file. (When more than one database document is open, more than one file name is listed.)
2. For the FIRST and LAST names to print on one line:
   a. Tab to the Fields box; use arrow keys to highlight the FIRST field.
   b. Strike Enter to make the selection. (The field appears on the word processing file screen.)
   c. Strike the Space Bar one time to insert a space between the first and last names.
   d. Insert field; highlight the LAST field in the Fields box.
   e. Strike Enter to make the selection. (The LAST name field appears on the same line as the FIRST name field.)
3. Strike Enter to move the cursor to the next line.
4. Insert Field; highlight and select the ADDRESS field from the Fields box.
5. Strike Enter to move the cursor to the next line.
6. For the city, state and ZIP Code to print on one line, adapt the procedure in Step 2 used to code the FIRST and LAST name fields on the same line.
7. Save the file.

WORKS MAC

1. With the database file open, create a new word processing document from the Field Menu; then key the form letter and locate the cursor at the first line of the letter address.
2. From the Edit Menu, select Prepare to Merge (⌘M). **Note:** Repeat this step for each field you select.
3. In the Merge Data Base Dialog box, select the correct database file. (When more than one database document is open, more than one field name is listed.)
4. In the Merge Field Dialog box, highlight FIRST; Return to select it.
   a. Depress the Space Bar one time.
   b. Prepare to Merge (⌘M); at the Merge Field Dialog box, highlight ADDRESS; Return to select it.
5. Return to move the I-beam to the next line.
6. ⌘M; at the merge Field Dialog box, highlight ADDRESS; Return to select it.
7. Return to move the I-beam to the next line.
8. For the city, state, and ZIP Code to print on one line, adapt the procedure in Step 4 used to code the FIRST and LAST name fields on the same line.
9. Save the file.

LABEL/REPORT PRINT FORMATS

The procedure to design label-style and report-style formats is similar to the procedure to design a form letter merge print format. The difference is that you do not key a form letter first. You simply code the commands to insert fields at the location desired.

Close:
Works DOS

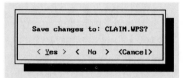

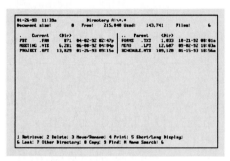

List Directory: WordPerfect

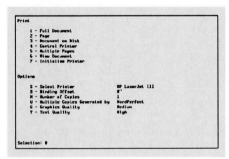

Print Screen: WordPerfect

prompt, if needed; key **N** at the *Exit WP:* prompt; (displays a clear screen); and begin keying the new document.

Closing (Saving) a File with Your IBM PC or Compatible Computer

Microsoft Works Software
When you want to remove a document from the desktop, close the document. During the close process, Works will let you save or delete this copy of the document or cancel the Close command if you have not saved the file or have made changes since you last saved the file. If you want to save this copy of the document on a disk, you should elect to save the changes. To use the Close command:
1. Depress and hold Alt; strike **F**. Release; strike **C** (chooses Close from the File Menu).
2. Strike Enter (selects the Yes option and Works closes the document and removes it from the desktop; the copy of the document on the current disk, if any, will be replaced by this copy).

WordPerfect 5.1 Software
When you want to remove a document from the desktop, save (or close) the document. During the save process, WordPerfect will let you save or delete this copy of the document or cancel the Save command. If you want to save this copy of the document on a disk, you should elect to save the changes. To use the Save command:
1. Strike **F7**; then choose Yes (selects the option to save the copy of the document)

2. At the *Document to be saved* prompt,
   a. Key the file name for the document if the document is being saved for the first time or if you want to change the file name.
   b. Strike Enter if the document is not being saved for the first time or you do not want to change the file name; then at the *Replace* prompt, key **Y** (replaces the copy of the document that is on the disk with this copy).
3. Select the desired option at the *Exit WP* prompt.

Printing a Document on Your IBM PC or Compatible Computer

Microsoft Works Software
To print a document using the default (preset) page setups:
1. Make certain the printer is turned on and ready for printing.
2. Depress and hold **Alt** and strike **P**; release, strike **P** again (chooses Print from the Print Menu).
3. Strike Enter (prints the document using the default print specifications).

WordPerfect 5.1 Software
To print a document using the default (preset) page setups:
1. Make certain that the printer is on and ready for printing.
2. Strike Shift **F7** (displays the Print Menu).
3. Key **1** (selects Option 1—entire document is to be printed).
4. Strike Enter (executes the Print command).

To print records from database files (and the database-like files of WordPerfect), a print format must be developed. A print format contains field merge code placeholders, as required by the software, that identify which fields will be merged. Placement of the field merge codes identify where the selected field contents will be located.

MERGE, LABELS, AND REPORTS

The Merge feature places selected database information within a form letter or other document according to the selection and placement of the field code placeholders. As a minimum, typical merging includes fields of a letter address.

WORDPERFECT

Two word processing files, a primary file and a secondary file, are merged. The primary file, saved with the .PF extension, contains the merge code information only, as for mailing labels, or the merge codes within a form letter. The secondary file, saved with the .SF extension, contains the database-like records (names, addresses, etc.). The files can be merged for printing in two ways: They can be merged to the screen and then printed; or they can be merged directly to the printer, bypassing the screen merge display. The screen merge sequence offers the option to view merged files before printing, and the merged document can be saved as a separate file. The merge directly to the printer sequence does not offer the View option nor the option to save as a separate file. For a lengthy merge, merging directly to the printer is more efficient.

WORKS DOS

Print formats are designed in word processing files that are created as new documents with the database file open. You design the print format in the word processing document by selecting and arranging the field codes in the location desired. To merge documents, you key the form letter or other document and then relocate the cursor to insert field codes where you want the fields to merge. For label- and report-style print formats, you key only the field codes and any needed spaces and hard returns to arrange the fields where you want them to print. That is, the word processing file contains only the field code information along with the character and line spacing that is needed to arrange the selected fields.

WORKS MAC

Print formats for document merges and label-style formats are designed in word processing files that are created as new documents with the database file open. You design the print format in the word processing document by selecting and arranging the field codes in the location desired. To merge documents, you key the form letter or other document and then relocate the cursor to insert field codes where you want the fields to merge. For label- and report-style print formats, you key the field codes and any needed spaces and hard returns to arrange the fields in the locations you want the field code information along with the character and line spacing that is needed to arrange the selected fields. Report-style formats are designed by making selections from the Report Menu in the database file.

MERGE PRINT FORMAT

The following sample provides the steps for creating and coding a form letter to merge database fields for a letter address.

FIELD NAME	field content
FIRST	first name
LAST	last name
ADDRESS	street address
CITY	city
STATE	state
ZIP	ZIP code

PART 1   Keyboarding

Block   A feature that defines a specific portion of text (word, phrase, sentence, paragraph) to be bolded, centered horizontally, copied, deleted, moved, or underlined (*see* Bold, Center, Undelete, Underline).

Bold   A feature that prints designated text darker than the rest of the copy to add emphasis; may be used as text is keyed or afterwards (*see* Block).

Center   A feature that centers lines of text horizontally; may be used as text is keyed or on existing text (*see* Block).

Cursor   A light on the screen that shows where the next keystroke will be keyed.

Default   Preset condition in software features such as Margins, Line Spacing, Tabs and Insert Mode; the operator may override these settings as part of formatting and keying a document.

Delete (text)   A feature that removes a segment of text (character, space, or word) by means of the Backspace or Delete key.

Document   Formatted information such as a letter, memo, report, table, or form. Document is also used interchangeably with the term file to denote any text.

Error   Any misstroke of a key; also any variation between source copy and displayed or printed copy; departure from acceptable format (arrangement, placement, and spacing).

File   Text stored on a disk.

File Name   Alphabetic or numeric characters (name) assigned to each file for identification purposes.

Hard Return   To move the cursor to beginning of the next line by striking the Return/Enter key (*see* Soft Return).

Insert Mode   Allows new text to be keyed into existing text; the default software mode (*see* Typeover Mode).

Line Spacing   A feature that allows operator to set the number of blank lines left between lines of text; usually single spacing (no blank lines) or double spacing (one blank line).

Margins   Specification of the number of inches left blank at the left and right of printed lines; also, at the top and bottom of printed pages.

Operator's Guide (User's Manual)   A set of instructions accompanying equipment or software that explains how the hardware/software features are made to work.

Print   To produce a paper (hard) copy of information displayed on a screen or saved on a disk.

Printer   A device attached to a computer that produces a paper (hard) copy of electronically stored text.

Proofread   To compare copy on a display screen or printout to the original or source copy and to correct errors (or mark them for correction); one of the steps in editing text.

Reveal Codes   A feature that displays text along with formatting codes for features such as Bold, Center, and Underline that were used in the text (WordPerfect).

Ruler Line   Line across top or bottom of screen that shows the position of the cursor in relation to the edges of a printed page; used to set left and right margins, tabs, and line spacing.

Scroll   A feature that makes room for more lines of copy by causing the first line to "disappear" off the top of the screen.

Soft Return   A feature that automatically moves the cursor to the beginning of the next line (*see* Word Wrap).

Software   A set of computer instructions; also called computer program.

Spacing   The number of blank line spaces between printed lines—usually indicated as SS (0), DS (1), or QS (3).

ABOUT PRINTING

The procedure for printing a file appears on p. 5. Before you print, you can preview the document on the screen by clicking the Print Preview box. Before you print, use Print Preview to check documents for changes in format that may be desirable.

ABOUT SHORTCUT KEYS

When you select various commands from the menus, you will note that some show the Apple command symbol (⌘) and a letter at the right edge. These key combinations represent shortcuts for executing the command. Shortcut keys are faster than pulling down a menu and making your selection. Many of the following shortcut commands can be found in a variety of software:

Select All = ⌘A
Copy selected part to clipboard = ⌘C
Open a new document = ⌘N
Open an existing document = ⌘O
Print = ⌘P
Paste in clipboard contents = ⌘V
Cut selected part to clipboard = ⌘X
Undo = ⌘Z

When you want to use a command that is selected (usually the default), strike Return rather than taking time to click the OK button. You can tell what is selected by the additional wide line around it, rather than a single thin line.

ABOUT WINDOW COMPONENTS AND FEATURES

Become familiar with window components and features by reviewing the following illustration and the labels.

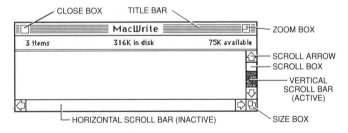

Activating Windows

When you want to activate a window on the desktop, click within it. The window is placed on top of the others, and its title bar has horizontal lines.

Close Box

The Close box is located at the left end of the title bar. Click the Close box when you want to close a window.

Horizontal/Vertical Scroll Bars

The vertical bars at the right side of the window and the horizontal bar at the bottom are called scroll bars. The scroll bars are shaded (active) when there are more items on the disk than can be displayed in the window. Within a document, scroll bars are also active when the document is longer or wider than one page.

Moving Windows

When more than one window is open on the desktop, one window may have to be moved so it does not hide the others. You may also need to move a window so that you can copy files or folders from it to another window. To move a window, locate the pointer in the title bar and drag it. An outline of the window moves with the pointer. When you release the mouse button, the window is displayed at the new location.

Scroll Box

When the scroll bars are active, a small white box, called a Scroll box, is displayed. Use the Scroll box to display other areas of the window. When you click the arrows at the end of the scroll bars, the Scroll box moves in the direction the arrow is pointing. When you click in the gray area of the scroll bar, the Scroll box jumps to the next window with each click. You also can move the Scroll box by dragging it along the scroll bar.

Size Box

The Size box is located at the lower-right corner of the window. Use the Size box to enlarge or reduce the window. Place the tip of the pointer in the Size box; then click and drag an outline of the window to change its size. When you release the mouse button, the window changes to the new size.

Title Bar

The bar across the top of the window is called the title bar. It displays the name of the window, such as the disk name or the folder name on the desktop, or the file name within a document. The title bar is active when the horizontal lines are displayed.

Zoom Box

The zoom box is located at the right end of the title bar. Click the Zoom box to enlarge the window instantly. Clicking the Zoom box a second time reduces the window to its original size.

Glossary, continued

Status Line   A display that shows location of the cursor, number of the screen in use, page of the document in process, line on the page being keyed, and position of the cursor; indicates whether bold, underline, and ALL CAPS features are activated (WordPerfect).

Tab   A feature that causes the cursor to skip across the screen when the tab key is struck to a point set by the operator or to points preset every five spaces (*see* Default).

Typeover Mode   Replaces existing text with newly keyed text (*see* Insert Mode).

Undelete   A feature that restores deleted text.

Underline   A feature that underlines text as it is keyed or existing text (*see* Block).

Word Wrap   A feature that permits an operator to key successive lines of text without having to strike the Return/Enter key at the end of each line (*see* Soft Return).

KEY TO ABBREVIATIONS USED IN KEYBOARDING AND COMPUTER APPLICATIONS

CS
Columnar spacing; space between columns of a table

DS
Double-space; double spacing

GWAM (*gwam*)
Gross words a minute; keyboarding rate in terms of standard (5-keystroke) words/minute

LM
Left margin

LS
Line spacing

PB
Page beginning

PE
Page ending

PI
Paragraph indent

QS
Quadruple-space; quadruple spacing

RM
Right margin

SM
Side margins

SS
Single-space; single spacing

~
Click, click on (Macintosh)

Clearing the Screen.   As you complete Keyboarding lessons—even the very first one—you may want to clear (erase) the computer screen occasionally. Commands (keys to strike) follow for WordPerfect, Works DOS, and Works MAC; use the command for the software you are using. Here's how to clear the screen:

WORDPERFECT (F7; N; N)

1. Strike the **F7** key.
2. At the prompt, strike the **N**(o) key.
3. At the prompt, strike **N**(o).

WORKS DOS (ALT, F; C; N; W [3.0, ENTER])

1. Press the **Alt** key; release it.
2. Strike the **F**(ile) key.
3. At the prompt, strike **C**(lose).
4. At the prompt, strike **N**(o).
5. At the prompt, strike **N**(ew).
6. At the prompt, strike (Ne)**W**.
7. Version 3.0: Strike Enter.

WORKS MAC (~ FILE; ~ CLOSE; NO; ~~ WP)

1. ~ (click mouse button on) File Menu.
2. ~ Close option.
3. At the prompt, select No.
4. ~~ (double click on) WP.

To continue initializing, select One-Sided if you are using a single-sided disk with an older model Macintosh system; select Two-Sided to initialize a double-sided disk. The following Dialog box appears:

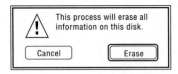

Select Cancel if you do not want to continue the initializing process.

Select Erase to continue. The following Dialog box appears:

Name the new disk by keying a title; then Return or select OK.

Printing Disk Directories

At the desktop, with the window active, select Print Directory from the File Menu; then follow the prompts. A printout of a disk directory lets you review the list of files on the disk without displaying it on the screen.

Renaming Disks

Rename disks at the desktop. First, double-click on the disk name to select it; key the new name (new name replaces previous name); then click anywhere outside the disk name to deselect.

QUITTING THE SOFTWARE APPLICATION

From the File Menu, select the Quit command.

ABOUT EDIT MENU

On the desktop, Edit Menu commands are available to edit the titles of disks, folders, documents, text in the Get Info Comment box, and text or graphics in some of the desk accessories. Within a document, the Edit Menu commands include others that are specific to the software you are using. Become familiar with the following frequently used commands:

Undo. Use this command to cancel the last editing or keying action. To cancel any previous action, the Undo command must be used before the next use of the mouse button.

Cut. Use this command after selecting a block of text or an object that you want to remove from one location and place in another within a document or in a different document. When you use the Cut command, the selected material is removed and placed in the clipboard. The clipboard is a temporary storage place.

Copy. Use this command after selecting a block of text or an object that you want to put in more than one location within a

document or in different documents. Unlike the Cut command, the Copy command leaves original material in the document; and a copy of it is placed in the clipboard.

Paste. Use this command to bring the contents of the clipboard into a document.

ABOUT FILES

Naming, saving, and copying files are basic operations. Paragraphs that follow also explain renaming files and using folders.

Copying Files

With the windows of the source and the destination disks open on the desktop, select and drag the document you want to copy to the window of the destination disk. To copy more than one document, highlight all documents to be copied (Shift Click); then drag to the window of the destination disk.

Naming and Renaming Files

Keep file names short, but descriptive. Descriptive names help to identify the contents of files.

Rename files at the desktop. With the list of files displayed, highlight the file name. Then key the new name (new name replaces previous name). Click anywhere outside the document name to deselect it.

Saving Files

Instructions for saving a document are given on p. 5 as part of the procedure to close a document. Save options are selected from the File Menu.

Save. The Save option allows you to save and continue working on a document after you save it. You should save frequently as you work. In case of a power failure, frequent saving will minimize the amount of work that is lost. The first time you save a document, you will be prompted to key a file name and to choose where the document is stored. If you do not change where the document is stored, it will be saved on the actual disk. As you work, any additional save commands you give will automatically update the document where it is saved.

Save as... Once a document has been saved, use the Save as... command to save it under a new name or in a different disk drive. Thus, you can keep an original file and an updated version of it, or you can save more than one copy of a file.

Using Folders

Macintosh folders, like paper file folders, are used to organize documents. Macintosh folders let you group related files into one location. You establish new folders on the desktop by activating the window of the disk where you want the folder and selecting New Folder from the File Menu. The name Empty Folder is highlighted when the new folder appears so that you can key the folder name replacing the words Empty Folder.

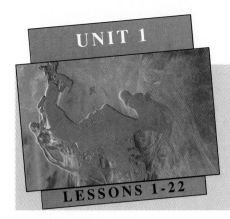

UNIT 1

LESSONS 1-22

Master Letter Keyboarding Technique

Learning Outcomes: After completing this unit, you will be able to

1. Operate the letter, punctuation, and service keys by touch (without looking) and with correct technique.
2. Key sentences and paragraphs, using all letters of the alphabet, with correct technique and acceptable speed.

LESSON 1 — HOME KEYS (ASDF JKL;)

Side margins (SM): Defaults; Line spacing (LS): single (SS)

1A ◆
GET READY TO KEY

1. Arrange work area as shown at right.
- alphanumeric (main) keyboard directly in front of chair; front edge of keyboard even with edge of table or desk
- monitor placed for easy viewing; disk drives placed for easy access
- word processing program and/or *Alphabetic Keyboarding* software within easy reach
- book behind or at right of keyboard; top raised for easy reading
- unneeded books and supplies placed out of the way
2. Turn on equipment (ON/OFF control of computer/monitor).
3. Load the software (follow the teacher's directions).

Properly arranged work area

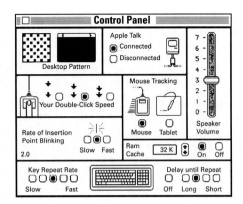

Find File. Select Find File when you can't remember the location of a file you have saved. Key the file name, and Find File will display information about the file and its location. If you don't remember the complete file name, you can key part of the name. Find File will list the names of all the files that contain the part you keyed. Highlight the correct file to display its location.

Key Caps. Select Key Caps when you want to locate special characters on your keyboard. This selection opens a replica of the keyboard and Key Caps appears in the menu bar. Pressing Shift, Option, Control, and combinations of these keys displays the special characters that are available in the typeface font that is selected. For example, in Chicago font, pressing the Option and striking 8 creates a bullet (·). Explore the special characters in various fonts by using the Key Caps Menu to select different fonts. If a special character is not available in the font you are using, return to your document; change to a font that includes the character; key the character; and then change back to your original font. The following illustration shows Key Caps in Chicago font with Option key pressed.

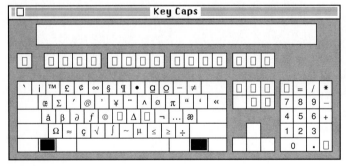

Note Pad. Select Note Pad when you want to key a reminder or a small amount of information. You can recall your note from the desktop or within a document. Your information is stored until you delete it.

Scrapbook. Select Scrapbook to store text, graphics, sounds, or other elements that you want to use in several documents.

ABOUT DISKS

The following paragraphs explain how to copy, eject, initialize, erase, and rename disks. Important information is provided also about deleting/recovering files and printing a disk directory.

Copying Disks

With the source (copy-from) disk and destination (copy-to) disk icons displayed on the desktop, drag the source disk icon over the destination disk icon. Keep in mind that any files on the destination disk will be replaced by the contents of the source disk.

Deleting and Recovering Files

To delete a file, select and drag the file to the trash can icon on the desktop. The trash can bulges a bit to show that something is in it and the file is no longer in its original window. The file remains in the trash can only until you do one of the following: empty the trash can (select the Empty Trash command from the Special Menu), shut down the system, open an application, eject the disk by dragging the on-screen icon to the trash, or copy a new file to the disk that contained the deleted file.

While the file is still in the trash can, it can be recovered by the following procedures: double-click on the trash can icon to open the trash window, then select and drag the file back to its original window; or select the file and then select the Put Away command from the File Menu.

Ejecting Floppy Disks

There are several ways to eject floppy disks from a disk drive. You can eject a floppy disk at the desktop by dragging the on-screen icon to the trash can. The icon disappears from the desktop, and the disk is ejected. This method clears the desktop of information about the disk. Note the important difference between dragging a disk icon to the trash can and dragging a file to the trash can: The disk is ejected, but the file is deleted.

Another method at the desktop is to select the disk icon and select the Eject command from the File Menu (or ⌘E). ⌘Shift 1 ejects the disk in the internal drive, and ⌘Shift 2 ejects the disk in the external drive. Only dragging the disk icon to the trash can removes the icon image. The other methods, including ejecting from an application, leave a shadow image on the desktop, and the computer does not recognize that the disk has been ejected. Work might be delayed by the Macintosh asking you to reinsert the disk for housekeeping purposes.

Initializing Disks

Before a computer can store a file on a disk, the disk must be prepared by a process called initializing or formatting. When you insert a disk that the Macintosh cannot read, it prepares to initialize the disk by displaying the following Dialog box:

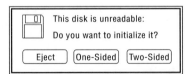

This message appears if the disk is unformatted, formatted for a computer other than Macintosh, damaged, or contains directory errors.

Select Eject to remove the disk from the drive without further action.

1B ◆
TAKE PROPER POSITION

The essential features of proper position are illustrated at right and listed below:
- fingers curved and upright over home keys
- wrists low, but not touching edge of table or frame of keyboard
- backs of hands parallel to slant of keyboard
- body erect, hips well back in chair
- feet on floor for balance

Proper position at keyboard

1C ◆
HOME-KEY POSITION

1. Locate the home keys on the chart: **f d s a** for left hand and **j k l ;** for right hand.
2. Locate the home keys on your keyboard. Place left-hand fingers on **f d s a** and right-hand fingers on **j k l ;** *with your fingers well curved and upright (not slanting).*
3. Remove your fingers from the keyboard; then place them in home-key position again, curving and holding them *lightly* on the keys.

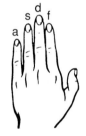

1D ◆
HOME KEYS AND SPACE BAR

1. Read the statement and study the illustrations at right.
2. Place your fingers in home-key position as directed in 1C, above.
3. Strike each letter key for the first group of letters in the line of type below the technique illustrations.
4. After striking **;** (semicolon), strike the Space Bar once.
5. Continue to key the line; strike the Space Bar once at the point of each arrow.

Keystroking technique
Strike each key with a light tap with the tip of the finger, snapping the fingertip toward the palm of the hand.

Spacing technique
Strike the Space Bar with the right thumb; use a quick down-and-in motion (toward the palm). Avoid pauses before or after spacing.

Space once

fdsajkl; f d s a j k l ; ff jj dd kk ss ll aa ;;

WHAT IS OS?

OS is an abbreviation for operating system. Without an operating system, a computer is a nonfunctioning piece of equipment. That is, the operating system instructs the computer to perform certain functions and to support the applications software, such as word processing, spreadsheet, and database programs.

The Macintosh OS gives you menus to guide you through the tasks needed. You select commands from the pull-down menus that are displayed in the menu bar at the top of the screen. With some selections the command is executed when you make the selection. With other selections you make choices by responding to prompts that are given before the command is executed.

THE APPLE MENU (🍎)

Consider the Apple Menu as a bonus. The selections in the Apple Menu provide valuable information, let you change printer control selections, make other changes, and give you several mini-applications that help you work more effectively. Become familiar with the following typical Apple Menu selections:

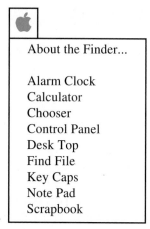

About the Finder...

The top item on the Apple Menu from the desktop is About the Finder ... . Select About the Finder ... from the desktop when you want information such as the finder version, system version, and memory size.

Within an application, the first item on the Apple Menu is About (application software name)... Select this option within an application when you want information such as the software version, copyright date, and registration.

About Desk Accessories

The Macintosh OS includes a list of useful miniapplications called desk accessories. They can perform many tasks to make your work more efficient. Desk accessories can be used on the desktop or within an application, such as within a word processing document. Desk accessories that come with the OS are installed automatically when the OS is installed. Other desk accessories—of the wide variety available—can be installed later.

Alarm Clock. Select Alarm Clock to display the time (as set by the Macintosh system clock). Click on the lever to display two additional panels.

To change the time, select the clock icon at the lower left. In the time panel, click on the part of the time you want to change (hour, minute, second, or AM/PM), then click on the up or down arrow or the AM/PM toggle to display the desired change.

Calculator. Click on the Calculator icon to display the calculator on the desktop or within an application when you want to make calculations. Place the result in the clipboard by selecting Cut or Copy from the File Menu; then Paste into your document.

Chooser. Select Chooser to change the printer selection if more than one printer is attached to your computer. Click on the icon of the printer you wish to select.

Control Panel. Select Control Panel when you want to change the Macintosh default settings. Settings you can change when General Resource is selected include the pattern of the desktop, the rate at which the insertion point blinks, the number of times menu items blink when selected, the double-click speed, the system time, the time scale (12- or 24-hour), the date, and the speaker volume. In addition, you can select and change settings for the keyboard, the mouse, and other peripherals.

1E ◆

RETURN AT LINE ENDINGS

To return the *cursor* to the left margin and move it down to the next line, strike the Return/Enter key (hard return).

Study the illustrations at right and return 4 times (quadruple-space) below the line you completed in 1D, p. 12.

Hard Return

Striking the Return/Enter key is called a "hard return." You will use a hard return at the end of all drill lines in this lesson and those that follow in this unit.

Reach the little finger of the right hand to the Return key or Enter key, tap the key, and return the finger quickly to home-key position.

1F ◆

PRACTICE HOME-KEYS/SPACING

1. Place your hands in home-key position (left-hand fingers on **f d s a** and right-hand fingers on **j k l ;**).
2. Key the lines once: single-spaced (SS) with a double space (DS) between 2-line groups. Do not key line numbers.

Fingers curved and upright

Down-and-in spacing motion

Strike the Return/Enter key twice at the end of a line to double-space (DS).

Strike Space Bar once to space.

```
1 j jj f ff k kk d dd l ll s ss ; ;; a aa jkl; fdsa
2 j jj f ff k kk d dd l ll s ss ; ;; a aa jkl; fdsa
```
Strike the Return/Enter key twice to double-space (DS).
```
3 a aa ; ;; s ss l ll d dd k kk f ff j jj fdsa jkl;
4 a aa ; ;; s ss l ll d dd k kk f ff j jj fdsa jkl;
                                                   DS
5 jf jf kd kd ls ls ;a ;a fj fj dk dk sl sl a; a; f
6 jf jf kd kd ls ls ;a ;a fj fj dk dk sl sl a; a; f
                                                   DS
7 a;fj a;sldkfj a;sldkfj a;sldkfj a;sldkfj a;sldkfj
8 a;fj a;sldkfj a;sldkfj a;sldkfj a;sldkfj a;sldkfj
```
Strike the Return/Enter key 4 times to quadruple-space (QS).

1G ◆

PRACTICE RETURN

each line twice single-spaced (SS); double-space (DS) between 2-line groups

Striking the Return/Enter key to return the cursor and space down one line is called a "hard return."

```
1 a;sldkfj a;sldkfj
                  DS
2 ff jj dd kk ss ll aa ;;
                        DS
3 fj fj dk dk sl sl a; a; asdf ;lkj
                                   DS
4 fj dk sl a; jf kd ls ;a fdsa jkl; a;sldkfj
                                             QS
```

Reach out with little finger; tap Return/Enter key quickly; return finger to home key.

B>**copy fi*.* c:**   (copies all Drive B files beginning with FI onto Drive C).

Delete or Erase   This command erases entire files from a disk or directory.

Examples
1. Change to disk drive that has file that is to be deleted.
2. Key **del frank** or key **erase frank** (deletes or erases the file named FRANK from the disk in the designated drive).

Directory Commands   A directory is a list of all files on a disk. A subdirectory is a list of files within a particular section of a disk. Variations of the basic command make the directory easier to read.

Example
1. If needed, change to the disk drive containing the files you want listed (see Changing Disk Drives command on p. 440).
2. Key **dir** (scrolls through the files in the directory on the disk).

Useful Variations of the Directory Command:

At B> or C>:
Key **dir a:** display files on Drive A.

Key **dir/p** to display screen-by-screen the files in a directory.

Key **dir/w** to display the files horizontally on the screen.

When you want to display a group of files that have common elements in their file names, use the so-called wildcard symbols (see Wildcard Symbols at right) in place of individual file names.

Examples   Display files with the same file name extension: Key **dir *.wk1** to display all files ending with .WK1.

Display files that begin with the same letter: Key **dir t*.*** to display all files beginning with the letter T.

Display all files that begin with the same letter and end with the same file name extension: Key **dir s*.ltr** to display files that begin with S and have file name extension .LTR.

Display all files that begin with the same letters, followed by any letter, and end with the same letters: Key **dir sm?th** to display all files in the directory that begin with SM, have any letter following SM, and end in TH.

Format   The format command initializes or prepares a disk for use on your computer. This command permanently erases any data on the disk; therefore, do not reformat a disk you have used unless you know you will not need any of those files.

Example
1. Change to C> prompt.
2. Insert disk to be formatted into Drive A.
3. Key **format a:** and follow the on-screen prompts.
4. Strike Enter.

Rename   The rename command allows you to change the name of any existing file.

Example
1. Change to the disk drive that has the file to be renamed.
2. Key **ren sara sarah** or key **rename sara sarah** (changes the name of the file named SARA to SARAH).

Type   The type command allows you to see the contents of files on your monitor. Files that are not "listable" will appear as encoded files that are illegible.

Example
1. Change to the disk drive that has the file to be displayed.
2. Key **type harry** (displays the contents of the file named HARRY).

Wildcard Symbols:

Wildcard symbols are useful in handling files with common elements in file names. Use a wildcard symbol to represent other characters in DOS commands. For example, the asterisk (*) represents a group of characters, and the question mark (?) represents only a single character. Wildcard symbols are used in the Change Directory and Copy commands, as shown on p. 358. These wildcards can be used with other DOS commands in this Appendix as well.

1. Key the lines once (without the numbers); strike the Return/Enter key twice to double-space (DS).
2. Rekey the drill at a faster pace.

Technique hint
Keep fingers curved and upright over home keys with right thumb just barely touching the Space Bar.

1. Exit the software according to the procedure in *User's Guide*.
2. If directed to do so, turn equipment off.
3. Store materials such as disks or textbook as the teacher directs.

Spacing hint
Space once after ; used as punctuation.

```
1 aa ;; ss ll dd kk ff jj a; sl dk fj jf kd ls ;a jf
                                                    DS
2 a a as as ad ad ask ask lad lad fad fad jak jak la
                                                    DS
3 all all fad fad jak jak add add ask ask ads ads as
                                                    DS
4 a lad; a jak; a lass; all ads; add all; ask a lass
                                                    DS
5 as a lad; a fall fad; ask all dads; as a fall fad;
```

Side margins (SM): Defaults; Line spacing (LS): single (SS)

R1A ◆

GET READY TO KEY

1. Arrange your work area (see p. 11).
2. Get to know your equipment (see pp. 4-8).
3. Use the default margins and spacing unless your teacher guides you in making format adjustments.
4. Take keyboarding position shown at right.

rmdir or **rd**   Remove Directory, eliminates a directory (delete all files first, then remove the directory or subdirectory). A subdirectory, or directory within a directory, is often used on hard drives to group related files so they can be located faster.

Working with Disks:

format   Initializes (prepares) a disk for use with DOS.

chkdsk   Verifies size, usage, and usability of a disk.

diskcopy   Formats a disk and copies the contents of one disk onto another disk.

BUILDING A DOS COMMAND

Step 1   Start at the operating system prompt, likely to be A>, B>, or C>, and key the command name.

Example   C>**dir** (shows a list of files on Drive C).

Step 2   Indicate what the command is to work on.

Examples   C>**dir a:** (shows a list of files on the disk in Drive A).

     C>**format b:** (initializes a disk in Drive B).

     A>**mkdir\fbla** (makes a new directory and names it FBLA.

     C>**chkdsk a:** (checks disk in Drive A).

Step 3   Indicate the end result you want.

Examples   C>**copy ames a:** (copies file named AMES from Drive C to Drive A).

     A>**ren ames smith** (renames AMES file on Drive A to SMITH).

     C>**del smith** (deletes SMITH file on Drive C).

Step 4   Execute the DOS command by striking Enter.

Punctuation Rules for DOS Commands:

1. Drive letters are always followed by a colon (:).
   Examples: a: b: c: d:

2. A period (.) always separates a file name and extension.
   Examples: SMITH.GAM   LETTER.HOM   TOM.MEM

3. The backslash (\) separates a directory from its subdirectory.
   Examples: c:\wp51   b:\123   c:\works

4. The backslash (\) also separates a directory from a file name.
   Examples: c:\wp51\ames   a:\123\raft.wk1   c:\117b.wks

ERROR MESSAGES

DOS commands may be keyed in uppercase (ALL CAPS) or lowercase. Spelling, spacing, and structure of the command must be exact or DOS will not accept the command and will respond by displaying "Bad command or file name." When this happens, check the spelling, spacing, and structure of the command carefully and reenter the command correctly. If the command still does not work, consult a DOS User's Guide.

If you get an error message stating "Disk error reading Drive x" with options to "Abort, Retry, or Ignore?", you probably have not inserted a disk into the drive or closed the drive latch. Correct the problem and strike **R** for Retry or select one of the other options before changing disks.

If you are attempting to access damaged data on a disk or to read an unformatted disk, you will get a message stating "General Failure reading Drive x" with options to "Abort, Retry, or Ignore?". Be certain the disk is the correct one and then strike **R** for Retry. If the computer cannot read the disk, strike **A** for Abort and then use the disk that contains the backup copy of the file, if you have one.

EXAMPLES OF COMMONLY USED DOS COMMANDS

The following examples are written for a computer system having DOS files stored on Drive C (the hard or fixed disk). If your system has the DOS files on another drive, substitute that drive's designation for C in the commands that follow, when appropriate.

Check disk   The check disk command is useful when trying to determine how much space has been used, how much space is left, and if there are any bad sections on a used disk.

Example
1. Go to C> prompt.
2. Insert disk to be checked into Drive A, if needed.
3. Key **chkdsk a:**.
4. Strike Enter.

Changing Disk Drives (Prompt):

This command is used when you want to use DOS to change from one disk drive to another.

From the current drive prompt, key the letter of the drive you want to change to and then key a colon (:).

Examples

Change From	Change To	Key	At
Drive C	Drive A	a:	C>
Drive A	Drive B	b:	A>
Drive B	Drive C	c:	B>
Drive C	Drive B	b:	C>

Copy   The copy command makes a copy of a disk file, copies files from one disk to another, or copies files from one section of a disk to another section (subdirectory) of that disk.

Examples   C>**copy james joe** (makes a duplicate of the file named JAMES and gives it a new name of JOE).

     A>**copy james c:** (copies JAMES onto Drive C disk).

     A>**copy *.* b:** (copies all Drive A files onto Drive B disk).

     C>copy ***.wks a:** (copies all Drive C files ending with .WKS extension onto Drive A disk).

REVIEW HOME-KEY POSITION

1. Locate the home keys on the chart: **f d s a** for left hand and **j k l ;** for right hand.
2. Locate the home keys on your keyboard. Place left-hand fingers on **f d s a** and right-hand fingers on **j k l ;** *with fingers well curved and upright (not slanting).*
3. Remove fingers from the keyboard; then place them in home-key position.

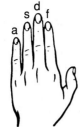  

REVIEW TECHNIQUES

Keystroke

Curve fingers over home keys. Strike each key with a quick-snap stroke; release key quickly.

Space

Strike the Space Bar with a quick down-and-in motion of the right thumb. Do not pause before or after spacing stroke.

Hard Return

Reach the right little finger to the Return/Enter key, strike the key, and return the finger quickly to home key.

Remember to use a hard return at the end of all drill lines. To double-space (DS), use two hard returns.

Key the lines once as shown (without the numbers), single-spaced (SS) with a double space (DS) between 2-line groups.

Strike Space Bar once to space.

```
1 f ff j jj d dd k kk s ss l ll a aa ; ;; fdsa jkl;
2 f ff j jj d dd k kk s ss l ll a aa ; ;; fdsa jkl;
```
Strike the Return key twice to double-space (DS).

```
3 j jj f ff k kk d dd l ll s ss ; ;; a aa asdf ;lkj
4 j jj f ff k kk d dd l ll s ss ; ;; a aa asdf ;lkj
```
DS

```
5 a;a sls dkd fjf ;a; lsl kdk jfj a;sldkfj a;sldkfj
6 a;a sls dkd fjf ;a; lsl kdk jfj a;sldkfj a;sldkfj
```
Strike the Return key 4 times to quadruple-space (QS).

IMPROVE HOME-KEY STROKING

1. Review the technique illustrations in R1C above.
2. Key the lines once as shown: single-spaced (SS) with a double space (DS) between 2-line groups.

Goal: To improve keystroking, spacing, and return technique.

```
1 f f ff j j jj d d dd k k kk s s ss l l ll a a aa;
2 f f ff j j jj d d dd k k kk s s ss l l ll a a aa;
```
DS

```
3 fj dk sl a; jf kd ls ;a ds kl df kj sd lk sa ;l j
4 fj dk sl a; jf kd ls ;a ds kl df kj sd lk sa ;l j
```
DS

```
5 sa as ld dl af fa ls sl fl lf al la ja aj sk ks j
6 sa as ld dl af fa ls sl fl lf al la ja aj sk ks j
```
QS

DISK OPERATING SYSTEM (DOS) COMMANDS

PURPOSES OF THIS APPENDIX

1. To give you an overview of the Disk Operating System called DOS.
2. To provide rules for naming files and keying DOS commands.
3. To acquaint you with DOS commands you may need to work with data on disks.

WHAT IS DOS?

DOS is an operating system that allows computer users like you to use the computer. An operating system is the software program that lets you start your computer at the beginning of each session; use your computer for word processing, database, and spreadsheets; and manage memory, disk storage, and files.

DOS is a specific type of disk operating system that is used on IBM PCs and IBM-compatible computers. PC-DOS is the IBM version of DOS and MS-DOS is Microsoft Corporation's version of DOS that is used on IBM-compatible computers. Since PC-DOS and MS-DOS are similar, this appendix will refer to these operating systems as DOS.

WHAT ARE THE FUNCTIONS OF DOS?

DOS serves three major functions. First, it is the software that your word processing, spreadsheet, and database software use to accept information from the keyboard (input), display information on the screen (output), and store files in the computer's main memory or on your disk. Without the operating system, each software application program would need to include a great many instructions to accomplish these tasks that are common to most applications.

Second, DOS interprets and executes commands that you enter and from the software packages that you use. Without this operating system, you would have no effective way of interacting with a DOS-based computer or controlling its activities.

Third, DOS enables you to manage files. It can be used to prepare (format) disks so that they can be used on your computer, name and rename files, delete and copy files, organize files so you can store and retrieve information easier, and display the files you have saved.

RULES FOR NAMING FILES

All information stored on a disk must be given a file name. When files are stored on an IBM PC or compatible, the file names must meet the following rules:

1. File names must be 1-8 characters long, have no spaces within the file name, and may have a 1- to 3-character extension.
2. File names may contain figures, even begin with a figure.
3. File names must not contain the following symbols or characters: period (.) unless it is used to separate the extension from the main part of the file name; backslash (\); less than (<); greater than (>); filter (¦); asterisk (*), question mark (?); diagonal (/); colon (:); or comma (,). Each of these symbols or characters has a special meaning in DOS and, therefore, cannot be used in file names.
4. The rules for naming the 1- to 3-character extensions are the same as for the 1- to 8-character file name, except you should not use the following extensions when naming your data files:

   .ALL .AUX .BAK .BAT .CHM .COM .CRS .DRS
   .EXE .FIL .FRS .IRS .PIC .PRS .SET .SYS .TUT
   .WK1 .WPK .WPM .WPS .WKS .WDB .WCM .VRS

   Each of these extensions means something specific in DOS, WordPerfect, or Microsoft Works.

DOS COMMANDS

DOS has many commands that enable you to work with information on your disks. Some commonly used DOS commands are named and described below. Then, the four steps in building a DOS command are listed. Finally, examples, with proper punctuation, are presented to give you practice using commands. This practice will help you when you need to use these commands or other DOS commands.

COMMONLY USED DOS COMMANDS

Controlling Settings on Your Computer:

date	Sets system date and uses the current date to "date stamp" edited files.
time	Sets system clock and uses the current time to "time stamp" all edited files.
prompt	Changes the A>, B>, C> or other disk drive prompt to indicate a path or display other information.

Working with Computer Files:

copy	Copies a file or group of files.
del or erase	Deletes a file or group of files.
rename or ren	Renames a file.
type	Displays contents of a file (cannot be edited).
dir	Lists the files (directory) that are on a disk.
backup	Copies hard disk files to floppy disks.
restore	Restores hard disk files from floppy disks.

Working with Directories (Subsections of Disks):

chdir or cd	Change Directory, changes from one directory (disk drive) to another.
mkdir or md	Make Directory, creates a subdirectory.

R1E ◆
IMPROVE RETURN TECHNIQUE

each line twice single-spaced (SS); double-space (DS) between 2-line groups

Technique goals
- curved, upright fingers
- quick-snap keystrokes
- down-and-in spacing
- quick return without spacing at line ending

Return without moving your eyes from the copy.

R1F ◆
KEY WORDS/ PHRASES

each line twice single-spaced (SS); double-space (DS) between 2-line groups

Technique goals
- curved, upright fingers
- eyes on copy in book or on screen
- quick-snap keystrokes
- steady pace

R1G ◆
END OF LESSON

1. Exit the software according to the procedure in *User's Guide*.
2. If directed to do so, turn equipment off.
3. Store disks, textbooks, etc., as the teacher directs.

```
1 a;sldkfj a;sldkfj
                           DS
2 a ad ad a as as ask ask
                           DS
3 as as jak jak ads ads all all
                           DS
4 a jak; a lass; all fall; ask all dads
                           DS
5 as a fad; add a jak; all fall ads; a sad lass
                           QS
```

 Correct finger curvature

 Correct finger alignment

 Down-and-in spacing motion

```
1 a jak; a jak; ask dad; ask dad; as all; as all ads
                                        Return twice to DS.
2 a fad; a fad; as a lad; as a lad; all ads; all ads
                                        DS
3 as a fad; as a fad; a sad lass; a sad lass; a fall
                                        DS
4 ask a lad; ask a lad; all jaks fall; all jaks fall
                                        DS
5 a sad fall; a sad fall; all fall ads; all fall ads
                                        DS
6 add a jak; a lad asks a lass; as a jak ad all fall
```

FORMATTING GUIDES INDEX

Refer to these pages for information about document formats not included in Appendix C.

HORIZONTAL CENTERING (without automatic center feature)

1. Space (strike the Space bar) to the center point (4.25" from left edge). **Note:** When the font or type size is 10 characters per inch (cpi), the center point is 4.2".
2. Backspace once for each 2 characters or spaces in line to be centered, omitting a single stroke at the end of a line. (For tables, backspace once for each 2 characters/spaces in the longest line of every column and for each 2 spaces between columns. Carry an odd character/space forward to the next column; drop an odd character/space at the end of the last column. See illustration.)
3. Begin keying where backspacing stops.

```
                    MAIN HEADING

                 Secondary Heading

These           Are           Column          Heads
xxxxxx          longest       xxxx            xxxxx
xxxx            item          longest         xxx
xxxxx           xxxxx         item            longest
longest         xxxxxx        xxxxx           item
item            xxxx          xxx             xxx

longest1234longest1234longest1234longest
```

VERTICAL CENTERING (without center page feature)

1. Count lines and blank line spaces in text to be centered.
2. Subtract lines in No. 1 from 66, the total number of lines on a sheet.
3. Divide by 2; if a fraction results, disregard it.
4. The result in No. 3 indicates the first line of text on the page. If necessary, convert this number to inches using the following chart.

```
 6 = 1.0"
 9 = 1.5"
12 = 2.0"
15 = 2.5"
18 = 3.0"
21 = 3.5"
24 = 4.0"
27 = 4.5"
30 = 5.0"
```

For numbers between 6 and 30 not listed in the left column, you may use the inches shown for the number above it. For example, if the result (No. 3) is 17, you may key the first line of text at 2.5". Doing so will place text slightly above exact center—in what is called *visual center* or *reading position*. For *exact center* in this example, space down (strike Return/Enter) twice from 2.5" to key the first line of text.

CENTERING COLUMN HEADINGS (optional)

1. From position in which column begins, space forward once for each 2 characters or spaces in the longest item in the column.
2. Backspace once for each 2 characters/spaces in column heading. Disregard an odd character.
3. Key the column heading at this position.

SM: Defaults; LS: SS

2A ◆
GET READY TO KEY

1. Arrange work area (see p. 11).
2. Turn on computer and monitor.

3. Select the software you will use: a tutorial such as *Alphabetic Keyboarding*, or word processing software such as WordPerfect, or integrated software such as Microsoft Works.

Your teacher may guide you through the appropriate steps for your equipment.

2B ◆
REVIEW HOME KEYS

each line twice single-spaced (SS): once slowly; again, at a faster pace; double-space (DS) between 2-line groups

all keys learned

```
1 a;sldkfj a; sl dk fj ff jj dd kk ss ll aa ;; fj a;
2 as as ad ad all all jak jak fad fad fall fall lass
3 a jak; a fad; as a lad; ask dad; a lass; a fall ad
```
Return 4 times to quadruple-space (QS) between lesson parts.

2C ◆
LEARN h AND e

Standard Plan for Learning New Keys (all lessons)

1. Find new key on chart, then on your keyboard.
2. Study reach-technique drawing for that key; read the caption below it to identify correct finger.
3. Reach to new key and back to home key a few times as you watch direction/distance of finger movement.

4. Key twice each line of the 3-line drill for learning that key.
5. When you finish the drill, double-space (DS); then learn and practice the second key in the same way.
6. Finally, key twice each line of the 3-line drill that combines the two new keys with other keys learned.

h *Right pointer finger*

e *Left middle finger*

Learn h ▼

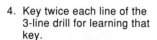

```
1 j j hj hj ah ah ha ha had had has has ash ash hash
2 hj hj ha ha ah ah hah hah had had ash ash has hash
3 ah ha; had ash; has had; a hall; has a hall; ah ha
```
Return twice to double-space (DS) after you complete the set of lines.

Learn e ▼

```
4 d d ed ed el el led led eel eel eke eke ed fed fed
5 ed ed el el lee lee fed fed eke eke led led ale ed
6 a lake; a leek; a jade; a desk; a jade eel; a deed
```

Combine h and e

```
7 he he he|she she she|shed shed|heed heed|held held
8 a lash; a shed; he held; she has jade; held a sash
9 has fled; he has ash; she had jade; she had a sale
```
Return 4 times to quadruple-space (QS) between lesson parts.

ELECTRIC KEYBOARD APPLICATIONS

Learning to key is of little value unless one applies it in preparing something useful--a record or document of some kind. Three basic kinds of software have been developed to assist those with keyboarding skill in applying their skill electronically.

Word Processing Software

Word processing software is "software specially designed to assist in the document preparation needs of an individual or business" (Clark et. al., 1990, 193). Word processing software permits the user to enter text, format it, manipulate or revise it, and print a copy. The software can be used to process a wide variety of documents such as letters, memos, reports, and tables.

This software has special features such as automatic centering and word wrap that reduce time and effort. In addition, it permits error corrections, format and sequence changes, and insertion of variables "on screen" before a copy is printed. These features increase efficiency by eliminating document rekeying.

Database Software

A database is "any collection of related items stored in computer memory" (Oliverio and Pasewark, 1989, 573). The

UNBOUND REPORT (PAGE 1)

---

data in a database may be about club members, employee payroll, company sales, and so on. Database software allows the user to enter data, retrieve and change it, or select certain data (such as an address) to be used in documents. Software users can manipulate and print data in report form for decision-making purposes.

Spreadsheet Software

"A spreadsheet is an electronic worksheet made up of columns and rows of data" (Oliverio and Pasewark, 1989, 489). Spreadsheet software applies mathematical operations to the data and prints reports that are useful in summarizing and analyzing business operations and in planning for the future.

Employment personnel look favorably upon job applicants who are familiar with these kinds of software and how they are used.

REFERENCES

Clark, James F., et. al., <u>Computers and Information Processing</u>. 2d ed. Cincinnati: South-Western Publishing Co., 1990.

Oliverio, Mary Ellen, and William R. Pasewark. <u>The Office</u>. Cincinnati: South-Western Publishing Co., 1989.

UNBOUND REPORT (PAGE 2) WITH REFERENCES

TAXES

Americans are taxed in order to raise revenues to finance governmental activities. Taxation has never been popular. Much time and energy have been devoted by the legislature trying to devise a system that requires everyone to pay his/her fair share. Taxes are generally based on the benefits received and/or on the ability to pay. Two of the most common revenue raising taxes are the personal income tax and the sales tax.

Personal Income Tax

The personal income tax is the tax individuals are required to pay on their earnings. Employers deduct this tax from employees' paychecks. When employees file their income tax returns, they will either receive a refund for any excess which has been paid or they will have to pay the balance due.

Personal income taxes have been the Federal Government's largest single source of revenue and a major source of state revenues as well. On the federal level, the personal income tax is a graduated tax, which means the more you make, the higher the percentage of your income you pay in taxes (Rachman and Mescon, 1987, 529).

With the Tax Reform Act of 1986, the highest tax an individual paid was 33 percent. The amount an individual pays changes with each tax reform. In the past, the top tax rate has been as high as 70 percent (Anrig, 1988, 56).

LEFTBOUND REPORT (PAGE 1)

Sales Taxes

The sales tax is another tax with which most people are familiar. It is a tax that is added to the retail price of goods and services. Two examples of this type of tax are as follows:

1. <u>General Sales Tax</u>. The general sales tax is a tax levied by most states on goods and services. The amount of tax and the specific goods and services that are taxed vary by state.

2. <u>Excise Tax (Selective Sales Tax)</u>. The excise tax is a state tax levied against specific items. Examples of items with an excise tax include tobacco, alcoholic beverages, and gasoline.

While the income tax is a tax based on the individual's ability to pay, the general sales tax and the excise tax are based on benefits received. For example, taxes collected on gasoline are used for highways. Individuals purchasing gasoline are those who benefit from the construction and maintenance of highways.

REFERENCES

Anrig, Greg, Jr. "Making the Most of 1988's Low Tax Rate." <u>Money</u>, February 1988, 56-57.

Rachman, David J., and Michael H. Mescon. <u>Business Today</u>. New York: Random House, 1987.

LEFTBOUND REPORT (PAGE 2) WITH ENUMERATIONS

2D ◆

IMPROVE TECHNIQUE

1. Key the lines once as shown: SS with a DS between 2-line groups.
2. Key the lines again at a faster pace.

Do not attempt to key the labels (home row, h/e), line numbers, or vertical lines separating word groups.

Space once after ; used as punctuation.

Fingers curved

Fingers upright

```
home  1 ask ask|has has|lad lad|all all|jak jak|fall falls
row   2 a jak; a lad; a sash; had all; has a jak; all fall
                                                         DS
h/e   3 he he|she she|led led|held held|jell jell|she shed
      4 he led; she had; she fell; a jade ad; a desk shelf
                                                         DS
all keys  5 elf elf|all all|ask ask|led led|jak jak|hall halls
learned   6 ask dad; he has jell; she has jade; he sells leeks
                                                         DS
all keys  7 he led; she has; a jak ad; a jade eel; a sled fell
learned   8 she asked a lad; he led all fall; she has a jak ad
```

L ESSON 3   I AND R

SM: Defaults; LS: SS

A time schedule for the parts of this lesson and lessons that follow is given as a guide for pacing your practice. If you key a drill in less than this amount of time, rekey selected lines.

3A ◆ 5'

GET READY TO KEY

Follow the steps on p. 11.

3B ◆ 7'

CONDITIONING PRACTICE

each line twice SS; DS between 2-line groups

Technique hints
1. Keep fingers upright and well curved.
2. Try to make each reach without moving hand or other fingers forward or downward.

Goals

First time: Slow, easy pace, but strike and release each key quickly.

Second time: Faster pace, move from key to key quickly; keep element or cursor moving steadily.

```
home   1 a;sldkfj a;sldkfj as jak ask fad all dad lads fall
keys                                          Return twice to DS.
h/e    2 hj hah has had sash hash ed led fed fled sled fell
                                                         DS
all keys  3 as he fled; ask a lass; she had jade; sell all jak
learned       Return 4 times to quadruple-space (QS) between lesson parts.
```

LESSON 3 ◆ I AND R **18**

ENVELOPES

ADDRESS PLACEMENT

Set a tab 2.5" from the left edge of a small envelope and 4" from the left edge of a large envelope. Space down about 2" from top edge of the envelope. Begin the address at the tab position.

USPS STYLE

Use the style recommended by United States Postal Service (USPS): block, SS, ALL CAPS, no punctuation. Place city name, 2-letter state abbreviation (a list follows on this page), and ZIP Code + 4 on last address line. One space precedes the ZIP Code + 4.

ATTENTION LINE

If an attention line is used, key it on the first address line, as recommended by USPS.

RETURN ADDRESS

Key a return address if plain envelopes are used: Begin on line 2 from top of envelope, 3 spaces from left edge. Use block, SS, caps and lowercase or USPS style.

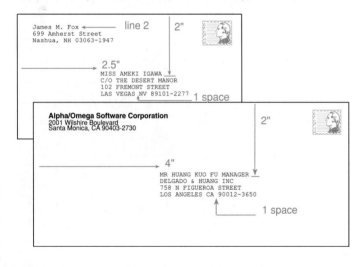

ADDRESSEE NOTATIONS

Key notations such as PERSONAL, PLEASE FORWARD, or HOLD FOR ARRIVAL a DS below the return address, 3 spaces from left edge. Key addressee notations in ALL CAPS.

MAILING NOTATIONS

Key notations such as REGISTERED, CERTIFIED, or SPECIAL DELIVERY a DS below the postage/stamp. (At least 3 blank line spaces must separate it and the envelope address.) Key mailing notations in ALL CAPS.

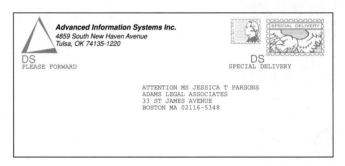

FOLDING AND INSERTING

Large envelopes (No. 10, 9, 7 3/4)
Step 1 With sheet face up, fold almost one third of sheet toward top; crease.
Step 2 Fold the top edge down to within 0.5" of this crease and crease again.
Step 3 Insert second crease into bottom of envelope.

Small envelopes (No. 6 3/4, 6 1/4)
Step 1 With sheet face up, fold bottom to 0.5" from top edge; crease.
Step 2 Fold the right third of sheet toward middle; crease again.
Step 3 Fold the left third of sheet to 0.5" from crease; crease once more.
Step 4 Insert last crease into bottom of envelope.

TWO-LETTER STATE ABBREVIATIONS

Alabama	AL	Illinois	IL	Nebraska	NE	South Carolina	SC
Alaska	AK	Indiana	IN	Nevada	NV	South Dakota	SD
Arizona	AZ	Iowa	IA	New Hampshire	NH	Tennessee	TN
Arkansas	AR	Kansas	KS	New Jersey	NJ	Texas	TX
California	CA	Kentucky	KY	New Mexico	NM	Utah	UT
Colorado	CO	Louisiana	LA	New York	NY	Vermont	VT
Connecticut	CT	Maine	ME	North Carolina	NC	Virgin Islands	VI
Delaware	DE	Maryland	MD	North Dakota	ND	Virginia	VA
District of Columbia	DC	Massachusetts	MA	Ohio	OH	Washington	WA
Florida	FL	Michigan	MI	Oklahoma	OK	West Virginia	WV
Georgia	GA	Minnesota	MN	Oregon	OR	Wisconsin	WI
Guam	GU	Mississippi	MS	Pennsylvania	PA	Wyoming	WY
Hawaii	HI	Missouri	MO	Puerto Rico	PR		
Idaho	ID	Montana	MT	Rhode Island	RI		

LEARN I AND R

1. Key each line twice SS (slowly, then faster); DS between 2-line groups.
2. Key each line once more.

Technique goals
- curved, upright fingers
- finger-action keystrokes
- quick return, eyes on textbook copy

i *Right middle* finger

r *Left pointer* finger

Learn i

```
1 k k ik ik is is if if did did aid aid kid kid hail
2 ik ik if if is is kid kid his his lie lie aid aide
3 a kid; a lie; if he; he did; his aide; if a kid is
                                                    DS
```

Learn r

```
4 f f rf rf jar jar her her are are ark ark jar jars
5 rf rf re re fr fr jar jar red red her her far fare
6 a jar; a rake; a lark; red jar; hear her; are dark
                                                    DS
```

Combine i and r

```
7 fir fir|rid rid|sir sir|ire ire|fire fire|air airs
8 a fir; if her; a fire; is fair; his ire; if she is
9 he is; if her; is far; red jar; his heir; her aide
```

Quadruple-space (QS) between lesson parts.

IMPROVE TECHNIQUE

1. Key the lines once as shown: SS with a DS between 2-line groups.
2. Key the lines again at a faster pace.

Technique goals
- curved, upright fingers
- finger-action keystrokes
- down-and-in spacing
- quick return, eyes on textbook copy

reach review
```
1 hj ed ik rf hj de ik fr hj ed ik rf jh de ki fr hj
2 he he if if all all fir fir jar jar rid rid as ask
                                                    DS
```

h/e
```
3 she she|elf elf|her her|hah hah|eel eel|shed shelf
4 he has; had jak; her jar; had a shed; she has fled
                                                    DS
```

i/r
```
5 fir fir|rid rid|sir sir|kid kid|ire ire|fire fired
6 a fir; is rid; is red; his ire; her kid; has a fir
                                                    DS
```

all keys learned
```
7 if if|is is|he he|did did|fir fir|jak jak|all fall
8 a jak; he did; ask her; red jar; she fell; he fled
                                                    DS
```

all keys learned
```
9 if she is; he did ask; he led her; he is her aide;
10 she has had a jak sale; she said he had a red fir;
```

MERKEL-EVANS, Inc.

1321 Commerce Street • Dallas, TX 75202-1648 • Tel. (214) 871-4400

November 10, 19--

Mrs. Evelyn M. McNeil
4582 Campus Drive
Fort Worth, TX 76119-1835

Dear Mrs. McNeil

The new holiday season is just around the corner, and we invite
you to beat the rush and visit our exciting Gallery of Gifts.
Gift-giving can be a snap this year because of our vast array of
gifts "for kids from one to ninety-two."

What's more, many of our gifts are prewrapped for presentation.
All can be packaged and shipped right here at the store.

A catalog of our hottest gift items and a schedule of holiday
hours for special charge-card customers are enclosed. Please
stop in and let us help you select that special gift or call us
if you wish to shop by phone.

We wish you happy holidays and hope to see you soon.

Cordially yours

Ms. Carol J. Suess, Manager

rj

Enclosures

BLOCK FORMAT, OPEN PUNCTUATION

DOCUMENT PROCESSING SPECIALISTS
6652 Remington Street
New Haven, CT 06517-1498
(203) 266-8215

April 16, 19--

Miss Linda S. LaValley
Vermillion Paper Products
5067 Blackstone Lane
Hartford, CT 06108-4913

Dear Miss LaValley:

MODIFIED BLOCK LETTER FORMAT/INDENTED PARAGRAPHS

This letter is arranged in modified block format with
indented paragraphs. The only difference between modified block
format and block format is that the dateline and the closing
lines (complimentary close, keyed name of the originator, and
his or her title) begin at the horizontal center point in modified block format.

Mixed punctuation (a colon after the salutation and a comma
after the complimentary close) is used in this letter. If an
enclosure is mentioned in the body of the letter, the word
Enclosure is keyed a double space below the reference notation,
flush with the left margin. Copy notations are placed a double
space below the enclosure notation or below the reference
notation if no enclosure has been indicated.

A copy of the block format letter is enclosed so that you
can compare the different formats. As you can see, either format presents an attractive appearance.

Sincerely yours,

Jeffrey R. McKinley
Word Processing Consultant

ph

Enclosure

c William L. Gray

MODIFIED BLOCK FORMAT, MIXED PUNCTUATION

SAILS FOR RENT

P.O. Box 1-230A
Honolulu, HI 96810-1230
(555) 166-1234
FAX (555) 166-1235

August 31, 19--

DIRECTOR OF SERVICES
HEMETT REGAL MAUI
KIHEI ROAD
WAILEA HI 96753-6612

SAILS FOR RENT CAN HELP BRING YOUR GUESTS BACK

"I love this place! Best vacation I've ever had; I'll be back
next year!" Are these the comments you hear from your departing
guests? Sails for Rent can help bring your guests back.

Sails for Rent can bring great recreational activities to your
magnificent Maui facilities--and more guests who return. When
you establish recreational activities at your hotel, you expand
the Hawaiian experiences of your guests. Your guests can learn
to windsurf right on the beach without getting wet! Scuba and
snorkeling safaris to Molokini Island can bring big adventures.
Call or write for more information on establishing a line with
Sails for Rent. Make a commitment to increase the number of
guests who return again and again.

Sails for Rent wants to help. You and selected members of your
staff can sample our services that you can offer to your guests.
Just call (555) 166-1234; then get ready for the aquatic time of
your life!

DANIELLE AUSTIN, MANAGER

rj

SIMPLIFIED BLOCK FORMAT

October 29, 19--

Student Leadership Program Committee

DALLAS JOHNSON TO ADDRESS ASSEMBLY

Dr. Dallas T. Johnson telephoned to say that he will be pleased
to address the special student assembly on March 10 on the topic

TEENAGE DRUG ABUSE

Dr. Johnson will use slides to present data on the incidence of
drug use among teenagers. He will use a short film to highlight
differences in attitudes and behavior before and after drug use.
Finally, a young adult who has undergone treatment at the Drug
Rehabilitation Center will tell us about her experiences with
drugs.

This assembly should be very interesting, but sobering.

Juan F. Ramirez

ph

MEMO: SIMPLIFIED FORMAT

SM: Defaults; LS: SS

4A ◆ 3'

REVIEW GET-READY PROCEDURES

1. Review the steps for arranging your work area (see p. 11).
2. Review the steps required to ready your equipment.
3. Take good keyboarding position:

- fingers curved and upright
- wrists low, but not touching frame of machine
- forearms parallel to slant of keyboard
- body erect, sitting back in chair
- feet on floor for balance

4B ◆ 5'

CONDITIONING PRACTICE

each line twice SS; DS between 2-line groups; if time permits, rekey selected lines

all keystrokes learned

```
1 a;sldkfj fj dk sl a; jh de ki fr hj ed ik rf fj a;
2 a if is el he la as re led fir did she has jak jar
3 he has fir; she had a jak; a jade jar; a leek sale
```
QS

4C ◆ 10'

IMPROVE SPACE-BAR TECHNIQUE

1. Key each line twice SS; DS between 2-line groups. Space *immediately* after keying a word; make the space a part of the word it follows.
2. Rekey lines 1-3.

Use down-and-in motion

Short, easy words

```
1 if is ha la ah el as re id did sir fir die rid lie
2 ad lad lei rah jak had ask lid her led his kid has
3 hah all ire add iris hall fire keel sell jeer fall
```
DS

Short-word phrases

```
4 if he|he is|if he is|if she|she is|if she is|as is
5 as he is|if he led|if she has|if she did|had a jak
6 as if|a jar lid|all her ads|as he said|a jade fish
```
QS

4D ◆ 10'

IMPROVE RETURN TECHNIQUE

1. Study the illustration at far right.
2. Key each line twice SS; DS between 2-line groups. Keep up your pace at the end of the line, return quickly, and begin the new line immediately.
3. Rekey the drill.

```
1 if he is;
2 as if she is;
3 he had a fir desk;
4 she has a red jell jar;
5 he has had a lead all fall;
6 she asked if he reads fall ads;
7 she said she reads all ads she sees;
8 his dad has had a sales lead as he said;
```
QS

Reach out and tap Return/ Enter

miner (n) one who removes minerals/ore from the earth; machine used for that purpose

minor (adj/n) lesser/smaller in amount, extent, or size; one under legal age

once (adj/conj) one time and no more; at any one time; at the moment when

ones (n) two or more things or people of loosely defined similarity

one (adj/pron) a single unit or thing

won (vb) past tense of win; gained a victory as in a game or contest; got by effort or work

passed (vb) past tense of pass; already occurred; moved by; gave an item to someone

past (adv/adj/prep/n) gone or elapsed; time gone by

peace (n) state of tranquility or quiet; a state of agreement within or between

piece (n/vb) a part of a whole; a fragment; to join; artistic composition

personal (adj) of, relating to, or affecting a person; done in person

personnel (n) a staff of persons making up a workforce in an organization

plain (adj/n) with little decoration; a large flat area of land

plane (n) an airplane or hydroplane

pole (n) a long, slender rounded piece of wood or other material

poll (n) a survey of people to analyze public opinion; a politician

poor (adj) having little wealth or value

pore (vb/n) to study carefully; a tiny opening in a surface

pour (vb) to make flow or stream; to rain hard

principal (n/adj) a chief or leader; of or relating to the most important thing or matter; capital (money) amount placed at interest

principle (n) a central rule, law, or doctrine

raise (vb/n) to lift up; to collect; an increase in amount, as of wages or salary

raze (vb) to tear down; to demolish

real (adj/n) genuine; not artificial

reel (n/vb) revolving device on which to wind lines; to turn round and round

right (adj) factual; true; correct

rite (n) customary form of ceremony; ritual

write (v) to form letters or symbols; to compose and set down in words, numbers, or symbols

rote (n/adj) use of memory with little thought; mechanical repetition

wrote (vb) past tense of write; composed and set down in words, numbers, or symbols

seam (n) the joining of two pieces

seem (vb) to give the impression of being

sew (vb) to fasten by stitches

so (adj/conj) in the same manner or way; in order that; with the result that

sow (vb) to plant seed; scatter; dispense

some (n/adv) unknown or unspecified unit or thing; to a degree or extent

sum (n/vb) the whole amount; the total; to find a total; summary of points

stationary (adj) fixed in a position, course, or mode; unchanging in condition

stationery (n) paper and envelopes used for processing personal and business documents

than (conj/prep) used in comparisons to show differences between items

then (n/adv) that time; at that time; next

threw (vb) past tense of throw; to fling; toss

through (prep) passage from one end to another; indicates a period of time or a range of space

to (prep/adj) used to indicate action, relation, distance, direction

too (adv) besides; also; to excessive degree

two (pro/adj) one plus one in number

vary (vb) change; make different; diverge

very (adv/adj) real; mere; truly; to high degree

waist (n) narrowed part of the body between chest and hips; middle of something

waste (n/vb/adj) useless things; rubbish; spend or use carelessly; nonproductive

wait (vb/n) to stay in place or pause; to serve as a waiter; act of waiting

weight (n/vb) amount something weighs; give relative importance to something

want (vb/n) to need or desire; lacking a required amount

won't (vb) will not

weak (adj) lacking strength, skill, or proficiency

week (n) a series of 7 days; a series of regular days within a 7-day period

wear (vb/n) to bear or have on the person; diminish by use; clothing

where (adv/conj/n) at, in, or to what degree; what place, source, or cause

whose (adj/pron) of or to whom something belongs

who's (contraction) who is

your (adj) of or relating to you as possessor

you're (contraction) you are

4E ◆ 10'

BUILD SPEED BY REPEATING WORDS

Every word in each line is shown twice. Practice a word the first time at an easy speed; repeat it at a faster speed.

1. Key each line once SS; DS below the third line. Use the plan suggested above.
2. Key each line again. Try to keep the cursor moving at a steady speed. QS (4 hard returns) at the end of the drill.

Technique hint
Think and say the word; key it with quick-snap strokes using the finger-tips.

Goal: to speed up the combining of letters

```
1 is is|if if|ah ah|he he|el el|irk irk|aid aid|aide
2 as as|ask ask|ad ad|had had|re re|ire ire|are hare
3 if if|fir fir|id id|did did|el el|eel eel|jak jaks
```

4F ◆ 12'

BUILD SPEED BY REPEATING PHRASES

1. Key each line once SS. Speed up the second keying of each phrase.
2. Key the lines once more to improve your speed.

Space with right thumb

Use down-and-in motion

Goal: to speed up spacing between words

```
1 ah ha|ah ha|if he|if he|as if|as if|as he|as he is
2 if a|if a|a fir|a fir|a jar|a jar|irk her|irks her
3 he did|he did|if all|if all|if she led|if she fled
4 a lad|a lad|if her|if her|as his aide|as his aides
```

LESSON 5   O AND T

SM: Defaults; LS: SS

5A ◆ 8'

CONDITIONING PRACTICE

each line twice SS (slowly, then faster); DS between 2-line groups

In this lesson and the remaining lessons in this unit, the time for the *Conditioning Practice* is changed to eight minutes. During this time you are to arrange your work area, ready your equipment for keying, and practice the lines of the *Conditioning Practice.*

Fingers curved

Fingers upright

```
home row   1 a sad fall; had a hall; a jak falls; as a fall ad;
3d row     2 if her aid; all he sees; he irks her; a jade fish;
all keys   3 as he fell; he sells fir desks; she had half a jar
learned
```
QS

accept (vb) to receive; to approve; to take
except (prep, vb) with the exclusion of; leave out

adapt (vb) to make fit; to adjust
adept (adj) skilled; thoroughly proficient

affect (vb) to produce a change in or have an effect on
effect (n) result; something produced by an agent or a cause

bases (n) plural of base or basis
basis (n) the fundamental ingredient of a thing or an idea

beat (vb) to strike repeatedly; to defeat
beet (n) a food plant with a dark red root

board (n/vb) a piece of thin sawed wood; daily meals offered for pay; group of managers; to get onto a bus, airplane, or ship
bored (vb/adj) pierced with a twisting or turning movement of a tool; weary and restless

buy (n/vb) to purchase; to acquire; a bargain
by (prep/adv) close to; via; according to; close at hand; at/in another's home or workplace

cease (vb) come to an end; discontinue; stop
seize (vb) to take hold of suddenly; to take by force; to take possession of

cents (n) specified portion of a dollar
sense (n/vb) meaning intended or conveyed; to perceive; ability to judge
since (adv/conj) after a definite time in the past; in view of the fact; because

choose (vb) to select; to decide
chose (vb) past tense of choose

cite (vb) use as support; commend; summon
sight (n/vb) ability to see; something seen; a device to improve aim
site (n) location

complement (n) something that fills, completes, or makes perfect
compliment (n,vb) a formal expression of respect or admiration; to pay respect or admiration

cooperation (n) working together willingly and harmoniously
corporation (n) a business entity that acts as an individual; a company; a firm

do (vb) to bring about; to carry out
due (adj) owed or owing as a debt; having reached the date for payment

done (adj) brought to an end; through; finished
dun (vb,n) to make demand for payment; a bill

fair (adj, n) just, equitable, beautiful or visually admirable; a competitive exhibition
fare (n) a charge for personal transportation

farther (adv) greater distance
further (adv) additional; in greater depth or extent

feat (n) an act or deed notable for its courage, skill, ingenuity, or endurance
feet (n) plural of foot, terminal part of legs; unit of measure equaling 12 inches; bottom

flew (vb) moved through the air
flue (n) a channel in a chimney

for (prep/conj) used to indicate purpose on behalf of; because of
four (n) two plus two in number; the fourth in a set or series

hear (vb) to gain knowledge of by the ear
here (adv) in or at this place; at or on this point; in this case

heard (vb) past tense of hear; perceived by the ear; listened attentively
herd (n/v) group of animals of one type; to guide into a group

hole (n) an opening in or through something
whole (adj/n) having all its proper parts; a complete amount or sum

hour (n) the 24th part of a day; a particular time
our (adj) of or relating to us as possessors

new (vb) past tense of know; understood; recognized truth or nature of
new (adj) novel; fresh; having existed for a short time; created in recent past

know (vb) to be aware of the truth or nature of; to have an understanding of
no (adv/adj/n) in no respect or degree; not so; indicates denial or refusal

lead (vb) to guide or direct; to be first
led (vb) past tense of lead

leased (vb/adj) granted use or occupancy or under contract in exchange for rent; something so used or occupied
least (adj) lowest in rank, size, or importance

lessen (vb) to cause to decrease; to make less
lesson (n) something to be learned; a period of instruction; a class period

lie (n/vb) an untrue or inaccurate statement; to tell an untrue story; to rest or recline
lye (n) a strong alkaline substance or solution

loan (n/vb) a sum of money lent at interest; to lend something of value
lone (adj) solitary; single; companionless

might (vb) used to express possibility, probability, or permission
mite (n) tiny insect; very little; a bit

LEARN O AND T

each line twice SS (slowly, then faster); DS between 2-line groups; key lines 7-9 again

o *Right ring* finger

t *Left pointer* finger

Learn o

1 l l ol ol do do of of so so lo lo old old for fore
2 ol ol of of or or for for oak oak off off sol sole
3 do so; a doe; of old; of oak; old foe; of old oak;

DS

Learn t

4 f f tf tf it it at at tie tie the the fit fit lift
5 tf tf ft ft it it sit sit fit fit hit hit kit kite
6 if it; a fit; it fit; tie it; the fit; at the site

DS

Combine o and t

7 to to|too too|toe toe|dot dot|lot lot|hot hot|tort
8 a lot; to jot; too hot; odd lot; a fort; for a lot
9 of the; to rot; dot it; the lot; for the; for this

QS

IMPROVE TECHNIQUE

1. Key the lines once as shown: SS with a DS between 2-line groups.
2. Key the lines again at a faster pace.

Technique goals
- curved, upright fingers
- quick-snap keystrokes
- down-and-in spacing
- quick return, eyes on textbook copy

reach review

1 hj ed ik rf ol tf jh de ki fr lo ft hj ed ol rf tf
2 is led fro hit old fit let kit rod kid dot jak sit

DS

h/e

3 he he|she she|led led|had had|see see|has has|seek
4 he led|ask her|she held|has fled|had jade|he leads

DS

i/t

5 it it|fit fit|tie tie|sit sit|kit kit|its its|fits
6 a kit|a fit|a tie|lit it|it fits|it sits|it is fit

DS

o/r

7 or or|for for|ore ore|fro fro|oar oar|roe roe|rode
8 a rod|a door|a rose|or for|her or|he rode|or a rod

DS

space bar

9 of he or it is to if do el odd off too for she the
10 it is|if it|do so|if he|to do|or the|she is|of all

DS

all keys learned

11 if she is; ask a lad; to the lake; off the old jet
12 he or she; for a fit; if she left the; a jak salad

BASIC GRAMMAR

■ Use a singular verb

1. With a singular subject.

The weather is clear but cold.

2. With an indefinite pronoun (*each, every, any, either, neither, one*) used as a subject.

Each of you is to bring a pen and paper.
Neither of us is likely to be picked.

3. With singular subjects linked by *or* or *nor*. If one subject is singular and the other is plural, however, the verb should agree with the closer subject.

Either Jan or Fred is to make the presentation.
Neither the principal nor the teachers are here.

4. With a collective noun (*committee, team, class, jury,* etc.) if the collective noun acts as a unit.

The jury has returned to the courtroom.
The committee has filed its report.

5. With the pronouns *all* and *some* (as well as fractions and percentages) when used as subjects if their modifiers are singular. Use a plural verb if their modifiers are plural.

All of the books have been classified.
Some of the gas is being pumped into the tank.

6. When *number* is used as the subject and is preceded by *the*; however, use a plural verb if *number* is preceded by *a*.

The number of voters has increased this year.
A number of workers are on vacation.

■ Use a plural verb

1. With a plural subject.

The blossoms are losing their petals.

2. With a compound subject joined by *and*.

My mother and my father are the same age.

■ Negative forms of verbs

1. Use the plural verb *do not* (or the contraction *don't*) when the pronoun *I, we, you,* or *they,* as well as a plural noun, is used as the subject.

You don't have a leg to stand on in this case.
The scissors do not cut properly.
I don't believe that answer is correct.

2. Use the singular verb *does not* (or the contraction *doesn't*) when the singular pronoun *he, she,* or *it,* as well as a singular noun, is used as the subject.

She doesn't want to attend the meeting.
It does not seem possible that winter's here.

■ Pronoun agreement with antecedents

1. A pronoun (I, we, you, he, she, it, their, etc.) agrees with its antecedent (noun represented) in person—person speaking, first person; person spoken to, second person; person spoken about, third person.

We said we would go when we complete our work.
When you enter, present your invitation.
All who saw the show found that they were moved.

2. A pronoun agrees with its antecedent in gender (feminine, masculine, or neuter).

Each of the women has her favorite hobby.
Adam will wear his favorite sweater.
The tree lost its leaves early this fall.

3. A pronoun agrees with its antecedent in number (singular or plural).

A verb must agree with its subject.
Pronouns must agree with their antecedents.
Brian is to give his recital at 2 p.m.
Joan and Carla have lost their homework.

4. When a pronoun's antecedent is a collective noun, the pronoun may be either singular or plural depending on whether the noun acts individually or as a unit.

The committee met to cast their ballots.
The class planned its graduation program.

■ Commonly confused pronoun sound-alikes

it's (contraction): it is; it has
its (possessive adjective): possessive form of *it*

It's good to see you; it's been a long time.
The puppy wagged its tail in welcome.

their (pronoun): possessive form of *they*
there (adverb/pronoun): at or in that place/used to introduce a clause
they're (contraction): they are

The hikers all wore their parkas.
Will he be there during our presentation?
They're likely to be late because of the snow.

who's (contraction): who is; who has
whose (pronoun): possessive form of *who*

Who's been to the movie? Who's going now?
I chose the one whose skills are best.

Note: Other commonly confused words are listed on pp. 433 and 434.

SM: Defaults; LS: SS

6A ◆ 8'

CONDITIONING PRACTICE

each line twice SS (slowly, then faster); DS between 2-line groups

all letters learned

home row 1 has a jak; ask a lad; a fall fad; had a jak salad;
o/t 2 to do it; as a tot; do a lot; it is hot; to dot it
e/i/r 3 is a kid; it is far; a red jar; her skis; her aide

QS

6B ◆ 20'

LEARN N AND G

each line twice SS (slowly, then faster); DS between 2-line groups; key lines 7-9 again

n *Right pointer finger*

g *Left pointer finger*

Learn n ▼

1 j j nj nj an an and and end end ant ant land lands
2 nj nj an an en en in in on on end end and and hand
3 an en; an end; an ant; no end; on land; a fine end

DS

Learn g ▼

4 f f gf gf go go fog fog got got fig figs jogs jogs
5 gf gf go go got got dig dig jog jog logs logs golf
6 to go; he got; to jog; to jig; the fog; is to golf

DS

Combine n and g

7 go go|no no|nag nag|ago ago|gin gin|gone gone|long
8 go on; a nag; sign in; no gain; long ago; into fog
9 a fine gig; log in soon; a good sign; lend a hand;

QS

6C ◆ 5'

IMPROVE RETURN TECHNIQUE

1. Key each line twice SS; DS between 2-line groups. Keep up your pace at the end of the line, return quickly, and begin new line promptly.
2. Rekey the drill.

1 she is gone;

2 he got an old dog;

3 she jogs in a dense fog;

4 she and he go to golf at nine;

5 he is a hand on a rig in the north;

QS

Reach out and tap Return/ Enter

■ **Use an exclamation mark**

1. After interjections.

Wow!   Hey there!   **What a day!**

2. After sentences that are emphatic.

"I won't go!" she said with determination.
How good it was to see you in New Orleans last
     week!

■ **Use a hyphen**

1. To join compound numbers from twenty-one to ninety-nine
that are keyed as words.

forty-six   fifty-eight   over seventy-six

2. To join parts of a compound adjective before a noun.

well-laid plans   six-year period
two-thirds majority

3. After each word or figure in a series of compound adjectives (suspended hyphenation).

first-, second-, and third-class reservations

4. To emphasize the spelling of a word.

s-e-p-a-r-a-t-e   G-a-e-l-i-c

5. To form compound nouns.

WLW-TV   teacher-counselor   AFL-CIO

■ **Use parentheses**

1. To enclose explanatory matter and added information.

The amendments (Exhibit A) are enclosed.

2. To enclose identifying letters or figures in lists.

Check these factors: (1) period of time, (2) rate of
     pay, and (3) nature of duties.

3. To enclose figures that follow spelled-out amounts to give
added clarity or emphasis (used mostly in legal documents).

The total award is five hundred dollars ($500).

■ **Use a question mark**

At the end of a sentence that is a direct question, but use
a period after a request in the form of a question.

What day do you plan to leave for Honolulu?
Will you mail this letter for me, please.

■ **Use quotation marks**

1. To enclose direct quotations.

He said, "I'll be there at eight o'clock."

2. To enclose titles of articles and other parts of complete
publications, short poems, song titles, television programs,
and unpublished works such as term papers and dissertations.

"Sesame Street"   "Chicago" by Sandburg
"Laura's Theme"   "Murder She Wrote"

3. To enclose special words or phrases or coined words.

"power up" procedure   "Murphy's Law"

■ **Use a semicolon**

1. To separate two or more independent clauses in a compound sentence when the conjunction is omitted.

Being critical is easy; being constructive is not so
     easy.

2. To separate independent clauses when they are joined by
a conjunctive adverb (*however*, *consequently*, etc.).

I can go; however, I must get excused.

3. To separate a series of phrases or clauses (especially if
they contain commas) that are introduced by a colon.

These officers were elected: Lu Ming, president;
     Lisa Stein, vice president; Juan Ramos, secretary.

4. To precede an abbreviation or word that introduces an
explanatory statement.

She organized her work; for example, putting work
     to be done in folders of different colors to indicate degrees of urgency.

■ **Use an underline**

1. With titles of complete works such as books, magazines,
and newspapers. (Such titles may also be keyed in ALL
CAPS without the underline.)

<u>Superwrite</u>   <u>The New York Times</u>   <u>TV Guide</u>

2. To call attention to special words or phrases (or you may
use quotation marks). **Note:** Use a continuous underline
unless each word is to be considered separately.

Stop keying <u>when time is called</u>.
Spell these words: <u>steel</u>, <u>occur</u>, <u>separate</u>.

Note: An italic font, if available, may be used instead of an
underline.

IMPROVE TECHNIQUE

1. Key the lines once as shown: SS with a DS between 2-line groups.
2. Key the lines again at a faster pace.

Technique goals
- curved, upright fingers
- quick-snap keystrokes
- down-and-in spacing
- quick return, eyes on text-book copy

reach review
1 a;sldkfj ed ol rf hj tf nj gf lo de jh ft nj fr a;
2 he jogs; an old ski; do a log for; she left a jar;
DS

n/g
3 an an|go go|in in|dig dig|and and|got got|end ends
4 go to; is an; log on; sign it; and golf; fine figs
DS

space bar
5 if if|an an|go go|of of|or or|he he|it it|is is|do
6 if it is|is to go|he or she|to do this|of the sign
DS

all keys learned
7 she had an old oak desk; a jell jar is at the side
8 he has left for the lake; she goes there at eight;
DS

all keys learned
9 she said he did it for her; he is to take the oars
10 sign the list on the desk; go right to the old jet

LESSON 7   LEFT SHIFT AND . (PERIOD)

SM: Defaults; LS: SS

Finger-action keystrokes

Down-and-in spacing

Quick out-and-tap return

CONDITIONING PRACTICE

each line twice SS (slowly, then faster); DS between 2-line groups

reach review
1 ed ik rf ol gf hj tf nj de ki fr lo fg jh ft jn a;

space bar
2 or is to if an of el so it go id he do as in at on

all keys learned
3 he is; if an; or do; to go; a jak; an oak; of all;
QS

SPACE-BAR/ RETURN TECHNIQUE

1. Key each line once SS; return and start each new line quickly.
2. Rekey the drill at a faster pace.

1 the jet is hers;
2 she has gone to ski;
3 he asked her for one disk;
4 all the girls left for the lake;
5 she is to take this list to his desk;
6 he is at the lake to ski if the fog lifts;
7 he is to see her soon if the jet lands at nine;
QS

■ Use an apostrophe

1. As a symbol for *feet* or *minutes* in forms and tables. (The quotation mark may be used as a symbol for *seconds* and *inches*.)

   12' x 16'   3'   54"   8'6" x 10'18"

2. As a symbol to indicate the omission of letters or figures (as in contractions).

   can't   wouldn't   Spirit of '76

3. To form the plural of most figures, letters, and words used as words rather than for their meaning: Add the *apostrophe* and *s*. In market quotations, form the plural of figures by the addition of *s* only.

   6's   A's   five's   ABC's   Century Fund 4s

4. To show possession: Add the *apostrophe* and *s* to a singular noun and plural noun that does not end in *s*.

   a man's watch   boy's bicycle   women's shoes

   Add the *apostrophe* and *s* to a proper name of one syllable that ends in *s*.

   Bess's Cafeteria   Jones's bill

   Add the *apostrophe* only after plural nouns ending in *s* and proper names of more than one syllable that end in *s* or *z*.

   boys' camp   Adams' home   Melendez' report

   Add the *apostrophe* and *s* to the last noun in a series to indicate joint or common possession by two or more persons; add the apostrophe to each of the nouns to show separate possession by two or more persons.

   Lewis and Clark's expedition
   the manager's and the treasurer's reports

■ Use a colon

1. To introduce an enumeration or a listing.

   These poets are my favorites: Shelley, Keats, and Frost.

2. To introduce a question or a long direct quotation.

   Let me raise an important question: Did you study for the test?

3. Between hours and minutes expressed in figures.

   10:15 a.m.   12:00   4:30 p.m.

■ Use a comma (or commas)

1. After introductory words, phrases, or clauses and after words in a series.

   If you can, visit Chicago, St. Louis, and Dallas.
   Although we were late, we caught the plane.

2. To set off short direct quotations.

   She said, "If you try, you can reach your goal."

3. Before and after appositives—successive words that refer to the same person, thing, or idea—and words of direct address.

   Clarissa, our class president, will give the report.
   I was glad to see you, Terrence, at the meeting.

4. To set off nonrestrictive clauses (not necessary to the meaning of the sentence), but not restrictive clauses (necessary to the meaning).

   Your report, which deals with the issue, is great.
   The girl who just left is my sister.

5. To separate the day from the year and the city from the state.

   July 4, 1996   New Haven, Connecticut

6. To separate two or more parallel adjectives—adjectives that modify the same noun separately. (Parallel adjectives could be separated by the word "and" instead of the comma.)

   a group of young, old, and middle-aged persons

   Do not use commas to separate adjectives that form a single element with the noun they modify (could not be separated by "and").

   a dozen large red roses   a small square box

7. To separate unrelated groups of figures that occur together and to separate whole numbers into groups of three digits each. (Exceptions: *policy*, *year*, *page*, *room*, *telephone*, and most *serial numbers* are shown without commas.) Commas are often omitted from values imported from spreadsheets.

   During 1993, 1,750 cars were insured under Policy 806423.
   page 1042   Room 1184   (213) 555-2626

   Also, large even numbers (1000, 20000) may be shown without a comma.

■ Use a dash

1. For emphasis.

   The icy road--slippery as a fish--was a hazard.

2. To indicate a change of thought.

   We may tour the Orient--but I'm getting ahead of my story.

3. To introduce the name of an author when it follows a direct quotation.

   "Hitting the wrong key is like hitting me."--Armour

4. For certain special purposes.

   Well--er--ah," he stammered.
   "Jay, don't get too close to the --." It was too late.

LEARN LEFT SHIFT AND PERIOD

each line twice SS (slowly, then faster); DS between 2-line groups; rekey each line

Left Shift *Left little* finger Shift, strike key, and release both in a quick 1-2-3 count.

. Period *Right ring* finger

Space twice after . at end of sentence.

Spacing hints
Space *once* after . used at end of abbreviations and following letters in initials. *Do not* space after . *within* abbreviations. Space *twice* after . at the end of a sentence except at line endings. There, return without spacing.

Learn Left Shift key ▼

```
1 a a Ja Ja Ka Ka La La Hal Hal Kal Kal Jae Jae Lana
2 Kal rode; Kae did it; Hans has jade; Jan ate a fig
3 I see that Jake is to aid Kae at the Oak Lake sale
```
                                                    DS

Learn . (period) ▼

```
4 l l .l .l fl. fl. ed. ed. ft. ft. rd. rd. hr. hrs.
5 .l .l fl. fl. hr. hr. e.g. e.g. i.e. i.e. in. ins.
6 fl. ft. hr. ed. rd. rt. off. fed. ord. alt. asstd.
```
                                                    DS

Combine Left Shift and .

```
7 I do.  Ian is.  Ola did.  Jan does.  Kent is gone.
8 Hal did it.  I shall do it.  Kate left on a train.
9 J. L. Han skis on Oak Lake; Lt. Haig also does so.
```
                                                    QS

IMPROVE TECHNIQUE

1. Key the lines once as shown: SS with a DS between 2-line groups.
2. Key the lines again at a faster pace.

Technique goals
* curved, upright fingers
* finger-action keystrokes
* quiet hands and arms
* down-and-in spacing
* out-and-down shifting
* quick out-and-tap return

Technique hint: Keep eyes on copy except when you lose your place.

abbrev./ initials
```
1 He said ft. for feet; rd. for road; fl. for floor.
2 Lt. Hahn let L. K. take the old gong to Lake Neil.
```
                                                    DS

3d row emphasis
```
3 Lars is to ask at the old store for a kite for Jo.
4 Ike said he is to take the old road to Lake Heidi.
```
                                                    DS

key words
```
5 a an or he to if do it of so is go for got old led
6 go the off aid dot end jar she fit oak and had rod
```
                                                    DS

key phrases
```
7 if so|it is|to do|if it|do so|to go|he is|to do it
8 to the|and do|is the|got it|if the|for the|ask for
```
                                                    DS

all letters learned
```
9 Ned asked her to send the log to an old ski lodge.
10 O. J. lost one of the sleds he took off the train.
```

CAPITALIZATION

■ Capitalize

1. The first word of every sentence and the first word of every complete direct quotation. Do not capitalize (a) fragments of quotations or (b) a quotation resumed within a sentence.

   She said, "Hard work is necessary for success."
   He stressed the importance of "a sense of values."
   "When all else fails," he said, "follow directions."

2. The first word after a colon if that word begins a complete sentence.

   Remember this: Work with good techniques.
   We carry these sizes: small, medium, and large.

3. First, last, and all other words in titles of books, articles, periodicals, headings, and plays, except words of three or fewer letters used as articles, conjunctions, or prepositions.

   Last of the Mohicans   "How to Buy a House"
   Saturday Review   "The Sound of Music"

4. An official title when it precedes a name or when used elsewhere if it is a title of distinction.

   President Lincoln   She is the Prime Minister.
   The doctor is in.   He is the class treasurer.

5. Personal titles and names of people and places.

   Miss Franks   Dr. Jose F. Ortez   San Diego

6. All proper nouns and their derivatives.

   Canada   Canadian Festival   France   French food

7. Days of the week, months of the year, holidays, periods of history, and historic events.

   Sunday   Labor Day   New Year's Day
   June   Middle Ages   Civil War

8. Geographic regions, localities, and names.

   the North   Upstate New York   Mississippi River

9. Street, avenue, company, etc., when used with a proper noun.

   Fifth Avenue   Avenue of the Stars   Armour & Co.

10. Names of organizations, clubs, and buildings.

    Girl Scouts   4-H Club   Carew Tower

11. A noun preceding a figure except for common nouns such as *line*, *page*, and *sentence*, which may be keyed with or without a capital.

    Style 143   Catalog 6   page 247   line 10

12. Seasons of the year only when they are personified.

    icy fingers of Winter   the soft kiss of Spring

NUMBER EXPRESSION

■ Use words for

1. Numbers from one to ten except when used with numbers above ten, which are keyed as figures. **Note:** Common business practice is to use figures for all numbers except those which begin a sentence.

   Was the order for four or eight books?
   Order 8 database books and 15 English books.

2. A number beginning a sentence.

   Fifteen persons are here; 12 are at home sick.

3. The shorter of two numbers used together.

   ten 50-gallon drums   350 five-gallon drums

4. Isolated fractions or indefinite amounts in a sentence.

   Nearly two thirds of the students are here.
   About twenty-five people came to the meeting.

5. Names of small-numbered streets and avenues (ten and under).

   1020 Sixth Street   Tenth Avenue

■ Use figures for

1. Dates and time, except in very formal writing.

   May 9, 1994   10:15 a.m.
   ninth of May   four o'clock

2. A series of fractions.

   Key 1/2, 1/4, 5/6, and 7 3/4.

3. Numbers following nouns.

   Rule 12   page 179   Room 1208   Chapter 15

4. Measures, weights, and dimensions.

   6 ft. 9 in. tall   5 lbs. 4 oz.   8 1/2" x 11"

5. Definite numbers used with the percent sign (%) but use *percent* (spelled) with approximations in formal writing.

   The rate is 15 1/2%.
   About 50 percent of the work is done.

6. House numbers except house number One.

   1915 - 42d Street   One Jefferson Avenue

7. Sums of money except when spelled for extra emphasis. Even sums may be keyed without the decimal.

   $10.75   25 cents $300
   seven hundred dollars ($700)

SM: Defaults; LS: SS

8A ◆ 8'

CONDITIONING PRACTICE

each line twice SS (slowly, then faster); DS between 2-line groups; practice each line again

Space once

reach review | 1 | ik rf ol ed nj gf hj tf .l ft. i.e. e.g. rt. O. J.
spacing | 2 | a an go is or to if he and got the for led kit lot
left shift | 3 | I got it. Hal has it. Jan led Nan. Kae is gone.

QS

8B ◆ 10'

RETURN TECHNIQUE

1. Key each pair of lines once as shown: SS with a DS between 2-line groups.
2. Repeat the drill at a faster pace.

Hint for Hard Return

Keep up your pace to the end of the line; return immediately; start the new line without pausing.

1 Nan has gone to ski;
2 she took a train at nine.

Keep eyes on copy as you return.

DS

3 Janet asked for the disk;
4 she is to take it to the lake.

DS

5 Karl said he left at the lake
6 a file that has the data she needs.

DS

7 Nadia said she felt ill as the ski
8 lift left to take the girls to the hill.

QS

8C ◆ 10'

BUILD SKILL: SPACE BAR/ LEFT SHIFT

each line twice SS; DS between 2-line groups

Goals

• to reduce the pause between words
• to reduce the time taken to shift/strike key/release when making capital letters

Down-and-in spacing

Out-and-down shifting

Space Bar (Space *immediately* after each word.)

1 if is an he go is or ah to of so it do el id la ti
2 an el|go to|if he|of it|is to|do the|for it|and so
3 if she is|it is the|all of it|go to the|for an oak

DS

Left Shift key (Shift; strike key; release both quickly.)

4 Lt. Ho said he left the skiff at Ord Lake for her.
5 Jane or Hal is to go to Lake Head to see Kate Orr.
6 O. J. Halak is to ask for her at Jahn Hall at one.

QS

Local area network (LAN): A communications network that connects microcomputers and other information processing equipment in a limited geographical area. See **Wide area network**.

Mainframe computer: A large computer that can process great amounts of data at very high speeds. See **Microcomputer** and **Minicomputer** .

Message center: A centralized telephone answering service that takes calls and messages for people who are unavailable to receive calls.

Microcomputer: A small desktop computer, less powerful than a mainframe computer or minicomputer. See **Mainframe computer** and **Minicomputer**.

Microwave signals: Straight-line radio signals used in short-distance voice and data communications.

Minicomputer: A midsized computer, less powerful than a mainframe computer and more powerful than a microcomputer. See **Mainframe computer** and **Microcomputer**.

Modem: An electronic device used to transmit digital data over an analog system. Modem is an acronym for MOdulator/DEModulator.

Multiplexing: A process whereby a common channel is made into two or more channels so several separate, individual signals can be transmitted simultaneously.

Network: A communications system that enables attached devices, such as computers and printers, to communicate with one another. See **Bus network**, **Local area network**, **Ring network**, **Star network**, and **Wide area network**.

Paging device: A portable analog radio receiver that beeps when someone tries to contact the person carrying the paging device.

Private Branch Exchange (PBX): A private telephone exchange system located on the user's premises used for on-site switching of incoming and some types of outgoing calls. See **Centrex service**.

Public Utilities Commissions (PUCs): State agencies that regulate communication services as well as other public utility services within a state.

Protocols: Agreed-on rules that regulate formats and procedures used in communications.

Ring network: A network that uses one cable to connect all networked devices so that a complete circle or loop is formed. See **Bus network** and **Star network**.

Satellite signals: Microwave signals transmitted by communication devices positioned above the earth.

Scanner: A device that "reads" keyed or handwritten characters and automatically copies them into a computer system.

Star network: A network that uses separate wires to connect all devices to a central computer that controls the network. See **Bus network** and **Ring network**.

Synchronous transmission: The process of transmitting characters in a block or a continuous stream. See **Asynchronous transmission**.

Telecommunications: Any process or system that transmits information from a sender to one or more distant receivers.

Telecommuting: Working at home on a workstation that enables the employee to communicate with the employer's computer without driving to and from work.

Teleconferencing: Having a conference between two or more people in different locations who are linked by a telecommunications system.

Telecourse: Instruction delivered to a site by a telecommunications system.

Telex: A worldwide message exchange service that produces hard copy of messages.

Terminal: A device that can communicate directly with a computer to accept or send data, usually equipped with a keyboard and display. See **Dumb terminal** and **Intelligent terminal**.

Twisted wire: A telecommunication line that has two wires.

VDT: Acronym for video display terminal; a computer monitor, for example.

Voice mail: A telephone service combining tone-signal telephone service and computer technology, allowing callers to leave messages that can be retrieved later by the recipient.

Voice processing: The technology that deals with having computers speak, store human voices, and react to human speech.

Wide area network (WAN): A communications network that connects microcomputers and other information processing equipment in a large geographical area. See **Local area network**.

IMPROVE KEYING SKILL

each line twice SS (slowly, then faster); DS between 2-line groups

Correct finger curvature

Correct finger alignment

Key words (*Think, say,* and *key* the words.)

1 an the did oak she for off tie got and led jar all
2 go end air her dog his aid rid sit and fir ask jet
3 talk side jell gold fled sign stir fork high shall

DS

Key phrases (*Think, say,* and *key* the phrases.)

4 to do|it is|of an|if he|is to|or do|to it|if he is
5 to aid|if she|he did|of the|to all|is for|is a tie
6 is to ask|is to aid|he or she|to rig it|if she did

DS

Easy sentences (Strike keys at a brisk, steady pace.)

7 Joan is to go to the lake to get her old red skis.
8 Les asked for a list of all the old gold she sold.
9 Laska said she left the old disk list on his desk.

LESSON 9   U AND C

SM: Defaults; LS: SS

CONDITIONING PRACTICE

each line twice SS (slowly, then faster); DS between 2-line groups

1 nj gf ol rf ik ed .l tf hj fr ki ft jn de lo fg l.

2 lo fir old rig lot fit gin fog left sign lend dike

3 Olga has the first slot; Jena is to skate for her.

QS

BUILD SKILL: SPACE BAR/ LEFT SHIFT

Key the lines once as shown: SS with a DS between 3-line groups. Keep hand movement to a minimum.

space bar

1 Ken said he is to sign the list and take the disk.
2 It is right for her to take the lei if it is hers.
3 Jae has gone to see an old oaken desk at the sale.

DS

left shift

4 He said to enter Oh. for Ohio and Kan. for Kansas.
5 It is said that Lt. Li has an old jet at Lake Ida.
6 L. N. is at the King Hotel; Harl is at the Leland.

QS

Analog signal: A continuous electronic signal used to transmit voice. See **Digital signal**.

ANSI: Acronym for American National Standards Institute.

ASCII: Acronym for American Standard Code for Information Exchange.

Asynchronous transmission: The process of transmitting characters one at a time and at random or varied intervals. See **Synchronous transmission**.

Automatic teller machine (ATM): A computer terminal that permits customers to complete certain banking transactions without the need to interface with a bank employee.

Automation: The use of machines to increase productivity by eliminating or reducing tasks done by humans.

Bandwidth: The range between the highest and lowest frequencies of a telecommunications channel that is used to carry information.

Baseband: Coaxial cable that carries only one signal at a time. See **Broadband**.

Baud rate: The speed at which data is transmitted over a line.

Bridge: An interconnection between two compatible computer networks that allows information to be transmitted between the networks. See **Gateway**.

Broadband: Coaxial cable that carries more than one signal at a time. See **Baseband**.

Bus network: A network that uses one cable to connect all devices on the network. See **Ring network** and **Star network**.

Cellular mobile telephone: A telecommunications device that uses low-power radio signals to transmit between mobile and/or stationary users.

Centrex service: A central office-based telephone system whereby the telephone company provides PBX-like services for a business. See **Private branch exchange**.

Circuit switching: The process of establishing and maintaining a communication path between a sender and receiver so information can be transmitted in a continuous stream.

Coaxial cable: Insulated copper wire used to transmit data.

Computer-assisted design (CAD): The use of computers to design products.

Computer-assisted instruction (CAI): The use of computers in the teaching and learning process.

Computer conferencing: The use of a computer keyboard and telecommunications facilities so conferees can key and then exchange messages with others who are connected to the system.

CRT: Acronym for cathode-ray tube; a computer screen.

Dedicated line: A point-to-point, leased telecommunications channel used only by one subscriber, often called a leased line or private line.

Digital signal: A series of discrete, discontinuous signals used to transmit data. See **Analog signal**.

Dumb terminal: A computer terminal that does not have its own processing power. See **Intelligent terminal**.

Electronic banking: The process of carrying on banking transactions without direct contact with banking employees; one example of electronic banking is the use of an **Automatic teller machine**.

Electronic mail (E-Mail): A computer data communications system for storing and delivering messages and documents without printing or sending hard (paper) copies.

Facsimile (Fax): The use of telephone lines and scanning technology to send text and images from one location to another.

FCC: Acronym for Federal Communications Commission.

Fiber-optic cable: Thin strands of clear glass or plastic that use light instead of electricity to transmit data.

Foreign exchange (fx) service: A dedicated telephone line that permits a caller in one location to call a distant location without a long-distance charge.

Full-duplex transmission: The act of sending data in two directions simultaneously (i.e., sending and receiving at once). See **Half-duplex transmission**.

Gateway: An interconnection between two incompatible computer networks that allows information to be transmitted between the networks. See **Bridge**.

Half-duplex transmission: The act of sending data in two directions but in only one direction at a time (i.e., sending or receiving, not both at once). See **Full-duplex transmission**.

Hardwiring: Using cables to link one computer with another computer.

Image communication: Sending pictures, charts, illustrations, and other graphics between computers and similar devices.

Intelligent terminal: A computer terminal that has its own processing power. See **Dumb terminal**.

ISO: Acronym for International Standards Organization.

LEARN U AND C

each line twice SS (slowly, then faster); DS between 2-line groups; repeat selected lines

U *Right pointer* finger

C *Left middle* finger

Learn u ▼

1 j j uj uj us us us jug jug jut jut due due fur fur
2 uj uj jug jug sue sue lug lug use use lug lug dues
3 a jug; due us; the fur; use it; a fur rug; is just
DS

Learn c ▼

4 d d cd cd cod cod cog cog tic tic cot cot can cans
5 cd cd cod cod ice ice can can code code dock docks
6 a cod; a cog; the ice; she can; the dock; the code
DS

Combine u and c

7 cud cud cut cuts cur curs cue cues duck ducks clue
8 a cud; a cur; to cut; the cue; the cure; for luck;
9 use a clue; a fur coat; take the cue; cut the cake
QS

IMPROVE TECHNIQUE

1. Key the lines once as shown: SS with a DS between 2-line groups.
2. Key the lines again at a faster pace.

Technique goals

- reach *up* without moving hands away from you
- reach *down* without moving hands toward your body
- use quick-snap keystrokes

3d/1st rows
1 in cut nut ran cue can cot fun hen car urn den cog
2 Nan is cute; he is curt; turn a cog; he can use it
DS

left shift and .
3 Kae had taken a lead. Jack then cut ahead of her.
4 I said to use Kan. for Kansas and Ore. for Oregon.
DS

key words
5 and cue for jut end kit led old fit just golf coed
6 an due cut such fuss rich lack turn dock turf curl
DS

key phrases
7 an urn|is due|to cut|for us|to use|cut off|such as
8 just in|code it|turn on|cure it|as such|is in luck
DS

all keys learned
9 Nida is to get the ice; Jacki is to call for cola.
10 Ira is sure that he can go there in an hour or so.

APPENDICES

SM: Defaults; LS: SS

10A ◆ 8'

CONDITIONING PRACTICE

each line twice SS (slowly, then faster): DS between 2-line groups

```
1 a;sldkfj a;sldkfj uj cd ik rf nj ed hj tf ol gf .l
2 is cod and cut for did end off got the all oak jug
3 Hugh has just taken a lead in a race for a record.
```
QS

10B ◆ 20'

LEARN W AND RIGHT SHIFT

each line twice SS (slowly, then faster); DS between 2-line groups; repeat each line

W *Left ring* finger

Right Shift *Right little* finger

Technique hint
Shift, strike key, and release both in a quick 1-2-3 count.

Learn w

```
1 s s ws ws sow sow wow wow low low how how cow cows
2 sw sw ws ws ow ow now now row row own own tow tows
3 to sow; is how; so low; to own; too low; is to row
```
DS

Learn Right Shift key

```
4 A; A; Al Al; Cal Cal; Ali or Flo; Di and Sol left.
5 Ali lost to Ron; Cal lost to Elsa; Di lost to Del.
6 Tina has left for Tucson; Dori can find her there.
```
DS

Combine w and Right Shift

```
7 Dodi will ask if Willa went to Town Center at two.
8 Wilf left the show for which he won a Gower Award.
9 Walt will go to Rio on a golf tour with Newt Lowe.
```
QS

10C ◆ 5'

REVIEW SPACING

each line once DS

Spacing hint
Do not space after an internal period in an abbreviation.

No space   Space once

```
1 Use i.e. for that is; cs. for case; ck. for check.
2 Dr. Wong said to use wt. for weight; in. for inch.
3 R. D. Roth has used ed. for editor; Rt. for Route.
4 Wes said Ed Rowan got an Ed.D. degree last winter.
```
QS

Activity 2: FAX FORM

1. Review the fax form you created for Sun Fun Cruises.

2. Draw two thumbnail sketches of a fax form that uses the logo and information from the Sails for Rent letterhead. It is OK to import appropriate parts of the Sun Fun Cruises fax form.

3. Select one sketch to duplicate for the fax form.

4. Open a new file, name it SAILSFAX, and create the fax form according to your sketch.

5. Save and print a copy.
   Works DOS 2.0: Draw a placeholder for the Sails for Rent logo on the printout.

A SSESSMENT FOR UNIT 43

Sun Fun Cruises is hosting a gala dinner event to promote their Caribbean cruises. You are to create an announcement for the event that is similar to this sample.

1. Key the information from the sample at left in Palatino, if possible, or in the font of your choice; experiment with font size and style to duplicate the text and the layout of the sample as much as possible (remember to save as you go).

2. Use the following graphic files from *Student's Template*
   a. Ship
   b. Tvltag
   c. Clock
   d. Suitcses

3. Key "*Your Name Here!*" in Zaph Chancery, 14 point bold, if possible; or key in your choice of font, bold italic.

4. Save as file ASSESS and print.
   Works DOS 2.0: Draw a placeholder for the graphic elements on the printout.

10D ◆ 17'

IMPROVE TECHNIQUE

1. Key the lines once as shown: SS with a DS between 2-line groups.
2. Key the lines again at a faster pace.

w and right shift

1 Dr. Rowe is in Tulsa now; Dr. Cowan will see Rolf.
2 Gwinn took the gown to Golda Swit on Downs Circle.
DS

n/g

3 to go|go on|no go|an urn|dug in|and got|and a sign
4 He is to sign for the urn to go on the high chest.
DS

key words

5 if ow us or go he an it of own did oak the cut jug
6 do all and for cog odd ant fig rug low cue row end
DS

key phrases

7 we did|for a jar|she is due|cut the oak|he owns it
8 all of us|to own the|she is to go|when he has gone
DS

all keys learned

9 Jan and Chris are gone; Di and Nick get here soon.
10 Doug will work for her at the new store in Newton.

LESSON 11   B AND Y

SM: Defaults; LS: SS

Fingers curved

Fingers upright

11A ◆ 8'

CONDITIONING PRACTICE

each line twice SS (slowly, then faster); DS between 2-line groups

reach review

1 uj ws ik rf ol cd nj ed hj tf .l gf sw ju de lo fr

c/n

2 an can and cut end cue hen cog torn dock then sick

all letters learned

3 A kid had a jag of fruit on his cart in New Delhi.
QS

11B ◆ 5'

IMPROVE TECHNIQUE

1. Key each line once SS; return and start each new line quickly.
2. On line 4, see how many words you can key in 30 seconds (30").

1 Dot is to go at two.
2 He saw that it was a good law.
3 Rilla is to take the auto into the town.
4 Wilt has an old gold jug he can enter in the show.
QS

gwam 1' | 1 | 2 | 3 | 4 | 5 | 6 | 7 | 8 | 9 | 10 |

A standard word in keyboarding is 5 characters or any combination of 5 characters and spaces, as indicated by the number scale under line 4.

***gwam* = gross words a minute**

To find 1-minute (1') *gwam*:

1. Note on the scale the figure beneath the last word you keyed. That is your 1' *gwam* if you key the line partially or only once.

2. If you completed the line once and started over, add the figure determined in Step 1 to the figure 10. The resulting figure is your 1' *gwam*.

To find 30-second (30") *gwam*:

1. Find 1' *gwam* (total words keyed).
2. Multiply 1' *gwam* by 2. The resulting figure is your 30" *gwam*.

7. Use arrow keys to locate cursor at beginning of next line.
8. Select **1**, Esc, → to draw the next line.
9. Repeat Steps 7 and 8 to draw the desired number of lines (to change line length at the *Repeat Value* prompt, key the new value).
10. Save as file FAXFORM; print.

196-197E ◆

IMPORT TEXT

Follow the steps at the right to complete the fax form.

Works DOS: Does not apply.

1. Open FAXFORM, if necessary, and import the letterhead graphics from file LTRHD.
2. Modify and move the letterhead graphics according to the sketch.
3. Print preview and adjust as needed.
4. Save and print.

OPTIONAL INTEGRATED ACTIVITY

WordPerfect and **Works MAC** only.

Load and print the word processing file OPTINT5 from *Student's Template*. Information for completing the Optional Integrated Activity is provided there.

PREPARE FOR ASSESSMENT

Activity 1: LETTERHEAD

SAILS FOR RENT

P.O. Box 1-230A
Honolulu, HI 96810-1230
(555) 166-1234
FAX (555) 166-1235

Danielle Austin at Sails for Rent furnished a sample of the firm's existing letterhead and asked you to design a new letterhead and a fax form. You are to use the company's logo of a sailboat along with the Sails for Rent name, address, and telephone and fax numbers. You may add lines, boxes, or other suitable graphics. Don't overdo the graphic elements, however.

1. Review the printout of the existing letterhead (shown at left).
2. Draw two thumbnail sketches for the new letterhead.
3. Select one sketch for the letterhead.
4. Open a new word processing file.
   Works DOS 2.0: Key the letterhead text.
   Other software: Import graphic SAILS (*Student's Template*), and create the letterhead according to your sketch.
5. Save as file SAILSLTR and print.
   Works DOS 2.0: Draw a placeholder for the Sails for Rent logo on the printout.

11C ◆ 20'

LEARN B AND Y

each line twice SS (slowly, then faster); DS between 2-line groups; practice selected lines again

b *Left pointer* finger

y *Right pointer* finger

Learn b ▼

1 f f bf bf fib fib rob rob but but big big fib fibs
2 bf bf rob rob lob lob orb orb bid bid bud bud ribs
3 a rib; to fib; rub it; an orb; or rob; but she bid
DS

Learn y ▼

4 j j yj yj jay jay lay lay hay hay day day say says
5 yj yj jay jay eye eye dye dye yes yes yet yet jays
6 a jay; to say; an eye; he says; dye it; has an eye
DS

Combine b and y

7 by by buy buy boy boy bye bye byte byte buoy buoys
8 by it; to buy; by you; a byte; the buoy; by and by
9 Jaye went by bus to the store to buy the big buoy.
QS

11D ◆ 17'

IMPROVE TECHNIQUE

1. Key the lines once as shown: SS with a DS between 2-line groups.
2. Key the lines again at a faster pace.

Technique goals
- reach *up* without moving hands away from you
- reach *down* without moving hands toward your body
- use quick-snap keystrokes

reach review
1 a;sldkfj bf ol ed yj ws ik rf hj cd nj tf .l gf uj
2 a kit low for jut led sow fob ask sun cud jet grow
DS

3d/1st rows
3 no in bow any tub yen cut sub coy ran bin cow deck
4 Cody wants to buy this baby cub for the young boy.
DS

key words
5 by and for the got all did but cut now say jut ask
6 work just such hand this goal boys held furl eight
DS

key phrases
7 to do|can go|to bow|for all|did jet|ask her|to buy
8 if she|to work|and such|the goal|for this|held the
DS

all letters learned
9 Kitty had auburn hair with big eyes of clear jade.
10 Juan left Bobby at the dog show near our ice rink.

gwam 1' | 1 | 2 | 3 | 4 | 5 | 6 | 7 | 8 | 9 | 10 |

DESIGN A FAX FORM

Complete the steps to design a fax form for Sun Fun Cruises.

1. On a separate sheet of paper, write the guide words you will use for the items listed under Guidelines for Fax Forms (p. 422).

2. Review the sample thumbnail sketches below for fax form.

3. Draw two additional thumbnail sketches on a separate sheet of paper.

4. Pick a thumbnail sketch (from your sketches or those below).

5. Open a new word processing file.

6. Select font, style, and size; then key the title, FAX TRANSMITTAL FORM, and the guide words you wrote in Step 1.

7. Draw the lines for the form following instructions for your software (bottom of page).

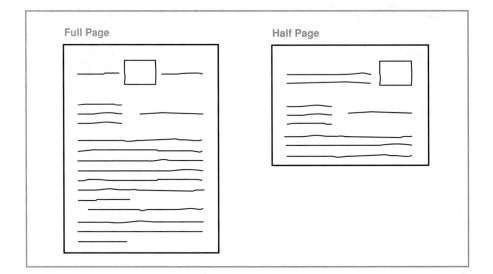

Full Page   Half Page

WORDPERFECT

1. Determine the number of characters in the line length needed (locate the cursor at the beginning of the line, note the location on the screen prompt, locate the cursor at the end of the line, again note the location on the screen prompt; the difference plus 1 is the number of characters in the line).

2. Locate the cursor at the beginning of the first line.

3. Select **1** from the Screen Line Draw Menu.

4. Esc; at the *Repeat Value* prompt, key the number of characters in the line length.

5. Press → to draw the line.

6. Select **6**—Move.

WORKS DOS

1. Key a line of underscores to the length desired.

2. Copy and place the line.

3. Copy two lines and place them; repeat by copying and placing four lines. (**Note:** It is faster to copy and place multiple lines than to place several lines one at a time.)

4. Save as FAXFORM and print.

5. Draw placeholders for the letterhead graphics on the printout.

WORKS MAC

1. Select the straight-line Draw tool.

2. Draw a line the desired length.

3. Copy and move the line you made in Step 2 if more than one line that length is needed.

4. Continue drawing or copying lines and moving them into place according to the sketch (if several lines are needed, group two or more lines and copy them; then align, group, and copy the expanded set of lines).

5. Save as FAXFORM and print.

(continued on next page)

SM: Defaults; LS: SS

Before you begin each practice session:

- Position your body directly in front of the keyboard (the b key should be at the center of your body). Sit erect, with feet on the floor for balance.
- Curve your fingers deeply and place them in an upright position over the home keys.
- Position the textbook or screen (if using *Alphabetic Keyboarding*) for easy reading (at about a 90° angle to the eyes).

Body properly positioned

Fingers properly curved

Fingers properly upright

12A ◆ 8'

CONDITIONING PRACTICE

each line twice SS (slowly, then faster); DS between 2-line groups; practice each line again

1 we ok as in be on by re no us if la do ah go C. J.
2 for us; in a jet; by the bid; cut his leg; to work
3 Fran knew it was her job to guide your gold truck.
QS

12B ◆ 12'

IMPROVE TECHNIQUE

1. Key the lines once as shown: SS with a DS between 2-line groups.
2. Key the lines again at a faster pace.

Down-and-in spacing

Out-and-down shifting

Space Bar (Space *immediately* after each word.)

1 an by win buy den sly won they than flay when clay
2 in a way|on a day|buy a hen|a fine day|if they win
DS
3 Jay can bid on the old clay urn he saw at the inn.
4 I know she is to be here soon to talk to the club.
DS

Shift keys (Shift; strike key; release both quickly.)

5 Lt. Su; Nan and Dodi; Karl and Sol; Dr. O. C. Goya
6 Kara and Rod are in Italy; Jane and Bo go in June.
DS
7 Sig and Bodie went to the lake with Cory and Lana.
8 Aida Rios and Jana Hardy work for us in Los Gatos.
QS

Works DOS:

1. Open a new file.

2. Select a font in italic and select a font size; then center the following address and telephone number on one line:

   1122 Cruise Way   Miami, FL 33133-1122   1-800-155-1122

3. Save as LTRHD and print.

196-197C ◆

FAX FORMS

Additional information appears in the Glossary, (pp. 371 and 372) and in Appendix A—Telecommunications Terms (pp. 427-428).

The use of facsimile (fax), an image of printed material that is transmitted over the telephone system, has increased rapidly. A variety of fax equipment is available. Faxes can be sent and received by computers, by combination fax/telephone machines, and by fax-only machines.

Many companies and individuals make fax transmissions regularly. A cover sheet is often used to identify details of the fax, such as the sender and the receiver. Forms with spaces to fill in the details (fax forms) are used for cover sheets. Copies are made of form copy masters (original printout). Specific information is entered on a copy each time a fax is sent. A fax form also can be saved as a computer file. To use, you open a copy of the file, key directly into the form and save as a new file, maintaining the original file for later use. The completed form, containing the message, could then be sent by telecommunications using a fax modem or printed and sent by a fax machine.

Guidelines for Fax Forms

Fax forms should include a place for:

- Sender's name, complete address, phone, fax phone.
- Receiver's name, fax phone.
- Date of fax.
- Subject of fax.
- Total pages, with indication whether the page count includes fax form or not.
- What to do if receiver does not receive the total number of pages.
- Space to write comments or messages.

12C ◆ 15'
IMPROVE SKILL

1. Key the lines once as shown: SS with a DS between 2-line groups.
2. Key the lines again at a faster pace.

Technique goals
- curved, upright fingers
- quiet hands and arms
- quick spacing—no pause between words
- finger-reach action to shift keys

 Finger-action keystrokes

 Down-and-in thumb motion

Think, say, and *key* words and phrases.

1 by dig row off but and jet oak the cub all got rid
2 ah she own dug irk buy cog jak for yet ask led urn
                                                      DS
3 of us|if the|all of|and do|cut it|he got|to do the
4 is to be|as it is|if we do|in all the|if we own it
                                                      DS

Strike keys at a brisk, steady pace (all letters learned).

5 Judy had gone for that big ice show at Lake Tahoe.
6 Jack said that all of you will find the right job.
                                                      DS
7 Cindy has just left for work at the big ski lodge.
8 Rudy can take a good job at the lake if he wishes.
                                                      QS

gwam 1' | 1 | 2 | 3 | 4 | 5 | 6 | 7 | 8 | 9 | 10 |

12D ◆ 15'
CHECK SKILL

1. Key each line once DS (return twice at the end of the line).
2. Take 20" writings; find *gwam.*

Goal: At least 15 *gwam*

20"	gwam									
	3	6	9	12	15	18	21	24	27	30

1 Al is to do it.
2 Di has gone to work.
3 Jan is to go to the sale.
4 Rog is to row us to your dock.
5 Harl has an old kayak and two oars.
6 She told us to set a goal and go for it.
7 It is our job to see just how high we can go.
8 Jake will go to the city to work on the big signs.
                                                      QS

E NRICHMENT ACTIVITY   REACH REVIEW

1. Key each line twice SS (slowly, then faster); DS between 2-line groups.
2. Rekey the drill for better control of reaches.

1 June had left for the club just as the news ended.
2 Bro led a task force whose goal was to lower cost.
3 Lyn knew the surf was too rough for kids to enjoy.
4 Ceil hikes each day on the side roads near school.

gwam 1' | 1 | 2 | 3 | 4 | 5 | 6 | 7 | 8 | 9 | 10 |

APPLICATION ACTIVITY

Read the information at the right, study the illustrations of the graphic elements and the letterhead, and complete the steps listed to create letterhead for the Sun Fun Cruises organization.

When you design letterhead with software, there are two ways the letterhead can be used. You can print the file for a copy master to reproduce copies of the letterhead, or you can key directly in the file. If you print the file for a copy master, copies of the letterhead could be made using a choice of colored ink.

When you key directly in a file, the printout includes both the letterhead and the text. If you key directly in a letterhead file, it is important to maintain the original file of the blank letterhead. You can maintain the original file either by copying it to a new name or saving the file with letter under a new name.

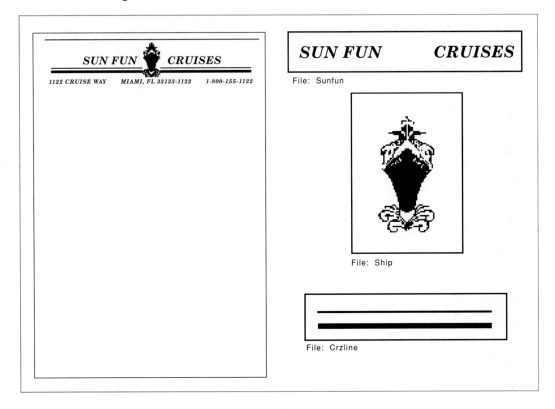

File: Sunfun

File: Ship

File: Crzline

WordPerfect and Works MAC
Works DOS: Go to top of p. 422.

1. Open a new file.

2. Import file SUNFUN from *Student's Template* and move it to the top of the page.

3. Import file SHIP from *Student's Template* and move it into place according to the illustration; if possible, group the graphic elements as you go.

4. Import the file CRZLINE and copy it.

5. Move the CRZLINE pieces into place according to the illustration.

6. Select a font in italic and select a font size; then center the following address and telephone number on one line:

   1122 Cruise Way   Miami, FL 33133-1122   1-800-155-1122

7. Move the address/phone information into place according to the illustration and adjust the space to align it as shown.

8. Preview and adjust if necessary.

9. Save as LTRHD and print.

SM: Defaults; LS: SS

13A ◆ 8'

CONDITIONING PRACTICE

each line twice SS (slowly, then faster); DS between 2-line groups

reach review 1 bf ol rf yj ed nj ws ik tf hj cd uj gf by us if ow

b/y 2 by bye boy buy yes fib dye bit yet but try bet you

all letters learned 3 Robby can win the gold if he just keys a new high.

DS

13B ◆ 20'

LEARN M AND X

each line twice SS (slowly, then faster); DS between 2-line groups; practice selected lines again

m *Right pointer* finger

X *Left ring* finger

Learn m

1 j j mj mj am am am me me ma ma jam jam ham ham yam

2 mj mj me me me may may yam yam dam dam men men jam

3 am to; if me; a man; a yam; a ham; he may; the hem

DS

Learn x

4 s s xs xs ox ox ax ax six six fix fix fox fox axis

5 xs xs sx sx ox ox six six nix nix fix fix lax flax

6 a fox; an ox; fix it; by six; is lax; to fix an ax

DS

Combine m and x

7 me ox am ax ma jam six ham mix fox men lax hem lox

8 to fix; am lax; mix it; may fix; six men; hex them

9 Mala can mix a ham salad for six; Max can fix tea.

QS

13C ◆ 5'

REVIEW SPACING WITH PUNCTUATION

each line once DS

▽ Do not space after an internal period in an abbreviation.

1 Mrs. Dixon may take her Ed.D. exam early in March.

2 Lex may send a box c.o.d. to Ms. Fox in St. Croix.

3 J. D. and Max will go by boat to St. Louis in May.

4 Owen keyed ect. for etc. and lost the match to me.

QS

PREPARE COPY MASTER

Follow the steps to prepare a copy master for the note-paper, using the disk graphic, in landscape 2-up.

Sample Thumbnail Sketches

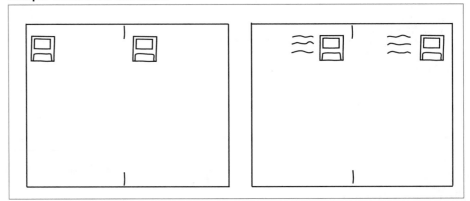

1. Review the sample thumbnail sketches above.

2. Draw two additional thumbnail sketches.

3. Pick one thumbnail sketch from your sketches or the text to design with the software.
   Works DOS 2.0: Pick a sketch to reproduce; write "my choice" beside it. Do not attempt the remaining steps.

4. Copy file NOTEPAPER to NOTE2 or open file NOTEPAPER and save as NOTE2.

5. With file NOTE2 open, change the page orientation to landscape.

6. Delete the horizontal guide marks.

7. Adjust the right margin.

8. Move the graphic units to desired locations.

9. Key vertical guide marks at the top and bottom center of the page by using the I key.

10. Print Preview and adjust as necessary.

11. Save and print.

LESSONS 196-197   PUBLISH LETTERHEAD AND FAX FORM

**196-197A ◆
CONDITIONING
PRACTICE**

each line twice SS

alphabet	1	Suzann gave the four new job descriptions to me to re-examine quickly.
figures	2	If you use F5-6091 rather than F25-7384, you can access the data file.
fig/sym	3	Kennedy & Nelson's last order (#2987), dated July 15, was for $31,640.
speed	4	Their problems with the forms may end when they go to see the auditor.

gwam 1' | 1 | 2 | 3 | 4 | 5 | 6 | 7 | 8 | 9 | 10 | 11 | 12 | 13 | 14 |

IMPROVE TECHNIQUE

1. Key the lines once as shown: SS with a DS between 2-line groups.
2. Key the lines again at a faster pace.

Technique goals

- reach *up* without moving hands away from you
- reach *down* without moving hands toward your body
- quiet hands and arms

3d/1st rows	1	by am end fix men box hem but six now cut gem ribs
	2	me ox buy den cub ran own form went oxen fine club
		DS
space bar	3	an of me do am if us or is by go ma so ah ox it ow
	4	by man buy fan jam can any tan may rob ham fun guy
		DS
key words	5	if us me do an sow the cut big jam rub oak lax boy
	6	curl work form born name flex just done many right
		DS
key phrases	7	or jam|if she|for me|is big|an end|or buy|is to be
	8	to fix|and cut|for work|and such|big firm|the call
		DS
all keys learned	9	Jacki is now at the gym; Lex is due there by four.
	10	Joni saw that she could fix my old bike for Gilda.

LESSON 14   P AND V

SM: Defaults; LS: SS

CONDITIONING PRACTICE

each line twice SS (slowly, then faster); DS between 2-line groups; if time permits, practice each line again

all letters learned

one hand	1	in we no ax my be on ad on re hi at ho cad him bet
phrases	2	is just|of work|to sign|of lace|to flex|got a form
all letters learned	3	Jo Buck won a gold medal for her sixth show entry.
		QS

IMPROVE RETURN TECHNIQUE

Key each 2-line sentence once as "Return" is called. SS; DS between sentences.

Goal: Reach end of each line just as "Return" is called.

Keep eyes on copy as you shift and as you return.

		gwam 30"|20"
1	Marj is to choose a high goal	12|18
2	and to do her best to make it.	12|18
	DS	
3	Gig said he had to key from a book	14|21
4	for a test he took for his new job.	14|21
	DS	
5	Alex knows it is good to hold your goal	16|24
6	in mind as you key each line of a drill.	16|24
	DS	
7	Nan can do well many of the tasks she tries;	18|27
8	she sets new goals and makes them one by one.	18|27
	QS	

195C ◆

DESIGN NOTE-PAPER 2-UP

1. Choose a thumbnail sketch from those shown on p. 418 or your sketches.
   Works DOS 2.0: Pick a sketch to reproduce; write "my choice" beside it. Do not attempt the remaining steps.

2. Open a new file; name it NOTEPAPER.

3. Import file DISK from the *Student's Template*.

4. Size the graphic and move it into place according to the thumbnail sketch.

5. Select a font and type size, then key the following:

   ...from the disk of

6. Move this text into place.
   Works DOS 3.0: Cannot overlay text on graphics; locate text close to graphic.

7. Select a font and type size, then key your name.

8. Move this text into place.

9. Insert a copy about halfway down on the page.

10. Save as file NOTEPAPER.

195D ◆

ADD GUIDE MARKS

Read the information at the right, then follow the steps to add guide marks for cutting copies of the notepaper apart.

Works DOS 2.0: Does not apply.

When copy masters are made for projects, guide marks are inserted to show where to cut. Most software designed for desktop publishing has grids and other tools to assist in aligning graphic elements and placing guide marks. Similar results can be produced with some integrated programs and high-level word processing programs.

1. Open file NOTEPAPER; locate the cursor at the top of the page.

2. Set horizontal guide marks.
   a. Locate the cursor on the line that is halfway down the page, then key a hyphen.
   b. Tab across to the right side of the page and key another hyphen.

3. Save.

195E ◆

ALIGN ELEMENTS

Follow the steps at the right to align the elements of the copy master.
Works DOS 2.0: Does not apply.

1. Open file NOTEPAPER; Print Preview to check placement of the graphic and text elements and the guide marks.

2. Adjust as necessary.

3. Preview and adjust again as needed for correct alignment.

4. Save and print.

LEARN P AND V

each line twice SS (slowly, then faster); DS between 2-line groups; practice selected lines again

p *Right little* finger

V *Left pointer* finger

Learn p ▼

1 ; ; p; p; pa pa up up apt apt pen pen lap lap kept
2 p; p; pa pa pa pan pan nap nap paw paw gap gap rap
3 a pen; a cap; apt to pay; pick it up; plan to keep
                                                         DS

Learn v ▼

4 f f vf vf via via vie vie have have five five live
5 vf vf vie vie vie van van view view dive dive jive
6 go via; vie for; has vim; a view; to live; or have
                                                         DS

Combine p and v

7 up cup vie pen van cap vim rap have keep live plan
8 to vie; give up; pave it; very apt; vie for a cup;
9 Vic has a plan to have the van pick us up at five.
                                                         QS

IMPROVE TECHNIQUE

1. Key the lines once as shown: SS with a DS between 2-line groups.
2. Key the lines again at a faster pace.

Technique goals
- reach *up* without moving hands away from you
- reach *down* without moving hands toward your body
- use quick-snap keystrokes
- keep action in fingers

reach review
1 vf p; xs mj ed yj ws nj rf ik tf ol cd hj gf uj bf
2 if lap jag own may she for but van cub sod six oak
                                                         DS

3d/1st rows
3 by vie pen vim cup six but now man nor ton may pan
4 by six but now may cut sent me fine gems five reps
                                                         DS

key words
5 with kept turn corn duty curl just have worn plans
6 name burn form when jury glad vote exit came eight
                                                         DS

key phrases
7 if they|he kept|with us|of land|burn it|to name it
8 to plan|so sure|is glad|an exit|so much|to view it
                                                         DS

all letters learned
9 Kevin does a top job on your flax farm with Craig.
10 Dixon flew blue jets eight times over a city park.

195A ◆
CONDITIONING PRACTICE
each line twice SS

alphabet 1 Biggi excluded a very quick jaunt to the new zoo from my travel plans.

figures 2 You can find answers to the 150-point text on pages 8, 32, 46, and 79.

fig/sym 3 Runner #3019 was first (49 min.) and runner #687 was second (52 min.).

speed 4 The rifleman saw my hand signal to go right at the fork by the shanty.

gwam 1' | 1 | 2 | 3 | 4 | 5 | 6 | 7 | 8 | 9 | 10 | 11 | 12 | 13 | 14 |

195B ◆
DRAW THUMB-NAIL SKETCHES

Review the information at the right, then follow the steps to draw thumbnail sketches.

Thumbnail sketches are small drawings that show the approximate placement for blocks of text and graphics of a publication. Drafting thumbnail sketches for a publication lets you review ways to produce the document more quickly than if you developed and printed sample layouts with the software. You can produce three or four thumbnail sketches very quickly, and then select one to use as a guide for reproducing with the software.

Sample Thumbnail Sketches for Notepaper

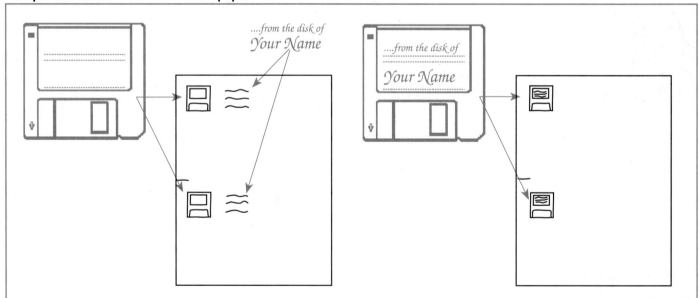

1. Review the sample thumbnail sketches for personalized notepaper. These sketches are drawn two per page (called 2-up). The sketches are placed so the margins will be equal for each copy when they are cut apart. (Guide marks for cutting sketches apart are shown in the sample above.)

2. Draw two different thumbnail sketches on a sheet of paper.

LESSON 15   Q AND , (COMMA)

SM: Defaults; LS: SS

15A ♦ 8'
CONDITIONING PRACTICE

each line twice SS (slowly, then faster); DS between 2-line groups; practice selected lines again

all letters learned 1 do fix all cut via own buy for the jam cop ask dig

p/v 2 a map; a van; apt to; vie for; her plan; have five

all letters learned 3 Beth will pack sixty pints of guava jam for David.

QS

15B ♦ 20'
LEARN Q AND , (COMMA)

each line twice SS (slowly, then faster); DS between 2-line groups; practice each line again

q *Left little* finger

, *Right middle* finger

Space once after , used as punctuation.

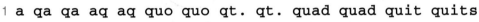

Learn q ▼

1 a qa qa aq aq quo quo qt. qt. quad quad quit quits

2 qa quo quo qt. qt. quay quay aqua aqua quite quite

3 a qt.; pro quo; a quad; to quit; the quay; a squad

DS

Learn , (comma) ▼

4 k k ,k ,k kit, kit; Rick, Ike, or I will go, also.

5 a ski, a ski; a kit, a kit; a kite, a kite; a bike

6 Ike, I see, is here; Pam, I am told, will be late.

DS

Combine q and ,

7 Enter the words quo, quote, quit, quite, and aqua.

8 I have quit the squad, Quen; Raquel has quit, too.

9 Marquis, Quent, and Quig were quite quick to quit.

QS

15C ♦ 5'
REVIEW SPACING WITH PUNCTUATION

each line once DS
▽ Space once after comma used as punctuation.

▽   ▽

1 Aqua means water, Quen; also, it is a unique blue.

2 Quince, enter qt. for quart; also, sq. for square.

3 Ship the desk c.o.d. to Dr. Quig at La Quinta Inn.

4 Q. J. took squid and squash; Monique, roast quail.

QS

SIZE GRAPHICS

Read the information at the right; then follow the instructions for your software to size graphics.

Graphics can be made larger or smaller using the same procedures as for bar and pie charts. Thus you can control the size of the graphic to fit the space available.

WORDPERFECT

1. Open file RACE, if necessary.
2. Import file CYCLIST.PCX from *Student's Template* using default graphic box size.
3. To resize the graphic before or after you import it:
   a. Select **1**—Figure, **2**—Edit, confirm Figure number 1.
   b. Select **7**—Size.
   c. Select **3**—Set Both.
   d. Key width = **5.5**; height = **4.0**. (Resize graphics either before or after you import them.)
4. Import and size file CALENDAR with width = 1.13"; height = 1.00".
5. Save.
6. Print View, adjust placement of graphics, if necessary.

WORKS DOS 2.0

Does not apply.

WORKS DOS 3.0

1. Open file RACE, if necessary.
2. Import file CYCLIST from *Student's Template*.
3. In Picture Format Menu, change the size to Height: 4.0"; Width: 5.5".
4. Import and size file CALENDAR to Height: 1.00"; Width: 1.13".
5. Save.

WORKS MAC

1. Open file RACE, if necessary.
2. Print Preview to check alignment of white box over filled box, and adjust location if necessary.
   a. Locate the Draw arrow tool on one of the handles.
   b. ~ and drag to size the box by stretching or shrinking it.
3. Check Print Preview frequently to locate and size the white box so that about equal amounts of the filled box form a border.
4. Import file CYCLIST from *Student's Template* and size graphic proportionally (press Shift while sizing) to approximately 5.5" wide and 4.0" high, then move into place.
5. Import file CALENDAR, size to approximately 1.125" wide and 1.0" high, and move into place.
6. Save.

ADD TEXT AND GRAPHIC

Follow the steps at the right to add text to the flier.

1. Open file RACE.
   Works DOS 2.0: Open a new word processing document and save as file RACE.

2. Select a font of your choice in bold (24 point size or very large size), then key the title: **Spring Break 75 Mile Race.** Using the same font in bold (18 point or a smaller size), key the subtitle: **Solvang to San Luis Obispo.**

3. Using the same font in normal (14 point type or a small size), key the flier information:

   Depart from Santa Ynez Mission.
   First rider off at 8 a.m.
   Draw lots for starting time.
   Flat to rolling hills, good blacktop roads.

4. Using 18 point bold Zaph Chancery if possible, or the font used in Step 2 in italic, key the sponsor information: **Sponsored by L'Polli Riders of the Universe.**

5. Save.

6. Print Preview, adjust if necessary.

7. Save and print.
   Works DOS 2.0: On the printout, draw placeholders for the border and graphic elements.
   Works DOS 3.0: Note that border does not print by graphics; on printout, draw lines connecting the border lines.

IMPROVE TECHNIQUE

1. Key the lines once as shown: SS with a DS between 2-line groups.
2. Key the lines again at a faster pace.

Technique goals
- reach *up* without moving hands away from you
- reach *down* without moving hands toward your body
- use quick-snap keystrokes

reach review
1 `qa .l ws ,k ed nj rf mj tf p; xs ol cd ik vf hj bf`
2 `yj gf hj quo vie pay cut now buy got mix vow forms`
DS

3d/1st rows
3 `six may sun coy cue mud jar win via pick turn bike`
4 `to go|to win|for me|a peck|a quay|by then|the vote`
DS

key words
5 `pa rub sit man for own fix jam via cod oak the got`
6 `by quo sub lay apt mix irk pay when rope give just`
DS

key phrases
7 `an ox|of all|is to go|if he is|it is due|to pay us`
8 `if we pay|is of age|up to you|so we own|she saw me`
DS

all letters learned
9 `Jevon will fix my pool deck if the big rain quits.`
10 `Verna did fly quick jets to map the six big towns.`

LESSON 16   REVIEW

SM: Defaults; LS: SS

Fingers properly curved

Fingers properly aligned

CONDITIONING PRACTICE

each line twice SS (slowly, then faster); DS between 2-line groups; practice each line again

review 1 `Virgil plans to find that mosque by six with Jack.`
shift keys 2 `Pam, Van, and McQuin should be in New Gate by two.`
easy 3 `Vi is to aid the girl with the sign work at eight.`
QS

gwam 1' | 1 | 2 | 3 | 4 | 5 | 6 | 7 | 8 | 9 | 10 |

KEY BLOCK PARAGRAPHS

each paragraph (¶) once SS; DS between ¶s; then key the ¶s again at a faster pace

Do not return at end of each line. The computer will return automatically with what is called a "soft return." You must, however, strike Return/Enter twice ("hard returns") at the end of ¶1 to leave a DS between ¶s.

gwam 1'

Paragraph 1

`When you strike the return or enter key at the end` 10
`of a line to space down and start a new line, this` 20
`process is called a hard return.` 26
DS

Paragraph 2

`If a machine returns at line ends for you, what is` 10
`known as a soft return or wordwrap is in use. You` 20
`must use a hard return, though, between paragraphs.` 30
QS

gwam 1' | 1 | 2 | 3 | 4 | 5 | 6 | 7 | 8 | 9 | 10 |

b. Select **2**—Line Draw.

c. Select **1**— | to draw a single straight line.

d. Use→ to draw across the top margin of page 1, ↓ to draw down right side margin of page 1, ← to draw across bottom margin of page 1, and ↑ to draw up left side margin of page 1; to erase at any time, select **5**—Erase, use the arrow key to erase; select—**1** to continue drawing.

3. Locate the cursor at top left corner of outline.

4. Fill with line pattern.

   a. Select Line Draw from Screen Menu if necessary.

   b. Select—Change, then select **3** (a wide pattern fill).

   c. Draw across top of page and down right side (a small amount of blank space is between the wide pattern and the line).

   d. Because the vertical pattern is not as wide as the horizontal pattern, draw three patterns on the sides as follows: on the bottom right side: ← one space, then ↑ to the top, ← one space, then ↓ ; use similar process for left side.

5. Locate the cursor in top left corner of wide pattern.

6. Draw an outline inside the wide pattern.

   a. Select Line Draw from Screen Menu if necessary.

   b. Select **1**— | .

   c. Draw outline inside the wide pattern.

7. Exit to the text screen.

8. Print View, adjust if necessary.

9. Save as file RACE.

2. Select Outline from the Borders Menu under Format and choose a Line style.

3. View and save as file RACE.

(note that the pattern you selected is displayed in the Draw Tools Fill box).

6. Place the draw tool cross at the top left corner of the screen, and drag to draw a box along the margins of the page.

7. Select the rectangle draw tool again, and select white-fill from the Fill Pattern Menu.

8. Place the draw tool cross inside the patterned box near the top left corner.

9. Draw a box that stretches close to the bottom right corner and displays nearly equal areas of the filled box and border.

10. Save as file RACE.

11. Explore overlaying graphics:

    a. Select the white box; then from Format, select Send to Back to send the white box behind the pattern-filled box (notice only the selected outline shows).

    b. From Format, select Bring to Front to bring the white box onto the pattern-filled box.

    c. Select the pattern-filled box; then bring the pattern-filled box to the front.

    d. From the Draw tool box, select the rectangle draw tool; then from the Fill Pattern Menu, select no-fill.

    e. Locate the draw tool on the pattern-filled box and draw a small box (pattern shows inside this box).

    f. Delete the box you made in Step e.

    g. Select and send the pattern-filled box to the back (the white box should be visible).

    h. Draw a small box on the white box with a different Fill Pattern.

    i. Select the original white box and send it to the back (the small pattern-filled box is on the large pattern-filled box).

    j. Select the small box and delete it.

    k. Send the pattern-filled box to the back.

    l. Do NOT resave.

16C ◆ 12'

BUILD SKILL: SPACE BAR/SHIFT KEYS

each line twice SS; DS between 4-line groups

Goals

- to reduce the pause between words
- to reduce the time taken to shift/strike key/release when making capital letters

Down-and-in spacing

Out-and-down shifting

Space Bar (Space immediately after each word.)

1 so an if us am by or ox he own jay pen yam own may
2 she is in|am to pay|if he may|by the man|in a firm
DS

3 I am to keep the pens in a cup by a tan mail tray.
4 Fran may try to fix an old toy for the little boy.
DS

Shift keys (Shift; strike key; release both quickly.)

5 J. V., Dr. or Mrs., Ph.D. or Ed.D., Fourth of July
6 Mrs. Maria Fuente; Dr. Mark V. Quin; Mr. T. C. Ott
DS

7 B. J. Marx will go to St. Croix in March with Lex.
8 Mae has a Ph.D. from Miami; Dex will get his Ed.D.
QS

16D ◆ 10'

IMPROVE SKILL

each line twice SS (slowly, then faster); DS between 4-line groups

Technique goals

- quick-snap keystrokes
- quick joining of letters to form words
- quick joining of words to form phrases

Think, say, and *key* words and phrases.

1 ox jam for oak for pay got own the lap via sob cut
2 make than with them such they when both then their
DS

3 to sit|an elf|by six|an oak|did go|for air|the jam
4 to vie|he owns|pay them|cut both|the quay|for they
DS

Strike keys at a brisk, steady pace.

all letters learned
5 I may have six quick jobs to get done for low pay.
6 Vicky packed the box with quail and jam for Signe.
DS

all letters learned
7 Max can plan to bike for just five days with Quig.
8 Jim was quick to get the next top value for Debby.
QS

16E ◆ 10'

CHECK SKILL

Take a 30" writing on each line; find *gwam*.
Goal: At least 18 *gwam*

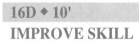

30" *gwam*

	2	4	6	8	10	12	14	16	18	20

1 I am to fix the sign for them.
2 Jaye held the key to the blue auto.
3 Todd is to go to the city dock for fish.
4 Vi paid the girl to make a big bowl of salad.
5 Kal may keep the urn he just won at the quay show.

	2	4	6	8	10	12	14	16	18	20

If you finish a line before time is called and start over, your *gwam* is the figure at the end of the line PLUS the figure above or below the point at which you stopped.

Spring Break 75 Mile Race

Solvang to San Luis Obispo

Depart from Santa Ynez Mission.
First rider off at 8 a.m.
Draw lots for starting time.
Flat to rolling hills, good blacktop roads.

Sponsored by L'Polli Riders of the Universe

IMPROVE TECHNIQUE

1. Key the lines once; SS with a DS between 2-line groups.
2. Key the lines again at a faster pace.

Technique goals
- curved, upright fingers
- quiet hands and arms
- steady keystroking pace

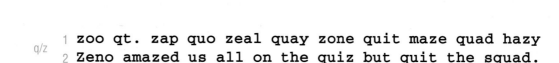

q/z

1 zoo qt. zap quo zeal quay zone quit maze quad hazy
2 Zeno amazed us all on the quiz but quit the squad.

p/x

3 apt six rip fix pens flex open flax drop next harp
4 Lex is apt to fix apple pie for the next six days.

v/m

5 vim mam van dim have move vamp more dive time five
6 Riva drove them to the mall in my vivid lemon van.

easy sentences

7 Glen is to aid me with the work at the dog kennel.
8 Dodi is to go with the men to audit the six firms.

alphabet

9 Nigel saw a quick red fox jump over the lazy cubs.
10 Jacky can now give six big tips from the old quiz.

LESSON 18   CAPS LOCK AND ? (QUESTION MARK)

SM: Defaults; LS: SS

18A ◆ 8'

CONDITIONING PRACTICE

each line twice SS; then a 1' writing on line 3; find *gwam*: total words keyed

alphabet 1 Lovak won the squad prize cup for sixty big jumps.
z/: 2 To: Ms. Mazie Pelzer; From: Dr. Eliza J. Piazzo.
easy 3 He is to go with me to the dock to do work for us.

gwam 1' | 1 | 2 | 3 | 4 | 5 | 6 | 7 | 8 | 9 | 10 |

18B ◆ 7'

KEY BLOCK PARAGRAPHS

Key each paragraph (¶) once; DS between ¶s; then key the ¶s again at a faster pace. Take a 1' writing on each ¶; find *gwam*.

To find 1-minute (1') *gwam*:

1. Note the figure at the end of your last complete line.
2. Note from the scale under the ¶s the figure below where you stopped in a partial line.
3. Add the two figures; the resulting number is your *gwam*.

Paragraph 1

gwam 1'

The space bar is a vital tool, for every fifth or   10
sixth stroke is a space when you key. If you use   20
it with good form, it will aid you to build speed.   30

Paragraph 2

Just keep the thumb low over the space bar. Move   10
the thumb down and in quickly toward your palm to   20
get the prized stroke you need to build top skill.   30

gwam 1' | 1 | 2 | 3 | 4 | 5 | 6 | 7 | 8 | 9 | 10 |

194A ◆
CONDITIONING PRACTICE
each line twice SS

alphabet 1 Pamela will acquire three dozen red vinyl jackets for the big exhibit.

figures 2 My teacher plans to have 75 test items from pages 289-306 for Unit 41.

fig/sym 3 Mai-Ling practiced the symbols $, ", %, &, and # in class on 10/25/91.

speed 4 The rich widow is to endow the sorority chapel on a visit to the city.

gwam 1' | 1 | 2 | 3 | 4 | 5 | 6 | 7 | 8 | 9 | 10 | 11 | 12 | 13 | 14 |

194B ◆
DESIGN GUIDELINES

Study the desktop publishing design guidelines listed at the right. In the remaining lessons, you will have opportunities to apply these guidelines to create professional-looking publications.

• Limit the use of typefaces to no more than two per publication. The use of too many typefaces interferes with readability.

• Serif typefaces are easier to read in smaller type sizes than sans-serif typefaces. The finishing strokes at the top and bottom (the "feet" on the letters) help to guide the eye across the line.

• Sans-serif typefaces (without finishing strokes) are more appropriate for larger type sizes than for small typefaces.

• Limit the use of ALL CAPS text, which is difficult to read.

• Limit the use of bold. Bold is best used for larger type sizes.

• Limit the use of italics. It is more difficult to read than normal type.

• Voids have value; that is, blank space on a page increases readability. Therefore, do not fill all the available space!

• Shading makes text more difficult to read. Don't do it!

• Use two or more columns rather than long lines of text.

• Use line length to enhance readability. Reading is faster when lines of text are short enough to be read in a single glance, without moving the eyes along the line of text. Lines should be long enough, however, to contain at least four words in whatever size type is used. Line length can be longer for large type than for small type.

• Limit the use of the underscore in desktop publishing; use bold rather than underscore. Underscoring makes text difficult to read.

194C ◆
LAYERING GRAPHIC ELEMENTS

Layering is stacking two or more graphic elements to create a desired illustration. The sequence in which the elements are layered is important. The sequence is arranged by selecting an element, and then sending it to the back or bringing it to the front of other elements.

Shapes created with draw tools, such as rectangles or circles, can be filled with a choice of patterns. You can select the fill pattern before you draw the shape; or you can change to a different fill pattern after the shape has been drawn. In addition to patterns, you can select solid fills. One solid fill is white, similar to a sheet of paper. When you bring a white shape to the front of other graphics, the other graphics are no longer visible. Another selection is clear or no-fill. Using clear or no-fill is like filling with glass or clear plastic. When you bring a clear shape to the front of other graphics, the other graphics are visible through the clear shape.

LEARN CAPS LOCK AND ?

each line twice SS (slowly, then faster); DS between 2-line groups; practice each line again

Caps Lock *Left little* finger

? Left shift; then *right little* finger

Depress Caps Lock to key a series of capital letters.

To release the Lock for lowercase letters, depress the Lock again.

Learn Caps Lock

1 Hal read PENTAGON and ADVISE AND CONSENT by Drury.
2 Oki joined FBLA when her sister joined PBL at OSU.
3 Zoe now belongs to AMS and DPE as well as to NBEA.

Space twice

Learn ? (question mark)

4 ; ; ?; ?; Who? What? When? Where? Why? Is it?
5 Who is it? Is it she? Did he go? Was she there?
6 Is it up to me? When is it? Did he key the line?

IMPROVE TECHNIQUE

1. Key the lines once; SS with a DS between 2-line groups.
2. Key the lines again at a faster pace.
3. Take a 1' writing on line 11 and then on line 12; find *gwam*.

Technique goals

* keep hands and arms quiet
* use finger-action keystrokes
* use Caps Lock to make ALL CAPS

Caps Lock/?
1 Did she join OEA?   Did she also join PSI and DECA?
2 Do you know the ARMA rules?   Are they used by TVA?

z/v
3 Zahn, key these words: vim, zip, via, zoom, vote.
4 Veloz gave a zany party for Van and Roz in La Paz.

q/p
5 Paul put a quick quiz on top of the quaint podium.
6 Jacqi may pick a pink pique suit of a unique silk.

key words
7 they quiz pick code next just more bone wove flags
8 name jack flax plug quit zinc wore busy vine third

key phrases
9 to fix|it is|to pay|to aid us|or to cut|apt to own
10 is on the|if we did|to be fit|to my pay|due at six

alphabet
11 Lock may join the squad if we have six big prizes.

easy sentence
12 I am apt to go to the lake dock to sign the forms.

gwam 1' | 1 | 2 | 3 | 4 | 5 | 6 | 7 | 8 | 9 | 10 |

To find 1' *gwam*: Add 10 for each line you completed to the scale figure beneath the point at which you stopped in a partial line. The total is your 1' *gwam*.

WORKS MAC

1. Open file POSTAL if necessary, and turn on Draw.
2. Select all three elements (the envelope address, the return address, and the envelope outline) with the pointer by drawing a box around them (handles show on all three elements). Selecting may be done by using Shift~, one element at a time.
3. With Draw on, group the elements by selecting Group Picture from Format Menu or use the key command (handles show only on the envelope, the largest element, not on all three elements).

193D ◆

CHANGE/REFOR-MAT GRAPHICS

Follow the steps at the right to make changes and to reformat in both portrait and landscape orientations.

1. Open file POSTAL if necessary.
2. Move envelope graphic and text for return address and envelope address to the bottom of the page.
   Works DOS 2.0: Move the blank lines for the envelope and the text to the bottom of the document.
3. DS between the paragraph and the list of states; delete extra blank lines if appropriate.
4. Save and print.
5. Change page orientation to landscape.
6. Adjust the line length of the introductory paragraph and move the envelope graphic approximately 1" to the right of the paragraph.
7. Reformat the list to three columns, deciding on the column breaks and the space between the columns.
   Works DOS: Use page breaks for column breaks.
8. Preview, adjust if necessary; save as POSTAL2, then print.

SM: Defaults; LS: SS

19A ◆ 8'

CONDITIONING PRACTICE

each line twice SS; then a 1' writing on line 3; find *gwam*: total words keyed

Caps Lock affects only the letter keys; shifted punctuation marks require the use of one of the Shift keys.

alphabet 1 **Zosha was quick to dive into my big pool for Jinx.**

Caps Lock 2 **Vi found ZIP Codes for OR, MD, RI, NV, AL, and PA.**

easy 3 **Ian kept a pen and work forms handy for all of us.**

gwam 1' | 1 | 2 | 3 | 4 | 5 | 6 | 7 | 8 | 9 | 10 |

19B ◆ 12'

LEARN TABULATOR

The tabulator (TAB) is used to indent the first line of ¶s. Most computer programs have preset tabs (called default tabs). Usually, the first default tab is set 5 spaces (0.5") to the right of the left margin and is used to indent ¶s (see copy below).

1. Locate the TAB key on your keyboard (usually at the upper left of the alphabetic keyboard).
2. Reach up to the TAB with the left little finger, depress the key firmly, and release it quickly. The cursor will move 5 spaces (0.5") to the right.

3. As you key each of the following ¶s, depress the TAB key firmly to indent the first line of each one. If you complete all ¶s before time is called, rekey them to master TAB technique.

Note: Two hard returns are required at end of each ¶.

Tab→ **The tab key is used to indent blocks of copy such as these.**

Tab→ **It should also be used for tables to arrange data quickly and neatly into columns.**

Tab→ **Learn now to use the tab key by touch; doing so will add to your keying skill.**

Tab→ **Strike the tab key firmly and release it very quickly. Begin the line without a pause.**

Tab→ **If you hold the tab key down, the cursor will move from tab to tab across the line.**

WORDPERFECT

1. Open file POSTAL, if necessary.
2. Select Edit Graphics from the Graphics Menu; key **N** at 8—Wrap Text Around Box; exit to text screen.
3. Locate the cursor within the upper left in the graphics box (the box disappears).
   a. Change font to Helvetica normal and size to 10 point, if possible, or change to your choice of font.
   b. Key your name and address for the return address.
4. Preview in print; adjust by inserting spaces and blank lines if necessary; repeat this step as needed to place return address in the correct location.
5. Locate the cursor at the approximate place for the envelope address; then key **Attention** (*teacher's title and first and last name*) followed by your school name and address.
6. Repeat Step 4 to align the envelope address.
7. Save.

WORKS DOS 2.0

1. Open file POSTAL, if necessary.
2. Print.
   a. On the printout, sketch a rectangle placeholder for an envelope graphic at the right margin of the blank space.
   b. With the sketch as a guide, use tabs and spaces to locate the cursor in the approximate place for the return address, then key your name and address; locate the cursor for the envelope address, then key **Attention** (*teacher's title and first and last name*), followed by your school name and address.

WORKS DOS 3.0

1. Open file POSTAL, if necessary.
2. From the Picture Format Menu, change space before and space after to 0.5 li each.
3. For the return address, key your name and address at the left margin above the graphic placeholder.
4. For the envelope address, key **Attention** (*teacher's title and first and last name*), followed by your school name and address.
5. Save and print.
6. On the printout, circle the return address and draw a line to indicate where it would be inserted on the illustration; then circle the envelope address and draw a line for it.

WORKS MAC

1. Open file POSTAL, if necessary, and turn on Draw. (**Note:** Text added to Draw mode is treated as graphics by the software, although the text looks the same as ordinary text. Text added in Draw mode is subject to Draw commands. When you add text elements to graphics, key the text in Draw Mode.)
2. Select the text tool from the Draw tools and locate the I-beam near the graphic (insert blank lines if necessary).
3. ~ to draw a text box for the return address.
4. Change font to Helvetica normal and size to 10 point, if possible, or change to your choice of font.
5. Key your name and address for the return address.
6. Select the pointer from the Draw tools.
7. Move the return address into position in the upper-left corner of the envelope.
8. Select text tool and draw a text box for the envelope address.
9. Change the font as in Step 4.
10. Key **Attention** (*teacher's title and first and last name*), followed by your school name and address.
11. Use the arrow tool to move the envelope address into position on the envelope; align so the street address and ZIP Code are aligned properly with the pointers.
12. Save.

193C ♦

GROUP THE GRAPHICS

(WORKS MAC ONLY)

Read the information at the right, then complete the steps listed to group the graphic and text elements.

Grouping graphic and text elements is a common feature of desktop publishing software. This feature is used to lock elements together before moving them to a new location. Unlock or ungroup the elements before making a change to any element. You can group the elements again by repeating the procedure.

19C ♦ 10'

IMPROVE TECHNIQUE

each pair of lines twice SS; DS between 4-line groups

tabulator	1 Tab → Indent five spaces the first line of a series
	2 of lines written as a paragraph.
shift-key sentences	3 The best dancers are: Ana and Jose; Mag and Boyd.
	4 Did Ms. Paxon send us the letter from Dr. LaRonde?
Caps Lock	5 Masami saw the game on ESPN; Krista saw it on NBC.
	6 The AMS meeting is on Tuesday; the DPE, on Friday.

19D ♦ 14'

BUILD SPEED

1. Key each pair of lines once; SS with a DS between pairs.
2. Take a 1' writing on each of lines 5-8; find *gwam* on each writing.
3. Take another 1' writing on line 7 and line 8 to improve speed.

Goal: At least 21 *gwam*

Think, say, and *key* words and phrases.

1 ad my we in be on at up as no are him was you gets
2 girl quay turn rush duty down maps rich laid spend

3 an ad|to fix|an oak|to get|the zoo|via jet|in turn
4 if they|to risk|by them|the duty|and paid|she kept

Key the words at a brisk, steady pace.

5 He is to aid the girls with the work if they wish.
6 Jan may go to the city for the bid forms for them.

7 He may go to the lake by dusk to do the dock work.
8 I did all the work for the firm for the usual pay.

gwam 1' | 1 | 2 | 3 | 4 | 5 | 6 | 7 | 8 | 9 | 10 |

19E ♦ 6'

CHECK SKILL

1. Key each ¶ once SS; DS between ¶s.
2. Take a 1' writing on each ¶; find *gwam* on each writing. (1' *gwam* = figure above the last word keyed.)

Note: These easy ¶s contain all letters.

¶1   Good form means to move with speed and quiet
control. My next step will be to size up the job
and to do the work in the right way each day.

¶2   To reach my goal of top speed, I have to try
to build good form. I will try for the right key
each time, but I must do so in the right way.

193A ◆
CONDITIONING
PRACTICE

each line twice SS

alphabet 1 I will need a pretty gift box for the quartz clock I have to send Jim.

figures 2 A school received 8,032 applications for 4,675 freshmen spots in 1989.

fig/sym 3 Jan said, "Buy Model #3746 or #1098 at a 25% discount at Frey & Sons."

speed 4 Diane and my busy neighbor may dismantle the shanty on the big island.

gwam 1' | 1 | 2 | 3 | 4 | 5 | 6 | 7 | 8 | 9 | 10 | 11 | 12 | 13 | 14 |

193B ◆

ADD TEXT TO GRAPHIC

Follow the steps at the right to place a graphic in an existing document and revise the document.

1. Open file POSTAL.

2. Import file ENVELOPE from *Student's Template*; if necessary, insert blank lines for the graphic.
   Works DOS 2.0: Insert several blank lines for a placeholder; later you will draw the envelope outline on a printout.

3. Delete the paragraph that describes standard abbreviations.

4. Change the title to: POSTAL SERVICE GUIDELINES FOR ADDRESSING MAIL; use ALL CAPS and bold.

5. Save.

With most software capable of importing graphics, you can add text to a graphic. For example, you will key a return address and envelope address (USPS style) in the graphics file illustrated below.

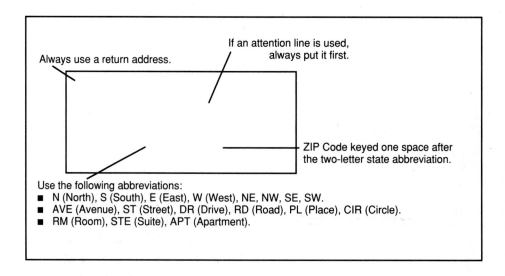

SM: Defaults; LS: SS

20A ◆ 8'

CONDITIONING PRACTICE

each line twice SS; then a 1' writing on line 3; find *gwam*

alphabet 1 Quig just fixed prize vases he won at my key club.

punctuation 2 Marcia works for HMS, Inc.; Juanita, for XYZ Corp.

easy 3 Su did vow to rid the town of the giant male duck.

gwam 1' | 1 | 2 | 3 | 4 | 5 | 6 | 7 | 8 | 9 | 10 |

20B ◆ 20'

IMPROVE TECHNIQUE

each line once SS; key each line again at a faster pace

Ask your teacher to check your keyboarding technique as you key the following lines.

Fingers curved

Fingers upright

Finger-action key-stroking

Down-and-in spacing

Reach review (Keep the fingers not used for reaching on home row.)

1 old led kit six jay oft zap cod big laws five ribs
2 pro quo|is just|my firm|was then|may grow|must try
3 Olga sews aqua and red silk to make six big kites.

Space-Bar emphasis (*Think*, *say*, and *key* the words.)

4 en am an by ham fan buy jam pay may form span corn
5 I am|a man|an elm|by any|buy ham|can plan|try them
6 I am to form a plan to buy a firm in the old town.

Shift-key emphasis (Reach *up* and reach *down* without moving the hands.)

7 Jan and I are to see Ms. Han. May Lana come, too?
8 Bob Epps lives in Rome; Vic Copa is in Rome, also.
9 Oates and Co. has a branch office in Boise, Idaho.

Easy sentences (*Think*, *say*, and *key* the words at a steady pace.)

10 Eight of the girls may go to the social with them.
11 Corla is to work with us to fix the big dock sign.
12 Keith is to pay the six men for the work they did.

gwam 1' | 1 | 2 | 3 | 4 | 5 | 6 | 7 | 8 | 9 | 10 |

20C ◆ 6'

THINK AS YOU KEY

Key each line once SS. In place of the blank line at the end of each sentence, key the word that correctly completes the adage.

1 All that glitters is not _____.
2 Do not cry over spilt _____.
3 A friend in need is a friend _____.
4 A new broom always sweeps _____.
5 A penny saved is a penny _____.

7. At the beginning of second paragraph to end of text, change the left margin to .125" (1/8" mark).

8. Change the style of the ¶ side headings to bold italic:
   Tip #1:   Tip #4:
   Tip #2:   Tip #5:
   Tip #3:

9. Change the first sentence following each Tip # to italic.

10. Move the graphic to the top left margin.
    Works DOS 2.0: Setting left margin at 2.75" leaves space for placeholder.

11. Size the graphic, if necessary.
    Works DOS 2.0: Does not apply.

12. Delete any extra blank lines at the top of the document.

13. Save as NEWS, replacing the existing file.

14. Print.

15. ***Works DOS 2.0:*** On the printout, draw a placeholder box in the blank space at the left of the title and first paragraph.

192E ♦

CHANGE TO NEW PAGE ORIENTATION

Read the information at the right, then follow the steps listed for your software to change the page orientation and to reformat text to the new orientation.

Page orientation, portrait (tall) and landscape (wide; sideways), provides flexibility to page layout. Portrait orientation is typically used for books, reports, and notebook handouts. The landscape orientation is becoming more common, however, now that software allows text to be arranged in several short, easy-to-read columns across an 11" sheet. With typewriters, lines of text are rarely displayed in columns, and wide lines of text in landscape orientation are difficult to read. When you plan page layouts for desktop publishing, consider page orientation as a design factor.

WORDPERFECT

1. With file NEWS open, locate the cursor at Home (the layout change occurs starting at the cursor).
2. From Format:
   a. Select **2**—Page.
   b. Select **7**—Paper Size/Type.
   c. Select Standard—Wide (11" x 8.5") if possible, or ask your teacher for information.
3. Exit to Format Menu and set right margin at 1.75" and other margins at 1".
4. Exit to the document.
5. Locate cursor at left margin of the second paragraph (under the graphic).
6. Reformat text to 2-column layout:
   a. right margin at 1.0".
   b. 0.25" between the columns.
7. Preview and adjust if necessary.
8. Save as NEWS2.
9. Print.

WORKS DOS

1. Open file NEWS, go to Page Setup & Margins, and change page length to 8.5" and page width to 11".
2. Locate cursor at the beginning of the second paragraph, then set right margin to 5.62" and left margin to 1".
3. Insert a page break halfway down the reformatted text.
4. Locate cursor at the beginning of the text on the second page; then set the left margin to 6.75" and the right margin to 1".
5. View the two pages and adjust if necessary.
6. Save as file NEWS2 and print.
   Version 2.0: On the printout, draw a placeholder for the graphic on the first page.

WORKS MAC

1. Open file NEWS.
2. From the File Menu, select Page Setup.
   a. Change page orientation to landscape (wide).
   b. Change all margins to 0.75"; then select OK.
3. Starting with the second paragraph (under the graphic), reformat in 2-column layout with the right margin at 9.5" and 0.25" between the columns.
4. Preview and adjust if necessary.
5. Save as NEWS2 and print.

IMPROVE SPEED

Take a 30" writing on each line; find *gwam*. Try to increase your speed.
Goal: At least 22 *gwam*

30" *gwam*

	2	4	6	8	10	12	14	16	18	20	22

1 He bid for the rich lake land.
2 Suzy may fish off the dock with us.
3 Pay the girls for all the work they did.
4 Quen is due by six and may then fix the sign.
5 Janie is to vie with six girls for the city title.
6 Duane is to go to the lake to fix the auto for the man.

	2	4	6	8	10	12	14	16	18	20	22

If you finish a line before time is called and start over, your *gwam* is the figure at the end of the line PLUS the figure above or below the point at which you stopped.

IMPROVE SPEED

1. Take a 1' writing on each paragraph (¶) SS; find *gwam* on each writing.
2. Using your better *gwam* as a base rate, select a practice goal and follow the procedures shown at the bottom of the page.

all letters used | E | 1.2 si | 5.1 awl | 90% hfw |

Tab→ How you key is just as vital as the copy you
work from or produce. What you put on paper is a
direct result of the way in which you do the job.

Tab→ If you expect to grow quickly in speed, take
charge of your mind. It will then tell your eyes
and hands how to work through the maze of letters.

GUIDED WRITING PROCEDURE

Select a practice goal

1. Take a 1' writing on ¶1 of a set of ¶s that contain superior figures for guided writings, as in 20E above.
2. Using the *gwam* as a base, add 4 *gwam* to determine your goal rate.
3. Choose from Column 1 of the table at the right the speed nearest your goal rate. At the right of that speed, note the ¹/₄' points in the copy you must reach to maintain your goal rate.

Quarter-minute checkpoints

gwam	¹/₄'	¹/₂'	³/₄'	Time
16	4	8	12	16
20	5	10	15	20
24	6	12	18	24
28	7	14	21	28
32	8	16	24	32
36	9	18	27	36
40	10	20	30	40

4. Note from the word-count dots and figures above the lines in ¶1 the checkpoint for each quarter minute. (Example: Checkpoints for 24 *gwam* are 6, 12, 18, and 24.)

Practice procedure

1. Take two 1' writings on ¶1 at your goal rate guided by the quarter-minute calls (¹/₄, ¹/₂, ³/₄, time).
   Goal: To reach each of your checkpoints just as the guide is called.
2. Take two 1' writings on ¶2 of a set of ¶s in the same way.
3. Take a 2' writing on the set of ¶s combined, without the guides.

Speed level of practice

When the purpose of practice is to reach out into new speed areas, use the *speed* level. Take the brakes off your fingers and experiment with new stroking patterns and new speeds. Do this by:

1. Reading 2 or 3 letters ahead of your keying to foresee stroking patterns.
2. Getting the fingers ready for the combinations of letters to be keyed.
3. Keeping your eyes on the copy in the book.

WORDPERFECT

1. Open file AUTO2; then press **Alt F9** to select Graphics Menu.
2. Select **1**—Figure, **2**—Edit, Figure Number **1**.
3. At the *Selection* prompt in the Definition Menu:
   a. Select **5**—Vertical Position, then key **1.25**; Enter.
   b. Select **6**—Horizontal position, then select **3**—Center; Enter.
4. Strike **F7** to return to the document.
5. View Document in Print to see graphic in box in new location.
6. Repeat Steps 1-5 to move the graphic to two additional locations.
7. Save.

WORKS DOS 2.0

Does not apply.

WORKS DOS 3.0

To move a picture, use procedure to move text: Highlight picture placeholder, select Move from Edit Menu, move cursor to new location, Enter. To align graphics (left, center, right), highlight the picture placeholder, select Picture from the Format Menu, and choose the alignment you want.

1. Open file AUTO2.
2. Highlight the picture placeholder.
3. From the Edit Menu, select Move.
4. Locate the cursor at the new location for the picture and Enter.
5. Change the alignment for the picture: Select picture placeholder; from the Format Menu, select Picture.
6. Select the alignment change and Enter.
7. Repeat Steps 2-6 to move the graphic to two additional locations.
8. Save.

WORKS MAC

To move a picture, use the procedure to move a chart.

1. Open file AUTO2; then turn on Draw.
2. Select and drag the graphic to a new location.
3. Repeat Step 2 to move the graphic to two additional locations.
4. Turn off the Draw tool.
5. Save.

192D ◆

APPLICATION ACTIVITY

Import word processing file NEWS, make the changes listed below right, and move the graphic. Study the illustration and, if necessary, review importing word processing files (173-174D, p. 376).

TIPS ON NIGHT DRIVING

by Diane Nelson

Have you ever noticed that night driving takes more skill than daytime driving? For one thing, you cannot see as far as you can in the daylight. For another, you cannot judge distances well.

Let's consider what is visible--and invisible--at night. On the highway, traffic is visible because headlights help identify the location of oncoming traffic.

1. Open file AUTO2, move the graphic to the top of the page, if necessary, and import the file NEWS below the graphic.
2. Change the text to Palatino font, if possible, or to a font of your choice.
3. Change the right margin so that it is 1.75" from the right edge of the page.
4. Change the title to bold caps and the justification to Left.
5. Change left margin for the title and the first paragraph to 2.75" from the left edge of the page.
6. DS below title and key "by Diane Nelson."

(continued on next page)

SM: Defaults; LS: SS

21A ◆ 6'
CONDITIONING PRACTICE

each line twice SS; then a 1' writing on line 3; find *gwam*

alphabet 1   Wusov amazed them by jumping quickly from the box.

spacing 2   am to│is an│by it│of us│an oak│is to pay│it is due

easy 3   It is right for the man to aid them with the sign.

gwam 1' │   1   │   2   │   3   │   4   │   5   │   6   │   7   │   8   │   9   │   10   │

21B ◆ 22'
RESPONSE PATTERNS

1. Key each pair of lines twice SS; DS between 4-line groups.
2. Take 1' writings on selected lines to increase speed; find *gwam*. Take another 1' writing on the slower line to increase your speed.

Practice hints

Balanced-hand lines:
Think, say, and *key* the words by word response at a fast pace.

One-hand lines:
Think, say, and *key* the words by letter response at a steady but unhurried pace.

Letter response
Many one-hand words (as in lines 3-4) are not easy to key. Such words may be keyed letter by letter and with continuity (steadily, without pauses).

Word response
Short, balanced-hand words (as in lines 1-2) are so easy to key that they can be keyed as words, not letter by letter. Think and key them at your top speed.

balanced hand
1   ah do so go he us if is of or to it an am me by ox
2   ha for did own the for and due pay but men may box

one hand
3   as up we in at on be oh ax no ex my ad was you are
4   ad ink get ilk far him few pop set pin far imp car

balanced hand
5   of it│he is│to us│or do│am to│an ox│or by│is to do
6   do the│and for│she did│all six│the map│for the pay

one hand
7   as on│be in│at no│as my│be up│as in│at him│saw you
8   you are│oil tax│pop art│you get│red ink│we saw him

balanced hand
9   The man is to go to the city and do the auto work.
10   The girl is to go by bus to the lake for the fish.

one hand
11   Jimmy saw you feed a deer on a hill up at my mill.
12   Molly sat on a junk in oily waters at a bare reef.

gwam 1' │   1   │   2   │   3   │   4   │   5   │   6   │   7   │   8   │   9   │   10   │

21C ◆ 8'
THINK AS YOU KEY

Key each line once SS. In place of the blank line at the end of each sentence, key the words that correctly complete the sentence. *You may add a sentence if you wish.*

1   My legal name is _____(first name, middle initial, last name)_____.
2   I am a (freshman, sophomore, junior, senior).
3   My favorite school subject is _____.
4   My favorite hobby or sport is _____.
5   I expect to use my keying skill later to _____.
6   The thing I like best about this course is _____.
7   The thing I like least about this course is _____.
8   My biggest problem in this course is _____.

IMPORT GRAPHIC FILE

Read the information at the right, then complete the steps for your software to import a graphic into a word processing document. If your software cannot import graphic files, you will draw a placeholder outline for the graphic on your printout.

Diane Nelson, manager of Wheels For Sale, wants her article on night driving printed to use as a handout. You will add a graphic and then print samples from which Diane will make a selection for the copy master.

WORDPERFECT

As with pie and bar charts, create a Graphics box to hold the image before importing graphics. List the directory before importing a graphic to identify the file name and extension.

1. List directory of *Student's Template* to verify that it contains file AUTO.PCX (.PCX is a graphics file extension); then open a new file, insert approximately 15 blank lines, and relocate the cursor at Home.
2. Press **Alt F9** to select Graphics Menu.
3. Select **1**—Figure.
4. Select **1**—Create at the *Figure* prompt.
5. At the *Selection* prompt in the Definition Menu:
   a. Select **1**—File name, key **AUTO.PCX**.
   b. Select **7**—Size, select **3**—Set Both; wide = 2.78 and high = 1.25.
6. Strike **F7** to return to the typing area; move cursor below Graphics box.
7. View Document to see graphics.
8. Save as file AUTO2.

WORKS DOS 2.0

Does not apply.

WORKS DOS 3.0

1. Open a new file.
2. Press **Alt, E, E** (from Edit Menu, select Insert Picture).
3. Select AUTO.PCX (.PCX is a graphics file extension) from *Student's Template*.
4. View document.
5. Save as file AUTO2.

WORKS MAC

1. Open file AUTO on *Student's Template*.
2. Select the graphic.
3. Copy to the clipboard.
4. Open a new word processing file and insert approximately 15 blank lines.
5. Paste in the graphic and save as file AUTO2.

Note: When you locate the cursor above the graphic in the document and insert blank lines, the blank lines are inserted above the graphic. When you locate the cursor on a line that is covered by the graphic, blank lines are inserted behind the graphic. When you locate the cursor below the graphic and insert blank lines, the graphic is not affected. The ability to move menu boxes is helpful when you want to work in an area of the screen covered by a menu box.

1. Open file AUTO2, turn on Draw.
2. Locate pointer at the top of Tool box within the Tools title rectangle.
3. Drag Tool box to a new location.
4. Drag Tool box back to its original location.

MOVE A GRAPHIC

Read the information at the right, then complete the steps for your software (p. 408) to move the graphic to a new location.

Graphics can be moved to different locations on a page and to different pages within a document. The process is the same as moving pie charts and bar graphs.

IMPROVE SPEED

LS: DS
Take 1' guided writings and 2' unguided writings; find *gwam* for each writing.

1' *gwam* goals
▽   17 = acceptable
▣   21 = average
☉   25 = good
◇   29 = excellent

all letters used | E | 1.2 si | 5.1 awl | 90% hfw

gwam 2'

Keep in home position all of the fingers not   5

being used to strike a key. Do not let them move   10

out of position for the next letters in your copy.   15

Prize the control you have over the fingers.   19

See how quickly speed goes up when you learn that   24

you can make them do just what you expect of them.   29

gwam 2' | 1 | 2 | 3 | 4 | 5 |

LESSON 22   KEYBOARDING SKILL BUILDING

SM: Defaults; LS: SS

CONDITIONING PRACTICE

each line twice SS; then a 1' writing on line 3; find *gwam*

alphabet 1 **Nat will vex the judge if she bucks my quiz group.**
punctuation 2 **Al, did you use these words: vie, zeal, and aqua?**
easy 3 **She owns the big dock, but they own the lake land.**

gwam 1' | 1 | 2 | 3 | 4 | 5 | 6 | 7 | 8 | 9 | 10 |

OUTSIDE REACHES

1. Key the lines once as shown: SS with a DS between 2-line groups.
2. Key the lines again to improve speed.

Technique goals
- fingers deeply curved and upright
- eyes on copy
- finger-action keystrokes
- hands and arms quiet, almost motionless

1 **ol po opt old owl apt pow lap pod pal low ape soap**
o/p/l 2 **a pol|old pal|oak pot|low post|top spot|is an opal**
3 **Lola is apt to opt for a job in the park all fall.**

4 **ws xs ox ow six own sow lax paw fox laws oxen swap**
w/s/x 5 **an ox|we saw|lax laws|two oxen|law exam|a faux pas**
6 **Lex will swap two onyx owls he owns for six swans.**

7 **za aq zap qt. adz quo zip aqua zone quit jazz quip**
a/z/q 8 **a zoo|an adz|zap it|aqua haze|zany quip|quiet jazz**
9 **Liza quit the zany jazz band for a quiet quay job.**

10 **Olive Penz packed my bag with six quarts of juice.**
alphabet 11 **Jud aims next to play a quick game with Bev Fritz.**
12 **Greta may just pack the box with five dozen quail.**
13 **Jacques Veloz keeps the new form by the tax guide.**

gwam 1' | 1 | 2 | 3 | 4 | 5 | 6 | 7 | 8 | 9 | 10 |

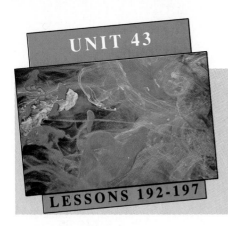

UNIT 43

LESSONS 192-197

Work With Desktop Publishing

Learning Outcomes: After completing this unit, you will be able to

1. Gain an understanding of selected desktop publishing features, and procedures.
2. Create, combine, and import graphics.
3. Use graphics to create various documents and forms.
4. Design page layouts from sample thumbnail sketches.

INTEGRATED FEATURE AND PROCEDURES GUIDE

COMPUTER GRAPHICS
DESKTOP PUBLISHING
IMPORT GRAPHICS

DESKTOP PUBLISHING

Desktop publishing is a system for producing professional-quality documents, either with or without graphics, using a computer, software, and a high-quality printer. Producing professional-quality documents includes learning and applying design guidelines for page layout.

COMPUTER GRAPHICS

Computer graphics includes a wide range of drawings, artwork, and photographs that are saved as computer files. Graphic software is available for creating graphics. Two common types of graphics software are bitmapped and object-oriented. Bitmap graphics, images created with many tiny dots, generally have jagged edges. The dots are called pixels, short for picture elements. Object-oriented graphics, created with lines and shapes, generally have smooth edges. Illustrations and drawings can be captured as files by scanners, and displays on the computer screen can be captured as files. Clip art, disks containing a variety of graphic designs, are available from many sources. The area of computer graphics is expanding rapidly.

IMPORT GRAPHICS

Importing graphics is similar to importing pie and bar charts created with spreadsheet software. To import graphics, the software used to create the graphics usually is not needed. The graphics software is necessary, however, to make changes to graphics.

LESSON 192   PUBLISH AN ARTICLE

192A ◆ CONDITIONING PRACTICE

each line twice SS (slowly, then faster); DS between 2-line groups

alphabet	1	Cody will acquire six blue jackets to give as door prizes to freshmen.
figures	2	I will fly 3,670 miles in May, 2,980 miles in June, and 1,450 in July.
fig/sym	3	Cookbook prices increased 14% from 7/1/89 to 6/30/90 in 25 bookstores.
speed	4	Claudia, the girl with the rifle, saw six turkeys by the lake at dusk.

gwam 1' | 1 | 2 | 3 | 4 | 5 | 6 | 7 | 8 | 9 | 10 | 11 | 12 | 13 | 14 |

RESPONSE PATTERNS

1. Key each set of lines twice SS (slowly, then faster); DS between 6-line groups.
2. Take 1' writings on selected lines; find *gwam* and compare rates.
3. Rekey the slowest line.

Combination response

Normal copy (as in lines 7-9) includes both word- and letter-response sequences.

Use *top* speed for easy words, *lower* speed for words that are harder to key.

letter response
1 be in as no we kin far you few pin age him get oil
2 see him|was nil|vex you|red ink|wet mop|as you saw
3 Milo saved a dazed polo pony as we sat on a knoll.

word response
4 ox if am to is may end big did own but and yam wit
5 do it|to cut|he got|for me|jam it|an owl|go by air
6 He is to go to the city and to do the work for me.

combination response
7 am at of my if on so as to be or we go up of no by
8 am in|so as|if no|is my|is up|to be|is at|is up to
9 Di was busy at the loom as you slept in the chair.

letter 10 Jon gazed at a phony scarab we gave him in a case.
combination 11 Pam was born in a small hill town at the big lake.
word 12 Keith is off to the lake to fish off the big dock.

gwam 1' | 1 | 2 | 3 | 4 | 5 | 6 | 7 | 8 | 9 | 10 |

CHECK/ IMPROVE SPEED

1. Take a 1' writing on ¶1; find *gwam*.
2. Add 2-4 *gwam* for a new speed goal; note ¼' checkpoints in table below.
3. Take two 1' guided writings on ¶1 to improve speed.
4. Key ¶2 in the same way.
5. Take a 2' writing on ¶s 1-2 combined; find *gwam*.
6. Take another 2' writing to improve speed.

Quarter-minute checkpoints

gwam	¼'	½'	¾'	Time
16	4	8	12	16
20	5	10	15	20
24	6	12	18	24
28	7	14	21	28
32	8	16	24	32
36	9	18	27	36
40	10	20	30	40

all letters used | E | 1.2 si | 5.1 awl | 90% hfw

gwam 2'

If you do not make your goal the first time,   5
do not give up or quit. Size up the task and try   10
it again in a new way. Try to focus on what will   15
help you make your rate the next time.   18

It may be that you need just to slow down in   23
order to speed up. That is to say, do not try so   28
hard to force your speed. Relax, read with care,   33
and just let the words flow from your fingers.   37

gwam 2' | 1 | 2 | 3 | 4 | 5 |

3. Create and import a pie chart from worksheet file 152B3 that represents the Oahu training course totals for the four-month period of January through April.
   a. Name the pie chart **JAN/APR TRAINING COURSES--OAHU**.
   b. Change the pie chart to a smaller size.
   c. Relocate the pie chart if necessary.

4. Create and import from worksheet file 152B3 a pie chart that represents the Maui training course totals for the four-month period of January through April.
   a. Name the pie chart **JAN/APR TRAINING COURSES--MAUI**.
   b. Change the pie chart to a smaller size.
   c. Relocate the pie chart if necessary.

5. Save and print.

TRAINING COURSE REPORT OVERVIEW

This report covers training courses on Oahu and Maui for the four-month period from January 1 through April 30. Pie charts display the percents for the training courses on the two islands. Detailed information on the full report and on proposals for increasing revenue from training courses will be presented at the next staff meeting.

JAN/APR TRAINING COURSES--OAHU

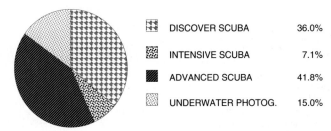

DISCOVER SCUBA	36.0%
INTENSIVE SCUBA	7.1%
ADVANCED SCUBA	41.8%
UNDERWATER PHOTOG.	15.0%

JAN/APR TRAINING COURSES--MAUI

DISCOVER SCUBA	34.0%
INTENSIVE SCUBA	13.0%
ADVANCED SCUBA	41.0%
UNDERWATER PHOTOG.	12.0%

24B ♦ 8'

REVIEW WORD PROCESSING FEATURES

Using the insert and typeover modes, make the changes to the conditioning practice sentences you just finished keying as shown at the right.

24C ♦ 20'

LEARN WORD PROCESSING FEATURES

Review the word processing features; study the command summary for the software you are using. Though letter-key commands appear as capitals, such as **Ctrl B** or ⌘ **U**, you will key lowercase letters.

Use the new word processing features to key the text at the right; use the center feature to center lines 7-10. Repeat activity to increase your skill at using the new features.

UNIT 2
LESSONS 23-25

Master Word Processing Features

Learning Outcomes: After completing this unit, you will be able to

1. Use cursor move, insert, and typeover features.
2. Use bold, underline, and center features.
3. Use status/ruler line and set line spacing.

LESSON 23   LEARN CURSOR MOVE, INSERT, AND TYPEOVER

SM: Defaults; LS: SS

23A ♦ 8'
CONDITIONING PRACTICE

each line twice SS; then three 1' writings on line 3; find *gwam*

alphabet 1   Marjax made five quick plays to win the big prize.

Caps Lock 2   Did you say to send the cartons by UPS or by USPS?

easy 3   I am to pay the six men if they do the work right.

gwam 1' | 1 | 2 | 3 | 4 | 5 | 6 | 7 | 8 | 9 | 10 |

23B ♦ 20'
LEARN WORD PROCESSING FEATURES

Cursor move

Being able to move the cursor quickly from one location to another in a document allows you to edit and revise copy/text in an efficient manner. You have already used the up and down arrow keys to move the cursor from line to line and the right and left arrow keys to move the cursor to the right or left one character at a time. Larger cursor movements can be made by using specific keys or key combinations or by using the mouse.

WordPerfect and Works DOS: The cursor can be moved to the beginning or end of the line and to the top or bottom of the screen by depressing a specific key or key combinations. (See Cursor Move Summary at the right.)

Works MAC: The cursor can be moved to any location of entered text by moving the I-beam pointer to the desired location and clicking and releasing the mouse. (The words *Click* and *Click on* are represented throughout this textbook by this symbol: ~.)

Cursor Move Summary

To move cursor to:	Word Perfect	Works/ DOS
Beginning of Line	Home, ←	Home
End of Line	Home, →	End
Top of Screen	Home, ↑	Ctrl PgUp
Bottom of Screen	Home, ↓	Ctrl PgDn
Right One Word	Ctrl →	Ctrl →
Left One Word	Ctrl ←	Ctrl ←

When a comma (,) separates the keys used, strike first key and then strike second key. When no comma separates commands, depress and hold first key while depressing second key.

Insert mode

New text can be inserted into existing text by using the insert mode, which is automatically on when you enter the software program. Move the cursor to the location where the new text is to be inserted and key the new text. When the insert mode is on, existing text will move to the right.

Typeover mode

The typeover mode allows you to replace current text with newly keyed text.

WordPerfect and Works DOS 3.0 (no typeover mode for Works 2.0): Depress the Ins key to change from the insert mode to the typeover mode. Move cursor to beginning of text to be replaced and key replacement text.

Works MAC: Move the I-beam to the beginning of the text to be replaced. Click (~) and hold as you drag (→) the I-beam over the text you want replaced. Release and key the replacement text.

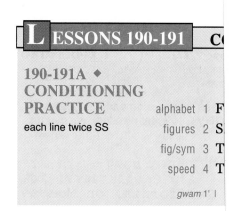

190-191A ◆ CONDITIONING PRACTICE

each line twice SS

alphabet	1	F
figures	2	S
fig/sym	3	T
speed	4	T

gwam 1' |

190B-191B ◆ APPLICATION ACTIVITIES

Activity 1

1. Open a new word processing documer PROM.
2. Key the following text, bold and center ing, and DS between heading and text

RECAP OF PROM ATTENDA

The following illustrations sh attendance for this year and last y that the pie charts display the p Seniors, Juniors, Sophomores, a men class members attending.

3. Import the pie chart from worksheet file
4. Insert two blank lines between the text chart.
5. Size and move the pie chart below the
6. Import the pie chart from worksheet file (This chart may appear on the second you size it.)
7. Size and move this pie chart to align w pie chart.
8. Save.

Activity 2

1. Study the sample at the right.
2. Open file PROM, if necessary.
3. At the end of the text, key the following

The bar chart displays the numb attending from each class.

4. Follow the steps listed for your softwar create and import a bar chart.

187-189D ◆ (cont.)

4. Import the pie chart from file 148D1 for conference participants; review procedures in 187-189B (p. 401) if necessary.
5. Adjust to fit on half a page.
6. Save and print.

187-189E ◆ IMPORT WORKSHEET DATA

1. Study the worksheet data at the right above.
2. Study the sample on p. 401.
3. Open file CONF, if necessary.

Conference Participants

Area	Number Attending
Northeast	155
Midwest	145
Southeast	175
West	135
Southwest	75
Foreign	15

4. Complete the steps listed for your software to import worksheet data for conference participants. (WordPerfect users will key the data.)

WORDPERFECT

1. In Home position, key the worksheet text (above right); bold the column titles.
2. From the Graphics Definition Menu:
   a. Change horizontal position to Left.
   b. Select **8**—Wrap Text Around Box, key **N** for (N)o.
   c. Return to the document.
3. Set tabs at 4.5" and 6".
4. Move the information you keyed in Step 1 to overlay on the right side of the pie chart (Word-Perfect printout will differ slightly from the sample).
5. Working between Print V and Reveal Codes, adjust the placement of the information.
6. Save and print.
7. Continue with the steps below.

WORKS DOS

1. Open worksheet file 148D1.
2. Select the cells in the worksheet including column titles for Area and Number Attending.
3. From the Edit Menu, select Copy.
4. Activate word processing file CONF.
5. Locate the cursor below the pie chart and strike Enter.
6. Continue with the steps below.

WORKS MAC

1. Open worksheet file 148D1.
2. Select cells from A1 through the final cell that contains information (DO NOT use Select All, which would select the entire worksheet).
   a. Copy to the clipboard.
   b. Activate file CONF.
   c. Paste in the spreadsheet text from the clipboard.
3. Continue with the steps below.

1. Make the following changes to the text you keyed (study the illustration again if necessary).
   a. Insert "list and" before "pie chart."
   b. Delete the "s" on shows.
   c. Insert "number and" before "percent."
2. Make the following changes to the worksheet text you imported.
   a. Delete the title "Conference Participants."
   b. Delete "Attending."
   c. Bold "Area" and "Number."

3. Tab and/or space the worksheet information to match the location shown on the sample or locate the worksheet information below and to the right of the pie chart.
4. Preview and adjust if necessary.
5. Save and print.

IMPROVE SPEED

Take 1' and 2' writings as your teacher directs you.

| all letters used | E | 1.2 si | 5.1 awl | 90% hfw |

gwam 2'

```
             .      2      .      4      .      6      .      8      .
        Many boys and girls have major goals in life        4
       10     .     12     .     14     .     16     .     18     .
that they hope to reach.  To hope is easy, but to           9
       20     .     22     .     24     .     26     .     28     .
get will take much effort.  Many of us have a lot          14
       30     .     32     .     34     .     36     .     38     .
of hope but lack the drive to do the needed work.          19
             .      2      .      4      .      6      .      8      .
        To reach a goal, we must first set up a plan       24
       10     .     12     .     14     .     16     .     18     .
of action.  Next, we must put that plan in motion          29
       20     .     22     .     24     .     26     .     28     .
step by step.  If we quit before we take the last          34
       30     .     32     .     34     .     36     .     38     .
step, we will not take the prize we wanted to win.         39
```

gwam 2' | 1 | 2 | 3 | 4 | 5 |

LESSON 25 STATUS/RULER LINE, LINE SPACING, AND MARGINS

SM: Defaults; LS: SS

25A ♦ 8'
CONDITIONING PRACTICE

each line twice SS; then three 1' writings on line 3; find *gwam*

alphabet 1 Kevin can fix the unique jade owl as my big prize.

capitalization 2 Rule: When : precedes a sentence, cap first word.

easy 3 Dodi is to make a visit to the eight island towns.

gwam 1' | 1 | 2 | 3 | 4 | 5 | 6 | 7 | 8 | 9 | 10 |

25B ♦ 22'

LEARN WORD PROCESSING FEATURES

Status/Ruler Line. In word processing software, a status or ruler line serves as a compass. Among other information, the status/ruler line shows the position of the cursor in relation to the edges of a printed page.

WORDPERFECT STATUS LINE

Information displayed in the lower right corner of screen telling you the location of the cursor. Indicates the Document (**Doc 1**) you are keying (either Doc 1 or Doc 2), the page (**Pg**) of the document you are keying, the line (**Ln**) on the page you are keying, and the position (**Pos**) of the cursor. Pos or POS number changes as the bold, underline, and ALL CAPS features are activated.

WORKS DOS STATUS LINE

Information displayed in the bar at the bottom of the screen telling you the total number of pages of the current document and the page where the cursor is presently located. Also shows when bold (**B**), underline (**U**), and italics (**I**) are turned on.

WORKS DOS AND MAC RULER LINE

Shows location of left and right margins. The cursor location can be seen in relation to the ruler line.

187-189B ◆ (cont.)

Open file EXPENSES, if necessary, then complete the steps listed for your software to import a pie chart into a word processing document.

WORDPERFECT

1. Insert several blank lines at the bottom of the document; then locate the cursor a DS below the last line of text.
2. Press **Alt F9**, **1**—Figure, **1**—Create.
   a. At the *Definition* prompt, define file 148B.PIC (pie chart from Unit 32).
   b. Center horizontally (**6**—Horizontal Position, **3**—Center).
3. Return to the document and add more lines if necessary.
4. Preview and save.

WORKS DOS

1. Open file 148B that you created in Unit 32.
2. Select file EXPENSES from the Window Menu.
3. Locate the cursor a DS below the last line of text.
4. Import the pie chart from the worksheet.
5. Preview and save.

WORKS MAC

1. Insert several blank lines at the bottom of the document.
2. Open worksheet file 148B, activate the pie chart, and copy it to the clipboard.
3. Activate file EXPENSES.
   a. Locate I-beam a DS below last line of text.
   b. Copy the chart from the clipboard.
   c. Move to align left edge of pie chart box with left margin.
4. Preview and save.

187-189C ◆

CHANGE SIZE OF PIE CHART

Size a pie chart the same way that you size a bar chart.

1. Open file EXPENSES, if necessary.
2. Review the sample.
3. Complete the steps listed for your software.

WORDPERFECT

1. From the Figure Graphics Menu, select **2**—Edit.
2. At the Definition Menu, select **7**—Size.
   a. Select **3**—Set Both.
   b. For wide, key **5**, Enter.
   c. For high, key **3.25**.
3. Return to the document, if needed. Add lines if necessary to view entire box.
4. Preview, save, and print.

WORKS DOS

1. Locate the cursor on the chart placeholder.
2. From the Format Menu, strike "a" to select Indents and Spacing.
3. At the Indent box, key
   a. left indent as **1"**.
   b. right indent as **1"**.
4. Key chart height as **3"**.
5. Preview, save, and print.

WORKS MAC

1. Turn on Draw; select pie chart, if necessary.
2. Locate arrow over black square at right bottom corner of box outline.
3. ~ and drag upward to the left, changing the size of chart.
4. Examine the chart for circular shape; if necessary, adjust to round.
5. Preview, save, and print.

187-189D ◆

APPLICATION ACTIVITY

1. Review the sample at the right.
2. Open a new word processing document and save as file CONF.
3. Select a font of your choice; then key and save the following information; center and bold the title.

GEOGRAPHIC AREA OF CONFERENCE PARTICIPANTS

Review the pie chart that shows the percent of conference participants from each of six geographic areas.

(continued on next page)

GEOGRAPHIC AREA OF CONFERENCE PARTICIPANTS

Review the list and pie chart that show the number and percent of conference participants from each of six geographic areas.

CONFERENCE PARTICIPANTS

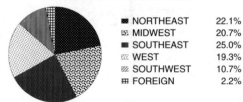

▨	NORTHEAST	22.1%
▧	MIDWEST	20.7%
▩	SOUTHEAST	25.0%
▨	WEST	19.3%
▨	SOUTHWEST	10.7%
▦	FOREIGN	2.2%

Line Spacing. You can set the number of blank lines left between lines of text with the spacing feature. Single spacing (SS) means there are no blank lines between text, while double spacing (DS) means there is one blank line left between lines of text.

WORDPERFECT

1. **Shift F8**; **L**(ine); **S**(pacing).
2. Key **1**, Return for single (Key **2**, Return for double).
3. Depress **F7**.

WORKS DOS

Ctrl 1 for Single Spacing.
Ctrl 2 for Double Spacing.

WORKS MAC

1. Format; Spacing.
2. Single (or Double).

Margins. Specification of the number of spaces (or inches) at the left and right of printed lines.

1. Review the wp features; study the specific commands on this page for the software you are using.
2. Change the left and right margin settings to 2".
3. Key the first paragraph in 25C below; return twice after keying the paragraph.
4. Change the spacing to double spacing (DS); change the margins to 1".
5. Key the second paragraph (25C); return twice after keying the paragraph.
6. Change the spacing to single spacing (SS); change the margins to 1.5" inches.
7. Key the two paragraphs again; return twice after keying the last paragraph.
8. Change the spacing to double spacing (DS); change the margins to the default settings.

WORDPERFECT

The default margin setting is 1". To change the margins to 2":
1. **Shift F8**; **L**(ine); **M**(argins).
2. Strike **2** (2" left margin), Return.
3. Strike **2** (2" right margin), Return.
4. Depress **F7**.

WORKS DOS

The default margin setting is 1.3" for the left margin and 1.2" for the right margin. To change the margins to 2":
1. **Alt, P**.
2. **M**(argins).
3. **Alt E**, strike **2** (2" left margin).
4. **Alt R**, strike **2** (2" right margin).
5. Return.

WORKS MAC

Underneath the ruler line are two triangles (▷ ◁). You can change the left (▷) and right (◁) margins by clicking and dragging the triangles to the desired location. The default margins are 1". To change the left margin to 2", click and drag (~ ←—) the ▷ to 1 on the ruler. To change the right margin to 2", click and drag (~ —→) the ◁ from 6.5 to 5.5 on the ruler.

The indent feature (■) is embedded inside the left margin. If you want the margin changed with no indent, you will need to drag both the ■ and the ▷ to the same location. If you want a 0.5" paragraph indention, drag the ■ five spaces past the ▷.

IMPROVE SPEED

Take 1' writings on each ¶ and 2' writings on both ¶s; find *gwam*.

REVIEW FEATURES

1. Rekey ¶1 and underline **many**, **quite**, and **more**; bold **proud**, **key**, and **prize**.
2. Rekey ¶2 and underline **short**, **use**, and **higher**.
3. Center and bold the last sentence in ¶1.
4. Center the last 5 words in ¶2 in ALL CAPS (omit the period).

all letters used │ E │ 1.2 si │ 5.1 awl │ 90% hfw

gwam 2'

. 2 . 4 . 6 . 8				

In the months and years ahead, you will have   4

many times to be proud of your new skill. If you   9

go on to college and then get a job, you may have   14

to key quite often. So build more skill to prize.   19

In a short while you will be able to key the   24

copy with just a little thought. By then you can   29

learn to format papers in proper style for actual   34

use. Make your next goal a higher level of skill.   39

gwam 2' │ 1 │ 2 │ 3 │ 4 │ 5 │

187-189A ◆
CONDITIONING
PRACTICE
each line twice SS

alphabet	1	Biggi excluded a very quick jaunt to the new zoo from my travel plans.
figures	2	You can find answers to the 150-point test on pages 8, 32, 46, and 79.
fig/sym	3	Runner #3019 was first (49 min.) and runner #687 was second (52 min.).
speed	4	The rifleman saw my hand signal to go right at the fork by the shanty.

gwam 1' | 1 | 2 | 3 | 4 | 5 | 6 | 7 | 8 | 9 | 10 | 11 | 12 | 13 | 14 |

187-189B ◆

IMPORT A PIE CHART

1. Study the sample below at the left.

2. Open a new word processing file and save as file EXPENSES (this file will be used again in this unit).

3. Key and save the information below at the right. Use margins for unbound report, but do not indent ¶s and use single spacing.

GOING IT ON YOUR OWN

Plan ahead! Before you go it on your own, examine the various monthly expenses that are likely. A good rule is to have savings enough for three to six months of expenses. Your monthly income should be enough to cover your monthly expenses--with a little to spare. You might wonder why you need savings to cover three to six months of expenses if your monthly income is more than enough to cover your monthly expenses. Look at it this way: Your savings is your backup resource that protects you from unexpected expenses.

You can count on major monthly expenses, such as food, rent, auto, clothes, and savings. Review the pie chart to see the typical relationship of these expenses. Gather information about expenses for food, rent, auto, and clothes in your community. This information will help you determine the amount you need for income and savings before going it on your own.

MAJOR MONTHLY EXPENSES

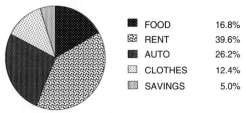

■	FOOD	16.8%
▨	RENT	39.6%
■	AUTO	26.2%
▧	CLOTHES	12.4%
▦	SAVINGS	5.0%

GOING IT ON YOUR OWN

Plan ahead! Before you go it on your own, examine the various monthly expenses that are likely. A good rule is to have savings for three to six months of expenses. Your monthly income should be enough to cover your monthly expenses--with a little to spare. You may wonder why you need savings to cover three to six months of expenses if your monthly income is more than enough to cover your monthly expenses. Look at it this way: Your savings is your backup resource that protects you from unexpected expenses.

You can count on major monthly expenses, such as food, rent, auto, clothes, and savings. Review the pie chart to see the typical relationship of these expenses. Gather information about expenses for food, rent, auto, and clothes in your community. This information will help you determine the amount you need for income and savings before going it on your own.

UNIT 3

LESSONS 26-28

Master Keyboarding/Word Processing Skills

Learning Outcomes: After completing this unit, you will be able to

1. Demonstrate better keying technique.
2. Demonstrate greater control of letter reaches and letter combinations.
3. Demonstrate improved speed on sentences and paragraphs.
4. Demonstrate mastery of basic word processing features.

L ESSON 26 | KEYBOARDING/WORD PROCESSING

SM: Defaults; LS: SS

26A ◆ 6'
CONDITIONING PRACTICE

each line twice SS;
DS between 2-line
groups; then a 1'
writing on line 3 for
speed

alphabet 1 Val may pack a box with prized fig jams for Quent.
punctuation 2 Space once after , and ; but twice after a : and ?
easy 3 Hand eight land forms to the man with auburn hair.

gwam 1' | 1 | 2 | 3 | 4 | 5 | 6 | 7 | 8 | 9 | 10 |

26B ◆ 10'

MASTER LETTER KEY

1. Key the lines once SS as shown; DS between 2-line groups.
2. Key the lines again to improve reach-stroke control.

A 1 Aida said her aunt gave her a pass to the theater.
B 2 Bobby did bobble the ball but made the big basket.

C 3 Cyd can make a quick copy of the check for a cent.
D 4 Donda did the drill at top speed for a good grade.

E 5 Ellen sent a check to each of the men on the crew.
F 6 Fran left half the forms in the file for the chef.

G 7 Gig used grit to gain his goal and get top grades.
H 8 Harv has high hopes that he can go to that school.

I 9 Inga is to sign the will this week and to file it.
J 10 Jean has a major job she enjoys with a just judge.

gwam 1' | 1 | 2 | 3 | 4 | 5 | 6 | 7 | 8 | 9 | 10 |

26C ◆ 10'

THINK AS YOU KEY

As you key the sentences shown at the right, replace the words in parentheses with the word or words that correctly complete the sentences.

1 The name of my best friend is ___(first name/last name)___ .
2 (He/She) lives in (name of city or community) .
3 (He/She) attends (name of school, name of city or town) .
4 Social activities we enjoy together are (name two or three) .
5 The things I like most about (her/him) are (name two or three) .
6 I met (name of friend) about (spell number) (years/months) ago.

APPLICATION ACTIVITIES

Activity 1

Compose a summary of the information provided. Study the sample at the top of the previous page *and* the information at the right. You are to create a summary in your own words; you are NOT to copy the sample.

Prepare a monthly notice to all Acme Department Store employees. Give a title to the notice about the February Sales Winner and the Sales Returns Winner. Show exact dollar amounts for the winners if necessary (review the worksheet for exact amounts). The top sales were made by John Neft. John's February sales topped runner-up Jason Smith's record by $75. Jack Peru had the lowest sales returns for February. Jack's low record of returns was significantly less than the records of others. As a separate item, ask other employees to congratulate these valuable Acme winners.

1. Open file ACME, if necessary.

2. Create a summary. Include these details:
   a. A title for the notice.
   b. The month to which the bar chart applies.
   c. The names of winners and the sales events.
   d. The dollar amounts for each winner.
   e. A request for congratulations from other employees.

Activity 2

Open file ACME, if necessary, and make the following changes.

1. Center and bold the title in ALL CAPS.

2. Bold the names of the winners.

3. Bold the request for congratulations.

4. Format the request for congratulations as a separate paragraph and move it to the end of the text if you did not key it that way.

MOVE A CHART

Review the sample on p. 398 again; then complete the steps listed for your software to move the bar chart.

WORDPERFECT

1. Reveal codes.
2. Select and delete the figure code.
3. Move the cursor between the main text and the request for congratulations and use the Enter key to add about 20 lines.
4. Strike **F1** for the Undelete Menu, then select **1**—Restore.
5. View, adjust the top and bottom space of the page by adding or deleting blank lines.
6. Save and print.

WORKS DOS

You move a graphic using the same procedures as for moving text.

1. Select the chart placeholder, select Move.
2. Locate the cursor between the main text and the request for congratulations.
3. Enter.
4. Preview document, adjust the top and bottom space of the page by adding or deleting blank lines.
5. Save and print.

WORKS MAC

1. Enter about 22 blank lines between the main text and the last paragraph (the request for congratulations).
2. Turn on Draw.
3. Select the graph.
4. Drag the graph below the text to the blank lines you inserted; if necessary, add more blank lines and move graph to center.
5. Adjust the top margin by deleting some of the blank lines at the top of the screen; Print Preview, adjust again if necessary.
6. Save and print.

26D ◆ 12'
IMPROVE/
CHECK SKILL

LS: DS

1. Key three 1' writings on ¶1; find *gwam* on each.
2. Key ¶2 in the same way.
3. Key two 2' writings on ¶s 1-2 combined; find *gwam* on each writing.

all letters used E | 1.2 si | 5.1 awl | 90% hfw

gwam 2'

```
            .      2      .      4      .      6      .      8
1       The level of your skill is a major item when       5
        10     .      12     .      14     .      16     .      18
2  you try to get a job.  Just as vital, though, may      10
        20     .      22     .      24     .      26     .      28     .
3  be how well you are able to express your thoughts      15
        30     .      32     .      34
4  and facts in written form.                              17
            .      2      .      4      .      6      .      8
5       It might amaze you to learn what it is worth      21
        10     .      12     .      14     .      16     .      18
6  to a company to find those who can write a letter      27
        20     .      22     .      24     .      26     .      28     .
7  or a report of quality as they key.  Learn how to      32
        30     .      32     .      34     .      36
8  do this while you are still in school.                  35
```

gwam 2' | 1 | 2 | 3 | 4 | 5 |

26E ◆ 12'
REVIEW FEATURES

1. Make the changes listed in the next column.
2. Reset SM: 1.5"; LS: DS.
3. Rekey the ¶s from the book, as directed in the third column.

Line 1 Change **major** to **vital**.
2 Change **Just as** to **Equally**.
3 Insert **just** after **be**.
6 Change **letter** to **report**.
7 Change **report** to **letter**.
8 Change **do this** to **compose**.

Center/**bold** the heading **COMPOSING AND KEYING**, then Return twice.
Make these changes as you key the paragraphs:
Line 1 Underline **major**.
7 Bold the last sentence in the ¶.

L ESSON 27 — KEYBOARDING/WORD PROCESSING

SM: Defaults; LS: SS

27A ◆ 6'
CONDITIONING PRACTICE

each line twice

alphabet 1 Jud Quick will buy the azure pin you gave Ms. Fox.
punctuation 2 Key these words; hex, lack, quiz, have, and zany.
easy 3 Ana may lend us a hand with the sign for the dorm.

gwam 1' | 1 | 2 | 3 | 4 | 5 | 6 | 7 | 8 | 9 | 10 |

27B ◆ 8'
MASTER LETTER KEY

1. Key the lines once SS as shown; DS between 2-line groups.
2. Key the lines again to improve reach-stroke control.

K 1 Kirk took a kid for a risky ride in the oak kayak.
L 2 Lena lost this list at the old mall when she fell.

M 3 Maxim made his mark on your swim team this summer.
N 4 Nina can lend a pen to the woman to sign the note.

O 5 Owen knows he is too old to be on our soccer team.
P 6 Paco put pepper on his pork chop and the new peas.

Q 7 Quen was quite quick to quiz my squad about squid.
R 8 Ruby worked on a report to be read by four jurors.

IMPORT BAR CHART

Read the information at the right and then complete the steps listed for your software. You will key the information and move the bar chart later in this unit.

Showing numeric information in graphic form makes it easy to understand. In 146B, p. 289, you created a bar chart from worksheet data. In this lesson, you include that bar chart in a report for Acme Department Store.

FEBRUARY SALES & SALES RETURNS WINNERS

John Neft is the Sales Winner of the monthly Top Sales contest. John's February sales of $750 topped runner-up Jason Smith by $75.

Jack Peru is the Sales Returns Winner with the lowest sales returns for February. Jack's low record of $50 in returns was significantly less than that of the other sales staff.

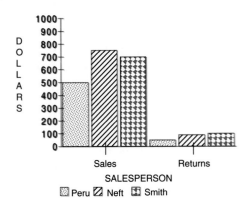

Notice to all employees: Be sure to congratulate these valued Acme winners!

WORDPERFECT

To import Lotus 1-2-3 spreadsheet chart files into WordPerfect documents, the files must have .PIC extensions (resave worksheet files as .PIC files if necessary). Worksheet chart file names in this unit, however, will be listed without the extension.

1. Open a new word processing document as file ACME; enter approximately 20 blank lines, then relocate cursor at Home.
2. Press **Alt F9** to select Graphics Menu.
   a. Select **1**—Figure.
   b. Select **1**—Create.
3. At the Definition Menu
   a. Select **1**—Filename and key 146B.PIC to select the worksheet chart file (created in Unit 32).
   b. Select **6**—Horizontal Position, then select **3**—Center.
4. Strike **F7** to return to the document.
5. If the graphic box is not totally visible, locate cursor at the end of the document and enter blank lines to display the graphic box.
6. View in Print.
7. Save.

WORKS DOS

Works DOS adds .WKS to worksheet file names; worksheet file names identified in this unit, however, will be listed without the extension.

1. Open a new word processing document as file ACME.
2. Open the worksheet file 146B (created in Unit 32).
3. From the Window Menu, select ACME to activate it.
4. From the Edit Menu, choose I (Insert Chart); use arrow key to select worksheet, move cursor to Chart 1, use arrow key to highlight, Enter to select (place-holder appears in document).
5. Print Preview (chart is visible).
6. Save.

WORKS MAC

1. Open the worksheet file 146B (created in Unit 32) , select the bar chart and copy to the clipboard.
2. Open a new word processing document and save as file ACME.
   a. Enter approximately 20 blank lines.
   b. Locate the cursor at Home.
   c. Paste in the bar graph from the clipboard, note that Draw is on.
   d. Turn off Draw.
3. Locate the I-beam at the end of the document; then enter additional blank lines, if needed, to locate the I-beam below the graph.
4. Print Preview.
5. Save.

IMPROVE SKILL

LS: DS

1. Key three 1' writings on ¶1; find *gwam* on each.
2. Key ¶2 in the same way.
3. Key two 2' writings on ¶s 1-2 combined; find *gwam* on each writing.

all letters used | E | 1.2 si | 5.1 awl | 90% hfw

Line

gwam 2'

```
        .      2      .      4      .      6      .      8      .
1          If you are moving with more control now than      5
        10   .   12      .   14      .   16      .   18      .
2  you were last week, you can be quite certain that        10
        20   .   22      .   24      .   26      .   28      .
3  you have shown growth in keying.  You can develop        14
        30   .   32      .   34      .   36      .   38      .
4  as fast as you desire if you will work with zest.        19
               .      2      .      4      .      6      .      8      .
5          For the next several days, put a little more      24
        10   .   12      .   14      .   16      .   18      .
6  effort into your work; then check the increase in        29
        20   .   22      .   24      .   26      .   28      .
7  speed.  You will find that just a bit more effort        34
        30   .   32      .   34      .   36      .   38      .
8  day by day can result in a much higher skill.            38
```

gwam 2' | 1 | 2 | 3 | 4 | 5 |

27D ◆ 12'

REVIEW FEATURES

1. Make the changes listed in the next column.
2. Reset SM: 1.5"; LS: DS.
3. Rekey the ¶s from the book as directed in the third column.

Line 1 Change **moving** to **keying**.
3 Insert **power** after **keying**.
5 Insert **just** after **put**.
7 Change **speed** to **skill**.
8 Change **skill** to **speed**.

Center/**bold** the title **EFFORT AND SKILL**; then Return twice.
Make these changes as you key the paragraphs:
Line 3 Underline **growth**.
5 **Bold** the next several days.

27E ◆ 10'

THINK AS YOU KEY

As you key the sentences, replace the words in parentheses with a word or words that best complete each sentence.

1 My ancestors __(are/were)__ originally from __(country, countries)__.
2 My __(first/last)__ name is __(African/Hispanic/Oriental/etc.)__.
3 When I finish school, I want to work as __(a/an)__ __(name of job)__.
4 If I go to college, I want to major in __(name of field of study)__.
5 I prefer this field of study because __(give reasons for choice)__.

L ESSON 28 KEYBOARDING/WORD PROCESSING

SM: Defaults; LS: SS

28A ◆ 6'
CONDITIONING PRACTICE

each line twice

alphabet 1 Rick Ziv saw you get the quaint box for Judy Palm.
punctuation 2 T.J. said that e.g. means for example; in., inch.
easy 3 Rico is to work with the man to fix the dock sign.

gwam 1' | 1 | 2 | 3 | 4 | 5 | 6 | 7 | 8 | 9 | 10 |

28B ◆ 14'

CHECK SKILL

1. Key each ¶ in 27C above, as directed there.
2. Key two 2' writings on ¶s 1-2 combined; find *gwam*.

Goals: Increase 4 *gwam* on 1' and 2 *gwam* on 2' writings.

UNIT 42

LESSONS 185–191

Use Graphics for Business Information

Learning Outcomes: After completing this unit, you will be able to

1. Import bar and pie charts into word processing documents.
2. Adjust the size of charts and move to new locations.
3. Import numeric worksheet data into word processing documents.
4. Create an abstract of information provided.

INTEGRATED FEATURE AND PROCEDURES GUIDE

ADJUST SIZE OF CHARTS
IMPORT BAR AND PIE CHARTS
IMPORT NUMERIC WORKSHEET
  DATA
MOVE CHARTS TO NEW LOCATIONS
SUMMARIZE AT THE KEYBOARD

IMPORT BAR AND PIE CHARTS

Bar and pie charts and other graphics, constructed from worksheet data, can be imported or inserted into word processing documents. Including graphics in a report makes numeric data easy to understand.

ADJUST SIZE OF CHARTS

You adjust or change the size of charts to fit the space that is available or to give visual balance. The word "size" is often used as a verb, meaning to adjust or change the size of graphic illustrations.

MOVE CHARTS TO NEW LOCATIONS

Charts can be moved to new locations within a document. Common procedures, depending on the software, are to select and drag, to enter locational data, or to copy and paste.

IMPORT NUMERIC WORKSHEET DATA

The numeric data used to create charts generally can be imported into word processing documents. More complete information is provided when graphics and the related numeric data are displayed together. The value of importing numeric data from the worksheet is that a variety of data can be selected and imported without the need to rekey it.

SUMMARIZE AT THE KEYBOARD

A summary contains the key points of a larger body of information. To create a summary, draw out main points as you read the information presented.

Instead of copying the points, compose text at the keyboard. That is, think as you write by keying.

As you read and comprehend information, write/key in your own words all the main points, not minor details.

Through frequent practice, you can learn to create summaries that are concise and clear.

LESSON 185-186   WORK WITH BAR CHARTS

185-186A ◆ CONDITIONING PRACTICE

each line twice SS
(slowly, then faster);
DS between 2-line
groups

alphabet 1 Peggy and Kami will enjoy a quiet, lazy bath after very hard exercise.

figures 2 Dave has 9,687 names and 12,534 addresses stored on one 80-track disk.

fig/sym 3 My electric bill was $135.98 (up 6%); my gas bill was $92.47 (up 10%).

speed 4 The auditor for a sorority cut by half the big goal for the endowment.

gwam 1' | 1 | 2 | 3 | 4 | 5 | 6 | 7 | 8 | 9 | 10 | 11 | 12 | 13 | 14 |

28C ◆ 8'

MASTER
LETTER KEYS

1. Key the lines once SS as shown; DS between 2-line groups.
2. Key the lines again to improve reach-stroke control.

S 1 **Sid said his sister has six silver charms to sell.**
T 2 **Tia got a taxi to the city square for the concert.**

U 3 **Uri is sure you will sue our county for a big sum.**
V 4 **Viv can have five vans of vivid color take voters.**

W 5 **Wes saw a bowl in the window and wished to own it.**
X 6 **Xerox the sixty tax forms; index them by tax year.**

Y 7 **You say you are not yet ready to dye the old yarn.**
Z 8 **Zoe saw a zebra nuzzle a lazy zebu at the new zoo.**

gwam 1' | 1 | 2 | 3 | 4 | 5 | 6 | 7 | 8 | 9 | 10 |

28D ◆ 12'

CHECK SKILL

LS: DS

1. Key two 1' writings on each of lines 1 and 2; find *gwam* on each writing.
2. Key a 1' writing on each of ¶s 1-3; find *gwam* on each.
3. Key a 2' writing on ¶s 1-3 combined; find *gwam*.
4. Key another 2' writing on the ¶s.

alphabet 1 **Lex Zahn will give a squad party for Buck Jamison.**
punctuation 2 **Lana and he may go with us to the big city social.**

gwam 1' | 1 | 2 | 3 | 4 | 5 | 6 | 7 | 8 | 9 | 10 |

all letters used | E | 1.2 si | 5.1 awl | 90% hfw

gwam 2'

Establish a daily work goal; then keep it in 5
mind while you practice. Work toward it by doing 10
expertly all that is within your power to try now. 14

You do not attain success easily or quickly. 19
It costs much time and effort. There is no magic 24
road to success, now or ever. It means hard work. 29

It is a good feeling to complete whatever we 34
start to do. A major sign of our success lies in 39
what we learn through the maze of vexing problems. 44

gwam 2' | 1 | 2 | 3 | 4 | 5 |

28E ◆ 10'

THINK AS
YOU KEY

1. Read each thought starter at the right and decide how you will complete it.
2. Key each sentence, completing it from your own thoughts.

1 **My two main goals in life are . . . .**
2 **Two things that give me great satisfaction in life**
  are . . . .
3 **I believe my two greatest strengths are . . . .**
4 **I believe my two greatest weaknesses are . . . .**
5 **The two things that I daydream most about are . . . .**

DRILL AND PRACTICE

1. Key each line twice SS (once slowly, then faster).
2. Key a 1' writing on each line.
3. Rekey slower lines for speed.

alphabet 1 Peter may quit cutting flax when jet black clouds cover the azure sky.

figures 2 On June 23 we served 461 hamburgers, 597 sodas, and 180 bags of chips.

fig/sym 3 Check #84 (dated 6/5) for $93 covers Invoice #275 less a 10% discount.

adjacent keys 4 Troy said he was at the arena for a pop concert when the lion escaped.

long reaches 5 Brenda checked both number columns twice before she plotted the curve.

combination 6 The panel agreed to award to the union the deed to the vast lake land.

speed 7 It is their wish to sign the amendment if he is to handle the problem.

gwam 1' | 1 | 2 | 3 | 4 | 5 | 6 | 7 | 8 | 9 | 10 | 11 | 12 | 13 | 14 |

IMPROVE/ CHECK SKILL

1. Key two 1' writings on each ¶; find *gwam*.
2. Key two 3' writings on ¶s 1-3 combined; find *gwam* and count errors.
3. Key a 5' writing on ¶s 1-3 combined; find *gwam* and count errors.

all letters/figures used | A | 1.5 si | 5.7 awl | 80% hfw | *gwam* 3' | 5'

	3'	5'
The two professors who are taking 35 students to study in foreign	4	3 43
countries met with the parents of the students on the night of Febru-	9	5 45
ary 19 in Room 612. The major purpose of the meeting was to give in-	14	8 48
formation to the parents of the students who were to study from March 16	18	11 51
to May 15 in Florence, Italy, and Vico Morote, Switzerland.	22	13 53
Every parent was informed that the group would be required to leave	27	16 56
O'Hare Airport (Chicago) on All World Flight #908 on the evening of	31	19 59
March 15. Flight #908 will go directly to Milan, Italy, where the group	36	22 62
will stay the first evening. After the trip to Milan, the students will	41	25 65
be taken to Florence where they will study until April 30.	45	27 67
On May 1 every student and teacher will take an express train to	49	30 70
Vico Morote, Switzerland, where they will remain until May 15. When	54	32 72
class is over on May 15, every student will take an overnight express	59	35 75
train to Frankfurt, Germany, for return on All World Flight #47. Flight	64	38 78
#47 is to land at O'Hare early in the evening on May 16.	67	40 80

gwam 3' | 1 | 2 | 3 | 4 | 5 |
5' | 1 | 2 | 3 |

UNIT 4

LESSONS 29-33

Master Figure-Key Operation

Learning Outcomes: After completing this unit, you will be able to

1. Operate the figure keys (top row) with correct technique by touch.
2. Key copy containing figures as well as words at acceptable speed.
3. Center lines of copy horizontally.

LESSON 29 · 8 AND 1

SM: Defaults; LS: SS

29A ◆ 6'
CONDITIONING PRACTICE

each line twice SS; then a 1' writing on line 3; find *gwam*

alphabet 1 Max was quick to fly a big jet plane over the frozen desert.

spacing 2 Any of them can aim for a top goal and reach it if they try.

easy 3 Nan is to go to the city hall to sign the land forms for us.

gwam 1' | 1 | 2 | 3 | 4 | 5 | 6 | 7 | 8 | 9 | 10 | 11 | 12 |

29B ◆ 18'

LEARN 8 AND 1

each line twice SS (slowly, then faster); DS between 4-line groups; practice each line again

8 *Right middle* finger

1 *Left little* finger

Learn 8

1 k k 8k 8k kk 88 k8k k8k 88k 88k Reach up for 8, 88, and 888.
2 Key the figures 8, 88, and 888. Please open Room 88 or 888.

Learn 1

3 a a 1a 1a aa 11 a1a a1a 11a 11a Reach up for 1, 11, and 111.
4 Add the figures 1, 11, and 111. Has just 1 of 111 finished?

Combine 8 and 1

5 Key 11, 18, 81, and 88. Just 11 of the 18 skiers have left.
6 Reach with the fingers to key 18 and 188 as well as 1 and 8.
7 The stock person counted 11 coats, 18 slacks, and 88 shirts.

APPLICATION ACTIVITY

Follow the steps at the right to complete this integrated application.

1. Open database file HOTELS(.SF) and verify arrangement in alphabetical order by hotel and island (arrange if necessary) and save.

2. Create a new word processing document, and key the introductory information below.
   a. Use 1" TM, LM, and RM; SS.
   b. Center each line.
   c. Bold the main heading.

SAILS FOR RENT
Kauai, Maui, and Oahu Hotels
Date (use today's date)

3. Save as HOTELIST.

4. Import database file HOTELS a DS below the introductory information.

5. Format in two-across columns and adjust the column length so that the information for each hotel is together in a column, not separated.

6. Save and print.

OPTIONAL INTEGRATED ACTIVITY

Load and print the word processing file OPTINT3 from the *Student's Template*. Complete the activity as outlined in the template.

A SSESSMENT FOR UNIT 41

Add a new record to database file SUPPLIER and import it into a new word processing document. Then format the list into two columns. Follow directions at the right.

1. Open database file SUPPLIER(.SF) and add the following record.

Bishop's Radiator Service
12775 Marathon Ave.
San Diego, CA 92123-4123
(619) 146-7711
Repair, clean, and replace radiators

2. Arrange in alphabetical order by supplier name and save.

3. Create a new word processing document; key the introductory information.

Wheels For Sale List of Suppliers

Suppliers hold the key to keeping your cars in outstanding condition in two ways--keeping them running and making them look pretty! Tell your suppliers that you saw them listed in <u>Rolling Wheels</u>.

4. Make the following changes, then save as SUPPLY.
   a. Use 1" TM, LM, and RM.
   b. Bold and center the title in ALL CAPS.
   c. DS below the title and below the body.
   d. Block paragraphs, SS.

5. Import database file SUPPLIER(.SF) a DS below the introductory information.

6. Format supplier name, complete address, and telephone number in two-across columns.

7. Save and print.

MASTER TECHNIQUE

1. Each pair of lines (1-6) twice SS (slowly, then faster); DS between 4-line groups.
2. A 1' writing on line 7 and on line 8; find *gwam* on each writing.

Technique goals

- reach *up* without moving the hand forward
- reach *down* without twisting the wrists or moving the elbows in and out

Row emphasis

home/3d	1 she quit	with just	that play	fair goal	will help	they did go
	2 Dru said you should try for the goal of top speed this week.
home/1st	3 hand axe	lava gas	can mask	jazz band	lack cash	a small flask
	4 Ms. Hamm can call a cab, and Max can flag a small black van.
figures	5 The quiz on the 18th will be on pages 11 to 18 and 81 to 88.
	6 Just 11 of the 118 boys got 81 of the 88 quiz answers right.
easy	7 Vi is to pay for the eight pens she laid by the audit forms.
	8 Keith is to row with us to the lake to fix six of the signs.

gwam 1' | 1 | 2 | 3 | 4 | 5 | 6 | 7 | 8 | 9 | 10 | 11 | 12 |

GUIDED WRITING

LS: DS

On each ¶, take a 1' writing to find base rate; then, 1' guided writings.

Quarter-minute checkpoints

gwam	1/4'	1/2'	3/4'	Time
16	4	8	12	16
20	5	10	15	20
24	6	12	18	24
28	7	14	21	28
32	8	16	24	32
36	9	18	27	36
40	10	20	30	40

all letters used E | 1.2 si | 5.1 awl | 90% hfw

gwam 2'

How much time does it take you to return at the end of   6
the line? Do you return with a lazy or a quick reach? Try   12
not to stop at the end of the line; instead, return quickly   18
and move down to the next line of copy.   21

How much time does it take you to strike the shift key   27
and the letter to make a capital? Just a bit more practice   33
will help you cut by half the time you are now using. When   39
you cut the time, you increase your speed.   43

gwam 2' | 1 | 2 | 3 | 4 | 5 | 6 |

LESSON 30   9 AND 4

SM: Defaults; LS: SS

CONDITIONING PRACTICE

each line twice

alphabet	1 Joby quickly fixed a glass vase and amazed the proud owners.
figures	2 She told us to add the figures 11, 88, 18, 81, 118, and 881.
easy	3 Ciel may make a bid on the ivory forks they got in the city.

gwam 1' | 1 | 2 | 3 | 4 | 5 | 6 | 7 | 8 | 9 | 10 | 11 | 12 |

IMPROVE SPEED: GUIDED WRITING

Practice again the two ¶s above, using the directions in 29D.

Goal: To improve your speed by 2-4 *gwam*.

MULTIPAGE COLUMN LAYOUTS

Review the samples. Then complete the steps for your software to create two-page two-column layout as shown using file POSTAL. This activity simulates using paper that is shorter than the standard 11" page.

TWO-LETTER STATE ABBREVIATIONS

Two-letter state abbreviations were developed by the Postal Service to help speed mail to its destination. These abbreviations can be read more quickly than the complete state name or most of the standard abbreviations. The two-letter abbreviation system is very simple--just two capital letters with no punctuation. For example, VA is the correct two-letter abbreviation for Virginia.

Alabama	AL	Idaho	ID
Alaska	AK	Illinois	IL
Arizona	AZ	Indiana	IN
Arkansas	AR	Iowa	IA
California	CA	Kansas	KS
Colorado	CO	Kentucky	KY
Connecticut	CT	Louisiana	LA
Delaware	DE	Maine	ME
Florida	FL	Maryland	MD
Georgia	GA	Massachusetts	MA
Hawaii	HI	Michigan	MI

Minnesota	MN	Oregon	OR
Mississippi	MS	Pennsylvania	PA
Missouri	MO	Rhode Island	RI
Montana	MT	South Carolina	SC
Nebraska	NE	South Dakota	SD
Nevada	NV	Tennessee	TN
New Hampshire	NH	Texas	TX
New Jersey	NJ	Utah	UT
New Mexico	NM	Vermont	VT
New York	NY	Virginia	VA
North Carolina	NC	Washington	WA
North Dakota	ND	West Virginia	WV
Ohio	OH	Wisconsin	WI
Oklahoma	OK	Wyoming	WY

WORDPERFECT

1. Retrieve POSTAL file if necessary.
2. Delete the second paragraph; leave a DS between the paragraph and the listing of states.
3. Reveal codes.
4. Delete [Col On] code preceding Alabama.
5. Turn off Reveal Codes.
6. Delete the page break after Missouri.
7. Insert page breaks after Hawaii, Michigan, and Oklahoma.
8. Locate cursor on A of Alabama.
9. Turn Columns On (**Alt F7, 1**—Columns, **1**—On).
10. Depress **Home, Home,** ↓.
11. Print the document.

WORKS DOS

1. Load file POSTAL.
2. Delete the second paragraph, then delete the page break.
3. Insert new page breaks after Hawaii, Michigan, and Oklahoma.
4. Print.
5. Cut and paste Column 2 (page 2), aligning it horizontally and vertically with Column 1; repeat the process to cut and paste Column 4 (page 4), aligning it with Column 3.

WORKS MAC

1. Load file POSTAL.
2. Delete the second paragraph, then locate the I-beam below the two columns.
3. Insert a page break; then use Return key to insert approximately 12 blank lines.
4. Turn on Draw and select the Text tool.
5. Draw two new column boxes below Columns 1 and 2.
6. Link the columns. Option ~ to link the left box as Column 3 and the right box as Column 4. (**Note**: that column boxes can be linked automatically by depressing Option while drawing the box.)
7. Shorten the first column box so it ends with Hawaii.
8. Shorten the second column box so it ends with Michigan.
9. Adjust the third column box so it ends with Oklahoma; adjust the fourth column for the remaining states.
10. Print.

LEARN 9 AND 4

each line twice SS (slowly, then faster); DS between 4-line groups; practice each line again

9 *Right ring finger*

4 *Left pointer finger*

Learn 9

use the letter "l"

1 l l 9l 9l ll 99 l9l l9l 99l 99l Reach up for 9, 99, and 999.
2 Key the figures 9, 99, and 999. Have only 9 of 99 finished?

Learn 4

3 f f 4f 4f ff 44 f4f f4f 44f 44f Reach up for 4, 44, and 444.
4 Add the figures 4, 44, and 444. Please study pages 4 to 44.

Combine 9 and 4

5 Key 44, 49, 94, and 99. Only 49 of the 94 joggers are here.
6 Reach with the fingers to key 49 and 499 as well as 4 and 9.
7 My goal is to sell 44 pizzas, 99 tacos, and 9 cases of cola.

MASTER TECHNIQUE: FIGURES

1. Key each line twice SS (slowly, then faster); DS between 2-line groups.
2. Key each line again to improve speed.

Figure sentences

use the figure "1"

1 Keep the fingers low as you key 11, 18, 19, 48, 94, and 849.
2 On March 8, 1991, 44 people took the 4 tests for the 8 jobs.
3 He based his May 1 report on pages 449 to 488 of Chapter 19.

CENTER LINES HORIZONTALLY

1. Center each line of Drill 1 horizontally (side to side), SS. Refer to 24C, p. 52, if necessary to recall the command for the center feature.
2. Space down 4 times and center each line of Drill 2 horizontally, SS.
3. Center Drill 3 in the same manner.
4. Change LM to 1.5" and LS to DS.
5. Repeat Steps 1-3.

1	to	2	a	3	I
	wish		the		work
	profit		their		handle
	problems		foreign		quantity
	amendments		committee		patient

7. Repeat Step 6 to draw a second column box beside the first box.
8. Link the columns by identifying the sequence of text flow from one column to the next.
   a. Select the Select tool (arrow).
   b. Option ~ the first column box to identify as Column 1.
   c. Option ~ the second column box to identify as Column 2.
9. Select the Text tool.
10. Locate the I-beam at the top of Column 1 box and paste in the list of states and abbreviations.
11. Choose the Select tool.
12. Locate the point of the Select tool at the bottom center handle of the Column 1 box outline; ~ and drag to change the column box size so that it is long enough to accommodate the first 25 states and abbreviations; the last 25 states should flow into the second column box.
13. Adjust the location of each column box to align and center them under the text information with about 1" of space between the two columns. Print.

181-184E ◆

EDIT TEXT IN COLUMNS

Complete the steps for your software to delete the standard abbreviations from the list of states columns and to adjust column space.

WORDPERFECT

Editing columns on separate pages, rather than side by side, is faster because the screen refreshes (displays changes) more quickly.

1. Retrieve file POSTAL, if necessary.
2. Reveal codes and delete the [Col ON] code preceding Alabama.
3. Delete AND STANDARD from the title.
4. Using the Tabular Column Delete feature, delete the standard abbreviations from the list.
5. Change the space between columns to 1.75".
6. Turn Column feature back on.
7. Depress **Home, Home, ↓**.
8. Print the document.
9. Save as POSTAL.

WORKS DOS

1. Load file POSTAL.
2. Delete AND STANDARD and the standard abbreviations.
3. Reset the tabs for the state names and two-letter abbreviations.
   a. Set a tab for the state names approximately 0.5" from the left margin.
   b. Set a tab for the two-letter abbreviations three characters after the longest state name.
4. Print a copy.
5. Follow your teacher's instructions or cut and paste the second column into position so that it aligns horizontally and vertically with the first column.

WORKS MAC

When you edit linked columns, the text adjusts after you deselect. When changes are made that affect the amount of text in the column, such as changing the size of the text or stretching a column, the text redistributes after the column is deselected.

1. Load file POSTAL.
2. Delete AND STANDARD and the standard abbreviations.
3. Reduce the length of the column boxes by approximately 0.5".
4. Adjust the positions of the columns horizontally so that they are centered under the narrative and have approximately 1.75" between them.
5. Print.

SM: Defaults; LS: SS

31A ◆ 6'
CONDITIONING PRACTICE
each line twice

alphabet 1 Roz may put a vivid sign next to the low aqua boat for Jack.

figures 2 Please review Figure 8 on page 94 and Figure 14 on page 189.

easy 3 Tien may fix the bus panel for the city if the pay is right.

gwam 1' | 1 | 2 | 3 | 4 | 5 | 6 | 7 | 8 | 9 | 10 | 11 | 12 |

31B ◆ 18'
LEARN 0 AND 5

each line twice SS (slowly, then faster); DS between 4-line groups; practice each line again

0 *Right little* finger

5 *Left pointer* finger

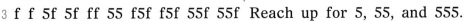

Learn 0 (zero) ▼

1 ; ; 0; 0; ;; 00 ;0; ;0; 00; 00; Reach up for 0, 00, and 000.

2 Snap the finger off the 0. I used 0, 00, and 000 sandpaper.

Learn 5 ▼

3 f f 5f 5f ff 55 f5f f5f 55f 55f Reach up for 5, 55, and 555.

4 Reach up to 5 and back to f. Did he say to order 55 or 555?

Combine 0 and 5

5 Reach with the fingers to key 50 and 500 as well as 5 and 0.

6 We asked for prices on these models: 50, 55, 500, and 5500.

7 On May 5, I got 5 boxes each of 0 and 00 steel wool for her.

31C ◆ 12'
IMPROVE TECHNIQUE: FIGURES

each line twice SS; DS between 2-line groups

Spacing note:
No space is left before or after : when used with figures to express time.

Capitalization note:
Most nouns before numbers are capitalized; exceptions include *page* and *line*.

No space

1 Flight 1049 is on time; it should be at Gate 48 at 5:50 p.m.

2 The club meeting on April 5 will be in Room 549 at 8:10 a.m.

3 Of our 185 workers in 1990, 14 had gone to new jobs by 1991.

4 I used Chapter 19, pages 449 to 458, for my March 10 report.

5 Can you meet us at 1954 Maple Avenue at 8:05 a.m. August 10?

6 Of the 59 students, 18 keyed at least 40 w.a.m. by April 18.

TWO-LETTER AND STANDARD STATE ABBREVIATIONS

Review the sample document at the right; then complete the steps for your software.

Two-letter state abbreviations were developed by the Postal Service to help speed mail to its destination. These abbreviations can be read more quickly than the complete state name or most of the standard abbreviations. The two-letter abbreviation system is very simple--just two capital letters with no punctuation. For example, VA is the correct two-letter abbreviation for Virginia.

Standard abbreviations have been used for many years for state names. Standard abbreviations are no longer correct for addressing envelopes or for inside letter addresses. Use the two-letter state abbreviations for these purposes.

Alabama	AL	Ala.		Montana	MT	Mont.
Alaska	AK	None		Nebraska	NE	Nebr.
Arizona	AZ	Ariz.		Nevada	NV	Nev.
Arkansas	AR	Ark.		New Hampshire	NH	N.H.
California	CA	Calif.		New Jersey	NJ	N.J.
Colorado	CO	Colo.		New Mexico	NM	N. Mex.
Connecticut	CT	Conn.		New York	NY	N.Y.
Delaware	DE	Del.		North Carolina	NC	N.C.
Florida	FL	Fla.		North Dakota	ND	N. Dak.
Georgia	GA	Ga.		Ohio	OH	None
Hawaii	HI	None		Oklahoma	OK	Okla.
Idaho	ID	None		Oregon	OR	Oreg.
Illinois	IL	Ill.		Pennsylvania	PA	Pa.
Indiana	IN	Ind.		Rhode Island	RI	R.I.
Iowa	IA	None		South Carolina	SC	S.C.
Kansas	KS	Kans.		South Dakota	SD	S. Dak.
Kentucky	KY	Ky.		Tennessee	TN	Tenn.
Louisiana	LA	La.		Texas	TX	Tex.
Maine	ME	None		Utah	UT	None
Maryland	MD	Md.		Vermont	VT	Vt.
Massachusetts	MA	Mass.		Virginia	VA	Va.
Michigan	MI	Mich.		Washington	WA	Wash.
Minnesota	MN	Minn.		West Virginia	WV	W. Va.
Mississippi	MS	Miss.		Wisconsin	WI	Wis.
Missouri	MO	Mo.		Wyoming	WY	Wyo.

WORDPERFECT

1. Retrieve POSTAL file if necessary and locate the cursor at the beginning of Alabama.
2. Press **Alt F7**, select **1**–Columns; select **3**–Define.
3. Select **3**–Distance between columns; change the number to 1" (margins for the columns are calculated automatically); Enter.
4. Enter to return to the columns prompt; then select **1**–On.
5. At the beginning of the line containing the twenty-sixth state, depress **Ctrl Enter** to establish end of first column.
6. Save as POSTAL.

WORKS DOS

1. Open file POSTAL.
2. Just above the twenty-sixth state name, insert a page break.
3. Print a copy.
4. Follow your teacher's instructions or use scissors (or a paper cutter) to cut out the column of state names and abbreviations on the second page and paste or tape it on the right side of the first page so that the columns are aligned horizontally and vertically.

WORKS MAC

1. Open file POSTAL.
2. Select and copy list of states and abbreviations to the clipboard.
3. Locate the I-beam a DS below text.
4. With Draw off, use the Return key to insert 50 blank lines.
5. Turn on Draw (⌘J) and select the Text tool from the Tools palette.
6. Put the I-beam about a DS below the text, drag to draw the column box, and hold down the Option key as you release the mouse button to display column number.

(continued on next page)

RESPONSE PATTERNS

1. Each pair of lines twice SS (slowly, then faster); DS between 4-line groups.
2. A 1' writing on line 2 and on line 4; find *gwam* on each writing.
3. Rekey the slower line.

letter response 1 face pump ever milk area jump vast only save upon safe union
2 As we were in a junk, we saw a rare loon feast on a crawdad.

word response 3 quay hand also body lend hang mane down envy risk corn whale
4 Tisha is to go to the lake with us if she is to do the work.

combination response 5 with only | they join | half safe | born free | firm look | goal rates
6 I sat on the airy lanai with my gaze on the sea to the east.

gwam 1' | 1 | 2 | 3 | 4 | 5 | 6 | 7 | 8 | 9 | 10 | 11 | 12 |

LESSON 32   7 AND 3

SM: Defaults; LS: SS

32A ◆ 6'
CONDITIONING PRACTICE

each line twice

alphabet 1 Gavin made a quick fall trip by jet to Zurich six weeks ago.
figures 2 Key 1 and 4 and 5 and 8 and 9 and 0 and 190 and 504 and 958.
easy 3 The man is to fix the big sign by the field for a city firm.

gwam 1' | 1 | 2 | 3 | 4 | 5 | 6 | 7 | 8 | 9 | 10 | 11 | 12 |

32B ◆ 18'

LEARN 7 AND 3

each line twice SS (slowly, then faster); DS between 4-line groups; practice each line again

7 *Right pointer finger*

3 *Left middle finger*

Learn 7
1 j j 7j 7j jj 77 j7j j7j 77j 77j Reach up for 7, 77, and 777.
2 Key the figures 7, 77, and 777. She checked Rooms 7 and 77.

Learn 3
3 d d 3d 3d dd 33 d3d d3d 33d 33d Reach up for 3, 33, and 333.
4 Add the figures 3, 33, and 333. Read pages 3 to 33 tonight.

Combine 7 and 3
5 Key 33, 37, 73, and 77. Just 37 of the 77 skiers have come.
6 Please order 7 Model 337 computers and 3 Model 737 printers.
7 On August 7, the 33 bikers left on a long trip of 377 miles.

FORMAT TEXT IN COLUMNS

Complete the steps for your software to reformat the text that was imported from the database file.

WORDPERFECT

Three column styles are available: Newspaper, Parallel, and Parallel with Block Protect. Newspaper style, the default style, will be used in this application. Newspaper style lets text flow continuously from column to column as it does in a newspaper article.

In WordPerfect, you have the options to display the columns side by side on the screen or to display the columns on separate pages. When you select the option to display the columns on separate pages, the columns will appear side by side on the printout.

You can have different column styles within a document. For each style, turn off columns, key the new column definition, and then turn on columns again. The steps are:

1. Determine the margins and the number of equal columns that you want on a page.
2. Locate the cursor where you want the first column to begin.
3. From the Columns/Table Menu, select Columns.
4. Select Define to display the Text Column Definitions Menu.
   a. For Newspaper, use default.
   b. For Parallel, select Type (**1**) to display the choice of columns, then select either Parallel or Parallel with Block Protect.
5. Key the number of columns and column widths; then Enter; the margins and spacing are automatically calculated.
6. Select On to turn on Columns feature.
7. Key or import the text.
8. Press **Ctrl Enter** to end a column and start a new one.
9. From Columns/Table Menu, select Off to turn off Columns feature.

WORKS DOS

Column capability is not a feature of Works DOS. To achieve column layouts, format the text in the desired column width; print a copy; then, using cut-and-paste techniques, cut out the text for the second column and paste or tape it on the printout so it is aligned with the first column. Continue in this manner for multiple columns.

WORKS MAC

Columns are created using a combination of word processing and the Text tool from the Tools palette. The steps are:
1. In word processing, with Draw off, use the Return key to insert blank lines for the text.
2. Turn on Draw (⌘J) and select the Text tool from the Tools palette.
3. For each column desired, locate the I-beam where you want the column to appear, drag to draw the column box, and hold down the Option key as you release the mouse button (displays a box with column number).
4. Identify the sequence of the text flow from one column to the next.
   a. Select the Select tool.
   b. Identify Column 1: Option ~ column box where text flow is to begin.
   c. Identify Column 2: Option ~ column box for text flow after Column 1.
   d. Continue in this manner to identify the sequence of the text flow into the column boxes.

32C ◆ 12'

IMPROVE TECHNIQUE: FIGURES

each line twice SS (slowly, then faster); DS between 2-line groups; practice each line again

3/7 1 Flights 337 and 377 will be replaced by Flights 733 and 737.
5/0 2 You had 500 books and 505 workbooks but returned 50 of each.
4/9 3 For the answer to Problem 94, see Unit 9, page 494, line 49.
1/8 4 Irv will be 18 on Tuesday, October 18; he weighs 181 pounds.
all figures 5 Key these figures as units: 18, 37, 49, 50, 73, 81 and 94.
learned 6 We sold 18 spruce, 37 elms, 49 maples, and 50 choice shrubs.

32D ◆ 14'

CENTER LINES

LS: DS
1. Center each line of Problem 1 (see 24C, p. 52).
2. Center the lines of Problem 2.
3. Center the heading of each part of Lesson 32. Example: Center Lines.

1 IMPORTANT TERMS

income tax

gross national product

balance of trade

consumer price index

national debt

social security

2 FBLA ANNOUNCES

NEW OFFICERS

Christopher Linden, President

Mary Ann Stokes, Vice President

ElVon Gibbs, Secretary

Carla Johnson, Treasurer

LESSON 33 — 6 AND 2

SM: Defaults; LS: SS

33A ◆ 6'
CONDITIONING PRACTICE

each line twice

alphabet 1 Jared helped Mazy quickly fix the big wood stove in the den.
figures 2 Bella lives at 1847 Oak Street; Jessi, at 5039 Duard Circle.
easy 3 They may make their goals if they work with the usual vigor.

gwam 1' | 1 | 2 | 3 | 4 | 5 | 6 | 7 | 8 | 9 | 10 | 11 | 12 |

33B ◆ 14'

CHECK TECHNIQUE

1. Key each of lines 1-10 twice SS as your teacher checks your keyboarding technique; DS between 4-line groups.
2. Take a 1' writing on line 11 and on line 12; find *gwam* on each writing.

finger reaches to top row
1 if 85 I am 17 I or 94 I me 737 I dot 395 I lap 910 I kept 8305 I corn 3947
2 In 1987, we had 305 workers; in 1991, we had a total of 403.

quiet hands and arms
3 Celia doubts if she can exceed her past record by very much.
4 Brian excels at softball, but many say he is best at soccer.

quick-snap keystrokes
5 Ella may go to the soap firm for title to all the lake land.
6 Did the bugle corps toot with the usual vigor for the queen?

down-and-in spacing
7 Coy is in the city to buy an oak chair he wants for his den.
8 Jan may go to town by bus to sign a work form for a new job.

out-and-down shifting
9 Robb and Ty are in Madrid to spend a week with Jae and Aldo.
10 Are you going in May or in June? Ellena is leaving in July.

easy sentences
11 Rick paid for both the visual aid and the sign for the firm.
12 Glena kept all the work forms on the shelf by the big chair.

gwam 1' | 1 | 2 | 3 | 4 | 5 | 6 | 7 | 8 | 9 | 10 | 11 | 12 |

Complete the steps for your software to reformat the text that was imported from the database file.

WORDPERFECT

Remove the end field codes, end record codes, and page breaks using search to replace as follows:

1. Retrieve file POSTAL (if necessary) and locate the cursor at the beginning of the line containing the first state, Alabama.
2. Search and replace the End Field code with nothing.
   a. Strike **Alt F2**, **N** (for No confirm).
   b. At the *Srch* prompt, (depress Delete key if any text follows →*Srch:* prompt), strike **F9** to enter End Field code, strike **F2**.
   c. At the *Replace with* prompt, strike **F2** again.
3. Again locate cursor at the beginning of the line containing the first state.
4. Search and replace the End Record and Page Break with a hard return.
   a. Press **Alt F2**, **N**.
   b. At the *Srch* prompt, delete current prompt, strike **Shift F9**, select **2—End Record**, strike **Ctrl Enter**, **F2**.
   c. At the *Replace with* prompt, Enter, strike **F2** again.
5. Delete the page break, column titles, and code commands for the state names and abbreviations that precede the first state.
6. Set left tabs at 1.6" and 2.1".
7. With cursor on Alabama, search and replace as follows to combine the state name, two-letter abbreviation, and standard abbreviation on the same line.
   a. **Alt F2**.
   b. Select Confirm: **Y**(es).
   c. Delete current prompt.
   d. Search for Hard Return (Enter, **F2**).
   e. Replace with Tab (Tab, **F2**).

(continued in next column)

WORDPERFECT (cont.)

   f. At the confirm? **No** (Yes) prompt:
      1. Depress **Y** (Yes confirm) when the cursor is located on two-letter or standard abbreviation lines.
      2. Depress **N** (No confirm) when the cursor is located on lines containing state names.
   You will repeat a **Y**, **Y**, **N** pattern for each of the 50 states. You can cancel search by depressing **F1** at any time. Any errors you make can be corrected at end of search.
8. Save as POSTAL.

WORKS DOS

You will combine the state name, two-letter abbreviation, and standard abbreviation on one line.

1. Open file POSTAL.
2. Delete the column titles for the state names and abbreviations.
3. Reset the tabs for the imported text as follows:
   a. Set a left tab for the state names .25" from the left margin.
   b. Set a left tab for the two-letter abbreviations at 1.6".
   c. Set a left tab for the standard abbreviations at 2.1".

WORKS MAC

You will combine the state name, two-letter abbreviation, and standard abbreviation on one line.

1. Open file POSTAL.
2. Delete the column titles for the state names and abbreviations.
3. Reset the tabs for the imported text.
   a. Begin the state names one character from the left margin.
   b. Begin the two-letter abbreviations three characters after the longest state name.
   c. Begin the standard abbreviations three characters after the two-letter abbreviations.

33C ◆ 12'
CHECK SPEED

LS: DS
Take 1', 2', and 3' writings, following your teacher's directions.

1' *gwam* goals

▽ 21 = acceptable
▫ 25 = average
⊙ 29 = good
◇ 33 = excellent

all letters used | E | 1.2 si | 5.1 awl | 90% hfw

| | | | | | | | | | | gwam | 2' | 3' |

Time and motion are major items in building our keying — 6 | 4

power. As we make each move through space to a letter or a — 12 | 8

figure, we use time. So we want to be sure that every move — 18 | 12

is quick and direct. We cut time and aid speed in this way. — 24 | 16

A good way to reduce motion and thus save time is just — 29 | 19

to keep the hands in home position as you make the reach to — 35 | 23

a letter or figure. Fix your gaze on the copy; then, reach — 41 | 27

to each key with a direct, low move at your very best speed. — 47 | 31

gwam 2' | 1 | 2 | 3 | 4 | 5 | 6 |
3' | 1 | 2 | 3 | 4 |

33D ◆ 18'

LEARN 6 AND 2

each line twice SS (slowly, then faster); DS between 2-line groups; practice each line again

6 *Right pointer* finger

2 *Left ring* finger

Learn 6 ▼

1 j j 6j 6j jj 66 j6j j6j 66j 66j Reach up for 6, 66, and 666.
2 Key the figures 6, 66, and 666. Have only 6 of 66 finished?

Learn 2 ▼

3 s s 2s 2s ss 22 s2s s2s 22s 22s Reach up for 2, 22, and 222.
4 Add the figures 2, 22, and 222. Review pages 2 to 22 today.

Combine 6, 2, and other figures

5 Key 22, 26, 62, and 66. Just 22 of the 66 scouts were here.
6 Reach with the fingers to key 26 and 262 as well as 2 and 6.

7 Key figures as units: 18, 26, 37, 49, 50, 62, 162, and 268.
8 The proxy dated April 26, 1990, was vital in Case No. 37584.

APPLICATION ACTIVITY

Format and key the information as shown at the right, using 1" LM and RM. DS below the heading. Insert two hard returns after the second paragraph. Save as file POSTAL.

TWO-LETTER AND STANDARD STATE ABBREVIATIONS

Two-letter state abbreviations were developed by the Postal Service to help speed mail to its destination. These abbreviations can be read more quickly than the complete state name or most of the standard abbreviations. The two-letter abbreviation system is very simple--just two capital letters with no punctuation. For example, VA is the correct two-letter abbreviation for Virginia.

Standard abbreviations have been used for many years for state names. Standard abbreviations are no longer correct for addressing envelopes or for inside letter addresses. Use the two-letter state abbreviations for these purposes.

IMPORT A DATABASE FILE

First, read about importing a database with your software. Specific directions at the bottom of the page will enable you to import a database.

WORDPERFECT

Retrieve the word processing file that will receive the secondary file containing the merge/end field/end record codes. Locate the cursor at the place where you want the secondary file inserted. Retrieve the secondary file into the current document by following the screen prompts. Reveal codes and delete the merge/end field/end record codes and page breaks using search to replace.

WORKS DOS

Open the database file and copy the part that is to be imported. Open or activate the word processing file and locate the cursor where you want to insert the database information. Strike Enter or select Edit Copy.

WORKS MAC

Open the database file and copy the part that is to be imported. Open or activate the word processing file, and locate the cursor where you want to insert the database information. Paste the database information.

Follow the steps for your software to import the database file STATES at the end of the word processing document POSTAL.

WORDPERFECT

1. Retrieve POSTAL file and locate the cursor a DS below the last paragraph.
2. Retrieve STATES.SF into POSTAL.
3. Save as POSTAL.

WORKS DOS

1. If necessary, go to List View and open the database file STATES; select all.
2. Select Edit Copy.
3. Open or activate the word processing file POSTAL.
4. Locate the cursor a DS below the last line of text in POSTAL.
5. Enter to insert the database copy. (You may have to wait as this step is completed.)

WORKS MAC

1. Open the database file STATES, select all, and copy.
2. Open or activate the word processing file POSTAL.
3. Locate the I-beam a DS below the last line of text in POSTAL.
4. Paste to insert the database copy.

Master Keyboarding/Word Processing Skills

Learning Outcomes: After completing this unit, you will be able to

1. Key all figures without looking at the keyboard.
2. Demonstrate improved technique on alphabetic copy.
3. Demonstrate higher speed on sentences and paragraphs.
4. Demonstrate mastery of basic word processing features.

LESSON 34   KEYBOARDING/WORD PROCESSING

SM: Defaults; LS: SS

34A ◆ 6'
CONDITIONING PRACTICE

each line twice SS;
then a 1' writing on
line 3; find *gwam*

alphabet 1   Linda may have Jack rekey parts two and six of the big quiz.
figures 2   Our house at 622 Gold Circle will be paid for June 26, 2006.
easy 3   Jena is to go to the lake towns to do the map work for them.

gwam 1' | 1 | 2 | 3 | 4 | 5 | 6 | 7 | 8 | 9 | 10 | 11 | 12 |

34B ◆ 10'

MASTER TECHNIQUE: FIGURES

each line once DS as shown

Fingers curved and
upright

Line
1   Twelve of the new shrubs have died; 38 are doing quite well.
2   Forty members have paid their dues, but 15 have not done so.
3   She ordered 2 word processors, 15 computers, and 3 printers.
4   Did he say they need 10 or 12 sets of 211 and 213 diskettes?
5   He will arrive on Paygo Flight 62 at 10:28 a.m. on March 21.
6   All candidates must be in Ivy Hall at 8:10 a.m. on August 1.
7   My home is at 9 Vernon Drive; my office, at One Weber Plaza.
8   Gladys Randolph is 5 ft. 6 in. tall and weighs 119 lbs. 6 oz.
9   Review Rules 1 to 22 in Chapter 6, pages 126 and 127, today.
10   All but 3 of the 18 boys keyed at least 32 gwam on April 15.

34C ◆ 9'

CHANGES

Using the lines keyed in 34B
above, make the changes
specified at the right.

Line 1   Change **Twelve** to **Eleven**, **38** to **39**.
2   Change **Forty** to **Fifty**.
3   Change **3 printers** to **5**.
4   Change **10** to **11**.
5   Change flight **#** to **64**, time to **11:08**.
6   Change **8:10** to **8:30**, **August 1** to **8**.

Line 7   Change **Vernon** to **Verdun**, **Plaza** to **Place**.
8   Change **Gladys** to **Glenda**, **119** to **118**.
9   Change pages **126** and **127** to **127** and **128**.
10   Change **3** to **2**, **32** to **34**.

Expand Integrated Applications Skills

Learning Outcomes: After completing this unit, you will be able to

1. Import database files into word processing documents.
2. Format text in columns.
3. Edit text in columns.

INTEGRATED FEATURE AND PROCEDURES GUIDE

EDIT TEXT IN COLUMNS
FORMAT TEXT IN COLUMNS
IMPORT DATABASE FILES

IMPORT DATABASE FILES

When you import a database file into a word processing document, the database information is converted to word processing. The procedure to import database files into a word processing document is similar to importing word processing files into word processing documents, which you accomplished in Unit 39.

FORMAT TEXT IN COLUMNS

With many word processing programs, you can change the format of existing documents into columns, or you can key a new document directly into columns. For word processing programs that do not feature column layout, you can achieve similar results manually using "cut-and-paste" techniques.

Cut-and-paste techniques have been used by graphic illustrators and others for years. It involves formatting the information in the desired width, printing a copy, cutting the printout apart, and pasting it in the desired sequence of columns. It is still a useful technique—though seldom used by professional illustrators these days—to overcome limitations of some software.

EDIT TEXT IN COLUMNS

Revising columnar text may not be a simple process, and you may have to wait for changes to appear correctly on the screen. Therefore, edit or revise a document as much as possible before you format it into columns.

LESSONS 181-184   INTEGRATE DATABASE AND WORD PROCESSING FILES

181-184A ◆ CONDITIONING PRACTICE

each line twice SS
(slowly, then faster);
DS between 2-line
groups

alphabet 1 Bryson may do exceptionally good work for the quartz industry in Java.
figures 2 The data are given in Figures 18-22 of Part 3, Chapter 7, pp. 459-460.
fig/sym 3 Reasoner & Smith's 10/13 Order #1947 was for 2 5/8-inch pine flooring.
speed 4 They lent the ancient ornament to their neighbor by the big city dock.

gwam 1' | 1 | 2 | 3 | 4 | 5 | 6 | 7 | 8 | 9 | 10 | 11 | 12 | 13 | 14 |

**REVIEW
TECHNIQUE**

1. Key each set of lines once SS as shown.
2. Key a 1' writing on line 16; find *gwam*.

Down-and-in
spacing motion

space bar	1	to my | is in | of the | to buy | for the | may sign | the form | pay them
	2	Kenton may sign the form at my farm for the corn and barley.
shift keys & Lock	3	Aida or Coyt; Hafner and Co.; Have you read OF MICE AND MEN?
	4	Frankie read LINCOLN by Vidal; Kate read ALASKA by Michener.
double letters	5	all off odd zoo jell door leek mess room cuff purr well fuzz
	6	Ann took off the desk a book of odd poems to keep at school.
adjacent keys	7	we opt has try open flew silk rent post suit lion went sport
	8	Kerry opted to rent a silk suit instead of to buy a new one.
long, direct reaches	9	any sum ice sun ace snub must curb dumb brim much snug brake
	10	Jenny spun on the ice, jumped the curb, and broke her thumb.
combination response	11	is we pen saw for was the mop turn were when fear hand nylon
	12	Eight of you are to work for him on the audit of a gas firm.
word response	13	toe own sue rug own man soap form they slam land their right
	14	They may name the auditor to chair their panel if they wish.
alphabet easy	15	Roz fixed the crisp okra, while Jane made unique beef gravy.
	16	Alfie is to go to work for the city to fix bus sign emblems.

gwam 1' | 1 | 2 | 3 | 4 | 5 | 6 | 7 | 8 | 9 | 10 | 11 | 12 |

**IMPROVE/
CHECK SPEED**

LS: DS

1. Two 1' writings on each ¶; find *gwam* on each writing.
2. A 2' writing on ¶s 1-2 combined; find *gwam*.
3. A 3' writing on ¶s 1-2 combined; find *gwam*.
4. Move cursor to beginning of first line in ¶1; reset margins at 1.5", spacing for SS.
5. Return twice; move cursor up to same position and center the heading WHAT IS SUCCESS?
6. Proofread and correct errors on screen.
7. Print the corrected copy.

all letters used | E | 1.2 si | 5.1 awl | 90% hfw |

gwam 2' | 3'

Success does not mean the same thing to everyone. For   6 | 4

some, it means to get to the top at all costs: in power, in   12 | 8

fame, and in income. For others, it means just to fulfill   18 | 12

their basic needs or wants with as little effort as required.   24 | 16

Most people fall within the two extremes. They work quite   30 | 20

hard to better their lives at home, at work, and in the social   36 | 24

world. They realize that success for them is not in being at   42 | 28

the top but rather in trying to improve their quality of life.   48 | 32

gwam 2' | 1 | 2 | 3 | 4 | 5 | 6 |
3' | 1 | 2 | 3 | 4 |

Use today's date

(Add codes for
letter address)

(Add salutation and code for first name)

You can still join the Sails for Rent Scuba Safari to sunken ships off the Big Island's northwest shores! Only a few openings are available for this outstanding trip. Call at once to make your reservation for the Sunken Ships Scuba Safari.

Don't miss this opportunity to join Enrico Piazza's Scuba Safari! Call 166-1234 to make your reservation before the Safari is sold out.

Sincerely

Danielle Austin, Manager

SM: Defaults; LS: SS

35A ♦ 6'
CONDITIONING
PRACTICE
each line twice

alphabet 1 Jung quickly baked extra pizzas for the film festival crowd.

figures 2 I moved from 3748 Oak Street to 1059 Jaymar Drive on May 26.

easy 3 She paid the big man for the field work he did for the city.

gwam 1' | 1 | 2 | 3 | 4 | 5 | 6 | 7 | 8 | 9 | 10 | 11 | 12 |

35B ♦ 10'

MASTER FIGURES

Key each line once DS. Then make the changes listed beneath the sentences.

Line

1 Units 5, 10, and 15 have 3 bedrooms, all others have 2.
2 More than twenty new houses have sold; ten condos have not.
3 At 8:10 p.m. on May 6, the curtain rises on Our Town.
4 Thirty members of the club have signed up; only 13 have not.
5 Ten of the books are now overdue; 26 have been returned.
6 We moved from 3947 Brook Road to 1750 Aspen Place on May 17.
7 For the answer to Problem 59, see unit 8, page 462, Line 13.
8 Our group sold 852 chili dogs, 497 sandwiches, 301 pies.
9 The letter dated June 26, 1993, was vital in Case no. 70583.
10 Several of the 43 workers chose not to take the flu shots.

Line 1 Change , after **bedrooms** to ;
2 Change ; to , and insert **but** before **ten**.
3 After **May 6** insert **and 7** (before the comma).
4 Change **13** to **12**.
5 Insert **new** after **the**.

Line 6 Change **Road** to **Lane**, **17** to **18**.
7 Cap **unit**; uncap **Line**.
8 Insert **and** before **301**.
9 Change **1993** to **1994**; cap **no**.
10 Delete **43**; bold **not**.

35C ♦ 10'

MASTER FEATURES

1. Key the ¶s once SS.
2. Move the cursor to the beginning of the first line and reset margins to 1.5", spacing to DS.
3. Make the changes listed below ¶s.
4. Proofread and correct errors.
5. Print your completed work with 1.5" side margins and DS.

Line

1   If you do not make your goal the first time, do not give
2 up or quit. Size up the task and try it again in a new way.
3 Try to focus on what will help you make your rate next time.

4   It may be that you need just to slow down in order to
5 speed up. That is to say, do not try so hard to force your
6 speed. Relax, read with care, and just let the words flow.

Line 1 Change **first** to **FIRST**.
3 Insert **the** after **rate**.

Line 4 Insert **will** after **you**.
6 Change **flow** to **flow** (typeover); insert **from your fingers**.

Activity 3

1. Use database file VACLIST(.SF) and word processing file FOLUP.
2. Merge print letters to people who live in San Diego.

OPTIONAL INTEGRATED ACTIVITY

Load and print the word processing file OPTINT2 on *Student's Template*. Follow directions provided in the file.

A SSESSMENT ACTIVITY FOR UNITS 39-40

A special scuba trip to be led by Enrico Piazza, director of the Maui Sails for Rent branch, still has openings. Danielle decided to promote this trip to people who recently participated in scuba activities. In her spare time, she keyed part of the information she wants to include. You are to key other information Danielle drafted, combine Danielle's file with the information that you keyed to create a new form letter, and selectively print letters.

1. Use the database file VACLIST(.SF).

2. Personalize the form letter on p. 387 by adding merge codes or placeholders. This letter is to be mailed to the hotel addresses.

3. Import the file RIC (*Student's Template*) after the first paragraph.

4. Print form letters to the people who participated in scuba activities on any of the islands.

35D ◆ 10'

MASTER RESPONSE PATTERNS

1. Key each line once SS.
2. Key a 1' writing on each of lines 7-9; find *gwam* on each writing.
3. Repeat Step 1.

letter response
1 dad hop few pop red you far kin gas oil vet mom get pan grew
2 be in | add up | my dad | you are | saw him | get mom | in case | sat upon

word response
3 ox too off zoo odd lay but cow pair with corn burn mend dorm
4 an ox | of us | to lay | he may | the cow | but when | for them | did turn

combination response
5 him zoo was off mop fix nip but hum wish pump dish milk than
6 he was | to mop | she saw | did hum | make fast | then grab | with facts

letter 7 As my case was set up, you saw him get only a few wage data.
word 8 Lana is to mend a map of the ancient lake town for the dorm.
combination 9 They are to fix by noon the pump at the oil rig on the hill.

gwam 1' | 1 | 2 | 3 | 4 | 5 | 6 | 7 | 8 | 9 | 10 | 11 | 12 |

35E ◆ 14'

IMPROVE/ CHECK SPEED

LS: DS

1. A 1' writing on each ¶; find *gwam* on each writing.
2. A 2' writing on ¶s 1-2 combined; find *gwam*.
3. A 3' writing on ¶s 1-2 combined; find *gwam*.
4. Center in bold the heading RESPONSE PATTERNS a quadruple space (QS) above your 3' writing.
5. Move the cursor to the top left of the screen; reset margins for 1.5" and spacing to DS.
6. Make the changes listed below the ¶s and correct any errors you made.
7. Print your corrected copy.

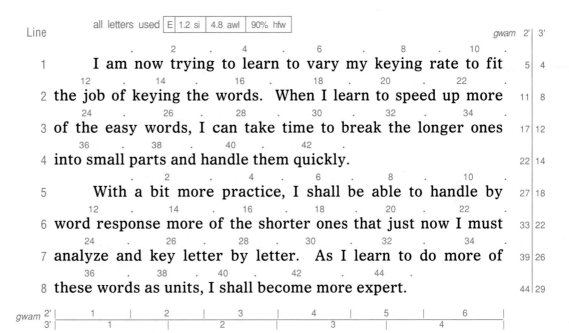

all letters used | E | 1.2 si | 4.8 awl | 90% hfw

Line

gwam 2' 3'

1 I am now trying to learn to vary my keying rate to fit   5 | 4
2 the job of keying the words. When I learn to speed up more   11 | 8
3 of the easy words, I can take time to break the longer ones   17 | 12
4 into small parts and handle them quickly.   22 | 14

5 With a bit more practice, I shall be able to handle by   27 | 18
6 word response more of the shorter ones that just now I must   33 | 22
7 analyze and key letter by letter. As I learn to do more of   39 | 26
8 these words as units, I shall become more expert.   44 | 29

gwam 2' | 1 | 2 | 3 | 4 | 5 | 6 |
3' | 1 | 2 | 3 | 4 |

Line 2 Insert **all** after **keying**; change **all** to **ALL.**
3 Change **longer** to **harder.**

Line 4 Insert **more** after **them.**
6 Change **more** to **many.**
8 Insert **short** after **these.**

APPLICATION
ACTIVITIES

Activity 1

1. If necessary, open the word processing file FIRSTLTR and the database file VACLIST(.SF).
   WordPerfect users will need to do a sort of the VACLIST.SF file, selecting those records that list snorkeling in Field 8. Use SNORKELING as the output file and merge with FIRSTLTR.

2. Merge print letters to people who participated in snorkeling on any island.

Activity 2

Danielle plans to send follow-up letters to Sails for Rent customers to their home addresses. The follow-up letter will include a discount coupon. The letter will also encourage customers to promote Sails for Rent to friends who plan to vacation in the Islands.

1. Use database file VACLIST(.SF).

2. Key the letter and merge codes or placeholders.

3. Save as file FOLUP; print.

(Use today's date)

(Codes for letter address at home)

REMEMBER YOUR GREAT ADVENTURES IN THE ISLANDS!

Songs of the Islands, sapphire seas, and fun in the sun--these memories help you remember your (code for Island) vacation. Now is not too soon to plan your next trip to the Islands! To get you started with Sails for Rent activities on your next trip, a $5 coupon is enclosed.

Here is how you can get more gift certificates! Tell your friends about Sails for Rent! Send us their names and addresses. We will send them our schedule of activities. Each time a friend participates in our activities, you will receive another $5 coupon, good for any activity at any location.

Sails for Rent invites you to come back to the Islands to get wet and add to your memories of adventure!

DANIELLE AUSTIN, MANAGER

SM: Defaults; LS: SS

36A ♦ 6'
CONDITIONING
PRACTICE
each line twice

alphabet 1 Zeno quickly packed my new bags for your next jet to Havana.
figures 2 Of 385 workers, 370 voted for the contract on June 26, 1994.
easy 3 Dixie may chair a panel of six girls to amend the bid forms.

gwam 1' | 1 | 2 | 3 | 4 | 5 | 6 | 7 | 8 | 9 | 10 | 11 | 12 |

36B ♦ 9'

CHECK
TECHNIQUE

each line once SS; rekey

Technique goals
- reach *up* without moving hands away from you
- use Caps Lock to make ALL CAPS
- space *immediately* after each word
- quick-snap keystrokes (all response levels)

figures 1 and 163 sob 295 rid 483 fog 495 hen 637 lap 910 own 926 span
2 Case 10463 may be found in Volume 27, Section 108, page 592.

shift keys 3 Pam and Zoe|Ron or Mark|Yancy and Sons|UPS and USPS|IDF, INC.
& Lock 4 The AMC Corp. ships to Maryland and Virginia largely by UPS.

space 5 to do| it is| or if| by the| for us| to end| and he| she is| am with
bar 6 Andy is to send me a copy of the poem he is to read to them.

letter 7 on at monk read plum fear jump grew look brag hunk care junk
response 8 Johnny read him rate cards on wage taxes set up at my union.

word 9 by zoo and may for men got pan curl vial born turn gush boxy
response 10 Tish may sign a work form to aid the auditor of a soap firm.

combination 11 may few men saw pan tax ham get jam rest lend hulk bush gaze
response 12 A few of them ate jam tarts with the tea she served at dusk.

gwam 1' | 1 | 2 | 3 | 4 | 5 | 6 | 7 | 8 | 9 | 10 | 11 | 12 |

36C ♦ 10'

CHECK SKILL

1. A 1' writing on each ¶; find *gwam* on each.
2. A 2' writing on ¶s 1-2 combined; find *gwam*.
3. A 3' writing on ¶s 1-2 combined; find *gwam*, count errors.

all letters used | E | 1.2 si | 5.1 awl | 90% hfw |

gwam 2' | 3'

You now know not just where each letter and figure key   5 | 4
is located but also how to strike it quickly in the correct   11 | 8
way. With additional practice of the right kind, you could   17 | 12
build your skills to the level of the expert.   22 | 15

Your skill in using a keyboard of an office machine is   27 | 18
a major one you will prize throughout your life. It should   33 | 22
open many doors to work of real worth. Build it high right   39 | 26
now in order to have many a future job offer.   44 | 29

gwam 2' | 1 | 2 | 3 | 4 | 5 | 6 |
3' | 1 | 2 | 3 | 4 |

FORM LETTER WITH MERGE CODES

Read the information at the right and then complete the steps.

Danielle wants to send discount coupons with a form letter to vacationers who participate in Sails for Rent activities. She believes that with a fast turnaround time between the activity and the mailing, most people will receive the letters before they leave the Islands. It will be a good reminder of the fun they experienced and will encourage them to come back to participate in other Sails for Rent activities before they leave the Islands. Danielle drafted a letter for people who participated in snorkeling and asked you to key it.

1. Key the letter below, inserting merge codes or placeholders for VACLIST database file.

2. Save as file FIRSTLTR; print.

(Use today's date)

(Codes or placeholders for letter address at hotel)

MAKE TIME FOR MORE FUN IN THE SUN

Sails for Rent invites you to get wet again--before you leave the Islands. Go sailing! Join a snorkeling safari again or just rent the equipment. Go windsurfing! Meet sea creatures in deep water on a scuba adventure--or enjoy any of the other great water activities we offer. There is still time to make reservations for the water adventure--or adventures--of your choice!

You no doubt noticed that members of the Sails for Rent staff are well-qualified. Our instructors are the best in the field of water recreation. Their goal is to help you have an excellent sea adventure--no matter what activity you select.

A certificate for a 10 percent discount is enclosed. Use it for more snorkeling or other fun in the sun with any Sails for Rent activity--on any Island!

DANIELLE AUSTIN, MANAGER

CHECK WORD PROCESSING SKILLS

LS: DS

1. Set margins for 1.5".
2. Clear the screen (p. 10); then center in bold the heading APPLIED KEYBOARDING; return twice.
3. Key the ¶s.
4. Make the changes given below the ¶s and correct any errors you may have made.
5. Move the cursor to the top of the screen (first line; first position); reset side margins for 1".
6. Insert hard returns so that the centered heading prints 2" from the top edge of sheet.*
7. Print the report.

*Note: Watch the status line (WordPerfect users). Works users: From the desired top margin (2"), subtract the default top margin for your software. The difference indicates how many hard returns you should insert (6 SS hard returns = 1"; 3 DS hard returns = 1").

¶1   Learning to key without wasting time or effort requires a great deal of practice of the proper kind.

¶2   I shall soon experience quite effective uses for my new skill. That is one of my major reasons for learning to key.

¶3   During the next few weeks, I shall master the keying of social and business papers. Perhaps, then, they will dub me a real operator.

¶4   Letters, reports, and tables are among the tasks I must master soon. According to one recent study, they are simple jobs that I must do very well.

¶5   My speed may indeed drop as I change from straight copy to job tasks. I must, therefore, remember to employ my best work habits for every job, whatever its size.

¶6   Learning to key is hard work; however, the skills built make the time well spent. If following a better method will speed progress, I will pursue it. I need sufficient ability to do a top job.

¶1   line 2, add s to kind.
¶2   line 1, insert keying after new.

¶3   line 3, change real to REAL.
¶4   line 3, insert learn to after must.

CREATE TEXT

1. From the thought starters given at the right, choose one for a short composition.
2. Compose a two paragraph theme at the keyboard.

1 I am (a/an/A/B/C/D) student because . . . (give reasons)
2 The most serious problem facing the United States today is . . . (give reasons)
3 The most serious problem facing me today is . . . (give reasons)
4 If I were guaranteed just one wish, I would wish for . . . (give reasons)
5 The public figure I admire most is . . . (give reasons)

WORDPERFECT

Use the same procedure used to complete 161-163G, p. 341. Make Key 2=5; use KAUAI5.SF, MAUI5.SF, and OAHU5.SF as the Output file for Sort: names.

1. Clear the screen; press **Ctrl F9**.
2. Select **1**—Merge.
3. At the prompt for the primary file, key the primary file for the island **(MAUILTR)**.*
4. At the prompt for the secondary file, key the secondary file for the island **(MAUI5.SF)**.

  * **Note:** If you save these files with a .PF extension, remember to use that extension to retrieve the file in the future.

WORKS DOS

1. Open the HOTELS database file and island word processing file (MAUILTR).
2. Activate the island word processing file, if necessary.
3. From the Print Menu, select Print Form Letters.
4. In the Databases box, select HOTELS (more than one file will show if more than one is open).
5. Enter or select OK.
6. At the Print dialog box, strike Enter.

WORKS MAC

1. Open the HOTELS database file and the island word processing file (MAUILTR).
2. From the Window Menu, activate the island word processing file to display it on the screen.
3. From the File Menu, select Print Merge.
4. At the Print dialog box, select appropriate options.
5. Return or ~ OK.

  Note: You can also print a single copy with the placeholders by selecting Show Field Names from the Edit Menu and then selecting Print from the Print Menu.

Use the HOTELS.(SF) database file you created earlier to merge print letters. See p. 341.

1. Merge files MAUILTR and HOTELS to print letters to hotels on Maui with ratings of ★★★★★.

2. Merge files KAUAILTR and HOTELS to print letters to hotels on Kauai with ratings of ★★★★★, following the steps above.

3. Merge files OAHULTR and HOTELS to print letters to hotels on Oahu with ratings of ★★★★★.

L ESSONS 179-180   APPLY DOCUMENT MERGES

179-180A ◆
CONDITIONING
PRACTICE
each line twice SS

alphabet 1 Major zero winds quickly exhausted four men, but they did not give up.

figures 2 Paul must study Section 2, pages 75-190, and Section 3, pages 246-380.

fig/sym 3 The $1,000 CMD Municipal 4 1/2% bonds, due 6/30/97, now sell for $958.

speed 4 Eight of the title firms may sign the amendment by the end of the day.

gwam 1' | 1 | 2 | 3 | 4 | 5 | 6 | 7 | 8 | 9 | 10 | 11 | 12 | 13 | 14 |

UNIT 6

LESSONS 37-39

Master Word Processing Features

Learning Outcomes: After completing this unit, you will be able to

1. Use block and delete/undelete features.
2. Use bold, underline, and center features for existing text.
3. Use copy and move features.

LESSON 37 — LEARN BLOCK AND DELETE/UNDELETE

SM: Defaults; LS: SS

37A ◆ 8'
CONDITIONING PRACTICE

each line twice SS; then three 1' writings on line 3; find *gwam*

alphabet 1 Cindy was pleased by the old quartz box Fran Majak gave her.
figures 2 I checked Items 23, 45, 67, and 89 on pp. 129, 130, and 156.
easy 3 When did the field auditor sign the audit form for the city?

gwam 1' | 1 | 2 | 3 | 4 | 5 | 6 | 7 | 8 | 9 | 10 | 11 | 12 |

37B ◆ 20'

LEARN WORD PROCESSING FEATURES

Delete/Undelete. Delete means to remove from text a segment of text such as a character or space, a word, a line, a sentence, or a defined block of text. Undelete means to restore deleted text.

Block. Block is a feature that defines a specific portion of text; used with the copy, move, and delete features. Cursor keys or mouse can be used to define (highlight) text to be deleted.

WORDPERFECT

character left of cursor	**Backspace**
character above cursor	**Del**
word	**Ctrl Backspace**
end of line	**Ctrl End**
end of page	**Ctrl PgDn**

To delete blocks of text, move cursor to beginning of text to be deleted. Depress **Alt F4** to turn block on; use arrow keys to highlight block of text to be deleted. Depress **Ctrl F4**, B(lock), D(elete). To undelete depress **F1**, R(estore).

WORKS DOS

character left of cursor	**Backspace**
character above cursor	**Del**
word	**Shift Ctrl →, Del**
end of line	**Shift End, Del**
end of page	**Shift Ctrl End, Del**

To delete blocks of text, move cursor to beginning of text to be deleted. Depress the shift key and strike the arrow keys to highlight the block of text to be deleted. Depress the **Del** key. To undelete, depress **Alt Backspace**.

WORKS MAC

character left of cursor	**Delete**
	(backspace)

To delete larger blocks of text, click (~) and drag (→ ↓ ← ↑) the I-beam over the text to be deleted. Depress the **Delete** (backspace) key. To undelete, depress ⌘ **Z**.

1. Review the word processing features; study the specific commands for the software you are using.
2. Key the paragraph at the right; underline and bold text as shown.
3. Using the most efficient method, delete all text that is bolded or underlined.
4. Proofread paragraph and correct any keying errors.
5. Delete the entire paragraph.
6. Undelete or restore the paragraph.

Speaking before a group **of people** can cause a great deal of anxiety for an individual. This anxiety is so extensive <u>that</u> it was ranked as the greatest fear among adults in a **recent** survey. Such fear suggests that <u>many</u> people would rather perish than **go before the public to** give a talk. Much of this fear <u>actually</u> comes from a lack of experience and training in giving **public** speeches. <u>People who excel in the area of public speaking have developed this unique skill through hard work.</u>

PRINT SELECTED PAGES

Study this description of printing selected pages. Step-by-step directions will be given to lead you through the process.

WORDPERFECT

At the Print Menu, select 5—Multiple Pages. To print a single page, key the page number at the *Page(s):* prompt. To print a sequence of pages, key the first page number, then a hyphen (-), then the ending page number. For example, key **4-6** to print pages 4 through 6. You can also print a combination of single pages and a series of pages by combining the groups of numbers. For example, key **1,4-6** to print page 1 and pages 4 through 6. You can also print a series of separate pages by inserting commas between page numbers.

WORKS DOS

At the Print Menu, select Print; then select Print Specific Pages. Select Pages; then key the page number at the *Pages:* prompt. You can print a range of pages by separating the page numbers with a colon (:) or hyphen (-). You also can print a series of separate pages by inserting commas between page numbers.

WORKS MAC

At the Print prompt, tab or locate the I-beam at the From box and key the beginning page number. Tab to the To box and key the ending page number. If you want to print only one page, key that page number in both boxes.

Print Selected Pages

Read the information at the right and then complete the steps. You will copy text, insert a page break, update, print a selected page, and block save a form letter for Oahu.

After reviewing the Kauai form letter, Danielle asked you to complete a form letter for Oahu.

1. Open file KAUAILTR.

2. Insert a page break at the end of the document (see Command Summary, pp. 449-452, if necessary).

3. Copy the letter within the file.

4. Change the second copy to make it a form letter for Oahu.
   a. Delete the middle paragraph.
   b. Import file OAHUWP as the middle paragraph.

5. Save.

6. Print page 2 of the Oahu letter (directions below for your software).

WORDPERFECT

a. Strike **Shift F7** (Print).
b. Key **5** (Multiple Pages).
c. Key **2** (for page 2).
d. Enter.

WORKS DOS

a. From the Print Menu, select Print; then select Print Specific Pages.
b. At the *Pages:* prompt, key **2** for page 2, Enter.

WORKS MAC

a. At the Print prompt, tab to the From box and key the number **2**.
b. Tab to the To box and key number **2** again.

7. Block save the Oahu letter as file OAHULTR.
8. Block delete the Oahu letter and the page break from the KAUAILTR file so that only the Kauai letter remains, then save.
9. Delete files KAUAIWP and OAHUWP; close file KAUOAHU.

37C ◆ 12'

CHECK/IMPROVE SPEED

LS: DS

Take 1' writings on each ¶ and 2' writings on both ¶s; find *gwam* on each writing.

all letters used	LA	1.4 si	5.4 awl	85% hfw

Line

		gwam 2'	3'
1	A vital difference exists between a job done right and	6	4
2	one done just about right. One is given approval while the	12	8
3	other is not. To receive full approval of the jobs you do,	18	12
4	recognize that just about right is not adequate. Attempt	23	16
5	now to do every task just right.	27	18
6	Before long you will try problems in which are applied	32	21
7	the seemingly little things that are crucial in learning to	38	25
8	key. Mastery of little things now is certain to make the	44	29
9	big jobs easier to do just right a little later. Knowledge,	50	33
10	skill, and purpose are the keys to your success.	55	36

gwam 2' | 1 | 2 | 3 | 4 | 5 | 6 |
3' | 1 | 2 | 3 | 4 |

37D ◆ 10'

REVIEW WORD PROCESSING FEATURES

1. Rekey the two paragraphs of 37C.
2. Make the changes outlined at the right.

Line 1 Delete vital.
2 Change just about to nearly.
3 Change of the jobs you do to of your work.
4 & 5 Delete the final sentence of ¶1.

Line 6 & 7 Delete in which are applied the seemingly little things.
9 Delete just right a little.
9 & 10 Delete the final sentence of ¶2.
Undelete the final sentence of ¶2.

L ESSON 38   BOLD, UNDERLINE, AND CENTER EXISTING TEXT

SM: Defaults; LS: SS

38A ◆ 8'
CONDITIONING PRACTICE

each line twice

alphabet 1 Jan Fox left my quiz show and gave back a prize she had won.
figures 2 Zoe set 5 new tab stops as follows: 15, 26, 38, 49, and 70.
easy 3 The city auditor may handle the penalty for the island firm.

gwam 1' | 1 | 2 | 3 | 4 | 5 | 6 | 7 | 8 | 9 | 10 | 11 | 12 |

38B ◆ 10'

REVIEW WORD PROCESSING FEATURES

Make the changes outlined at the right to the sentences you keyed for 38A.

Tom
Jan Fox left my the quiz show and gave back a prize she had won.
adele five s   6 4 6 8   64
Zoe set 5 new tab stops as follows: 15, 26, 38, 49, and 70.
reduce   Marsha's paying late
The city auditor may handle the penalty for the island firm.

Study this procedure for your software to save a block of text, but do not attempt the steps now. First, what do you think the procedure will involve?

WORDPERFECT

1. Block the text to be saved.
2. Strike **F10** to save.
3. At the *Block name:* prompt, key the name of the file where you want the block of text saved.
4. Strike Enter.

WORKS DOS

Select text; from the Edit Menu select Copy; open a new word processing document. Strike Enter to copy the text into the new document. To name the file, select Save As from the File Menu and key the name at the *Save file as:* prompt.

WORKS MAC

Select text; cut or copy to the clipboard; open a new word processing file; paste the text from the clipboard; save under new file name.

COPY FILE/SAVE NEW FILE

Danielle asked you to adapt the updated Maui letter for a form letter to Kauai hotels.

1. Open the *Student's Template* file KAUOAHU.

2. Block save the paragraph for Kauai as file KAUAIWP as follows:

WORDPERFECT

a. Block the text to be saved.
b. Strike **F10** to save.
c. At the *Block name:* prompt, key the name of the file where you want the block of text saved (KAUAIWP).
d. Strike Enter.

WORKS DOS

a. Position the cursor at the beginning of text to be selected.
b. From the Select Menu, select Text.
c. Highlight the appropriate text.
d. From the Edit Menu, select Copy.
e. From the File Menu, select Create New File.
f. Create a new word processing document.
g. Enter (the text will automatically copy into the new document).
h. To name the file, select Save As from the File Menu and key the name KAUAIWP at the *Save file as:* prompt.

WORKS MAC

a. Select text.
b. Cut or copy to the clipboard.
c. Open a new word processing file and paste the text from the clipboard.
d. Save as KAUAIWP.

3. Block save the paragraph for Oahu as file OAHUWP, repeating the steps above.

4. Copy the file MAUILTR to a new file and name it KAUAILTR.

5. Open file KAUAILTR.

6. Change the file to make it a form letter for Kauai as follows:
   a. Delete the middle paragraph.
   b. Import file KAUAIWP to KAUAILTR as the middle paragraph (see p. 376).

7. Save and print.

Take 1' writings on each ¶ and 2'
writings on both ¶s; find *gwam*
on each writing.

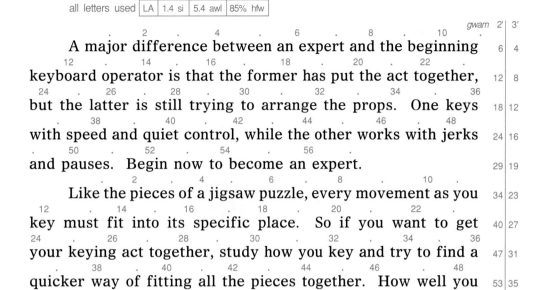

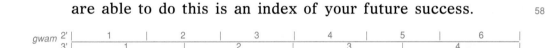

Bold and Underline Existing Text. Text can be bolded or underlined after it is keyed by using the block feature to highlight text and then using the specific software commands for underlining or bolding.

WORDPERFECT

1. Move cursor to beginning of text to be bolded or underlined.
2. Depress **Alt F4** to turn block on, use cursor keys to highlight text to be changed.
3. Depress **F6** to bold highlighted copy, or depress **F8** to underline highlighted copy.

WORKS DOS

1. Move cursor to beginning of text to be bolded or underlined.
2. Use Shift and arrow keys to highlight text to be changed.
3. Depress **Ctrl B** to bold highlighted copy, or depress **Ctrl U** to underline highlighted copy.

WORKS MAC

1. Move I-beam pointer to beginning of text to be bolded or underlined.
2. Click and drag (~ → ↓ or ← ↑) I-beam over the text you want changed.
3. Depress ⌘ **B** to bold highlighted copy, or depress ⌘ **U** to underline highlighted copy.

Center Existing Text. Existing text can be centered by using the specific software centering command.

WORDPERFECT

With the cursor at the beginning of text to be centered, depress **Shift F6**.

WORKS DOS

With the cursor positioned any place on the line to be centered, depress **Ctrl C**.

WORKS MAC

With the cursor positioned any place on the line to be centered, click on (~) **Format**, drag (→) to **Justification**, drag (→) to **Center**, release.

Information at the right applies to WordPerfect only.

Reveal Codes. You can display on the screen the WordPerfect formatting codes by depressing the reveal codes keys (Alt F3). This will display where you have instructed the WordPerfect program to do such things as bold [BOLD], underline [UND], and center [CENTER]. Uppercase [BOLD] shows the beginning of the code; lowercase [bold] shows the ending of the code. Formatting features can be deleted by moving the cursor over the code and depressing the Del key.

Ms. Anita Filippini ~ *ALL CAPS*
Director of Services ~
Hemett Regal Maui ~ *(code for hotel)*
425 Kihei Rd. ~ *(code for address)*
Wailea, HI 96753-9711 ~ *(code for City, State, ZIP)*

Dear Ms. Filippini ~

SAILS FOR RENT CAN HELP BRING YOUR GUESTS BACK
BRINGING YOUR GUESTS BACK!

"I love this place. Best *are* vacation I've ever had; I'll be back next year!" ~~Is this~~ *these* the comment~~s~~ you hear from your departing guests? Sails for Rent can help make this happen.

will want to
Sails for Rent can bring great recreational activities *to your* to your magnificent Maui facilities--and ~~more~~ guests who return! When you establish Sails for Rent recreational activities at your hotel, you expand the Hawaiian experiences of your guests. Your guests, for example, can learn to windsurf right on the beach without getting wet. Scuba and snorkeling safaris to Molokini Island usually bring big adventures. Call or write for more information on establishing a link with Sails for Rent. Make a commitment to increase the number of guests who return again and again.

that you can offer to your guests
Sails for Rent wants to help. You and selected members of your staff can sample our services. Just call (555) 166-1234; ~~and~~ get ready for the aquatic time of your life! *then*

~~Sincerely~~

Danielle Austin, Manager
~~KayAnn Nelson, Director~~

COPY A FILE/ BLOCK SAVE

Study these steps for your software to copy a file, but do not actually do the steps now. Directions will be given again as needed.

WORDPERFECT

1. List the directory of files.
2. Key **N** for Name search; key the name of the file that you want to copy; Enter (highlights the file name).
3. Select **8** to select copy from the menu at the bottom of the screen.
4. At the *Copy this file to:* prompt, key the new file name; Enter.

WORKS DOS

Note: A file cannot be copied when it is open.

1. From the File Menu, select File Management, then select Copy File.
2. At the *File to copy:* prompt, highlight the name of the desired file in the Files List box; Enter.
3. At the *New file name:* prompt, key the new file name; Enter.
4. Strike Esc.

WORKS MAC

1. From the File Menu, select Save As.
2. At the *Save Document As:* prompt, key the new name; select the correct drive if you are storing on a different drive.

1. Key lines 1-4 at the right. Do *not* bold or underline the copy as you key.
2. Use the block feature to bold and underline the copy as shown at the right. Center line 4.

1 **Jo's** birthday is on **Sunday**, <u>May 2</u>; mine is on **Monday**, <u>May 3</u>.

2 The next **FBLA** meeting is on **Thursday**, June 15, at <u>12:30</u> p.m.

3 The **Hixons** moved from <u>3748 Key Street</u> to <u>1629 Vivian Street</u>.

4 **Sandra Mackey, President**

LESSON 39 — LEARN COPY AND MOVE

SM: Defaults; LS: SS

39A ◆ 8'
CONDITIONING PRACTICE
each line twice

alphabet 1 Jay knew Bix and Gavin had perfect papers on my weekly quiz.

figures 2 On May 26, 15 girls and 7 boys keyed Lessons 38, 39, and 40.

easy 3 Nancy is to handle all title forms for the eight auto firms.

gwam 1' | 1 | 2 | 3 | 4 | 5 | 6 | 7 | 8 | 9 | 10 | 11 | 12 |

39B ◆ 7'
REVIEW FEATURES

Bold and underline existing text from the above conditioning practice as shown at the right.

1 **Jay** knew <u>Bix</u> and <u>Gavin</u> had **perfect papers** on my <u>weekly</u> quiz.

2 On <u>May 26</u>, 15 girls and 7 boys keyed <u>Lessons 38, 39, and 40</u>.

3 <u>Nancy</u> is to handle <u>all</u> **title forms** for the <u>eight auto firms</u>.

39C ◆ 23'
LEARN FEATURES

Move. The move feature takes text from one location and places it in another.
Copy. The copy feature duplicates text from one location and places it in another.

WORDPERFECT

Move
1. Place cursor at beginning of text to be moved.
2. Depress **Alt F4** to turn block on; use arrow keys to highlight desired text.
3. Depress **Ctrl F4**.
4. Depress **B**(lock); depress **M**(ove).
5. Move cursor to new text position; strike Return.

Copy
1. Place cursor at beginning of text to be copied.
2. Depress **Alt F4** to turn block on; use cursor keys to highlight desired text.
3. Depress **Ctrl F4**; depress **B**(lock); depress **C**(opy).
4. Relocate cursor at position where you want copied text placed.
5. Strike Return.

WORKS DOS

Move
1. Move cursor to beginning of text to be moved.
2. Depress Shift key and use arrow keys to highlight text to be moved.
3. Depress **Alt, E, M**.
4. Position cursor at location where you want text moved to; strike Return.

Copy
1. Move cursor to beginning of text to be copied.
2. Depress Shift key and use arrow keys to highlight text to be copied.
3. Depress **Alt, E, C**.
4. Position cursor at location where you want copied text placed and strike Return.

WORKS MAC

Move
1. Move cursor to beginning of text to be moved.
2. Use I-beam to highlight text desired.
3. Use mouse to click on (~) **Edit**; drag (→) to **Cut** and release (or use ⌘ **X**).
4. Position cursor at location where you want to place text.
5. Click on (~) **Edit**; drag (→) to **Paste** and release (or use ⌘ **V**).

Copy
1. Move cursor to beginning of text to be copied; highlight text to be copied.
2. Click on (~) **Edit**; drag to **Copy** and release (or use ⌘ **C**).
3. Position cursor at location where you want copied text to be placed.
4. Click on (~) **Edit**; drag to **Paste** and release (or use ⌘ **V**).

RENAME A FILE

Read the information below for your software, but do not attempt these steps now. More specific directions follow on the page for actually renaming a file.

WORDPERFECT

1. Strike **F5;** Enter to list the directory of files.
2. Highlight the file to rename.
3. Key **3** or **M** for Move/Rename.
4. At the *New name:* prompt, key the new name and Enter.

WORKS DOS

A file cannot be renamed when it is open.

1. From the File Menu, select File Management, then select Rename, Enter.
2. At the *File to rename:* prompt, highlight the desired file in the Files List box; Enter.
3. At the *New file name:* prompt, key the new name; Enter.
4. Strike Esc.

WORKS MAC

1. Display the list of files on the screen.
2. Highlight the file name.
3. Key the new name; Return.

Read the information at the right and then complete the steps to rename a file and convert an existing document to a form letter.

Danielle Austin plans to send letters to selected hotels on Oahu, Maui, and Kauai to promote establishing Sails for Rent recreational centers at their facilities. She asked you to convert a letter to a simplified block style form letter. Because hotels in the Islands have frequent changes of personnel for the position of Director of Services, Danielle wants the letter addressed to Director of Services (not to include a name). The simplified block format is appropriate in this case because it eliminates the need for a salutation. (Refer to p. 321 or p. 435 if necessary.)

1. Rename file HOTELLTR (on *Student's Template*) to MAUILTR, following the steps below.

WORDPERFECT

a. List the directory of files.
b. Highlight HOTELLTR.
c. Select **3**—Move/Rename.
d. At the *New Name:* prompt, key **MAUILTR**; Enter.

WORKS DOS

a. From the File Menu, select File Management.
b. Select Rename File, Enter.
c. In the Files List box, highlight HOTELLTR; Enter.
d. At the *New File Name:* prompt, key the name as **MAUILTR**, Enter; then Esc.
e. Open the file MAUILTR.

WORKS MAC

a. Open HOTELLTR.
b. From the File Menu, select Save As.
c. At the prompt, key **MAUILTR**; Return.

2. Make the changes marked on the printout (top of p. 380).

3. Insert the appropriate codes or placeholders necessary for your software to merge HOTELIST database and this word processing file. (Review print formats and printing in 157C, p. 320, if necessary.)

4. Spell-check, proofread, save, and print.
   WordPerfect: Save as a primary file.
   Note: You should already have developed the habit of spell-checking and proof-reading your work. Instructions to spell-check and proofread will no longer be given.

Exercise 1

1. Key the listing of cities and states as shown at the right. Return twice after keying the last entry.
2. After you key the list, use the move feature to alphabetize the listing by city.
3. Use the copy feature to copy the list and place a copy of the list a double space below the first listing.
4. Use the move feature to alphabetize the second listing by state.

Exercise 2

1. Key the ¶s at the right.
2. Use move feature to:
   a. move ¶1 to end.
   b. move ¶3 to beginning.
   c. move first sentence of ¶2 to end of ¶2.

Boise, Idaho
Scottsdale, Arizona
Portland, Oregon
Logan, Utah
Los Angeles, California
Seattle, Washington
Reno, Nevada

¶1 If you have any questions about any of the furniture you looked at yesterday, please call me.

¶2 As I indicated, Wilson's Department Store is committed to customer satisfaction. In the meantime, you may be interested in looking over the brochures of furniture that are enclosed. If a set particularly interests you, we could order it. You would be under no obligation to buy the set if it does not meet your expectations when it arrives.

¶3 Discussing your furniture needs with you yesterday was enjoyable. I checked with the department manager, and the next shipment of furniture should arrive within a few weeks. Eight new styles of dining room sets were ordered. When the shipment arrives, I will call you.

39D ◆ 12'

CHECK/IMPROVE SPEED

LS: DS

Take 1' writings on each ¶ and 2' writings on both ¶s; find *gwam* on each writing.

all letters used | LA | 1.4 si | 5.4 awl | 85% hfw

gwam 2' | 3'

It is okay to try and try again if your first efforts do 6 | 4
not bring the correct results. If you try but fail again and 12 | 8
again, however, it is foolish to plug along in the very same 18 | 12
manner. Rather, experiment with another way to accomplish the 24 | 16
task that may bring the skill or knowledge you seek. 30 | 20

If your first attempts do not yield success, do not quit 35 | 23
and merely let it go at that. Instead, begin again in a bet- 41 | 27
ter way to finish the work or develop more insight into your 47 | 31
difficulty. If you recognize why you must do more than just 54 | 36
try, try again, you will work with purpose to achieve success. 60 | 40

gwam 2' | 1 | 2 | 3 | 4 | 5 | 6 |
     3' | 1 | 2 | 3 | 4 |

UNIT 40

LESSONS 175-180

Work With Form Letters

Learning Outcomes: After completing this unit, you will be able to

1. Rename, copy, and backup documents.
2. Save text blocks as new documents.
3. Convert existing documents to form letters and merge print.
4. Print selected pages.

INTEGRATED FEATURE AND PROCEDURES GUIDE

BLOCK SAVE
CONVERT DOCUMENT TO FORM LETTER
COPY AND BACKUP A FILE
PRINT SELECTED PAGES
RENAME A FILE

RENAME A FILE

When you rename a file, the procedure depends on the software you are using. With some software, you select the rename function, key the current name of the file at the prompt, and then key the new name at the next prompt. With other software, you display the file names on the screen, highlight the file you want to change, and key the new name, replacing the original one. In all cases, the file is not duplicated. That is, you have just one copy of the document.

COPY AND BACKUP A FILE

When you copy a file, the original file remains and a new file appears. One reason to copy a file is to create a backup of it. Backup files are made so that you have copies of files without the need to key them again if something happens to the original file. Usually, a backup file is copied as the same name as the original file, but to a different disk. It is a good idea to make backup copies of important files and to store the backup copies in a different location from the original files.

When keeping the original file intact is important, a copy of the file should be saved using a different name. You can then maintain the original file and revise/edit the copy. Because the file names are different, both files could be saved on the same disk, even though the original contents are identical.

BLOCK SAVE

When you block save, you select or highlight a block of text and then save the selected text as a new document.

CONVERT DOCUMENT TO FORM LETTER

Converting a document to a form letter and merging it with a database mailing list is a simple process. For each of the variables (information that would not be the same in each letter), such as name and address, you replace the existing information with merge codes or place-holders. For example, you would replace the letter address by replacing the name with the codes or placeholders for the name (first name, last name) and replacing the street address, city, state, and ZIP with the appropriate codes for them.

PRINT SELECTED PAGES

When you are working with multipage documents, most modern software lets you select which pages to print. Several choices are available. You can print a single page, pages not in sequence, pages in sequence, or a combination of these. With some software, you insert a comma between single pages that are not in sequence, and you insert a hyphen (-) between pages in sequence. With other software, you key page numbers at the Print Menu prompts for printing pages in sequence, and you repeat the process for each single page.

L ESSONS 175-178 | WORK WITH DOCUMENT MERGES

**175-178A ◆
CONDITIONING
PRACTICE**

each line twice SS
(slowly, then faster);
DS between 2-line
groups

alphabet 1	Maja was to have five pens and extra clips in a kit for your big quiz.
figures 2	Sandy was 25 years old when she moved to 4360 Rosegarden Road in 1987.
fig/sym 3	She arrived at 12:47 a.m. on Flight #860 (Gate 38) with 59 classmates.
speed 4	Pam kept the big emblem in a fir box by the enamel bowls on the shelf.

gwam 1' | 1 | 2 | 3 | 4 | 5 | 6 | 7 | 8 | 9 | 10 | 11 | 12 | 13 | 14 |

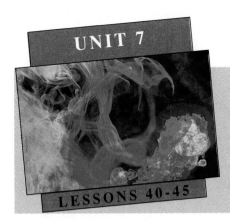

Master Symbol-Key Operation

Learning Outcomes: After completing this unit, you will be able to

1. Key copy containing symbols, using proper technique with correct fingers.
2. Key script (handwritten) copy and copy containing figures at a high percentage of your straight-copy speed.

LESSON 40 / AND $

SM: Defaults; LS: SS

40A ◆ 6'
CONDITIONING PRACTICE

each line twice SS; then a 1' writing on line 3; find *gwam*

alphabet 1 Di will buy from me as prizes the six unique diving jackets.
figures 2 The January 17 quiz of 25 points will test pages 389 to 460.
easy 3 Both of us may do the audit of the work of a big title firm.

gwam 1' | 1 | 2 | 3 | 4 | 5 | 6 | 7 | 8 | 9 | 10 | 11 | 12 |

40B ◆ 18'

LEARN / AND $

each line twice SS (slowly, then faster); DS between 4-line groups; practice the lines again

Technique hint
Do not space between a figure and the / or the $ sign.

/ *Right little* finger

$ Shift; then *left pointer* finger

Learn / (diagonal) ▼

1 ; ; /; /; ;; // ;/; ;/; 2/3 4/5 and/or We keyed 1/2 and 3/4.
2 Space between a whole number and a fraction: 7 2/3, 18 3/4.

Learn $ (dollar sign) ▼

3 f f $f $f ff $$ f$f f$f $4 $4 for $4 Shift for $ and key $4.
4 A period separates dollars and cents: $4.50, $6.25, $19.50.

Combine / and $

5 I must shift for $ but not for /: Order 10 gal. at $16/gal.
6 Do not space on either side of /: 1/6, 3/10, 9 5/8, 4 7/12.
7 We sent 5 boxes of No. 6 3/4 envelopes at $11/box on June 2.
8 They can get 2 sets of disks at $49.85/set; 10 sets, $39.85.

stet

Those helpful headlights, however, also can be a problem. ~~Oncoming headlights tend to draw our attention directly to them.~~ When we look directly at oncoming headlights, they seem to attract us like a magnet and blind us to everything else! It is as though ~~we are~~ hypnotized by those oncoming headlights and we are drawn toward them!

it takes time for When we look directly into the headlights of oncoming traffic, our eyes take a while to adjust so that we can see once the oncoming traffic has moved past us. If you

¶ Night Driving Tip #1 are on a two-lane road, watch the right side of the road-- not the oncoming headlights. Often, a line identifies the right edge of the lane. If you are on a multilane road, watch the right marking for the lane in which you are driving. You will find that your eyes quickly adjust to the darkness once the oncoming traffic has passed.

¶ Night Driving Tip 3 Be alert for animals that might run in front of you. In city driving, be alert for dogs and cats. Watch for a number of other critters, ~~in addition to dogs and cats,~~ in the country, such as deer, cows, horses, rabbits, squirrels, and skunks. *All* ~~Any~~ of these animals might sud-

be invisible until they denly appear in your headlights. Stopping in time is critical, especially when the animal is large. While quick stopping is important, there is an even more impor- tant issue--you must maintain your position in the lane without swerving. Just as in daytime driving, it is vital that you do not turn the steering wheel sharply in an attempt to miss a critter. That action will likely put your car into a skid and cause a much more serious accident. The important action to remember is that you attempt to stop while you maintain your position in the lane.

Other drivers can become a problem *∧ when you drive* ~~driving~~ at night. For example, drivers who are tired or who are under the influence of various substances that reduce driving abil- ity are more likely to be involved in head-on collisions than drivers who are alert. Conditions that reduce driv- ing ability are generally more common at night than in

¶ Night Driving Tip 5 the daytime. Drive defensively. That is, be alert to oncoming cars that might be heading toward you! Con- stantly anticipate dangerous situations when you are driving and have a plan in mind. As you are driving, for example, study the shoulder of the road to determine if it is wide enough for your car if an oncoming car is heading toward you.

**OPTIONAL
INTEGRATED
ACTIVITY**

Load and print the word processing file OPTINT1 on the *Student's Template*. Follow the directions given in the file.

MASTER SKILL

1. Key each set of lines twice: first slowly; then at a faster pace.
2. Take a 1' writing on line 6, then on line 8. Find *gwam* on each; then compare rates.
3. As time permits, key the slower line again.

figures
1 Keep your hands steady as you key 46, 57, 182, 193, and 750.
2 Ask for 16 men to work on Job 5749 at Pier 28 on January 30.

fig/sym
3 Space once between a whole number and a fraction: 8 1/2 oz.
4 I paid $195 for a 4 by 6 rug and $87 for 3 vases on June 20.

word response
5 jay aid oak the may she and but fix both fish also when make
6 Jemal may go to the lake dock with eight of the men to fish.

combination response
7 own was men saw hay are did pen get form were hand jump duty
8 Jane keeps a set of cards in a box on a shelf in the garage.

gwam 1' | 1 | 2 | 3 | 4 | 5 | 6 | 7 | 8 | 9 | 10 | 11 | 12 |

40D ◆ 16'

MASTER TECHNIQUE

1. Center each of lines 1-5 using the center feature (see 24C, p. 52); DS.
2. QS and key each of lines 6-11 once SS; DS between 2-line groups.
3. Rekey the drill.

Quick-snap keystroke

center lines
1 WORD PROCESSING TERMS
2 automatic centering
3 delete and insert
4 store and retrieve
5 global search and replace

space bar
6 by us of an am to go by an urn of elm to pay she may and jam
7 Karen is to pay the man for any of the elm you buy from him.

Caps Lock
8 They are to see the musical play INTO THE WOODS on Saturday.
9 HBO will show THE KING AND I on Monday, May 13, at 8:30 a.m.

alphabet 10 Sprague is amazed at just how quickly he fixed the blue van.
figures 11 Invoice No. 2749 totals $163.85 plus $4.20 shipping charges.

gwam 1' | 1 | 2 | 3 | 4 | 5 | 6 | 7 | 8 | 9 | 10 | 11 | 12 |

LESSON 41 % AND -

SM: Defaults; LS: SS

41A ◆ 6'
CONDITIONING PRACTICE
each line twice

alphabet 1 Lopez knew our squad could just slip by the next five games.
figures 2 Check Numbers 267, 298, 304, and 315 were still outstanding.
easy 3 Dixie works with vigor to make the theory work for a profit.

gwam 1' | 1 | 2 | 3 | 4 | 5 | 6 | 7 | 8 | 9 | 10 | 11 | 12 |

41B ◆ 16'

MASTER TECHNIQUE

1. Key lines 1-11 of 40D, above, once each as shown.
2. Take a 1' writing on line 7 and on line 10 of 40D.

Goals:
- to refine technique
- to increase speed

IMPORTING WORD PROCESS-ING FILES

Read the information at the right and then complete the steps listed for your software.

Diane reviewed your printout of her night driving article and marked several revisions. She also originated additional information for the article and asked you to combine the files and then to make more revisions.

1. Import *Student's Template* file DRIVE into file NEWS.

WORDPERFECT

a. Retrieve file NEWS.
b. Locate the cursor at the beginning of the third paragraph.
c. Retrieve file DRIVE into current document.

WORKS DOS

a. Open files NEWS and DRIVE.
b. With file DRIVE active, Select All.
c. Select Edit Copy.
d. From Window Menu, activate file NEWS.
e. Locate the cursor at the beginning of the third paragraph and strike Enter or Edit Copy.

WORKS MAC

a. Open files NEWS and DRIVE.
b. With file DRIVE active, Select All, and copy to clipboard.
c. Activate file NEWS, locate I-beam at the beginning of the third paragraph, and paste.

2. Block move the second paragraph of the inserted file to the location specified in the file and delete text as indicated in the merged file.

3. Revise as indicated on the text copy (below and on p. 377) and then make the following changes.
   a.   SS with DS between paragraphs.
   b.   Add side heading tips before paragraphs as indicated.
   c.   Top and bottom margins 1.5".

4. Set page numbering to print at top right margin (see 103B, p. 187).

5. Suppress page number on page one as follows.

WORDPERFECT

a. From the Format Menu, select Page.
b. Select Suppress (this page only), *Suppress Page Numbering* **Y**(es).

WORKS DOS

a. Select Headers and Footers from the Print Menu.
b. Select No header on first page.

WORKS MAC

a. Select Format Menu.
b. Select Title Page.

6. Spell-check and proofread, save, and print.

7. Correct errors if necessary, then print again.

Tips on Night Driving

Have you ever noticed that night driving takes more skill than daytime driving? For one thing, you cannot see as far as you can in the daylight. For another, you cannot judge distances as well.

Let's consider what is visible--and invisible--at night. On the highway, traffic is visible because head-lights help to identify the location of oncoming traffic.

(continued on next page)

LEARN % AND -

each line twice SS (slowly, then faster); DS between 4-line groups; practice the lines again

% Shift; then *left pointer* finger

- *Right little* finger

Technique hint
Do not space between a figure and the %, nor before or after - or -- (dash) used as punctuation.

Learn % (percent sign) ▼

1 f f %f %f ff %% f%f f%f 5% 5%   Shift for the % in 5% and 15%.
2 Do not space between a number and %: 5%, 75%, 85%, and 95%.

Learn - (hyphen) ▼

3 ; ; -; -; ;; -- ;-; ;-; 4-ply I use a 2-ply tire on my bike.
4 I gave each film a 1-star, 2-star, 3-star, or 4-star rating.

Combine % and -

5 He can send the parcel by fourth-class mail at a 50% saving.
6 A dash is two unspaced hyphens--no space before or after it.
7 The new prime rate is 12%--but you have no interest in that.
8 You need 60 signatures--51% of the members--on the petition.

41D ◆ 10'

BUILD SKILL TRANSFER

LS: DS
Take 1' writings on each ¶; find and compare *gwam*. Try for a higher *gwam* on additional writings.

To find *gwam*, use the 1' *gwam* for partial lines in ¶s 1 and 2, but *count* the standard words (5 characters/spaces) in a partial line in ¶ 3.

all letters/figures used | LA | 1.4 si | 5.4 awl | 85% hfw

gwam 1'

You should try now to transfer to other types of copy   11
as much of your straight-copy speed as you can. Handwritten   23
copy and copy in which figures appear tend to slow you down.   35
You can increase speed on these, however, with extra effort.   48

An immediate goal for handwritten copy is at least 90%   11
of the straight-copy rate; for copy with figures, at least   23
75%. Try to speed up balanced-hand figures such as 26, 84,   35
and 163. Key harder ones such as 452 and 890 more slowly.   47

Copy that is written by hand is often not legible, and   11
the spelling of words may be puzzling. So give major atten-   23
tion to unclear words. Question and correct the spacing used   35
with a comma or period. You can do this even as you key.   47

gwam 1' | 1 | 2 | 3 | 4 | 5 | 6 | 7 | 8 | 9 | 10 | 11 | 12 |

Be alert for animals that might run in front of you. In city driving, be alert for dogs and cats. Watch for a number of other critters, in addition to dogs and cats, in the country, such as deer, cows, horses, rabbits, squirrels, and skunks. Any of these animals might suddenly appear in your headlights. Stopping in time is critical, especially when the animal is large. While quick stopping is important, there is an even more important issue--you must maintain your position in the lane without swerving. Just as in daytime driving, it is vital that you do not turn the steering wheel sharply in an attempt to miss a critter. That action will likely put your car into a skid and cause a much more serious accident. The important action to remember is that you attempt to stop while you maintain your position in the lane.

Other drivers can become a problem driving at night. For example, drivers who are tired or who are under the influence of various substances that reduce driving ability are more likely to be involved in head-on collisions than drivers who are alert. Conditions that reduce driving ability are generally more common at night than in the daytime. Drive defensively. That is, be alert to oncoming cars that might be heading toward you! Constantly anticipate dangerous situations when you are driving and have a plan in mind. As you are driving, for example, study the shoulder of the road to determine if it is wide enough for your car if an oncoming car is heading toward you.

173-174C ◆

IMPORTING FILES/ SUPPRESSING PAGE NUMBERS

WORDPERFECT

Importing Files. Open the word processing file that will receive the other file; locate the cursor at the place where you want the second file inserted; retrieve desired file into current document by following the screen prompts.

Suppressing Page Numbers. From the Format Menu, select in sequence Page, Suppress (this page only), *Suppress Page Numbering*, **Y**(es).

WORKS DOS

Importing Files. Importing word processing files to other word processing documents is similar to copying text within a document. Select the information you want to copy, then select Edit Copy. To copy information to another file, open the file or select it from the Window Menu if it is already open. Move the cursor to where you want to insert the copied information and strike Enter or select the Edit Copy command again.

Suppressing Page Numbers. From the Print Menu, select Headers and Footers; then select No header on first page, Enter.

WORKS MAC

Importing Files. Importing word processing files to other word processing documents is similar to copying text within a document. Select the information you want to copy and copy it to the clipboard. To import to another file, open at the file or activate it if it is already open. Move the I-beam to where you want to insert the copied text and paste the text into the document.

Suppressing Page Numbers. When you select Title Page from the Format Menu, the page number will not print on the first page of the file.

SM: Defaults; LS: SS

42A ◆ 6'
CONDITIONING PRACTICE
each line twice

alphabet	1	Racquel just put back five azure gems next to my gold watch.
figures	2	Joel used a comma in 1,203 and 2,946 but not in 583 and 750.
easy	3	The auto firm owns the big signs by the downtown civic hall.

gwam 1' | 1 | 2 | 3 | 4 | 5 | 6 | 7 | 8 | 9 | 10 | 11 | 12 |

42B ◆ 10'
MASTER ALPHANUMERIC COPY

Key the ¶ once DS at an easy pace with particular attention to figures and symbols. Take 2' and 3' writings.

gwam 2' | 3'

In one class of 16 students, 100% reached a speed of 28 — 6 | 4

words a minute or higher on a 3-minute writing by the middle — 12 | 8

of December. The worst speed was 28, the best 64, the class — 18 | 12

average 39.5. The error range was 0-6 with an average of 3. — 24 | 16

Students could use the backspace/erase key to correct errors — 30 | 20

as they keyed. Over 79% of the students earned an A or a B. — 36 | 24

42C ◆ 18'
LEARN # AND &

each set of lines twice SS (slowly, then faster); DS between groups; practice the lines again

= number/pounds
& = ampersand (and)
Do not space between # and a figure; space once before and after & used to join names.

Shift; then *left middle* finger

& Shift; then *right pointer* finger

Learn # (number/pounds)

1 d d #d #d dd ## d#d d#d 3# 3# Shift for # as you enter #33d.
2 Do not space between a number and #: 3# of #633 at $9.35/#.

Learn & (ampersand)

3 j j &j &j jj && j&j j&j 7& 7& Have you written to Poe & Son?
4 Do not space before or after & in initials; i.e., CG&E, B&O.

Combine # and &

5 Shift for # and &. Recall: # stands for number and pounds.
6 Names joined by & require spaces; a # sign alone does, also.
7 Letters joined by & are keyed solid: List Stock #3 as C&NW.
8 I bought 20# of #830 grass seed from Locke & Uhl on March 4.

173-174A ◆
CONDITIONING
PRACTICE

each line twice SS
(slowly, then faster);
DS between 2-line
groups

alphabet 1 Jacques has asked to be given one week to reply to this tax quiz form.

figures 2 What is the sum of 9 and 12 and 39 and 40 and 48 and 57 and 60 and 93?

fig/sym 3 The amount I paid is $25,640.78, with 5% sales tax and 13% excise tax.

speed 4 She may go with them down the lane to the shale rocks by the big lake.

gwam 1' | 1 | 2 | 3 | 4 | 5 | 6 | 7 | 8 | 9 | 10 | 11 | 12 | 13 | 14 |

173-174B ◆

APPLICATION
ACTIVITY

Read the information at the
right and then complete the
steps listed. Note that file
names are provided without
extensions.

You are the editor for the next edition of *Rolling Wheels,* Wheels For Sale's newsletter. Diane, the manager, drafted an article on night driving on her typewriter at home. She asked you to key the draft in word processing and print a copy.

1. Key from the draft of the article (below and on next page); you will use this file later.
   a. Use default margins.
   b. DS.
   c. Indent paragraphs using the default tab.
   d. Center the title in ALL CAPS.

2. Correct any errors you make as you key.

3. Use spell check and correct any spelling errors.

4. Save as file NEWS; print.

5. Proofread, revise if necessary; print again.

Tips on Night Driving

Have you ever noticed that night driving takes more skill than daytime driving? For one thing, you cannot see as far as you can in the daylight. For another, you cannot judge distances as well.

Let's consider what is visible--and invisible--at night. On the highway, traffic is visible because headlights help to identify the location of oncoming traffic. Those helpful headlights, however, also can be a problem. Oncoming headlights tend to draw our attention directly to them. When we look directly at oncoming headlights, they seem to attract us like a magnet and blind us to everything else! It is as though we are hypnotized by those oncoming headlights and we are drawn toward them! When we look directly into the headlights of oncoming traffic, our eyes take a while to adjust so that we can see once the oncoming traffic has moved past us. If you are on a two-lane road, watch the right side of the road-- not the oncoming headlights. Often, a line identifies the right edge of the lane. If you are on a multilane road, watch the right marking for the lane in which you are driving. You will find that your eyes quickly adjust to the darkness once the oncoming traffic has passed.

(continued on next page)

BUILD SKILL TRANSFER

LS: DS

Take 1' writings on each ¶ and compare *gwam* on straight copy and statistical copy.

Goal: To transfer at least 75% of your straight-copy speed to statistical copy.

To determine % of transfer:
¶2 *gwam* ÷ ¶1 *gwam*

all letters/figures used | LA | 1.4 si | 5.4 awl | 85% hfw

Figures appear often in personal and business documents. It is vital, therefore, that you learn to key them rapidly. If you will just keep your hands in position and reach with your fingers, you will soon be amazed at your ability to key all figures with ease.

Learn to read and key figures in distinct groups. For example, read 165 as one sixty-five and key it that way. Tackle the longer sequences in like manner. Read 1078 as ten seventy-eight and handle it as 2 units. Try this trick for 2493, also.

LESSON 43   (AND)

SM: Defaults; LS: SS

CONDITIONING PRACTICE

each line twice

alphabet 1 Jacques could win a prize for eight more dives by next week.

figures 2 In 1987, Sam had only 150 computers; as of 1993, he had 264.

easy 3 The girls paid for the eight antique urns with their profit.

gwam 1' | 1 | 2 | 3 | 4 | 5 | 6 | 7 | 8 | 9 | 10 | 11 | 12 |

CHECK SKILL

Take 2' and 3' writings DS on both ¶s; find *gwam* and circle and count errors. Take another 3' writing:

0-6 errors—speed
7+ errors—control

gwam	¹/₄'	¹/₂'	³/₄'	Time
20	5	10	15	20
24	6	12	18	24
28	7	14	21	28
32	8	16	24	32
36	9	18	27	36
40	10	20	30	40
44	11	22	33	44
48	12	24	36	48

all letters used | LA | 1.4 si | 5.4 awl | 85% hfw

gwam 2' 3'

When you need to adjust to a new situation in which new people are involved, be quick to recognize that at first it is you who must adapt. This is especially true in an office where the roles of workers have already been established. It is your job to fit into the team structure with harmony.

Learn the rules of the game and who the key players are; then play according to those rules at first. Do not expect to have the rules modified to fit your concept of what the team structure and your role in it should be. Only after you become a valuable member should you suggest major changes.

6	4
12	8
18	12
24	16
30	20
6	23
12	27
18	31
24	36
30	39

gwam 2' | 1 | 2 | 3 | 4 | 5 | 6 |
     3' | 1 | 2 | 3 | 4 |

Get Started With Integrated Applications

Learning Outcomes: After completing this unit, you will be able to

1. Import (combine) word processing files.
2. Apply page numbering techniques.

**INTEGRATED FEATURE AND
PROCEDURES GUIDE**

APPEND AND IMPORT FILES
PAGE NUMBERING TECHNIQUES

APPEND AND IMPORT FILES

Appending files means to combine files by inserting another file at the end of a document. Importing files also involves combining files. The difference is that when you import a file, you are not limited to inserting it at the end of the receiving file but can insert it at any location.

Appending and importing word processing documents lets you combine word processing files without rekeying them. When you combine word processing files, you are integrating the files, word processing to word processing.

You open the document that will receive another file, locate the cursor/insertion point at the place where you want the other file inserted; and then key the software commands to bring in the other file. Using this procedure, it is possible to import a number of word processing files to specific locations within the receiving file.

PAGE NUMBERING TECHNIQUES

When you understand how pages of a document are numbered, you can produce professional-looking documents.

Multipage documents may be printed on only one side of a sheet (called "single-sided") or on both sides (called "back-to-back" or "double-sided"). Options for placement of page numbers include the top or bottom of the page at the center or at the margin.

When you turn the pages of a leftbound document that is printed back-to-back, you see two pages opposite each other (called "facing pages"). When facing pages are numbered at the margin, the location of page numbers differs for facing pages. Left-hand pages have numbers located at the left margin, and right-hand pages have numbers located at the right margin. Page one (and all odd-numbered pages) are right-hand pages of documents printed back-to-back, and page two (and all even-numbered pages) are left-hand pages.

A major section of a document—such as a chapter in a long report or unit of a textbook—should begin at the top of a right-hand page. Sometimes you may have to leave a blank left-hand page in order to do this. When this is the case, the blank left-hand page is counted but generally does not have a page number printed on it.

Suppress Page Number on First Page.
In a multipage document, the first page usually does not have a printed page number. A feature of modern word processing software is the ability to suppress (stop it from printing) the page number on the first page. If the document has several sections, numbers generally are not printed on the first page of each section.

Suppress Page Numbers Within a Document. The ability to suppress page numbers within a document is not yet common to all software. There are ways to omit a page number within a document even though the software does not have a suppress feature. If you want to suppress the page number on the first page of each section of a long document, each section may be saved as a separate file. When your software has draw capability, you can hide the page number by drawing a no-line, white-filled box over it. Another way to achieve similar results, though somewhat old-fashioned, is simply to use correction fluid on the printout to block out the page number.

43C ◆ 18'

LEARN (AND)

each set of lines twice SS (slowly, then faster); DS between groups; practice the lines again

Do not space between ( ) and the copy they enclose.

(Shift; then *right ring* finger

) Shift; then *right little* finger

Learn ((left parenthesis) ▼

use the letter "l"
1 l l (l (l ll ((l(l l(l 9(9(Shift for the (as you key (9.
2 As (is the shift of 9, use the l finger to key 9, (, or (9.

Learn) (right parenthesis) ▼

3 ; ;);); ;;)) ;); ;); 0) 0) Shift for the) as you key 0).
4 As) is the shift of 0, use the ; finger to key 0,), or 0).

Combine (and)

5 Hints: (1) depress shift; (2) strike key; (3) release both.
6 Tab steps: (1) clear tabs; (2) set stops; and (3) tabulate.
7 Her new account (#495-3078) draws annual interest at 6 1/2%.

43D ◆ 14'

MASTER TECHNIQUE

1. Center each of lines 1-5 DS using the center feature (see 24C, p. 52).
2. QS and key each of lines 6-13 once SS; DS between 2-line groups.
3. Rekey the drill.

1
2
center lines 3
4
5

Dental Services, Inc.
Announces New Dental Center
in
Eastwood Circle Mall
Opening the First of March

letter response
6 upon ever join save only best ploy gave pink edge pump facts
7 You acted on a phony tax case only after a union gave facts.

word response
8 visit risks their world field chair proxy throw right eighty
9 Lana may sign the form to pay for the giant map of the city.

combination response
10 also fast sign card maps only hand were pair link paid plump
11 To get to be a pro, react with zest and care as the pros do.

alphabet 12 Shep quickly coaxed eight avid fans away from the jazz band.
fig/sym 13 Of 370 students, only 35 (9.46%) failed to type 18-20 w.a.m.

Glossary, continued

Two-up   Printing two copies on the same page. The copies are then cut apart. Copies are aligned so that the margins are the same when the copies are cut apart.

Typeface   The name of the unique appearance of the characters that are printed, such as Helvetica or New Century Schoolbook.

' AND "

SM: Defaults; LS: SS

44A ◆ 6'
CONDITIONING
PRACTICE
each line twice

alphabet 1 Bowman fixed prized clocks that seven judges say are unique.

figures 2 Only 1,470 of the 6,285 members were at the 1993 convention.

easy 3 She lent the field auditor a hand with the work of the firm.

gwam 1' | 1 | 2 | 3 | 4 | 5 | 6 | 7 | 8 | 9 | 10 | 11 | 12 |

44B ◆ 18'

LEARN ' (APOSTROPHE) AND " (QUOTATION MARK)

Depress the left shift before striking ".

Learning procedures

1. Locate new symbol on appropriate keyboard above.
2. Key twice SS the appropriate pair of lines given at right; DS between pairs.
3. Repeat Steps 1 and 2 for the other new symbol.
4. Key twice SS lines 5-8.
5. Rekey the lines with which you had difficulty.

Capitalization note:
Capitalize the first and all important words in titles of publications.

'/" *Right little finger*

Learn ' (apostrophe) ▼

1 ; ; '; '; ;; " ;'; ;'; it's he's I'm I've It's hers, I see.

2 I'm not sure if it's Hal's; but if it's his, I'll return it.

Learn " (quotation mark) ▼

3 ; ; "; "; ;; "" ;'; ;'; "Keep on," she said, but I had quit.

4 I read "Ode on a Grecian Urn," "The Last Leaf," and "Trees."

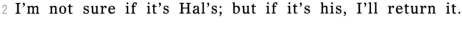
Combine ' and "

5 "If it's Jan's or Al's," she said, "I'll bring it to class."

6 "Its" is an adjective; "it's" is the contraction of "it is."

7 Miss Uhl said, "To make numbers plural, add 's: 8's, 10's."

8 O'Shea said, "Use ' (apostrophe) to shorten phrases: I'll."

PART 5

Integrated Software Applications

Append Files   Combine files by inserting one file at the end of another.

Back-to-Back Pages   Pages that are printed on both sides.

Bitmapped Graphics   Graphics that are created with pixels.

Bring to Front/Send to Back   Commands that allow the sequence of layered graphic elements to be changed.

Clip Art   Illustrations available on computer disks or in books.

Copymaster   An original printout that is used to reproduce copies.

Cut-and-Paste   Attaching cutout pieces of graphics or text to complete a page.

Draw Programs   Computer programs used to create or change object-oriented graphic files.

Draw Tools   A menu of special tools used to key text, create graphics, and draw and fill shapes.

Fill Patterns   A selection of patterns, in addition to solid black or white, used to fill enclosed spaces, such as rectangles and circles.

Font   The appearance of printed characters. A font consists of the typeface name (such as Palatino), the style or appearance (such as bold or italic), and the size (such as 10 point).

Group Graphic Elements   The ability to lock several graphic elements together in relation to each other.

Import (file)   Combine files by inserting one file within another.

Layering Graphic Elements   Stacking two or more graphic elements to create a desired illustration.

Object-Oriented Graphics   Graphics that are created with lines and shapes.

Page Layout   The placement of graphics and text on a page.

Page Orientation   The layout of a page as portrait (tall/vertical) or landscape (wide/horizontal).

Paint Programs   Computer programs used to create or change bitmapped graphic files.

Pasteup   Combining text and/or graphic elements by manually attaching them in place on a page.

Pixel   The tiny dots on a computer screen. The term pixel is short for *picture element*.

Placeholder   An outline of the space needed for graphics or text that will be added later.

Send to Back   (*see* Bring to Front)

Serif   The finishing strokes on the ends of letters (*see* illustration below).

Sans Serif   Without serifs or finishing strokes on the ends of letters (*see* illustration below).

Ascenders extend above Mean line

Mean line

Baseline

Descenders extend below Baseline

Serif Typeface   abcdefghij

Sans Serif Typeface   abcdefghij

Size Graphics   Changing the size of a graphic, such as a bar chart or pie chart or line drawing. Graphics are sized either in proportion to the original or skewed (distorted) from the original.

Thumbnail Sketches   Small drawings that show approximate placement for the graphic and text elements on a page.

FIGURES/ SYMBOLS

1. Key lines 1-10 at a slow but steady pace.
2. Key each line again; try to speed up the keying of figures and figure/symbol groups.

Figure review

1 I became 18 last month. I have a brother 8 and a sister 11.
2 Of the 98 test problems, she got 84 right and only 14 wrong.
3 She said to key 19, 48, and 50 quickly but 45 and 89 slowly.
4 On May 30, 58 boys came to camp; by July 19, we had only 47.
5 Of 20 persons, 9 keyed 38 or more; 6, 35 to 37; 5, 31 to 34.

Symbol review

6 Use / to make fractions: 1/2, 1/4; $ for dollars: $5, $10.
7 We offer discounts of 20% and 30% on our 2- and 4-ply tires.
8 Poe & Sons bought #1748 and #2936 L&M siding for Site #5026.
9 The railway sign said to (1) Stop, (2) Look, and (3) Listen.
10 Mr. Ho said: "It's your goal; don't stop 'til you make it."

MASTER TECHNIQUE

1. Key each pair of lines once as shown: SS with a DS between pairs.
2. Take two 1' writings on line 11 and on line 12; find *gwam* on each writing.
3. Rekey the slower line.

Technique goals

* curved, upright fingers
* quick-snap keystrokes
* quiet hands and arms

shift-key sentences
1 He and Vi crossed the English Channel from Hove to Le Havre.
2 J. W. Posner has left Madrid for Turin for some Alps skiing.

fig/sym sentences
3 I signed a 20-year note--$67,495 (at 13.8%)--with Coe & Han.
4 Order #29105 reads: "16 sets of Cat. #4718A at $36.25/set."

adjacent-key sentences
5 We spent a quiet week at the shore prior to the open season.
6 If we buy her coffee shop, should we buy the gift shop, too?

long-reach sentences
7 My niece has a chance to bring the bronze trophy back to us.
8 Ced once had many mussels but not since the recent harvests.

alphabetic sentences
9 Pam was quickly given the bronze trophy by six fussy judges.
10 Quent got six big jigsaw puzzles from the very dapper clerk.

easy sentences
11 Did he rush the rotor of the giant robot to the island firm?
12 The busy girl works with a fury to fix the signals by eight.

gwam 1' | 1 | 2 | 3 | 4 | 5 | 6 | 7 | 8 | 9 | 10 | 11 | 12 |

L ESSON 45   – AND *

SM: Defaults; LS: SS

CONDITIONING PRACTICE

each line twice

alphabet 1 Quig was just amazed by the next five blocks of his players.
figures 2 On October 20, 1993, the 187 members met from 5 to 6:45 p.m.
easy 3 Keith may hang the sign by the antique door of the big hall.

gwam 1' | 1 | 2 | 3 | 4 | 5 | 6 | 7 | 8 | 9 | 10 | 11 | 12 |

MASTER TECHNIQUE

1. Key lines 1-12 of 44D, above, once SS as shown; DS between pairs.

2. Take two 1' writings on line 11 and one on line 12; find *gwam* on each writing.

Goals:
* to refine technique
* to increase speed

ASSESSMENT ACTIVITIES

Activity 1

Retrieve template file T169 and use it and the following directions to print a list that includes the fields named FIRST, LAST, STREET, CITY, and YEAR. Complete the directions in the most efficient order for your software and keep an unchanged copy of T169 on the disk.

1. Add this record.

Field	Field Name	Field Entry
1	LAST	Webster
2	FIRST	Joshua
3	STREET	214 East Valley Rd
4	CITY	Pittsburgh
5	STATE	PA
6	ZIP	15243

2. Delete the record for Titan.
3. Sort for members from Pittsburgh with ZIP Codes higher than 15230.

4. Insert a field named GRAD.
5. Insert these years in the GRAD field for the Pittsburgh members with ZIP Codes higher than 15230: Chin—1978; Sampson—1984; Yulheist—1993; Webster—1993.
6. Move the field named FIRST so it is to the left of the field named LAST.
7. **WordPerfect and Works DOS:** Print a horizontally centered list of Pittsburgh members with ZIP Codes higher than 15230 with these fields in this order: FIRST, LAST, STREET, CITY, and GRAD. Arrange the list from the earliest year to the most recent. Format the FIRST and LAST fields for bold print and leave at least 0.25" between fields. Save the list as 172B1 and close the file.

   Works MAC: Prepare a horizontally centered report of the Pittsburgh members with ZIP Codes higher than 15230 arranged by last name from A to Z. Print these fields in this order: FIRST, LAST, STREET, CITY, and GRAD. Format the FIRST and LAST fields for bold print and leave at least 0.25" between fields. Save the list and the report as 172B1 and close the file.

Activity 2

Retrieve T169 and use it and the following directions to prepare labels.

1. Refer to Activity 1, No. 1, as needed to review the fields in T169.

2. Prepare labels for members from Aliquippa and Clairton. The labels will be the members' first and last names on Line 1 and the city on Line 2.
3. Name and save the labels as 172B2.
4. Print the labels one-across and then close the files.

Activity 3A (For WordPerfect users only)

Retrieve template file T169 and use it and the following directions to prepare a report. Complete the directions in the most efficient order.

1. The report is to include only members for Aliquippa and Pittsburgh grouped by city and then alphabetically (A-Z) by last name within each city group.
2. Prepare a horizontally centered list of Aliquippa and Pittsburgh members with these fields in this order: FIRST, LAST,

CITY, and ZIP. Refer to Activity 1, No. 1, as needed to review the fields in T169.
3. Leave one space between the first and last names and three spaces between the other fields.
4. Insert a bold, centered title—**MEMBERS FROM ALIQUIPPA AND PITTSBURGH.**
5. Insert centered column headings—**NAME, CITY, ZIP CODE.**
6. Print one copy of the report.
7. Save the report as 172B3A and clear the screen.

Activity 3B (Works DOS and MAC users only)

Retrieve template file T169 and use it and the directions that follow to prepare a report. Complete the directions in the most efficient order.

1. The report is to include only the members from Aliquippa and Pittsburgh grouped by city and then arranged alphabetically (A to Z) by last name within each city group.
2. Include these fields in this order: FIRST, LAST, STREET, and CITY.
3. Leave at least two spaces between the fields.
4. Bold all field headings.
5. Add a bold title—**MEMBERS FROM ALIQUIPPA AND PITTSBURGH.**

6. **Works DOS:**
   a. Delete all default calculations in the Summary line except the one in the CITY field.
   b. Insert NUMBER: as a label in the summary line in the STREET field.
   c. Right-align the NUMBER: label and left-align the COUNT value in the Summ CITY row.
   d. Add a blank line above and below the labels and values in the summary lines.
   e. Bold the labels and values in the summary lines.

   Works MAC: Prepare a report that lists the Aliquippa and Pittsburgh members with last names arranged from A to Z within each group.
7. Print one copy of the report; center it visually horizontally.
8. Save the database file and report as 172B3B; close the file.

FILE MAINTENANCE

If instructed by your teacher, erase all database files from your disk except those that begin with T and these files: HOTELS, POSTAL, STATES, and SUPPLIER.

45C ◆ 18'
LEARN _ (UNDERLINE) AND * (ASTERISK)

Underline: Key _ (the shift of -) with the *right little finger*. Depress the left shift before striking _.

Asterisk: Key * (the shift of 8) with the *right middle finger*. Depress the left shift before striking *.

Learning procedures

1. Locate new key on appropriate keyboard above. Read the reach technique given below the keyboard.
2. Key twice SS the lines given at right; DS between pairs. Use the underline feature to underline words as you key lines 5 and 6.
3. Repeat Steps 1 and 2 for the other new key.
4. Key twice SS lines 5-6.
5. Rekey the lines with which you had difficulty.

Learn __ (underline)

1 ; ; _; _; ;; __ ;_; ;_; I _ _ _ _ _ go there; she _ _ _ _ go also.
2 They _ _ _ to visit _ _ _ _ _ aunt, but _ _ _ _ _ cousin _ _ at school.

Learn * (asterisk)

3 k k *k *k kk ** k*k k*k She used * for a single source note.
4 All discounted items show an *, thus: 48K*, 588*, and 618*.

Combine __ and *

5 Use an * to mark often-confused words such as <u>then</u> and <u>than</u>.
6 *Note: Book titles (like <u>Lorna Doone</u>) are often underlined.

45D ◆ 12'
CHECK/ IMPROVE SKILL

LS: DS
Take 1', 2', and 3' writings as directed by your teacher.

gwam	¼'	½'	¾'	Time
20	5	10	15	20
24	6	12	18	24
28	7	14	21	28
32	8	16	24	32
36	9	18	27	36
40	10	20	30	40
44	11	22	33	44
48	12	24	36	48

all letters used | LA | 1.4 si | 5.4 awl | 85% hfw

gwam 2' 3'

One reason we learn to key is to be able to apply that 6 4
skill as we format personal and business documents--letters, 12 8
reports, and tables, for example. Your next major goal will 18 12
be to learn the rules that govern how we arrange, place, and 24 16
space the most commonly used documents. 28 18

In one way or another, we must memorize the features 33 22
that distinguish one style of letter or report from another. 39 26
Our ability to retain in our minds the vital details will 45 30
help us place and space documents quickly and avoid having 51 34
to look up such facts as we key letters or reports. 56 37

gwam 2' | 1 | 2 | 3 | 4 | 5 | 6 |
3' | 1 | 2 | 3 | 4 |

Activity 2

Retrieve T168 and follow the directions to prepare labels.

1. Refer to Activity 1, No.1, as needed to review the fields in T168.
2. Prepare labels for the infielders only. (The labels will have the infielder's first and last names on Line 1 and INFIELDER on Line 2.)

3. Name and save the labels as 171B2.
4. Print the labels one-across and close the file.

Activity 3A (For WordPerfect users only)

Retrieve template file T168 and use it and the directions that follow to prepare a report. Complete the directions in the most efficient order.

1. The report is to include only pitchers and catchers grouped by position and then alphabetically (A to Z) by last name within each position group.
2. Prepare a horizontally centered list of pitchers and catchers with those fields in this order: FIRST, LAST, POSITION,

SPEED, AVG, and GRANT. Refer to Activity 1, No. 1 as needed to review the fields in T168.

3. Leave one space between the first and last names and three spaces between the other fields.
4. Insert a bold, centered title—**BASEBALL ROSTER**.
5. Insert centered column headings—**NAME, POSITION, SPEED, AVERAGE, GRANT**.
6. Print one copy of the report.
7. Save the report as 171B3A and clear the screen.

Activity 3B (Microsoft Works DOS and MAC users only)

Retrieve template file T168 and follow the directions to prepare a report. Complete the directions in the most efficient order.

1. The report is to include only the pitchers and catchers grouped by position and then alphabetically (A to Z) by last name within each position group.
2. Include these fields in this order: LAST, FIRST, POSITION, SPEED, and AVG.
3. Leave at least two spaces between the fields.
4. Bold all field headings.
5. Add a bold title—**ROSTER OF PITCHERS AND CATCHERS**.
6. Change the AVG field heading to AVERAGE.
7. Format the Speed numbers as Fixed with 2 decimal places and the Average numbers as Fixed with 3 decimal places.
8. **Works DOS**
   a. Delete all default calculations in the Summary line except the one in the FIRST field.
   b. Insert NUMBER: as a label in the summary line in the LAST field.

c. Insert AVERAGES: as a label in the summary line in the POSITION field.
d. Use the =AVG(SPEED) and =AVG(AVG) to compute the average for the SPEED and AVG fields, respectively.
e. Add a blank line above and below the labels and values in the summary lines.
f. Left-align the COUNT value; right-align the AVERAGES: label.
g. Bold the numbers and values in the summary lines.

Works MAC
Prepare a report that lists the pitchers and catchers with last names arranged from A to Z within each position group.

9. Print one copy of the report that appears centered horizontally.
10. Save the database file and report as 171B3B; close the file.

LESSON 172   ASSESS DATABASE SKILLS

172A ♦ CONDITIONING PRACTICE

each line twice

alphabet 1	Mia will quickly award grand prizes to five exhibitors in Jaquar Hall.
fig/sym 2	Line 45 on page 76 and lines 12 and 30 on page 189 need to be revised.
keypad 3	17 28 39 456 789 123 417 528 639 174 285 396 714 825 936 01 02 030 040
speed 4	They may blame both of them for the six problems with the eight autos.

gwam 1' | 1 | 2 | 3 | 4 | 5 | 6 | 7 | 8 | 9 | 10 | 11 | 12 | 13 | 14 |

Master Keyboarding/Word Processing Skills

Learning Outcomes: After completing this unit, you will be able to

1. Demonstrate improved technique on alphanumeric copy.
2. Key rough-draft copy at acceptable levels of speed and control.
3. Demonstrate greater mastery of the word processing features you learned previously .

LESSON 46 — KEYBOARDING/WORD PROCESSING

SM: Defaults; LS: SS

46A ♦ 6'
CONDITIONING PRACTICE

each line twice SS; then a 1' writing on line 3; find *gwam*

alphabet 1 Jarvis will take the next big prize for my old racquet club.

fig/sym 2 My income tax for 1993 was $5,274.60--up 8% over 1992's tax.

speed 3 A neighbor paid the girl to fix the turn signal of the auto.

gwam 1' | · 1 | 2 | 3 | 4 | 5 | 6 | 7 | 8 | 9 | 10 | 11 | 12 |

46B ♦ 15'

MASTER LETTER KEYS

1. Key line 1 at a brisk pace. Note the words that were awkward for you.
2. Key each of the awkward words three times at increasing speed.
3. Key line 2 at a steady fluent rate.
4. Key each of the other pairs of lines in the same way.

A/N
1 an and pan nap any nag ant man aunt land plan hand want sand
2 Ann and her aunt want to buy any land they can near the inn.

B/O
3 bow lob bog rob boy mob gob fob bob body robe boat born glob
4 Bobby bobbed in the bow of the boat as the boys came aboard.

C/P
5 cup cop cap pack copy cape cope pick pecks clips camps claps
6 Cap can clip a copy of the poem to his cape to read at camp.

D/Q
7 did quo quid ride quit road quiz paid aqua dude squid squads
8 The dude in an aqua shirt did quit the squad after the quiz.

E/R
9 or re ore per are her red peer here rent fore leer sore very
10 Vera read her book report to three of her friends at school.

F/S
11 if is fish fuss soft furs self fast fans sift surf fist fees
12 Floss said that fish on this shelf is for fast sale at half.

G/T
13 get got tag togs grit gilt gust tang right guilt fight ghost
14 Garth had the grit to go eight rounds in that fight tonight.

H/U
15 hue hut hub hurt shut shun huge hush brush truth shrug thugs
16 Hugh said four burly thugs hurled the man off the huge dock.

I/V
17 vie vim give view five vein dive vial vice vigor voice alive
18 Vivian made her five great dives with visible vim and vigor.

J/W
19 jay wow jet own jab town just will jest when joke what judge
20 Jewel jokes with your town judge about what and who is just.

K/X
21 oak fix kid fox know flax walk flex silk oxen park axle work
22 Knox fixed an oak axle on a flax cart for a kid in the park.

L/Y
23 lay sly try ply all pry lei ally only rely reply truly fully
24 Dolly truly felt that she could rely fully on only one ally.

M/Z
25 may zoo man zam zone make fuzz mama jazz maid jams game zoom
26 Zoe may make her mark in a jazz band jam session at the zoo.

UNIT 38

LESSONS 171-172

Assess Database Skills

Learning Outcomes: After completing this unit, you will have

1. Reviewed database software features used to prepare databases and print lists, labels, and/or reports.
2. Demonstrated skill in using database software to prepare databases, lists, labels, and/or reports.

LESSON 171 ◆ PREPARE FOR ASSESSMENT

171A ◆ CONDITIONING PRACTICE

each line twice, then 30" timings on selected lines; exit wp; access db

alphabet	1	Jacky and Paul thawed the frozen quiche in that box seven minutes ago.
fig/sym	2	I will take routes 136, 279, 468, and 51 to get to Jane's beach house.
keypad	3	11 44 77 22 55 88 33 66 99 00 10 40 70 20 50 80 30 60 90 101 202 3030
speed	4	Rod may work with a busy neighbor to fix or dismantle the small rifle.

gwam 1' | 1 | 2 | 3 | 4 | 5 | 6 | 7 | 8 | 9 | 10 | 11 | 12 | 13 | 14 |

171B ◆ REVIEW ACTIVITIES

Activity 1

Retrieve template file T168 and use it and the following directions to print a list that includes the fields named FIRST, LAST, POSITION, and ERA, in that order. Complete the directions in the most efficient order for your software and keep an unchanged copy of T168 on the disk.

1. Add this record.

Field	Field Name	Field Entry
1	LAST	Fairly
2	FIRST	Joshua
3	POSITION	Pitcher
4	THROWS	Right
5	BATS	Right
6	SPEED	5.2
7	AVG	.000
8	GRANT	500

2. Delete the record for Piroli.

3. Sort for pitchers who throw right handed.
4. Insert a field named ERA.
5. Insert these ERAs for the right-handed pitchers: Tony Corteze—6; Mark Hiber—1.15; Ralph Nix—3.25; Craig Wilson—4; Ken Wiltrout—8.25; and Joshua Fairly—.000.
6. Move the field named FIRST so that it is to the left of the field named 6LAST.
7. **Works DOS and WordPerfect:** Print a horizontally centered list of the right-handed pitchers with these fields in this order: FIRST, LAST, POSITION, THROWS, ERA that is arranged from the lowest ERA to the highest. Format the ERA field for 3 decimal places and leave at least 0.25" between each field. Save the list as 171B1 and close the file.

   Works MAC: Prepare a report of right-handed pitchers with these fields in this order: FIRST, LAST, POSITION, THROWS, and ERA that lists the last names from A to Z. Format the ERA field for 3 decimal places and leave at least 0.25" between fields. Save the list and the report as 171B1 and close the file.

IMPROVE SKILL

LS: DS

Take 1' guided writings and 2' and 3' unguided writings, following your teacher's directions. Save the copy for use in 46D; print the copy.

all letters used | LA | 1.4 si | 5.4 awl | 85% hfw

gwam	2'	3'

What is it that makes one person succeed and another — 5 | 4

fail when the two seem to have about equal ability? Some — 11 | 7

have said that the difference is in the degree of motivation — 17 | 11

and effort each brings to the job. Others have said that an — 23 | 16

intent to become excellent is the main difference. — 28 | 19

At least four items are likely to have a major effect — 5 | 22

on our success: basic ability, a desire to excel, an aim — 11 | 26

to succeed, and zestful effort. If any one of these is ab- — 17 | 30

sent or at a low point, our chances for success are lessened. — 23 | 34

These features, however, can be developed if we wish. — 29 | 38

gwam	2'	1	2	3	4	5	6
	3'	1		2		3		4

gwam	1/4'	1/2'	3/4'	1'
20	5	10	15	20
24	6	12	18	24
28	7	14	21	28
32	8	16	24	32
36	9	18	27	36
40	10	20	30	40
44	11	22	33	44
48	12	24	36	48
52	13	26	39	52
56	14	28	42	56

PROOFREAD YOUR COPY

1. Note the kind of errors marked in the illustrated ¶ at right.
2. Note how the proofreader's marks above the copy are used to make corrections in the ¶.
3. Proofread the printout of the 3' writing above and mark for correction each error you made.
4. Clear the screen (see p. 10).
5. Center FEATURES OF SUCCESS so that it will print 2" from the top of a sheet.
6. QS and rekey the ¶s from your rough draft (printout); correct all errors.

= space ∧ = insert ⊂ = close up ⌐ = delete ∿ = transpose (tr)

Line 1   Sucess does not mean thesame thing to every one.

2 For some, it means to get the top att all costs: in

3 power, in fame, and in income. For others it means juts

4 to fulfill thier basic needs or or wants with as little

5 effort required.

Line 1	Line 2	Line 3	Line 4	Line 5
1 Omitted letter	1 Omitted word	1 Misstroke	1 Transposition	1 Omitted word
2 Failure to space	2 Added letter	2 Omitted comma	2 Added word	
3 Faulty spacing	3 Faulty spacing	3 Transposition		

After completing Steps 1-6, make these changes:

1. In ¶1, line 3, change *degree* to **amount**.

2. In ¶2, line 1, change *major* to **vital** and underline it.

3. In ¶2, line 4, change *point* to **level**.

4. Proofread your copy on screen and correct any errors you find.

5. Move the cursor to the beginning of the text; reset

the left margin only at 1.5" and line spacing for SS.

6. Print the paragraph.

Activity 4
Key the spreadsheet and then follow the directions to complete it.

1. Use the following equation to determine Purchases Needed: =IF(C6-B6>0,C6-B6,0).
2. Use the following equation in F6 to determine total cost: =D6*E6.
3. Format Columns B, C, and D with commas and no decimal places.
4. Format Columns E and F as money with 2 decimal places.
5. Format column widths so there are at least 2 spaces between columns and the worksheet fits attractively on 8 1/2" x 11" paper.
6. Center and bold the column headings.
7. Bold the title.
8. Insert a Total line two lines below the last line and use the following equation to compute the Total Cost: =SUM(F6:F15).
9. Print one copy of the worksheet.
10. Save the file as 169B4 and close the file.

PURCHASING PROJECTIONS TO END OF YEAR					
Product	Present Inventory	Expected Needs	Purchases Needed	Cost/ Item	Total Cost
A-222	30000	44000		1.05	
A-222E	55500	77600		1.15	
A-433	49875	65000		1.34	
A-433E	33200	88250		1.39	
B-224	25000	20000		1.67	
B-224E	55750	62000		1.72	
C-666	45000	40000		1.73	
C-666E	32900	59000		1.78	
D-555	45000	25000		1.95	
D-555E	95000	96000		2	

Activity 5
Assume you are Chuck, one of the players who received the letter and itinerary that was processed in Activity 3. Use the word processing software to compose a response to Ms. Demmet. Your response should indicate that you can be part of the caravan on January 15 but not on the second day. Give what you believe is a valid reason for not being able to participate on January 16. Save your letter as 169B5.

SM: Defaults; LS: SS

47A ♦ 6'
CONDITIONING PRACTICE

each line twice

alphabet 1 Bevis had quickly won top seed for the next games in Juarez.

fig/sym 2 THE DIAMOND CAPER (Parker & Sons, #274638) sells for $19.50.

speed 3 Shana may make a bid for the antique bottle for the auditor.

gwam 1' | 1 | 2 | 3 | 4 | 5 | 6 | 7 | 8 | 9 | 10 | 11 | 12 |

47B ♦ 12'
MASTER TECHNIQUE

1. Each line twice SS; DS between 4-line groups.
2. Take a 1' writing on each of lines 6, 8, and 10; find gwam on each.
3. Rekey the two lines on which you had the lowest gwam.

shift keys 1 Jane and Robb go to a New Year's party with Donna and Spiro.

2 R. J. Appel was paid by the Apollo Insurance Co. of Jackson.

space bar 3 It is up to me to do my best in each try to make a new goal.

4 Andy may use his pen to sign the form for a job in the city.

letter response 5 A tax rate was set in my area only after we set a case date.

6 We are free only after we get him set up on a tax rate case.

combination response 7 I shall bid on the antique vase only if I regard it as rare.

8 You are to sign all of the artwork you turn in to be graded.

word response 9 He is to do the work for both of us, and she is to pay half.

10 The girl with the titian hair owns the title to the autobus.

gwam 1' | 1 | 2 | 3 | 4 | 5 | 6 | 7 | 8 | 9 | 10 | 11 | 12 |

47C ♦ 12'
KEY FROM ROUGH DRAFT

1. Read the two ¶s shown at the right; check the proofreader's marks using the key below.
2. On a clear screen (p. 10) key the ¶s DS, correcting the errors marked in the copy.
3. Make the on-screen changes specified below the ¶s.

Although the copy lines in your book are even at the right margin they maynot be when you key them. The reason for this is that type used by a printer is not uniform in width as is that on your equipment. Be sure to recognize this.

Do not think that just because your copy is even at the right, it contains no errors. To be sure that your work is correct, you must check it to see that each character and space is an exact match with the copy from which you work.

Proofreader's Marks

- ℰ delete (take out)
- ∧ insert
- # add space
- ⌒ close up
- ⁓ transpose

1. In ¶1, line 1, change *book* to **text** and underline it.
2. In ¶2, line 3, change *correct* to **perfect** and bold it.
3. Proofread your copy on screen and correct any errors you made.

4. Center VARIABLE VS. UNIFORM SPACING so that it will print 2" from the top edge of sheet and 4 lines (QS) above the first line of the ¶.

5. Reset side margins for 1.5", line spacing to SS.
6. Print; then mark corrections with proofreader's marks.

Activity 3
Access wp and then follow the instructions below to prepare a table and form letters (modified block format).

1. Retrieve template files T169B3A and T169B3B and make the changes indicated (and others as needed) in the letter and table at the right.
2. Prepare a primary file (169B3A.PRI) and a secondary file (169B3A.SEC) that can be merged so the letter can be sent to the three people named at the bottom of the letter. The salutation (following *Dear*) and address for each letter is

Manager:
609 Menees Lane
Madison, TN 37115-5807

Chuck:
317 Adair Road
Jackson, TN 38305-2912

Jim:
6700 Forest Road
Columbus, GA 31907-3011

3. Date each letter January 6.
4. Save the merged file as 169B3.

Dear

The ~~itinerary~~ schedule for this month's Gold Caravan has been set for January 15 and 16, the two days you have agreed to represent the ~~club~~ GOLD baseball team. I have enclosed a copy of the schedule for the two days ~~so you can see the~~ *and stores at which* and have listed the location you will appear.

Please ~~report come to~~ be in my office by ~~11:30~~ 11:15 a.m. on January 15 so we can have a ~~short~~ luncheon meeting to review the purpose of the *public apparances* caravan and the schedule.

We ~~plan to~~ will all leave the stadium in one car at 12:30 *p.m.* to drive to the first *location* ~~appearance~~.

Sincerely, *Ms. Susan M. Demmet, Director, Promotions and Marketing*

MADISON GOLD CARAVAN SCHEDULE *

January			
15	~~11:45 a.m.~~ *1:00 p.m.*	Green City Hall	*Altmants* ~~Harvey's~~
15	4:00 p.m.	Crestmont Village	The Sport Spot
15	7:30 p.m.	East Shopping Mall	Everetts
16	~~1:00 p.m.~~ *11:30 a.m.*	Five Points	Athlete's Wear
16	2:30 p.m.	Westend Village	Oscar's Corner
16	5:45 p.m.	High Point Center	*DVJ Clothing* ~~The Wilson~~
16	~~7:45~~ *8:00* p.m.	Southland Mall	Big League's

The members ~~of the~~ caravan are Manager, Al S. Rojah, and players, Chuck H. Mravic, and Jim R. Alberti. The driver is Ted S. Botts.

47D ◆ 20'

CHECK/IMPROVE SKILL

LS: DS

1. Take 3', 2', and 1' writings as directed by your teacher. On 1' *guided* writings, try to improve either speed (increase goal rate) OR accuracy (reduce goal rate). Goal chart, p. 87.

2. On a clear screen (see p. 10), center the heading PLANNING MESSAGES so that it will print 2" from the top of a sheet;* QS; then rekey the ¶s as a short report; correct all errors.

*Works users: Remember to consider default top margin. See Note in 36D, p. 71.

gwam 2' | 3'

Planning is the first step in composing a message. The | 6 | 4

plan should include a goal, what you want to accomplish. It | 12 | 8

also should include a list of the points you will use to con- | 18 | 12

vince the reader of your point of view or of the action you | 24 | 16

want taken. The list should be arranged in logical sequence. | 30 | 20

Your goal is the major idea behind the topic sentence. | 36 | 24

The topic sentence is often stated first, followed next by | 41 | 28

facts and ideas that support it. You may instead decide to | 47 | 32

work up to the main idea at the end. In either case, you | 53 | 35

itemize the information and tie it to the main thought. | 59 | 39

gwam 2' | 1 | 2 | 3 | 4 | 5 | 6 |
3' | 1 | 2 | 3 | 4 |

LESSON 48 — KEYBOARDING/WORD PROCESSING

SM: Defaults; LS: SS

48A ◆ 6'
CONDITIONING PRACTICE

each line twice

alphabet 1 Zoe quickly made six jugs of punch to serve by the new pool.

fig/sym 2 We got a discount of 10% on Invoice #1837; only 5% on #2946.

speed 3 They wish us to make a copy of an ancient map of the island.

gwam 1' | 1 | 2 | 3 | 4 | 5 | 6 | 7 | 8 | 9 | 10 | 11 | 12 |

48B ◆ 15'

MASTER TECHNIQUE

1. Key lines 1-7 twice each: first slowly; then faster.
2. Take a 1' writing on each of lines 8, 9, and 10; find *gwam* on each.

figures 1 By May 25 in 1993 we had planted 475 trees and 1,608 shrubs.

fig/sym 2 Al asked, "How much is due by May 28 on Account #4039-1657?"

shift keys 3 Marla Appel and Pat Coe will play Nan Epps and Larry Sparks.

space bar 4 Any of you can go by the inn for a swim in the pool at noon.

one hand 5 My war on waste at a union mill was based upon minimum data.

long reach 6 Myna said I must curb at once my urge to glance at my hands.

adjacent key 7 Coila hoped for a new opal ring to wear to her next concert.

double letters 8 Bobby will sell the cookbook for a little less than it cost.

combination 9 He may join us for tea at the pool if he wishes to see them.

balanced hand 10 Did they make the right title forms for the eight big firms?

gwam 1' | 1 | 2 | 3 | 4 | 5 | 6 | 7 | 8 | 9 | 10 | 11 | 12 |

169-170A ◆ CONDITIONING PRACTICE
each line twice

alphabet	1	Stacks of judo magazines were piled very high on the exquisite tables.
fig/sym	2	By 6:45 p.m. on May 28 the men had branded all but 19 of the 730 cows.
keypad	3	40 10 70 407 410 714 825 936 520 630 127 238 319 492 583 671 47 83 980
speed	4	Enrique may wish he had vigor when he duels with the haughty neighbor.

gwam 1' | 1 | 2 | 3 | 4 | 5 | 6 | 7 | 8 | 9 | 10 | 11 | 12 | 13 | 14 |

169-170B ◆ APPLICATION ACTIVITIES

Activity 1

Retrieve template file T168 and make the following changes:

1. Delete the THROWS, BATS, SPEED, and GRANT fields.
2. Add two fields to the left of AVG: AT BAT and HITS.
3. Delete the Seko record.
4. Clear all numbers in the AVG field.
5. Key the equation **=HITS/AT BAT** in the AVG field (formatted as fixed with 3 decimal places).
6. **Works DOS:** Display an alphabetical list (A to Z) of the records for infielders.

   Works MAC: Sort the records in ascending alphabetical order (A to Z) by last name within each playing position group; arrange position groups in alphabetical order.
7. Enter the following numbers in the AT BAT and HITS fields for each infielder

Corteze	45	13
Drnach	23	6
LaQunito	49	22
Niklevicz	21	6
Nix	75	28
Pixel	72	24
Vish	65	15
Volmer	15	2
Yenchi	25	8

8. Add the following record:

   Tom Stanovich

   Infielder

   At Bat: 3

   Hits: 0

9. Sort the infielder list by AVG in descending order.
10. **Works DOS:** If needed, format the AVG field to Fixed with 3 decimal places.

    Works MAC: Create a report of infielders only.
11. Add a header: **INFIELDER AVERAGES.**
12. Print one copy of the infielder list.
13. Save the infielder list (**Works DOS** saves the report and database) as 169B1 and close the file.

Activity 2

Retrieve template file T169 and use the instructions that follow to prepare a report. Preview all instructions before you begin, since it is not necessary to complete them in order.

1. Include only those members in Pennsylvania.
2. Group by city (from A to Z) and by last name (A to Z) within cities.
3. Delete the FIRST and ZIP fields.
4. Use approximately 12 spaces for the LAST field, 20 for STREET, 12 for CITY, and 6 for STATE.
5. Bold all field headings.
6. **Works DOS:** Delete all counts between groups except between the CITY field; add **MEMBERS FROM CITY:** in Column B in the Summ CITY row; left align the count; and add a blank line above and below the count in the Summ CITY row.

   Works MAC: Create a report of PA cities.
7. Add a centered title—**PENNSYLVANIA MEMBERS.**
8. Change the LAST field heading to LAST NAME.
9. Print one copy of the report.
10. Save the file and report as 169B2 and close the file.

CHECK SKILL

LS: DS
1. Take 1', 2', and 3' writings finding *gwam* and circling errors after each.
2. On a clear screen, center in bold TECHNIQUES AND SPEED; QS.
3. Key the ¶s as a short report; correct all errors.
4. Move the cursor to the beginning of the heading line; insert hard returns as needed to place the heading 2" from the top.

all letters used | LA | 1.4 si | 5.4 awl | 85% hfw

	gwam 2'	3'
As you work for higher skill, remember that how well you	8	4
key fast is just as important as how fast you key. How well	12	8
you key at any speed depends in major ways upon the technique	18	12
or form you use. Bouncing hands and flying fingers lower the	24	16
speed, while quiet hands and low finger reaches increase speed.	31	20
Few of us ever reach what the experts believe is perfect	36	24
technique, but all of us should try to approach it. We must	42	28
realize that good form is the secret to higher speed with	48	32
fewer errors. We can then focus our practice on the improve-	54	36
ment of the features of good form that will bring success.	60	40

gwam 2' | 1 | 2 | 3 | 4 | 5 | 6
3' | 1 | 2 | 3 | 4

MASTER SKILL: ROUGH DRAFT

1. Key a 2' writing on the ¶, DS, making the marked changes as you key.
2. Proofread your copy; circle errors; and find *gwam*.
3. Key another 2' writing; try to increase your speed.

∧ = insert
⌀ = delete
= add space
∿ = transpose
⌒ = close up

all letters used | LA | 1.4 si | 5.4 awl | 85% hfw

	gwam 2'
When you key from marked copy, read just a litle ahead	6
of where your keying. Doing this will keep you from missing	12
changes that must be made. Learn to reconize quickly the	18
correction simbols so that you don't have to reduce speed	24
or stop toread. Expect to copy rough-draft at about eighty	30
five per cent of your straight copy speed.	35

COMPOSE (CREATE) AS YOU KEY

LS: DS; PB: line 13
1. Select a topic from those given at right.
2. Compose one or two ¶s giving your plans (or point of view) regarding the topic.
3. Edit your copy: add, delete, move, or copy words, phrases, and sentences until the ¶(s) says just what you want it to say.
4. Proofread your copy; mark corrections with proofreader's marks.
5. Prepare a final draft with errors corrected.

1 My future education plans

2 The job I want and why

3 Why I want to excel

4 Why I do not care to be No. 1

5 How to reduce teenage drinking

6 My plans for a future career

7 Why cheating is wrong

8 How to reduce teenage drug use

9 My plans for next summer

10 How I do my homework

Note: In later lessons, choose different topics and practice composing as you key.

e. Extend the highlight through Column E.

f. Press **Alt, E, E**.

5. Insert desired summary statistics:

a. Insert =AVG in Columns F and G. Move cursor to =SUM in Column F in the Summ POSITION row.

b. Key **Alt, E, S** (selects Insert Field Summary from the Edit Menu).

c. Move cursor to highlight Speed in the dialog box (selects Speed as field that will be used in the calculation).

d. Press **Alt A** (selects the built-in function for computing averages).

e. Strike Enter.

f. Move cursor to =SUM in Column G in the Summ POSITION row (selects the cell where the next calculation is to occur).

g. Repeat Steps b through e, substituting AVG for SPEED when selecting the field contents to average.

h. Use Print Preview (**Alt, P, V,** Enter) to see the calculations for the three fields after each grouping. Strike Esc when done (returns to report definition).

6. Insert labels to describe the answers calculated in the Summ POSITION row:

a. Insert NUMBER: to the left of the =COUNT answers. Move the cursor to Column B in the Summ POSITION row (the cell that will hold the label).

b. Key **NUMBER**: (enters the label).

c. Add AVERAGES: to the left of the first =AVG answer. Move the cursor to Column D in the Summ POSITION row.

d. Key **AVERAGES:** and then strike Enter.

e. Use Print Preview to observe the addition of these two labels at the end of each grouping. Strike Esc to return to report definition.

7. Left align the =COUNT answer in the Summ POSITION row:

a. Highlight =COUNT in the Summ POSITION row (specifies the cell to be formatted).

b. Press **Alt, T, S, L** and then strike Enter (selects Left from the Style option in the Format Menu).

8. Format all numbers in the SPEED field as Fixed with two decimal places.

9. Format all numbers in the AVG field as Fixed with three decimal places.

10. Insert a blank line between each grouping:

a. Highlight a cell in the first Summ Report row (specifies where the blank line will be inserted).

b. Press **Alt, E, I** (selects Insert Row/Column from the Edit Menu).

c. If needed, key **R** and then strike Enter (selects Row from the dialog box).

d. Use cursor to highlight Summ Position in the dialog box (specifies the type of line to be inserted).

e. Strike Enter (inserts a blank row below each grouping).

11. Print one copy of the report after making formatting changes needed to make the report attractive.

12. Save the report and database file as 168C and close the file.

c. ~ Print.

d. Observe the subtotals at the end of each grouping and at the end of the report and the horizontal placement.

e. ~ Cancel (returns to report definition screen).

9. Make necessary changes to left and right margins to have the list horizontally centered.

10. Insert **1995 RAMS BASEBALL POSITION ROSTER** as a bold header.

11. Print one copy of the report.

12. Save the report and database file as 168C and close the file.

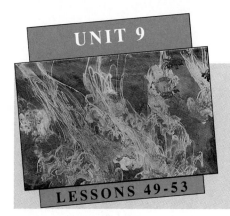

UNIT 9

LESSONS 49-53

Master Numeric Keypad Operation

Learning Outcomes: After completing this unit, you will be able to

1. Operate the keypad of a computer with proper technique: fingers well curved and upright over home keys.
2. Enter all-figure copy at acceptable speed with good control by touch (minimum of looking).

 **ESSON 49**   **4/5/6/0**

49A ◆
GET ACQUAINTED WITH 10-KEY PAD

Figure keys 1-9 are in standard locations on numeric keypads of computers and 10-key calculators.

The zero (0 or Ø) key location may vary slightly from one keyboard to another.

The illustrations at the right show the location of the figure keys on selected computer keyboards.

Note: To use the keypad, the Num (number) Lock must be turned on.

Macintosh LCII numeric keypad

IBM PC

49B ◆
CORRECT OPERATING POSITION

1. Position yourself in front of the computer—body erect, both feet on floor for balance.
2. Place this textbook at the right of the keyboard.
3. Curve the fingers of the right hand and place them on the numeric keypad:
   pointer finger on 4
   middle finger on 5
   ring finger on 6
   thumb on 0

1. Retrieve T168 and switch to List View, if needed.
2. Create a report (Press **Alt**, **V**, **N** and strike Enter).

Version 2.0
   a. Display the report definition by striking Esc.
   b. Add a title by highlighting the cell at the intersection of Column A in Row 1 (Intr Report row).
   c. Key **1995 RAMS BASEBALL POSITION ROSTER** (enters the title).
   d. Strike Enter.
   e. Delete the GRANT field by highlighting =GRANT and keying **Alt, S, C** (choose Columns from the Select Menu).
   f. Key **Alt, E, D** (selects Delete Row/Column from the Edit Menu).
   g. Use ← key as needed to display the remaining fields that are to be in the report.

Version 3.0
   a. Key **1995 RAMS BASEBALL POSITION ROSTER** in the Report Title box (enters the report title).
   b. Strike Tab (moves cursor to LAST, the first field name, in the Fields in Database box).
   c. Key **Alt A** (adds field named LAST to the Fields in Report box so this field will be included in the report).
   d. Repeat Step c as needed to add the fields named FIRST, POSITION, THROWS, BATS, SPEED, and AVG.
   e. Strike Enter (selects OK in the New Report dialog box and displays the Report Statistics dialog box).
   f. Since no statistics are to be included at the end of the report, strike Enter (displays the report specified).
   g. Strike Esc (displays the report definition based on the selections you made).

3. Sort the records by position and alphabetically from A to Z within positions:
   a. Press **Alt, S, O** (selects Sort Records from the Select Menu).
   b. Key **POSITION** in the first sort field.
   c. *Version 2.0*
      Key **Alt G, Alt H** (instructs software to insert a summary row every time the first letter of the last name changes).
      Version 3.0
      Key **Alt G** (instructs software to insert a summary row every time the first letter of the position name changes).
   d. Key **Alt 2** and then **LAST** in the second sort field.
   e. Key **Alt 3** and then **FIRST** in the third sort field.
   f. Strike Enter (notice that Works created a line of equations in a row titled Summ POSITION).

4. Delete unwanted field summary statistics:
   a. Delete =COUNT in Columns A and B; Highlight =COUNT in Column A of the Summ POSITION row and then key **Alt, S, E** (selects Cells from the Edit Menu).
   b. Use → key to extend the highlight through Column B (designates the statistics to be deleted).
   c. Press **Alt, E, E** (selects Clear from the Edit Menu).
   d. Delete =COUNT in Columns D and E. Highlight =COUNT in Column D of the Summ POSITION row and then key **Alt, S, E**.

1. Retrieve T168 and switch to Show List, if needed.
2. Sort the records alphabetically from A to Z by position and alphabetically from A to Z within positions:
   a. Highlight the field named LAST, select Sort from the Organize Menu, ~ A to Z button, and ~ OK.
   b. Highlight the field named POSITION, select Sort from the Organize Menu, ~ A to Z button, and ~ OK.
3. Format all numbers in the SPEED field as fixed with two decimal places.
4. Format all numbers in the AVG field as fixed with three decimal places.
5. Format the GRANT field to Dollars with no decimal places.
6. Create a report that does not contain the THROWS and BATS fields:
   a. Select New Report from the Report Menu.
   b. Drag THROWS and BATS field to the right of the GRANT.
   c. Move Right Edge Marker to right edge of GRANT field.
7. Insert subtotals at the end of each position grouping and at the end of the report:
   a. Highlight the field named GRANT (specifies the numeric field to be subtotalled).
   b. Choose Sum This Field from the TotalsPage Menu.
   c. Highlight the field named POSITION (specifies the field on which the subtotals are to be based).
   d. Select Take a Sub-Total on Field Change from the TotalsPage Menu.
8. Preview the report to see the subtotals, totals, and arrangement:
   a. Select Print from the File Menu.
   b. If needed, ~ Print Preview box.

(continued on next page)

(continued on next page)

ENTER DATA USING HOME KEYS: 4, 5, 6, 0

Complete the drills as directed below, entering the numbers in columns, as shown, on your word processing software; but do not key the totals.

When you can operate the keypad by touch—Lesson 53 completed—determine whether your word processing software contains a calculator (math function). If so, repeat Lessons 49-53 using the math function. Check your totals against the printed totals. Reenter the data whenever you do not get the correct total.

1. Turn equipment, including Num Lock, "on".
2. Curve the fingers of your right hand and place them upright on home keys:
   pointer finger on 4
   middle finger on 5
   ring finger on 6
   little finger on + bar
   thumb on 0 or Ø (zero)
3. Using the special Enter key to the right of the keypad, enter data in Drill 1a as follows:
   4 Enter
   4 Enter
   4 Enter
   Strike Enter

Note: Ignore any decimal (.) or comma (,) that may appear in an entry or total figure.

4. Enter and check Columns b, c, d, e, and f in the same way.
5. Using the special Enter key to the right of the keypad, enter data in Drill 2a as follows:
   44 Enter
   44 Enter
   44 Enter
   Strike Enter
6. Continue Drill 2 and complete Drills 3-5 in a similar manner. In Drills 4 and 5, strike 0 (zero) with the *side* of your right thumb.

Technique cue

Strike each key with a quick, sharp stroke with the *tip* of the finger; release the key quickly. Keep the fingers curved and upright; the wrist low, relaxed, and steady.

Drill 1

a	b	c	d	e	f
4	5	6	4	5	6
4	5	6	4	5	6
4	5	6	4	5	6
12	15	18	12	15	18

Drill 2

a	b	c	d	e	f
44	55	66	44	55	66
44	55	66	44	55	66
44	55	66	44	55	66
132	165	198	132	165	198

Drill 3

a	b	c	d	e	f
44	45	54	44	55	66
55	56	46	45	54	65
66	64	65	46	56	64
165	165	165	135	165	195

Drill 4

a	b	c	d	e	f
40	50	60	400	500	600
40	50	60	400	500	600
40	50	60	400	500	600
120	150	180	1,200	1,500	1,800

Drill 5

a	b	c	d	e	f
40	400	404	406	450	650
50	500	505	506	540	560
60	600	606	606	405	605
150	1,500	1,515	1,518	1,395	1,815

168C ◆

FIELD SUMMARIES

Read the information at the right about field summaries in reports and study the illustration below. Then complete the activities for your software.

Database reports can be enhanced by including totals, counts, and/or other statistics at the end of the report and/or at the end of each grouping within a report. For example, an employee salary report might print the salaries for each department (if the report is grouped by departments) as well as the total salaries for all employees.

WORKS DOS

When Works DOS prepares a report, it inserts introductory rows, record rows, and summary rows. Works provides and names a summary line for each grouping in the report. The summary rows between breaks are named SUMM (field name) and those at the end of the report are named SUMM Report. Summary rows can be added or deleted; partial rows can be deleted. When Works automatically provides statistics, the count (=COUNT) is used for text fields; the total (=SUM) is used for numeric fields. In addition, you can insert summary rows to create blank lines between groupings.

WORKS MAC

With Works MAC you can enhance your report by using the TotalsPage Menu to select numeric fields that can be totaled or subtotaled. As shown below, the TotalsPage Menu has four options:

1. Sum This Field is used to total all the numbers in a field.
2. Take a Sub-Total on Field Change is used to subtotal the numbers for each grouping within a field.
3. Take a Sub-Total on 1st Char is used to subtotal the numbers each time the first character in a specified field changes.
4. New Page After Total is used to start a new page after each subtotal is printed.

1. **Intr. Report.** Intr (for introductory) Report rows are used for report titles and blank lines at the beginning of the report.
2. **Intr. Page.** Intr Page rows are used for column headings that print at the top of each page and blank lines below the headings.
3. **Record.** Record rows are used to print text for each record in the report.
4. **Summ.** Summ field name rows (POSITION in the example) are used to print the statistic used or text that is to appear (COUNT and AVG are statistics used in this example).
5. **Sum Report.** Sum Report rows are used to print statistics used at the end of the report (COUNT and AVG are statistics used in this example).

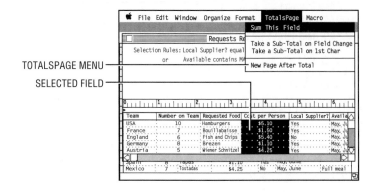

TOTALSPAGE MENU —
SELECTED FIELD —

THE REPORT DEFINITION

```
                 A        B       C          D

1 → Intr Report
    Intr Report   LAST    FIRST   POSITION   SPEED
2 → Intr Page
    Intr Page
3 → Record        =LAST   =FIRST  =POSITION  =SPEED
4 → Summ POSITION =COUNT(LAST)               =AVG(SPEED)
5 → Summ Report
    Summ Report   =COUNT(LAST)               =AVG(SPEED)
```

50A ◆

IMPROVE HOME-KEY TECHNIQUE

Enter the columns of data listed at the right as directed in Steps 1-6 on p. 92.

a	b	c	d	e	f
4	44	400	404	440	450
5	55	500	505	550	560
6	66	600	606	660	456
15	165	1,500	1,515	1,650	1,466

50B ◆

LEARN NEW KEYS: 7, 8, 9

Learn reach to 7

1. Locate 7 (above 4) on the numeric keypad.
2. Watch your pointer finger move up to 7 and back to 4 a few times *without striking keys*.
3. Practice striking 74 a few times as you watch the finger.
4. With eyes on copy, enter the data in Drills 1a and 1b.

Learn reach to 8

1. Learn the middle-finger reach to 8 (above 5) as directed in Steps 1-3 above.
2. With eyes on copy, enter the data in Drills 1c and 1d.

Learn reach to 9

1. Learn the ring-finger reach to 9 (above 6) as directed above.
2. With eyes on copy, enter the data in Drills 1e and 1f.

Drills 2-4

Practice entering the columns of data in Drills 2-4 until you can do so accurately and quickly.

Drill 1

a	b	c	d	e	f
474	747	585	858	696	969
747	777	858	888	969	999
777	474	888	585	999	696
1,998	1,998	2,331	2,331	2,664	2,664

Drill 2

a	b	c	d	e	f
774	885	996	745	475	754
474	585	696	854	584	846
747	858	969	965	695	956
1,995	2,328	2,661	2,564	1,754	2,556

Drill 3

a	b	c	d	e	f
470	580	690	770	707	407
740	850	960	880	808	508
704	805	906	990	909	609
1,914	2,235	2,556	2,640	2,424	1,524

Drill 4

a	b	c	d	e	f
456	407	508	609	804	905
789	408	509	704	805	906
654	409	607	705	806	907
987	507	608	706	904	908
2,886	1,731	2,232	2,724	3,319	3,626

50C ◆

UNEQUAL DIGITS

Enter single, double, and triple digits in columns as shown, left to right. The computer will align the digits automatically.

a	b	c	d	e	f
4	90	79	4	740	860
56	87	64	56	64	70
78	68	97	78	960	900
90	54	64	60	89	67
4	6	5	98	8	80
232	305	309	296	1,861	1,977

g. Strike Enter (selects OK in the Report Statistics dialog box and displays the report specified).

h. Strike Esc (displays the report definition based on the selections you made).

4. Format numbers in GRANT field as Currency with no decimal places:
   a. If needed, use the ⇥ key to make the GRANT field appear in the report definition.
   b. Highlight =GRANT in the Record row (marks the field to be formatted).
   c. Press **Alt**, **T**, **U** (selects Currency from the Format Menu).
   d. Key **0** and strike Enter (designates no decimal places).

5. Change GRANT field width to 9:
   a. If needed, highlight =GRANT in the Record row (marks the field to be changed).
   b. Press **Alt**, **T**, **W**, **9**.
   c. Strike Enter.

6. Sort the records alphabetically from Z to A:
   a. Press **Alt**, **S**, **O** (selects Sort Records from the Select Menu).
   b. Key **LAST** in the first sort field.
   c. Press **Alt B** (selects descending order).
   d. *Version 2.0:* Key **Alt G**, **Alt H** (instructs software to insert a summary line every time the first letter of the last name changes). *Version 3.0:* Key **Alt G**, **Alt I** (instructs software to insert a summary line every time the first letter of the last name changes).
   e. Key **Alt 2** and then **FIRST** in the second sort field.
   f. Key **Alt D** (selects descending order).
   g. Strike Enter (notice that Works created a line of equations in a row titled SUMM LAST. This represents the automatic feature of WORKS that lists the number of entries (=COUNT) in each break group when the field contents is text and the total (=SUM) when the field contents is numbers. To see how this is reported use Print Preview at this time [**Alt P**, **V**, Enter]. When done previewing, strike Esc).

7. Delete the SUMM LAST lines:
   a. Move highlight to a cell in the SUMM LAST row.
   b. Press **Alt**, **E**, **D**, **R** (deletes the break between groups and the statistics between groups).

8. Change the margins of the report to make it visually attractive by making changes to the settings in the Page Setup & Margins option in the Print Menu.

9. Print one copy of the report.

10. Save the report and database file as 168B and close the file.

9. Key a header (title):
   a. If needed, select Page Setup from the File Menu.
   b. ~ Header box and key **&B1995 RAMS BASEBALL ROSTER** (enters and bolds the header).
   c. ~ OK.

10. Preview the list:
    a. Select Print from the File Menu.
    b. ~ Print Preview if needed.
    c. ~ Print box.
    d. If arranged attractively, ~ Print. If additional changes need to be made to have it arranged attractively, ~ Cancel and make necessary changes in Page Setup dialog box.

11. Print one copy of the report.

12. Save the report and database file as 168B and close the file.

51A ◆

REINFORCE REACH STROKES

Enter the columns of data listed at the right as directed in Steps 1-6 on p. 92.

	a	b	c	d	e	f	g
	44	74	740	996	704	990	477
	55	85	850	885	805	880	588
	66	96	960	774	906	770	699
	165	255	2,550	2,655	2,415	2,640	1,764

51B ◆

LEARN NEW KEYS: 1, 2, 3

Learn reach to 1

1. Locate 1 (below 4) on the numeric keypad.
2. Watch your pointer finger move down to 1 and back to 4 a few times *without striking keys.*
3. Practice striking 14 a few times as you watch the finger.
4. With eyes on copy, enter the data in Drills 1a and 1b.

Learn reach to 2

1. Learn the middle-finger reach to 2 (below 5) as directed in Steps 1-3 above.
2. With eyes on copy, enter the data in Drills 1c and 1d.

Learn reach to 3

1. Learn the ring-finger reach to 3 (below 6) as directed above.
2. With eyes on copy, enter the data in Drills 1e, 1f, and 1g.

Drills 2-4

Practice entering the columns of data in Drills 2-4 until you can do so accurately and quickly.

Drill 1

	a	b	c	d	e	f	g
	414	141	525	252	636	363	174
	141	111	252	222	363	333	285
	111	414	222	525	333	636	396
	666	666	999	999	1,332	1,332	855

Drill 2

	a	b	c	d	e	f	g
	114	225	336	175	415	184	174
	411	522	633	284	524	276	258
	141	252	363	395	635	359	369
	666	999	1,332	854	1,574	819	801

Drill 3

	a	b	c	d	e	f	g
	417	528	639	110	171	471	714
	147	280	369	220	282	582	850
	174	285	396	330	393	693	936
	738	1,093	1,404	660	846	1,746	2,500

Drill 4

	a	b	c	d	e	f	g
	77	71	401	107	417	147	174
	88	82	502	208	528	258	825
	99	93	603	309	639	369	396
	264	246	1,506	624	1,584	774	1,395

51C ◆

ENTER DATA WITH COMMAS

Enter the data in Columns a-g. (Even though number data often include commas to separate hundreds from thousands, do not enter them.)

	a	b	c	d	e	f	g
	14	25	36	17	28	39	174
	174	285	396	197	228	339	285
	1,014	2,025	3,036	9,074	1,785	9,096	1,736
	1,740	2,850	3,960	4,714	8,259	6,976	3,982
	7,414	8,250	9,636	1,417	2,528	3,639	2,803
	753	951	321	283	173	357	196
	1,474	2,585	3,696	4,974	5,285	6,398	1,974
	2,785	3,896	4,914	8,795	6,836	7,100	8,200
	15,368	20,867	25,995	29,471	25,122	33,944	19,350

WORKS DOS

1. Retrieve database file T168 on *Student's Template* and use it to create a report with a title, three fields (LAST, FIRST, and GRANT), with names listed from Z to A with a break when the first letter of the LAST field changes.
2. If needed, change to List View and study the field names and entries to become familiar with the database.
3. Create a report.

Version 2.0

   a. Press **Alt**, **V**, **N** (selects New Report from the View Menu) and strike Enter (displays the report).

   b. Display the report definition by striking Esc.

   c. Add a title by highlighting the cell at the intersection of Row 1 (Intr Report) and Column A (designates the beginning point of the title).

   d. Key **1995 RAMS BASEBALL ROSTER** and strike Enter (enters the report title).

   e. Delete the POSITION, THROWS, BATS, SPEED, and AVG fields by highlighting = POSITION and pressing **Alt**, **S**, **E** (chooses Cells from the Select Menu).

   f. Use → to extend highlight through the = AVG column (marks the fields to be deleted on this report).

   g. Press **Alt**, **E**, **D** (selects Delete Row Column from the Edit Menu).

   h. Key **C** (selects Column from the dialog box).

   i. Strike Enter.

   j. Use ← as needed to show the remaining three fields that are to be in the report. (Go to Step 4 on next page.)

Version 3.0

   a. Press **Alt**, **V**, **N** (selects New Report from the View Menu and displays the New Report dialog box).

   b. Key **1995 RAMS BASEBALL ROSTER** in the Report Title box (enters the report title).

   c. Strike the Tab key (moves cursor to LAST, the first field name in the Fields in Database box).

   d. Press **Alt A** (adds field LAST to the Fields in Report box so this field will be included in the report).

   e. Repeat Step d twice to add the fields named FIRST and GRANT to the Fields in Report box.

   f. Strike Enter (selects OK in the New Report dialog box and displays the Report Statistics dialog box).

WORKS MAC

1. Retrieve database file T168 on *Student's Template* and use it to create a report with a title, three fields (LAST, FIRST, and GRANT), with names listed from Z to A with a break when the first letter of the LAST field changes.
2. If needed, change to Show List and study the field names and entries to become familiar with the database.
3. Format numbers in GRANT field as money with 0 decimal places:

   a. Highlight the field named GRANT.

   b. Select Set Cell Attributes from the Format Menu.

   c. ~ Numeric, ~ Dollar, key **0**, and strike Return.

4. Change GRANT field width to about 9 spaces by moving the pointer to the vertical line to the right of the field name GRANT (a cross will form) and drag it to the right about 4 spaces.
5. Sort the records by last name from Z to A.
6. Create a report by choosing Select New Report from the Report Menu (displays the report definition).
7. To prepare a report that will print only the LAST, FIRST, and GRANT fields:

   a. Move the GRANT field so that it is to the right of the FIRST field, ~ the field name GRANT, drag the pointer to the left until the POSITION field is highlighted, and then release the mouse button.

   b. Place the Right Edge Marker (the black triangle below and near the right side of the ruler) above the vertical line separating the GRANT and POSITION fields by dragging it to the left.

8. Set margins so that the list will be horizontally centered when printed:

   a. Note that the distance from the Left Edge Marker to the Right Edge Marker is about 2.5". Therefore, to have it horizontally centered, you will need to set the left margin at 3" and the right margin so that it is not more than 3".

   b. Select Page Setup from the File Menu.

   c. Key **3** in the Left Margin box (sets LM at 3").

   d. Key **2** in the Right Margin box (sets RM smaller than 3").

(continued on next page)

(continued on next page)

52A ◆

REVIEW KEY LOCATIONS

Enter the columns of data listed at the right as directed in Steps 1-6 on p. 92.

a	b	c	d	e	f	g
44	55	66	714	414	525	636
14	25	36	825	474	585	696
74	85	96	936	400	500	600
132	165	198	2,475	1,288	1,610	1,932

52B ◆

IMPROVE FACILITY

Enter the data listed in each column of Drills 1-3.

Note: If you are using the math function of your word processing software, remember to check your totals against the printed totals.

Drill 1

a	b	c	d	e	f	g
14	19	173	1,236	1,714	4,174	4,074
25	37	291	4,596	2,825	5,285	5,085
36	18	382	7,896	3,936	6,396	6,096
74	29	794	5,474	7,414	1,400	9,336
85	38	326	2,975	8,525	2,500	8,225
96	27	184	8,535	9,636	3,600	7,114
330	168	2,150	30,712	34,050	23,355	39,930

Drill 2

a	b	c	d	e	f	g
1	3	40	123	114	1,004	8,274
14	36	50	789	225	2,005	9,386
174	396	70	321	336	3,006	7,494
2	906	740	456	774	7,004	1,484
25	306	360	174	885	8,005	2,595
285	20	850	285	996	9,006	3,686
805	50	960	396	500	5,005	6,006
1,306	1,717	3,070	2,544	3,830	35,035	38,925

Drill 3

a	b	c	d	e	f	g
126	104	107	707	4,400	3,006	1,714
786	205	208	808	5,000	2,005	2,825
324	306	309	909	6,600	1,004	3,936
984	704	407	1,700	7,000	9,006	7,144
876	805	508	2,800	8,800	8,005	8,255
216	906	609	3,900	9,000	7,004	9,366
3,312	3,030	2,148	10,824	40,800	30,030	33,240

52C ◆

ENTER DATA WITH DECIMALS

Enter the data in Columns a-f, placing the decimals as shown in the copy.

a	b	c	d	e	f
1.40	17.10	47.17	174.11	1,477.01	10,704.50
2.50	28.20	58.28	285.22	2,588.02	17,815.70
3.60	39.30	69.39	396.33	3,996.03	20,808.75
4.70	74.70	17.10	417.14	4,174.07	26,909.65
5.80	85.80	28.20	528.25	5,285.08	30,906.25
6.90	96.90	39.30	639.36	6,396.06	34,259.90
24.90	342.00	259.44	2,440.41	23,916.27	141,404.75

167E ◆

ADD LABELS
TO FORMS

Works DOS Only

Read the information at the right about adding labels and then complete the steps.

A label is any descriptive text (usually titles or instructions) that appears in every record. The label is not part of a field and it is displayed only when Form View is used. Labels can be entered before or after records are created.

WORKS DOS

1. Retrieve 167C and change to Form View, if needed.
2. Position the highlight in Field 1 on any record and press **Alt, E, I** (inserts a line in the record where the label is to be inserted).
3. Use cursor key to move to left edge of record, if needed (marks the left margin of the label).
4. Key **FAMILY AUTO REPORT** (enters the label).
5. Strike any cursor key.
6. Use cursor key to move highlight to beginning of the line below the last field in the record.
7. Key **JIM SMITH IS THE PERSON AUTHORIZED TO REVISE THIS DATABASE**.
8. Strike any cursor key.
9. Scroll through the other records and see that the title and instructions are included on each record.
10. Switch to List View and note that the list does not contain either label.
11. Change to Form View and print the first record.
12. Save the database file as 167E and close the file.

L ESSON 168   REVIEW AND ENHANCE REPORT FORMAT SKILLS

168A ◆
CONDITIONING
PRACTICE

each line twice

alphabet 1 Kevin justified his low quiz score by explaining his unusual problems.

fig/sym 2 She accumulated 2,453 miles in June, 989 in July, and 1,706 in August.

keypad 3 47 58 69 41 52 63 456 789 123 447 558 698 474 585 696 417 428 639 4070

speed 4 Diana and the visitor can handle the problems of the eighth amendment.

gwam 1' | 1 | 2 | 3 | 4 | 5 | 6 | 7 | 8 | 9 | 10 | 11 | 12 | 13 | 14 |

168B ◆

REVIEW REPORT
FORMAT SKILLS

Read the information at the right about reports and then complete the activities for your software.

In an earlier unit, you learned how to customize a report to make it more meaningful and easier to read and understand. To customize the report, you learned to sort information into meaningful groups, add meaningful titles and headers, set left and right margins, align column entries, format numbers, insert or delete blank rows or columns, and delete fields not needed for the report. This lesson reviews many of these routines.

53A ◆
REVIEW KEY LOCATIONS

Enter the columns of data listed at the right.

a	b	c	d	e	f	g
477	588	707	107	41.6	141.4	936.6
417	528	808	205	52.9	252.5	825.6
717	825	909	309	63.3	393.3	719.4
1,611	1,941	2,424	621	157.8	787.2	2,481.6

53B ◆
IMPROVE FACILITY

Enter the data listed in each column of Drills 1-4.

Note: When using the math function, enter each column of data a second time (bottom to top). If you get the same total twice, you can "assume" it is correct. If you get a different total the second time, reenter the data until you get two totals that match.

Drill 1

a	b	c	d	e	f	g
5	77	114	5,808	1,936	9,300	6,936
46	89	225	3,997	2,825	8,250	3,896
3	78	336	9,408	3,796	10,475	7,140
17	85	725	5,650	8,625	7,125	4,874
28	98	825	3,714	9,436	12,740	2,515
9	69	936	2,825	8,514	12,850	8,360
10	97	704	6,796	4,174	9,674	1,794

Drill 2

a	b	c	d	e	f	g
99	795	1,581	1,881	2,642	4,573	2,185
67	657	1,691	1,991	2,772	4,683	3,274
88	234	1,339	2,202	2,992	5,477	9,396
96	359	1,221	2,432	3,743	6,409	4,585
84	762	1,101	3,303	3,853	6,886	5,872
100	485	1,144	4,650	4,714	7,936	6,903

Drill 3

a	b	c	d	e	f
1,077	3,006	5,208	7,104	1,774	7,417
1,400	3,609	5,502	8,205	2,885	8,528
1,700	3,900	5,205	9,303	3,996	9,639
2,008	4,107	6,309	7,407	4,174	3,936
2,500	4,400	6,600	8,508	5,285	5,828
2,805	1,704	6,900	9,609	6,396	4,717

Drill 4

a	b	c	d	e	f
1.4	14.00	170.40	1,714.70	7,410.95	1,147.74
2.5	17.00	170.43	2,825.80	8,520.55	2,258.88
3.6	25.00	250.90	3,936.90	9,630.65	3,369.93
7.4	28.00	288.50	4,747.17	10,585.78	7,144.74
8.5	36.00	369.63	5,878.25	11,474.85	8,255.85
9.6	39.00	390.69	6,969.39	12,696.95	9,366.63

Does your word processing software have a calculator function? If so, learn how to use it. Then complete Lessons 49-53 a second time using the calculator and checking your totals against the printed totals.

FIND DATA QUICKLY

Read the information at the right about finding data quickly and then complete the steps for your software.

Sometimes you need to locate specific data quickly in a database.

Works DOS: You can use a question mark (?) or an asterisk (*) to search a database for records whose contents are similar, but not exactly the same. These symbols are called wildcards. The question mark (?) represents any single character in the same position in a word as the question mark. For example, if you want to find a particular name but are unsure whether the spelling is Metson, Metsen, or Metsan, key **mets?n** in the Search For box and Works will find and list all records with any of the three names. The asterisk (*) is used for any number of characters in that same position. For example, if you key **m*n** in the Search For box, Works will find all words that begin with "m" and end with "n," such as Metson, Metsen, Mean, Metsan, Moon, and Metterson.

Works MAC: You can use Find Field from the Organize Menu repeatedly to find each entry containing the data (for example, all entries with the name Smith), or you can use Match Records to display a list of all records containing the data (for example, a list of all records containing the name Smith).

WORKS DOS

1. In file 167C switch to List View.
2. Search for records that have family name of Smart, Smirt, Smert, or Smurt:
   a. Press **Alt, S, S** (selects Search from the Select Menu).
   b. Key **sm?rt** in the Search For box (enters the wildcard search).
   c. Press **Alt A** (specifies that all records in the database are to be searched).
   d. Strike Enter (executes the search and lists the records found).
      Note: Two records should be listed—Smart and Smert.
3. Search for records that contain the letter "a":
   a. Press **Alt, S, S**.
   b. Key **a*** (enters the wildcard search).
   c. Press **Alt A** (specifies that all records in the database are to be searched).
   d. Strike Enter (executes the search of the entire database even though only two records are visible in List View, and lists the records found).
      Note: Three records should be listed—Smega, Smart, and Adametz.
4. Search for records that contain "sm":
   a. Press **Alt, S, S**.
   b. Key **sm*** (enters the wildcard search).
   c. Press **Alt A**.
   d. Strike Enter (five records should be listed).
5. Save the last list as 167D and close the file.

WORKS MAC

1. In file 167C switch to Show List.
2. Find each entry that contains SME
   a. Select Find Field from the Organize Menu.
   b. Key **SME** in the dialog box (designates the information to be located).
   c. ~ Find Next or strike Return (highlights the next occurrence of SME in the database).
   d. Select Find Field from the Organize Menu.
   e. ~ Find Next or strike Return (highlights the next occurrence of SME in the database).
   f. Repeat Steps d and e until an alert box appears and indicates that all occurrences of SME have been found.
   g. ~ OK or strike Return.
3. Display a list of all records that contain SM in an entry:
   a. Select Match Records from the Organize Menu.
   b. Key **SM** (enters the information that is to be found and listed).
   c. ~ OK or strike Return (lists five records that have SM in the name).
4. Save the last list as 167D and close the file.

UNIT 10

LESSONS 54-57

Master Keyboarding/Word Processing Skills

Learning Outcomes: After completing this unit, you will be able to

1. Demonstrate improved technique on alphanumeric copy.
2. Demonstrate improved speed and control on straight-copy paragraphs.
3. Demonstrate greater transfer of straight-copy speed.
4. Demonstrate improved mastery of word processing features.

L ESSON 54   KEYBOARDING/WORD PROCESSING

54A ♦ 6'
CONDITIONING PRACTICE

each line twice SS; then a 1'
writing on line 3; find *gwam*

alphabet 1   Jevon was quick to fix my prized urn, the big clock for you.
fig/sym 2   I paid $19.75 (20% off) for the book, $6.48 for 3 notebooks.
speed 3   Nancy did fix the bicycle and got to the lake dock by eight.

gwam 1' | 1 | 2 | 3 | 4 | 5 | 6 | 7 | 8 | 9 | 10 | 11 | 12 |

54B ♦ 15'
MASTER LETTER KEYS

1. Key line 1 at a brisk pace. Note the words that were awkward for you.
2. Key each of the awkward words three times at increasing speed.
3. Key line 2 at a steady fluent rate.
4. Key each of the other pairs of lines in the same way.
5. If time permits, rekey selected lines.

Fingers curved

Fingers upright

A/B
1   also club plan burn slam curb make brim alto slab mask bring
2   Alan is an able backup, but he broke an elbow on that block.

C/D
3   corn glad dock cent make pick door hack slid curl rode crude
4   Candice did pick a nice gold medal for the best ice dancers.

E/F
5   else flow melt soft lend firm able cuff made fuss rent fight
6   Effie took off at the desert airfield for her final mission.

G/H
7   gush high grin bush that slug hand grip huge sang this angle
8   Garth might get high marks on his tests at the target range.

I/J
9   idle just item jail file jerk isle joke time jell find major
10   Jinx just joked about finding a major job in their jet firm.

K/L
11   kale lake silk like walk lack bilk flak link milk lark slack
12   Kyle will check all books of the big silk maker at the lake.

M/N
13   make nape mend name pens lame land lamb plan came mane snake
14   More men, women, and children may visit the mall next month.

O/P
15   open poem soap post spot poet opal hope flop rope poor topic
16   Orpha took top prize at the pool party as polo team captain.

Q/R
17   quit rush quay rock aqua rich quad park quiz roam quid quart
18   Quin quit her squad after a quirky rise in our quartz quota.

S/T
19   sold turn loss fort sham torn span them just mash dent shape
20   Tasha said that their sale is surely the best of the season.

U/V
21   undo vote much have sure move push vain rust pave such views
22   Vaughn must review very fully your various views on visuals.

W/X
23   wish flax vent flux slow axle owns axis down oxen fowl toxin
24   Xerxes will show why new excise tax laws will vex wax firms.

Y/Z
25   your quiz buys jazz duty zeal many zest pity doze city prize
26   Lizzy was truly puzzled by the zeal and zest of my baby boy.

Read the information at the right about using functions. Use this information to create a database and then complete the steps below for your software.

Works, like most other database software, has built-in equations. Using a built-in function (equation) saves time because it reduces the need to construct and key equations. In this lesson, you will use the SUM function to add a series of fields and the COUNT function to determine the number of entries in each record. These functions, used in Part 3—Spreadsheet Applications, can be used in databases.

FAMILY	AUTO1	AUTO2	AUTO3	AUTO4
WILSON	8000	4000		
DEITZ	25000	18500	14500	2000
SMERT	14000			
SOERGEL	14000	13000	5000	
SMART	30200	17500		
SMOCK	21000	11600	6000	1200
ADAMETZ	8000			
SMITH	55000	15000	1000	
SMEGA	12500	11000	7500	

WORKS DOS

1. Add a field at the right and name it VALUE by keying **Alt**, **E**, **N**, **VALUE**.
2. Add a field at the right and name it NO.AUTOS by keying **Alt**, **E**, **N**, **NO. AUTOS**.
3. Highlight the first cell in the VALUE field and key **=SUM(AUTO1,AUTO2, AUTO3,AUTO4)** to use the SUM function to find the total value of the autos in each record. Note that the equation is automatically copied to and the computation is made for each record in the database.
4. Highlight the first cell in the NO. AUTOS field and key **=COUNT (AUTO1,AUTO2,AUTO3,AUTO4)** to use the COUNT function to find the number of cars in each family.
5. Format the VALUE field to money with no decimal places:
   a. Highlight the first cell in the VALUE field.
   b. Press **Alt**, **S**, **F**.
   c. Press **Alt**, **T**, **U**, **0** (zero) and strike Enter.
6. Sort the records by the number of autos (in descending order):
   a. Press **Alt**, **S**, **O**.
   b. Key **NO.AUTOS**.
   c. Press **Alt B** and strike Enter.
7. Save the database as 167C, but do NOT close the file.

WORKS MAC

1. Add a field at the right and name it VALUE by selecting Add New Field from the Edit Menu and keying **VALUE**.
2. Add a field at the right and name it **NUM AUTOS**.
3. Highlight the field named VALUE and then select Set Field Attributes from the Format Menu (first step in entering a formula).
4. ~ Numeric and then Computed.
5. ~ Dollars, key **0**, and strike Return (formats field for dollars with no decimal places).
6. Key **SUM(AUTO1,AUTO2,AUTO3, AUTO4)** to the right of the = (equal) sign in the Entry Bar (uses the SUM function to find the total value of the autos in each record). Note that the equation is automatically copied to and the computation is made for each record in the database.
7. Highlight the field named NUM AUTOS and then select Set Field Attributes from the Format Menu.
8. ~ Numeric and then Computed.
9. ~ Fixed, key **0**, and strike Return (formats field for Fixed with no decimal places).
10. Key **COUNT(AUTO1,AUTO2,AUTO3, AUTO4)** to the right of the = sign in the Entry Bar (uses the COUNT function to find the number of cars in each family).
11. Sort the records by the number of autos (in descending order):
    a. Highlight a cell in the NUM AUTOS field.
    b. Select Sort from the Organize Menu.
    c. ~ 9 to 0 in the dialog box (selects descending order).
    d. ~ OK or strike Return.
12. Save the database as 167C, but do NOT close the file.

IMPROVE/CHECK SPEED

LS: DS

1. A 1' writing on ¶1, then a 1" writing on ¶2; find *gwam* on each.
2. A 2' writing on ¶s 1-2 combined; find *gwam*.
3. A 3' writing on ¶s 1-2 combined; find *gwam* and count errors.

gwam	¼'	½'	¾'	1'
20	5	10	15	20
24	6	12	18	24
28	7	14	21	28
32	8	16	24	32
36	9	18	27	36
40	10	20	30	40
44	11	22	33	44
48	12	24	36	48
52	13	26	39	52
56	14	28	42	56

all letters used | LA | 1.4 si | 5.4 awl | 85% hfw

gwam 2' | 3'

An excellent performance shows the true concern of the   5 | 4
performer for the task. It gives one a feeling of personal   11 | 8
triumph and prompts us as a matter of habit to do our best.   18 | 12
Really successful men and women take great delight in their   24 | 16
work and pursue it with a lot of dedication.   28 | 19

A factor common to all who succeed is the need to have   5 | 22
a good job recognized by others. If good work goes without   11 | 26
notice, the desire to excel may be reduced. Lucky, indeed,   18 | 30
are those who can study their own performance, evaluate its   24 | 34
quality, and do what must be done to improve.   28 | 37

gwam 2' | 1 | 2 | 3 | 4 | 5 | 6 |
3' | 1 | 2 | 3 | 4 |

SKILL TRANSFER: SCRIPT

LS: DS

1. A 2' writing on ¶s 1-2 combined; find *gwam*.
2. A 3' writing on ¶s 1-2 combined; find *gwam* and count errors.
3. Then make changes as listed below right.

all letters used | LA | 1.4 si | 5.4 awl | 85% hfw

gwam 2' | 3'

Line		
1	Those who have pencils but no erasers can never make a	5 / 4
2	mistake. They must never, of course, try anything of great	11 / 8
3	importance either. Don't be ashamed of making an error now	17 / 12
4	and then, but try not to make the same one again and again.	23 / 16
5	Follow this excellent rule to become a careful worker.	29 / 19
6	As you try to develop your typing power, you will make	5 / 23
7	quite a few errors when you try out new or improved methods.	11 / 27
8	of stroking. Just as in other skills, though, many of your	17 / 31
9	errors will fall away as you further your ability. Realize,	23 / 35
10	also, that even the best workers often need erasers.	29 / 39

Changes

Line 1 Change **those** to **people**.
2 Delete **great**.
3 Change **don't** to **do not**.
4 Underline **same**.

Line 6 Change **typing** to **keying**.
8 Change **though** to **however**.
9 Change **fall away** to **drop out**.
10 Bold the last sentence (see 38D, p. 74).

REMOVE INFORMATION

Read the paragraph at the right about removing information from a database and then complete the steps for your software.

Works lets you remove information by deleting, clearing, and/or cutting. When Delete is used, the information and its formatting is eliminated. When Clear is used, the information is eliminated; but its formatting remains so that any new information you key has the same format. When Cut (a feature of Works MAC) is used, the information removed is placed on the clipboard and may be pasted in another location. In this lesson, you will learn to remove entries in adjacent cells, records, and fields with a database list. Information can also be removed when working with forms and reports.

WORKS DOS	WORKS MAC
1. Retrieve file 166D.	1. Retrieve file 166D.
2. If needed, change to List View.	2. If needed, change to Show List.
3. Delete a Field—Delete the FIRST name field:	3. Delete a Field—Delete the FIRST name field:
a. Position the highlight in a cell in the FIRST field.	a. ~ the field named FIRST (selects the field to be deleted).
b. Press **Alt**, **S**, **F** (chooses Field from the Select Menu).	b. Select Delete Field from the Edit Menu (deletes the field).
c. Press **Alt**, **E**, **D** (chooses Delete Record/Field from the Edit Menu).	4. Delete a Record—Delete the Danoff record:
d. Strike any cursor key.	a. ~ Record Selector box at the left of the Danoff record (marks the record to be deleted).
4. Delete a Record—Delete the Danoff record:	b. Select Cut from the Edit Menu (cuts the record and moves remaining records up one row).
a. Position the highlight in a cell in the Danoff record.	5. Clear a Group of Adjacent Cells—Clear the first two cells in the LAST name and STREET fields:
b. Press **Alt**, **S**, **R** (chooses Record from the Select Menu).	a. Highlight the first two cells in the first two rows of the LAST name and STREET fields (designates the cells to be cleared).
c. Press **Alt**, **E**, **D** (chooses Delete Record/Field from the Edit Menu).	b. Select Clear from the Edit Menu (removes the information and leaves blank cells).
d. Strike any cursor key.	6. Formulas—Formulas cannot be removed (cut, cleared, or deleted) from individual records in a database. If the formula needs revision, display its contents in the Entry Bar and make the necessary changes. If the formula needs to be eliminated from the database, delete the entire field. Delete the COMMISSION field that contains the formula:
5. Clear a Group of Adjacent Cells—Clear the first two cells in the LAST name and STREET fields:	a. Highlight the field named COMMISSION.
a. Highlight the first cell record 5 (designates the upper-left cell in the group to be cleared).	b. Select Delete Field from the Edit Menu.
b. Press **Alt**, **S**, **E** (chooses Cells from the Select Menu).	7. Save as 167B.
c. Highlight the cells that are to be cleared.	
d. Press **Alt**, **E**, **E** (chooses Clear from the Edit Menu).	
e. Strike any cursor key.	
6. Clear a Formula—Clear the formula in the COMMISSION field:	
a. Highlight the COMMISSION field (designates the field that contains the formula to be cleared).	
b. Key =	
c. Strike Enter (clears the formula and answers in all applicable records).	
7. Save as 167B.	

 **ESSON 55** | KEYBOARDING/WORD PROCESSING

SM: Defaults; LS: SS

55A ◆ 6'
CONDITIONING PRACTICE
each line twice

alphabet 1 Javitz had him quickly bring six sets of new plastic knives.
fig/sym 2 My taxes (1994) were $1,832 on a $116,570 home on Elm Place.
speed 3 Their city neighbor owns the dock and half of the rich land.

gwam 1' | 1 | 2 | 3 | 4 | 5 | 6 | 7 | 8 | 9 | 10 | 11 | 12 |

55B ◆ 19'
IMPROVE/CHECK TECHNIQUE

1. Key lines 1-21 once SS; DS between 3-line groups.
2. Key a 1' writing on each of lines 22-26; find *gwam* and compare rates on the five writings.

Technique goals
- fingers deeply curved and upright
- eyes on copy
- finger-action keystrokes
- hands and arms quiet, almost motionless

word response
1 by with then worn they make corn pens them vigor their right
2 of the | for us | if she is | by the end | pay them for | work with us
3 I shall make a big name panel to hang by a door of the hall.

combination response
4 to my of him for you they were pale pink torn card goal rates
5 to him | see me | if we may | if you did | she fed them | then you got
6 The men are to fix a water pump for the big pool in the gym.

double letters
7 all ill odd ebb hall mass fizz sell cuff purr flee good need
8 is odd | lay off | too big | all men | toss the | will pay | a good putt
9 Ann will sell all her old school books at a good price, too.

adjacent keys
10 as top was open were ruin very tray coin mask soil rent port
11 ask her | we went | top post | new coin | buy art | oil well | last week
12 Jered was to open a coin shop in an old store at the square.

long, direct reaches
13 my gym fun mud ice sum run any curb nice must many hunt glum
14 hum it|had fun|hot sun|any gym|must run|my thumb|bring a mug
15 Ceci had much fun at the gym and the ice center this summer.

outside reaches
16 apt quo now zap opt low sap was pal aqua soap flax span slow
17 as low | was apt | now all | pro quo | will stop | polo pony | slow play
18 Laska is apt to play a top game of polo if the pony is well.

figures & symbols
19 25% $483.10 #36790 PO #472-413859 Model #1600LS 2-floor plan
20 May 9|less 5%|30 books|2-ply forms|Invoice #81746|Orr & Chin
21 She said: "You must keep your ____ on the copy as you key."

alphabet 22 Rob may vex a top judge with his quick flips and zany dives.
fig/sym 23 Fifty dollars ($50) is due on Account #291-4836 by August 6.
combination 24 You are to visit a gas firm with my auditor if you are free.
double letters 25 Ann will see that all the books are passed out before class.
word 26 Six of the antique firms may lend us a hand with the social.

gwam 1' | 1 | 2 | 3 | 4 | 5 | 6 | 7 | 8 | 9 | 10 | 11 | 12 |

55C ◆ 5'
REVIEW CENTERING

On a clear screen, center DS each line given at right so that the first line would print 2" from the top edge. Refer to p. 10 and p. 52.

READING LIST

Lord of the Flies

To Kill a Mockingbird

A Raisin in the Sun

APPLICATION ACTIVITY

Use the information at the right and the directions below to create a database.

1. Format the numeric columns as money without decimal places.
2. Add a new field at the right; name it PER REC. Format it as Percent with no decimal places, and use the following formula in it to compute the percent received:
   =Amount Received/ Amount Pledged
3. Sort the file by percent received in descending order and save it as 166E1.
4. Query the 166E1 file for all people who have given 80% or more of their pledge.

   Works DOS: Key >=80% in the PER REC field after keying **Alt, V, Q**.

   Works MAC: Select Record Selection from the Organize Menu and install this rule: PER REC is greater than or equal to 80%.
5. Print a list of those donors who have given 80% or more and then save the list (database will be saved automatically) as 166E2.

NAME	AMOUNT PLEDGED	AMOUNT RECEIVED
ALICE GOMORY	750	701
DIANE ALDRIDGE	1500	1258
DONALD ESPINOSA	2500	2400
GREGG FOSTER	350	350
JONATHAN AKERVIK	2250	1760
MARCIA KELLY	1675	1342
MARY WHITNER	1600	1625
MICHAEL McCOSKEY	2305	2205
NANCY SCNEIDER	1775	1660
ORLANDO MARTINEZ	750	730
REBECCA JOHNSTON	2000	1000
ROGER McDONALD	1875	550
RUTH PETERSON	1200	500

L ESSON 167 REMOVE INFORMATION, SEARCH, USE FUNCTION

167A ◆ CONDITIONING PRACTICE

each line twice

alphabet 1 Dr. Zisk told us to keep quiet just before the physics exam was given.

fig/sym 2 Jason hit .418 in May, .257 in June, .360 in July, and .409 in August.

keypad 3 11 22 33 44 55 66 77 88 99 00 117 128 139 114 225 336 477 588 699 4560

speed 4 The ornament on their oak mantle is a small antique ivory lamb or cow.

gwam 1' | 1 | 2 | 3 | 4 | 5 | 6 | 7 | 8 | 9 | 10 | 11 | 12 | 13 | 14 |

CHECK SPEED

LS: DS
1. A 2' writing on ¶s 1-2 combined; find *gwam*.
2. A 3' writing on ¶s 1-2 combined; find *gwam* and count errors.

all letters used | A | 1.5 si | 5.7 awl | 80% hfw

	gwam 2'	3'
If success is vital to you, you have distinct	5	3
advantage over many people who have no particular feeling	10	7
one way or the other. The desire to succeed is helpful, for	17	11
it causes us to establish goals without which our actions	22	15
have little or no meaning. Success may not necessarily	28	19
mean winning the big prize, but it does mean approaching a	34	22
goal.	35	23
It is foolish, of course, to believe that we can all be	40	27
whatever we wish to become. It is just as foolish, though,	46	31
to wait around hoping for success to overtake us. We should	52	35
analyze our aspirations, our abilities, and our limitations.	58	39
We can next decide from various choices what we are best	64	43
equipped with effort to become.	67	45

gwam 2' | 1 | 2 | 3 | 4 | 5 | 6
3' | 1 | 2 | 3 | 4

SKILL TRANSFER: ROUGH DRAFT

LS: DS
1. A 2' writing on ¶s 1-2 combined; find *gwam*.
2. A 3' writing on ¶s 1-2 combined; find *gwam* and count errors.
3. Key another 3' writing on ¶s 1-2 to improve speed.

	gwam 2'	3'
It is ~~very~~ *extremely* important to use ~~exceeding~~ *extra* care in addressing	6	4
envelopes. By doing so you will make it easier for the mail	12	8
to be ~~sorted~~ *processed* quickly. Because of # the automation ~~employed~~ *being used*	18	12
with mail to day, ~~various~~ *certain* requirements have to be met to assure	25	16
~~quick~~ *rapid* processing.	27	18
The correct ~~format~~ and placement of the ~~letter~~ *return* address	32	21
and destination address on the envelope are ~~quite~~ *very* important.	38	25
Just as ~~crucial~~ *important* as the correct placement and format of the	44	29
addresses is the ZIP code. # If it is not ~~shown,~~ ~~all~~ *included* your mail	50	34
~~won't~~ *will not* be delivered as ~~rapidly.~~ *nearly fast.*	54	36

LESSON 55 ◆ KEYBOARDING/WORD PROCESSING **100**

WRITE
FORMULAS

Read the information at the right about writing formulas and then complete the steps for your software.

1. If needed, retrieve 166C.
2. Use the following field names to add three fields to the database file.
   a. RATE (this field name designates the commission rate the person is being paid).
   b. SALES (this field name designates the amount of the person's sales).
   c. COMMISSION (this field name designates the amount of commission each person receives; it is the field in which a formula will be entered).

One of the primary uses of database formulas is to calculate the contents of one field on the basis of the contents of one or more other fields. For example, mathematical values are calculated by keying a formula (equation) into a field (cell) you choose. Each formula must be preceded by an equal sign (=). You can have only one formula in a database field, and that formula is then automatically entered into all records. When applicable information is keyed into a new record, the formula automatically creates a value for that field in the new record.

WORKS DOS

1. Key **=rate*sales** as the first cell entry in the COMMISSION field and strike Enter (this formula will calculate the commission for each person based on the information that is keyed into the RATE and SALES fields).
2. Key the following values into the RATE and SALES fields for the person designated. (Note that the commission is automatically calculated for each record as the values are entered even though the formula was entered only in the first record.)

Elaine Wilson:	.06	$125,000
Surin Bajwa:	.08	90,575
Ellen Wilson:	.055	135,095
Frances Danoff:	.0575	143,945
Cory Gentile:	.07	95,675
Lorita Perez:	.075	101,755
Celia Thomas:	.0775	99,995
Bobbi Unis:	.0725	105,970

3. Format the RATE field as percents with two decimal places; format the SALES and the COMMISSION fields as Currency with no decimal places.
4. Save the file as 166D and close the file.

WORKS MAC

1. Select the COMMISSION Field and then select Set Field Attributes from the Format Menu.
2. ~ Numeric in the Type column of the dialog box (designates that the field will be a numeric field).
3. ~ the Computed box in the lower-left corner of the dialog box (designates that the field will be a computed field).
4. ~ Dollar and key **0** (formats the field as Dollar with no decimal places).
5. ~ OK or strike Return (returns you to list window and places an = (equal) sign in the Entry Bar).
6. Key **rate*sales** to the right of the = (equal) sign (enters the formula needed to calculate the commission for each person on the basis of information that is keyed in the RATE and SALES fields).
7. Strike Return.
8. Key the following values into the RATE and SALES fields for the person designated. (Note that the commission is automatically calculated for each record as the values are entered even though the formula was entered only in the first record.)

Elaine Wilson:	.06	$125,000
Surin Bajwa:	.08	90,575
Ellen Wilson:	.055	135,095
Frances Danoff:	.0575	143,945
Cory Gentile:	.07	95,675
Lorita Perez:	.075	101,755
Celia Thomas:	.0775	99,995
Bobbi Unis:	.0725	105,970

9. Format the RATE field as Percent with two decimal places; format the SALES field as dollar with no decimal places.
10. Save the file as 166D and close the file.

SM: Defaults; LS: SS

56A ◆ 6'
CONDITIONING PRACTICE
each line twice

alphabet 1 Dezi will quickly bring me guava to have six pints of juice.

fig/sym 2 Account #27401 was overdue by $395.63; #38192, by $1,284.95.

speed 3 They paid the firm for the land to make a lake for the town.

gwam 1' | 1 | 2 | 3 | 4 | 5 | 6 | 7 | 8 | 9 | 10 | 11 | 12 |

56B ◆ 10'
IMPROVE TECHNIQUE

1. Key lines 1-10 once SS; DS between 2-line groups.
2. Key a 1' writing on line 11, then on line 12; find *gwam* on each writing.

word response
1 pair auto maps fuel sick born laid coal body duty land goals
2 by them | to wish | am paid | if they | it also | she kept | held it for

combination response
3 also upon auto area hand ever owns data half only dial after
4 to eat | for only | the pump | due date | own data | and join | may test

double letters
5 ooze burr peel good jazz food full door cuff miss toss glass
6 do miss | to peel | so tall | is good | am full | all jazz | toss a ball

adjacent keys
7 same stop mere suit poem foil more guys flew poet coin train
8 he was | ask her | pop art | top post | you were | few weeks | was quick

long, direct reaches
9 must peck much nice hunt deck many nuts sums plum lace juice
10 a gym | any ice | my deck | my lace | must curb | any doubt | zany dance

word 11 Eight men own the ancient island and may make it a city zoo.
combination 12 The ink firm may join my panel to fix a toxic waste problem.

gwam 1' | 1 | 2 | 3 | 4 | 5 | 6 | 7 | 8 | 9 | 10 | 11 | 12 |

56C ◆ 10'
WORD PROCESSING

1. Clear the screen (p. 10) and key the ¶s given at right DS.
2. In line 1, change *every person* to **everyone**.
3. In line 2, change *serve* to **be**.
4. In line 4, insert **all** after *that*.
5. In line 5, underline each.
6. In line 7, change *athletic* to **playing**.
7. In line 10, delete *from all*.
8. Move the last sentence of ¶2 to the end of ¶1 (see 39C, p. 75).
9. Move the sentences on lines 4 and 5 (*Realize that . . . they play.*) to the end of ¶2.
10. Center in bold the heading WINNING TAKES EFFORT so that it will print 2" from top edge of sheet and a QS above first ¶.
11. Proofread and correct errors.
12. Print.

Line

1 It is a satisfying feeling to be a winner. Every person
2 prefers to serve on a winning team. Although the prize might
3 not be worth either the time or effort involved, the desire to
4 excel may justify both. Realize that team members must meet
5 the requirements for a winning exhibition each time they play.
6 An office work force is a team, also; and the same basic
7 principles apply there as apply on an athletic field. A major
8 difference, however, is that in the office the rewards are in-
9 creased pay and promotions instead of trophies and letters.
10 Winning is fun on any team, but winning takes effort from all.

Works DOS and Works MAC

Key the first two records shown below in a database file that you create. Use LAST, FIRST, STREET, CITY, and STATE as the five field names. Key the field names in ALL CAPS.

Record 1
Wilson Elaine
225 West Avenue
Toledo OH

Record 2
Bajwa Surin
834 Euclid Street
Erie PA

Record 3
Wilson Ellen
225 West Avenue
Toledo OH

Record 4
Danoff Frances
45 Scott Lane
Detroit MI

Record 5
Gentile Cory
358 North Street
Detroit MI

Record 6
Perez Lorita
44 Wilson Avenue
Detroit MI

Record 7
Thomas Celia
1900 State Street
Detroit MI

Record 8
Unis Bobbi
1397 East Street
Detroit MI

WORKS DOS

1. If needed, change to List View.
2. Since the third record is very similar to the first record, use the Copy feature to enter it:
   a. Highlight the first field of the first record (marks the first record as the one to be copied).
   b. Press **Alt**, **S**, **R** (chooses Record from the Select Menu).
   c. Press **Alt**, **E**, **C** (selects Copy from the Edit Menu).
   d. Highlight the upper-left cell of the area into which you want to place the copy.
   e. Press Enter (places the copy in the designated area).
3. Edit the third record so that it reads Ellen instead of Elaine.
4. Key the fourth record.
5. Key the first three fields of the last four records (the Copy feature will be used in the next steps to enter the city and state to reduce keying time).
6. Highlight the fourth field of the fourth record and press **Alt**, **S**, **E** (chooses Cells from the Select Menu).
7. Extend the highlight over the fourth and fifth fields of records 4 through 8 (designates the cells that are to be copied and to receive copies).
8. Press **Alt**, **E**, **F** (selects Fill Down from the Edit Menu).
9. Strike any cursor key.
10. Save the file as 166C but do not clear the screen.

WORKS MAC

1. If needed, change to Show List.
2. Since the third record is very similar to the first record, use the Copy feature to enter it:
   a. ~ Record Selector box at the left of the first record (designates that the first record is the one to be copied).
   b. Select Copy from the Edit Menu.
   c. Move the pointer to the upper left cell of the area into which you want to place the copy.
   d. Select Paste from the Edit Menu.
3. Edit the third record so it reads Ellen instead of Elaine.
4. Key the fourth record.
5. Key the first three fields of the last four records (the Copy and Paste features will be used in the next steps to enter the city and state to reduce keying time).
6. Highlight the fourth and fifth fields of Record 4 (designates the cells that are to be copied).
7. Select Copy from the Edit Menu.
8. Highlight the fourth and fifth fields of Record 5 (designates the cells that will receive the copy).
9. Select Paste from the Edit Menu (places the copy into the selected cells).
10. Highlight the fourth and fifth fields of Records 4 and 5 (designates the cells that are to be copied).
11. Select Copy from the Edit Menu.
12. Highlight the fourth field of Record 6 (designates the upper-left cell that will receive the copy).
13. Select Paste from the Edit Menu (places the copy into the selected cells).
14. Save the file as 166C but do not clear the screen. Switch to Show View, if needed.

56D ◆ 12'

IMPROVE/CHECK SPEED

LS: DS

1. Key a 1' writing on each ¶; find *gwam* on each.
2. Key a 2' writing on ¶s 1-2 combined; find *gwam*.
3. Key a 3' writing on ¶s 1-2 combined; find *gwam* and count errors.
4. Key another 3' writing for speed.

all letters used | A | 1.5 si | 5.7 awl | 80% hfw

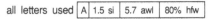

	gwam 2'	3'
Words are the building blocks of effective writing. The	6	4
better we put our ideas into words, the more likely we are to	12	8
persuade the reader to do what we ask. If our letters ramble,	18	12
are not clear, or exhibit poor grammar, we increase the like-	24	16
lihood of having our ideas rejected and our requests denied.	30	20
Any weak letter can be improved by rewriting so that the	36	24
final copy quickly conveys its basic ideas in a clear, exact	42	28
manner. The reader should not then need to puzzle over its	48	32
meaning. All features of style and content should be designed	54	36
to enhance the meaning instead of to distract from it.	60	40

56E ◆ 12'

SKILL TRANSFER: STATISTICAL COPY

LS: DS

1. Key a 2' writing on ¶s 1-2 combined; find *gwam*.
2. Key a 3' writing on ¶s 1-2 combined; find *gwam*.
3. Divide 3' rate by your 3' rate in 56D above. If you did not transfer at least 75% of your straight-copy speed, key another 3' writing on the statistical copy.

all letters used | A | 1.5 si | 5.7 awl | 80% hfw

	gwam 2'	3'
The 50 most-used words account for 46% of the total of	6	4
all words used in a study of 4,100 letters, memorandums, and	12	8
reports. The first 100 account for 53%; the first 500, 71%;	18	12
the first 1,000, 80%; and the first 2,000, just under 88%.	24	16
Of the first 7,027 most-used words (accounting for 97%	29	19
of all word uses), 209 are balanced-hand words (26% of all	35	23
uses) and 284 are one-hand words (14% of all uses). So you	41	27
see, practice on these words can help to increase your rate.	47	32

Format the entries in the PERCENT RAISE field as Percents with one decimal place.

WORKS DOS	WORKS MAC
1. Highlight the entry in the PERCENT RAISE field in one of the records. 2. Press **Alt, T, P, 1**, and strike Enter (selects Percent from the Format Menu, sets decimal places at 1, and enters the format command).	1. ~ PERCENT RAISE field name. 2. Select Set Field Attributes from the Format Menu. 3. ~ Numeric. 4. ~ Percent (selects desired format). 5. Key **1** (sets decimal places). 6. ~ OK or Return.

Format the entries in the YEARS EMPLOYED field as Fixed with one decimal place.

WORKS DOS	WORKS MAC
1. Highlight the entry in the YEARS EMPLOYED field in one of the records. 2. Press **Alt, T, X, 1**, and strike Enter (selects Fixed from the Format Menu, sets decimal places at 1, and enters the format command).	1. ~ YEARS EMPLOYED field name. 2. Select Set Field Attributes from the Format Menu. 3. ~ Numeric. 4. ~ Fixed (selects desired format). 5. Key **1**. 6. ~ OK or Return.

Format the entries in the HOURS WORKED WITHOUT AN ACCIDENT field with commas and no decimal places.

WORKS DOS	WORKS MAC
1. Highlight the entry in the HOURS WORKED WITHOUT AN ACCIDENT field in one of the records. 2. Press **Alt, T, C, 0**, and strike Enter (selects Comma from the Format Menu, sets decimal places at 0, and enters the format command). 3. Close the file without saving it.	1. ~ field HOURS WORKED WITHOUT AN ACCIDENT. 2. Select Set Field Attributes from the Format Menu. 3. ~ Numeric. 4. ~ General (selects desired format). 5. Key **0**. 6. ~ Commas in the Style column (selects comma format). 7. ~ OK or Return. 8. Close the file without saving it.

166C ♦

COPY INFORMATION

Read the information at the right about copying database information. Complete the steps listed on p. 353 for your software.

You can copy the contents and formats of any record, field, or cell in your database. In Form View or window, you can copy an entire record to a new location. In List and Report Views or windows, you can copy the contents of one or more records, fields, or cells. The Copy feature saves time. For example, if you have several records with the same city and state, instead of keying the city and state repeatedly, key it once and then copy it to the other records. In this lesson, you will copy records and cells while working in List View or window.

L ESSON 57

57A ◆ 6'
CONDITIONING PRACTICE

each line twice

SM: Defaults; LS: SS

alphabet 1 Jacques was to find her by six to have a big pizza and milk.
fig/sym 2 Key: "No space after symbol in $140.39, #275-648, or I'll."
speed 3 Sign the form to pay them for the antique chair and the urn.

gwam 1' | 1 | 2 | 3 | 4 | 5 | 6 | 7 | 8 | 9 | 10 | 11 | 12 |

57B ◆ 19'

MASTER LETTER KEYS

1. Key line 1 at a brisk pace. Note the words that were awkward for you.
2. Key each of the awkward words three times at increasing speed.
3. Key line 2 at a steady fluent rate.
4. Key each of the other pairs of lines in the same way.
5. Make changes as listed under the sentences.
6. Copy lines 1-8 below the text on your screen (see 39C, p. 75).
7. Move line 6 below line 8, line 4 below line 6, line 2 below line 4. (Lines of text will be in this order: A-D, W-Z.)
8. Delete blank lines between the lines of text (see 37B, p. 72).

A/Z
1 ah zoo zap lazy hazy jazz haze zany azure gauze plaza pizzas
2 Zoe had a pizza at the plaza by the zoo on a lazy, hazy day.

B/Y
3 by buy boy buoy bony byte bury body maybe hobby buddy shabby
4 Abby may be too busy to buy me a book for my long boat ride.

C/X
5 ox cot lax cow mix cod fox cut flax lock crux cord oxen lack
6 Doax caught six cod to fix lunch for his six excited scouts.

D/W
7 do ow doe owe did own down wild sown would drown wield drawn
8 Wilda would like to own the wild doe she found in the woods.

E/V
9 eel van eve even very have envy move movie every heavy event
10 Evan will give us the van to move the five very heavy boxes.

F/U
11 of us fur fun surf furl cuff flub ruff full buff awful bluff
12 All four of us bought coats with faux fur collars and cuffs.

G/T
13 go it got tug get tog tag goat gong right tough eight though
14 Eight guys tugged the big boat into deep water to get going.

H/S
15 she his has shut wash shot this mash push those short thrust
16 Marsha wishes to show us how to make charts on the computer.

I/R
17 if or fir rid ire sir rim firm ride hire riot rise fire iron
18 Kirt can rise above his ire to rid the firm of this problem.

J/Q
19 jay quo just aqua jest quit joke quad jute quay major quotas
20 Quen just quietly quit the squad after a major joint injury.

K/P
21 pa key pen kit pan oak opt ken keep peck kept pack park pick
22 Kip packed a backpack and put it on an oak box on the porch.

L/O
23 lo old low fold slow gold flow cold loan hold coil sold soil
24 Lolita is wearing a royal blue skirt and a gold wool blouse.

M/N
25 am an man ham pan may nap many moan name norm omen main hymn
26 Many of the men met in the main hall to see the new manager.

Changes

Line 2 Bold Zoe.
4 Underline book.
6 Change his to the.
10 Delete very; change boxes to machines.
12 Change faux to fake.
14 Bold and underline eight guys.
16 Change wishes to wants and charts to graphs.

18 Change can to must and underline it.
22 Change packed to closed.
24 Change is to was and blouse to shirt.
26 Change Many to Most, main to union, and manager to steward.

Comma. The Comma option displays numbers with a comma between every third (from right) whole number and the next number. Decimals are displayed to the extent specified by the user; negative numbers are placed in parentheses.

Percent. The Percent option displays the percent equivalent of a number. A percent sign (%) is written after the number, and the number of decimal places to be written can be specified by the software user. Negative percents are displayed with a minus sign.

1. Use the information below to create a database. Use these field names: EMPLOYEE, EMPLOYEE #, HOURLY RATE, PERCENT RAISE, YEARS EMPLOYED, and HOURS WORKED WITHOUT AN ACCIDENT.
2. Format the entries in the HOURLY RATE field as money with 2 decimal places.

Record 1	Record 2	Record 3
James Smith	Harriet Silio	Jane Yuhouse
324563	426984	555908
5.78	6.17	5.68
.04	.055	.052
1.3	2.2	3
2600	4100	5742

Record 4	Record 5	Record 6
Marita Ruiz	Chu Chiang	Gerald Newton
556021	873584	554921
6.35	6.15	5.95
.06	.045	.06
4.5	3.2	3.9
3563	5475	4714

WORKS DOS

1. Press **Alt, V, F** or **Alt, V, L** (selects Form or List from the View Menu).
2. Highlight the entry in the HOURLY RATE field in one of the records (selects the field that is to be formatted).
3. Press **Alt, T, U**, and strike Enter (selects Currency from the Format Menu, accepts the default setting for decimal places, and enters the format command).

WORKS MAC

1. Select Show List from the Format Menu.
2. ~ HOURLY RATE field name (selects the field to be formatted).
3. Select Set Field Attributes from the Format Menu.
4. ~ Numeric in the Type column of the dialog box (specifies the field is made up of numbers).
5. ~ Dollar in the Display column (selects desired format).
6. ~ OK or Return.

CHECK SPEED/ CONTROL

LS: DS

1. Key a 1' writing on each ¶; find *gwam* on each.
2. Key a 2' writing on ¶s 1-2 combined; find *gwam*.
3. Key a 3' writing on ¶s 1-2 combined; find *gwam* and count errors.

| all letters used | A | 1.4 si | 5.4 awl | 85% hfw |

		gwam 2'	3'
Many students argue that there just is not enough time		5	4
to do everything they are supposed to do. Others, however,		11	8
seem to accomplish everything demanded with time still left		17	12
to embark on activities they merely choose to pursue. What		23	16
can cause us to differ so in how we analyze and spend time?		29	20
If you are among those students for whom time does not		35	23
seem adequate, ask a few critical questions and answer them		41	27
honestly. Do you write a schedule of vital activities then		47	31
stick to it, for example? If choices are essential, do you		53	35
do required tasks first? Master yourself to master time.		59	39

gwam 2' | 1 | 2 | 3 | 4 | 5 | 6 |
3' | 1 | 2 | 3 | 4 |

WORD PROCESSING SKILLS

1. Key the text at the right as an unbound report DS with a 2" top margin (TM) and side margins (SM) of 1".
2. Compose a third ¶ telling why you are learning to key and how you expect to use your skill.
3. Proofread, correct errors on screen, and print your completed work.

KEYBOARDING: AN ESSENTIAL SKILL

Often it has been said that everybody should learn how to key. Even though that may be stretching the truth, no one was ever penalized for knowing how. An office worker must know how to key, of course; but keying can be quite a help in personal and professional communication as well.

Keying specialists are working in private and public offices of every kind. They have a wide variety of duties, too. Not only do they have to prepare letters of all types; they also compile and key reports, arrange and key tables, and fill in many types of forms.

the software automatically creates a value for that field in the new record.

Works DOS

Key the = (equal) and the formula (or function) in the first cell of the field where the answer is to appear.

Works MAC

Select Set Field Attributes from the Format Menu; ~ Numeric in the Type column of the dialog box; ~ the Computed box in the lower-left corner of the dialog box; if desired, set format for the field; ~ OK; key the formula (or function) to the right of the = (equal) sign in the Entry Bar; strike Return.

REMOVE INFORMATION

Works lets you remove information by deleting, clearing, and/or cutting. When Delete is used, the information and its formatting is eliminated. When Clear is used, the information is eliminated; but its formatting remains so that any new information you key has the same format. When Cut (a feature of Works MAC) is used, the information removed is placed on the clipboard and may be pasted in another location. Within a database list, entries may be removed from adjacent cells, records, and files. Information can be removed when you are working with forms and reports.

Works DOS

Select the information you want to delete; choose the Clear or appropriate Delete option from the Edit Menu (**Alt, E**); if dialog box appears, respond appropriately to prompt.

Works MAC

If needed, change to List View; select the information to be deleted, cleared, or cut; choose the Cut, Clear, or Delete Field from the Edit Menu.

L ESSON 166   FORMAT NUMBERS; COPY, DELETE, AND COMPUTE

166A ◆ CONDITIONING PRACTICE

each line twice, then 30" timings on selected lines; exit wp; access db

alphabet 1 Mr. Garvey told Jay to pick up six dozen roses for the awards banquet.

fig/sym 2 Gains of 5.09 and 6.15 the last two days put the Dow Jones at 1842.37.

keypad 3 44 55 66 77 88 99 11 22 33 00 456 654 798 987 123 312 40 50 60 70 5090

speed 4 They may blame the six girls for the problem with the neighbor's auto.

gwam 1' | 1 | 2 | 3 | 4 | 5 | 6 | 7 | 8 | 9 | 10 | 11 | 12 | 13 | 14 |

166B ◆

Read the information at the right about formatting numbers and then complete the steps for your software.

WordPerfect users: Go to Unit 38, p. 368.

Numbers in a database can be formatted in various ways before or after they are entered into the database. The following formats are commonly used in databases:

Fixed. The Fixed option displays a fixed number of decimal points that are specified by the software user. Negative numbers are displayed with a minus sign (-).

Currency. The Currency option places a $ before each value, commas after the thousands and millions places in applicable cell entries, and the number of decimal places specified by the software user. Negative numbers are placed in parentheses by the software.

General. The General option is the software default value display; it does not include commas. It displays decimals when they are present and a minus sign to indicate negative numbers.

(continued on next page)

Assess Keyboarding/Word Processing Skills

Learning Outcomes: After completing this unit, you will be able to

1. Demonstrate correct technique and acceptable speed and control as you key straight copy, script, and rough-draft copy.
2. Demonstrate that you can center individual lines horizontally.
3. Demonstrate that you can proofread and correct errors in your copy.
4. Computer users: Demonstrate proper use of word processing features.

LESSON 58   PREPARE FOR ASSESSMENT

SM: Defaults; LS: SS

58A ◆ 6'
CONDITIONING PRACTICE

each line twice SS; then a 1' writing on line 3; find *gwam*

alphabet 1 Jocko will place a high bid for my next prized antique vase.

fig/sym 2 Ora asked, "Wasn't R&N's check #285067 deposited on 1/4/93?"

speed 3 When did the field auditor sign the audit form for the city?

gwam 1' | 1 | 2 | 3 | 4 | 5 | 6 | 7 | 8 | 9 | 10 | 11 | 12 |

58B ◆ 19'

CHECK/IMPROVE TECHNIQUE

1. Key lines 1-15 once SS; DS between 3-line groups.
2. Key a 1' writing on each of lines 16-21; find *gwam* on each writing.
3. Key another 1' writing on each of lines 19-21; find *gwam* on each writing.

spacing
1 by man fry men boy jam may pan city slam body trim duty dorm
2 Clem is to stay for only a day or two at an inn on the quay.
3 Many a boy wants to make the team, but only a few can do so.

shifting
4 Mabel or Sophi; Martin or Tobias; Larry Epson or Janet Spahn.
5 Ms. Alexis Epworth said that she saw Jan Spinx in Nantucket.
6 Coach Jason Parker will speak to the Gridiron Club in March.

adjacent keys
7 Buy the three silver coins we saw in the new shop yesterday.
8 We hope to open a new pottery store in the square next week.
9 Pop saw his sister swim into choppy water off Misty's Point.

long, direct reaches
10 Myrna now doubts that anyone at my gym can out jump my niece.
11 Cecil must race for any medal to curb any doubts anyone had.
12 Nyles is to serve a nice iced drink to my aunt and my niece.

figures/ symbols
13 I went to work at #4956 Holt Road on January 27 at 8:30 a.m.
14 A 32-inch screen costs $760 while a 19-inch costs only $485.
15 She said: "Buy 250 of J&B Preferred at $364.87 on June 19."

letter response 16 John was in a great act on my union stage after you saw him.
word response 17 I wish to pay the auditor for the good work he did for them.
combination 18 I gave the best grade to the girl with the best work of art.

letter 19 Jim was up at my mill after you saw him act on a union case.
word 20 The eight girls wish to pay for their half of the lake dock.
combination 21 Di may see my aunt at a bazaar to be held at the union hall.

gwam 1' | 1 | 2 | 3 | 4 | 5 | 6 | 7 | 8 | 9 | 10 | 11 | 12 |

3. Move cursor to highlight the desired field name (the one to be used in the calculation) in the dialog box.
4. Select the desired built-in function (**Alt** and desired letter).
5. Strike Enter.

Insert labels to describe numbers in the SUMM row:

1. Move the cursor to a cell in the SUMM row where you want to place the label.
2. Key the label and strike any cursor key.

Insert Blank Line Between Groupings:

1. Highlight a cell in the SUMM row where the blank line is to be inserted.
2. Select Insert Row/Column from the Edit Menu (**Alt, E, I**).
3. If needed, select Row from the dialog box.
4. Strike Enter.

Works MAC

Use the TotalsPage Menu to select numeric fields that can be totaled or subtotaled. This menu has four options: Sum This Field (totals all the numbers in a field); Take a Sub-Total on Field Change (subtotals the numbers for each grouping within a field); Take a Sub-Total on first Char (subtotals the numbers each time the first character in a specified field changes); and New Page After Total (starts a new page after each subtotal is printed).

If needed, switch to a report window, ~ the field name of the numeric field that you want totaled and/or subtotaled; choose Sum This Field from the TotalsPage Menu; if subtotals are desired, ~ the field name of the field on which the subtotals will be based and then choose Take a Sub-Total on Field Change or Take a Sub-Total on 1st Char from the TotalsPage Menu.

FIND DATA QUICKLY

Sometimes you need to locate specific data quickly in a database.

Works DOS

With Works DOS you can use a question mark (?) or an asterisk (*) to search a database rapidly for records that have similar, but not the same, contents. These symbols are called wildcards. The question mark (?) represents any single character in the same position in a word as the question mark. The asterisk (*) is used for any number of characters in that same position.

Select Search from the Select Menu; key the letters and the appropriate wildcard symbol (? or *) in the Search For box; select All records or Next record in the dialog box; and strike Enter.

Works MAC

Use Find Field from the Organize Menu repeatedly to find each entry containing the needed data (for example, all entries with the name Smith), or you can use Match Records to display a list of all records containing the data (for example, a list of all records containing the name Smith).

To find each occurrence one at a time, switch to List window, if needed; choose Find Field from the Organize Menu; key the search information in the dialog box; ~ Find Next; repeat as needed until an alert box appears and indicates that all occurrences of the data have been found; ~ OK.

To display a list of all records that contain the search information, choose Match Records from the Organize Menu; key the search information in the dialog box; if desired, ~ Search Text Fields Only box; ~ OK.

FORMAT NUMBERS

Numbers in a database can be formatted in various ways before or after they are entered into the database. Frequently used formats are Fixed, Currency (or Dollar), General, Comma, and Percent.

Works DOS

Select the number(s) you want to format; select the desired format from the Format Menu (**Alt, T**); if needed, key desired decimal places; choose OK.

Works MAC

Select the number(s) you want to format; select Set Cell Attributes from the Format Menu; ~ appropriate buttons in dialog box; if needed, set decimal places; ~ OK.

LABELS

A label is descriptive text (usually titles or instructions) that appears in every record. The label is not part of a field and it is displayed only when Form View is used. Labels can be entered before or after records are created.

Works DOS

Change to Form View, if needed; highlight Field 1 on any record and select Insert Line from the Edit Menu (Press **Alt, E, I**); position cursor where label is to begin; key the label; strike any cursor key.

FORMULAS AND FUNCTIONS

Formulas and functions are used to calculate the contents of a field on the basis of the contents of one or more other fields. Mathematical values are calculated in a field that you designate by keying a formula (an equation you write) or function (an equation written into software) into that field or cell. Each formula or function must be preceded by an equal sign (=). You can have only one formula or function in a database field, and that formula or function is then automatically entered into all records. When applicable information is keyed into a new record,

(continued on next page)

CHECK/IMPROVE SKILL

LS: DS

Take a 1' writing on each ¶; find *gwam*. Try to key this *gwam* on a 2' writing (both ¶s). End with a 3' writing; find *gwam*; circle errors.

gwam	¼'	½'	¾'	1'
20	5	10	15	20
24	6	12	18	24
28	7	14	21	28
32	8	16	24	32
36	9	18	27	36
40	10	20	30	40
44	11	22	33	44
48	12	24	36	48
52	13	26	39	52
56	14	28	42	56

all letters used | LA | 1.4 si | 5.4 awl | 85% hfw

gwam 2' | 3'

All of you make an error now and then in performing an   6 | 4
act like driving a car, doing the high jump, or playing the   12 | 8
piano. Keying is no different. To err is human. The more   18 | 12
difficult the activity, the greater the opportunity to make   24 | 16
errors. Do not expect all your work to be correct now.   29 | 19

Do not infer from this, though, that the more mistakes   35 | 23
you make, the more human you are. A lot of your errors are   41 | 27
merely chance; why you make them is a real puzzle. Others,   47 | 31
however, are known to be due to lack of attention, improper   53 | 35
reading, and bad techniques. Try to reduce the latter.   59 | 39

gwam 2' | 1 | 2 | 3 | 4 | 5 | 6
3' | 1 | 2 | 3 | 4

SHORT REPORT

SM: 1.5"; LS: DS
PI: 0.5" ; TM: 2"

1. Center the heading in ALL CAPS.
2. Key the report DS, correcting errors as you key.
3. Proofread on screen and correct all errors you find.
4. Make the following changes:
   a. Bold **Ethics** in line 1.
   b. Underline <u>No</u> at the end of ¶2.
   c. Delete *and group* near the end of ¶1.
   d. Insert **or values** after *principles* in line 1, ¶1.
5. Change LS to SS. (Remember to move the cursor to the beginning of the first line.)

COMPUTER ETHICS

QS (2 DS)

Ethics has been defined as a set of moral principles that are designed to guide human conduct. Dealing with what is good and bad, ethics represents a pattern of personal and group conduct that is acceptable to society.

If somebody in one business breaks into computer files of another company to seek information in order to obtain a competitive advantage, would you judge that to be moral conduct? If an employee of one firm gives privileged data to someone in another firm to give the latter firm an advantage, do you view that as being moral conduct? Your answer to both questions should be "No."

In a similar situation, a student who uses someone else's data disk to print a copy of assigned work as his or her own is not being ethical. Generally, one who breaks a rule of acceptable conduct, whether at work or at school, is guilty of violating the code of ethical behavior.

Enhance Microsoft Works Database Skills

Learning Outcomes: After completing this unit, you will be able to

1. Format numbers and copy and delete information.
2. Calculate by writing formulas or using functions.
3. Insert labels.
4. Perform a wildcard search.
5. Add and delete summary fields to reports.

DATABASE FEATURE AND COMMAND GUIDE

COPY INFORMATION
FIELD SUMMARIES
FIND DATA QUICKLY
FORMAT NUMBERS
FORMULAS AND FUNCTIONS
LABELS
REMOVE INFORMATION

The database features and commands listed alphabetically and explained in this section are presented in Unit 37. This feature and command guide can be used to preview the topics presented in the unit or as an easy-to-locate reference to review features and commands while working in this or another unit.

COPY INFORMATION

You can save time by copying the contents and formats of any record, field, or cell in your database. In Form View or window, you can copy an entire record to a new location. In List and Report Views or windows, you can copy the contents of one or more records, fields, or cells.

Works DOS

Select the record, field, or cell you want to copy; choose Copy from the Edit Menu (Press **Alt, E, C**); move the highlight to where you want the copy inserted; choose the desired copy feature from the Edit Menu (**Alt, E**).

Works MAC

From a List window, highlight the entries you want to copy; choose Copy from the Edit Menu; move the highlight to where you want the copy inserted; choose Paste from the Edit Menu.

FIELD SUMMARIES

Database reports can be enhanced by including subtotals, totals, counts, and/or other statistics at the end of the report and/or at the end of each grouping within a report.

Works DOS

When Works DOS prepares a report, it inserts introductory rows (Intr) for report titles and column headings, record rows for the field contents, and summary rows. The summary rows can be used for calculating totals, averages, or other statistics about the records included in the report. Summary rows can also be inserted to create blank lines between the groupings. Works DOS will provide and name a summary line for each grouping you create for a report. Works DOS names the summary rows between breaks SUMM (field name) and the end-of-report summary line SUMM Report. You can add additional summary lines as desired, or delete entire lines or partial lines as desired. Works DOS automatically includes calculations in summary lines at the end of each break. A count (=COUNT) is provided for fields that have text; a total (=SUM) is provided for fields that have numbers.

Works MAC

Insert a Summary Line after Groupings:

1. Switch to Report. View and display the report definition.

2. Select Sort Records from the Select Menu (**Alt, S, O**).
3. Key the name of the first sort field; select Ascend or Descend; turn on the Break check box to create a grouping; turn on the first Letter check box if you want a grouping only after the first letter of the sort field changes, or turn off this box if you want groupings whenever there is a change in any part of the sort field.
4. If desired, specify a second and third sort field.
5. Choose OK.

Delete Unwanted Field Summary Statistics:

1. Select the unwanted statistic(s) in the appropriate SUMM row.
2. Select Clear from the Edit Menu (Press **Alt, E, E**).

Insert Desired Summary Statistics:

1. Move cursor to the cell in the appropriate SUMM row where the statistic is to be inserted.
2. Select Insert Field Summary from the Edit Menu (**Alt, E, S**).

(continued on next page)

SM: Defaults; LS: SS

59A ◆ 6'
CONDITIONING
PRACTICE
each line twice

alphabet 1 Jake led a big blitz which saved the next play for my squad.
fig/sym 2 Beth has ordered 26 5/8 yards of #304 linen at $7.19 a yard.
speed 3 Good form is the key if all of us wish to make the big goal.

gwam 1' | 1 | 2 | 3 | 4 | 5 | 6 | 7 | 8 | 9 | 10 | 11 | 12 |

59B ◆ 20'

CHECK SKILL

LS: DS
1. Take a 1' writing on each ¶; find *gwam* on each writing.
2. Take a 2' writing on ¶s 2-3 combined; find *gwam*.
3. Take two 3' writings on ¶s 1-3 combined; find *gwam* and circle errors on each.

Record your rate for use in later lessons.

If time permits, key the ¶s as a short report, centering in bold the heading EXCELLENCE to print 2" from the top and inserting a QS below it. Make the following changes:
1. In line 4 of ¶1, change *though* to **however**.
2. At the end of ¶1, change *sufficient* to **enough**.
3. In line 4 of ¶2, underline Really.
4. In line 1 of ¶3, change *all* to **those** and *the* to **a**.
5. Proofread; correct all errors.

all letters used | LA | 1.4 si | 5.4 awl | 85% hfw |

gwam 2'| 3'

A desire to excel is a quality that forces us to try to improve our own performance and to surpass that of others. All our major achievements have been sparked by a desire to improve. The desire, though, had to be turned into a series of right actions. Desire alone was not sufficient.

An excellent performance shows the real concern of the performer for the task. It gives one a feeling of personal success and causes all as a matter of habit to do our best. Really successful men and women take great delight in their work and pursue it with a lot of satisfaction.

A factor common to all who succeed is the need to have a good job recognized by others. If good work goes without notice, the desire to excel will be reduced. Lucky, indeed, are people who can study their own performance, recognize its quality, and do what must be done to improve it.

gwam	2'	3'
	6	4
	12	8
	18	12
	24	16
	29	20
	34	23
	40	27
	46	31
	52	35
	57	38
	63	42
	69	46
	75	50
	80	54
	87	57

gwam 2' | 1 | 2 | 3 | 4 | 5 | 6 |
3' | 1 | 2 | 3 | 4 |

164-165F ◆

PRINT THREE-ACROSS LABELS

Read the information at the
right and then complete the
steps listed for your software.

The office supply company where Danielle places her orders sent a complimentary
supply of three-across mailing labels. Danielle asked you to use them to print mailing
labels for vacationers at hotels on Maui and Kauai. (You may print on paper instead of
mailing labels.)

WORDPERFECT

1. Create a word processing
    document for a primary file and
    name it LABEL3.PF.
2. Select Macro (**Alt F10**) and key
    Labels at the prompt or follow
    your teacher's instructions.
3. Select the label and printer
    specified by your teacher (a
    typical label is Number 5160
    Avery; typical printer selections
    at the Location prompt is to
    select **1** if your printer uses
    continuous form paper; select **2** if
    your printer has more than one
    bin of paper; select **3** if your
    printer uses separate sheets of
    paper).
4. Insert the field codes for the
    database fields requested.
5. Save as primary file name
    LABEL3.PF and exit.
6. Open file VACLIST.SF and
    activate the Sort feature.
7. Use VACMAUI.SF for the output
    file name.
8. **7**-Type; **1**-Merge.
9. In the Sort Secondary Merge File
    Menu:
    a. Use ISLAND field location for
        Key1 information.
    b. For **4**-**S**elect, key the state-
        ment **KEY1=MAUI**.
    c. Exit; then **1**-Perform Action.
10. Clear screen.
11. Merge LABEL3.PF and
    VACMAUI.SF; print.
12. Repeat Steps 6-11 by adapting
    the information to Kauai and
    name the Kauai secondary file
    VACKAUAI.SF.

WORKS DOS

1. Open word processing merge
    document LABEL2 and name it
    LABEL3.
2. Open VACLIST database file; go
    to List View.
3. Press **Alt S I** to Show All Records.
4. To print Maui and Kauai labels,
    hide the records for Oahu:
    a. Highlight the records for Oahu.
    b. Press **Alt S, H** (select Hide
        record from Select Menu) to
        hide records (note that only
        Maui and Kauai records are
        displayed).
5. Open file LABEL3 and press **Alt
    P, L** (from the Print Menu, select
    Labels). *Version 3.0* go to list
    below.
Version 2.0
    a. Change Horizontal label;
        spacing to Horizontal 2.75".
    b. Change left and right margins
        to .25"; (if your printer will not
        print .25" margins, change to
        .5" margins and the horizon-
        tal spacing to 2.5").
    c. Select **T** (Test).
Version 3.0
    a. Change number of labels
        across page to 3.
    b. Accept default for Label
        Spacing, and Page Size &
        Label Margins.
    c. Test print.
6. Make corrections if necessary;
    then print.
7. From Window Menu, select file
    VACLIST.
8. Press **Alt S I** to show all records.

WORKS MAC

1. Open file VACLIST.
2. From the Organize Menu, select
    Record Selection.
    a. Highlight ISLAND field (equals
        is highlighted).
    b. Key **Maui** for the record
        selection and install (or is
        activated).
    c. Key **Kauai** and Return (note
        that only Maui and Kauai
        records are displayed).
3. With VACLIST file open, create a
    new word processing merge
    document as file name LABEL3.
4. Set up custom page, 2.75" paper
    (label) width, no gaps between
    pages, 1" paper (label) height;
    set margins and page length
    (review procedure in 164-165E, if
    necessary).
5. Set right indent triangle to 7.75".
6. Use font, type size, and style you
    want, or use defaults.
7. Set tabs at 2.75" and 5.0".
8. Prepare to merge; insert place-
    holders and spaces.
9. Select Multiple Labels (Edit
    Menu); copy and paste first line
    at tabs for three-across; repeat
    for other lines; copy and past
    labels to fill page.
10. Print Merge, preview to check;
    print labels for vacationers on
    Maui and Kauai.

OPTIONAL DATA-BASE ACTIVITY

Load and print the word processing file OPTDB3 on *Student's Template*. Directions are
included in the file.

59C ◆ 12'

CHECK SKILL: SCRIPT

LS: DS

Take 2' and 3' writings, circling errors on 3' writings. Figure the percentage of your straight-copy skill transferred to script copy (divide 3' *gwam* on this writing by 3' *gwam* on 59B).

Goal: 90%

all letters used | LA | 1.4 si | 5.4 awl | 85% hfw

gwam 2' | 3'

Many workers fail to get ahead, yet they do not seem to | 6 | 4
realize quite why this is so. They believe they should get | 12 | 8
a promotion or salary increment simply because they are | 17 | 11
next in line. What they fail to understand is that to deserve a | 24 | 16
better job, competence counts more than being next in line. | 30 | 20

As you get promoted, more will be required of you than | 35 | 23
mere job competence, although that is vital. You must get | 41 | 27
along with other people even when they may not desire to get | 47 | 31
along with you. Working harmoniously with others is a major | 53 | 35
test of leadership, so begin learning to do this right now. | 59 | 39

59D ◆ 12'

CHECK SKILL: ROUGH DRAFT

LS: DS

Take 2' and 3' writings, circling errors on 3' writings. Figure the percentage of your straight-copy skill transferred to rough-draft copy (divide 3' *gwam* on this writing by 3' *gwam* on 59B).

Goal: 80%

all letters used | LA | 1.4 si | 5.4 awl | 85% hfw

gwam 2' | 3'

Pick   for studying.   Have
Set a definite time and place to study. Arrange all | 5 | 4
                    s   easy
books and paper within your reach. You will understand and | 12 | 8
                                a
recall better what you reed if you out line it or underline | 17 | 12
        key   Equally
each important statement. Important is to read for meaning | 24 | 16
                                            in the book
and not merely just to cover so many pages. | 28 | 19
    Many   serious
    Some students have grave learning difficulties and do | 34 | 22
                    #   that
not know why. The fault may be they do not use the proper | 40 | 27
study habits. When they realize this they should get help | 46 | 31
in learning how to study. Doing so may help them acquire | 52 | 35
exact   lead to
study habits that can bring good work and success. | 58 | 38

WORDPERFECT

1. Clear screen.
2. Select Macro (**Alt F10**) and key **Labels** at the *Insert Macro* prompt or follow your teacher's instructions.
3. Select the label and printer specified by your teacher (a typical label is Number 5161 Avery; typical printer selection at the *Location* prompt is to select **1** if your printer uses continuous form paper; select **2** if your printer has more than one bin of paper; select **3** if your printer uses separate sheets of paper.
4. Insert the eight field codes for TITLE FIRST NAME LAST NAME HOTEL
   (HOTEL) ADDRESS
   (HOTEL) CITY STATE ZIP
5. Save as primary file LABEL2.PF and exit.
6. Open file VACLIST.SF and activate the Sort feature.
7. Use VACOAHU.SF for the *Output file for sort:*.
8. **7**-Type; **1**-Merge.
9. In the Sort Secondary Merge File Menu:
   a. Use the ISLAND field location for **Key1** information.
   b. For **4**-Select, key the statement **Key1=Oahu**.
   c. Exit; then **1**-Perform Action.
10. Clear screen.
11. Merge print LABEL2.PF and VACOAHU.SF.
12. Print.

WORKS DOS

1. Open word processing merge document LABEL1 and name it LABEL2.
2. Open VACLIST database file; go to List View; if necessary, sort the ISLAND field in alphabetical order.
3. Hide the records for Maui and Kauai:
   a. Highlight one cell of each record for Maui and Kauai (note that when only one cell is highlighted, the Hide function will select and hide an entire record).
   b. Press **Alt S, H** (select Hide record from Select Menu) to hide records (note that only Oahu records are displayed).
4. Open file LABEL2; then press **Alt P, L** (from the Print Menu, select Labels). *Version 3.0* users go to list below.

Version 2.0
   a. Select VACLIST database file if more than one database files are open.
   b. Change Horizontal label spacing to Horizontal 3.0".
   c. Change number of labels across page to 2.
   d. Test print; make corrections if necessary.
   e. Accept default margins and page size.

Version 3.0
   a. Select VACLIST database file if more than one database file is open.
   b. Change number of labels across page to 2.
   c. Accept default for Label Spacing, and Page Size & Label Margins.
   d. Test print; make corrections if necessary.
5. Update if necessary, then Print.
6. From Window Menu, select file VACLIST.
7. Press **Alt S I** to show all records.

WORKS MAC

1. Open the VACLIST database file.
2. From the Organize Menu, select Record Selection.
   a. Highlight ISLAND field, equals.
   b. Key **Oahu** (note that only Oahu records are displayed).
3. With Vaclist file open, create a new word processing document as file name: LABEL2.
4. Select Page Setup (File Menu).
   a. ~ Custom Size.
   b. ~ No Gaps Between Pages.
   c. Use default (standard paper size).
   d. Set margins as follows: left .25"; right .125"; top, 0; bottom, 0.
5. Change font to your choice (type size 10 points; 6 lines per inch).
6. Set tab on ruler at 2.75".
7. Prepare to merge (Edit Menu); insert the placeholders and spaces; Show Field Data to see information.
8. Select Multiple Labels (Edit Menu).
9. Copy the first line; ~ at the end of the line, tab, then paste (the information from the next record will appear):

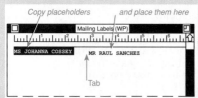

10. Return; then insert placeholders for the additional lines.
11. Strike Return to locate I-beam at beginning of line 7.
12. Select and copy the six lines; paste at the beginning of line 7.
13. Paste additional labels to fill one page.
14. With the LABEL2 file active, select Print Merge from the File Menu.
15. Print preview to check; then print labels for vacationers on Oahu.

LESSON 60 — ASSESS WORD PROCESSING SKILLS

SM: Defaults; LS: SS

60A ◆ 6'
CONDITIONING PRACTICE
each line twice

alphabet	1	Jacki had won first place by solving my tax quiz in an hour.
fig/sym	2	Our 1993 profit was $58,764 (up 20% from the previous year).
speed	3	Roddy may sign the six forms and work with the city auditor.

gwam 1' | 1 | 2 | 3 | 4 | 5 | 6 | 7 | 8 | 9 | 10 | 11 | 12 |

60B ◆ 12'
CHECK CENTERING

1. Beginning 2" from top edge, center DS *each line* of Announcement 1 horizontally; correct errors as you key.
2. Space down 4 DS; then center SS *each line* of Announcement 2 horizontally; correct errors as you key.

Announcement 1

FUND-RAISING AUCTION
Student Activity Center
Central High School
Saturday, March 9
Catered Dinner at 6:30 p.m.
Auction at 8 p.m.
Reservation Required: 555-4027

Announcement 2

SENIOR CLASS OFFICERS DS

Ella Mae Flores, President
Shawn Bennett, Vice President
Kathryn Richardson, Treasurer
Cyril Jackson, Secretary
Rita Metz/Jon Hicks, Historians

60C ◆ 12'
CHECK WORD PROCESSING SKILL

Using the word processing features you have learned, key the lines given at the right DS. Be guided by the numbered statements above the sentences.

Do not key the numbers or letters used to identify the sentences.

1 Key the following sentence as shown:

Angela will fly to Florida on Thursday.

2 Make the following changes using the insert mode:

Angela will fly to Florida on Thursday, *Veterans Day.* [insert: *Childs*, *Miami,*]

3 Make these additional changes using typeover mode as necessary:

Angela Childs will fly to Miami, Florida, on ~~Thursday,~~ [*Dr.* *our new principal,* *Monday*]
~~Veterans~~ Day. [*Labor*]

4 Key the following sentences; **bold** and underline as you key.

a <u>As the Crow Flies</u>, by Jeffrey Archer, was published in 1991.

b She said that **don't** means <u>do not</u> and **doesn't** means <u>does not</u>.

c Ms. Lindsay said to **bold** and ALL CAP the heading EXCELLENCE.

d A book title may be shown in ALL CAPS <u>and</u> **bold** for emphasis.

e Key <u>Time</u>, a magazine, in cap and lowercase and <u>underline</u> it.

f Mr. Mendez said to center the talk title on a separate line:

WORD PROCESSING: KEY TO THE FUTURE

Mr. Cedric Brown, 5959 Airdrome St., Los Angeles, CA 90039-1174; Boogie Board; First Class Inns, P.O. Box 27050, Honolulu, Oahu, HI 96810-7050; use today's date

Mr. Keido Iwasaki, 2505 Cypress St., Eureka, CA 95502-4132; Windsurf; Hemett Regal Maui, Kihei Rd., Wailea, Maui, HI 96753-6612; use yesterday's date

Ms. Lee Gallagher, 91203 E. Borden, San Marcos, CA 92096-9657; Snorkel; Hemett Regal Maui, Kihei Rd., Wailea, Maui, HI 96753-6612; use today's date

Mr. Preben Christensen, 6995 Balboa, San Diego, CA 92122-6742; Scuba; Vacations Plus Kauai, 3000 Kapule Hwy., Lihue, Kauai, HI 96766-5411; use tomorrow's date

164-165D◆

APPLICATION ACTIVITY

Mailing Labels

1. Design a label print format; select and arrange the fields as shown at the right.
2. Print one-across mailing labels for all vacationers. Use a sheet of paper if you do not have labels.

Note: The alignment of the paper or labels in the printer affects how the printout appears on the page.

Title First name Last name (3 fields)
Hotel
(Hotel) address
(Hotel) city state ZIP (3 fields)

164-165E◆

PRINT TWO-ACROSS LABELS

Read the information at the right and then complete the steps listed for your software.

Danielle ordered a supply of two-across mailing labels and asked you to print labels, using the VACLIST file, to vacationers who are staying on Oahu. Use the label print format from 164-165D.

(continued on next page)

CHECK WORD PROCESSING SKILL

SM: 1"; LS: DS; TM: 2"
PI: 0.5"

1. Center the heading MATURITY.
2. QS (2 hard returns) and key the ¶s DS. Correct the marked errors and any errors you make as you key.
3. After completing the report, make the changes listed below, using the word processing features you have learned:

Bold the heading.
In ¶1, line 2, change *yet* to **but**.
In ¶2, line 1, change *attempt* to **try**.
In ¶2, line 7, underline <u>flight</u> and <u>fight</u>.
In ¶2, transpose the last two sentences (use move feature).
In ¶3, line 1, delete the first sentence and the word *so*; change *begin* to **Begin**.
In ¶3, line 2, change *face up to* to **confront**.
In ¶3, last line, change *conflict* to **problems**.

4. Proofread your copy and correct any errors you find.
5. Change left margin to 1.5"; print your completed report.

MATURITY

Not all adults are mature. (adult) Some have grown up bodies and childish minds, yet it requires maturity to ajust (d) to others with out expecting them to do all the adjusting. No one lives without choming in (to) contact with others. So conflicts come and will keep on coming until all men (people) realize that they have to work forthe (#) solution of the problems instead of being the cheif cause of them.

Problems come to us (all of) eventually. How we attempt to solve it (them) is a clue to our maturity or the lack of it. We may run from (away) some problems and fight back at some critics, but this this is the immature way of handling dificulties (f). Wether (h) we are young or old, our imaturity (m) is showning when we try to solve problems (re difficulties) through flight or fight.

"You can run, but you cannot hide." So begin learning to face up to problems and try to find ways to resolve conflict without flight or fight. Learn to communicate (talk) and reason with those who are in conflict with you. By (Through) a mature process of "give and take" comes the solutions to conflict.

Mr. Ben Finnegan, 5555 E. Cheyenne Pl., Sunnyvale, CA 94088-4757; Windsurf; First Class Inns, Lahina Harbor, Lahina, Maui, HI 96761-6623; use yesterday's date

Ms. Johanna Cossey, 441 Alisal Rd., Salinas, CA 93901-3664; Windsurf; Vacations Plus Waikiki, P.O. Box 27320; Honolulu, Ohau, HI 96815-7320; use tomorrow's date

Mr. Christopher Daniels, 2220 Elkwood, Canoga Park, CA 91304-2523; Windsurf; Anahola Beach Hotel, Kuhio Hwy., Anahola, Kauai, HI 96703-2113; use today's date

Ms. Fran Diaz, 17 Lincoln St., Fountain Valley, CA 92728-1007; Scuba; Hemett Regal Maui, Kihei Rd., Wailea, Maui, HI 96753-6612; use yesterday's date

164-165C ◆

APPLICATION ACTIVITY

Add Records

A list of additional vacationers was provided by Danielle. She wants the information keyed as additional records in the vacation list database.

1. Open file VACLIST.
2. Key records for additional vacationers.
3. Save.

Additions

Ms. Hai Le, 1404 Rosecrans Ave., San Diego, CA 92106-2245; Sea-Board; Vacations Plus Kauai, 3000 Kapule Hwy., Lihue, Kauai, HI 96766-5411; use tomorrow's date

Mr. Raul Sanchez, 1704 Euclid, San Diego, CA 92115-1141; Snorkel; First Class Inns, P.O. Box 27050; Honolulu, Oahu, HI 996810-7050; use today's date

Mrs. Juanita Romero, 6001 Pacific Ave., Riverside, CA 92506-6721; Snorkel; Hemett Regal Maui, Kihei Rd., Wailea, Maui, HI 96753-6612; use tomorrow's date

Ms. Beth Lazarus, 4666 Ingraham, San Diego, CA 92103-5412; Boogie Board; Vacations Plus Kauai, 3000 Kauple Hwy., Lihue, Kauai, HI 96766-5411; use today's date

Ms. Paula Di Napoli, 89565 Marlinda Dr., Santee, CA 92071-2275; Snorkel; Vacations & More, Hwy. 32, Kahului, Maui, HI 96732-1032; use today's date

Mr. Yuan Lim, 8202 San Carlos, San Diego, CA 92114-2254; Snorkel; First Class Inns, Lahina Harbor, Lihanai, Maui, HI 96761-6623; use yesterday's date

(continued on next page)

MASTER TECHNIQUE: SPACING

1. Key each pair of lines once SS; DS between pairs.
2. Check accuracy of spacing with punctuation marks.
3. Key each pair of lines again, spacing properly after each punctuation mark.

period/question
1 Why are they not here? The meeting is at 7. All know that.
2 I want a dozen roses. How much are they? May I mix colors?

comma
3 Ms. Reid, the store manager, asked Max, Flo, and me to help.
4 When roll was called, Hatch, Parker, and Ross were not here.

semicolon/colon
5 We made three stops: Tampa, FL; Key West, FL; San Juan, PR.
6 CLUB MEETING: date, May 19; time, 7:45 p.m.; place, Room 8.

abbreviations/initials
7 Drs. Rosa M. and Juan P. Ruiz begin house calls at 4:15 p.m.
8 Jean has a Ph.D. from Cornell; D. K., a D.B.A. from Indiana.

parentheses
9 Is the space after . following initials (a) 1, (b) 2, (c) 3?
10 Is the space after : in stating time (a) 0, (b) 1, or (c) 2?

hyphen
11 Words such as one-fifth and self-service always require a -.
12 A compound adjective like 4-ply or 12-foot requires a - too.

gwam 1' | 1 | 2 | 3 | 4 | 5 | 6 | 7 | 8 | 9 | 10 | 11 | 12 |

CHECK/IMPROVE SKILL

LS: DS

1. Take 1' writings on each ¶ and 2' and 3' writings on both ¶s. Find *gwam*, circle errors for each writing.
2. For 1' guided writings, use the better 1' *gwam* in Step 1 as your base rate.

gwam	¼'	½'	¾'	Time
20	5	10	15	20
24	6	12	18	24
28	7	14	21	28
32	8	16	24	32
36	9	18	27	36
40	10	20	30	40
44	11	22	33	44
48	12	24	36	48
52	13	26	39	52
56	14	28	42	56
60	15	30	45	60

all letters used | A | 1.5 si | 5.7 awl | 80% hfw

gwam 2' | 3'

One of the great hazards in social and medical science | 6 | 4
lies in pretending that we know exactly what is best for an | 12 | 8
individual, a couple, or a group. People vary so much that | 18 | 12
the utmost we can expect is a series of general or specific | 24 | 17
guidelines that have been tested and proven quite effective | 30 | 20
in careful research with large numbers of individuals. | 35 | 23

Education is a social science, and teaching people how | 40 | 30
to key is not an exception. Good teaching, like developing | 46 | 31
solid learning material, depends upon a set of major guides | 52 | 35
or rules that are based on the findings of careful research | 58 | 40
into how learners acquire a skill most easily. This is why | 64 | 43
a teacher knows best what and how a student should practice. | 70 | 47

gwam 2' | 1 | 2 | 3 | 4 | 5 | 6 |
3' | 1 | 2 | 3 | 4 |

164-165A ◆
CONDITIONING PRACTICE
each line twice

alphabet 1 Fay Bok's new zoo job requires her to do seven or eight complex tasks.

fig/sym 2 The cost of Model #40-79 is $352 plus 6% sales tax and 18% excise tax.

keypad 3 174 285 396 471 582 693 714 825 936 456 789 123 500 808 4090 6070 9050

speed 4 The official goal of the spa downtown is to get my body in good shape.

gwam 1' | 1 | 2 | 3 | 4 | 5 | 6 | 7 | 8 | 9 | 10 | 11 | 12 | 13 | 14 |

164-165B ◆
APPLICATION ACTIVITY

Create Database

Read the information at the right; then create a vacation list database. You will use this file for additional database activities and in Part 5—Integrated Software Applications.

The recreational business that Danielle manages offers equipment rentals and activities, such as snorkeling trips and windsurfing lessons. Because of limited rental equipment, only a small number of participants can take tours or lessons at one time. Therefore, most local customers make reservations for these activities. Vacationers coming to the Islands often make reservations, too.

To determine equipment needs, the manager must have reservations confirmed the day before. Thus, people who were placed on waiting lists can be told when last-minute openings for activities or rental equipment are available.

A variety of information is needed to fill these last-minute openings. Not only names and Island addresses are needed. For vacationers, having their home addresses is vital, too.

1. Create a new database file; use file VACLIST.SF (**WordPerfect**) or VACLIST (**Works**). Remember, you will use the file again.
2. Review the list of vacationers (beginning below and continuing on p. 344) to determine the field sequence.
3. Decide on a field name for each of the following 15 fields and key in ALL CAPS:
   customer first, last name, and title (3 fields)
   activity
   date of activity (MM/DD/YY)
   island
   hotel
   hotel address
   hotel city
   hotel state
   hotel ZIP
   home address
   home city
   home state
   home ZIP
4. Key field contents:
   a. Use USPS style for addresses.
   b. Key the activity field in lowercase.
   c. Key digits for the month, day, and year. (January 9, 1994, would appear as 01/09/94.)
   d . Key the island names with initial caps only.

List of Vacationers

Dr. Jane Burleson, 56029 Cedar St., Mt. Shasta, CA 96067-4512; Snorkel; Hemett Regal Maui; Kihei Rd., Wailea, Maui, HI 96732-6612; use today's date

(continued on next page)

MASTER TECHNIQUE

1. Key each pair of lines twice SS: first slowly; then faster. DS between 2-line groups.
2. Key a 1' writing on line 11, then on line 12; find *gwam* on each.

alphabetic sentences	1 Virg fixed a unique bronze sculpture he won at my junk shop.
	2 Vic was pleased with a quartz jewelry box Karen got for him.
figures/ symbols	3 Didn't she say Invoice #9480 was for $376 (plus 5 1/2% tax)?
	4 Ramo & Lo used * to identify "best buys": #17285*; #30496*.
long, direct reaches	5 Marilyn can carve many unique pieces out of onyx and marble.
	6 Herbie doubts if any of my dancers must bring bronze medals.
adjacent keys	7 Very few workers will try for a top spot in the local union.
	8 Over twenty people opted for a review to avoid a short quiz.
combination response	9 We got an award for the extra work we did on the stage sets.
	10 Handle the oil with care and test it when you get to a pump.
word response	11 Did the busy man rush the six bus panels to the firm by air?
	12 They wish to go to the city to visit the busy field auditor.

gwam 1' | 1 | 2 | 3 | 4 | 5 | 6 | 7 | 8 | 9 | 10 | 11 | 12 |

CHECK/ IMPROVE SKILL

Take 3', 2', and 1' writings, following your teacher's directions. On 1' *guided* writings work to improve speed (increase goal rate) OR accuracy (reduce goal rate).

gwam	¼'	½'	¾'	Time
20	5	10	15	20
24	6	12	18	24
28	7	14	21	28
32	8	16	24	32
36	9	18	27	36
40	10	20	30	40
44	11	22	33	44
48	12	24	36	48
52	13	26	39	52
56	14	28	42	56
60	15	30	45	60

all letters used | A | 1.5 si | 5.7 awl | 80% hfw

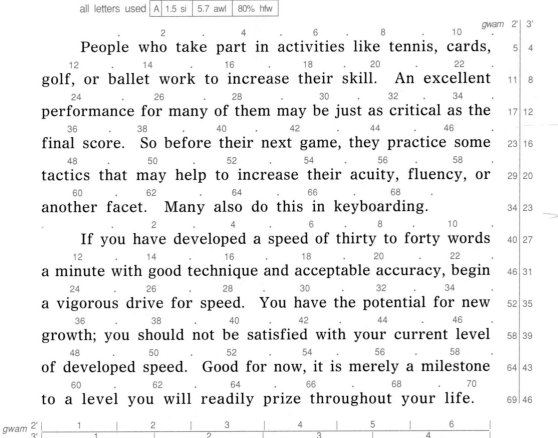

	gwam 2'	3'
People who take part in activities like tennis, cards,	5	4
golf, or ballet work to increase their skill. An excellent	11	8
performance for many of them may be just as critical as the	17	12
final score. So before their next game, they practice some	23	16
tactics that may help to increase their acuity, fluency, or	29	20
another facet. Many also do this in keyboarding.	34	23
If you have developed a speed of thirty to forty words	40	27
a minute with good technique and acceptable accuracy, begin	46	31
a vigorous drive for speed. You have the potential for new	52	35
growth; you should not be satisfied with your current level	58	39
of developed speed. Good for now, it is merely a milestone	64	43
to a level you will readily prize throughout your life.	69	46

gwam 2' | 1 | 2 | 3 | 4 | 5 | 6 |
3' | 1 | 2 | 3 | 4 |

161-163H ◆ (cont.)

Initially, no label selection options will appear in the Format: Paper Size/Type Screen unless previously created. You will need to complete the procedure shown below to create label sizes that will then become part of the Format: Paper Size/Type Screen options.

3. From the Edit Menu, insert the database fields that are needed.
4. From the Print Menu, select Print Labels.
5. Select the database file that you want to print in label format.
   a. Make changes to label spacing and number of labels across page if needed.
   b. Select Print or Test.
   c. Make changes to margins, page size, and page number, or accept the defaults.
   d. Print View, print.

placeholders in a layout that matches your labels. You can change the font, type size, and type style in the Format Menu or use the defaults.

To print mailing labels, open the database document you want to use and the word processing document that contains the print setup. Activate the word processing document, then complete the steps to Print Merge (from the File Menu).

161-163I ◆

PRINT ONE-ACROSS LABELS

Read the information at the right and then complete the steps listed for your software. Print on plain paper if mailing labels are not available.

Danielle asked you to print mailing labels for the HOTEL database in the following arrangement:

HOTEL
ADDRESS
CITY STATE ZIP

Note: The margins of labels are affected by the alignment of the label sheet in the printer.

WORDPERFECT

1. Clear screen.
2. Select Macro (**Alt F10**) and key **Labels** at the *Macro* prompt.
3. Select the label and printer specified by your teacher. (Typical printer selection at the *Location* prompt is to select **1** if your printer uses continuous form paper; select **2** is your printer has more than one paper bin; select **3** if your printer uses separate sheets of paper.)
4. Follow the screen prompts. (The label will be installed in the Format: Pager Size/Type Menu for you to select whenever you need it.)
5. Insert the field codes for HOTEL, ADDRESS, CITY, STATE, and ZIP.
6. Save as primary field LABEL1.PF and exit.
7. Merge LABEL1.PF with HOTELS.ST.
8. Print.

WORKS DOS

1. Create a new word processing merge document and name it LABEL1 (for one-across mailing label).
2. Press **Alt E F** (or **A**) to insert the field names in the order requested.
3. Press **Alt P L** (from the Print Menu, select Labels) and select file HOTELS if more than one database file is open.
4. Set up the label.

Version 2.0
   a. Accept defaults for label spacing (vertical, 1"; horizontal, 3.5") and number of labels across page (1).
   b. Press **Alt T** to select Test.
   c. Accept default margins and page size.

Version 3.0
   a. Accept defaults for Across and Down page, Label Spacing, and Page Size & Label Margins.
   b. Select Test (**T**).

5. Make corrections if necessary; print.

WORKS MAC

1. Create a new word processing merge document as file name LABEL1 (for one-across mailing label).
2. From Format Menu, select Spacing, 6 Lines per inch; insert placeholders for fields needed.
3. From File Menu, select Page Setup.
4. ~ Custom Size option.
5. In Paper Width box, key **3.5** for the width of label.
6. ~ No Gaps Between Pages.
7. In the Paper Height text box, key **1.0** for the label height.
8. Set margins as follows: .25 left; .125 right; 0 top; 0 bottom. (**Note:** Margins are affected by alignment of label in the printer.)
9. Return or ~ OK.
10. Open the HOTELS database file and activate LABEL1 (as with mail merge, database and word processing merge documents must be open with word processing document active).
11. Select your choice of font; change type size to 10 if necessary; set Spacing at 6 lines per inch.
12. From the Edit Menu, select Prepare to Merge; insert the placeholders.
13. Print Preview, make corrections if necessary; Print Merge.

PART 2

Word Processing Applications

Backup Disk   A duplicate of a disk to be used if something happens to the original disk.

Block   A feature that defines a specific portion of text (word, phrase, sentence, paragraph) to be bolded, centered horizontally, copied, deleted, moved, or underlined (*see* Bold, Center, Copy, Delete, Undelete, Move, Underline).

Bold   A feature that prints designated text darker than the rest of the copy to add emphasis; may be used as text is keyed or afterwards (*see* Block).

Center   A feature that centers lines of text horizontally; may be used as text is keyed or on existing text (*see* Block).

Center Page (top to bottom)   A feature that automatically places text on a page so that the top margin is equal to the bottom margin (WordPerfect).

Command   An instruction to a computer.

Command Keys   Keys used to instruct a computer to perform a particular action.

Copy   A feature that duplicates text from one location and places the duplicated text at another location.

Cursor   A light on the screen that shows where the next keystroke will be keyed.

Decimal Tab   A feature that uses a tab setting to align numbers at the decimal point (*see* Tab).

Default   Preset condition in software features such as Margins, Line Spacing, Tabs and Insert Mode; the operator may override these settings as part of formatting and keying a document.

Delete (file)   A procedure that removes a document (file) from a disk to free up disk space and make management of the remaining files easier.

Delete (text)   A feature that removes a segment of text (character, space, or word) by means of the Backspace or Delete key or (line, sentence, or paragraph) by means of the Block feature.

Directory   A listing of files stored on a disk.

Document   Formatted information such as a letter, memo, report, table, or form. Document is also used interchangeably with the term file to denote any text.

Document Retrieval   A procedure that displays a document again after it has been saved or stored for the purpose of editing and/or printing.

Document View   A feature that displays a page or pages of a document so that operator may see the format before printing the document.

Error   Any misstroke of a key; also any variation between source copy and displayed or printed copy; departure from acceptable format (arrangement, placement, and spacing).

Extension   Additional characters added to a file name to further identify a file.

File   Text stored on a disk.

File Name   Alphabetic or numeric characters (name) assigned to each file for identification purposes.

Flush Right   A feature that moves the cursor to the right margin. Cursor remains at right margin with keyed text being pushed to the left.

Font   A print (character) style (size and appearance).

Hanging Indent   A feature that positions the first line of a segment of text at the left margin (or other point) and indents the remaining lines a specified number of spaces to the right; frequently used with enumerated items.

WORDPERFECT

1. Retrieve HOTELS.SF and activate the Sort feature.
2. Use KAUAI.SF for the output file name.
3. **7**-Type; **1**-Merge.
4. In the Sort Secondary Merge File Menu,
   a. Key the location information for ISLAND for **K**ey**1**.
   b. Key the location information for HOTEL RATING for **K**ey**2**; exit.
   c. **4**-**S**elect to state that Key 1 = Kauai and Key 2 is greater than or equal to 4; key the statement: **Key1=Kauai* Key2>=4**.
   d. Exit; then **1**-Perform Action.
5. Activate the Sort feature again to create an alphabetical listing for Maui. (Use MAUI.SF for the output file; then change the Select statement for Key1 to Maui; exit; Perform Action. Repeat procedure for Oahu, using OAHU.SF for the output file name.)
6. Clear screen.
7. Merge HOTELIST.PF with KAUAI.SF; delete the other two islands from the main heading; print. Repeat this step to create a hotel list for Maui and Oahu.

WORKS DOS

1. Open the HOTELS database file.
2. From View, Select Query.
   a. In the RATING field, key >="********".
   b. In the ISLAND field, key ="OAHU".
3. Open word processing file HOTELS.
4. Select Print Form Letter from the Print Menu to print the records for Oahu.
5. From the Window Menu, activate the HOTELS database file.
6. Change the rule for island selection for Maui.
   a. From the View Menu, select Query.
   b. Select ISLAND field.
   c. From Edit Menu, select Clear Field Contents.
   d. Key ="Maui".
7. From the Window Menu, activate word processing file HOTELIST; merge print the records for Maui.
8. Merge print the records for Kauai by Repeating Steps 6 and 7 for Kauai.

WORKS MAC

1. Open the HOTELS database file, sort alphabetically by hotel name.
2. Install rule for RATING.
   a. From the Organize Menu, select Record Selection.
   b. Select RATING field (equals, the default statement, is already highlighted).
   c. In Record Comparison Information, key ******** and select Install Rule.
   d. In Record Comparison Information, key ********* and select Install Rule (note both ratings can be selected with one command by using the "is greater than or equal to" selection rule).
3. Install rule for ISLAND.
   a. Select ISLAND field.
   b. Select equals.
   c. In the Record Comparison Information, key **Oahu** and choose Select (automatically installs rule).
4. Open word processing file HOTELIST.
5. Merge print the records for Oahu.
6. From the Window Menu, activate the HOTELS database file and change island selection rule to Maui.
   a. From the Organize Menu, select Record Selection.
   b. Select Delete Rule (deletes the last entered rule).
   c. Select ISLAND field; select equals.
   d. In the Record Comparison Information, key Maui and choose Select.
7. Activate HOTELIST; merge print the records for Maui.
8. Merge print records for Kauai by adapting Steps 6 and 7.

161-163H ◆

PRINT MAILING LABELS

WORDPERFECT

The LABELS file in WordPerfect contains macros for several labels. You can select macros to use and they will be added to the Format Paper Size/Type Menu for future selection.

WORKS DOS

To print mailing labels:

1. Open the database document you want to use.
2. Create a new word processing document.

WORKS MAC

To print mailing labels, create a word processing document; change the options in the Page Setup dialog box to match the measurement of your mailing labels; and use field

(continued on next page)   (continued on next page)   (continued on next page)

Glossary, continued

Hard Return To move the cursor to the beginning of the next line by striking the Return/Enter key (*see* Soft Return).

Hyphenation A feature that automatically divides words between syllables to give a more even right margin.

Indent A feature that sets a tab that serves as a temporary left margin (*see* Tab).

Insert Mode Allows new text to be keyed into existing text; the default software mode (*see* Typeover Mode).

Justification A feature that allows text to be aligned at the left and/or right margins.

Left Tab A feature that places text to the right of the tab (*see* Tab).

Line Spacing A feature that allows operator to set the number of blank lines left between lines of text; usually single spacing (no blank lines) or double spacing (one blank line).

Macro A feature that allows operator to record often-used words, phrases, sentences, or paragraphs and, later, insert them into documents simply by depressing the macro definition key(s).

Margins Specification of the number of inches (or spaces) left blank at the left and right of printed lines; also, at the top and bottom of printed pages.

Move A feature that takes a designated block of text from one location and places it in another location (*see* Block).

Operator's Guide (User's Manual) A set of instructions accompanying equipment or software that explains how the hardware/software features are made to work.

Page Break A feature that ends a page and begins a new page; inserted automatically (soft) when text exceeds a page; inserted manually (hard) to force the software to start a new page.

Page Numbering A feature that places a page number on each page of a document.

Print To produce a paper (hard) copy of information displayed on a screen or saved on a disk.

Printer A device attached to a computer that produces a paper (hard) copy of electronically stored text.

Print Preview (*see* Document View)

Proofread To compare copy on a display screen or printout to the original or source copy and to correct errors (or mark them for correction); one of the steps in editing text.

Rename File A procedure that allows operator to assign a new file name to a file that has been saved or stored.

Reveal Codes A feature that displays text along with formatting codes for features such as Bold, Center, and Underline that were used in the text (WordPerfect).

Right Tab Places text to the left of the tab (*see* Tab).

Ruler Line Line across top or bottom of screen that shows the position of the cursor in relation to the edges of a printed page; used to set left and right margins, tabs, and line spacing.

Save A software function that records keystrokes on a disk so that the information may be retrieved later.

Search to Find A feature that locates a specified series of keystrokes or word(s) in a document.

Search to Replace A feature that locates a specified series of keystrokes in a document and replaces them with another series of keystrokes.

Soft Return A feature that automatically moves the cursor to the beginning of the next line (*see* Word Wrap).

Software A set of computer instructions; also called computer program.

Sort A feature that arranges text in a specific order, such as alphabetically or numerically.

Spacing The number of blank line spaces between printed lines—usually indicated as SS (0), DS (1), or QS (3).

Spell Check A feature that checks text for misspelled words against a dictionary included in the software.

Status Line A display that shows location of the cursor, number of the screen in use, page of the document in process, line on the page being keyed, and position of the cursor; indicates whether bold, underline, and ALL CAPS features are activated (WordPerfect).

Tab A feature that causes the cursor to skip across the screen when the tab key is struck to a point set by the operator or to points preset every five spaces (*see* Default; *see* Decimal Tab, Left Tab, and Right Tab).

Table Formatting Feature A feature that allows the keyboard operator to specify the number of rows and columns in a table to create a shell. Text keyed in the shell is automatically arranged in table format (WordPerfect).

Typeover Mode Replaces existing text with newly keyed text (*see* Insert Mode).

Undelete A feature that restores deleted text (*see* Delete [text]).

Underline A feature that underlines text as it is keyed or existing text (*see* Block).

Vertical Centering Placing text on a page so that the top margin is equal to the bottom margin (*see* Center Page).

Word Wrap A feature that permits an operator to key successive lines of text without having to strike the Return/Enter key at the end of each line (*see* Soft Return).

READ ABOUT
SELECTION CRITERIA

WORDPERFECT

Using the Sort Secondary Merge selections, you can include up to nine selection criteria. Identify selection criteria by defining field type, field location, line of the field, and location of word within the line. Then you key a Select statement that identifies the action for each Key and the connecting action between the Keys. For example, the Select statement in the following illustration indicates that records will be selected in which the fifth field contains the word Kauai and the second field is greater than (>) or equal to (=) 4. You save the selected records as a new secondary merge file and then merge print with a primary file. Study the illustration.

WORKS DOS

Open the database file, then open a new report by selecting New Report from the View Menu. Select Query from the View Menu and key the selection criteria in the appropriate field. The following operations can be used for selection: = Equal, <> Does not equal, > Greater than, < Less than, < = Less than or equal to, >= Greater than or equal to.

For example, < + indicates that records will be selected if the specified field is less than or equal to XXX. Continue until all selection criteria have been keyed. To print, open the word processing merge file; insert field name placeholders where appropriate; and merge print the records by selecting Print Labels or Print Form Letter from the Print Menu.

WORKS MAC

Open the database file, then open a new report. From the Organize Menu, select Record Selection; then highlight the field name to select it. Key the field contents in the Record Comparison Information box and ~ Install. The **And** and **Or** selectors let you link multiple selection rules. When you use **And** between two selection rules, only those records that satisfy both rules are selected. When you use **Or** between two selection rules, those records that satisfy either selection rule are selected. Note that records might match both selection criteria; however, when you use **Or**, a match of both is not required. Make other selections, if necessary. Each additional rule refines the definition of the records that are selected.

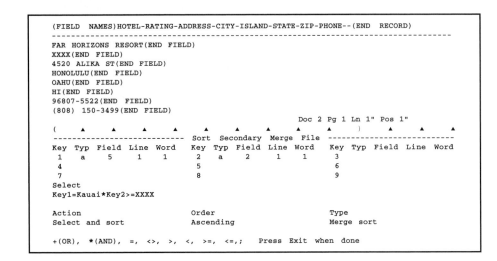

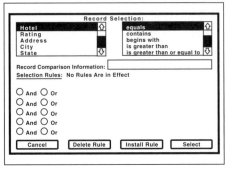

161-163G ◆

USE MULTIPLE
SELECTION
CRITERIA

Read the information at the right and then complete the steps listed on p. 341 for your software.

Danielle asked you to print a list of four- and five-star hotels in alphabetical order for each island.

1. Center a title for each of the three lists as follows: (ISLAND NAME) HOTELS RATED ★★★★.
2. Selectively print only the hotels rated with four or five stars (★★★★ or ★★★★★).

Glossary, continued

KEY TO ABBREVIATIONS USED IN KEYBOARDING AND COMPUTER APPLICATIONS

CS
Columnar spacing; space between columns of a table

DS
Double-space; double spacing

GWAM (*gwam*)
Gross words a minute; keyboarding rate in terms of standard (5-keystroke) words/minute

LM
Left margin

LS
Line spacing

PB
Page beginning

PI
Paragraph indent

QS
Quadruple-space; quadruple spacing

RM
Right margin

SM
Side margins

SS
Single-space; single spacing

~
Click, click on (Macintosh)

APPLICATION ACTIVITY

Change Records

Hint: Use the Search feature to locate the text to be changed (see p. 180 if necessary).

Danielle received the annual update for hotel listings and noted some changes for some of the hotels in the database. Key the changes given below. Correct any errors that you might have made; save.

Star Rating Changes
　　Fantasy Inn ★★
　　First Class Inns, Kauai ★★★
　　Heavenly Beach Hotel ★★★★
　　Waikiki West Beach Hotel ★★★★

Name Changes
　　Queen Elaina Hotel/Waikiki to Queen Elaina Waikiki Hotel
　　Vacations Plus Maui to Vacations & More

Phone No. Change—Anahola Beach Hotel—4008

USE MULTIPLE SORT

Read the information at the right and then complete the steps listed below for your software.

Danielle asked for an alphabetized list of the hotels on the islands. She would like a first-level sort by hotel names with a second-level sort by island (see p. 335). Danielle asked that you print the fields in the following sequence (DS between records):
　　HOTEL
　　RATING
　　ADDRESS
　　CITY STATE ZIP
　　PHONE

WORDPERFECT

Up to nine sorts can be defined using the Merge/Sort command. To sort the secondary file (HOTELS.SF) first by hotel and then by island, do the following:

1. Open HOTELS.SF and activate the Sort feature.
2. At the Sort Menu, select **7**-Type; **1**-Merge to keep the lines in each record together.
3. Enter the sort information in **K**eys **1** and **2**. The HOTEL field location will be used for Key 1 information and the ISLAND field location will be used for Key 2 information.
4. Select **1**-Perform Action.
5. Clear screen.
6. Create a primary file (file name: HOTELIST.PF). Center and bold the title **KAUAI, MAUI, & OAHU** in ALL CAPS.
7. Add merge commands that insert field contents and print records continuously without page breaks between records (see p. 325, Step 5, if necessary); save; clear screen.
8. Merge HOTELIST.PF with HOTEL2.SF.

WORKS DOS

Up to three fields can be sorted at a time. For the first field, enter information for the first-level sort; for the second field, enter information for the second-level sort. When more than two sorts are necessary, repeat the process to sort additional fields.

1. Open the HOTELS database file and show in List View to see results.
2. Sort Records (**Alt S, O**) in ascending order as follows:
　a. First field: HOTEL field.
　b. Second field: ISLAND field.
3. Create a new word processing file and name it HOTELIST. Center and bold the title **KAUAI, MAUI, & OAHU HOTELS** in ALL CAPS.
4. Insert field names (**Alt, E, F** or **Alt, E, A**) as placeholders in the order requested above; add space between fields on same lines.
5. Print View, update if necessary; print.

WORKS MAC

You select a field to sort and complete each sort, one at a time. Start by sorting the lower-level fields and progressing in order to the first-level sort.

1. Open the HOTELS database file.
2. Sort HOTEL field, then sort Island field.
3. Create a word processing merge file (file name, HOTELIST).
4. From the Edit Menu, select Prepare to Merge; insert the field placeholders in the order requested; remember to add a space between fields that are on the same line; note that placeholders can be set in either Show Field Names or Show Field Data (selected from the Edit Menu).
5. Print Preview, update if necessary; print.

Master Correspondence Formatting

Learning Outcomes: After completing this unit, you will be able to

1. Format personal-business letters in block style.
2. Format simplified memos.
3. Format business letters in block style.

FORMATTING GUIDES

Parts of a Letter

The parts of a letter are illustrated in the block format models shown on pp. 118 (personal-business letter) and 128 (business letter). Block format (style) means that all lines of a letter (or memorandum) begin at the left margin (LM). The parts are described below in order of their occurrence.

All parts described are not required for every letter. The subject line, reference initials, enclosure notations, and copy notations are special letter parts that may or may not be part of a letter. Regardless of which special letter parts are used, key them in the order given with a DS above and below.

Return address. The return address consists of a line for the street address and one for the city, state, and ZIP Code of the sender. Leave a 2" top margin and key the street address (or post office box or route number) on the first line beneath the 2" top margin (remember 1" default). Key the city, state abbreviation, and ZIP Code a single space (SS) below the street address. No return address is keyed for business letters, since they are keyed on letterhead stationery that includes the sender's company name and address.

Date. Key the date (month, day, and year) a SS below the last line of the return address. For *business letters* place the date on the first line beneath the 2" top margin.

Letter address. Begin the letter address on the fourth line space (QS) below the date.

Salutation. Key the salutation a double space (DS) below the letter address. The models (pp. 118 and 128) are keyed with *open punctuation;* no punctuation follows the salutation.

Subject line. A subject line (optional) identifies the topic of the letter. It is placed a DS below the salutation in ALL CAPS.

Body. Begin the letter body a DS below the salutation or a DS below the subject line when a subject line is used. Block the paragraphs of the body and SS them with a DS between paragraphs.

Complimentary close. Key the complimentary close a DS below the last line of the body. With *open punctuation*, no punctuation follows the complimentary close.

Name of writer. Key the name of the writer of the message a QS below the complimentary close. The name may be preceded by a personal title such as Miss, Mrs., or Ms. to indicate how a female prefers to be addressed in a response. For business letters, the writer's business title may follow the name on the same line, preceded by a comma, or may be placed on the next line.

Reference initials. If the keyboard operator is not the writer of the message, the operator's initials (lowercase) are keyed a DS below the writer's name or title.

Enclosure notation. An enclosure notation indicates that something other than the letter is included in the envelope. When appropriate, key the word *Enclosure* or *Enclosures* a DS below the reference initials (if used) or a DS below the name of the writer.

Copy notation. If a copy of the letter is to be sent to someone other than the addressee, the letter c (lowercase), followed by a space and the recipient's name, is placed a DS below the enclosure notation. If two people are to receive copies, both names are placed on the same line with a comma

and space between them or aligned vertically.

FORMATTING GUIDES

Parts of a Simplified Memo

Simplified memorandums are often used as a quick and easy means of written communication. (See model memorandum on p. 124.) The parts of simplified memorandums are described below in order of their occurrence.

Date. Key the date (month, day, and year) on the first line beneath the 2" top margin.

Name of addressee. Key the name(s) of recipients a QS below the date. No personal title(s) should be used before the name(s), but an official title (such as Principal or President) may follow a name, preceded by a comma.

Subject. The subject line specifies the topic discussed in the memo. Key the subject line in ALL CAPS a DS below the name of the addressee.

Body. Block the paragraphs in the body a DS below the subject line. SS the paragraphs with a DS between them.

Name of writer. Key the name of the writer a QS below the last line of the body. A personal title does not precede the name, but an official title may follow it, preceded by a comma.

Reference initials. If the keyboard operator is not the writer of the message, key the operator's initials (lowercase) a DS below the name of the writer.

Attachment/enclosure notation. If a supporting document is attached to the memo, key the word *Attachment* a DS below the name of the writer (or below the reference initials, if any). If the enclosure is not attached to the memo, use the word *Enclosure* rather than *Attachment.*

Spouting Horn Lodge   ★★★★
152 rooms. 7 suites. Adjacent to Spouting Horn State Park (Lawaii Rd, Koloa, Kauai, HI 96756-8110). All rooms have lanais, some with ocean view. All suites have ocean view. Pool. Restaurants in nearby Koloa Town. (808) 155-1234

Hemett Regal Kauai   ★★★★★
235 rooms, 26 suites. On the cliffs at Princeville (Ka Haku Rd, Princeville, Kauai, HI 96761-5527). All rooms have lanais, some with ocean view. All suites have ocean view. 3 pools; 2 spas. 3 restaurants. (808) 125-8913

Hemett Regal Maui   ★★★★★
265 rooms, 20 suites. On the beach near Wailea (Kihei Rd, Wailea, Maui, HI 96753-6612). All rooms have lanais, some with ocean view. All suites have ocean view. 2 pools and 1 spa. 3 restaurants. (808) 157-9135

Hemett Regal Waikiki   ★★★★★
240 rooms. 24 suites. On the beach at Waikiki (P.O. Box 1910, Honolulu, Oahu, HI 96815-1910). All rooms have lanais, some with ocean view. All suites have ocean view. Giant pool. 3 restaurants. (808) 135-7913

Tropical Paradise Inn   ★★★★
245 rooms, 30 suites. On the beach at Hana Bay (Hana Hwy., Hana, Maui, HI 96713-2204). All rooms have lanais, some with ocean view. All suites have ocean view. 3 pools and 2 spas in tropical garden setting. 2 restaurants. (808) 198-5318

Far Horizons Resort   ★★★★
261 rooms, 30 suites. Near the beach at Waikiki (4520 Alika St., Honolulu, Oahu, HI 96837-5522). All rooms have lanais, some with ocean view. All suites have ocean view. Pool and spa. 2 restaurants. (808) 150-3499

Waikiki West Beach Hotel   ★★★
120 rooms, 15 suites. On the beach at Waikiki (P.O. Box 3731, Honolulu, Oahu, HI 96815-3731). All rooms have lanais, some with ocean view. All suites have ocean view. Pool. Restaurant. (808) 145-3198

Queen Elaina Hotel/Waikiki   ★★★
140 rooms, 14 suites. Near the beach at Waikiki (P.O. Box 29, Honolulu, Oahu, HI 96815-0029). All rooms and suites have lanais, some with ocean view. Pool. Restaurants nearby. (808) 166-8686

Sandy Beach Resort   ★★
75 rooms. 6 suites. Adjacent to Palauea Beach (8990 S. Kihei Rd., Kihei, Maui, HI 96753-6655). All rooms and suites have lanais and ocean views. Pool. Restaurants nearby. (808) 117-0192

61A ◆
CONDITIONING PRACTICE

each line twice SS; DS between 2-line groups; then three 1' writings on line 4; find *gwam;* clear screen

alphabet	1	With quick jabs and deft parries, a young boxer amazed several people.
figures	2	Yuki keyed 51 letters, 84 envelopes, 37 tags, 92 labels, and 60 cards.
fig/sym	3	He's given me the numbers and prices: #16392, $48.30; #14593, $75.95.
speed	4	It is their duty to sign the amendment if he is to handle the problem.

gwam 1' | 1 | 2 | 3 | 4 | 5 | 6 | 7 | 8 | 9 | 10 | 11 | 12 | 13 | 14 |

61B ◆
LEARN WORD PROCESSING FEATURES

1. Study the specific commands for the software you are using.
2. Use the view feature to look at the full-page layout of the conditioning practice that you keyed for 61A.

Document View/Print Preview. The view/preview feature allows you to see the document format of a page or pages before printing the document.

WORDPERFECT

Shift F7

6—View Document

F7 (to return to input screen)

Options
1—100%
2—200%
3—Full page
4—Facing pages

Cursor keys can be used to move around the view document screen. Striking the PgDn key allows you to view the next page of the document.

WORKS DOS

Alt, P

PreView

Alt P

Options
Strike PgUp or PgDn for previous or next page.

Depress Esc to return to input screen.

WORKS MAC

⌘ **P**

~ print preview if not on. (When print preview is on, you print from the print preview screen. When it is not on, you print from the print screen.)
~ print.

Options
Cancel—to return to input screen
Previous—to go to previous page
Next—to go to next page
Print—to print document

~ the magnifying glass once to enlarge copy; ~~ to return to print preview screen.

3. Remove the text (61A) from the screen (clear screen).

Clear Screen. The clear screen feature allows you to remove text from the input screen without saving it.

WORDPERFECT

F7

N(o)

N(o)

WORKS DOS

Alt

F(ile)

C(lose)

N(o)

N(ew)

Ne**(w)** (Return after w for Version 3.0.)

WORKS MAC

~ File

~ Close

No

~~ WP

First Class Inns ✱✱
120 rooms. In central Kapaa (Olehana Road at Hwy. 56, Kapaa, Kauai, HI 96746-2154). All rooms have lanais. Pool; swimming at local beaches. Restaurants nearby. (808) 199-2378

First Class Inns ✱✱
184 rooms. In central Lahaina (Lahaina Harbor, Lahaina, Maui, HI 96761-6623). All rooms have lanais. Pool; swimming at local beaches. Restaurants nearby. (808) 183-4321

Anahola Beach Hotel ✱
30 rooms. On Anahola Bay (Kuhio Hwy., Anahola, Kauai, HI 96703-2113). All rooms have lanais, some with ocean view. Pool. Restaurants in nearby Anahola. (808) 186-4208

Fantasy Inn ✱✱✱
205 rooms, 12 suites. Near the beach at Waikiki (5420 Umi St., Honolulu, Oahu, HI 96820-7255). All rooms have private lanais, some with ocean view. All suites have ocean view. Pool and spa. 2 restaurants. (808) 191-8273

Paradise Resort Hotel ✱✱✱✱
310 rooms, 40 suites. On the beach at Waikiki (P.O. Box 1777, Honolulu, Oahu, HI 96825-1777). All rooms have lanais, some with ocean view. All suites have ocean view. Pool and spa. 4 restaurants. (808) 142-4590

Heavenly Beach Hotel ✱✱✱✱✱
180 rooms, 20 suites. On the point at Kaanapali (Heavenly Beach Rd., Kaanapali, Maui, HI 96761-6144). All rooms and suites have lanais and ocean views. 3 pools in tropical garden settings. 3 restaurants. (808) 197-5323

161-163C ◆

APPLICATION ACTIVITY

Add Records

The following information represents 12 more records for the Hotels database. Add these records, selecting field contents from the information provided; save.

Vacations Plus Kauai ✱✱✱
94 rooms. Near Kalapaki Beach (3000 Kapule Hwy., Lihui, Kauai, HI 96766-5411). All rooms have lanais. Pool. Restaurants nearby. (808) 168-0246

Vacations Plus Maui ✱✱✱
152 rooms. One-half mile from the beach (Hwy. 32, Kahului, Maui, HI 96732-1032). All rooms have lanais. Pool. Restaurants nearby. (808) 146-8024

Vacations Plus Waikiki ✱✱✱
180 rooms. 3 blocks from Waikiki Beach (P.O. Box 27320, Honolulu, Oahu, HI 96815-7320). Some rooms have lanais, some have ocean views. Pool. Restaurants nearby. (808) 124-6802

(continued on next page)

WordPerfect Users
The default setting for justification is *full* (both left and right margin justified). To change the justification setting to left justified (as in the illustration), do the following:

Shift F8
Line
Justification
Left
Return
Return

		words in parts	total words
Return address	2274 Cogswell Road 2" TM	4	4
	El Monte, CA 91732-3846	9	9
Date	October 15, 19--	12	12

Quadruple-space (QS)

Letter address	Mrs. Alice M. Wiggins	16	16
	11300 Lower Azusa Road	21	21
	El Monte, CA 91732-4725	26	26

Double-space (DS)

Salutation   Dear Mrs. Wiggins — DS   29   29

NOVEMBER 18 PTA MEETING — DS   5   34

Body   The El Monte PTA is devoting its next meeting to the important   17   47
topic "Computer Literacy." The meeting is on November 18 and   30   59
begins at 7 p.m. — DS   33   63

Our speaker will be Dr. Mark C. Gibson. For the past several   46   75
years, he has written the "Personal Computer" column in the   58   87
Los Angeles Post. His talk will combine wisdom and wit. — DS   69   99

To assure Dr. Gibson a large audience, we are asking selected   82   111
members to bring as guests two parents who are not active mem-   94   124
bers of our group. Please use the enclosed return card to   106   135
give me the names of your guests by November 1. — DS   116   145

I shall appreciate your assistance. — DS   123   152

(1" LM)   (1" RM)

Complimentary close   Cordially yours — QS   3   156

Laura J. Marsh

Writer	Ms. Laura J. Marsh — DS	7	159
Enclosure notation	Enclosure — DS	9	161
Copy	c Shelby Taylor	12	164

Letter Spacing Summary
Three blank line spaces (a quadruple space) separate date from letter address and complimentary close from keyed name of writer. A double space separates all other letter parts.

All models are shown in 10-pitch type with 1" side margins, photo-reduced.

161-163A ◆ CONDITIONING PRACTICE

each line twice SS (slowly, then faster); DS between 2-line groups; keypad, return after each number

alphabet 1 Jerry's big mistake was to list seven dozen xylophones for quick sale.

fig/sym 2 The 6% interest amounted to $190 on account # 12-35-470 and #12-48-903.

keypad 3 .6 .9 9.6 10.3 14.95 20.49 34.79 46.39 57.69 61.95 72.93 183.99 196.39

speed 4 Their field hand works in the cornfield down by the lake by the docks.

gwam 1' | 1 | 2 | 3 | 4 | 5 | 6 | 7 | 8 | 9 | 10 | 11 | 12 | 13 | 14 |

161-163B ◆ APPLICATION ACTIVITY

Create a Database

Read the information at the right. Then create and save a database for Hawaiian hotels on the islands of Oahu, Maui, and Kauai. Review p. 313 if necessary. **Note:** You will use this file for additional database activities and in Part 5—Integrated Software Applications.

File names:

WordPerfect: HOTELS.SF
Works: HOTELS

Danielle Austin is the manager of Sails for Rent, a recreational business with locations on three Hawaiian Islands—Oahu, Maui, and Kauai. She requested the development of a database for selected hotels on the three islands. After the database is completed, letters will be sent to the hotels promoting the recreational activities. Danielle provided a printout of hotel information (below and p. 337). The city is listed first, then the island, then the state. For example, in the first record below, Lihue is the city and Kauai is the island.

1. Design and save a database. (**WordPerfect users**: Create a secondary merge file.) Remember, you will use this file again.
2. Use the following field names:
   - HOTEL
   - PHONE
   - ISLAND
   - ADDRESS
   - CITY
   - STATE
   - ZIP
   - RATING
3. Determine the sequence of the fields. (**Hint:** When the fields are in the same sequence as the source information, keying the field contents can be done faster, because you don't have to hunt for information to be keyed.)
4. Extract and key the field contents as you read the hotel information provided; use USPS style.
   WordPerfect: For RATING field contents (shown as ✶ following the hotel name), key the letter X.
   Works: For RATING field contents (shown as ✶ following the hotel name), key asterisk (✶).

Kalalau Beach Resort   ✶✶✶✶✶
24 private cottages; 1 week minimum stay. On the beach (P.O. Box 1000, Lihue, Kauai, HI 96766-1000). All cottages have lanais, ocean views, and private pools. Accessible only by helicopter or boat from Lihue. Chef Rick's Gourmet Restaurant. (808) 197-5311

First Class Inns   ✶✶
218 rooms. In central Waikiki (P.O. Box 27050, Honolulu, Oahu, HI 96810-7050). All rooms have lanais. Pool; swimming at local beaches. Restaurants nearby. (808) 146-2246

(continued on next page)

PERSONAL-BUSINESS LETTERS

SM: Defaults

1. Study the formatting guides for letters on p. 116 and the model personal-business letter illustrating block format on p. 118. Note the vertical and horizontal placement of letter parts and the spacing between them.

2. Format and key a copy of the letter on p. 118. Correct your errors as you key. Proofread document on screen and use the view feature to check the format of the letter before saving the letter under the file name WIGGINS.

3. Format and key Letters 2 and 3 shown below. Save Letter 2 under RYAN and Letter 3 under TUTOR.

Letter 2	words
5802 Lehman Drive	4
Colorado Springs, CO 80918-1123	10
October 20, 19-- _{QS}	14
Ms. Lorna K. Ryan, Director	19
Placement Services, Inc.	24
350 E. Colfax Avenue	28
Denver, CO 80203-6285 _{DS}	33
Dear Ms. Ryan _{DS}	36

October 20, 19-- QS

Ms. Lorna K. Ryan, Director
Placement Services, Inc.
350 E. Colfax Avenue
Denver, CO 80203-6285 DS

Dear Ms. Ryan DS

Today's _Times Star_ quotes you as saying in a recent talk that "more workers fail as a result of personal traits than because of weak technical skills." DS

I want to quote this statement in a paper I am writing titled "Why Beginning Workers Fail," and I would like to know the research studies to which you referred so that I can include them in my reference list. DS

If you will send me the research references you used to support your statement, I shall be most grateful. I am sure the references will be of great help to me in preparing my paper. DS

Sincerely yours QS

Edward R. Shields

Letter 3

2405 Siesta Avenue
Las Vegas, NV 89121-2683
October 22, 19--

Learning Tutor, Inc.
752 S. Bascom Avenue
San Jose, CA 95128-3605

Ladies and Gentlemen

On October 8, I ordered from your fall catalog a copy of MATH TUTOR IX (Catalog #A2937) designed for use on the Eureka GS. I have had the diskette a week.

I followed the booting instructions step by step but am unable to boot the program on my Eureka GS. I took the diskette to the store where I bought my computer, but the manager could not boot the program on the same model computer.

Will you please check the booting instructions in the user's guide to see if they are correct. If they are, please send a replacement diskette and I will return the faulty one to you.

Sincerely yours

Miss Ellen M. Marcos

LESSON 62   PERSONAL-BUSINESS LETTERS

62A ◆
CONDITIONING PRACTICE
each line twice

alphabet	1	Jan was very quick to fix many broken zippers for the bright children.
figures	2	The shipment included 162 sofas, 179 lamps, 104 desks, and 385 chairs.
fig/sym	3	Order the roll-top desks (57" x 26" x 48") from Hermann's for $391.50.
speed	4	Rick may wish to go downtown by bus to pay a visit to a busy rug firm.

gwam 1' | 1 | 2 | 3 | 4 | 5 | 6 | 7 | 8 | 9 | 10 | 11 | 12 | 13 | 14 |

UNIT 36

LESSONS 161-165

Expand Your Database Skills

Learning Outcomes: After completing this unit, you will be able to

1. Use multiple selection criteria.
2. Sort on multiple fields.
3. Print mailing labels 1-, 2-, and 3-across.

DATABASE FEATURE AND PROCEDURES GUIDE

MAILING LABELS
MULTIPLE SELECTION CRITERIA
MULTIPLE SORTS

MULTIPLE SELECTION CRITERIA

Most database software lets you set up multiple selection criteria. This ability gives you greater control to retrieve information. For example, multiple selection criteria could be used by a large company to help employees establish car pools. The company could provide a printed list of employees who work the same hours at the same location and live near each other.

MULTIPLE SORTS

Databases may be sorted by more than one field. For example, you could sort a database of hotels by state, by city, and by hotel name. Following this sort, a printed list of the hotels would show the states arranged in alphabetical order, cities within each state arranged in alphabetical order, and hotels within each city also arranged in alphabetical order. In this example, the state field is considered the first-level sort, the city field is the second-level sort, and the hotel field is the third-level sort. The sequence in which the fields are sorted makes a difference in the outcome.

When you want data sorted by more than on field, usually you can follow the screen prompts to enter the sort requirements. Generally, you enter information for the first-level (highest level) sort and then continue by entering information for each lower level. You execute the sort command after entering all information about the sort requirements, and the software performs all the sorts in one operation. If the database software cannot handle multi-level sorts, you usually can achieve the same results by sorting one field at a time. In either case, you must identify what you want for the final outcome—what field controls the overall arrangement (first- or highest-level), the next (second-level), and so forth. For software that requires sorting a field at a time, generally you begin by entering information to sort the lowest-level field and progress in order up to the first- or highest-level field.

In the example of a hotels database, you would first sort the hotel field (third-level); next, sort the city field (second-level); and then sort the state field (first-level). This sequence would print a list with states in alphabetical order, cities for each state in alphabetical order, and the hotels for each city in alphabetical order.

MAILING LABELS

Printing mailing labels is a common use of database files. Mailing labels are available in a wide range of sizes. Each size requires a different print layout so that names and addresses print within the space limitations. While many sizes are available, standard sizes are typical for one- and two-across forms feed (also called tractor feed) labels and sheets of three-across labels. Standard labels are approximately 1" by 3.5". Fan-fold 11" strips contain 11 one-across labels and 22 two-across labels. Standard three-across label sheets are 8.5" x 11" and contain 33 labels (3 across by 11 down). When font sizes that print six lines to an inch are used, typical three- and four-line addresses can fit easily on the label. Larger labels should be used with larger font sizes and with addresses that require more than four or five lines of data.

Pressure adhesive labels are most commonly used today. Special sheets of labels are available to use with copy machines. The procedure is simple: First you print master pages of names and addresses in the same layout as the labels; then you copy the master pages onto sheets of labels.

LEARN WORD PROCESSING FEATURES

SM: Defaults

Document Retrieval. After a file has been saved, the document can be displayed again. Once a file is retrieved, any of the word processing features learned may be used to change the document. The edited document may be saved under the same file name or a different one.

WORDPERFECT

1. **Shift F10**.
2. Key name of document to be retrieved: WIGGINS.
3. Return.

Alternate Retrieval Method
1. **F5**. If the correct drive letter is displayed, strike Enter. If not, key letter of desired drive, followed by : (colon) and strike Enter.
2. Use cursor keys to highlight file name (WIGGINS).
3. Depress **1** or **R**(etrieve).

WORKS DOS

1. **Alt, F**.
2. **O**(pen) Existing File.
3. File to open: WIGGINS.

You can key in the file name or you can use the up and down arrow keys to scroll the Files List. When using the Files List, depress the Return key once you have the desired file name highlighted.

Note: If you are using a computer with a hard disk drive, you may have to change disk drives by depressing **Alt I** and using the up and down arrow keys to highlight the desired drive. Depress the Return key to select a highlighted drive.

WORKS MAC

1. ⌘ **O**.
2. ~~ on the file you want to retrieve (WIGGINS).

If you don't see the file you want to retrieve in the file listings, use up and down arrow keys to move to the file name. File names are listed alphabetically. Once you have the desired file name highlighted, ~~ on it to retrieve file.

Note: If you are using a computer with a hard disk drive, you may have to click on Drive to change disk drives.

Formatting Task: Retrieve the letter to Wiggins that you keyed in Lesson 61, p. 118, and make the changes shown at the right. WordPerfect users should save the letter under the file name GALEN. When you save the document under GALEN, you will have two files. The WIGGINS file will remain as it was before you made the changes; the GALEN file will be the document with the changes made.

Works DOS and Works MAC users should use the **Save as** command when resaving the document. If the **Save** command is used, the letter to Wiggins will be replaced by the letter to Galen.

Change the letter address to:

Mr. Jon Galen
Silverbay Avenue
El Monte, CA 91732-6782

Paragraph 1:
bold El Monte PTA
change Computer Literacy to Teenage Drug Abuse
change November 18 to January 25
underline 7 p.m.

Paragraph 2:
change Dr. Mark C. Gibson to Dr. Rebecca Linton
change he to she
change Personal Computer to Teen Talk
change His to Her

Paragraph 3:
change Dr. Gibson to Dr. Linton
underline two parents
change November 1 to January 3

Page Break. Your software program will automatically insert a page break when the amount of text exceeds a page. You can manually insert a page break to force the software to start a new page. For example, if you were going to key two letters and save them in the same file—as you will do in 62C—a page break would be used to separate the two letters in the file.

WORDPERFECT

Ctrl Return.

WORKS DOS

Ctrl Return.

WORKS MAC

~ **Format**; drag to **Insert Page Break**.

DRILL PRACTICE

1. Key each line twice SS (once slowly, then faster).
2. Key a 1' writing on each line.
3. Rekey slower lines for speed.

alphabet 1 Marvin, the tax clerk, was puzzled by the quaint antics of the judges.

figures 2 The shop is 278.4 meters long, 90.6 meters wide, and 13.5 meters high.

fig/sym 3 Su paid a $72.48 premium on a $5,000 insurance policy (dated 6/13/91).

Caps Lock 4 The AVA convention will be in Los Angeles; ABCA will convene in Omaha.

underline 5 Do not use <u>then</u> when you mean <u>than</u>, <u>vise</u> for <u>vice</u>, or <u>their</u> for <u>there</u>.

adjacent keys 6 We stopped asking the questions and quietly assisted the poor teacher.

speed 7 Did the chair signal the man to name the auditor of the downtown firm?

gwam 1' | 1 | 2 | 3 | 4 | 5 | 6 | 7 | 8 | 9 | 10 | 11 | 12 | 13 | 14 |

IMPROVE CHECK SKILL

1. Key two 1' writings on each ¶; find *gwam*.
2. Key two 3' writings on ¶s 1-3 combined; find *gwam* and count errors.
3. Key a 5' writing on ¶s 1-3 combined; find *gwam* and count errors.

all letters used A | 1.5 si | 5.7 awl | 80% hfw   gwam 3' | 5'

Being able to communicate well is one of the leading keys to the	4	3 43
success of any business. Information must move outside a business and	9	5 45
up, down, and sideways within a business so people can use acquired	14	8 48
facts to make good decisions. The report is one medium that a business	18	11 51
can use to relay information in internal and external directions.	23	14 54
A business report is generally thought to be a written message that	27	16 56
is used to make business decisions. To be of value, the message must be	32	19 59
based on factual information rather than fancy and should be presented	37	22 62
in a format that is easy to read, consistent in style, neat, and free of	42	25 65
keying and language skills errors.	44	26 66
Business reports can be done in many formats. Informal ones can	48	29 69
utilize a letter or memo style. Progress, proposal, annual, or other	53	32 72
major reports are often done in a formal style. These formal reports	58	35 75
have a required style for margins, spacing, and headings and often have	62	37 77
parts such as a title page, a table of contents, and an abstract.	67	40 80

gwam 3' | 1 | 2 | 3 | 4 | 5 |
gwam 5' | 1 | 2 | 3 |

62C ◆

PERSONAL-BUSINESS LETTERS

SM: Defaults
File name: L62C

Document 1

1. Format the material at the right as a personal-business letter from **Willis R. Lowenstein**.
2. After you key Document 1, insert a page break and key Document 2.

Document 2

1. Format and key the handwritten copy (below, right) as a personal-business letter in block style.
2. Use **your own return address**; date the letter **October 25** of the **current year**.
3. Address the letter to: **Shutterbug Shops, Inc. 812 Olive Street St. Louis, MO 63101-4460**
4. Use **your name** in the closing lines.

Document 3

Reformat Document 1 with these changes:

1. Use **November 20, 19--** as the date.
2. Address the letter to: **Mr. Charlton Schmidt 5489 Snow Road Cleveland, OH 44122-7117**
3. Bold **Congratulations** at the end of ¶1.
4. Underline serious in ¶2.

	words
22149 West chester Road	5
Cleveland, OH 44122-3756	10
November 15, 19--	13
QS	
Mr. Trevor L. DeLong	18
5202 Regency Drive	21
Cleveland, OH 44129-2756	27
Dear Trevor	29

A news item in the Shaker Heights <u>Gazette</u> says that you are 42
to be graduated from Case Western Reserve at midyear 53
with honors no less. Congratulations. High, 61
When you were a student at Woodmere, I worried that you 73
might never put your potential to work in a serious way. But 86
evidently you have been able to continue your athletic 97
goals and at the same time pursue an academic major suc- 108
cessfully. I am glad you have done credit to us at Wood- 119
mere. We are quiet proud of you. 126

What are your plans after graduation? Whatever your goals, 138
your former teachers at Woodmere wish you well. I would 149
enjoy a note from you which I would share with the others. 161

Cordially yours 165

	words
	opening lines 25
Ladies and Gentlemen	29
The enclosed copy of my credit card statement shows that you	42
have not yet issued a credit for the Lycon Camera (Catalog	53
#C288) that I returned to you more than three weeks ago.	65
Will you please check to see whether a credit of $137.95 has	77
now been issued; and, if not, see that it is issued promptly.	90
I wish to pay the invoice less the appropriate credit.	101
Sincerely yours /Enclosure	106

LESSON 63   PERSONAL-BUSINESS LETTERS

63A ◆
CONDITIONING PRACTICE

each line twice

alphabet	1	The blitz vexed the famous quarterback whose game plan just went awry.
figures	2	Today we keyed 40 letters, 15 reports, 369 orders, and 278 statements.
fig/sym	3	Make finger reaches (hands quiet) to key 303#, 126.95%, and $1,475.98.
speed	4	He may hand me the clay and then go to the shelf for the die and form.

gwam 1' | 1 | 2 | 3 | 4 | 5 | 6 | 7 | 8 | 9 | 10 | 11 | 12 | 13 | 14 |

DRILL PRACTICE

1 Key each line twice SS (once slowly, then faster).
2. Key a 1' writing on each line.
3. Rekey slower lines for speed.

alphabet 1 Liquid oxygen fuel was used to give this big jet rocket amazing speed.

figures 2 We proofread 275 letters, 18 reports, 369 invoices, and 40 statements.

fig/sym 3 Rizzo & Lewis wrote Check #728 for $301.95 and Check #745 for $648.50.

Caps Lock 4 Please buy Cody and Kaye these books by Gore Vidal: LINCOLN and BURR.

underline 5 Do we have the magazine Phi Delta Kappan and PC World in our library?

long reaches 6 The rainy day became sunny after we ate lunch under a big bright umbrella.

speed 7 Rich may make the goal if he works with vigor and with the right form.

gwam 1' | 1 | 2 | 3 | 4 | 5 | 6 | 7 | 8 | 9 | 10 | 11 | 12 | 13 | 14 |

IMPROVE/ CHECK SKILL

1. Key two 1' writings on each ¶; find gwam.
2. Key two 3' writings on ¶s 1-3 combined; find gwam and count errors.
3. Key a 5' writing on ¶s 1-3 combined; find gwam and count errors.

all letters used | A | 1.5 si | 5.7 awl | 80% hfw

gwam 3' | 5'

Appearance, which is often defined as the outward aspect of someone | 5 | 3 42

or something, is quite important to most of us and affects just about | 9 | 6 45

every day of our lives. We like to be around people who and things which | 14 | 8 47

we consider attractive. Because of this preference, appearance is a | 19 | 11 50

factor in almost every decision we make. | 21 | 13 52

Appearance often affects our selection of food, the place in which | 26 | 15 54

we live, the clothes we purchase, the car we drive, and the vacation we | 31 | 18 57

schedule. For example, we usually do not eat foods which are not visu- | 35 | 21 60

ally appealing or buy clothing that we realize will be unattractive to others | 41 | 24 63

who are important to us. | 42 | 25 64

Appearance is important in business. People in charge of hiring | 47 | 28 67

almost always stress the importance of a good appearance. Your progress | 51 | 31 70

in a job or career can be affected by how others judge your appearance. | 56 | 34 73

It is not uncommon for those who see but do not know you to evaluate | 61 | 36 78

your abilities and character on the basis of your personal appearance. | 65 | 39 78

gwam 3' | 1 | 2 | 3 | 4 | 5 |
gwam 5' | 1 | 2 | 3 |

63B ◆
PERSONAL-BUSINESS LETTERS

SM: Defaults
File name: L63B

Letter 1
1. Format and key the handwritten copy as a personal-business letter in block style.
2. The return address:
   3988 Bancroft Court
   Roswell, GA 30075-9082
3. Use the current date.
4. The letter address:
   Mr. Martin Fehr
   Fehr Computer Products
   829 Silverwood Drive
   Atlanta, GA 30349-4217
5. Use **your name** in the closing lines and supply an **Enclosure** notation.
6. Save as L63B (file name).

Dear Mr. Fehr | 31

Last week when I was in Atlanta, I purchased the | 41
"Quality System" software package from your store. When | 52
I tried to use the software, I found that there was | 62
no user's manual. | 66

Please send me the manual as soon as possible so | 76
that I will be able to install the software. I've | 86
enclosed a copy of the receipt which contains the | 96
identification numbers for the software. | 104
Sincerely yours | 107

Error detection: Review the procedures outlined below for your software for using spell check. Use the spell check to find any errors you may have missed while keying the document. You will still need to proofread the document; the spell check only checks for the spelling of words, not content. If you keyed *you* instead of *your*, for example, the spell check would not detect the error.

Spell Check. Spell check is a feature in a word processing program that checks text for misspelled words.

WORDPERFECT

1. Depress **Ctrl F2**.
2. Select Option: **1**—Word
   2—Page
   3—Document
3. If highlighted word is spelled correctly, either depress **1** *Skip once* or **2** *Skip*. If highlighted word is incorrectly spelled, either key the letter preceding the correct word from those offered or depress **4** and *Edit* the spelling of the highlighted word. (To exit in the middle of the spell-check program, depress **F1** three times.)

WORKS DOS

1. Move cursor to the location where you want to start spell check.
2. Depress **Alt, O**.
3. Strike **S**.
4. If highlighted word is spelled correctly, depress **Alt I** or strike Return. If highlighted word is incorrectly spelled, either depress **Alt S** to get suggestions for the correct spelling (↓ to highlight; strike Return) or key the correct spelling of the highlighted word and strike Return. (Replacement word appears beneath Replace with.)
5. Strike Return to exit spell check.

Note: When a word, such as a proper name or technical term, appears several times in a document, depress **Alt G** to instruct spell check to ignore that word each time.

WORKS MAC

1. ~ **Spell** and drag to **Correct Spelling**.
2. If highlighted word is spelled correctly, ~ **Skip**. If highlighted word is incorrectly spelled, either select replacement word from dictionary listing by ~~ on correct spelling *or* key correct spelling of highlighted text and depress Return key. (Replacement text will appear in Replace with box as you key corrected spelling of highlighted word.)

(continued, p. 123)

APPLICATION ACTIVITY

Selectively print a list of the full state names for all states where you have visited or lived; center and bold a title of your choice in ALL CAPS.

OPTIONAL DATA-BASE ACTIVITY

Load and print the word processing file OPTDB2 from *Student's Template*. Follow directions on the printout.

63B ♦ (cont.)

1. Process Letters 2 and 3 as personal-business letters.
2. Use the spell-check feature after keying the documents and then proofread before saving each document.

Letter 2	words
5209 W. Grand Avenue	4
Chicago, IL 60639-3372	9
October 23, 19--	12

Dr. Dallas T. Johnson — 17
Drug Rehabilitation Center — 22
4056 W. Melrose Street — 27
Chicago, IL 60641-2940 — 32

Dear Dr. Johnson — 35

With the approval of the principal of Columbus — 44
High School, the Student Leadership Club is — 53
sponsoring a series of assembly programs this — 62
year dealing with student problems in learn- — 71
ing and life. One of these student assemblies — 81
will address the serious problem of teenage drug — 90
abuse. — 92

As chair of the program committee, I would es- — 101
pecially like you, or a member of your staff, to — 111
talk to us on this timely topic. A presentation — 121
similar to the one you made last year on local — 130
TV would be ideal. — 134

Can you give us 45 minutes of your time on — 143
Friday, March 10, at 10:15 a.m. We need your — 152
help, and we will appreciate it. If you prefer — 162
to call, my telephone number (after 4 p.m.) is — 171
555-2048. — 173

Sincerely yours — 176

Juan F. Ramirez — 179

Letter 3	words
11300 Lower Azusa Road	5
El Monte, CA 91732-4725	10
October 24, 19--	13

Ms. Laura J. Marsh — 17
2274 Cogswell Road — 21
El Monte, CA 91732-3846 — 26

Dear Ms. Marsh — 29

How fortunate you are to have Dr. Mark C. — 37
Gibson as a speaker for the November 18 meet- — 46
ing of the El Monte PTA. If he speaks as well — 55
as he writes, your meeting will be a success. — 65

Because I strongly support the effort El Monte — 74
schools are making to assure computer liter- — 83
acy for all students, I would like to bring three — 93
guests, not two, to the meeting. All three names — 103
are listed on the enclosed card. If the limit is — 113
two guests per member, please let me know. — 122

We need parental support for the computer lit- — 131
eracy program to be the success it should be. — 140
You are to be commended for arranging this — 149
informative program for us. — 155

Cordially yours — 158

Mrs. Alice M. Wiggins — 162

Enclosure — 164

USE SELECTION CRITERIA

Note: Only one field, the full state name field, is printed and only seven states are listed.

Complete the steps listed for your software to print selectively only those full state names for states that do not have a standard abbreviation.

WORDPERFECT

1. Retrieve file STATES.SF, the secondary merge file; then press **Ctrl F9**; select **2**–Sort.
2. Strike Enter to accept *Input file to sort: (Screen)*.
3. At the *Output file for sort: (Screen)* prompt, key **NONE.SF**; Enter.
4. At the Sort Menu, select **7**–Type; select **1**–Merge to keep the lines in each record together.
5. Make selections:
   a. Select **3**–Keys.
   b. At Key **1**, accept the default **a** (for alphanumeric) by striking Enter.
   c. Strike–**3** to select Field 3 (the location of the standard abbreviation field).
   d. Depress **F7** to accept defaults (1) for Line and Word (to select line 1 of field 3 and the first word of the field 3 contents).
6. Select **4**–Select; key **Key1= None**; strike Enter.
7. Select **5**–Action; select **2**–Select Only.
8. Select **1**–Perform Action.
9. Clear screen.
10. Copy STATES2.PF as STATES3.PF.
11. Retrieve STATES3.PF file; Reveal Codes and make the following changes:
    a. From line 5, delete {FIELD}CAPITALS~.
    b. Strike **PgUp**; delete the tabs; set a new center tab at 3.25".
    c. On line 1, center and bold in ALL CAPS the title **STATES WITHOUT STANDARD ABBREVIATIONS.**
    d. Delete line 3 (see Item b).
    e. Save as STATES3.PF; clear screen.
12. Merge STATES3.PF with NONE.SF.
13. Document View, make changes if necessary; print.

WORKS DOS

1. Open the STATES database file; in List View, copy Report3 to Report4; open Report4 if necessary and update as follows:
   a. Center new header in ALL CAPS: **STATES WITHOUT STANDARD ABBREVIATIONS**.
   b. Delete all fields but FULL using the Edit Menu (delete rows/columns, select column; for adjacent columns, use the Select feature to select more than one at a time). **Note:** Fields are not deleted from the database but only from this report.
   c. Insert FULL field contents on Row 3 (*3.0* —line 4), Column A (note that no column title is used).
   d. Format Column A to center align field contents.
2. Print Preview; if necessary, adjust field width and margins to accommodate the header and display only field FULL (the full state name); Esc or print.
3. Press **Alt V**, select Query.
   a. Tab to standard abbreviation field.
   b. Key **="None"**.
   c. Strike Enter, then press **F10** to return to the report List.
4. Print Preview; adjust if necessary; print.

WORKS MAC

1. Open file STATES; go to List View, copy Report2 (the copy becomes Report3).
2. Update Report3 as follows:
   a. From the Format Menu, select any font.
   b. Center and bold the new header in ALL CAPS: **STATES WITHOUT STANDARD ABBREVIATIONS**.
   c. Change the top margin to 1".
   d. Change the right and left margins to 2.3".
3. Increase the STATE field size to the right page edge marker (it will be the only field that is printed).
4. From the Organize Menu select Record Selection:
   a. ~ the field STANDARD.
   b. In the Record Comparison box, key **None**.
   c. Return or ~ select.
5. Preview; change the type size to 12 and preview again.
6. If necessary:
   a. Change the margins to accommodate the larger type.
   b. Adjust the size of the field.
   c. Change the header size.
7. Preview again, make adjustments if necessary; print.

LESSON 64 SIMPLIFIED MEMORANDUMS

64A ◆ CONDITIONING PRACTICE

each line twice

alphabet	1	Five excellent joggers pounded quickly along the beach in a warm haze.
figures	2	They replaced at cost 50 plates, 78 knives, 194 forks, and 362 spoons.
fig/sym	3	The Roe & Son check, dated May 17, should be $45.39 instead of $62.80.
speed	4	She may cycle to the city to go to the ancient chapel by the big lake.

gwam 1' | 1 | 2 | 3 | 4 | 5 | 6 | 7 | 8 | 9 | 10 | 11 | 12 | 13 | 14 |

Memo 1

2" TM · 1" LM · 1" RM

		words in parts	total words
Date	October 29, 19-- QS	3	3
Addressee	Student Leadership Program Committee DS	11	11
Subject	DALLAS JOHNSON TO ADDRESS ASSEMBLY DS	18	18
Body	Dr. Dallas T. Johnson telephoned to say that he will be pleased	13	31
	to address the special student assembly on March 10 on the topic DS	26	44
	TEENAGE DRUG ABUSE DS	30	47
	Dr. Johnson will use slides to present data on the incidence of	42	60
	drug use among teenagers. He will use a short film to highlight	55	73
	differences in attitudes and behavior before and after drug use.	69	86
	Finally, a young adult who has undergone treatment at the Drug Re-	82	100
	habilitation Center will tell us about her experiences with drugs. DS	95	113
	This assembly should be very interesting, but sobering. QS	106	125
	Juan F. Ramirez		
Writer	Juan F. Ramirez, Principal DS	6	130
	dc	6	131

160A ◆
CONDITIONING PRACTICE

each line twice

alphabet 1 Margy expected pop quizzes on the new books and five journal articles.

fig/sym 2 Anna's canceled checks (#398 & #401) showed he paid for Model #25-769.

keypad 3 981-4726 781-5047 513-871-4629 303-271-3846 615-762-8493 216-351-4602

speed 4 To their dismay, the townsman kept the fox and the dog in the kennels.

gwam 1' | 1 | 2 | 3 | 4 | 5 | 6 | 7 | 8 | 9 | 10 | 11 | 12 | 13 | 14 |

160B ◆
READ ABOUT SELECTION CRITERIA

Read the information at the right and the selection criteria information for your software.

The term selective print is used whenever the contents of database fields are selected to match specific information. The specific information for a selective print is called the selection criteria. Selection criteria give you powerful control of records in a database. You make selections based not only on fields but also the field contents. With the selection criteria identified for the field and field contents, any field can be selected to print (or not to print) for those records that match the selection criteria.

WORDPERFECT

Important preliminary steps for selecting records are to:

1. Identify the location of the field containing selection criteria.
2. Identify the type of field contents (alphanumeric or numeric).
3. Identify the location of the line within the field.
4. Identify the location of the word within that line.

Note: The line and word information must be entered even if there is only one line with one word in the field.

WORKS DOS

Use the Select Search command or define query in View Query command. The Select Search command finds records that match only one condition, such as a specific last name. The View Query command finds records that meet more than one condition, such as a last name and a city. The View Query command displays the form with blank fields. View Query requirements (called formulas) are keyed into blank fields instead of field contents. The sample formula >=P (greater than or equal to P) would find records in which field contents begin with P through Z. In List View, you can search the entire database or only selected fields or records. In Form View, you can search the entire database. The following symbols represent selections:

=	exact match
<>	not equal to
>	greater than
<	less than
>=	greater than or equal to
<=	less than or equal to
&	and
:	or
~	not

WORKS MAC

When you select Record Selection from the Organize Menu, a list of selection criteria is displayed as comparison phrases, such as *equals*, *contains*, *begins with*, and *is greater than*. The comparison phrases are used as the selection criteria.

64B ◆
SIMPLIFIED MEMORANDUMS

File name: L64B
SM: 1"
TM: 2"

1. Study the formatting guides for simplified memos on p. 116 and the model memo illustrating the simplified format on p. 124. Note the vertical and horizontal placement of memo parts.

2. Format and key a copy of the memo on p. 124. Correct your errors as you key. Center **TEENAGE DRUG ABUSE** as shown.
3. Process Memos 2 and 3 (below). Insert a page break after each memo.

4. Use spell check and proofread to detect any remaining errors.
5. Save the memos under L64B.

Memo 2

	words
October 24, 19-- QS	3
All Seniors DS	6
CHOOSING A COLLEGE OR UNIVERSITY DS	12
A voluntary assembly for seniors is planned for	22
3 p.m. next Friday, November 5, in the cafete-	31
ria. The purpose is to give you information and	41
answer your questions about choosing and get-	50
ting into the college or university of your choice	60
upon graduation. DS	64
Each guest speaker will summarize entrance	72
requirements and opportunities at his or her	81
college or university. A question/answer period	91
will follow. You may direct your questions to	101
the person of your choice: Miss Micaela Stokes	110
of Central Community College, Dr. Louise	118
Bolan of Midland State University, or Mr. John	128
Hawkes of Metropolitan College of Business. DS	137
If you plan to attend, sign your name below. QS	146
Melissa Briggs, Senior Class President	154

Memo 3

	words
October 28, 19--	3
Leon Deitz	6
FOREIGN EXCHANGE STUDY	10
On Thursday, November 15, Mr. Earl Bosma	18
of Rotary International will be here to discuss	28
the foreign study program with prospective	37
exchange students.	41
The meeting will be at 11:15 a.m. in Conference	50
Room A of Tredwell Library. After the general	60
session, Mr. Bosma will visit with each applicant	70
separately. Your appointment is at 2:30 p.m.	79
Please be prompt for these meetings and bring	88
all your application materials with you.	97
Eileen P. Roth, Assistant Principal	104
xx (Use your own initials for reference.)	104

L ESSON 65 — SIMPLIFIED MEMORANDUMS

65A ◆
CONDITIONING PRACTICE
each line twice

alphabet 1 Jacki saw five prime quail and two big foxes down by the old zoo lake.
figures 2 We had 36 work tables, 247 office chairs, and 85 office desks in 1990.
fig/sym 3 The bookcase (36" x 59" x 14 1/2") is on sale at the Mart for $178.50.
speed 4 The busy visitor may work with usual vigor to form a key social panel.

gwam 1' | 1 | 2 | 3 | 4 | 5 | 6 | 7 | 8 | 9 | 10 | 11 | 12 | 13 | 14 |

CUSTOMIZE REPORT FORMATS

Read the information at the right and then complete the steps listed for your software.

You can customize report formats to print unique layouts. When customized printouts are needed, creative report designs can be used to meet a variety of layout requirements.

WORDPERFECT

1. Retrieve STATES2.PF, Reveal Codes and delete the tabs. If necessary, review 77B on p. 147. Key **C** at desired position on DOS line for a center tab.
2. Set new tabs as follows: right tab at 2.75"; left tab at 3.75".
3. On line 1, key (ALL CAPS and bold) a new centered title: **LIST OF STATES AND CAPITALS**.
4. Delete the text on line 3 and do the following:
   a. Tab, bold the column heading **States**.
   b. Tab, bold the column heading **Capitals**.
5. In line 5, delete the {FIELD} code and field names that identify the two fields, but remember, do not delete: {LABEL}top~.
6. With the cursor on line 5 after the tilde (~), Tab, **Shift F9**, select Field, key **FULL,** Enter.
7. Tab, **Shift F9**, select Field, key **CAPITALS**, Enter.
8. Save.
9. Merge with STATESCAP.SF; Document View; make corrections if necessary; print.

WORKS DOS

1. Open file STATES; go to List View.
2. With the cursor in Column 1, add a field to function as a spacer.
   a. Add field: **Alt, E, I**(nsert) Record/Field, **F**(ield), Enter.
   b. **Alt, E, N**, name the new field **AND**, Enter.
   c. Change field width to 5.
3. Choose New Report from the View Menu.
4. *Version 2.0:* Select and change Report3 so FULL is in column A; AND is in Column B; and field CAPITALS is in Column C:
   a. Select the column (locate cursor in column to be moved, **Alt, Select, Column**).
   b. **Alt, Edit, Move** to select move function; move cursor to new location; Enter.
   Version 3.0: Insert field contents:
   a. Locate cursor in Column A on line 5; then press **Alt, E, O** (Insert Field Contents), and select FULL.
   b. Locate cursor in Column B on line 5; then press **Alt, E, O**, and select AND.
   c. Locate cursor in Column C on line 5; then press **Alt, E, O**, and select CAPITALS.
5. Format fields (columns) as follows:
   a. Flush right: FULL field.
   b. Flush left: CAPITALS field.
6. Align columns titles in first row:
   a. Right-align Column A (column title **States**).
   b. Center and bold Column B (column title **And**).
   c. Left-align and bold Column C (column title **Capitals**).
7. Center the new header in ALL CAPS: **LIST OF STATES AND CAPITALS.**
8. Preview; adjust field widths and margins center visually.
9. Print.

WORKS MAC

1. Open file STATES and go to List View.
2. Change the name of the CAPITALS field to **Capitals**, in bold.
3. Add a new field and name it **AND**, in bold (it will function as a spacer and will not have field contents).
4. Format the fields as follows:
   a. Flush right: FULL.
   b. Flush left: CAPITALS.
   c. Center the new field AND; reduce field size to have only a small space before and after the field title.
5. Open Report2; then follow the steps to print the FULL, AND, and CAPITALS fields:
   a. Move the AND field to the right of the FULL field.
   b. Move the CAPITALS field to the right of the AND field.
   c. Adjust the FULL and CAPITALS fields, aligning the fields to the right page edge marker.
6. Center and bold the new header in ALL CAPS: **LIST OF STATES AND CAPITALS.**
7. Preview; adjust if necessary to center visually; print.

65B ◆
SIMPLIFIED MEMORANDUMS

File name: L65B

1. Review the formatting guides for simplified memos on p. 116 and the model memo on p. 124.
2. Format and key the three memos at the right.
3. When no date is given, use the current date.
4. For Memo 3, use **Keyboarding Students** as the addressee.
5. Spell-check each document.
6. Proofread and correct remaining errors before saving.

Proofreader's Marks

∧	= insert
#	= add space
∽	= transpose
ℯ	= delete
◡	= close up
≡	= capitalize

Memo 1

	words
November 4, 19--	3
Accounting Department	8

SELECTION OF NEW ACCOUNTING DEPARTMENT MANAGER — 17

As most of you have heard by now, last week Marsha Mobley announced her — 32
intent to retire at the end of this year. In keeping with company policy, — 47
President Norwood prefers to have the position filled by a current employee. — 62

If you are interested in applying for the position, submit an updated resume — 78
and letter of application to the personnel office before November 21. It is — 93
our intent to have the position filled by December 1 so that the new man- — 108
ager will have the opportunity of working with Ms. Mobley for a month be- — 122
fore she retires. — 126

Sophia Ramirez, Personnel — 131

xx — 132

Memo 2

words

Adrian S. Comstock | OFFICE TECHNOLOGY SYMPOSIUM — 12

Information on the "Fifth Annual Office Technology Symposium" is enclosed. — 28
I attended last year's symposium and found it very beneficial. Since we — 42
have been allocated money for upgrading the word processing department, I — 57
plan to attend again this year. — 64

There is enough money in the budget to pay the expenses for two people to — 78
attend. Since you will be involved in upgrading the word processing center, — 94
you may be interested in attending. If you are, please let me know before — 109
the end of the month so I can make the necessary arrangements. — 122

Harriet D. Steinman | xx | Enclosure — 128/137

Memo 3

words

opening lines — 7

AUTOMATICLY [AL] CONTROLLED RIGHT MARGINS — 15

Some machines have built-in software that control[s the] right mar- — 28
gin; others, such as computers, depend upon[#]a separate software — 41
disk to[ℯ] control how the lines end. — 48

However the ri[∽]hgt margin is controll[ed,] though, you can override — 61
the defaults ◡to change a line ending. adding [a word] or dividing a — 74
wr[∽]od may make the right margin [less] ragged.[# ≡] You must fol◡low the — 87
proce[ℯ]dure in your user's guide to make line-ending changes. — 99

Liang Chih, *Keyboarding Teacher* — 106

xx — 106

WORDPERFECT

1. Retrieve STATES2.PF; Reveal Codes and delete the tabs.
2. Move cursor to Home position and set new tabs as follows: center tab at 2.2"; left tab at 4.0".
3. Delete the text on line 3 and enter the following:
   a. Tab; bold and key the column title **Two Letters**.
   b. Tab; bold and key the column title **States**.
4. In line 5, delete {FIELD}FULL~ {FIELD}TWO~ {FIELD}STANDARD~
5. With the cursor on line 5 after the tilde (~), Tab, **Shift F9**, select Field; key **TWO**, the name of two-letter abbreviation field; Enter.
6. Tab; **Shift F9**, select Field, key **FULL**, the name of full state name field; Enter.
7. Save as STATES2.PF.
8. Merge with STATES.SF; Document View; make corrections if necessary; print.

WORKS DOS

1. Open file STATES, from View Menu select Report2, Esc.
2. Make the following changes in the report definition:
   a. Center new header in ALL CAPS, **LIST OF TWO-LETTER ABBREVIATIONS AND STATES**.
   b. Set width of Column A to **28**.
   c. Set width of Column B to **15**.
   d. Column C does not change.
   e. Set left and right margins at 1.9".
3. Insert column titles:
   a. Center column title, **Two Letters**, in first row of Column A.
   b. Center column title, **States**, in first row of Column B.
4. Insert field contents:
   a. Locate cursor in Column A on line 5 (*Version 3.0:* line 4); then press **Alt**, **E**, **O** (Insert Field Contents), and select Two.
   b. Locate cursor in Column B on line 5 (4); then press **Alt**, **E**, **O**, and select Full.
5. Print Preview; adjust field width and/or margins if necessary for visual balance (only the abbreviations and two-letter full state names are displayed); print.

WORKS MAC

1. Open file STATES, go to List View.
2. Select Report2 and make the following changes:
   a. Locate the pointer in the Two Letters field name to show the hand; ~ and drag the field to the left of the STATES field to change the sequence.
   b. Adjust the field lengths to end at the right page edge marker.
3. Change the header to **LIST OF TWO-LETTER ABBREVIATIONS AND STATES**; center and bold in ALL CAPS.
4. Preview, adjust field sizes if necessary for visual balance; print.

159D ♦

APPLICATION ACTIVITY

1. Open/retrieve STATES (STATES.SF).
2. Add fields 4 and 5 for the following (see p. 317 if needed):
   a. State capitals with field name CAPITALS.
   b. States where you have lived or visited with field name VISITED.
3. Key the list of capitals for each state.

4. Key the letter **X** in the VISITED field for states where you have lived or visited. (**WordPerfect users:** Insert X followed by {END FIELD} code for states visited; for states not visited, insert {END FIELD} code as a placeholder.)
5. Save file as STATECAP(.SF).

States	Capitals	States	Capitals	States	Capitals
Alabama	Montgomery	Louisiana	Baton Rouge	Ohio	Columbus
Alaska	Juneau	Maine	Augusta	Oklahoma	Oklahoma City
Arizona	Phoenix	Maryland	Annapolis	Oregon	Salem
Arkansas	Little Rock	Massachusetts	Boston	Pennsylvania	Harrisburg
California	Sacramento	Michigan	Lansing	Rhode Island	Providence
Colorado	Denver	Minnesota	St. Paul	South Carolina	Columbia
Connecticut	Hartford	Mississippi	Jackson	South Dakota	Pierre
Delaware	Dover	Missouri	Jefferson City	Tennessee	Nashville
Florida	Tallahassee	Montana	Helena	Texas	Austin
Georgia	Atlanta	Nebraska	Lincoln	Utah	Salt Lake City
Hawaii	Honolulu	Nevada	Carson City	Vermont	Montpelier
Idaho	Boise	New Hampshire	Concord	Virginia	Richmond
Illinois	Springfield	New Jersey	Trenton	Washington	Olympia
Indiana	Indianapolis	New Mexico	Santa Fe	West Virginia	Charleston
Iowa	Des Moines	New York	Albany	Wisconsin	Madison
Kansas	Topeka	North Carolina	Raleigh	Wyoming	Cheyenne
Kentucky	Frankfort	North Dakota	Bismark		

LESSON 66 BUSINESS LETTERS/ADDRESSING ENVELOPES

66A ◆ CONDITIONING PRACTICE

each line twice

alphabet 1 Barth was given a big prize for completing six quick high jumps today.
figures 2 The inventory includes 96 pamphlets, 1,827 books, and 3,450 magazines.
fig/sym 3 The #329 item is sold by Janoch & Co. for $875.46 (less 10% for cash).
speed 4 The key to proficiency is to name the right goals, then work for them.

gwam 1' | 1 | 2 | 3 | 4 | 5 | 6 | 7 | 8 | 9 | 10 | 11 | 12 | 13 | 14 |

66B ◆ FORMAT LETTER PARTS

Drill 1

1. Begin return address 2" from top edge.
2. After keying the salutation, insert 14 hard returns to begin closing lines.

Drill 2

1. Study the business letter formatting guides on p. 116; check each placement point with the model letter on p. 128 and with the copy in Drill 2 at right.
2. Key the drill, inserting hard returns as shown.

Drill 1: Personal-Business Letter

3204 Mount Holly Road
Charlotte, NC 28216-3746
November 10, 19-- (Return 4 times)

Mrs. Juanita L. Ruiz
1859 Boston Road
Springfield, MA 01129-3467 DS

Dear Mrs. Ruiz DS

Space down 14 times (hard returns).

Cordially yours (Return 4 times)

Ms. Gloria C. Ainsley DS

Enclosure

Drill 2: Business Letter

November 10, 19-- (Return 4 times)

Attention Mr. Kevin J. Marx
Kendall Computers, Inc.
733 Marquette Avenue
Minneapolis, MN 55402-1736 DS

Ladies and Gentlemen DS

WORD PROCESSING EQUIPMENT ORDER DS

Space down 14 times (hard returns).

Sincerely yours (Return 4 times)

Evan L. Ritchey, Director
Word Processing Center DS

tbh DS

Enclosure DS

c Miss Mary E. Durbin

66C ◆ FORMAT BUSINESS LETTERS

File name: L66C

1. Format and key the letter shown on p. 128.
2. Proofread and correct errors before saving the document.
3. If time permits, take a 2' writing on the opening lines (date through subject line); then a 1' writing on the closing lines (complimentary close to the end).

b. Highlight file to be copied (STATES1.PF).
c. Select **8-Copy.** At the *Copy this file to:* prompt, key file name of the copy (STATES2.PF); strike Enter.
2. Retrieve STATES2.PF.
3. At beginning of document, clear all tabs and set new tabs: center tab at 3.25"; right tab at 6.25".
4. Reveal Codes, delete any unnecessary codes.
5. On line 1, center and rekey the same title, in ALL CAPS and bold.
6. Change the column headings, using uppercase and lowercase letters, as follows:
   a. Key the word **States** for FULL column heading (full state name column).
   b. Key the words **Two Letters** for TWO column heading (two-letter abbreviation column).
   c. Key the word **Standard** for STANDARD column heading (standard abbreviations column).
7. Save as STATES.PF.
8. Merge STATES2.PF with STATES.SF; Document View; make corrections if necessary; print.

report definition; Press **F10** to return to List or Form View.

1. Open file STATES, go to List View.
2. Press **Alt, V**, select Reports; with Report1 highlighted, Tab to Name and key **Report2**; Tab to Copy; Enter, Esc or Done.
3. Select Report2 if necessary, delete first two rows (title is deleted):
   a. At row, press **Alt, S**(select), **R**(row or record), press **Shift** and ↓ to select second row.
   b. Press **Alt, E**(dit), **D**(elete) Row/Column or Record/Field to delete Intr Report lines or Record/Field Title lines.
4. Delete last two rows by adapting the procedure in Step 3 to delete Summ Report lines.
5. Key centered header in ALL CAPS: **LIST OF STATES AND ABBREVIATIONS** (same as keying headers in word processing: select Headers & Footers from Print Menu; in the Headers box, key &C to center, then key the title and Enter).
6. Change the left and right margins: **Alt, P** (Print), **M** (Page Setup & Margins), left margin 1.4"; right margin 1.5"; Enter.
7. Change width of Column A to **22** (**Alt, T, W**).
8. Change width of Column B to **12**.
9. Center Column B: highlight a cell in column, then **Alt, T** (Format), **S**(tyle), **C**(enter), Enter. *Version 3.0:* Highlight a cell in the column; then **Alt, S, C** to select the column; and then **Alt, T** (Format), **S**(tyle), **C**(enter), Enter.
10. Align Column C at the right by adapting procedure in Step 9.
11. Print Preview; adjust margins or column width if necessary to print on one page; print.

3. To flush right (align at right edge) the field STANDARD: from Format Menu, select Field Attributes; ~ Right button.
4. Select Change Field Names from the Edit Menu (the field name is the column heading); use upper-case and lowercase letters.
   a. Change the first field name (FULL) to **States**.
   b. Change the second field name (TWO) to **Two Letters**.
   c. Change the third field name (STANDARD) to **Standard**.
5. Copy the report print format as follows:
   a. From the Report Menu, select Duplicate Report.
   b. ~ the report name: States Report1.
   c. Return or ~ OK (automatically becomes Report2).
6. In States Report2, select Page Setup from the File Menu and complete the following:
   a. Change the header to ALL CAPS, bold.
   b. Change the top margin to .65".
   c. Change the bottom margin to 0.
   d. Return or ~ OK.
7. Change type size to 10 (under Format in Report Menu).
8. Adjust the size of the fields to right margin marker.
9. Print Preview (the complete list should be displayed), review the steps if changes are necessary; print.

SELECT FIELDS

Read the information at the right and then complete the steps listed for your software.

Report print formats control which fields are selected and the sequence in which they are arranged on the printout. You are to print selected two-letter abbreviations and the state names.

MERKEL-EVANS, Inc.

1321 Commerce Street • Dallas, TX 75202-1648 • Tel. (214) 871-4400

Date November 10, 19-- 2" TM   QS | 4 | 4

Letter address
Mrs. Evelyn M. McNeil | 8 | 8
4582 Campus Drive | 12 | 12
Fort Worth, TX 76119-1835 | 17 | 17
DS

Salutation Dear Mrs. McNeil | 20 | 20
DS

Body The new holiday season is just around the corner, and we invite | 13 | 33
you to beat the rush and visit our exciting Gallery of Gifts. | 26 | 45
Gift-giving can be a snap this year because of our vast array of | 38 | 58
gifts "for kids from one to ninety-two." | 47 | 67
DS

What's more, many of our gifts are prewrapped for presentation. | 64 | 80
All can be packaged and shipped right here at the store. | 71 | 91
DS

1" LM 1" RM

A catalog of our hottest gift items and a schedule of holiday | 84 | 104
hours for special charge-card customers are enclosed. Please | 96 | 117
stop in and let us help you select that special gift, or call us | 109 | 129
if you wish to shop by phone. | 115 | 135
DS

We wish you happy holidays and hope to see you soon. | 126 | 146
DS

Complimentary close Cordially yours | 3 | 149
QS

Carol J. Suess

Writer's name and title Ms. Carol J. Suess, Manager | 9 | 155
DS

Reference initials rj | 9 | 155
DS

Enclosure notation Enclosures | 11 | 157

WordPerfect Users

To turn on the automatic hyphenation feature, do the following:

Shift F8
Line
Hyphenation
Yes
Return
Return

158C ◆ (cont.)

LIST OF STATES AND ABBREVIATIONS

FULL	TWO	STANDARD

{LABEL}TOP~{FIELD}FULL~ {FIELD}TWO~ {FIELD}STANDARD~
{END IF}{NEXT RECORD}{GO}TOP~

   j. Reveal Codes to check entries; modify if necessary; and save as file—STATES1.PF.

   k. Clear screen.

6. Merge (**Ctrl F9, 1**—Merge). STATES1.PF and file STATES.SF.
7. Document View (**F7, 6**); make corrections if necessary; print.

8. With the cursor on the first line in Column A, key the title: **LIST OF STATES AND ABBREVIATIONS**; Enter.
9. Access Print Preview to verify that the title and all three fields appear; review the steps to adjust field widths if necessary; print.
10. Save.

L ESSON 159   FIELD SELECTIONS

159A ◆ CONDITIONING PRACTICE

each line twice

alphabet 1 A new expert may organize both journal displays quickly for the event.

fig/sym 2 D & L Shops cashed in Policy #2847-08 for $15,986 on October 30, 1994.

keypad 3 00 10 20 30 40 50 60 70 80 90 100 200 300 400 500 600 700 800 900 1000

speed 4 Make the panel suspend the pay of their city officials as the penalty.

gwam 1' | 1 | 2 | 3 | 4 | 5 | 6 | 7 | 8 | 9 | 10 | 11 | 12 | 13 | 14 |

159B ◆ ALIGN FIELD CONTENT AND EDIT

Read the information at right and then complete the steps listed for your software to align field contents and change selected field names.

You can adjust a print format by controlling subtle details of a printout. You will improve the printout of the database file STATES by aligning the field contents and printing records for all 50 states, using a copy of the STATES file.

WORDPERFECT

Field names are aligned in the primary file. During merge, the field contents of the secondary file are changed to the format of the fields in the primary file.

1. Copy STATES1.PF as STATES2.PF (The procedure for copying a file follows.)
   a. Press F5; Enter.

(continued on next page)

WORKS DOS

While in the Report definition screen, move the cursor to line 5 (line 4) in the desired column; then from the Format Menu, select Style (**Alt, T, S**); use arrow keys to select alignment desired; Enter or select OK.

To view an existing report definition: from View, select the report; Enter to view additional pages; Esc to the

(continued on next page)

WORKS MAC

Select the field that is to be aligned; from the Format Menu, select Set Field Attributes. . .; ~ alignment desired; Return or ~ OK.

1. Open database file STATES; show List View.
2. To center field TWO: ~ the field; from Format Menu select Field Attributes; ~ Center button.

(continued on next page)

DELETE A FILE

Delete the following files from your disk:

WIGGINS	GALEN
RYAN	L62C
TUTOR	L63B

Deleting a File. When a file is no longer needed, it should be deleted (removed) from the disk. Doing so frees up disk space and makes it easier to manage the remaining files.

WORDPERFECT

1. Depress **F5**. *
2. Strike Return (see note below).
3. Use arrow keys to highlight file to be deleted.
4. Strike **D**(elete).
5. Strike **Y**(es).
6. Depress **F7** to return to input screen.

* Note: If the file to be deleted is not on the default drive, you will have to change disk drives after you depress F5.

WORKS DOS

1. Depress **Alt**, **F**.
2. Strike **F**(ile Management).
3. Strike **D**(elete File).
4. Strike Return.
5. Use arrow keys to highlight file to be deleted.
6. Strike Return twice.
7. Strike the Esc key.

WORKS MAC

1. Select File.
2. Select Delete.
3. ~ file to be deleted.
4. ~ delete.
5. ~ **OK**.

ADDRESS ENVELOPES

1. Study the guides at right and the illustrations below.
2. Format a small (No. 6 ¾) and a large (No. 10) envelope for each of the addresses. Use your own return address on the small envelopes.

MISS AMEKI IGAWA
C/O THE DESERT MANOR
102 FREMONT STREET
LAS VEGAS NV 89101-2277

MR HUANG KUO FU
   MANAGER
DELGADO & HUANG INC
758 N FIGUEROA STREET
LOS ANGELES CA 90012-3650

Envelope address
Set a tab 2.5" from the left edge of a small envelope and 4" from the left edge of a large envelope.

Space down about 2" from top edge of the envelope. Begin the address at the tab position.

U. S. Postal Service Style
Use block style, SS. Use ALL CAPS; omit punctuation. Place city name, 2-letter state abbreviation, and ZIP Code + 4 on last address line. One space precedes the ZIP Code + 4.

Return address
Use block style, SS, and caps and lowercase or ALL CAPS. Begin on line 2 from top of envelope, 3 spaces from left edge.

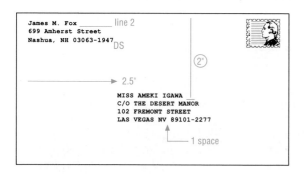

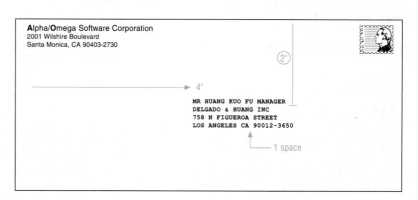

For columns, field codes are entered at tab settings. Titles and column headings can be keyed in the screen-merged document or in the primary file for one-page documents.

1. Clear the screen.
2. On the first line, clear all tabs; set relative tabs as follows: left tab at 3.0"; left tab at 4.5".
3. On the first line, bold and center the main heading: **LIST OF STATES AND ABBREVIATIONS**.
4. Key column headings on line 3. Key **FULL**; tab, then key **TWO**; tab, then key **STANDARD**.
5. Add merge commands that insert field contents and print records continuously without page breaks between records as follows:
   a. Locate cursor at beginning of line 5, from Format (**Shift F9**), select **6**–More; highlight {LABEL}label~; Enter.
   b. At *Enter Label*, key **TOP**, Enter.
   c. Press **Shift F9**, select Field, key **FULL**; Enter.
   d. Tab to first stop; press **Shift F9**; select Field; key **TWO**; Enter.
   e. Tab to next stop; **Shift F9**; select Field; key **STANDARD**, strike Enter twice.
   f. Press **Shift F9**; select **6**–More, key the letter **e** (the first letter of END); highlight (END IF); Enter. (The fast way to locate the cursor within the command list—and near or on the command you want—is to key the first letter of the command. Doing so locates the cursor on the first command with that letter. Use arrow keys to highlight the correct command.)
   g. Press **Shift F9**, select **6**–More, key the letter **n** (for Next), highlight {NEXT RECORD}; Enter.
   h. Press **Shift F9**; select **6**–More; key the letter **g**; highlight {GO}label; Enter.
   i. At the *Enter Label*; key **TOP**; Enter (software goes to the top of the next record) Sample of screen:

(continued on next page)

Intr Page/Title. Introductory page or title rows are used for top of page introductory information and column headings. For column headings, use either the field names or any column heading.

Record/Headings. Record or heading rows are used for information that determines the fields included in the report. Record rows can be sorted in groupings of records.

Sum Report/Summary. Summary report or summary rows are used for summary statistics, such as calculating totals and averages. Use these rows to create the breaks for groupings of records.

1. Open database file STATES; go to List View.
2. Press **Alt, V**; select New Report; Esc to display Report definition screen. *Version 3.0*: **Alt, V**; select New Report; at *Title* strike Enter to bypass it.
3. Insert field names:
   a. Locate cursor in Column A on line 3, **Alt, Edit**, Insert Field Names (**Alt, E, N**); select (highlight) FULL; Enter.
   b. Locate cursor in Column B on line 3, then **Alt, E, N** and select TWO; Enter.
   c. Locate cursor in Column C on line 3, then **Alt, E, N** and select STANDARD; Enter.
4. Insert field contents:
   a. Locate cursor in Column A on line 5 (*Version 3.0:* line 4), then press **Alt, E, O** (Insert Field Contents), and select FULL.
   b. Locate cursor in Column B on line 5 (4), then press **Alt, E, O**, and select TWO.
   c. Locate cursor in Column C on line 5 (4), then press **Alt, E, O**, and select STANDARD.
5. Locate cursor on any row in Column A, press **Alt, T, W** (to select Format, Column Width), change column width to **18**; Enter or select OK.
6. Move cursor to any row in Column B and change column width to **16**.
7. Change width of Column C to **18**.

(continued on next page)

field length in List View: locate the I-beam over the end of field FULL, then ~ and drag the field end to change it).
4. Change the size of field TWO, the two-letter abbreviation field, to the 3.5" mark, change the size of field STANDARD to the length of the right edge marker. (The right edge marker is automatically established by the left and right margins you set in the Page Setup Menu. To get correct spacing on printouts, always size the fields you want to print so that the right edge of the final field is aligned with the right edge marker.)
5. Center and bold the title, **LIST OF STATES AND ABBREVIATIONS,** in the Header box in the same way you entered headers in word processing. (From the File Menu, select Page Setup; locate the I-beam in the Header box; &C to center and &B to bold; key the title of the report. Do not insert spaces after the center and bold commands.)
6. Return or ~ OK.
7. Print Preview to verify; review the steps to make changes if necessary; print.

LESSON 67   BUSINESS LETTERS

67A ◆
CONDITIONING PRACTICE
each line twice

alphabet 1 Monkeys in the quaint park watched a fat lizard devour six juicy bugs.

figures 2 The telephone number for your 120 N. Lotus Drive location is 378-4569.

fig/sym 3 The rates varied from 15 1/2% to 17 1/4% on loans from $98 to $36,500.

speed 4 Kay may make an authentic map of the ancient city for the title firms.

gwam 1' | 1 | 2 | 3 | 4 | 5 | 6 | 7 | 8 | 9 | 10 | 11 | 12 | 13 | 14 |

67B ◆
BUSINESS LETTERS

1. Format and key the letters below in block style with open punctuation (shown).

2. Spell-check and proofread before saving the documents.

Letter 1
File name: DAHMS

	words
November 12, 19--	4
Miss Carmen J. Blanco, Chair	9
Business Education Department	15
Dolphin Vocational High School	22
104 N. Andrews Avenue	26
Fort Lauderdale, FL 33301-2859	32
Dear Miss Blanco	36

Your order for six Genesis GS computers and | 45
two printers is being processed. We are pleased | 54
to include you in the growing number of users | 64
of this quality equipment. | 69

We plan to deliver and install these machines at | 79
three o'clock on November 18 to avoid disrupt- | 88
ing classroom activities. Please let me know if | 98
this date and time are convenient for you. | 107

Only a few minutes are required to install the | 116
equipment, but we want to test two or three | 125
programs to be certain that everything is work- | 134
ing properly. | 137

Please telephone me at the number shown above | 147
to confirm or change the appointment. | 154

(words in body: 121)

Sincerely yours	158
Kermit L. Dahms, Sales Manager	164
xx	164
c DeRon S. Jackson	168

Letter 2
File name: THOMPSON

	words
November 12, 19--	4
Mr. Duane R. Burk, Office Manager	10
Huesman & Schmidt, Inc.	15
662 Woodward Avenue	19
Detroit, MI 48226-1947	24
Dear Mr. Burk	27

Thank you for letting our representative, Miss | 36
Tina Chun, discuss with you and your staff our | 46
new line of landscaped office modules. | 54

Using in-scale templates, Miss Chun has rede- | 63
signed the general work area of your word | 71
processing center. Her mock-up offers you | 80
important features: ideal use of space in indi- | 89
vidual workstations, stationary panels to create | 99
private work areas without a feeling of cloister, | 109
and traffic patterns that are least disruptive | 118
to others. | 121

May we show you this portable display and dis- | 130
cuss the low cost of improving the productivity | 140
and harmony of your office staff. A color photo- | 149
graph of the mock-up is enclosed. Please call | 159
me to set a convenient date and time for us to | 168
spend about an hour with you. | 174

(words in body: 149)

Sincerely yours	178
Virgil P. Thompson	181
Assistant Sales Manager	186
xx	187
Enclosure	189

1. Open a new database file; refer to pages 313 and 314 if necessary.
2. Key the field names; use default field size:
   FULL (for the full state name)
   TWO (for the two-letter abbreviation)
   STANDARD (for the standard abbreviation)
3. Key the field contents from the list that is provided.
4. Save as file name: STATES. (**WordPerfect users:** Save as secondary file STATES.SF. You will use this file later).

FULL	TWO	STANDARD	FULL	TWO	STANDARD
Alabama	AL	Ala.	Montana	MT	Mont.
Alaska	AK	None	Nebraska	NE	Nebr.
Arizona	AZ	Ariz.	Nevada	NV	Nev.
Arkansas	AR	Ark.	New Hampshire	NH	N.H.
California	CA	Calif.	New Jersey	NJ	N.J.
Colorado	CO	Colo.	New Mexico	NM	N. Mex.
Connecticut	CT	Conn.	New York	NY	N.Y.
Delaware	DE	Del.	North Carolina	NC	N.C.
Florida	FL	Fla.	North Dakota	ND	N.Dak.
Georgia	GA	Ga.	Ohio	OH	None
Hawaii	HI	None	Oklahoma	OK	Okla.
Idaho	ID	None	Oregon	OR	Oreg.
Illinois	IL	Ill.	Pennsylvania	PA	Pa.
Indiana	IN	Ind.	Rhode Island	RI	R.I.
Iowa	IA	None	South Carolina	SC	S.C.
Kansas	KS	Kans.	South Dakota	SD	S. Dak.
Kentucky	KY	Ky.	Tennessee	TN	Tenn.
Louisiana	LA	La.	Texas	TX	Tex.
Maine	ME	None	Utah	UT	None
Maryland	MD	Md.	Vermont	VT	Vt.
Massachusetts	MA	Mass.	Virginia	VA	Va.
Michigan	MI	Mich.	Washington	WA	Wash.
Minnesota	MN	Minn.	West Virginia	WV	W. Va.
Mississippi	MS	Miss.	Wisconsin	WI	Wis.
Missouri	MO	Mo.	Wyoming	WY	Wyo.

158C ♦

REPORT PRINT FORMATS

Read the information at the right. Then complete the steps listed for your software to design a print format and print a report. You will use the STATES file in later lessons.

You can produce a variety of printouts from a database by creating different print formats. The number of print formats that can be saved at one time is limited by the software. You can always delete a format, however, when you need to add a new one.

Two kinds of print formats are report formats and label formats. Report formats generally are used to print records in the form of a table; that is, with the field contents in columns across the page. Label formats generally are used to print records down the page, such as for mailing labels. In this lesson, you work with report formats; you will work with label formats in later lessons.

Remember to save frequently as you work and to save before printing, even when save instructions are not given. When you are instructed to save and no additional information is given, save by updating the file.

WORDPERFECT

Primary merge files are used to print reports from information in secondary files, similar to merging form letters. Each primary file created for a secondary merge file generates a different printout according to the field codes and selections.

(continued on next page)

WORKS DOS

Row types in Works DOS include the following: You can delete or add rows of each type.

Intr Report (*2.0*)/Title (*3.0*). Introductory rows are used to add titles that will print on first page only.

(continued on next page)

WORKS MAC

1. Open database file STATES; go to List View.
2. From the Report Menu, select New Report.
3. Change the size of field FULL to the 1.5" mark on the ruler. (The process is similar to changing the

(continued on next page)

Letter 3

File name: SABIN
Retrieve Letter 1 and use the word processing features you have learned to make the changes outlined at the right.

Send the letter to: Mrs. Ellen Sabin, Chair
Business Education Department
Riverside High School
968 Blakely Drive
Cleveland, OH 44143-1342

Mrs. Sabin ordered eight Genesis GS computers and three printers. The equipment will be delivered on November 25 at four o'clock.

67C ♦

RENAME A FILE

Letter 1 should have been saved under the name of the addressee (Blanco), rather than under the name of the sender (Dahms). Using the rename feature outlined below, save the Dahms letter under BLANCO. The same is true for Letter 2. Save the Thompson letter under BURK.

Rename File. At times, you may want to change the name of an existing file. To rename a file, follow the instructions outlined for your particular software.

WORDPERFECT

1. Depress **F5** (select disk drive if necessary).
2. Strike Return.
3. Use arrow keys to highlight file to be renamed.
4. Strike **M**(ove/Rename).
5. Key new file name; strike Return.
6. Depress **F7**.

WORKS DOS

1. Use **Alt**, **F**.
2. Strike **F**(ile Management).
3. Strike **R**(ename); strike Return.
4. Use arrow keys to highlight file to be renamed.
5. Strike Return.
6. Key new file name.
7. Strike Return; strike Esc.

WORKS MAC

With the file open, select the Save As command in the File Menu. Key new file name and strike Return key. (Document is saved under the new name, leaving the old file intact. If you do not want the document saved under both names, delete the old file.)

L ESSON 68   BUSINESS LETTERS

68A ♦
CONDITIONING
PRACTICE
each line twice

alphabet	1	Brave jockeys and large quarter horses whiz past farmers in box seats.
figures	2	Your Order No. 648 calls for 103 chairs, 29 typewriters, and 75 desks.
fig/sym	3	She wired them $365 on May 29 for the items ordered on Invoice #40187.
speed	4	Cy may be the right man to blame for the big fight in the penalty box.

gwam 1' | 1 | 2 | 3 | 4 | 5 | 6 | 7 | 8 | 9 | 10 | 11 | 12 | 13 | 14 |

UNIT 35

LESSONS 158-160

Work With Print Formats and Records

Learning Outcomes: After completing this unit, you will be able to

1. Print selected and sequenced fields in report format.
2. Align field content and edit.
3. Print specific records by applying selection criteria.

DATABASE FEATURE AND PROCEDURES GUIDE

ALIGNING FIELD CONTENTS
REPORT PRINT FORMATS
SELECTION CRITERIA

REPORT PRINT FORMATS

Report printouts generate tables that display the field contents in columns. A report print format is used whenever a columnar display of the records is needed.

ALIGNING FIELD CONTENTS

Most database software lets you align the field contents at the left margin or right margin or to center it.

SELECTION CRITERIA

Database records that match specific qualifications can be selected for printing. The specific qualifications are called the selection criteria. Selection criteria for a mailing list, for example, might be to select and print only the records that have a particular ZIP code.

Making selections with the Print Format feature differs from making selections with Merge feature. With the Merge feature, two files are generally required—the database file and the word processing file containing the merge code information. When you design a print format with some software, only the database file is needed because you access and choose the selection criteria within the database options. Your selections are saved with the database file as a report format and can be used again at a later time.

LESSON 158 REPORT PRINT FORMATS

**158A ◆
CONDITIONING PRACTICE**

each line twice SS (slowly, then faster); DS between 2-line groups; keypad, return after each number

alphabet 1 Buzz expects to take his good vehicle for quick journeys on warm days.

fig/sym 2 I made Check #948 payable to O'Hare & O'Brian for $156.07 on April 23.

keypad 3 000 101 202 303 404 505 606 707 808 909 1010 2020 3030 4040 5050 60606

speed 4 Their men are in good shape to box with vigor to the end of the fight.

gwam 1' | 1 | 2 | 3 | 4 | 5 | 6 | 7 | 8 | 9 | 10 | 11 | 12 | 13 | 14 |

**158B ◆
APPLICATION ACTIVITY**

Read the information at the right and then complete the steps on the next page to create a "states" database.

The two-letter state abbreviation system was developed by the U.S. Postal Service to speed mail delivery. The two letters are in caps and no punctuation is used with them. As you examine the two-letter abbreviations, you will discover that some of the abbreviations are the first two letters of the state name (AL for Alabama). Others are the first and last letters (CT for Connecticut). Some could be either the first two letters or the first and last letters, for example, CA for California. The two-word state names, such as New York, are the first letters of each word. Some states are exceptions and do not follow any of these patterns.

BUSINESS LETTERS

File name: L68B
Proofread and correct errors before saving documents.

Letter 1

Format and key the letter at the right. Review Drill 2, p. 127 for placement of attention and subject lines if necessary.

words

November 14, 19-- | Attention Sales Manager | Business Management   12
Systems | 748 S. Market Street | Tacoma, WA 98402-1365 | Ladies and   25
Gentlemen | IMPROVE SALES BY 10 PERCENT   33

If you could close 10 percent more sales a year, would you spend a day of   48
your time to learn how? If so, we want to welcome you to   59

SUCCESS BY VISUAL PERSUASION   65

This special seminar is designed for high-level managers like you who want   80
quick, easy ways to prepare visual presentations that are a cut above the   95
chalkboard and flipchart. Using a lecture/electronic technique, a seminar   110
leader will show you how to use built-in outlining, drawing, and charting tools.   127
You will even learn how to get full-color effects in overheads and slides.   142

To improve your sales by 10 percent a year, read the enclosed brochure   156
about the seminar; then complete and return the registration card. You will   171
be glad you did.   (143)   175

Sincerely yours | Robert L. Marsh, Director | xx | Enclosure   186

Letter 2

1. Format and key the letter at the right.
2. Use the U.S. Postal Service address style as shown. (See 66E, p. 129.)

Letter 3

Make the following changes to Letter 2:

Date: **November 17, 19--**

Address (in the style shown):
Mr. Edwin C. Phipps
Elmwood Vocational School
1262 Asylum Avenue
Hartford, CT 06105-2828

Salutation: supply one

Subject: **WORLD CHAMPIONS**

Copy notation: **c Ms. Eloise M. Rozic**

words

November 16, 19--   4

MISS JANELLE A QUIN   8
CENTRAL HIGH SCHOOL   12
1000 LINCOLN AVENUE   16
EVANSVILLE IN 47714-2330   21

Dear Miss Quinn   24

Thank you for conveying the interest of your students in the   36
keying speeds achieved by those who have won international   48
typewriting contests.   52

Margaret Hama won the last international contest, held   64
in 1941. She keyed for an hour on an electric typewriter   75
at a speed of 149 net words a minute (errors penalized).   87
The next highest speed was attained by Albert Tangora, who   99
won the 1923 contest on a manual typewriter at the rate of   110
147 words a minute.   115
Although later claims have been laid to the title "World   126
Champion Typist," the international contests were discon-   137
tinued during World War II and, to our knowledge, have not   149
been resumed.   152

Good luck to you and your students as you seek champion-   163
ship speed.   (141)   166
Sincerely yours   169

Mrs. Allison K. Boyles   173
Educational Director   178

xx   178/195

OPTIONAL DATA-BASE ACTIVITY

Load and print the word processing file OPTDB1 on the *Student's Template* for information about the Optional Database Activity. Directions for this activity are included in the file.

WORDPERFECT: SORT MENU OPTIONS

1. Perform Action is used to begin sorting or selecting after choices have been entered.

2. View is used to scroll through the input document that is displayed.

3. Keys are the words, fields, or phrases within a record that are used to sort and/or select specific items in a document.

4. Select is used to enter a statement that specifies the records that you want to include in the sorting.

5. Action is selected only if you have entered a select statement in Option 2 of the Sort Menu.

6. Order is selected to sort in Ascending (1) or Descending (2) order.

7. Type is selected to set the kind of sort; selections are Merge (1), used to keep database records that end with {End Record} commands together during sorts; Line (2), used when each line is a separate chunk of information; and Paragraph (3), used for information or a block of information that ends with two or more hard returns.

69A ◆
CONDITIONING
PRACTICE
each line twice

alphabet 1 Jacques has asked to be given one week to reply to this tax quiz form.

figures 2 Raul must study Section 2, pages 75-190, and Section 4, pages 246-380.

fig/sym 3 The new rate on Glenn & Taylor's $2,856 note (due 4/13/97) is 10 1/2%.

speed 4 Jo may sign the usual form by proxy if they make an audit of the firm.

gwam 1' | 1 | 2 | 3 | 4 | 5 | 6 | 7 | 8 | 9 | 10 | 11 | 12 | 13 | 14 |

69B ◆

IMPROVE
LETTER SKILL

File name: L69B

1. Format and key the letters below in block style with open punctuation.

2. Spell-check and proofread before saving documents.

Letter 1   words

899 Farmers Loop Road	4
Fairbanks, AK 99712-3647	9
November 18, 19--	12
Attention Customer Service	18
Outergear, Inc.	21
1354 Market Street	25
San Francisco, CA 94103-2746	31
Ladies and Gentlemen	35

On October 30, I ordered from your winter cata-   44
log a Heavyweight Fleece Tee Shirt (#M628).   53
Although the packing slip and the printed plastic   63
bag label clearly state that the shirt is a large,   73
the shirt label shows that the size is medium.   83
Large was the size I ordered.   89

Because I have had a similar experience twice   98
in the past, my confidence in your ability to fill   108
my orders accurately is reduced. To avoid the   118
nuisance and expense of packaging and return-   126
ing the shirt, I will keep it to use as a gift.   136

Will you please caution your packers or the   145
appropriate manufacturers to check sizes and   154
colors more carefully before placing garments   163
in prelabeled bags. I'm certain that the extra   173
care will make your other customers happier,   182
too.   (words in body: 147)   183

Sincerely yours   186

Roland C. Marshall   190

Letter 2   words

November 18, 19--	4
Mr. Leslie D. Banks	8
George Washington High School	14
2165 E. 2700 South Street	19
Salt Lake City, UT 84109-3720	25
Dear Mr. Banks	28

Your question about the effect of word process-   37
ing equipment on the need for keying accuracy   46
is a good one.   50

Accuracy of documents processed is just as   58
vital now as ever before. The ease with which   68
keying errors can now be corrected, however,   77
has shifted the emphasis from number of input   86
errors made to skill in finding and correcting   95
these errors.   98

A major weakness of those who take employ-   106
ment tests is their inability to detect and correct   117
the errors they make. Therefore, we suggest   126
that employee training should emphasize proof-   135
reading and error correction rather than error-   144
free initial input.   148

A grading system rewarding efficient proofread-   158
ing and correction skills instead of penalizing   167
errors of initial input is worthy of your serious   177
consideration.   (words in body: 152)   180

Sincerely yours   184

Ms. Audrey M. Lindsay   188
Employment Office Manager   193

xx   194/214

APPLICATION ACTIVITY

Read the information at the right and then complete the activity. (Refer to procedures used for 157C. See Appendix F, pp. 446-448, also.)

1. Key the form letter at right and save as file name: **DBLTR.**
2. Enter merge codes for the letter address fields in the SUPPLIER database:
   SUPPLIER
   ADDRESS
   CITY STATE ZIP
   See p. 320—
   WordPerfect: Steps 2-6.
   Works DOS: Steps 2-9.
   Works MAC: Steps 3-9.
3. Merge and print the letters. See p. 320—
   WordPerfect: Steps 9-13.
   Works DOS: Step 10.
   Works MAC: Step 10.

Diane provided a copy of a form letter that she wants to send to the suppliers. She requested a sample printout of the letter merged with a supplier name and address from the database.

Current date

SUPPLIER
ADDRESS
CITY STATE ZIP

ADD YOUR NAME TO OUR LIST!

Suppliers hold the key to keeping vehicles in outstanding condition in two ways: keeping them running and making them look good! Our customers are always eager to get a copy of our list of suppliers each time it is updated.

We want to keep your name on the list. Please send a note saying you want to stay on the list for another year. Without your request, we cannot keep your firm on the list. I look forward to hearing from you.

DIANE NELSON, MANAGER

xx

Form Letter

69C ♦
CREATE TEXT
File name: L69C

1. Compose at the keyboard 1 or 2 paragraphs on one of the questions at the right. DS paragraph(s).
2. Edit your copy, marking corrections and changes to improve sentence structure and organization.
3. Prepare the final copy.

Questions

If you received a check for $100,000 in the mail today, what would you do with it?

What qualities do you think an employer would look for in a prospective employee?

Would you buy a stereo on credit? Explain.

69D ♦
IMPROVE SKILL
File name: L69D

all letters used | LA | 1.4 si | 5.4 awl | 85% hfw

gwam 2'

Whether you key documents for personal or for business — 5
use, much of the copy will be in handwritten or rough-draft — 11
form. So adjust your speed in order to do work of quality. — 18
Seize the next opportunity to prove that you can handle both — 24
kinds of copy without too great a loss in speed and control. — 30
With practice, you can process such copy with speed and ease. — 36

LESSON 70   BUSINESS LETTERS

70A ♦
CONDITIONING PRACTICE
each line twice

alphabet 1 Jack answered many questions about the exact value of each topaz ring.
figures 2 On Monday, November 14, 1988 I bought pattern numbers 32A57 and 60B94.
fig/sym 3 The 1992 cost ($414) was 15 percent greater than the 1987 cost ($360).
speed 4 The neighbor's dog was with the girl by the big sign in the cornfield.

gwam 1' | 1 | 2 | 3 | 4 | 5 | 6 | 7 | 8 | 9 | 10 | 11 | 12 | 13 | 14 |

70B ♦
ASSESS FORMATTING SKILLS

File name: L70B
1. Format and key Documents 1-3 (at right and on p. 135).
2. Proofread and correct errors before saving documents.

Document 1
Simplified Memo
Date: **November 13, 19--**
Addressee: **DeRon Jackson**
Subject: **APPOINTMENT FOR GENESIS INSTALLATION**
Writer's name: **Kermit L. Dahms**
Reference: your initials

words

opening lines 16

Miss Blanco of Dolphin Vocational High School called to con- — 28
firm the appointment for you to install the six Genesis GS — 39
computers and two printers in her word processing lab. — 52
The appointment is at 3 p.m. on Friday, November 18. — 64

Be sure to take the three user's manuals for the basic — 78
software programs we are providing. Miss Blanco wants — 90
three of her teachers to have a brief hands-on demonstration — 101
of the basic operating procedures. — 108

closing lines 111

WORDPERFECT

1. Create a new document as a primary file.
2. Press **Shift F9**; select **1—Field**; key SUPPLIER at *Enter Field*; Enter to select. Enter again to move cursor to the next line.
3. Repeat Step 2 to key the **PHONE**, the field you named for parts/ services field, and **ADDRESS** fields on separate lines.
4. To print the CITY, STATE, and ZIP fields on the same line with one space between each field, do the following:
   a. Press **Shift F9**; select **1—Field**.
   b. Key **CITY** at *Enter Field;* strike Enter, strike space bar one time.
   c. Press **Shift F9**; select **1—Field**.
   d. Key **STATE** at *Enter Field;* strike Enter; strike space bar one time.
   e. Press **Shift F9**; select **1—Field**; key ZIP at *Enter Field*; strike Enter.
5. Strike Enter twice to leave a blank line, then press **Shift F9**.
6. Select **4—Page off** so that each record will not print on a separate page but rather will print as a continuous list. Your screen should look like this:
   {FIELD}SUPPLIER~
   {FIELD}PHONE~
   {FIELD} **(The name you gave PARTS/SERVICES field followed by ~ should be displayed.)**
   {FIELD}ADDRESS~
   {FIELD}CITY~ {FIELD}STATE~ {FIELD}ZIP~

   {Page Off}
7. Save as a primary file using file name: MERGSUPP.PF (for Merge Supplier Primary File).
8. Clear the screen.
9. Press **Ctrl F9**; select **1—Merge**.
10. At the *Primary file:* prompt key MERGSUPP.PF or retrieve the file using board commands (Enter).
11. At the *Secondary file:* prompt key SUPPLIER.SF or retrieve the file using board commands (Enter).
12. Save as file name: LIST.
13. View the document before printing; update if necessary, then print the document.

WORKS DOS

1. With the SUPPLIER.WDB file on the screen, create a new word processing document from the File Menu (*2.0:* **Alt**, **F**, **N**, **W**—*3.0:* **N**, **W**, Enter).
2. From the Edit Menu, select Insert Field. *3.0:* Select Insert Database Field.
3. In the databases box, move the cursor to SUPPLIER.WDB if necessary; then Tab to the Fields box.
4. If necessary in the Fields box, highlight the SUPPLIER field, using arrow keys or the space bar. (Use the arrow keys to highlight other fields when you need to select them.)
5. Strike Enter to make the selection (field appears on the word processing file screen). **Note:** A field must be highlighted to select it.
6. Strike Enter to move the cursor to the next line in the word processing document.
7. Repeat Steps 3–6 to select the PHONE field, the field that you named for the parts and services, and the ADDRESS field.
8. For the city, state, and ZIP Code to print on one line:
   a. Repeat Steps 3 and 4.
   b. In the Fields box, select the CITY field. Strike Enter to make the selection.
   c. Strike the space bar one time to insert a space between CITY and STATE fields. Because the STATE field should appear on the same line, DO NOT strike Enter.
   d. Repeat the steps to select the STATE field, and strike the space bar one time.
   e. Again, without striking Enter, repeat the steps to select the ZIP Code field.
9. Save the word processing file as file name: LIST.
10. From the Print Menu, select Print Labels in this instance (select Print Form letter when appropriate); Enter to accept defaults through the other screens; print the document.

WORKS MAC

1. Open file SUPPLIER-DB.
2. With SUPPLIER-DB on the screen, create a new word processing document from the File Menu.
3. From the Edit Menu, select Prepare to Merge (⌘ M).
4. At the Merge Data Base dialog box, select SUPPLIER-DB. (When more than one database document is open, more than one file name is listed.)
5. At the Merge Field dialog box, select SUPPLIER.
6. Return or ~ the Merge button.
7. Repeat Steps 3–6 for the PHONE, PARTS/SERVICES field that you named, and ADDRESS fields.
8. For the city, state, and ZIP Code to print on one line:
   a. Repeat Steps 3 and 4.
   b. In the Fields box, select the CITY field.
   c. Strike Return to make the selection; then strike the space bar one time.
   d. Without striking Return, repeat the steps to select the STATE field.
   e. Strike the space bar one time.
   f. Again, without striking Return, repeat the steps to select the ZIP Code field.
9. Save as file name: LIST-WP.
10. Print Preview; update if necessary, then print the document.

Document 2
Personal-Business Letter

2274 Cogswell Road | El Monte, CA 91732-3846 | December 3, 19-- | Mrs. Alice   14
M. Wiggins | 11300 Lower Azusa Road | El Monte, CA 91732-4725 | Dear Mrs.   28
Wiggins   30

Thanks to you and other PTA members who brought guests, our November 18   44
meeting was a tremendous success. Dr. Gibson was overwhelmed by the   58
high level of interest in computer literacy shown by parents of our students.   74

You will be pleased to know that two of the guests you brought have now reg-   89
istered to become regular PTA members. The total new-member registra-   103
tion was nine.   106

The other officers of the El Monte PTA join me in appreciation of the active   121
role you are taking this year.   128

Cordially yours | Ms. Laura J. Marsh   134

Document 3
Business Letter

December 4, 19-- | Mr. Duane R. Burk, Office Manager | Huesman & Schmidt,   14
Inc. | 662 Woodward Avenue | Detroit, MI 48226-1947 | Dear Mr. Burk   27

Miss Chun and I certainly enjoyed our discussions with you last week. We   41
are highly pleased that you have given us an opportunity to work with you to   57
maximize your office space.   63

Based upon your plan to regroup certain personnel, Miss Chun is reworking   77
her design to accommodate the changes. That work should be completed   91
next week. At that time, we shall also have a firm bid to show you.   105

Would next Friday at ten o'clock be a convenient time for us to show you the   121
new plans? If not, please suggest another date and time.   132

Sincerely yours | Virgil P. Thompson | Assistant Sales Manager | xx   (105)   145

Document 4
Simplified Memo

Date: **December 4, 19--**
Addressee: **Vincente W. Lugo**
Subject: **NEW SERVICE CONTRACT FOR OFFICE EQUIPMENT**
Writer: **Danielle E. Bogarde**
Reference: your initials

Document 5

Make a copy of Document 2 and then make these changes.
Address the letter to:

Mr. Jon Galen
22 Silverbay Avenue
El Monte, CA 91732-6782

Change the date to **February 1**
Make these changes in ¶1:
November 18 to **January 25**
Dr. Gibson to **Dr. Linton**
computer literacy to **teenage drug abuse**

opening lines 15

¶ We have just signed a new service contract with the   25
Lee & Perin Company. Henceforth, they will clean, service,   37
and repair all our keyboarding and word processing   48
equipment.   50
¶ L & P has asked me to notify all supervisors that only   61
L & P personnel should do internal cleaning or make repairs   72
on any typewriter, computer, or word processor. When service   85
is required, please call 555-8590 to make your request.   96
¶ Make sure everyone under your supervision knows   106
about this change.   110

closing lines 114

157A ◆
CONDITIONING
PRACTICE

each line twice

alphabet	1	Mary's five quaint, prized jugs and their six bowls broke into pieces.
fig/sym	2	Di (5/19/74) is my oldest sister; Lea (6/30/82) is my youngest sister.
keypad	3	85-749612-301 96-857432-10 74-859613-20 93-142586-07 96-253617-41 8293
speed	4	He may sign the usual form by proxy if they make an audit of the firm.

gwam 1' | 1 | 2 | 3 | 4 | 5 | 6 | 7 | 8 | 9 | 10 | 11 | 12 | 13 | 14 |

157B ◆

SORT A DATABASE

Read the information at the right and then complete the steps listed for your database software to sort the database. **WordPerfect Users**: See the list of Sort Menu options on p. 322 before taking the steps below.

The suppliers database will be used in a variety of ways. For the first use, the list will be sorted alphabetically by the suppliers' names.

Usually when a database has been sorted and saved, you are not able to rearrange it in the original order. You save the sorted file under a new file name whenever you need both the original and the sorted files.

WORDPERFECT

1. With the SUPPLIER.SF file open and the cursor in SUPPLIER field name, press **Ctrl F9**; then select **2—Sort**.
2. Strike Enter to select default: *Input file to sort: (Screen).*
3. Strike Enter to replace the input document on the screen with the output document.
4. At the Sort Menu, select **7—Type**.
5. Select **1—Merge**, select **6—Order**, select Order: **1—Ascending**, select **1—Perform Action**.
6. Save (original order not needed).

WORKS DOS

You can sort in either view. If you sort in List View, however, you can verify the sort because the sorted records are displayed on the screen.

1. With the SUPPLIER file open and in List View, press **Alt, S, O** to select Sort Records.
2. In the first field box, key **Supplier** if necessary.
3. Select Ascend order if necessary.
4. Enter.
5. Save (original order not needed).

WORKS MAC

1. With the SUPPLIER file open, ~ name field title or any item in SUPPLIER field.
2. ⌘ A; or from the Organize Menu, select Sort.
3. Return to select default A to Z.
4. Save (original order not needed).

157C ◆

DESIGN PRINT FORMAT

Read the information at the right and then complete the steps listed on the next page for your database software. Make a practice of saving a file before printing it. Thus, if something happens to a file when it is sent to the printer, you can open a copy that is current.

A printout of the supplier database is needed. Diane wants to use it as a reference to look up telephone numbers and to check the parts and services that the suppliers provide. She asked for the printout to be in this order:

SUPPLIER
PHONE
PARTS/SERVICES (the field you named)
ADDRESS
CITY STATE ZIP

Master Keyboarding Skills

Learning Outcomes: After completing this unit, you will be able to

1. Demonstrate improved response patterns and service-key operation.
2. Key straight-copy paragraphs with higher speed and improved control.
3. Demonstrate improved skill transfer to script and rough-draft copy.

LESSON 71   KEYBOARDING SKILLS

SM: Defaults; LS: SS

71A ◆ 6'
CONDITIONING PRACTICE

each line twice SS; two 1'
writings on line 4

alphabet 1 Zoya picked a bouquet of vivid flowers growing next to the jungle gym.

figures 2 Order 196 was for 38 vests, 72 jackets, 40 skirts, and 25 plaid suits.

fig/sym 3 I said, "The quiz covering pages 35-149 and 168-270 will be on May 5."

speed 4 She is to pay the six firms for all the bodywork they do to the autos.

gwam 1' | 1 | 2 | 3 | 4 | 5 | 6 | 7 | 8 | 9 | 10 | 11 | 12 | 13 | 14 |

71B ◆ 12'
MASTER TECHNIQUE: SERVICE KEYS

each set of lines twice (once
slowly, then faster)

Space bar (quick down-and-in thumb motion)

1 by us | in a pan | to a man | if any of | to the boy | of the firm | he may try it
2 Many of the men and women may vote to delay action on a new wage plan.

Shift keys (finger reaches to shift keys)

3 Panama City | Latin America | Dubuque, Iowa | Madrid, Spain | Adams & Sons Co.
4 Have Spencer & Co. of Laramie ship the boots to J. D. Yates in Boston.

Underline and Caps Lock (quiet hands and arms)

5 <u>Modern Maturity</u>, a publication of AARP, is for people fifty and older.
6 Kirk's book COMPUTER USE should be reviewed soon in <u>The Balance Sheet</u>.

71C ◆ 15'
COMPARE SKILL

1. Key the drill twice as shown.
2. Key a 1' writing on each line; find *gwam* on each.
3. As time permits, key the four slowest lines again.

balanced hand 1 He is apt to make the men go to the island for the coalfish and clams.

double letters 2 Kellee saw three little rabbits hopping between rows looking for food.

3d row 3 Three of our territory reporters were told to type their trade report.

adjacent key 4 Every owner was there to report the trade union's prior point of view.

outside reach 5 Paul won all six top regional prizes last season for his zealous play.

one hand 6 Polly saw a few deserted cats on a battered crate in a vacated garage.

shift keys 7 Janie saw Karen, Lauren, Ellen, and Claudia while she was in Columbus.

figures 8 Her phone number is 836-9572; her address is 3014 Jefferson Boulevard.

gwam 1' | 1 | 2 | 3 | 4 | 5 | 6 | 7 | 8 | 9 | 10 | 11 | 12 | 13 | 14 |

156C ◆

CHANGE FIELD SIZES

Works Users Only
Read the information at the right and then complete the steps listed for your database software.

In database software, such as Microsoft Works, field sizes can be changed when the database is originated or at a later time. The main advantage of using default field sizes when you create a database file is that you can key the field names faster when you do not stop to change the default field size. Once all the field names have been keyed, the field sizes can be changed as needed.

Why decrease the field size? Advantages of decreasing the field size are to display more fields on the multiple-record screen and to make efficient use of the file space required for the database.

An advantage of increasing the field size is to allow the contents of fields to be fully visible. When it is desirable to view the full field contents, check the copy to identify the longest entry in multiple-records layout; then increase the field size to accommodate the longest entry.

WORKS DOS

Field size can be changed in List or Form View. (Field size changes in one layout do not affect the other layout.)

1. Move cursor highlight to desired field.
2. Press **Alt T** for Format; in List View, select Field Width (in Form View, select Field Size).
3. Key the new width (**15**), Enter.
4. Increase and decrease the field sizes for fields you determine need adjusting.
5. Save.

WORKS MAC

Field size can be changed in Form or List View. (Field size changes in one layout do not affect the other layout.)

1. Move I-beam to top right edge of the field name box of desired field.
2. ~ and drag the edge of the field name box to the desired size; then release mouse button (+ symbol appears until mouse button is released).
3. Increase and decrease the field sizes for fields you determine need adjusting.
4. Save.

156D ◆

UPDATE RECORDS

Read the information at the right and then complete the steps listed for your database software.

Database records can be updated easily because the process is similar to updating a word processing document. You are to make these changes and save. (Remember to use USPS style.)

1. *Classic Salvage* to **Classic Auto Salvage.**
2. P.O. Box for Midwest Body Parts to **155** and last 4 digits of ZIP to **0155.**
3. Phone for Import Auto Supply to **(714) 198-7070.**
4. City name for Sports Truck Accessories to **San Diego**, ZIP to **92130-4322.**
5. Correct any errors that you might have made.

WORDPERFECT

1. Open SUPPLIER.SF file.
2. Locate the cursor at the place where changes are to be made.
3. Use Insert/Typeover key as needed to make corrections.

WORKS DOS

1. Open SUPPLIER.WDB if necessary.
2. Locate the cursor highlight on the field contents to be changed.
3. Key the new information (new information replaces old information).
4. Use Enter or arrow key to enter new information; then save.

WORKS MAC

1. Open SUPPLIER-DB if necessary.
2. Locate the cursor highlight on the field contents to be changed.
3. Key the new information (new information replaces old information).
4. Return or arrow key to enter new information; save.

71D ◆ 17'
IMPROVE SKILL

1. Take a 1' unguided writing and two 1' guided writings on each ¶.
2. Take a 2' and a 3' writing on ¶s 1-3 combined; find *gwam*. Record *gwam* for future reference.
3. If time permits, key another 3' writing; find *gwam*, count errors.

gwam	¼'	½'	¾'	1'
20	5	10	15	20
24	6	12	18	24
28	7	14	21	28
32	8	16	24	32
36	9	18	27	36
40	10	20	30	40
44	11	22	33	44
48	12	24	36	48
52	13	26	39	52
56	14	28	42	56

all letters used | A | 1.5 si | 5.7 awl | 80% hfw

	gwam 2'	3'
People in business are concerned about what is communicated by the	6	4
written word. As they write memos, letters, and reports, they may plan	14	9
for the content but may not plan for the image of the message. Experts,	21	14
however, realize that neglecting the way a document looks can be costly.	29	19
Many times a written piece of correspondence is the only basis on	35	23
which a person can form an impression of the writer. Judgments based on	42	28
a first impression that may be formed by the reader about the writer	50	33
should always be considered before mailing a document.	54	36
The way a document looks can communicate as much as what it says.	62	41
Margins, spacing, and placement are all important features to consider	69	46
when you key a document. A quality document is one that will bring the	75	50
interest of the reader to the message rather than to the way it appears.	83	55

gwam 2' | 1 | 2 | 3 | 4 | 5 | 6 | 7 |
3' | 1 | 2 | 3 | 4 | 5 |

LESSON 72 — KEYBOARDING SKILLS

SM: Defaults; LS: SS

72A ◆ 6'
CONDITIONING PRACTICE

each line twice SS; two 1" writings on line 4

alphabet 1 A judge will quiz expert witnesses before he makes any vital decision.

figures 2 Please order 1,520 pencils, 894 pens, 350 file boxes, and 76 dividers.

fig/sym 3 Order #5-207 (May 24) from Kline & Co. totals $98.56, less 2/10, n/30.

speed 4 It is a civic duty to handle their problem with proficiency and vigor.

gwam 1' | 1 | 2 | 3 | 4 | 5 | 6 | 7 | 8 | 9 | 10 | 11 | 12 | 13 | 14 |

72B ◆ 18'
CHECK SKILL

1. Key 1', 2', and 3' writings on 71D above as directed there. (Record *gwam*.)

1' Goal: 3 *gwam* increase
2' Goal: 2 *gwam* increase
3' Goal: 1 *gwam* increase

2. Key selected lines of 71B and 71C, page 136, to improve technique.

156A ◆
CONDITIONING PRACTICE
each line twice

alphabet	1	Jeanne may use twelve quart tins for packing the extra zucchini bread.
fig/sym	2	Here & Now (Vol. 17, No. 12) was rated the #1 magazine in a 1992 poll.
keypad	3	00-463971-852 20-748596-13 30-964715-82 40-851739-26 00-789456-12 4729
speed	4	Their field hand works in the cornfield down by the lake by the docks.

gwam 1' | 1 | 2 | 3 | 4 | 5 | 6 | 7 | 8 | 9 | 10 | 11 | 12 | 13 | 14 |

156B ◆

ADD A FIELD

Read the information at the right and then complete the steps listed below for your software.

Most database software lets you add fields to a record. Diane decided it would be helpful to include the parts and services that are provided by each of the suppliers. She requested the addition of a new field to the SUPPLIER database file. You should decide the name; add it for the new field; then key the field information for each supplier.

Lichen Motors: MG parts and accessories

Classic Salvage: Used parts for American classic cars

Parts-4-Less: Mail-order domestic parts

Sports Truck Accessories: New accessories for sports trucks

North County Auto Parts: Domestic car parts

British Spares, Ltd.: Parts for classic and modern British cars

Import Auto Supply: Foreign car parts

Classic Parts Locators: Locates foreign and domestic car parts

Harry's Hot Line: Parts-locating service for dealers

Midwest Body Parts: Domestic classic car parts

Wally's Warehouse: Discount foreign and domestic car parts

The Detailing Doctor: Detail car supplies

The Safety Shop: Automotive safety items

Mobile Mechanics: Mobile automotive repair service

Best Auto Salvage: Rare and unusual car parts, used

WORDPERFECT

1. Retrieve SUPPLIER.SF file and locate the cursor where the new field is to be inserted in the list of fields, taking care not to separate the tilde (~) from the preceding field name.
2. Depress **Shift F9**, 1—Field; at the *Enter Field* prompt, key the name, then Enter.
3. Relocate the cursor at Home so the new field will be recognized.
4. In the first record, insert a blank line at the new field location; verify by checking the screen prompt.
5. Key the information for the new field, press **F9** to end field; if an extra line is inserted in this step, delete it.
6. Relocate cursor and repeat Steps 4 and 5 for each record.
7. Save.

WORKS DOS

1. If necessary, strike **F9** for List View; locate the cursor where the new field is to be inserted.
2. Press **Alt E** to display the Edit Menu.
3. Strike **I** to select Insert Record/Field.
4. Strike **F** to select Insert Field.
5. Strike Enter to add the field (new field is added at the location of the cursor).
6. To name the field, press **Alt E**.
   a. Key **N** to select Field Name.
   b. Key the field name in the dialog box; Enter.
7. Press **F9,** if necessary, for List View; then locate the cursor on the new field for Lichen Motors; key the field contents.
8. Strike ↓ to move to the new field in the next record; key the contents.
9. Repeat Steps 7 and 8 to key all records.
10. Save.

WORKS MAC

1. From the Edit Menu, select Add New Field.
2. Key the new field name in the dialog box.
3. Strike Return or ~ the Add Field button (the new field is added after the last field).
4. Key the field contents in List View.
5. Save.

SKILL TRANSFER: SCRIPT

1. Key a 1' writing on each ¶; find *gwam*.
2. Key a 2' and a 3' writing on ¶s 1-2 combined; find *gwam* on each.
3. Compare 1', 2', and 3' rates with those attained on the straight copy in 72B on the preceding page.

Goal: 90% of straight copy *gwam* on each length of writing.

all letters used | A | 1.5 si | 5.7 awl | 80% hfw

	gwam 1'	2'	3'

Workers on the job have to plan their workdays and organize their work so that all duties are done in a timely fashion. As a result, much is being said about teaching students to prioritize work. The truth is that novice office workers have only limited opportunities to set their own priorities; rather, priorities are often set for them.

For example, in a word processing center a supervisor receives the work from various document writers. He or she then assigns the work to keyboard operators on the basis of their workloads and in the sequence of immediacy of need. Even a private secretary is often told by the "boss" which work is urgent and which may not be needed immediately.

gwam	1'	2'	3'
	9	5	3
	20	10	7
	30	15	10
	38	19	13
	48	24	16
	57	29	19
	68	34	23
	9	38	26
	18	43	29
	27	48	32
	37	53	35
	46	57	38
	55	62	41
	65	66	44
	70	69	46

SKILL TRANSFER: ROUGH DRAFT

1. Key a 1' writing on each ¶; find *gwam*.
2. Key a 2' and a 3' writing on ¶s 1-2 combined; find *gwam* on each.
3. Compare 1', 2', and 3' rates with those attained on the straight copy in 72B on the preceding page.

Goal: 80% of straight copy *gwam* on each length of writing.

all letters used | A | 1.5 si | 5.7 awl | 80% hfw

You must work very hard to build a high skill; it is not bestowed. No magic plan nor simple system will help you obtain maximum keyboarding skill. To build a high skill, you must spend extra energy, devote many hours to developing proper technique on copy containing ideas for growth, and use the most effective work methods each and every time you practice.

No simple skill building activity will supply the variety of experience that will yield maximum progress and skill. Sometimes the object of practice is to reach for speed; at other times, the purpose maybe to practice at a slower rate to lower the number of errors. Learn now to employ each kind of technique with equal zest.

gwam	1'	2'	3'
	11	5	4
	23	11	8
	35	17	12
	47	23	16
	59	29	20
	71	36	24
	11	41	27
	24	47	32
	36	53	36
	48	59	40
	60	66	44
	66	69	46

ADD RECORDS

Read the information at the right and then complete the steps listed for your software.

Database software lets you add records to a database file. Diane provided an additional list of companies for the suppliers database.

Load the file if necessary, and key the records (USPS style) for the additional suppliers as directed in the steps below. Remember to save the file frequently as you work in case there is a power failure.

Wally's Warehouse
19876 Sports Arena Blvd.
San Diego, CA 92122-6578
(619) 146-4678

The Detailing Doctor
403 Doubletree Rd.
La Mesa, CA 92041-7298
(619) 178-6345

The Safety Shop
21987 Mission Ave.
Vista, CA 92083-5472
(619) 178-4444

Mobile Mechanics
9705 Vista Del Sol
San Diego, CA 92115-7544
(619) 166-7878

Best Auto Salvage
3508 Bayside St.
Mission Beach, CA 92109-4473
(619) 115-1209

WORDPERFECT

1. Locate the cursor at the end of the SUPPLIER.SF file after the page break (**Home**, **Home**, ↓). **Note:** The field is identified at the left bottom of the screen.
2. Continue with steps for keying records that you used to key the original records (remember to end fields with the end field command, **F9**; and end records with the end record command, **Shift F9**, select **2—End Record**).
3. Save.

WORKS DOS

1. Use your choice of Form or List View.
   a. If you use Form View, locate cursor at the end of the last field in last record, press Tab to get a new blank form.
   b. If you use List View, locate cursor in the first cell of the first blank record.
2. Key the field information for that cell.
3. Continue with steps for keying records that you used to key the original records. (If you use List View, at the end of the last field of a record, press ↓ and then **Home** to move cursor quickly to first cell of next record.)
4. Save.

WORKS MAC

1. Use your choice of Form or List View.
   a. In Form View, locate I-beam at the end of the last field in last record, press Tab.
   b. In List View, locate cursor in the first field of the first blank record.
2. Key the field information for that field.
3. Continue with steps for keying records that you used to key the original records.
4. Save.

UNIT 14

LESSONS 73-78

Master Report Formatting

Learning Outcomes: After completing this unit, you will be able to

1. Format and key unbound reports.
2. Format and key reference lists.
3. Format and key title pages.
4. Format and key topic outlines.

UNBOUND REPORT FORMAT

Many short reports are prepared without covers or binders. Such reports are called unbound reports. If they consist of more than one page, the pages are fastened together in the upper left corner by a staple or paper clip.

Standard Margins

Unbound reports are formatted with standard 1-inch (1") side margins (SM). A top margin of 2" is customarily used on the first page of unbound reports. Remember the 1" default top margin.

A 1" bottom margin is recommended. Because the internal spacing of report parts varies, a bottom margin of exactly 1" is often not possible. For that reason, a bottom margin of at least 1" is acceptable.

Page Numbering

The first page of an unbound report is usually not numbered. On the second and subsequent pages, there is a 1" top margin. If a default top margin of 1" is being used, place the page number on the first line of the input screen. A DS is left below the page number.

Internal Spacing of Reports

A QS is left between the report title and the first line of the body. Multiple-line titles are DS. A DS is left above and below side headings and between paragraphs, which are usually DS but may be SS when specified.

Internal Citations

References used to give credit for quoted or paraphrased material are cited in parentheses in the report body. This internal citation method of documentation is rapidly replacing the footnote method because it is easier and quicker. Internal citations should include the name(s) of the author(s), the year of publication, and the page number(s) of the material cited.

Quotation marks are used for direct quotes but not for paraphrased material. An ellipsis (. . .) is used to indicate any material omitted from a quotation:

"Many changes are occurring today in office organization . . . and technology" (VanHuss and Daggett, 1990, 1).

Reference Lists

All references cited in a report are listed alphabetically by author surnames at the end of a report (usually on a separate page) under the heading REFERENCES. A QS appears between the heading and the first reference. The reference page uses the same top margin and side margins as the first page of the report, but a page number is included at the RM, 1" from the top of the page.

Each reference is SS with a DS between references. The first line of each reference begins at the LM; other lines are indented 0.5". If the reference list appears on the last page of the report body, a QS is left between the last line of copy and the heading REFERENCES.

155C ◆

SINGLE- AND MULTIPLE- RECORD LAYOUTS

Works Users Only
Read the information at the right and then complete the steps listed for your software.

Most database software lets you move between viewing a single record and viewing multiple records.

WORKS DOS

1. At the Form screen, the two ways to display the List screen are
   a. Press **F9**.
   b. From View Menu select List.
2. At the List screen, the two ways to display the Form screen are
   a. Press **F9**.
   b. From View Menu select Form.
3. Practice moving between single- and multiple-record layouts several times using both ways. Which way is faster?

WORKS MAC

1. At the Form screen, the three ways to display the List screen are
   a. ~~ in a blank area of the screen.
   b. Press ⌘ **L**.
   c. From Format Menu, select List.
2. At the Grid or List screen, three ways to display the Form screen are
   a. ~~ in a blank area of the screen.
   b. Press ⌘ **F**.
   c. From Format Menu, select Show Grid.
3. At the List screen to display a record in Form View, ~~ the box to the left of a record.
4. Practice moving between single- and multiple-record layouts several times using the different ways. Which way is faster?

155D ◆

MOVE AROUND IN A DATABASE

Read the information at the right and then study the information for your software. Practice moving around in the database file on your computer screen.

There are several ways to move to a new location on the screen. Some methods take more keystrokes than others. Practice the fastest methods, those using fewer keystrokes, until they become automatic.

WORDPERFECT

Use the rapid cursor move methods that you learned in word processing. See p. 50.

WORKS DOS

Move	Key(s)	View
One field left or right	← or →	List
Next line or field	↓ or ↑	Both
Left-most field	Home	List
Right-most field	End	List
Left edge	Home	Form
Right edge	End	Form
Down one window	Page Down	Both
Up one window	Page Up	Both
First record	Ctrl + Home	Both
Last record	Ctrl + End	Both
Next record	Ctrl + Page Down	Form
Previous record	Ctrl + Page Up	Form

WORKS MAC

Move	Key(s)	View
Down one field	Return	Form
Up one field	Shift + Return	Form
Down in same field, next record	Return or ↓	List
Up in same field, previous record	Shift + Return or ↑	List
Right one field	Tab or →	Both
Left one field	Shift + Tab or ←	Both
Next record from last field	↓	List
Previous record from first field	↑	List

73A ◆
CONDITIONING PRACTICE

each line twice SS; then three 1' writings on line 4; find *gwam*; clear screen

alphabet 1 Pamela Jaworski inquired about the exact size of the very large house.

figures 2 Flight 687 from Boston will arrive at 10:45 a.m. on May 29 at Gate 13.

fig/sym 3 The 5% sales tax on Order #394 is $16.80; for Order #202 it is $17.50.

speed 4 The haughty man may signal with a giant emblem or with the usual sign.

gwam 1' | 1 | 2 | 3 | 4 | 5 | 6 | 7 | 8 | 9 | 10 | 11 | 12 | 13 | 14 |

73B ◆
CENTER LINES HORIZONTALLY

Center each of the lines at the right horizontally. Start the first line 2" from the top of the page. DS between lines.

WordPerfect: Shift F6
Works DOS: Ctrl C
Works MAC: Format, Justification, Center

HORIZONTAL CENTERING
Equal Left and Right Margins
Half of Copy to Left of Center
Half of Copy to Right of Center
Variance of One or Two Spaces Acceptable

73C ◆
REPORT AND REFERENCE LIST

File name: L73C

1. Study the report formatting information on p. 139.
2. Format and key the model report and references shown on pp. 141-142. Correct your errors as you key.

Note: Depending on the software you are using, line endings may be different from those of the model.

73D ◆
TITLE PAGE

File name: L73D

A cover or title page is prepared for many reports. Using the following guides, format a title page for the report you prepared in 73B.

1. Center the title in ALL CAPS 2" from the top.
2. Center your name in capital and lower-case letters 5" from the top.
3. Center the school name a DS below your name.
4. Center the current date 9" from the top.

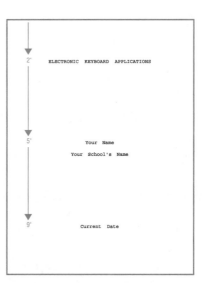

```
2"    ELECTRONIC  KEYBOARD  APPLICATIONS




5"              Your  Name
            Your  School's  Name




9"             Current  Date
```

Import Auto Supply
7105 Malvern Ave.
Anaheim, CA 92805-2318
(714) 198-7373

Classic Parts Locators
21098 E. Overland Rd.
Boise, ID 83707-1776
(208) 122-6061

Harry's Hot Line
23456 N. Military Wy.
Seattle, WA 98111-7315
(206) 196-2211

Midwest Body Parts
P.O. Box 1555
Oklahoma City, OK 73159-1555
(405) 188-9000

WORDPERFECT

1. Retrieve SUPPLIER.SF file.
2. Depress **Home**, **Home**, ↓ .
3. Key the field contents (LICHEN MOTERS) in the SUPPLIER field of the first record; press **F9** to insert {END FIELD} command.
4. Continue to key field contents for the first record, pressing **F9** after each field.
5. With the cursor on the line below last field contents, press **Shift F9**; select **2**—End Record.
6. Continue to key field content for each record by repeating Steps 3-5.
7. Save.

WORKS DOS

1. Locate the cursor highlight to the right of SUPPLIER.
2. Key the first supplier name and press Tab (moves cursor highlight to next field).
3. Key the address field contents and press Tab.
4. Continue keying field contents for all fields of all records. (When Tab is pressed after last field, a new blank form appears.)
5. Save.

WORKS MAC

1. Key the SUPPLIER field contents (LICHEN MOTORS) for the first record. (When you key the field contents, the information appears in the Entry Bar at the top of the screen, not in the field. The Cancel box (5) and the Enter box (3) are located at the right of the Entry Bar.)
2. To enter what you keyed, strike Return or ~ the Enter box.
3. Continue keying the fields for each record. (A new blank form appears after the last field of a record is entered.)
4. Save.

L ESSON 155   RETRIEVE, MOVE AROUND, ADD RECORDS

155A ◆ CONDITIONING PRACTICE

each line twice

alphabet	1	Six glazed rolls with jam were quickly baked and provided free to all.
fig/sym	2	The 0-384 MC costs $196.75, and the 300/1200 Baud modem costs $265.89.
keypad	3	185 296 374 429 536 619 700 1,749 2,850 3,964 4,711 5,822 6,933 10,450
speed	4	Their red autobus turns to visit the busy shantytown dock by the lake.

gwam 1' | 1 | 2 | 3 | 4 | 5 | 6 | 7 | 8 | 9 | 10 | 11 | 12 | 13 | 14 |

155B ◆

RETRIEVE A FILE

Read the information at the right and then retrieve the file listed for your software.

When you retrieve a database file in an integrated software package, the procedure is similar to retrieving a word processing file. As you worked with word processing files, you learned to activate your data disk when you saved and retrieved files. Remember to do this for database lessons. *Instructions to activate your data disk drive will not be given in the lessons that follow.*

WORDPERFECT

Retrieve secondary merge file SUPPLIER.SF.

WORKS DOS

Retrieve database file SUPPLIER.WDB.

WORKS MAC

Retrieve database file SUPPLIER-DB.

Title ELECTRONIC KEYBOARD APPLICATIONS 2" TM

QS (Space down 2 DS.)

Report
body   Learning to key is of little value unless one applies it in   19

preparing something useful--a record or document of some kind.   31

Three basic kinds of software have been developed to assist those   45

with keyboarding skill in applying their skill electronically. DS   57

Side
heading Word Processing Software DS   67

Word processing software is "software specially designed to   79

assist in the document preparation needs of an individual or   91

Internal business" (Clark et al., 1990, 193). Word processing software   104
citation

permits the user to enter text, format it, manipulate or revise   117

it, and print a copy. The software can be used to process a wide   130

variety of documents such as letters, memos, reports, and tables. DS   143

This software has special features such as automatic center-   155

ing and word wrap that reduce time and effort. In addition, it   168

1" LM   permits error corrections, format and sequence changes, and   180   1" RM

insertion of variables "on screen" before a copy is printed.   193

These features increase efficiency by eliminating document   204

rekeying. DS   207

Side
heading Database Software DS   214

A database is "any collection of related items stored in   225

Internal computer memory" (Oliverio and Pasewark, 1989, 573). The data in   238
citation

a database may be about club members, employee payroll, company   251

sales, and so on. Database software allows the user to enter   263

At least 1"

Model is shown in
10-pitch type, photo-
reduced.

WORDPERFECT

You will create this file as a secondary merge file and save as file name SUPPLIER.SF (.SF for secondary file).

1. Clear the screen.
2. Press **Shift F9**.
3. Select **6**—More to get the Merge Codes commands.
4. Strike **F** and scroll down one line to select {FIELD NAMES} name1~...nameN~~; strike Enter.
5. At the *Enter Field 1:* prompt, key SUPPLIER, the first field name; strike Enter.
6. Continue keying each field name at the *Enter Field* prompt. Strike Enter after each field is keyed.
7. After keying the last field name, strike Enter at the next *Enter Field* prompt to stop entering field names and identify the end of the record.

   Field names can be separated after the tilde (~) so that each field name is on a separate line. Field names placed on separate lines are easier to review. If so, the last field name and the End Record command are separated between the two tildes.
8. Save (file name: SUPPLIER.SF).

WORKS DOS

Works DOS uses the terms field and cell interchangeably. You will create this database file in Form View and save as file name SUPPLIER. Works adds extension .WDB (WDB = Works Database). List View works nearly the same as Form View. You will use List View later.

1. From the File Menu, select Create New File.

Version 3.0: Select Create a New File from the Opening Menu.

2. Select New Database; move to Form View, if necessary (**Alt**, **V**, **F**).
3. Press **Alt**, **E**, **S** to select Insert Record from Edit.
4. Key the first field name followed by colon (:), Enter.

Version 3.0: Key first field name followed by colon (:),↓.

5. Enter again to accept defaults for field width and height.
6. Key the other field names using Steps 4 and 5.
7. Save As (file name: SUPPLIER).

WORKS MAC

You will create this database file in Form View and save as file name: SUPPLIER-DB (Supplier Database). You will use List View later.

1. From the File Menu, select New.
2. Select database icon.
3. Key each field name over highlighted word <Untitled>.
4. Accept displayed field sizes.
5. Return after each entry.
6. To end entering field names, ~<Done>.
7. Save (file name SUPPLIER-DB).

154C ◆

ADD RECORDS

Read the information at the right and then complete the steps listed for your database software.

Use U.S. Postal Service style (ALL CAPS, no periods or commas) to key the information from the following list of records. In Works, data keyed is in the field, even when it does not show on the screen.

Lichen Motors
14567 Hollister Ave.
Santa Barbara, CA 93102-9567
(805) 165-8801

Classic Salvage
1000 Mira Mesa Blvd.
El Cajon, CA 92022-0882
(619) 134-5445

Parts-4-Less
23456 Rover Rd.
Portland, OR 97210-2156
(503) 144-9090

Sports Truck Accessories
2101 Oceanside St.
Oceanside, CA 92118-1822
(619) 178-6363

North County Auto Parts
9876 Carmel Mountain Rd.
Oceanside, CA 92054-5186
(619) 177-4567

British Spares, Ltd.
P.O. Box 24567
Middlebury, VT 05753-4567
(802) 109-0025

(continued on next page)

total words

Page number

2

DS

data, retrieve and change it, or select certain data (such as an   276

address) to be used in documents. Software users can manipulate   289

and print data in report form for decision-making purposes.   302

DS

Side heading   Spreadsheet Software   310

DS

"A spreadsheet is an electronic worksheet made up of columns   322

Internal citation   and rows of data" (Oliverio and Pasewark, 1989, 489). Spread-   334

sheet software applies mathematical operations to the data and   347

prints reports that are useful in summarizing and analyzing busi-   360

1" LM   ness operations and in planning for the future.   1" RM   370

DS

Employment personnel look favorably upon job applicants who   382

are familiar with these kinds of software and how they are used.   395

QS (Space down 2 DS.)

REFERENCES   397

QS, then change to SS.

List of references   Clark, James F., et al. Computers and Information Processing.   417
2d ed. Cincinnati: South-Western Publishing Co., 1990.   428

DS

Oliverio, Mary Ellen, and William R. Pasewark. The Office.   442
Cincinnati: South-Western Publishing Co., 1989.   452

Unbound Report, Page 2

73E ◆

WORD PROCESSING ACTIVITIES

Retrieve file L73B and bold the headings in the report. If you need to, refer to 62B, p. 120.

Delete the following files from your disk (refer to 66D, p. 129 if necessary):
BLANCO   BURK
L68B   L69C
L69B

L ESSON 74   UNBOUND REPORTS

74A ◆

CONDITIONING PRACTICE

each line twice

alphabet 1 Morgan Sanchez was frequently invited to exhibit her artwork in Japan.

figures 2 We purchased 3,148 of her 7,260 shares on Thursday, December 15, 1992.

fig/sym 3 Frederick & Gilbertson paid me $635,000 for the 460 acres on 12/17/89.

speed 4 She may make us visit the big chapel in the dismal city on the island.

gwam 1' | 1 | 2 | 3 | 4 | 5 | 6 | 7 | 8 | 9 | 10 | 11 | 12 | 13 | 14 |

order, the records are rearranged quickly according to the specifications. A list of 100 names and addresses, for example, can be sorted by ZIP Code in seconds. If you save a database file after sorting it, the original order of the records will be lost. To keep the original order and preserve the original file, the sorted database file must be saved under a different file name after sorting.

MERGING

You can merge or insert database information into word processing documents. For example, names and addresses from a database file can be automatically inserted (merged) into a form letter. Merge codes or placeholders are keyed in the form letter to tell the data-base which fields to merge and where to insert them.

PRINT FORMATS

Before you can print, you must identify the fields that you want and design a layout or arrangement for the printout. This information is called the print format. Common choices of layout are the label-style format, such as for mailing labels, and the report-style (also called table-style) format, such as printouts across a page.

Most database programs justify or close up any extra space in a field so that extra spaces do not appear between items that are printed on the same line. For example, the same number of spaces would appear between the first names Alberta and José and the last name, although the first names are not the same length. The unused space in the first name field would be eliminated in the case of José. When spaces are needed between fields that are printed on the same line, the spaces can be added in the field or in the print format. Review the following example of adding spaces in a print format for a mailing label (note spaces between FIRST NAME/LAST NAME, CITY/STATE, and STATE/ZIP fields):

FIRST NAME: LAST NAME:
ADDRESS:
CITY: STATE: ZIP:

L ESSON 154   CREATE A DATABASE

154A ◆
CONDITIONING PRACTICE

each line twice SS (slowly, then faster); DS between 2-line groups; (keypad, return after each number)

alphabet 1 Gwen's six jumpers quickly seize every chance to practice before dawn.

fig/sym 2 Sam will pay $1,954 for the 16-MHz EP/37 PC which is 80286 compatible.

keypad 3 14   17 41 71   25   28 52 82 36 39 63 93 85 471 582 693 456 789 123 496 572

speed 4 They may do the handiwork for the panel with the usual vigor and rush.

gwam 1' | 1 | 2 | 3 | 4 | 5 | 6 | 7 | 8 | 9 | 10 | 11 | 12 | 13 | 14 |

154B ◆

CREATE AND SAVE A DATA-BASE FILE

Read the information at the right and then complete the steps listed on p. 313 for your database software.

One of the major advantages of using a database program is the ability to retrieve information easily. A carefully planned database can be used to retrieve information for a variety of uses. For example, an auto parts company can use a database to record sales, accumulate a reorder list, and maintain an accurate inventory. When a customer needs a particular part, the supply on hand can be checked quickly.

Wheels For Sale, a San Diego used-car firm, deals with several suppliers. The suppliers sell car parts and provide related services. Diane, the manager, asked you to create a database to help Wheels For Sale manage the list of suppliers.

    Field Names
    SUPPLIER
    ADDRESS
    CITY
    STATE
    ZIP
    PHONE

74B ◆
REPORT WITH LONG QUOTATION

File name: L74B

Document 1
Report
Format and key the report shown at the right and on the next page as a 2-page unbound report, DS. Correct errors as you key.

Long Quotations
When keying quotations of more than 3 typed lines, SS and indent them 0.5" from the LM. Leave a DS above and below them.

To indent a block of text 0.5" from the left margin do the following:

WordPerfect
Depress **F4** at beginning of the paragraph.

Works DOS
1. Depress **Alt, T**.
2. Strike **A** (spacing).
3. Change the left indent to 0.5".
4. Strike Enter. After keying the long quotation, return to start the next line.
5. Reset the left indent to 0.

Works MAC
1. Drag the left margin (and paragraph indent) 0.5" to the right.
2. Key the long quotation; return to start the next line.
3. Drag the left margin back (to the left) 0.5".

TYPEWRITERS: AN ENDANGERED SPECIES? — 7

For well over a decade, experts in office automation — 18
have predicted the demise of the typewriter. In their view — 30
the computer is destined to take over the word processing — 42
role enjoyed by the typewriter for over a century. Yet, a — 53
recent report (Fernberg, 1989, 49-50) indicates that elec- — 65
tronic typewriter shipments over the last three years aver- — 76
aged about a billion dollars a year. Further, the Computer — 88
and Business Equipment Manufacturers' Association projects — 100
that the annual growth rate will remain constant at 1.5 per- — 112
cent over the next five years. With sales holding steady at — 124
over a million units a year, the electronic typewriter does — 136
not appear endangered. It is likely here to stay--and for — 148
good reasons. — 151

Typewriter Familiarity — 160

Virtually anyone who has learned to key can sit down at — 171
the electronic typewriter and within a few minutes operate it — 184
with amazing ease and speed. According to Paez (1985, 55): — 196

SS {
A familiar keyboard, which requires fewer keystrokes and — 207
has a simpler, less code-intensive user interface, makes — 219
the transition to a high-end typewriter much easier than — 230
the transition to a personal computer with the same func- — 241
tions. — 243

Typewriter Flexibility — 252

An electronic typewriter can preform some function com- — 263
puters cannot, but a personal computer (PC) cannot be used as — 275
a mere typewriter (nor should it be). Perhaps that is why — 287
one large survey found that 85 percent of secretaries who use — 299
PCs also use typewriters. Using microchip technology, sophis- — 312
ticated electronic typewriters can perform many of the auto- — 324
matic functions and editing functions of which computers are — 336
capable. — 338

Automatic Functions. Among the features of electronic — 353
typewriters are automatic centering, returning, right-margin — 365
justifing and hang-indenting. These features are available on — 378
computers as well, but some users of both kinds of equipment — 390
say that the typewriter is more "user friendly." — 400

Editing Functions. Some electronic typewriters permit — 415
operators to backspace/delete, insert copy, move copy from — 426
one place to another, and search and replace specific words or — 439
terms in a document. Some are equiped with templates that — 451
make form fill-in easy; others permits the merging of in- — 462
formation from diferent sources. All these functions are — 474
performed without needing to rekey documents. — 482

(continued, p. 144)

UNIT 34

LESSONS 154-157

Get Started With Database Software

Learning Outcomes: After completing this unit, you will be able to

1. Access database software, create, save, and retrieve database files.
2. Add and update records.
3. Make changes to database forms and change field sizes.
4. Sort records and print merged files.

DATABASE FEATURE AND PROCEDURES GUIDE

ADDING RECORDS
FORMS, FIELDS, AND RECORDS
HELP FEATURE
MERGING
MODIFY DATABASE FORMS
PRINT FORMATS
SEQUENCE OF FIELDS
SINGLE- AND MULTIPLE-RECORD
  SCREENS
SORTING
UPDATING RECORDS
WHAT IS A DATABASE?

The paragraphs below and at the top of p. 312 give an overview of Unit 34. Read the material before starting Lesson 154. Read the paragraphs again any time you need to review database applications.

WHAT IS A DATABASE?

A database is a computerized filing system that is used to organize and maintain a collection of data. Examples of databases are lists of names and addresses, such as the list for telephone directories and the list for card catalogs in a school library.

FORMS, FIELDS, AND RECORDS

Database forms are computerized versions of paper forms, such as a job application form or a class registration form. On a printed form, you fill in the blanks with the information that is needed, such as your name and address. When you complete the form, it becomes a record of your information. In a database form, the blanks are called fields, and fields have names. Field names for a mailing list, for example,

include name, address, city, state, and ZIP Code of each person or company. When you fill in the blanks by keying the data for each field, the form becomes a record. A form and a record for a mailing label database might look like this:

Blank Form	Record (filled in form)
FIRST NAME:	FIRST NAME: ANDREA
LAST NAME:	LAST NAME: KAPPAN
ADDRESS:	ADDRESS: 1123 MARATHON DR
CITY:	CITY: SAN DIEGO
STATE:	STATE: CA
ZIP:	ZIP: 92123-4515

SEQUENCE OF FIELDS

Fields should be arranged in the same order as the data in the source document (paper form from which data is keyed). This sequence reduces the time needed to key the field contents and to maintain the records.

SINGLE- AND MULTIPLE-RECORD SCREENS

With database software you can move between single- and multiple-record screens. In other words, you can choose to view only one or more than one record at a time.

HELP FEATURE

When you are using the database application, the Help feature explains various database commands and procedures.

ADDING RECORDS

Once you create a database file and key the records, you can key additional records easily. They can be added at

the end of the file or inserted within the existing records.

UPDATING RECORDS

Updating or making changes to existing database records is similar to updating word processing documents.

MODIFY DATABASE FORMS

When necessary, you can modify a database form. For example, if a new field is needed, it can be added and then the field information for each record can be keyed. Also, a field can be deleted. When a field is deleted, however, ALL the information in that field for ALL the records is deleted.

As you become experienced with designing and using databases, you will likely develop insight into some of the common changes in needs that occur. This insight can be used when you plan new databases so that you can avoid unnecessary modifications.

SORTING

The Sort function controls the sequence of the records. Typical options are to sort in ascending or descending order of words (alphabetically) or numbers (numerically). Ascending order is from A to Z and from 0 to 9; descending order is the reverse—from Z to A and 9 to 0. Consider that ascending order is like taking an up elevator from the first floor to the top floor of a building; descending order, the reverse, is like taking the down elevator from the top floor to the first floor.

When a field is selected and a sort is specified, such as numeric in ascending

74B ◆ (cont.)

Document 2
Reference Page
Format and key a reference page from the information at the right.

Document 3
Title Page
Format and key a title page for the report. Use your name, your school name, and the current date.

Document 4
Use the move feature to move the final side heading (*Typewriter Sophistication*) and the last ¶ of text. Place this text below the first ¶ of the report.

Typewriter Sophistication | 492

    Electronic typewriters range from low-end machines with | 503
limited features and without editing windows to high-end | 514
machines with full-page displays, diskete storage, and com- | 526
plete text-editing capabilities. The price range varies with | 539
the number of advanced features included. Some machines are | 551
upgradable so that the apropriate level of sophistocation | 563
can be obtained without replacing machines. | 572

REFERENCES | 574

Audion, Mark. "Using Electronic Typewriters: The Basics, | 584
    Plus. . . ." *Today's Office*, July 1986, 55-64. | 597

Fernberg, Patricia M. "Electronic Typewriters: Understanding | 610
    the Product." *Modern Office Technology*, March 1989, | 625
    48-50. | 627

Paze, Patricia. "Typewriters: Technology with an Easy | 638
    Touch." *Today's Office*, September 1985, 55-72. | 650

LESSON 75   UNBOUND REPORTS

75A ◆ CONDITIONING PRACTICE

each line twice

alphabet 1   Jackson believed he might maximize profits with a quality sales force.

figures 2   Jo's social security number, 504-18-2397, was recorded as 504-18-2396.

fig/sym 3   Invoice #689 (dated 10/24) for $3,575 was paid on Tuesday, November 1.

speed 4   Their neighbor may dismantle the ancient ricksha in the big cornfield.

gwam 1' | 1 | 2 | 3 | 4 | 5 | 6 | 7 | 8 | 9 | 10 | 11 | 12 | 13 | 14 |

75B ◆ FORMAT ENUMERATED ITEMS

File name: L75B

Document 1
Report
Format and key the copy at the right and on the next page as an unbound report. Place the reference list below the last line of copy on page 2 of the report. Correct errors as you key.

words

BASIC STRATEGIES FOR EFFECTIVE STUDY | 7

    Effective learning depends upon good study habits. Efficient study skills | 22
do not simply occur; they must first be learned and then applied consis- | 37
tently. Good study strategies include a preset time for study, a desirable | 52
place to study, and a well-designed study plan. | 62

A Time for Study | 68

    All of us think we have more things to do than we have time to do, and | 82
studying gets shortchanged. It is important to prepare a schedule of daily ac- | 98
tivities that includes time slots for doing the studying we have to do. Within | 114
each study slot, write in the specific study activity; for example, "Read Unit 6 | 130
of accounting; do Problems 1-5." Keep the schedule flexible so that it can be | 146
modified after you assess your success in meeting your study goals within | 161
each time slot. | 164

(continued, p. 145)

words

A Place to Study 171

Choose the best place to study and use the same one every day. Doing so 185 will help to put you in a study mood when you enter that place. According to 201 Usova (1989, 37), "The library is not always a desirable place to study." Choose 217 a place that has the fewest distractions such as people traffic, conversation, 233 telephone, TV, and outside noises. Study is usually best done alone and in the 249 absence of sights and sounds that distract the eye and ear. In your chosen 264 quiet place, force the mind to concentrate on the task at hand. 277

A Plan for Study 284

Research on the effects of specific study skills on student performance 298 (Dansereau, 1985, 39) suggests that the following study tactics help to im- 313 prove academic performance. 319

1. Skim a unit or a chapter, noting headings, topic sentences, key words, 334 and definitions. This overview will clue you to what you are about to 348 study. 350

2. As you read a unit or chapter, convert the headings into questions; then 365 seek answers to those questions as you read. 374

3. If you own the book, use color marking pens to highlight important 389 ideas: headings, topic sentences, special terms, definitions, and support- 403 ing facts. If you don't own the book, make notes of these important ideas 418 and facts. 421

4. After you have completed a unit or chapter, review the highlighted 435 items (or your notes which contain them). 444

5. Using the headings stated as questions, see if you can answer those 458 questions based on your reading. 465

6. Test yourself to see if you can recall definitions of important terms and 480 lists of supporting facts or ideas. 488

A high correlation exists between good study habits and good grades for 502 the courses taken in school. 508

Enumerated Items
1. Block a series of numbered items 0.5" from the LM.
2. SS each item, but DS between items and above and below the series.
3. Use the procedures outlined in 74B on p. 143 for indenting.

Document 2
Title Page
Format and key a title page for the report using your name, your school name, and the current date.

REFERENCES 510

Dansereau, D.F. "Learning Strategy Research." <u>Thinking and Learning</u> 529
<u>Skills</u>. Vol. l. Hillsdale, NJ: Lawrence Erlbaum, 1985, 21-40. 543
Usova, George M. <u>Efficient Study Strategies</u>. Pacific Grove, CA: Brooks/ 563
Cole Publishing Company, 1989. 569

LESSON 76 | UNBOUND REPORTS

76A ◆
CONDITIONING PRACTICE
each line twice

alphabet 1 The vast Cox farm was just sold by the bank at quite an amazing price.
figures 2 Their firm constructed 340 of the 560 new homes between 1987 and 1992.
fig/sym 3 Martin paid Invoice #382 ($56.79 with a 5% discount) with Check #1084.
speed 4 The girls and the maid may go downtown to pay for the six giant signs.

gwam 1' | 1 | 2 | 3 | 4 | 5 | 6 | 7 | 8 | 9 | 10 | 11 | 12 | 13 | 14 |

PART 4

Database Applications

Database Report A report that organizes and summarizes database information for printing. Database reports are updated automatically if the database information changes.

Field Each item of a database form, such as first name and last name. Sometimes called cells or categories.

Form A computer version of a printed form.

Formula A mathematical expression that defines the relationship among two or more fields or cells in a database.

Function A built-in formula that performs a calculation automatically when it is used in a formula. SUM, AVG, COUNT, MIN, and MAX are examples of frequently used functions.

Introductory Page Rows Lines in a database report used for column headings and any following blank lines that are to be printed at the top of each page of a report.

Introductory Report Rows Lines in a database report used for the report title(s) and blank lines that follow the last title line.

Label Print Format A format used to print selected fields in a specified sequence, as for mailing labels.

Merge Codes In the merge process, these codes tell the software where to insert or merge each variable, such as a name and address within a letter.

Multiple-Record Layout Information in each record displayed on a single line in table format (*see* Single-Record Layout).

Print Format Specifies the sequence and arrangement of the fields to be printed.

Record A blank form that is completed with information for each field.

Record Rows Lines in a database report used to print text for each record included in the report.

Report Definition A table layout that displays the field contents in columns.

Report View An option that allows a user to create or view a database report.

Search Criteria Defining exactly what database information is wanted.

Selection Criteria Specific qualifications that are defined for selecting records that match the specified requirements.

Single-Record Layout Information in a single record displayed (*see* Multiple-Record Layout).

Sort Arranging information in alphabetical or numerical order in ascending order (smallest to largest number or A to Z) or descending order (largest to smallest number or Z to A).

Summary Rows Lines in a database report used to print the desired statistical data or text that is to appear at the end of each grouping and/or at the end of the report, including any desired blank lines.

Wildcard Characters In a database search, the characters that allow retrieval of information when the complete or exact search criteria are not known. Also a file name specifier used to find all files that contain a specific character or set of characters in the file name.

Zoom A command to switch between the multiple-record layout and the single-record layout.

UNBOUND REPORT

words

READING FOR KEYBOARDING AND FORMATTING   8

When learning to key, format, and process documents, a major portion of one's time is spent reading. Two different reading processes are used in learning: reading for meaning and reading for "copy getting."   16 25 35 44 50

Reading for Meaning   58

When one reads an explanation and description of a document format or directions for completing a keying task, the purpose of reading is to process information and to acquire meaning or understanding (de Fossard, 1990, 1). Such reading requires focusing on the content: its organization, sequence, ideas, terms, and facts. The objective is to assimilate them, store them, and recall them in proper order for later use. Reading for meaning is very important when learning terms, concepts, and procedures. Such reading is preferably done with speed followed by review.   66 75 85 94 103 113 123 133 142 151 160 170 172

Reading for Copy Getting   182

When one reads a drill or document for the purpose of copying it by means of a keyboard, one reads to "get the copy" to feed through the brain at the speed the fingers are able to record it by striking the keys (West, 1983, 130). The purpose is not to understand the   191 200 210 219 227 236

words

message or to get meaning from it; rather, the purpose is to reproduce the message character for character. In initial learning, this process is done on a letter-by-letter basis. As skill grows, however, the process begins to include "chains" of letters and short words that are perceived and responded to as units. Rarely, though, can a keyboard operator feed the fingers more than one or two words at a time unless the words are short.   245 254 264 274 283 292 301 310 319 324

Reading for copy getting requires that the speed of reading be synchronized with the fingers' ability to make the keystrokes required to reproduce the words. In this process, the mind is concerned with the form and sequence of the letters and words, not with the meaning of the message the letters and words convey. This kind of reading must be done at a slower pace that is deliberate but harmonious.   333 342 352 361 371 380 389 398 405

REFERENCES   407

de Fossard, Esta. Reading in Focus. 3d ed. Cincinnati: South-Western Publishing Co., 1990.   420 428 430

West, L. J. Acquisition of Typewriting Skills. 2d ed. Indianapolis: Bobbs-Merrill Educational Publishing, 1983.   446 455 459

EDITING ACTIVITY

File name: L76C

Retrieve file L74B and edit the first paragraph to agree with the text at the right. Save updated file under L76C.

For over a decade, office automation experts have speculated about the demise of the typewriter. In their view, the computer will assume the word processing role held by the typewriter for more than a century. Ironically, a recent report (Fernberg, 1989, 49-50) indicates that electronic typewriter sales over the last three years averaged about a billion dollars each year.

L ESSON 77   UNBOUND REPORTS

77A ◆
CONDITIONING PRACTICE

each line twice

alphabet 1 For the next two weeks you could save the big quilts for major prizes.

figures 2 Kane received 1,845 votes; Kennedy, 973 votes; and Mertins, 602 votes.

fig/sym 3 Their bill came to $68.19 ($47.63 for paper and $20.56 for envelopes).

speed 4 Their neighbor on the cozy island is the chair of the sorority social.

gwam 1' | 1 | 2 | 3 | 4 | 5 | 6 | 7 | 8 | 9 | 10 | 11 | 12 | 13 | 14 |

DRILL AND PRACTICE

1. Key each line twice SS (once slowly, then faster).
2. Key a 1' writing on each line.
3. Rekey slower lines for speed.

alphabet	1	Gomez jokes expertly with a friend but can be very shy and very quiet.
figures	2	The data are given in Figures 26 and 27 of Part 14, Unit 39, page 50.
fig/sym	3	Invoice #14729 was paid by Byron & Gibb's check (#6058) on January 13.
Shift keys	4	Donald, Tom, Jan, and I all live on Park Haven Court, two blocks away.
Space Bar	5	Sean may meet his mom at noon at an inn by a big park in the old city.
adjacent keys	6	They were there when the popular soprano with the operatic voice sang.
speed	7	Eighty of the men may work for the island firms if they make a profit.

gwam 1' | 1 | 2 | 3 | 4 | 5 | 6 | 7 | 8 | 9 | 10 | 11 | 12 | 13 | 14 |

IMPROVE/ CHECK SKILL

1. Key two 1' writings on each ¶; find *gwam*.
2. Key two 3' writings on ¶s 1-3 combined; find *gwam* and count errors.
3. Key a 5' writing on ¶s 1-3 combined; find *gwam* and count errors.

all letters used | A | 1.5 si | 5.7 awl | 80% hfw

gwam 3' | 5'

Character is often described as a person's combined moral or ethical strength. Most people think it is like integrity, which is thought to be a person's ability to adhere to a code or a set standard of values. If a person's values are accepted by society, others are likely to view her or him as having a somewhat high degree of integrity.

You need to know that character is a trait that everyone possesses and that it is formed over time. A person's character reflects his or her definition of what is good or just. Most children and teenagers mold their character through the words and deeds of parents, teachers, and other adults with whom they have regular contact.

Existing character helps mold future character. It is important to realize that today's actions can have a lasting effect. For that reason, there is no better time than now to make all your words and deeds speak favorably. You want them to portray the things others require of people who are thought to possess a high degree of character.

3'	5'
5	3 44
9	6 47
14	8 49
19	11 52
23	14 55
27	16 57
32	19 60
37	22 63
42	25 66
45	27 68
50	30 71
54	33 74
59	36 77
64	38 79
68	41 82

gwam 3' | 1 | 2 | 3 | 4 | 5 |
5' | 1 | 2 | 3 |

WORD PROCESSING FEATURES

File name: L77B

1. Study the information at the right about the tab feature.
2. Complete the drills below.

Tab. A tab is a feature that causes the cursor to skip across the screen to a point set by the operator or to the default tabs preset every 0.5". Three types of tabs (left, right, and decimal) align copy for easy reading. A left tab places text to the right of the tab. A right tab places text to the left of the tab. A decimal tab aligns numbers at the decimal point.

WORDPERFECT

1. Depress **Shift F8**.
2. Strike **L**(ine).
3. Strike **T**(ab Set).
4. Depress Home, Home, ← .
5. Depress **Ctrl End** (clears tabs).
6. Key number for new tab and strike Return for each tab to be set. If a Decimal or Right tab is desired, key the first letter of the desired type (D or R) after keying number and striking Return key.
7. Depress **F7** twice.

Notes: Tabs can be set for relative or absolute by adjusting **T**(ype) in the tab command list. The default is set for relative: Tabs are measured from the left margin and will change automatically when the left margin is changed.

A single tab can be deleted by moving the cursor to the tab and striking the Delete or Backspace key.

WORKS DOS

1. **Alt, T**.
2. Strike **T**(abs).
3. **Alt A** (clears existing tabs).
4. Key number for new tab setting.
5. Strike Return.
6. If you wish to change the alignment (left, right, decimal), use arrow keys to make new selection. Once you have all selections made, strike Return.
7. After you finish keying tab settings, depress **Alt D** to return to input screen.

Note: Preset tabs to the left of a newly set tab are automatically removed when the new tab is set.

WORKS MAC

1. Move the pointer to the position just beneath the ruler where you want a tab set.
2. To set a left tab ~; to set a right tab ~~; and to set a decimal tab ~~~.

Notes: A tab can be removed by dragging the tab set down into the text and releasing the mouse button.

Preset tabs to the left of a newly set tab are automatically removed when the new tab is inserted.

Drill 1

1. Clear the screen.
2. Following the procedure outlined above for your software, set a left tab at 1", 3", and 5".
3. Key the information at the right.
4. Insert a page break.

1st tab (left)	2d tab (left)	3d tab (left)
Mary Smith	June 20	1956
Jose Martinez	September 8	1961
Roberto Sanchez	February 7	1966
Leo Vang	April 15	1965
Marsha Cey	July 2	1959

Drill 2

1. Clear all existing tabs using the procedure outlined above for your software.
2. Set a left tab at 1", a decimal tab at 4", and a right tab at 6".
3. Key the information at the right.
4. Save file.

1st tab (left)	2d tab (decimal)	3d tab (right)
Jay Chang	125.00	Senior
Tim Ellickson	95.25	Junior
Vladamar Getz	88.90	Freshman
Mike Lofton	63.75	Sophomore
Mary Skidmore	180.50	Junior
Maria Valdez	92.75	Sophomore

ASSESSMENT ACTIVITIES

Activity 1

Prepare a worksheet.

1. Key the information at the right in the cells designated.
2. Move the rows as needed to arrange them in alphabetic order.
3. In A6, use the IF function to compare the average of the numbers in Column B to the average of Column C. IF statements follow.
   Lotus:
   @IF(@AVG(B1.B5)>@AVG(C1.C5),@AVG(B1.B5),@AVG(C1.C5))
   Works DOS:
   =IF(AVG(B1:B5)>AVG(C1:C5),AVG(B1:B5),AVG(C1:C5))
   Works MAC:
   =IF(AVERAGE(B1:B5)>AVERAGE(C1:C5),AVERAGE(B1:B5), AVERAGE(C1:C5))
4. In B6 and C6, use the AVG (AVERAGE) function to average B1 through B4 and C1 through C4, respectively, to verify the accuracy of the IF function.

	A	B	C
1	Erie	5976	6017
2	Detroit	4829	5104
3	Boise	5741	5296
4	Houston	6975	6854

5. Multiply each number in Column C by the number in B4 and put the result in the adjacent cell in Column D.
   a. Use a formula that makes reference to B4 absolute.
      Lotus: +C1*$B$4
      Works: =C1*$B$4
   b. Copy the formula to other rows in Column D.
6. Change B4 to **9000** to change all values in Column D.
7. Copy all entries in Column B to Column E.
8. Display all formulas in the worksheet.
9. Widen all columns, except A, to display the entire formula or number.
10. Save the worksheet as 153B1.

Activity 2

Prepare a worksheet and a bar chart.

1. Key the information at the right as a worksheet.
2. Arrange the rows in alphabetic order.
3. Compute the total deliveries for each carrier, for each week, and for all carriers.
4. Create a bar chart showing the carriers along the x-axis and the deliveries for each week along the y-axis.
5. Key **NEWSPAPER DELIVERIES** as the title, **CARRIER** as the x-axis title, and **DELIVERIES** as the y-axis title.
6. Lotus users only: Save the chart as a PIC file named 153B2.
7. Save the worksheet as 153B2.

	A	B	C	D	E	F
1	Carrier	Week 1	Week 2	Week 3	Week 4	Total
2						
3	Sue Block	235	257	259	264	
4	Raul Luez	278	281	274	289	
5	Li Chu	292	288	281	277	
6						
7	Totals					

Activity 3

Prepare a worksheet and a pie chart.

1. Key the information at the right as a worksheet.
2. Create a pie chart. Include a title and label and shade each wedge; if possible, explode the smallest wedge of the chart.
3. Save the worksheet as 153B3 (Lotus users should save the chart as a PIC file named 153B3).

	A	B
1	VOTER REGISTRATION	
2		
3	District 15	24,950
4	District 18	26,727
5	District 23	30,508
6	District 35	21,063

FILE MAINTENANCE

If instructed by your teacher, erase all spreadsheet files from your disk except those that begin with T and these files: 146B, 148D1, 148D2, 148D3, and 152B3.

File name: L77C
SM: 1"; TM: 2"

Outline 1
1. Review the information at the right.
2. Format and key the outline.

WordPerfect and Works DOS
Tabs are relative to the left margin. For example, a relative tab set at 0.5 is one-half inch from wherever the left margin is set. Set tabs at 0.5", 0.9", and 1.3".

Works MAC
Each mark on the ruler is 1/8". Set tabs at 3/8", 5/8", and 7/8".

Outline 2
Format and key the outline shown at the right.

Space forward once from margin

1st tab

2nd tab

3rd tab

```
                    SPACING TOPIC OUTLINES
                                         QS
I.   VERTICAL SPACING          ←—— DS
     A.  Title of Outline
         1.  Two-inch top margin
         2.  Followed by 3 blank line spaces (QS)
     B.  Major Headings
         1.  First major heading preceded by a QS; all
             others preceded by 1 blank line space (DS)
         2.  All followed by a DS
         3.  All subheadings single-spaced (SS)
                                               DS
II.  HORIZONTAL SPACING
                       DS
     A.  Title of Outline Centered over the Line of Writing
     B.  Major Headings and Subheadings
         1.  Identifying Roman numerals at left margin (periods
             aligned) followed by 2 spaces
         2.  Identifying letters and numbers for each subsequent
             level of subheading aligned below the first word of
             the preceding heading, followed by 2 spaces
```

Hard return and then *tab 3 times*

```
                    EMPLOYMENT COMMUNICATIONS
                              QS
I.   PERSONAL DATA SHEET

     A.  Personal Information                    lc
         1.  Name, address, and Telephone number      if needed
         2.  Social Security number (work permit number)
         3.  Personal interests:  hobbies/recreational interests
     B.  Educational Information
         1.  Schools attended and dates of attendance
         2.  Special areas of study; activities; awards received
     C.  Work Experience
         1.  Jobs held; what you experienced; commendations
         2.  Volunteer work
DS   D.  References (Teachers, Work Supervisors)
II.  LETTER OF APPLICATION

     A.  Source of Information about Job Opening
     B.  Expression of Interest in Being Interviewed for the Job
     C.  Brief Summary of Work Skills and How They Fit the Job
         1.  Special courses that are applicable to the job
         2.  Work experiences make you qualified for the job
     D.  Request for Interview that

III. THANK-YOU LETTER FOLLOWING INTERVIEW
     A.  Appreciation for Courtesies Shown During Company Visit
DS   B.  Positive Impressions of Company and Employees
     C.  Expression of Continued Interest in the Job
```

Activity 2

Use the information at the right to construct a worksheet and then create a pie chart. Include a title and label and shade each wedge; if possible, explode the largest wedge.

	A	B	C	D
1	FAN ATTENDANCE BY GEOGRAPHIC AREA			
2				
3		NUMBER		
4	AREA	OF FANS		
5				
6	NORTH	523,437		
7	SOUTH	675,981		
8	EAST	437,899		
9	WEST	775,914		

Activity 3

Prepare a worksheet and bar chart.

1. Retrieve file 150B2.
2. Create a bar chart that shows the total income for each training course for each month.
   a. Chart the training courses along the x-axis and the monthly income along the y-axis.
   b. Key **TRAINING COURSE IN-COME** as the title.
   c. Key **COURSE** as the x-axis title.
   d. Key **INCOME** as the y-axis title.
   e. Lotus: Save the chart as PIC file 1SLBAR.
      Works DOS: Rename Chart1 to 1SLBAR.
3. Copy the labels in B1 through G7 to a block in which the upper-left cell is

	J	K	L	M
1				
2				
3	9000	7050	9140	6120
4	3000	3000	3000	3000
5	8750	10100	10940	8000
6	3200	2450	3450	1975

J1 (if needed, extend the line through the end of the last column).
4. Clear the values in J3 through M6.
5. Key the information above in the cells designated.
6. Add two rows at the top of the worksheet.
7. In B1, key **OAHU**; in J1 key **MAUAI**.

8. Format numbers as dollars (no cents) with commas.
9. Format column widths and headings appropriately.
10. Save the worksheet and chart as 152B3 for use in Part 5 (Integrated Software Applications) of this textbook.

LESSON 153   ASSESS SPREADSHEET AND CHARTING SKILLS

153A ♦
CONDITIONING
PRACTICE

each line twice

alphabet 1 Robert kept examining the size and quality of the very choice jewelry.
figures 2 He scored 94, 75, 82, 64, and 100 on the quizzes for an average of 83.
keypad 3 41 52 63 47 58 69 70 80 90 404 505 606 101 202 303 707 808 909 500 600
speed 4 The eight giant signs are downtown by the city chapel by the big lake.

gwam 1' | 1 | 2 | 3 | 4 | 5 | 6 | 7 | 8 | 9 | 10 | 11 | 12 | 13 | 14 |

78A ◆
CONDITIONING PRACTICE

each line twice

alphabet	1	Everyone except Zelda Jenkins will be required to go to the math fair.
figures	2	Jo's Nursery sold 370 trees and 458 shrubs between May 29 and June 16.
fig/sym	3	The checks written on 8/4 ($81.52) and 9/3 ($68.70) were not recorded.
speed	4	The box with the emblem of the bugle is on the mantle by the fishbowl.

gwam 1' | 1 | 2 | 3 | 4 | 5 | 6 | 7 | 8 | 9 | 10 | 11 | 12 | 13 | 14 |

78B ◆

ASSESS SKILL: UNBOUND REPORTS

File name: L78B

1. Format and key the report in unbound style.
2. Format the reference list on a separate sheet.

REFERENCES

Hamel, Ruth. "Making Summer Earnings Work for You." USA Weekend, 2-4, June 1989, 10-11.

Kushner, John. How to Find and Apply for a Job. Cincinnati: South-Western Publishing Co., 1989.

3. Prepare a title page using your name, school name, and the current date.

words

THE IMPORTANCE OF WORK EXPERIENCE   7

A part-time or summer job pays more than money. Although the money 20
earned is important, the work experience gained has a greater long-term 35
value when one applies for a full-time job after graduation from school. Job 50
application forms (the application blank and the personal data sheet) ask you 66
to list jobs you have held and to list as references the names of individuals 82
who supervised your work. As one young person was heard to remark, "You 96
can't get a job without experience and you can't get experience without a 111
job." That dilemma can be overcome, however, by starting to work early in 126
life and by accepting simpler jobs that have no minimum age limit and do not 141
require experience. 146

Jobs Teens Can Do 153

Start early at jobs that may not pay especially well but help to establish a 168
working track record: baby-sitting, delivering newspapers, mowing lawns, 183
assisting with gardening, and the like. Use these work experiences as spring- 198
boards for such later jobs as sales clerk, gas station attendant, fast food 213
worker, lifeguard, playground supervisor assistant, and office staff assistant 229
(after you have developed basic office skills). As you progress through these 245
work exploration experiences, try increasingly to get jobs that have some re- 260
lationship to your career plans. If, for example, you want a career involving 276
frequent contact with people--as in sales--seek part-time and summer work 291
that gives you experience in dealing with people (Hamel, 1989, 10). 305

How to Handle Yourself on the Job 318

Whatever the job you are able to get, the following pointers will help you 333
succeed in getting a good recommendation for the next job you seek. 347

1. Be punctual. Get to work on time and return from lunch and other 361
breaks promptly. 364

2. Get along well with others. Do your job well and offer to assist others 380
who may need help. Take direction with a smile instead of a frown. 394

3. Speak proper English. Teenage jargon is often lost on the adults who 408
are likely to be your supervisors. 416

4. Dress the part. Observe the unwritten dress code; dress as others on 430
the job do. Always be neat and clean. 438

references 487

152A ◆ CONDITIONING PRACTICE
each line twice

alphabet 1	Mr. Zahn will ask very specific questions before judging the exhibits.
figures 2	Only 32 of the 64 computers were replaced in 1990 with the B758 model.
keypad 3	4 7 1 471 5 8 2 582 6 9 3 693 14 74 25 85 36 96 147 258 369 0 40 50 60
speed 4	The formal social for the visitor is to be held in the ancient chapel.

gwam 1' | 1 | 2 | 3 | 4 | 5 | 6 | 7 | 8 | 9 | 10 | 11 | 12 | 13 | 14 |

152B ◆ REVIEW ACTIVITIES

Activity 1
Prepare a worksheet.

1. Key the information below in the cells designated.

	A	B
1	1400	1457
2	1548	1632
3	2496	2387
4	4513	4397
5	2835	2854

2. In A8, use an IF statement to compare the sum of Column A to the sum of Column B. If A is larger, print the sum of A; if A is not larger, print the sum of B. IF statements follow.

   Lotus:
   @IF(@SUM(A1.A5)>@SUM(B1.B5),@SUM(A1.A5),@SUM(B1.B5))

   Works:
   =IF(SUM(A1:A5)>SUM(B1:B5), SUM(A1:A5),SUM(B1:B5))

3. In A6 and B6, use the SUM function to add A1 through A5 and B1 through B5, respectively, to verify the accuracy of the IF function.

4. Multiply each value in Column B by the value in A1 and print the result in the adjacent cell in Column C.
   a. Write a formula in C1 that makes A1 an absolute cell address.
      Lotus: **+B1∗$A$1**
      Works: **=B1∗$A$1**
   b. Copy the formula to other rows in Column C.
5. Add the numbers in each row for Rows 1 through 6; divide each row's sum by B5; and print each result in the adjacent cell of Column D.
   a. Write a formula in D1 that makes the reference to B5 absolute.
      Lotus: **+SUM(A1.C1)/$B$5**
      Works: **=SUM(A1:C1)/$B$5**
   b. Copy the formula to other rows in Column D.
6. How much do the values in D1 and D2 change if the value of B5 is increased to 3000?
   a. Key (do not copy) the numbers in D1 and D2 into cells E1 and E2, respectively.
   b. Change the value in B5 to **3000**.
   c. In F1 and F2 use a formula that prints the differences between D1 and E1, D2 and E2, respectively.
7. Change the value of B5 to **6000**.
8. Display the formulas in the cells.
9. Widen all Columns B through F so that the entire formula appears.
10. Copy the values in A1 through A5 to Column F making F4 the upper cell.
11. Save the worksheet as 152B1.

Master Keyboarding Skills

Learning Outcomes: After completing this unit, you will be able to

1. Demonstrate improved response patterns and use of service keys.
2. Demonstrate improved technique and speed on statistical copy.
3. Key straight-copy paragraphs with higher speed and improved control.

L ESSON 79   KEYBOARDING SKILLS

SM: Defaults; LS: SS

79A ◆ 6'
CONDITIONING PRACTICE

each line twice SS; then two 1' writings on line 4; find *gwam*

alphabet 1 Cho just dropped a quaint pink vase we got on sale for my next bazaar.
figures 2 What is the sum of 16 3/8 and 27 4/5 and 49 1/2 and 10 2/3 and 17 1/6?
fig/sym 3 There is a credit (on 9/3) of $418.23 and a debit (on 9/25) of $76.02.
speed 4 He may go with them to a small town by the lake to do the work for us.

gwam 1' | 1 | 2 | 3 | 4 | 5 | 6 | 7 | 8 | 9 | 10 | 11 | 12 | 13 | 14 |

79B ◆ 24'

MASTER TECHNIQUE

1. Key lines 1-20 twice as shown.
2. Key a 1' writing on each of lines 21-24; find *gwam* on each writing.
3. Rekey selected lines.

fig/sym 1 5/8" hose | $13.75 rebate | 6.5% tax | 60-watt bulb | May 27, 1994 | 8-day clock
2 Our check (#2947) for $1,263.85 covers your 4/18/95 Invoice #302-4847.
alphabet 3 axe pax zoo bid jug sue wit name club have quit from works small might
4 Zelma quickly made six jugs of punch to serve by the new pool at noon.
bottom row 5 am ban zam fax jab cash lamb java mass band sack mask flax black smash
6 Malana can send a flash on a fax machine she has in a small black van.
third row 7 owe you pet wit let kit top quo row pro your quit spot hurt left story
8 Porter should take the top spot if he will just go for his goal daily.
adjacent keys 9 ask pop saw ore sop news open true suit part aids buys blew silk stalk
10 Opal said that more than forty people were asked to join the new club.
long, direct reaches 11 sum ice sun ace gun deck spun nice must smug buns myth curb vice bring
12 Alice must curb any doubt she harbors about my zany and new ice dance.
double letters 13 off all odd fee keen ally meek fell seek foot jell roof been tell roll
14 Lee is keen to tell all about a fall he took from a little abbey roof.
one hand 15 limp card join best pool ever upon area hull case jump data milk start
16 John set up a data card on a red oil pump at my mill as you are aware.
balanced hand 17 city shall right their slant visit shelf tight ivory curls fight shale
18 Jane may pay for the chair with the profit she got for an antique urn.
balanced & one hand 19 the pop hay few pay set she him bit hip they test with grew then start
20 Drew was to get a neighbor to start my car or to tow it to the garage.
combination response 21 Brad is to serve on a panel at the union to set up the rates for work.
22 We shall bear right at the fork in the wood to a grass knoll and rest.
word response 23 Helen may row to the island with a neighbor girl to dig for big clams.
24 Clancy may wish to do the audit for the panel chair for the usual pay.

gwam 1' | 1 | 2 | 3 | 4 | 5 | 6 | 7 | 8 | 9 | 10 | 11 | 12 | 13 | 14 |

151B ◆ (cont.)

5. Copy the B22 formula to C22, E22, and F22.
6. In D10, compute the % change in applications by using (B10–C10)/C10 in a formula.
7. Copy the D10 formula to appropriate rows in Column D.
8. In G10, compute the % change in acceptances by using (E10 – F10)/F10 in a formula.
9. Copy the G10 formula to appropriate rows in Column G.
10. Format all numbers to have commas and Columns D and G as Percent with 1 decimal place.
11. Establish appropriate column widths and right-align all column headings.
12. Draw a line in Rows 6, 9, and 21.
13. Save the worksheet as 151B2.

	A	B	C	D	E	F	G	H
1	ADMISSION REPORT							
2								
3	YEAR-TO-DATE COMPARISON OF APPLICATIONS RECEIVED AND ACCEPTANCES							
4								
5		APPLICATIONS			APPLICATIONS			
6								
7		THIS	LAST	%	THIS	LAST	%	
8	PROGRAM	YEAR	YEAR	CHANGE	YEAR	YEAR	CHANGE	
9								
10	ACCOUNTING	274	256		175	183		
11	ADMIN MGT	155	143		98	101		
12	BUS TEACH ED	55	49		32	30		
13	ECONOMICS	33	32		28	25		
14	ENGLISH	97	99		66	71		
15	FINANCE	12	10		7	6		
16	HEALTH ADMIN	35	30		22	20		
17	MANAGEMENT	265	254		212	215		
18	MARKETING	174	183		135	155		
19	SPORT MGT	66	52		44	32		
20								
21	TOTALS							

Activity 3

Prepare a worksheet.

1. Key the information at the right.
2. Delete Jim Skolski's name and scores from the electronic grade book.
3. Add Jim Jarvis between Gomez and Martinez and record scores of 70 on Test Three, 75 on Test Four, and 74 on Test Five.
4. In G8, compute Berryman's average score.
   Lotus: **@AVG(B8.F8)**
   Works DOS: **=AVG(B8:F8)**
   Works MAC: **=AVERAGE(B8:F8)**
5. Copy the formula to appropriate rows.
6. In B16, compute the average score on Test One (refer to average functions in Step 4) and then copy this formula to C16 through F16.
7. In B17, compute the minimum score on Test One and then copy this formula to C17 through F17.
   Lotus: **@MIN(B8.B14)**
   Works: **=MIN(B8:B14)**
8. In B18, compute the maximum score on Test One and then copy this formula to C18 through G18.
   Lotus: **@MAX(B8.B14)**
   Works: **=MAX(B8:B14)**
9. Formats: numbers fixed with one decimal point; column widths to 6 spaces; right-align column headings in B-G.
10. Draw lines in Rows 4, 7, and 15.
11. Save the worksheet as 151B3.

	A	B	C	D	E	F	G
1	ELECTRONIC GRADE BOOK						
2							
3	MICROCOMPUTER APPLICATIONS COURSE--19--						
4							
5		TEST	TEST	TEST	TEST	TEST	TEST
6	STUDENT	ONE	TWO	THREE	FOUR	FIVE	AVG
7							
8	JIM BERRYMAN	85	81	71	77	65	
9	SUSAN CLARKSON	91	84	87	93	86	
10	RUTH FORD	71	65	78	75	71	
11	SARA GOMEZ	97	99	100	92	94	
12	JAMES MARTINI	78	84	81	76	88	
13	JIM SOLSKI	68	75	79	83	84	
14	HARRY THOMPSON	97	92	85	95	98	
15							
16	AVERAGE SCORE						
17	LOW SCORE						
18	HIGH SCORE						

IMPROVE/ CHECK SKILLS

1. Key two 1' writings on each ¶; find *gwam* on each writing.
2. Key two 2' writings on ¶s 1-3 combined; find *gwam* on each.
3. Key two 3' writings on ¶s 1-3 combined; find *gwam* and count errors on each. Record *gwam* on each length writing for future use.

gwam	¼'	½'	¾'	1'
20	5	10	15	20
24	6	12	18	24
28	7	14	21	28
32	8	16	24	32
36	9	18	27	36
40	10	20	30	40
44	11	22	33	44
48	12	24	36	48
52	13	26	39	52
56	14	28	42	56

all letters used | A | 1.5 si | 5.7 awl | 80% hfw

	gwam 2'	3'
Human relations skills on the job are very critical in terms of	6	4
how you will be perceived by peers as well as by superiors. During	13	9
your early weeks at work, you will be sized up quickly by coworkers.	20	14
How they observe and evaluate you will help to determine whether your	27	18
work experience will be pleasant, successful, and valuable.	33	22
Be cautious at first and do not align yourself closely with any	40	26
of the cliques that often develop in the workplace. Show understand-	46	31
ing and be courteous to everybody, but don't take sides in a dispute	53	36
that may occur between members of any group of workers. Show that you	60	40
can think for yourself, but don't convey your ideas too freely.	67	45
Look, listen, and learn before you take an active part in the poli-	73	49
tics of the workplace. Let the older, experienced workers be the agents	80	54
of change. Study and learn from them and carefully notice what seems	88	59
to cause their successes or failures. As you develop on a job, all	95	68
positive human relations skills will be rewarded.	99	71

gwam 2' | 1 | 2 | 3 | 4 | 5 | 6 | 7 |
3' | 1 | 2 | 3 | 4 | 5 |

LESSON 80   KEYBOARDING SKILLS

SM: Defaults; LS: SS

CONDITIONING PRACTICE

each line twice SS; then two 1' writings on line 4; find *gwam*

alphabet 1	Al criticized my six workers for having such quick tempers on the job.
figures 2	Add 14 meters 25 centimeters, 89 meters 36 centimeters, and 70 meters.
fig/sym 3	Both start today (6/7): Tina Ho at $421.89/wk.; Vic Kuo at $10.53/hr.
speed 4	It is the wish of all of us to lend a hand to the visitor to the city.

gwam 1' | 1 | 2 | 3 | 4 | 5 | 6 | 7 | 8 | 9 | 10 | 11 | 12 | 13 | 14 |

IMPROVE/ CHECK SKILLS

1. Key 1', 2', and 3' writings on 79C above as directed there. Record 3' *gwam* for future reference.

1' Goal: 3 gwam increase
2' Goal: 2 gwam increase
3' Goal: 1 gwam increase

2. Key selected lines of 79B, p. 150, to improve technique.

151A ◆ CONDITIONING PRACTICE

each line twice

alphabet	1	Seven new boys qualified through expert knowledge of jazz dance music.
figures	2	Ms. Tedd excluded Chapters 19 and 20, pages 378 to 465, from the exam.
keypad	3	74 285 396 1,736 1,974 2,803 3,982 4,561 5,672 6,145 7,400 8,523 9,420
speed	4	She bid on the field by the lake as the right land for the big chapel.

gwam 1' | 1 | 2 | 3 | 4 | 5 | 6 | 7 | 8 | 9 | 10 | 11 | 12 | 13 | 14 |

151B ◆ ASSESSMENT ACTIVITIES

Activity 1

Prepare a worksheet.

1. Key the information below in the cells designated.

	A	B
1	656	1756
2	539	3458
3	6593	1283
4	3920	1305
5	6543	2943

2. Insert a blank row at 4 and in A4 key **3000**; in B4, **4000**.
3. Insert a blank column at B and in Cells B1 through B6 key **500**, **600**, **700**, **800**, **900**, and **1000**, respectively.
4. In D1, subtract A1 from B1.
5. In D2, divide B1 by A2.
6. In D3, multiply B4 by A1.
7. In D4, add A6 and B6.
8. In D5, add B4 to A3 and then divide that sum by A5.
9. In E1, use the SUM function to add A1 through B6.
10. In E2, use the AVG (AVERAGE for Works MAC users) function to compute the average score for Cells B1 through B6.
11. In E3, use the MIN function to identify the minimum value in Columns A and B.
12. In E4, use the MAX function to identify the maximum value in Columns A and B.
13. In E5, compute the average of the cells in Columns A and B.
14. Edit D2 so B3 is divided by A4.
15. Edit D3 so that A1 is multiplied by A2.
16. Draw a line to separate Row 3 and Row 4.
17. In E7, use the COUNT function to identify the number of values in Columns B through D that are below the line.
18. Format all column widths to 13 spaces.
19. Format numbers as dollars with commas and no cents and columns to width of 8 spaces.
20. If needed, edit the horizontal line so that it extends from Column A through Column E.
21. Save the worksheet as 151B1.

Activity 2

Prepare a worksheet.

1. Format a worksheet so that Column A is 15 spaces wide and Columns B through I are 6 spaces wide.
2. Key the information at the top of p. 304; headings in Columns B through I should be left aligned.
3. Add a row between 12 and 13; starting at Column A, key this information:
   A—**COMP INFO SYS**; B—**76**; C—**65**; E—**54**; F—**S**.
4. In B22, compute the total applications for This Year
   Lotus: **@SUM(B10.B20)**
   Works: **=SUM(B10:B20)**

80C ◆ 12'

MASTER TECHNIQUE

1. Key each line once.
2. Key a 1' writing on line 2, then on line 16; find *gwam* on each writing.

alphabet review	1	oz. mix cow van big quiz jest road felt ship they sick zone held flank
	2	Suzi can equal a track record by jumping twelve feet at the next meet.
fig/sym review	3	$106 net │ 4 or 5% rebate │ LG&E bill │ (See Note.*) │ Pay #93748 plus 2% tax.
	4	This rug (12' x 13'6") was $814.95, but it is now on sale for $710.50.
Shift keys & Lock	5	FOR RENT: 5-rm. apt.--ACE Realty/FOR SALE: 7-rm. house--Rogers, Inc.
	6	Ain't Misbehavin' is playing at MARX THEATER at Playhouse in the Park.
adjacent keys	7	spot poise quite clash threw parts train jewel slope truly silks there
	8	True poise is to remain calm as others in a clash noisily make points.
Space Bar	9	by own jam pay then them flay than city born duty dorm gown they storm
	10	It is the duty of the firm to pay the women for all the work they did.
double letters	11	toss buzz puff fuss mutt flee fell hurry folly stuff wooly fuzzy jetty
	12	Abby tossed the ball to the wooly little mutt running about the jetty.
combination response	13	may eat │ the war │ for him │ she bet │ pay you │ and data │ their case │ they dread
	14	The data form in the trade case may be held secret by a state auditor.
word response	15	flap urns corn same both rush also risks goals flair spend their right
	16	Eighty of the city firms may form a panel to handle the fuel problems.

gwam 1' | 1 | 2 | 3 | 4 | 5 | 6 | 7 | 8 | 9 | 10 | 11 | 12 | 13 | 14 |

80D ◆ 12'

STATISTICAL COPY

1. Key a 1' writing on each ¶; find *gwam*.
2. Key a 2' writing on ¶s 1-2 combined; find *gwam*.
3. Key a 3' writing on ¶s 1-3 combined; find *gwam*.
4. Compare the 3' *gwam* with that attained in 80B, p. 151.
5. Key another 3' writing on the slower kind of copy.

Goal: 70% transfer

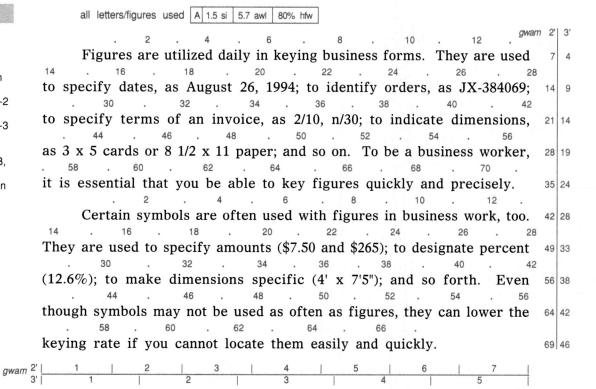

all letters/figures used │ A │ 1.5 si │ 5.7 awl │ 80% hfw │

	gwam 2'	3'
Figures are utilized daily in keying business forms. They are used	7	4
to specify dates, as August 26, 1994; to identify orders, as JX-384069;	14	9
to specify terms of an invoice, as 2/10, n/30; to indicate dimensions,	21	14
as 3 x 5 cards or 8 1/2 x 11 paper; and so on. To be a business worker,	28	19
it is essential that you be able to key figures quickly and precisely.	35	24
Certain symbols are often used with figures in business work, too.	42	28
They are used to specify amounts ($7.50 and $265); to designate percent	49	33
(12.6%); to make dimensions specific (4' x 7'5"); and so forth. Even	56	38
though symbols may not be used as often as figures, they can lower the	64	42
keying rate if you cannot locate them easily and quickly.	69	46

gwam 2' | 1 | 2 | 3 | 4 | 5 | 6 | 7 |
     3' | 1 | 2 | 3 | 4 | 5 |

Activity 2

Prepare a worksheet.

1. Format a worksheet so that Column A is 20 spaces wide and Columns B through G are at least 7 spaces wide.
2. Key the information at the right; headings in Columns B through G should be right aligned.
3. In F3 find the average income for Discover Scuba (B3 through E3).
   Lotus:　　　**@AVG(B3.E3)**
   Works DOS: **=AVG(B3:E3)**
   Works MAC: **=AVERAGE(B3:E3)**
4. Copy F3 formula to appropriate rows in Column F.
5. In G3 compute the total income for Discover Scuba (B3 to G3).
   Lotus:　**@SUM(B3.E3)**
   Works: **=SUM(B3:E3)**
6. Copy G3 formula to appropriate rows in Column G.
7. In B7 compute the total income for January (Column B).
   Lotus:　**@SUM(B3.B6)**
   Works: **=SUM(B3:B6)**
8. Copy B7 formula to Columns C through G.
9. Format all values to dollars with commas (no cents).
10. Draw a line between Rows 6 and 7.
11. Save the worksheet as 150B2 for use in Lesson 152.

	A	B	C	D	E	F	G
1	Training Courses	January	February	March	April	Average	Total
2	---------------------------						
3	Discover Scuba	8000	7150	8120	6980		
4	Intensive Scuba	3000	0	0	3000		
5	Advanced Scuba	7900	9875	10270	7110		
6	Underwater Photog.	3500	2800	3850	2450		
7	Total Income						

Activity 3

Prepare a worksheet.

1. Key the information at the right.
2. Add your name between Loebb and Ruiz with sales of $198,456 for last month and $203,455 this month.
3. Compute the total sales for last month and this month by using the SUM function and print the results in the proper columns in the TOTALS row.
4. Use cell references for (This Month – Last Month) / Last Month in a formula to compute the percent change for Jim Harris and record the answer in the proper row in the PERCENT CHANGE column.
5. Copy the percent change formula to appropriate rows in the PERCENT CHANGE column.
6. Format the numbers, column widths, and column headings appropriately.
7. Draw lines to make the worksheet easier to read.
8. Save the worksheet as 150B3.

	A	B	C	D
1	CHANGE IN SALES PERFORMANCE FROM LAST MONTH			
2				
3		LAST	THIS	PERCENT
4	SALESPERSON	MONTH	MONTH	CHANGE
5				
6	JIM HARRIS	112456	105696	
7	SUSAN LOEBB	139655	154205	
8	ROSCOE RUIZ	125384	152670	
9	SANDRA DAYES	90543	85430	
10	MARY CLANCY	153456	135869	
11	RITA MORINA	50304	60357	
12				
13	TOTALS			

Master Simple Table Format

Learning Outcomes: After completing this unit, you will be able to

1. Format and key 2- and 3-column tables.
2. Align numbers of varying lengths.

PARTS OF A SIMPLE TABLE

A table is a systematic arrangement of data, usually in rows and columns. Tables range in complexity from those with only two columns and a main heading to those with several columns and special features. The tables in this unit are limited to those with the following parts:

1. Main heading (title) in ALL CAPS
2. Secondary heading in capital and lowercase letters
3. Column headings (blocked)
4. Body (column entries)
5. Source note
6. Total line

HORIZONTAL/VERTICAL PLACEMENT OF TABLES

Tables are placed on the page so that the left and right margins (LM, RM) are approximately equal and the column spacing (CS), or number of spaces between columns, is exactly equal. This means about half the characters and spaces in each line are at the left of horizontal center; about half are at the right.

Tables prepared on separate sheets are placed so that the top and bottom margins are approximately equal. This means about half the lines are above vertical center; about half are below. Tables that are placed slightly above vertical center ("reading position") are considered to look more appealing than those that are placed at or below exact vertical center. Short, simple tables are usually double-spaced (DS) throughout, but single-spaced (SS) column entries for longer tables are acceptable.

ALIGNING DATA IN COLUMNS

Words in columns are aligned at the left. Figures, however, are usually aligned at the right or at the decimal point. With computer software, aligning is done automatically by setting a decimal or a right alignment tab.

HORIZONTAL CENTERING

The center feature used for centering lines of text between the left and right margins also may be used for centering columns. The operator must key the longest line in the table (longest entry in each column, plus space between columns). The center feature places half of this line to the left of center point and half to the right. The tab positions are determined by text in this line.

VERTICAL CENTERING

Vertical centering involves subtracting the number of lines of text (including blank line spaces) from the number of lines available on the sheet and dividing the remaining number of unused lines equally between the top and bottom margins. WordPerfect software has a feature that performs this procedure automatically. On Works software, the operator must figure the number of lines in the top margin and insert hard returns above the first line of text.

	HEISMAN TROPHY WINNERS	Main heading	
	(Best College Football Player of the Year)	Secondary heading	
Column headings	Year	Player	College
	1984	Doug Flutie	Boston College
	1985	Bo Jackson	Auburn
Body	1986	Vinny Testaverde	Miami (Fla.)
	1987	Tim Brown	Notre Dame
	1988	Barry Sanders	Oklahoma State
	1989	Andre Ware	Univ. of Houston
	1990	Ty Detmer	BYU
	1991	Desmond Howard	Michigan
Source note	Source: _The World Almanac_, 1993.		

UNIT 33

LESSONS 150-153

Assess Spreadsheet Skills

Learning Outcomes: After completing this unit, you will have

1. Reviewed spreadsheet features used to prepare worksheets.
2. Reviewed spreadsheet features used to prepare bar and pie charts.
3. Demonstrated your skill in using spreadsheet software to prepare worksheets and charts.

L ESSON 150   PREPARE FOR ASSESSMENT

150A ◆ CONDITIONING PRACTICE

each line twice; then
30" timings on
selected lines;
exit wp; access ss

alphabet	1	Jerry met his quota for seventy new wax paper and zip-lock bag orders.
figures	2	I had sold 48 hot dogs, 35 hamburgers, 72 candy bars, and 1,960 sodas.
keypad	3	456 789 123 414 415 416 525 526 524 636 635 634 747 858 9693 8582 7471
speed	4	The girls in the sorority dorms pay for the autobus to go to the town.

gwam 1' | 1 | 2 | 3 | 4 | 5 | 6 | 7 | 8 | 9 | 10 | 11 | 12 | 13 | 14 |

150B ◆ REVIEW ACTIVITIES

Activity 1

Use the information below to create a worksheet and then complete the steps to review many spreadsheet features.

	A	B
1	100	1100
2	200	1200
3	400	1400
4	500	1500

1. Insert a blank row at 3; in A3 key **300** and in B3, **1300**.
2. Insert a blank column at B and in Cells B1 to B5, respectively, key **600**, **700**, **800**, **900**, and **1000**.
3. In D1, subtract B1 from C1.
4. In D2, divide C2 by B1.
5. In D3, multiply B1 by B2.
6. In D4, add B4 and B5.

7. In D5, add B4 to C2 and then divide that sum by B1.
8. In E1, use the SUM function to add B1 through C5.
9. In E2, use the AVG (AVERAGE for Works MAC users) function to compute the average score for Cells B1 through D3.
10. In E3, use the MIN function to identify the minimum value in Cells B1 through D4.
11. In E4, use the MAX function to identify the maximum value in Cells B1 through D5.
12. In E5, compute the average value in Cells C1 through D5.
13. Edit D2 so that C2 is divided by B3.
14. Edit D3 so that B4 is multiplied by B2.
15. Draw a line to separate Row 1 from Row 2.
16. In F1, use the COUNT function to identify the number of values in Columns B through E that are below the line.
17. Format columns as dollars and cents, 13 spaces wide.
18. Delete Column A.
19. If needed, edit the horizontal line so it that is a solid line extending from Column A through Column F.
20. Save the worksheet as 150B1.

HORIZONTAL CENTERING

WORDPERFECT

1. Turn the centering feature on (**Shift F6**).
2. Key the longest entry from the first column.
3. Space over the amount of space to be left between the first and second column.
4. Key the longest entry from the second column. (If more than two columns, repeat Steps 3 and 4 for each additional column.)
5. Write down the Position (**Pos**) number where tab stops will be set for each column. (For relative tabs, subtract 1" for left margin.)
6. Delete the centered line.
7. Clear existing tabs (review p. 147).
8. Set tabs at the beginning of each left aligned column, at the decimal point for each decimal aligned column, and at the right for each right aligned column.
9. Set for DS: **Shift F8**, **L**(ine), **S**(pacing), **2**, **F7**, **F7**.
10. Turn on vertical centering feature as outlined below.
11. Key the table.

WORKS DOS

1. Key the longest entry from the first column.
2. Space over the amount of space to be left between the first and second column.
3. Key the longest entry from the second column. (If more than two columns, repeat Steps 2 and 3 for each additional column.)
4. Center the keyed line (**Ctrl C**).
5. Clear existing tabs (**Alt**, **T**; **T**; **Alt A**).
6. Set tabs at the beginning of each left aligned column, at the decimal point of each decimal aligned column, and at the right of each right aligned column.
7. Change spacing to DS (**Ctrl 2**).
8. Delete the centered line.
9. Key the main and secondary headings and strike Return.
10. Change justification to left (**Ctrl L**).
11. Key the table.
12. Center table vertically as outlined below.

WORKS MAC

1. Key the longest entry from the first column.
2. Space over the amount of space to be left between the first and second column.
3. Key the longest entry from the second column. (If more than two columns, repeat Steps 3 and 4 for each additional column.)
4. Center the line (**Format, Justification, Center**).
5. Set tabs at the beginning of each left aligned column, at the decimal point of each decimal aligned column, and at the right of each right aligned column.
6. Delete the centered line.
7. Set spacing to DS.
8. Key the main and secondary headings and strike Return.
9. Change justification to left.
10. Key the table.
11. Center table vertically as outlined below. (Set spacing to SS before inserting the hard returns.)

VERTICAL CENTERING

WORDPERFECT

The feature used for vertical centering is called the center page feature or the top/bottom feature:
1. Place the cursor at upper left on the page (Pos 1, Line 1).
2. Use **Shift F8**.
3. Strike **P**(age).
4. Strike **C**(enter).
5. Choose **Y**(es); **F7**.

WORKS DOS

1. Count the number of lines to be used to key the table (include blank lines).
2. Subtract lines needed from 54 total lines available. (There are 66 lines on a sheet of paper. When the default top and bottom margins of 1" are deducted, 54 lines remain.)
3. Divide the remainder by 2 to determine page beginning (PB). If the number that results ends in a fraction, drop the fraction. If an odd number results, use the next lower even number.
   Example for table on p. 155:
   Lines available = 54
   Total lines to be used for table = $\dfrac{13}{41}$
   $41 \div 2 = 20\frac{1}{2}$
   PB = line 20
4. If SS, insert 19 hard returns, starting at top of screen (line 1); if DS, insert 9 hard returns, starting at top of screen (line 2).

WORKS MAC

The number of lines on a page varies by the font and point size used:
1. Key the table, beginning on the first line of the screen.
2. Determine the number of lines left on the page below the table by inserting/counting hard returns until a soft page break appears.
3. Divide the number of returns by 2.
4. Place the cursor at the beginning of the document and insert the number of returns determined in Step 3.

Alternative method: The default setting (Geneva, 12 point, 1" top and bottom margins) leaves 40 lines for copy.
1. Count the number of lines to be used to key the table (include blank lines).
2. Subtract this number from 40.
3. Divide the remainder by 2. (If the number that results ends in a fraction, drop the fraction.)
4. Insert this number of hard returns.
   Example for table on p. 155:
   Lines available = 40
   Total lines to be used for table = $\dfrac{13}{27}$
   $27 \div 2 = 13\frac{1}{2}$
   Lines in top margin = 13
   PB = 14

LESSON 149 — APPLY SPREADSHEET CHARTING SKILLS

149A ◆ CONDITIONING PRACTICE
each line twice

alphabet	1	Eight quick joggers wanted very badly many prizes and expensive gifts.
figures	2	Nearly 250 pupils and 146 adults attended the game which we won 997-83.
keypad	3	10 200 407 1,474 2,585 3,696 4,714 5,825 6,939 4,741 5,852 6,963 4,560
speed	4	Nancy is to make an official bid for title to the authentic dirigible.

gwam 1' | 1 | 2 | 3 | 4 | 5 | 6 | 7 | 8 | 9 | 10 | 11 | 12 | 13 | 14 |

149B ◆ APPLICATION ACTIVITIES

Activity 1
Use the information at the right to prepare a worksheet and a bar chart. Add a title; label each axis; and provide a legend if needed.
File name: 149B1

Activity 2
Use the information at the right to prepare a worksheet and a pie chart. Add a title, label each wedge, and shade all wedges. Lotus and Works DOS users: Explode the wedge representing common stocks and add a subtitle.
File name: 149B2

Activity 3
Use the worksheet from Activity 2 to create a bar chart. Present the market value and cost of each type of investment. Add a title; label each axis; and provide a legend if needed. Lotus and Works DOS users are to add a subtitle.
File name: 149B3

Activity 4
Use information in the paragraph at the right to create a worksheet and a pie chart. Add a title; label each wedge; and shade all wedges. Lotus and Works DOS users: Explode the soda sales wedge.
File name: 149B4

A FOUR-YEAR LOOK AT TREF STOCK PRICES

Year	Stock Price
1	$5.35
2	$4.79
3	$4.98
4	$5.89

THE AMERICAN EAGLE FUND

For Period Ending December 31

Investment	Market Value	Cost
Common stocks	$1,954,983	$1,321,964
Long-term bonds	$ 945,000	$1,004,351
Short-term bonds	$ 236,982	$ 212,956
Preferred stocks	$1,345,925	$1,232,007

On November 30, the Riverside High Soccer Boosters prepared a report of sales in the refreshment booth at the soccer field: $550 from hot dog sales, $375 from candy, $490 from coffee, $750 from pizza, and $275 from soda.

81A ♦
CONDITIONING PRACTICE

each line twice SS; DS
between 2-line groups;
then three 1' writings
on line 4; find *gwam*;
clear screen

alphabet 1 Jacob was quite puzzled when Mr. Grifey told us to take the exam over.

figures 2 There are 1,503 engineering majors; 879 are males and 624 are females.

fig/sym 3 My 1992 property tax increased by 6.75% ($241); I paid $3,580 in 1991.

speed 4 Helen owns the six foals and the lame cow in the neighbor's hay field.

gwam 1' | 1 | 2 | 3 | 4 | 5 | 6 | 7 | 8 | 9 | 10 | 11 | 12 | 13 | 14 |

81B ♦
REVIEW HORIZONTAL CENTERING

Horizontally center each of the lines at the right. If necessary, review horizontal centering feature before you begin: 24C, p. 52, also, 38D, p. 74.

CENTERING CONCEPTS

Horizontal: side to side

Vertical: top to bottom

Horizontal center: half left; half right

Vertical center: half top; half bottom

81C ♦
FORMAT A TWO-COLUMN TABLE

File name: L81C

Table 1

1. Study the procedures for vertical and horizontal centering given for your software on page 154.
2. Format and key the model copy at the right. Leave 1" between columns (CS: 1").

Table 2

The yearbook staff has added an **Assistant Business Manager (Mitchell Chang)**. Prepare another table reflecting the new staff member.

YEARBOOK STAFF

Editor-in-Chief	Susan Druhan
Assistant Editor	Elizabeth Poole
Business Manager	Robert Banks
Photography/Layout	Denise Richardson
Advertising/Sales	Diane Blust
Advisor	Anthony Diaz

Note: Numbers 1-7 selects different patterns; Numbers 0 and 8 specify that the wedge is to be clear. In C9 the 105 specifies that the corresponding wedge (savings) is to be exploded (100) and shaded (5). The cells used to indicate shading (the B range in the Range Setting box) can be any blank range of cells on your worksheet that is the same size as the A range that makes up the wedges of the pie.

2. Key **/**, **G**, strike **F2**, and key **T**, **P** (indicates that a pie chart is to be created).
3. Key **R**, **X** (the X range contains the labels for the individual wedges).
4. Key **A5.A9** (identifies the labels for the wedges).
5. Tab to highlight A and if needed, key **B5.B9** (contains the numbers that determine the size of each wedge).
6. Tab to highlight B; key **C5.C9** and strike Enter (identifies the range of cells that controls the pattern and determines whether to explode a specific wedge).
7. Key **L**, **T**, **F** (establishes that the first title will be keyed).
8. Key **MAJOR MONTHLY EXPENSES** and strike Enter, Enter, Enter (records the title for the chart and returns you to the Graph Menu).
9. Key **V**.
10. When done viewing the chart, return to the Graph Menu by striking any key.
11. Key **Q** (selects the Quit option from the Graph Menu).
12. Save the worksheet as 148C.

6. Press **Alt**, **V**, **1** (displays Chart1 with a title).
7. When done viewing the chart, strike Esc.
8. Press **Alt**, **T**, **D** (selects Data Format from the Format Menu).
9. If needed, highlight 1 in Slices column in dialog box.
10. Press **Alt P**, highlight Dense, and strike **Alt F** (specifies that Slice 1 is to be formatted with Dense print).
11. Highlight 2, press **Alt P**, highlight Sparse, and press **Alt F** (specifies that Slice 2 is to be formatted with Sparse print).
12. Highlight 3, press **Alt P**, highlight Medium, and press **Alt F** (specifies that Slice 3 is to be formatted with Medium print).
13. Highlight 4, press **Alt P**, highlight Sparse, and press **Alt F**.
14. Highlight 5, press **Alt E** (turns on the Explode box); and press **Alt F** (specifies that Slice 5—Savings—is to be exploded).
15. Highlight 5, press **Alt P**, highlight Medium, and press **Alt F**.
16. Press **Alt D** (selects Done in the dialog box and returns you to the View Chart Menu).
17. Press **Alt**, **V**, **1** (displays Chart1 with shading and exploded wedge).
18. Save the file as 148C.

APPLICATION ACTIVITIES

Activity 1

Use the information at the right to construct a worksheet and then create a pie chart to present the information. Add a title, include a subtitle (Lotus and Works DOS users only). Label each wedge, shade all wedges, and explode the Foreign wedge (Lotus and Works DOS users only).

File name: 148D1

Activity 2

Use the information at the right to construct a worksheet and then create a pie chart to present this year's attendance. Add a title, label each wedge, shade all wedges. Lotus and Works DOS users should add the subtitle and explode the Senior wedge.

File name: 148D2

Activity 3

Use the worksheet and pie chart created in Activity 2. Revise the pie chart to reflect last year's attendance.

File name: 148D3

CONFERENCE PARTICIPANTS

By Geographic Area

Area	Number Attending
Northeast	155
Midwest	145
Southeast	175
West	135
Southwest	75
Foreign	15

PROM ATTENDANCE

By Class and Year

Class	Last Year	This Year
Seniors	132	128
Juniors	154	144
Sophomores	66	54
Freshmen	12	18

82A ◆ CONDITIONING PRACTICE

each line twice

alphabet 1 Mozambique was the place Karen most enjoyed visiting in exotic Africa.

figures 2 South High School had 350 graduates in 1986 and 284 graduates in 1987.

fig/sym 3 Order #3845-6079 was damaged during shipment by J&B Express on May 21.

speed 4 The lame lapdog may wish to dognap on the burlap by the antique chair.

gwam 1' | 1 | 2 | 3 | 4 | 5 | 6 | 7 | 8 | 9 | 10 | 11 | 12 | 13 | 14 |

82B ◆ REVIEW CENTERING

File name: L82B

1. Review vertical and horizontal centering steps on p. 154 for your software.
2. Using the model table on p. 155, see how quickly you can format and key the copy.
3. Proofread and correct errors before removing the table from your screen.
4. Check work for proper format. Are the top and bottom margins about equal? Are the left and right margins about the same width? If not, review the centering procedures on p. 154 once more.

82C ◆ TABLES WITH MAIN HEADINGS

File name: L82C

Table 1

Format and key the information at the right as a table. Center vertically and horizontally; leave 1" between columns (CS: 1").

words

PERSONNEL RECORD		
Employee Name	Jorge L. Ortega	9
Street Address	1624 Melody Drive	16
City	Midwest City	20
State	OK	21
ZIP Code	73110-2856	25
Telephone	733-1958	29

(PERSONNEL RECORD — 3)

Table 2

Format and key the information at the right as a table. Center vertically and horizontally; leave 1.5" between columns (CS: 1.5").

Table 3

Copy table; then reformat. Leave 2" between columns. Change the title to **WORDS COMMONLY MISSPELLED**.

COMMONLY MISSPELLED WORDS		
accommodate	corporate	10
adequate	customer	13
appropriate	electrical	18
categories	eligible	22
committee	employees	26
compliance	immediately	30
compliment	implemented	35
correspondence	international	41

(COMMONLY MISSPELLED WORDS — 5)

LOTUS

Retrieve file 148B if it is not displayed and use it to create a pie chart.

1. Key **/**, **G**.
2. Strike **F2** and then key **T**.
3. Key **P** (indicates that a pie chart is to be created).
4. Key **R**.
5. Key **A** (indicates that the A range, the wedges in the pie, is to be established).
6. Key **B5.B9** (establishes data range for pie chart).
7. Strike Enter twice (displays the Graph Menu).
8. Key **V** (selects the View option from the Graph Menu).
9. When done viewing the chart, return to the Graph Menu by striking any key.
10. Key **Q** (selects the Quit option from the Graph Menu).
11. Save the worksheet as 148B.

WORKS DOS

1. Retrieve file 148B if it is not displayed, and use it to create a pie chart. Highlight A5 and then press **Alt, S, E** (selects Cells from the Select Menu).
2. Highlight cells A5 to B9 (selects the information that is to be included in the chart. The words in Column A will be used to label each wedge of the pie, the numbers in Column B will become the pie wedges).
3. Press **Alt, V, N** (selects New Chart from the View Menu and then draws and displays the information as a bar chart and names the chart).
4. When done viewing the chart, strike Esc (returns you to the worksheet).
5. Press **Alt, T, P** (selects Pie from the Chart Format Menu so that you can change the bar chart to a pie chart).
6. Press **Alt, V, 1** (displays Chart1 as a pie chart with a label for each wedge).
7. Strike Esc.
8. Save the worksheet and chart as 148B.

WORKS MAC

Retrieve file 148B if it is not displayed and use it to create a pie chart.

1. ~ Chart and choose New Pie Chart (displays the Pie Chart Definition box).
2. If needed, drag the box so it doesn't hide the worksheet.
3. In the Chart Title box, key **MAJOR MONTHLY EXPENSES** (specifies the chart title).
4. In the Plot Values in Column box, key **B** (specifies that the numbers in Column B will be the slices in the pie chart).
5. In the From Row box, key **5** (specifies that the first slice will be found in Row 5).
6. In the Through Row box, key **9** (specifies that the last slice of the pie chart will be found in Row 9).
7. If needed, in the Column of Values Titles, key **A** (specifies that the titles for the slices will be found in Column A).
8. ~ Plot It! box in the lower right corner.
9. When done viewing the chart, ~ the Close box.
10. Save the worksheet as 148B.

ENHANCE PIE CHARTS (LOTUS AND WORKS DOS USERS ONLY)

Read the information at the right and then complete the steps below and on p. 299 for your ss software.

Each wedge of a pie chart can have a different pattern or shade and can be labeled to improve the readability of the chart. Lotus and Works DOS enable you to explode individual wedges (separate them from the rest of the pie).

LOTUS

Retrieve ss file 148B; create a pie chart with shaded wedges and explode the savings wedge of the pie chart.

1. In C5, key **1**; in C6, **2**; in C7, **3**; in C8, **4**; in C9, key **105**. (This range of cells, C5.C9, will be entered as the B range in the Range box of the Graph Settings box later. The number entered in each cell specifies a particular pattern for each wedge.)

WORKS DOS

In file 148B revise the pie chart.

1. Press **Alt, S, E**.
2. If needed, highlight cells A5 through B9.
3. Press **Alt, V, 1, Esc**.
4. Press **Alt, D, T** (selects Titles from the Data Menu).
5. Key **A1** and strike Enter (specifies that the contents of A1˜ will be the title of the chart).

(continued on next page)

(continued on next page)

83A ◆
CONDITIONING PRACTICE
each line twice

alphabet	1	They are moving to a new development just back of the Vasquez complex.
figures	2	Between 1987 and 1993 there were 203,564 recorded births in our state.
fig/sym	3	The balance due on Account #2849 after the 10% down payment is $3,756.
speed	4	The proficient auditor was in dismay due to the problem with an audit.

gwam 1' | 1 | 2 | 3 | 4 | 5 | 6 | 7 | 8 | 9 | 10 | 11 | 12 | 13 | 14 |

83B ◆
ALIGN FIGURES

File name: L83B

Drill 1
Center horizontally the drill at the right; SS; CS: 1".

Drill 2
Center horizontally the drill at the right; DS; CS: 1.5".

Set a *right* tab at the end of each column to align the figures.

492	1640	2288
63	930	826
110	4610	1049
374	475	638
85	928	1177
211	2017	405

83C ◆
TABLES WITH SECONDARY HEADINGS

File name: L83C

Table 1
Center table vertically and horizontally; CS: 1"; DS all headings and column entries.

words

BASIC UNITS OF METRIC MEASURE		6
Units and Names		9
Unit of length	meter (m)	14
Unit of mass (weight)	kilogram (kg)	21
Unit of temperature	kelvin (K)	28
Unit of time	second (s)	32
Unit of electrical current	ampere (A)	40
Unit of luminous intensity	candela (cd)	48
Unit of substance	mole (mol)	54

Table 2
Center table vertically and horizontally; CS: 1.5"; DS all headings and column entries.

SUMMER SCHOOL COURSE OFFERINGS		6
Summer 19--		9
Computer Basics	June 22	13
Integrated Software	June 29	19
Desktop Publishing	July 6	24
Spreadsheet Basics	July 13	30
Graphics	July 20	33
Database Fundamentals	August 8	39
Word Processing	August 10	44

Activity 3

Use the information at the right to prepare a worksheet and a bar chart. Add a title, subtitle, axis titles, and legends. Save the worksheet and chart as 147E3. Works MAC users omit the secondary title.

GAME ATTENDANCE

By Class and Year

Class	Last Year	This Year
Seniors	141	137
Juniors	150	144
Sophomores	66	50
Freshmen	15	19

L ESSON 148   CONSTRUCT PIE CHARTS

148A ◆
CONDITIONING PRACTICE

each line twice

alphabet 1 Gwen just froze the bread, chickens, pork, veal, quiche, and six yams.

figures 2 Sheila was told to call Ruth around 5:30 p.m. at 264-8498 or 264-710.

keypad 3 000 100 200 300 400 500 600 700 800 900 1010 2020 3030 4040 5050 6060

speed 4 An auditor on the panel did not sign a key element of the small audit.

gwam 1' | 1 | 2 | 3 | 4 | 5 | 6 | 7 | 8 | 9 | 10 | 11 | 12 | 13 | 14 |

148B ◆

CREATE A PIE CHART

1. Use the expense information at the right to prepare a worksheet and then save it as 148B.
2. Learn about pie charts: A pie chart compares parts (each value in a range of values) to a whole (the sum of the parts) by making each part of the whole a wedge of the pie.
3. Study the illustration at the far right to learn the major parts of a pie chart.
4. Follow the steps for your ss software (next page) to create a pie chart using the information in the worksheet prepared in Step 1.

MAJOR MONTHLY EXPENSES

Item	Expense
Food	$ 150
Rent	$ 400
Auto	$ 285
Clothes	$ 125
Savings	$ 50
Total	$1010

(1)

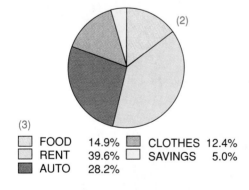

MAJOR MONTHLY EXPENSES

FOOD 14.9% CLOTHES 12.4%
RENT 39.6% SAVINGS 5.0%
AUTO 28.2%

1. First or main title
2. Wedge or slice
3. Wedge or slice titles

83D ◆
CREATE AS YOU KEY

File name: L83D

1. Select three of the questions and compose a response. Number your responses and DS between paragraphs.
2. Edit your copy, making corrections and changes to improve sentence structure and organization.
3. Prepare the final copy.

Questions

What would you like to be doing five years from now?

Do your grades accurately reflect your ability? Explain why or why not.

Are you considering further education? Explain why or why not.

What are your major accomplishments in life?

If you could travel anywhere in the world, where would you go? Explain why.

LESSON 84   TABLES

84A ◆
CONDITIONING PRACTICE

each line twice

alphabet 1 Making a yearly budget was a very unique experience for Jonathan Zorn.

figures 2 There were 386 blue, 274 green, and 159 yellow lights on the 10 trees.

fig/sym 3 Computer Model #364-A8 sells for $1,250; Model #365-A7 sells for $995.

speed 4 I may work with the city on their problems with the city turn signals.

gwam 1' | 1 | 2 | 3 | 4 | 5 | 6 | 7 | 8 | 9 | 10 | 11 | 12 | 13 | 14 |

84B ◆
BUILD SKILL IN FORMATTING TABLES

CS: 1"; DS all lines
File name: L84B

Using Table 2 on p. 157 (83C), see how quickly you can format and key the copy.

1. Review vertical/horizontal centering steps on p. 154 if necessary.
2. Check work for proper placement. Are the LM and RM about the same width? Are the top and bottom margins about equal? Is there 1.5" between columns?

84C ◆
FORMAT THREE-COLUMN TABLES

File name: L84C
Block column headings as shown.

Table 1
CS: 1"; DS

Keying Total Lines

1. Underline the last figures in the columns so that the underlines extend over the *Total* figures and $. (Turn underline on; strike Space Bar.)
2. DS below the underlined figures.
3. Indent the word "Total" 0.5"; key the totals; align figures at decimals.

			words
UNITED WAY CONTRIBUTIONS			5
(In Thousands)			8
Department	Goal	Final	16
Accounting	$ 2.5	$ 3.0	22
Credit	2.0	2.3	25
Human Resources	3.8	3.9	30
Management Information	1.3	1.4	36
Manufacturing/Shipping	5.6	7.1	42
Marketing/Sales	9.4	10.2	47
Purchasing	2.0	2.7	51
Word Processing	2.0	2.8	58
Total	$28.6	$33.4	63

147D ◆ (cont.)

(Lotus continued)

the worksheet at this point, especially when you have made changes to it or have not saved it since the chart was created).

13. Key **I**, **Q**, **Y** (exits spreadsheet program and returns to the Lotus Menu so you can move to Printgraph).

14. Highlight Printgraph and strike Enter (accesses the utility print program).

15. Highlight Image-Select and strike Enter (lets you select the chart you want to print).

16. Highlight Chart1 and strike Enter (selects Chart1 as the chart file to be printed).

17. Key **A** (selects Align from the Printgraph Menu).

18. Check your printer to make sure it is ready to print.

19. Key **G** (selects Go from the Printgraph Menu).

20. When printing has stopped, strike **P** (selects Page option from the Printgraph Menu so the paper in the printer will advance).

21. Key **E** (selects Exit from the Printgraph Menu and exit the utility print program).

22. Key **Y** (verifies that you want to end the printing session).

23. Key **E** (selects Exit from the Lotus Menu and returns you to the operating system).

24. View the chart that has been printed and close the file.

147E ◆

APPLICATION ACTIVITIES

Activity 1

Use the information at the right to prepare a worksheet and a bar chart. Add a chart title, axis titles, and legend for the data ranges. Save the worksheet and chart as 147E1.

ENROLLMENT REPORT

Class	Females	Males
Freshman	155	142
Sophomore	150	148
Junior	159	151
Senior	153	147

Activity 2

Use the information at the right to prepare a worksheet and a bar chart. Add a chart title, axis titles, and legend for the data ranges. Save the worksheet and chart as 147E2. Works MAC users do not chart the data for Murray.

PITCHER RECORDS

Pitcher	Victories	Losses
Batiste	8	2
Murray	10	8
Ruiz	15	11
Hammel	5	8
Yu Chin	13	2

84C ◆ (cont.)

Table 2
CS: 1"; DS
DS above and below the 1.5"
rule before the source note.

	HEISMAN TROPHY WINNERS		5
	(Best College Football Player of the Year)		13
Year	Player	College	21
1984	Doug Flutie	Boston College	27
1985	Bo Jackson	Auburn	32
1986	Vinny Testaverde	Miami (Fla.)	39
1987	Tim Brown	Notre Dame	44
1988	Barry Sanders	Oklahoma State	51
1989	Andre Ware	Univ. of Houston	57
			61
	Source: The World Almanac, 1990.		71

Table 3
CS: 1"; DS
Using the information at the
right, update Table 2.
(Total words: 80)

1990	Ty Detmer	BYU	61
1991	Desmond Howard	Michigan	67
			71
	Source: The World Almanac, 1993.		81

L ESSON 85 — TABLES

85A ◆
CONDITIONING PRACTICE
each line twice

alphabet 1 Marquis Becks enjoyed expanding his vast knowledge of Arizona history.

figures 2 Games of 36, 28, 24, and 21 gave Brian a 1990 season average of 27.25.

fig/sym 3 Stone Realty sold the houses on Lots #3 & #6 for $87,950 and $104,200.

speed 4 The proficient man was kept busy with the problem with the city docks.

gwam 1' | 1 | 2 | 3 | 4 | 5 | 6 | 7 | 8 | 9 | 10 | 11 | 12 | 13 | 14 |

85B ◆
BUILD SKILL: TABLES
File name: L85B

Using Table 2 above, see how quickly you can format and key the copy.

1. Review vertical/horizontal centering on p. 154 if necessary.

2. Check work for proper placement. Are the LM and RM about the same width? Are the top and bottom margins about equal?

85C ◆
MANAGE FILES
Refer to 66D, p. 129 if necessary before deleting files.

Delete the following files:
L70B   L74B
L73B   L75B
L73D   L76B

PRINT A CHART
(OPTIONAL)

1. Read the information at the right about printing a chart.
2. Complete the steps listed for your ss software to print the bar chart in file 147C.

Charts can be printed separately or imported into other software packages, such as word processing, and then printed as a chart to enhance the word processing text. In this lesson, you will learn to print charts as separate documents. To print a chart, your computer must have a graphics card, and your printer must be capable of printing graphics.

LOTUS

Save the chart as a chart or graph file and then use a utility program called Printgraph to print the chart.

1. Quit the ss software and return to the appropriate directory prompt at the operating system level.
2. Key **LOTUS** (enables you to access and move between 1-2-3 and Printgraph. When you access 1-2-3 by keying **123**, the utility program named Printgraph cannot be used).
3. Highlight 1-2-3 and strike Enter.
4. Retrieve ss file 147C (the worksheet contains the chart you will print).
5. Key **/**, **G**, **V** (lets you view the chart filed with this worksheet).
6. Strike any key (returns to the Graph Menu).
7. Highlight Save in the Graph Menu and strike Enter (lets you name and save the chart file separately so it can be printed).
8. Strike Esc as many times as needed (usually twice) so that you can specify the directory letter of your data disk and key : after the directory letter (usually A:).
9. After the colon, key **CHART1** (names the chart file Chart1. Lotus will add .PIC as an extension to this chart file name, and CHART1.PIC will be displayed when you list the files in your directory).
10. Strike Enter.
11. Key **Q** (lets you Quit the Graph Menu).
12. *Optional:* Save the worksheet (it is generally a good idea to save

WORKS DOS

Use the Print option while in Chart View to print the chart.

1. Retrieve ss file 147C (the worksheet contains the chart you will print).
2. Check your printer to make sure it is ready to print.
3. Press **Alt**, **V**, **1** (lets you view the chart that is to be printed).
4. Strike Esc (returns to the Chart View menu).
5. Press **Alt**, **P**, **P** (selects Print from the Print menu).
6. Strike Enter (chooses default setting for number of copies to be printed and begins the printing process).
7. When printing has stopped, close the file.

WORKS MAC

Select Print Window from the File option.

1. Retrieve ss file 147C (the worksheet contains the chart you will print).
2. ~ Chart and choose Select Chart Definition.
3. Highlight the desired chart and ~ OK.
4. ~ Plot It! box.
5. Check your printer to make sure it is ready to print.
6. ~ File and select Print Window.
7. When printing has stopped, close the file.

(continued on next page)

85D ♦
BUILD SKILL: TABLES

File name: L85D

Table 1
CS: 1.5"; DS

PLAYS MOST OFTEN STAGED BY HIGH SCHOOLS		
(Times Produced by Schools Surveyed)		15
You Can't Take It with You	42	21
Bye Bye Birdie	35	25
Arsenic and Old Lace	31	30
Guys and Dolls	27	33
The Music Man	24	37

Source: International Thespian Society.

Table 2
CS: 1"; DS

Table 3
CS: 1"; DS
Reformat or rekey Table 2. Delete the first row of information.
Include the following information:
1990 Lionel Simmons   LaSalle
1991 Larry Johnson   UNLV
1992 Christian Laettner Duke
Change source to **The World Almanac, 1993**.
(Total words: 83)

JOHN R. WOODEN AWARD WINNERS		
(Best College Basketball Player of the Year)		15
Year	Player	College
1984	Michael Jordan	North Carolina
1985	Chris Mullin	St. John's
1986	Walter Berry	St. John's
1987	David Robinson	Navy
1988	Danny Manning	Kansas
1989	Sean Elliott	Arizona

Source: The World Almanac, 1990.

		words
		6
		15
		22
		30
		37
		43
		49
		55
		61
		65
		75

LESSON 86   PREPARE FOR ASSESSMENT: TABLES

86A ♦
CONDITIONING PRACTICE

each line twice

alphabet 1 Max would ask very specific questions before analyzing the job issues.

figures 2 Test scores of 84, 93, 75, 62, and 100 gave Marcia an average of 82.8.

fig/sym 3 Jane wrote checks #807 & #794 for $1,650.03 and $212.50, respectively.

speed 4 He owns both the antique bottle and the enamel bottle on their mantel.

gwam 1' | 1 | 2 | 3 | 4 | 5 | 6 | 7 | 8 | 9 | 10 | 11 | 12 | 13 | 14 |

86B ♦
PREPARE FOR ASSESSMENT

File name: L86B

To prepare for assessment in Lesson 87, format and key each of the tables on pp. 161 and 162 according to the directions given with the problems. Refer to centering procedures for your software on p. 154 as needed.

LOTUS

1. Retrieve ss file 147B if it is not displayed.
2. Key **/**, **G**, **O**.
3. Strike **F2**.
4. Key **L** (selects and displays the Graph Legends and Titles box).
5. Key **T** (selects the Titles box).
6. Key **F** (establishes that main title will be keyed).
7. Key **ACME DEPARTMENT STORE**.
8. Tab to highlight Second (establishes that the secondary title will be keyed).
9. Key **April Sales Report**.
10. Tab to highlight x-axis (establishes that a title for the x-axis will be keyed).
11. Key **SALESPERSON** (enters the x-axis title).
12. Tab to highlight y-axis (establishes that a title for the y-axis will be keyed).
13. Key **DOLLARS**; strike Enter (enters the y-axis title).
14. Key **L** (selects Legends from the Option Menu).
15. Key **A** (establishes that the first legend will be keyed).
16. Key **SALES** (enters the legend for Data Range A).
17. Tab to highlight B (establishes that the second legend will be keyed).
18. Key **RETURNS** and strike Enter three times (enters the legend for Data Range B and returns to the Graph Menu).
19. Key **Q** (quits the Option Menu).
20. Key **V** (allows you to view the chart with the legends added).
21. Strike any key (returns to Graph Menu).
22. Key **Q** (quits the Graph Menu).
23. Save the worksheet and chart as 147C.

WORKS DOS

1. Retrieve ss file 147B if it is not displayed. If you are in View Chart, press **Alt**, **V**, **S** (returns to View Spreadsheet).
2. Highlight A5 and press **Alt**, **S**, **E**.
3. Highlight cells A5 to C9 (selects the information, including the column headings needed to generate a legend for the two data ranges included in the chart).
4. Press **Alt**, **V**, **1** (displays Chart1 with a legend for the two data ranges).
5. When done viewing the chart, strike Esc.
6. Press **Alt**, **D**, **T** (selects Titles option from the Data Menu in Chart View).
7. Key **A1** (specifies that the contents of A1 are to be used as the chart title).
8. Tab or key **Alt S** (moves the cursor to the subtitle line).
9. Key **A3** (specifies that the contents of A3 are to be used as the subtitle).
10. Tab or key **Alt X** (moves the cursor to the x-axis line).
11. Key **A5** (specifies that the contents of A5 are to be used as the title for the x-axis).
12. Tab or key **Alt Y** (moves the cursor to the y-axis line).
13. Key **DOLLARS** (specifies the title for the y-axis).
14. Strike Enter.
15. Press **Alt**, **V**, **1** (displays Chart1 with a title, subtitle, and titles for each axis).
16. Strike Esc.
17. Save the worksheet and chart as 147C.

WORKS MAC

1. Retrieve ss file 147B if it is not displayed.
2. ~ Chart and choose Select Chart Definition (displays the charts you have created).
3. Highlight the desired chart and strike Enter (displays the dialog box settings or the chart).
4. *Optional:* Uncover the worksheet (~ Title Bar and drag box until it no longer hides the worksheet).
5. In the Chart Title box, key **ACME DEPARTMENT STORE** (specifies the title for the chart).
6. In the Vertical Scale Title box, key **DOLLARS** (specifies the title for the y-axis).
7. In the Horizontal Scale Title box, key **SALESPERSON** (specifies the title for the x-axis).
8. If needed, ~ the Draw Grid box to turn it on and then ~ the Label Chart box to turn it on).
9. Confirm that all other Chart Definition settings are correct.
10. ~ Plot It! box in the lower-right corner.
11. When done viewing the chart, ~ the Close box.
12. Save the worksheet and chart as 147C.

Table 1
CS: 1.5"; DS

words

OTHER OFTEN MISSPELLED WORDS   6

installation	previously	11
judgment	prior	14
monitoring	pursuant	18
opportunity	received	22
permanent	recommendation	27
personnel	reference	31
participants	similar	35
patient	successful	39
possibility	sufficient	43

Table 2
CS: 1.5"; DS

WESTERN SALES REPRESENTATIVES   6

State	Representative	
		14
Idaho	Chen, Jung	19
Utah	Carlton, Brenda	23
Washington	Fishback, Mary	27
Montana	O'Connor, Thomas	32
Nevada	Schofield, Robbin	37
Colorado	Hartstein, Susan	41
California	Van Noy, Adrian	46
Oregon	Moore, Brent	51
Wyoming	Buckholtz, Martin	57

Table 3
CS: 1"; DS

TOP TEN SALES REPRESENTATIVES   6

June 19- -   8

Sales Rep	Sales	Country	
			17
Karin Cox	$99,930	Austria	22
Sylvie Perillat	99,560	France	28
Jose Teixeira	98,288	Brazil	34
Martin McMillian	97,458	United States	41
Carlos Rosales	89,381	Nicaragua	48
Soon Choi	78,613	Hong Kong	53
Yumiko Kimura	65,980	Japan	58
Torbjorn Bengtsson	56,391	Sweden	65
Jennifer Walton	48,975	United States	72
Sauri El-Shawi	46,928	Egypt	78

Source: July 15, 19- - Sales Report.   82

89

11. Strike Enter.
12. Key **G** (selects Grid from the Options Menu).
13. Key **H** (places an X in the horizontal grid lines box to include horizontal lines on the chart).
14. Strike Enter, Enter (returns to the Graph Menu).
15. Key **V** (displays the chart with grid lines). When done viewing the chart, strike any key.
16. Key **Q**.
17. Name and save the worksheet and chart as 147B.

6. Press **Alt**, **V**, **1** (Chart1 is displayed with grid lines).
7. When done viewing the chart, strike Esc.
8. Save the worksheet and chart as 147B.

5. In the From Column box, key **B**; in the To Column box, key **C** (specifies the information to be charted is in Columns B and C).
6. In the Data Legends in Column box, key **A** (specifies that the legend for the data to be charted is in Column A).
7. In the Horizontal Titles in Row box, key **5** (specifies that the horizontal titles for the data to be charted is in Row 5).
8. ~ the circle to the left of Numeric.
9. ~ the Maximum box and key **1000** (sets the maximum number for the y-axis slightly higher than the highest number in the data to be charted).
10. If needed, ~ the Minimum box and key **0**.
11. If an X appears to the left of Draw Grid, ~ the X to turn on Draw Grid.
12. If the box to the left of Label Chart is empty, ~ the box to turn on Label Chart.
13. ~ Plot It! box in the lower-right corner.
14. When done viewing the chart, ~ the Close box.
15. Save the worksheet and chart as 147B.

147C ◆

ADD TITLES AND LEGENDS

Read the information at the right about titles and legends on bar charts. Complete the steps for your ss software listed on p. 294.

Titles can be added at the top of a chart and beside each axis, and grid lines can be printed to make the chart more understandable. A legend, identifying the data type represented by each bar can be included below the x-axis, if needed.

86B ◆ (cont.)

Table 4
Arrange Table 2 alphabetically by state.

Table 5
Arrange Table 2 alphabetically by representatives' last names.

WordPerfect—Sort Feature
1. Highlight text to be sorted (**Alt F4**).
2. Depress **Ctrl F9** to activate the sort definition screen. The default setting is for an Alphabetic Line Sort in Ascending Order.
3. Strike **3** (Keys) and use the right arrow key to move over to the field (the first column).
4. Key the number **2** for the field. (The left margin is the first field, although no text is keyed at the left margin.)
5. Depress **F7**, **1** (Perform action). (The column will be sorted by state.) To sort representatives' last names, repeat this procedure. In Step 4, key the number **3** (second column) for the field.

Works DOS and Works MAC
1. Copy Table 2.
2. Use the move feature to alphabetize by state.
3. Repeat these steps for Table 5.

LESSON 87   ASSESSMENT: TABLES

87A ◆
CONDITIONING PRACTICE
each line twice

alphabet 1 Their equipment manager always kept an extra five-dozen jumper cables.

figures 2 The total attendance for 1993 was 87,652, about a 40 percent increase.

fig/sym 3 The desk (#28A935) and chair (#73Z146) are usually sold for over $700.

speed 4 Sue owns the wheelchair in the shanty at the end of the big cornfield.

gwam 1' | 1 | 2 | 3 | 4 | 5 | 6 | 7 | 8 | 9 | 10 | 11 | 12 | 13 | 14 |

87B ◆

ASSESS SKILL: TABLES

File name: L87B
Table 1
CS: 1.5"; DS

		words
AL Batting		
THE LEADERS		5
Through July 4		8
Puckett, Twins	.345	12
Alomar, Blue Jays	.336	16
Molitor, Brewers	.322	21
E. Martinez, Mariners	.318	26
Knoblauch, Twins	.311	30
Ventura, White Sox	.309	35
Bordick, Athletics	.308	40
Baerga, Indians	.307	44
Miller, Royals	.307	48
Harper, Twins	.306	52
		56
Source: Star Tribune, July 6, 1992		64

147A ◆ CONDITIONING PRACTICE

each line twice

alphabet	1	Buffi was told to try to keep singing until her next major vocal quiz.
figures	2	Tony Mason had 702 points, 451 rebounds, and 436 assists from '92-'93.
keypad	3	141 704 252 805 363 906 189 178 245 265 363 625 987 654 3210 4785 5974
speed	4	Their proficient robot with a giant hand and eye can fix the problems.

gwam 1' | 1 | 2 | 3 | 4 | 5 | 6 | 7 | 8 | 9 | 10 | 11 | 12 | 13 | 14 |

147B ◆

BAR CHART WITH TWO DATA RANGES

Use the information at the right to construct a worksheet; then complete the steps listed for your ss software.
File name: 147B

ACME DEPARTMENT STORE

April Sales Report

Salesperson	Sales	Returns
Peru	$600	$60
Neft	$850	$105
Smith	$525	$175

LOTUS

1. In file 147B, record the beginning and ending cells of the data to be displayed (A7 and C9) in a bar chart.
2. Key **/**, **G**.
3. Strike **F2**.
4. Key **T**, **B**, and **R**.
5. Key **X** (selects the option to establish the x-axis data range).
6. Key **A7.A9** (sets the data range).
7. Tab to highlight A (selects the option to establish the first y-axis data range).
8. Key **B7.B9** (sets the data range).
9. Tab to highlight B (selects the option to establish the second y-axis data range).
10. Key **C7.C9** (sets the data range).

WORKS DOS

1. In file 147B, highlight A5 and press **Alt, S, E**.
2. Highlight cells A5 to C9 (selects the data to be included in the chart). The data in Column A will be charted on the x-axis and the data in Columns B and C will be charted as two data ranges on the y-axis.
3. Press **Alt, V, N, Esc** (creates Chart1 and then clears the screen).
4. Press **Alt, O, Y** (selects y-axis from the Choose Options Menu).
5. Press **Alt G** and strike Enter (turns on Grid Lines for the y-axis).

WORKS MAC

1. In file 147B, ~ Chart and select New Series Chart (displays the Series Chart dialog box).
2. To uncover the worksheet, ~ anywhere on the dialog box title bar and drag the box.
3. ~ the circle to left of Bar chart in the Type of Chart column (specifies that a bar chart is going to be created).
4. In the Values to Be Plotted column, key the numbers of the rows that contain data to be charted in each box. For this chart:

   In the 1st Row box, key **7**.
   In the 2nd Row box, key **8**.
   In the 3rd Row box, key **9**.

(continued on next page)　　　(continued on next page)　　　(continued on next page)

words

Table 2
CS: 1"; DS

STATEHOOD ... 2

(Last 10 States to Join) ... 7

Montana	November 8, 1889	12
Washington	November 11, 1889	18
Idaho	July 3, 1890	22
Wyoming	July 10, 1890	26
Utah	January 4, 1896	30
Oklahoma	November 16, 1907	36
New Mexico	January 6, 1912	41
Arizona	February 14, 1912	46
Alaska	January 3, 1959	51
Hawaii	August 21, 1959	55

Table 3
CS: 0.5"; DS

∧ insert

sp spell out

δ delete and close

WORD SKATING CHAMPIONS ... 6
(insert) L FIGURE

Year	Men	Women	
			12
1985	Aleksandr Fadev, USSR (e)	Katerina Witt, E. Germany (a)	22
1986	Brian Boitano, USA	Debbi Thomas, USA	31
1987	Bryan Orser, (Can.) sp. (i)	Katarina Witt, E. Germany (w)	41
1988	Brian Boitano, USA	Katarina Witt, E. Germany	51
1989	Kurt Browning, Canada	Midori Ito, Japan	60

_____ ... 90

Source: <u>The World Almanac</u>, 1990. (4) ... 100

1990	Kurt Browning, Canada	Jill Trenary, USA
1991	Kurt Browning, Canada	Kristi Yamaguchi, USA
1992	Viktor Petrenko, Ukraine	Kristi Yamaguchi, USA
1993	Kurt Browning, Canada	Oksona Baiul, Ukraine

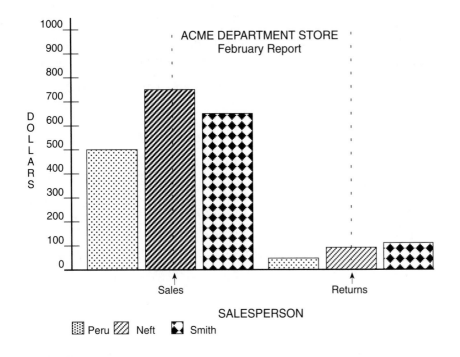

12. If an X appears in the box to the left of Draw Grid, ~ the X to turn off Draw Grid. If the box to the left of Label Chart is empty, ~ the box to turn on Label Chart.
13. ~ Plot It! box in the lower-right corner (plots the chart using the settings you keyed in the dialog box and displays the chart).
14. When done viewing the chart, ~ on the Close box (displays the worksheet).
15. Save the worksheet as 146B in the normal manner. (The chart is automatically named Untitled Chart 1). The chart is saved as part of the worksheet file and will be displayed after the worksheet is retrieved if you:

~ Chart; choose Select Chart Definition; and choose Untitled Chart 1.

146C ◆

APPLICATION ACTIVITIES

Use the following information to construct two worksheets. Create a bar chart to present the information in each worksheet. Save each bar chart as part of the worksheet.

Activity 1 (File name: 146C1)

Activity 2 (File name: 146C2)

Works MAC: Use information for only the first four salespersons in Activity 2, since Works MAC cannot have more than four rows of information in a bar chart.

VICTORIES BY PITCHER

Pitcher	Victories
Batiste	8
Ruiz	15
Hammel	5
Yu Chin	13

MAY AUTO SALES

Salesperson	Autos Sold
Lalli	5
Danko	8
Lewis	3
Harris	6
Justi	10
Wills	7

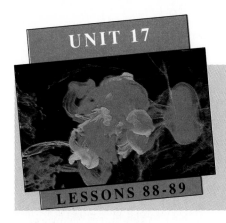

Master Keyboarding Skills

Learning Outcomes: After completing this unit, you will be able to

1. Demonstrate improved technique on service keys.
2. Demonstrate improved response patterns.
3. Key straight-copy paragraphs with higher speed and improved control.

LESSON 88 · KEYBOARDING SKILLS

SM: Defaults; LS: SS

88A ◆ 6'
CONDITIONING PRACTICE

each line twice SS; two 1' writings on line 4; clear screen

alphabet	1	Jaye paid the exotic woman a quarter each for three black gauze veils.
figures	2	Sales slip 7294 lists 36 pencils, 15 pens, 10 disks, and 8 ruled pads.
fig/sym	3	Check #165 (dated 8/4) for $39 covers Invoice #720 less a 5% discount.
speed	4	Glenn may work with the auditor to fix the audit of the big city firm.

gwam 1' | 1 | 2 | 3 | 4 | 5 | 6 | 7 | 8 | 9 | 10 | 11 | 12 | 13 | 14 |

88B ◆ 12'
MASTER TECHNIQUE: SERVICE KEYS

each set of lines twice (one slowly, one faster)

Space bar (quick down-and-in thumb motion)
1 by pan any sum buy man coy ran lay slam duty turn city clam harm shady
2 The boy ran by a shady park on his way to the city dock to buy a fish.

Shift keys (finger reaches to shift keys)
3 Rogers & Sons | Boston, Mass. | Yale or Harvard | J.A. Jarvis Co. | Voss Lake
4 Both Martha and Paul Appleton will leave for Brooks College in August.

Underline and Caps Lock (quiet hands and arms)
5 new ZIP Code | no if's, and's, or but's | You are to read OF MICE AND MEN.
6 He said to replace MUST with should throughout my guide for employees.

gwam 1' | 1 | 2 | 3 | 4 | 5 | 6 | 7 | 8 | 9 | 10 | 11 | 12 | 13 | 14 |

88C ◆ 15'
RESPONSE PATTERNS

1. Key the drill twice as shown.
2. Key a 1' writing on each of lines 3, 6, and 9; find *gwam* on each.

letter response	1	were pump edge join gave milk bear pink fact upon draw jump ever union
	2	red ink	get him	draw up	bad milk	gave him	draw upon	ever join	beat him
	3	As we are aware, my union drew upon a few area data in a gas tax case.

word response	4	with they them make than when also work such form then wish paid their
	5	rich girl	pays half	they also	busy firm	auto fuel	turn down	city panel
	6	I paid the busy girls to make the six bus signs for the big city firm.

combination response	7	the pin	big ads	aid him	for oil	got you	oak bed	tie pin	and him	pay up
	8	fuel test	busy area	city cars	held fast	then join	when safe	both serve
	9	John is to sign the card and join the union with the rest of the crew.

gwam 1' | 1 | 2 | 3 | 4 | 5 | 6 | 7 | 8 | 9 | 10 | 11 | 12 | 13 | 14 |

LOTUS

1. Retrieve file 146B (if not displayed) so that the data can be used to create a bar chart. Record on a sheet of notepaper: "Chart information begins in Cell A3, ends in Cell B5."
2. Key **/, G** (selects the Graph option from the Main Menu and displays a Graph Settings box).
3. Strike **F2** (activates the box so you can define or change settings).
4. Key **T** (selects the Type option from the Settings box).
5. Key **B** (indicates that a bar chart is to be created).
6. Key **R** (selects the Ranges option from the Settings box).
7. Tab to highlight X (selects the option to establish the x-axis, the horizontal axis, data range).
8. Key **A3.A5** (sets the data range from A3—the name of the first salesperson to A5—the name of the last salesperson. (Names in each cell in A3.A5 display below the x-axis line.)
9. Tab to highlight A (moves the cursor to A, which is the range that will be used to establish the vertical or y-axis).
10. Key **B3.B5** (sets the data range from B3, sales of the first salesperson, through B5, sales of the last salesperson. Displays labels in increments along y-axis).
11. Strike Enter, Enter (returns to Graph Menu).
12. Key **V** (selects View Chart option from the Graph Menu).
13. When done viewing the chart, strike any key (displays to the Graph Menu and Settings box again).
14. Key **Q** (selects Quit from the Graph Menu).
15. Name and save the worksheet as 146B in the normal manner (the chart is automatically saved as part of the worksheet file). The chart can be retrieved by keying **/, G, V** after the worksheet has been retrieved.

WORKS DOS

1. Retrieve file 146B (if not displayed) so that the data can be used to create a bar chart.
2. Highlight A3 and press **Alt, S, E** (selects Cells from the Select Menu).
3. Highlight cells A3 to B5 (selects the data to be included in the chart). Data in Column A will be charted on the x-axis, the horizontal axis; the data in Column B will be charted on the y-axis, the vertical axis.
4. Key **Alt, V, N** (selects New Chart from the View Menu and draws, displays, and assigns Chart1 as the chart's name).
5. When done viewing the chart, strike Esc (returns to the worksheet).
6. Key **Alt, V, 1** (displays Chart1 again). The name Chart1 could be changed to a more descriptive name, but leave it Chart1 for now).
7. Strike Esc.
8. Key **Alt, F, S** and save the file as 146B in the usual manner (the chart is automatically saved as part of the worksheet file). The chart can be retrieved by keying **Alt, V, 1** after the worksheet has been retrieved.

WORKS MAC

1. Retrieve file 146B (if not displayed) so that the data can be used to create a bar chart.
2. ~ Chart; select New Series Chart (displays the Series Chart Dialog box).
3. To uncover the worksheet, ~ anywhere on the dialog box's title bar and drag the box.
4. ~ the button beside Bar chart in the Type of Chart column (specifies that a bar chart is to be created).
5. In the Values to Be Plotted column, key the numbers of the rows that contain the data to be charted. For 146B:

   In the 1st Row box, key **3.**
   In the 2nd Row box, key **4.**
   In the 3rd Row box, key **5.**
   (These three boxes specify the numbers to be plotted along the vertical or y-axis).
6. In both From Column box and To Column box, key **B** (specifies that Column B is to be charted.) **Note:** When any box contains an undesired row number or column letter, highlight the number or letter and key the correct number or letter. The cursor can be moved from box to box with the Tab key or mouse.
7. For legends in the Data Legends in Column box, key **A** (specifies that the legend for the data to be charted is in Column A).
8. For titles, in the Horizontal Titles in Row box, key **1** (specifies that the horizontal title for the data to be charted is in Row 1).
9. ~ button beside Numeric (turns Numeric on and Semi-Logarithmic off).
10. ~ the Maximum box and key **1000** (sets maximum value on the y-axis at 1000).
11. If needed, ~ the Minimum box and key **0** (indicates that the values on the y-axis will begin at 0).

(continued on next page)

88D ♦ 17'

IMPROVE SKILL

1. Take a 1' unguided writing and two 1' guided writings on each ¶.
2. Take a 2' and a 3' writing on ¶s 1-3 combined; find *gwam*.

gwam	¼'	½'	¾'	1'
20	5	10	15	20
24	6	12	18	24
28	7	14	21	28
32	8	16	24	32
36	9	18	27	36
40	10	20	30	40
44	11	22	33	44
48	12	24	36	48
52	13	26	39	52
56	14	28	42	56

all letters used | A | 1.5 si | 5.7 awl | 80% hfw

gwam 2' | 3'

What is a job? In its larger sense, a job is a regular duty, role, 6 | 5
or function that one performs for pay. Therefore, when you apply for 14 | 9
and accept a job, you accept responsibility for completing a series of 21 | 14
specified tasks such as record keeping, word processing, and data entry. 28 | 19

What is a career? A career is a broad field in business, profes- 34 | 23
sional, or public life that permits one to progress in successive steps 42 | 28
up the job ladder. Whatever the tasks performed, one may have a career 49 | 33
in law, in health services, in education, or in business, for example. 56 | 37

It should be very clear that a career may include many jobs, each 62 | 42
with different ability requirements. Realize, however, that many of the 70 | 47
jobs leading to increasing success in most careers are better done with 77 | 51
greater ease by people who have built a high level of keying skill. 84 | 56

gwam 2' | 1 | 2 | 3 | 4 | 5 | 6 | 7 |
3' | 1 | 2 | 3 | 4 | 5 |

L ESSON 89   KEYBOARDING SKILLS

SM: Defaults; LS: SS

89A ♦ 6'

CONDITIONING PRACTICE

each line twice SS; two 1' writings on line 4

alphabet	1	Tex just received quite a sizable rebate check from the wagon company.
figures	2	Order these books: 12 copies of TM37; 16, TM104; 18, BK59; 10, OM285.
fig/sym	3	He said, "Say figures in units: 326, 3-26; 1067, 10-67; 4859, 48-59."
speed	4	Pamela may lend them the map of the ancient lake town if they wish it.

gwam 1' | 1 | 2 | 3 | 4 | 5 | 6 | 7 | 8 | 9 | 10 | 11 | 12 | 13 | 14 |

89B ♦ 12'

MASTER TECHNIQUE: SERVICE KEYS

each set of lines twice (once slowly; then faster)

Space bar (quick down-and-in thumb motion)

1 All the men on the quay may go by bus to the town on the lake to work.
2 Jan may do key work for the six men on the audit of the big city firm.

Shift keys (finger reaches to shift keys)

3 Spiro and Jacki left with Epson and Lana for a trip to Padua and Rome.
4 Mars leaves for Bora Bora in March; Nancy goes to Lake Worth in April.

Underline and Caps Lock (quiet hands and arms)

5 We read a review of the book THE FIRM in the magazine Books in Review.
6 Underline the title of a magazine, Ebony; CAP a book title, WHIRLWIND.

146A ◆ CONDITIONING PRACTICE

each line twice;
then 30" timings
on selected lines;
exit wp; access ss

alphabet	1	Vera quickly justified the six itemized party food bills while dining.
figures	2	He flew 3,250 miles on Monday, 1,896 on Tuesday, and 475 on Wednesday.
keypad	3	100 400 700 200 500 800 300 600 900 107 208 309 407 508 609 4107 63094
speed	4	An off-duty ensign got sick with the toxic virus and was to go to bed.

gwam 1' | 1 | 2 | 3 | 4 | 5 | 6 | 7 | 8 | 9 | 10 | 11 | 12 | 13 | 14 |

146B ◆ CREATE, VIEW, SAVE BAR CHARTS

1. Use the information at the right to construct a worksheet.
2. Study the illustration and accompanying key below to learn the major parts of a bar chart.
3. Complete the steps listed on p. 290 for your ss software to create, view, and save a bar chart.

		Sales	Returns
1	Salesperson	Sales	Returns
2			
3	Peru	500	50
4	Neft	750	95
5	Smith	675	105

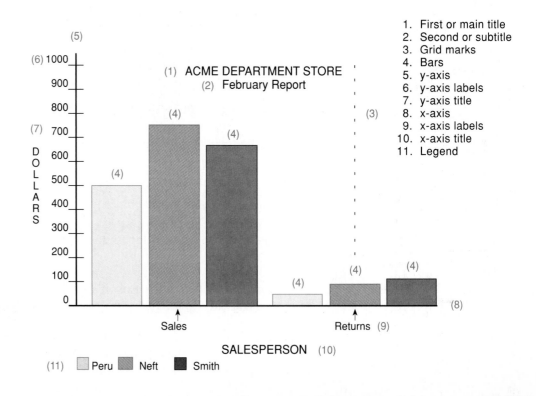

1. First or main title
2. Second or subtitle
3. Grid marks
4. Bars
5. y-axis
6. y-axis labels
7. y-axis title
8. x-axis
9. x-axis labels
10. x-axis title
11. Legend

KEYSTROKING PATTERNS

1. Key each set of 2 lines twice (once slowly, then faster).
2. Key a 1' writing on each of lines 9 and 10; find *gwam* on each.

Adjacent-key reaches (fingers curved and upright)

1 Luis was the last guy to be weighed in before stadium practice opened.
2 We are to open a shop by the stadium to offer the best sporting goods.

Long, direct reaches with same finger (quiet hands and arms)

3 Myra broke my gym record to receive a bronze medal at the county meet.
4 Eunice brought a recorder to music hall to record my recital of hymns.

Double letters (quick repeat strokes)

5 Perry was puzzled by the quizzical look of a shopper at the city mall.
6 Ellen shipped all the zoology books to the new school office as asked.

Balanced- and one-hand words (combination response)

7 Freda may fix the bicycle after she gets off work at my cafe at eight.
8 Lonny read the amendment to the union panel at noon at the union hall.

Balanced-hand sentences (word response)

9 Both of them may also wish to make a formal bid for the big auto firm.
10 I wish to do the work so the girls may go with them to make the signs.

gwam 1' | 1 | 2 | 3 | 4 | 5 | 6 | 7 | 8 | 9 | 10 | 11 | 12 | 13 | 14 |

IMPROVE/ CHECK SKILL

1. Take a 1' unguided and two 1' guided writings on each ¶.
2. Take a 2' and 3' writing on ¶s 1-3 combined; find *gwam*.

gwam	1/4'	1/2'	3/4'	1'
20	5	10	15	20
24	6	12	18	24
28	7	14	21	28
32	8	16	24	32
36	9	18	27	36
40	10	20	30	40
44	11	22	33	44
48	12	24	36	48
52	13	26	39	52
56	14	28	42	56

all letters used | A | 1.5 si | 5.7 awl | 80% hfw

gwam 2' | 3'

In deciding upon a career, learn as much as possible about what 6 | 4
individuals in that career do. For each job class, there are job re- 14 | 9
quirements and qualifications that must be met. Analyze these tasks 20 | 13
very critically in terms of your personality and what you like to do. 27 | 18

A high percentage of jobs in major careers demand education or 33 | 22
training after high school. The training may be very specialized, re- 41 | 27
quiring intensive study or interning for two or more years. You must 48 | 32
decide if you are willing to expend so much time and effort. 54 | 36

After you have decided upon a career to pursue, discuss the choice 60 | 40
with parents, teachers, and others. Such people can help you design a 68 | 45
plan to guide you along the series of steps required in pursuing your 74 | 49
goal. Keep the plan flexible and change it whenever necessary. 81 | 54

gwam 2' | 1 | 2 | 3 | 4 | 5 | 6 | 7 |
3' | 1 | 2 | 3 | 4 | 5 |

3. Key **T**; key desired titles (first, second, x-axis, and y-axis) in Titles box.
4. Key **L**; key desired legends in Legends box.
5. As needed, complete Steps 1 through 8 above.

Printing a Chart

1. Access spreadsheet software (key **LOTUS**).
2. If chart has not been saved as a PIC file, display worksheet; access Graph Menu (*I*, **G**); select Save option; identify desired directory; name chart; strike Enter; key **Q** (quit) 1-2-3.
3. Highlight Printgraph; Enter.
4. Highlight Image-Select; Enter.
5. Highlight name of chart to be printed; Enter.
6. Prepare printer; key **A**, **G** (start printing).
7. When printing stops, key **P**, **E**, **Y**, and **E** (ends session).

Using Patterns and Exploding Wedges in a Pie Chart

1. Create pie chart in usual manner; display the worksheet.
2. Find a blank area (usually the column next to the last data range you will chart) that will be the B data range. The number of cells in this area must equal the number of values in the A data range, which is the number of wedges in the pie chart.
3. Enter a number **1** to **8** in each cell of the B data range. The numbers represent patterns for filling in wedges of the pie. Entering 8 or leaving the cell blank will give a clear wedge.
4. Explode (separate) one or more wedges of the pie: add 100 to the value in the B data range.
5. If necessary, make the chart you want to change to be the current chart.
6. Key *I*, **G** (displays Graph Settings box); strike F2.
7. Select B in Ranges box; specify B range; Enter.
8. View the chart (optional).

Printing a Chart

1. Retrieve worksheet; view chart (Press **Alt**, **V** and select desired chart); Esc (accesses Chart View Menu).
2. Press **Alt**, **P**, **P** (selects Print from Print Menu).
3. Strike Enter (accepts default number of copies) or change number; strike Enter (prints).
4. When printing has stopped, close file.

Specifying Patterns and Exploding Wedges in a Pie Chart

1. Create and view pie chart in the usual manner; Esc.
2. Press **Alt**, **T**, **D**.
3. Select pattern for each wedge (slice): Highlight wedge/slice number; highlight desired pattern in dialog box.
4. Explode (separate) a wedge: Press **Alt E** (turns on Exploded option) .
5. Press **Alt D** (returns to View Chart Menu).
6. ~ Bar Chart in the Type of Chart column.

12. Turn Label Chart **on/off** as desired.
13. ~ Plot It! box in lower right corner; view the chart.
14. ~ Close box.

Adding Titles and Legends to Bar Charts

1. Retrieve worksheet, ~ Chart; and choose Select Chart Definitions.
2. Select desired chart (displays the Chart Definitions dialog box).
3. Key title of chart in Chart Title box; key title for y-axis in Vertical Scale Title; title for x-axis in Horizontal Scale Title box.
4. Turn on Label Chart, if needed.
5. ~ Plot It! and proceed normally.

Creating, Viewing, and Saving Pie Charts with Titles and Legends

1. Retrieve worksheet; choose New Pie Chart from Chart Menu (displays the Pie Chart Definition box).
2. In Chart Title box, key title of pie chart.
3. If needed, in Plot Values in Column box, key letter of column that contains numbers that are to be in pie chart.
4. In From Row box, key number of row that contains first number to be included in pie chart.
5. In Through Row box, key number of row that contains the last number to be included in pie chart.
6. If needed, in Column of Values Titles, key letter of the column that contains the names you want to use as titles for wedges of pie chart.
7. ~ Plot It! box; proceed as usual.

Printing Charts

1. Prepare printer.
2. Retrieve worksheet, ~ Chart; choose Select Chart Definitions.
3. Select desired chart.
4. ~ on Plot It! box.
5. Select Print Window from File Menu.
6. When printing stops, close file if desired.

Ritter Realty Company

Learning Outcomes: As you complete this unit, you will

1. Apply your knowledge of document formats.
2. Demonstrate your ability to prepare documents from script and rough-draft copy.
3. Practice following general directions to complete a variety of keyboarding tasks.
4. Apply many of the word processing features learned.

RITTER REALTY COMPANY

A Word Processing Simulation

Before you begin the documents on pp. 168-174, read the following copy. When planning your work, refer to the formatting guides given here to refresh your memory about the proper formatting of memos, letters, tables, and reports.

BACKGROUND

To discover if you might like a career in real estate, you are working part time for Ritter Realty. Besides assisting the realtors with showings, you also work for the Branch Manager, Ms. Jessica Sampson, in Ritter's main office.

Each year, Ritter Realty sponsors a Parade of Homes. The Parade of Homes is a showing open to the general public of newly constructed homes that feature the latest innovations in the housing industry. This year the company will be inviting former clients to attend a private showing prior to the Parade of Homes. Most of the documents to be prepared will be about the Parade of Homes and the private showing. The work will include the processing of memos, tables, letters, and a report.

Directions for each document are given by Ms. Sampson. Use the date included

on the instructions for all correspondence requiring a date. Ms. Sampson likes the closing lines of all her letters to read as follows:

Sincerely

Ms. Jessica A. Sampson
Branch Manager

Ms. Sampson has given you a copy of "A Quick Guide to Document Formats," which summarizes the basic features of formats used by Ritter Realty Company. Refer to this guide as needed when processing the various documents.

You will supply appropriate parts of documents when necessary. You will use your own initials for reference.

If the directions and the "Quick Guide" summary are not sufficiently detailed, use what you have learned when making formatting decisions.

You are expected to produce error-free documents, so proofread and correct your work carefully.

A QUICK GUIDE TO DOCUMENT FORMATS

Memos
Side margins: 1"
Format: Simplified
Spacing: QS below date and last paragraph. DS below other parts of memo and between paragraphs.
Date: 2" top margin
Subject: ALL CAPS

Letters
Side margins: 1"
Spacing: SS with DS between paragraphs
Format: Block with open punctuation
Date: 2" top margin

Tables
Placement: Centered
Vertical spacing: DS throughout
Horizontal spacing: 0.5" or 1" between columns
Headings: Blocked

Reports
Format: Unbound with internal citations
Side margins: 1"
First page top margin: 2"
Second page top margin: 1"
Bottom margin: 1" (or as near as possible)
Spacing: DS text; SS quotations and lists
References: On separate sheet

Use Spreadsheet Graphics

Learning Outcomes: After completing this unit, you will be able to

1. Create bar charts with one and two data ranges.
2. Create pie charts.
3. View, save, and print charts.
4. Enhance charts with titles, legends, grid lines, and data formats.

SPREADSHEET CHARTING FEATURE AND COMMAND GUIDE

The guide on this page and the next two pages give a preview of topics presented in Unit 32. Use it whenever you need to look up features and commands.

CHARTING

Spreadsheet software provides options to create a variety of graphs and charts, including bar charts (see illustration on p. 289) and pie charts (see p. 297). The type of chart has to be selected; parts of the chart must be defined. Charts can be kept as part of the worksheet file, printed as separate files, and/or inserted into documents prepared with word processing and other applications software. When charts are kept as part of the worksheet file (the method used in this unit), values in the chart change automatically whenever worksheet data are changed.

LOTUS

Creating, Viewing, and Saving Charts

1. Retrieve worksheet file.
2. Key **/**, **G**, **F2** (edits Graph Settings box).
3. Key **T**; select type of chart.
4. Key **R**; key the data range(s) to be used in x-axis and y-axis.
5. Strike Enter twice (returns to Graph Menu).
6. Key **V** (view the chart); any key (returns to Graph Menu).
7. Key **Q** (quit Graph Menu).
8. Name and save worksheet in normal manner (chart automatically saved in same file).

Adding Titles and Legends to Charts

1. Complete Steps 1 through 4 (previous section).
2. Key **L** (displays Legends and Titles box).

(continued on next page)

WORKS DOS

Creating, Viewing, and Saving Charts

1. Retrieve worksheet file.
2. Press **Alt**, **S**, **E**; highlight information to be charted on the x- and y-axes.
3. Press **Alt**, **V**, **N** (view new chart). To view a chart that has been created, press **Alt**, **V**; select desired chart. If a Pie Chart is wanted, strike Esc; press **Alt**, **T**, **P**; and then **Alt**, **V**; and select desired chart.
4. Strike Esc (returns to worksheet).
5. Press **Alt**, **F**, **S** (saves worksheet and chart).

Adding Titles and Legends to Charts

1. Complete Steps 1 through 3 (previous section).
2. Strike Esc (clears screen).
3. Press **Alt**, **D**, **T** (selects Titles option from Data Menu in Chart View).
4. Enter cell address of each desired title or key the desired information for each title (Chart Title, Subtitle, x-axis, and y-axis) and strike Enter.
5. Optional: Press **Alt**, **V**; select desired chart (view the chart).

(continued on next page)

WORKS MAC

Creating, Viewing, and Saving Bar Charts with Titles and Legends

1. Retrieve worksheet file.
2. ~ Chart; select New Series Chart.
3. ~ Bar Chart in the Type of Chart column.
4. In Values to be Plotted column, key numbers of rows that contain the data to be charted.
5. In the From Column box, key letter of first column to be charted; in To Column, key letter of last column to be charted.
6. For legend, in Data Legends in Column box, key letter of column that contains legends for data to be charted.
7. For title, in the Horizontal Titles in Row box, key number of row that has titles for data to be charted.
8. ~ Numeric (or Semi-Logarithmic).
9. ~ Maximum box; key number slightly higher than maximum value to be charted.
10. If needed, ~ Minimum box; key 0 (y-axis value begins at 0).
11. Turn Draw Grid **on/off** as desired (x in box to left of Draw Grid indicates it is on).

(continued on next page)

90-96A
CONDITIONING
PRACTICE

each line twice SS; then three 1' writings on line 4; find *gwam*; clear screen

alphabet 1 Judy quickly spent all her extra money on a new puzzle before leaving.

figures 2 Order No. 78966 was for 140 disks, 30 printer ribbons, and 25 manuals.

fig/sym 3 March sales ($366,680) were 24% higher than February sales ($295,700).

speed 4 The big social for their neighbor may also be held in the city chapel.

gwam 1' | 1 | 2 | 3 | 4 | 5 | 6 | 7 | 8 | 9 | 10 | 11 | 12 | 13 | 14 |

90-96B ◆

Documents 1-3

Message from JESSICA SAMPSON

Key the attached memos.

The first memo goes to All Agents. Use PARADE OF HOMES SCHEDULE for the subject line.

The second memo goes to Mary Carlson, Sales Agent. Use REFRESHMENTS FOR PARADE OF HOMES as the subject line.

The third memo goes to John Morgan, Broker. Use ELECTRONIC MAIL as the subject line. JS 5/12

¶ The response from former home buyers who are interested in the private showing of this year's Parade of Homes has been excellent. Meeting with past customers to determine if we can be of further assistance to them with their housing requirements is a real opportunity for us. All of the individuals invited have been in their present homes for over five years and <u>may be</u> ready to consider the purchase of a new home.
¶ Michi will be coordinating schedules for the two days of the private showing. We should have your schedule ready within the next two or three days. A meeting will be held on <u>May 20</u> at <u>8:30 a.m.</u> to discuss specific details for the Parade of Homes.

¶ Mary, last month when we were discussing some of the details for the Parade of Homes private showing, you indicated that you would be willing to handle the arrangements for refreshments. I would like to take you up on that offer if it still stands.
¶ Please stop by my office sometime this week so that we can discuss a few of the specifics.

John, the information on electronic mail you brought back from the convention in Miami was intriguing. When you have a few minutes, stop by my office and let's discuss the applications that you think may be of value to our office.

Activity 3

Use the following information and directions to prepare a worksheet.

1. The members of the Business Club at Reed High have just completed their dance marathon to support muscular dystrophy, and you have been asked to create a worksheet that reports:
   a. Names of the members (in alphabetical order) with each member's expected and actual donations (see chart at right).
   b. Club's total expected and actual donations.
   c. Percent of total donations that each member donated.
2. Each member whose actual donation equals or exceeds the expected donation is to receive a $5 gift certificate. Use an IF statement to show who will receive a certificate.
3. Format the worksheet appropriately.
4. Save the worksheet as 144B3.

Activity 4

Use wp software to compose a letter to the **Muscular Dystrophy Association (Fulton Building, Pittsburgh, PA 15233-0569)**. The letter is to accompany the Business Club's donation (check). The letter should include all appropriate letter parts and should identify the Business Club at Reed High School, the number of members who raised donations, the activity used to raise the donations, and the amount of money raised. Use your name as the sender; use this title: **President, Reed High Business Club**. Save the letter as 144B4.

Member	Expected Donations	Actual Donations
Jamie Harris	$100	$135
Susie Woo	$125	$149
Bill Diaz	$125	$100
Bob Carter	$150	$175
John Ripcai	$150	$135
Sandy Doer	$150	$165
Mary Barr	$100	$105
Sam Efram	$125	$120
Harry Wilson	$100	$90
June Simms	$150	$175
Mary Harris	$125	$150
Lin Chung	$125	$135
Millie Brown	$100	$85
Peg Tilison	$125	$115
Don Perez	$150	$175

KEYBOARDING WORKSHOP

STATISTICAL COPY

all letters used | A | 1.5 si | 5.7 awl | 80% hfw

1. Select a goal: Accuracy—reduce errors by one on each writing. Speed—increase *gwam* by 3 on each writing.
2. Take three 3' writings; determine errors and *gwam*.

	gwam 1'	3'
The sales report for the quarter ending September 31 indicated that	14	4
sales for Easy-Korec Blue Correctable Film ribbon (Stock #B193) were	27	9
down by 40%, while sales of all other ribbons were up by an average of	41	14
15%. To boost sales of B193 ribbons, the selling price will be reduced	56	19
during the next quarter from $7.50 to $4.49 per ribbon (a 40% discount).	71	24
Also, a four-color display board emphasizing that the B193 ribbon can be	85	28
used as a replacement ribbon for TJK-133 and XRT-159 will be available	100	33
to all salespersons in the region.	106	35

gwam 1' | 1 | 2 | 3 | 4 | 5 | 6 | 7 | 8 | 9 | 10 | 11 | 12 | 13 | 14 |
gwam 3' | | 1 | | 2 | | 3 | | 4 | | 5 | |

Message from JESSICA SAMPSON

*Retrieve the Document filed as **HOMEMORT** and make the changes shown at the right. Insert A and B as shown below.*

JS
5/13

Insert A

Rate	Monthly Payment
8.0%	$ 7.34
9.0	8.05
10.0	8.78
11.0	9.53
12.0	10.29
13.0	11.07

Insert B

1. Loan origination fees.
2. Mortgage insurance application fee.
3. Appraisal fee.
4. Credit report fee.
5. Loan discount (points).

To place a table within the body of a report, take these steps:
1. DS above and below the table; SS the body of the table.
2. Clear all tabs.
3. Determine and set a tab for each column of the table. (The table must be centered within the margins of the report.)
4. After keying the table, reset the tab for the paragraph indention before keying the remainder of the report.

2" Top Margin — Caps, Center, and Bold

Home Mortgage — QS

　　Many types of creative financing for home loans are offered by financial institutions. However, the two most common types of mortgages are the fixed-rate mortgage and the adjustable-rate mortgage. ⟩ DS

Fixed-Rate Mortgage The interest rate of a fixed-rate mortgage remains the same for the duration of the loan. Even if economic conditions change, the interest rate cannot be adjusted. this can be an advantage or disadvantage, depending on whether interest rates are increasing or decreasing. The table below (Wyllie, 1988, 301) illustrates the amount of a monthly mortgage payment on a 30-year loan per $1,000 borrowed. For example, The monthly payment for a $50,000 loan for 30 years at 10 percent would be $439 ($8.78 x 50 = $439).

INSERT A

　　One percentage point can make a sizeable difference in the amount paid each month. It is to a borrowers advantage to check with several financial institutions to find the best interest rate available. when analyzing interest rates, however, a buyer should keep in mind that there are variable closing costs associated with securing a loan. These costs may include the following:

INSERT B

Adjustable-Rate Mortgage

　　Another common type of mortgage offered by most financial institutions is the adjustable-rate mortgage.

An adjustable-rate mortgage is a loan with an interest rate that can be adjusted up or down an agreed-upon number of times during the life of the loan. The interest rate is usually tied to changes in a monetary index, such as the interest rates on U.S. Treasury securities or the rates financial institutions must pay their depositors or investors. (Green, 1988, 441)

REFERENCES

Wyllie, Eugene D., et al. *Consumer Economics*. 11th ed. Cincinnati: South-Western Publishing Company, 1988.

Green, D. Hayden, *Consumers in the Economy*. 2nd ed. Cincinnati: South-Western Publishing Co., 1988.

144-145A ◆
CONDITIONING PRACTICE
each line twice

alphabet	1	The Arizona firm will quote a very good price for the jet's black box.
figures	2	Of the 13,748 people who entered this year's 10k race, 9,652 finished.
keypad	3	456 789 123 404 9,363 8,252 7,141 6,393 5,282 4,171 3,693 2,582 11,471
speed	4	Profit is no problem for the sorority social when it is held downtown.

gwam 1' | 1 | 2 | 3 | 4 | 5 | 6 | 7 | 8 | 9 | 10 | 11 | 12 | 13 | 14 |

144-145B ◆

APPLICATION ACTIVITIES

Activity 1

Key the worksheet at right. Use the directions to complete the worksheet.

1. Format the columns, putting 2 or 3 spaces between each pair.
2. Format all rate and pay columns as Currency/Dollars with 2 decimal places.
3. Compute the total hours for each employee. (In G6, use the SUM function to add Cells B6 through F6 and then copy G6 to other rows in G.)
4. Compute Regular Pay for each employee. (In I6, multiply G6 x H6 and then copy I6 to other rows in I.)
5. Compute Overtime Pay for each employee. In J6, use the following formula:
   Lotus:
   @IF(G6>40,(G6–40)∗H6∗1.5,0)
   Works:
   =IF(G6>40,(G6-40)∗H6∗1.5,0)
6. Copy J6 to other rows in J.
7. Compute Total Pay. (In K6, add I6 and J6 and then copy K6 to other rows in K.)
8. Insert a column between A and B and assign an ID No. to each employee, starting at 105. Each employee thereafter is to be assigned a number 5 higher than the preceding employee. Center the ID No.'s and use ID No. as the column heading.

9. Key AVERAGE at A18; compute an average for each column, beginning with Column C, and show each average on Row 18 below its respective column. The formula for the average is
   Lotus: **@AVG(C6.C16)**
   Works DOS: **=AVG(C6.C16)**
   Works MAC: **=Average(C6:C16)**

10. Insert a row between 1 and 2 and then draw a horizontal line.
11. Save the worksheet as 144B1.

	A	B	C	D	E	F	G	H	I	J	K
1	PAYROLL JOURNAL										
2	FOR WEEK ENDING JUNE 15, 19--										
3								Hrly	Reg	Ovtm	Tot
4	Employee	Mon	Tue	Wed	Thu	Fri	Hrs	Rate	Pay	Pay	Pay
5											
6	J. Abel	8	8	8	8	10		6.8			
7	B. Clark	8	6	8	8	10		6.4			
8	C. Diaz	9	8	8	10	8		7.1			
9	D. Efra	8	8	8	8	8		8.5			
10	F. Grant	9	8	7	8	9		7.8			
11	J. Jones	7	8	8	8	8		6.4			
12	H. Means	9	9	9	9	9		6.8			
13	K. Napes	7	8	8	8	10		7.1			
14	K. Porto	6	8	8	8	8		7.8			
15	R. Silski	8	8	8	8	8		8.5			
16	T. Ulia	8	8	8	8	8		6.4			

Activity 2

Retrieve wp file T144B2 from *Student's Template*. Make the following changes.

1. Format as a leftbound report with separate reference page.
2. Center, bold, underline and ALL CAP the main heading.
3. Bold and underline side headings and paragraph headings.
4. SS and block the long quotation at the paragraph indent point.
5. Search for *which* and replace with **that** unless it's preceded by a comma.
6. Search for *microcomputers* and replace with **computers**.
7. Move Item 5 to No. 3 and renumber accordingly.
8. Reverse the order of the "advantages" and "disadvantages" paragraphs.
9. Run spell check and then proofread for meaning.
10. Number pages at the top right except page 1.
11. Save as 144B2.

Document 5

Message from JESSICA SAMPSON

Here are the names of three more clients that Jeff Grayson would like invited to the private showing. A copy of the original letter is attached. Prepare a letter to each client for me to sign.

Mr. and Mrs. Chi Shen
1288 Paramount Lane
Houston, TX 77067-4310

Ms. Marjorie S. Butler
3198 Rosedale Circle
Houston, TX 77004-7120

Mr. Kevin N. King
2982 Spring Field Road
Houston, TX 77062-1312

*JS
5/14*

May 1, 19--

Mr. and Mrs. Jason R. Walton
1825 Victoria Drive
Houston, TX 77022-1903

Dear Mr. and Mrs. Walton

The 19-- Parade of Homes will be held **June 7-21**. This year we are planning something new. A limited number of our previous home buyers from Ritter Realty are being invited to participate in a private showing prior to the public opening of the Parade of Homes.

The private showing will give Ritter Realty agents the time needed to point out the many fine features of the quality homes being shown this year and to answer any questions you may have. With so many people taking part in the Parade of Homes, it is difficult to give our preferred customers the attention they deserve during the days the homes are shown to the public.

If you are interested in this free showing, sign and return the enclosed card. We look forward to showing you the outstanding homes built for this year's home show.

Sincerely

Jessica A. Sampson

Ms. Jessica A. Sampson
Branch Manager

xx

Enclosure

_____

Document 6

Message from JESSICA SAMPSON

Please send the attached letter to:

Mr. Nelson C. Decker
Lakeside National Bank
2310 North Main Street
Houston, TX 77009-4612

*JS
5/14*

Here is a copy of an article *on streamlining the mortgage process* which may be of interest to you. *It appeared in* ~~from~~ the April issue of Mortgage Banking. ~~It has~~ several good su*g*gestions for ways of cutting the time between the application ~~date~~ *are presented* and ~~the~~ closing dates. *recently* As I mentioned to you last week, we have had several customers who ~~are~~ *were* quite concerned about the length of time that ~~it is currently taking~~ *was required* for *the* processing *of* their loans. I will be interested in your reaction to the article.

Sincerely

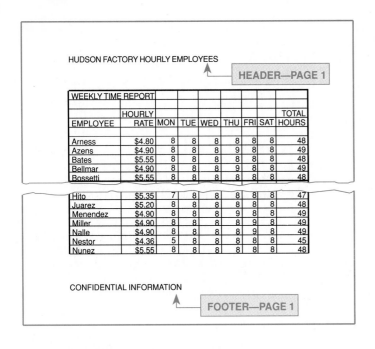

WEEKLY TIME REPORT								
EMPLOYEE	HOURLY RATE	MON	TUE	WED	THU	FRI	SAT	TOTAL HOURS
Arness	$4.80	8	8	8	8	8	8	48
Azens	$4.90	8	8	8	9	8	8	49
Bates	$5.55	8	8	8	8	8	8	48
Bellmar	$4.90	8	8	8	9	8	8	49
Bossetti	$5.55	8	8	8	8	8	8	48
Hito	$5.35	7	8	8	8	8	8	47
Juarez	$5.20	8	8	8	8	8	8	48
Menendez	$4.90	8	8	8	9	8	8	49
Miller	$4.90	8	8	8	8	9	8	49
Nalle	$4.90	8	8	8	8	9	8	49
Nestor	$4.36	5	8	8	8	8	8	45
Nunez	$5.55	8	8	8	8	8	8	48

CONFIDENTIAL INFORMATION

FOOTER—PAGE 1

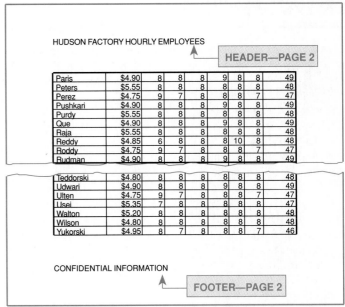

Paris	$4.90	8	8	8	9	8	8	49
Peters	$5.55	8	8	8	8	8	8	48
Perez	$4.75	9	7	8	8	8	7	47
Pushkari	$4.90	8	8	8	9	8	8	49
Purdy	$5.55	8	8	8	8	8	8	48
Que	$4.90	8	8	8	9	8	8	49
Raja	$5.55	8	8	8	8	8	8	48
Reddy	$4.85	6	8	8	8	10	8	48
Roddy	$4.75	9	7	8	8	8	7	47
Rudman	$4.90	8	8	8	9	8	8	49
Teddorski	$4.80	8	8	8	8	8	8	48
Udwari	$4.90	8	8	8	9	8	8	49
Ulten	$4.75	9	7	8	8	8	7	47
Usei	$5.35	7	8	8	8	8	8	47
Walton	$5.20	8	8	8	8	8	8	48
Wilson	$4.80	8	8	8	8	8	8	48
Yukorski	$4.95	8	7	8	8	8	7	46

CONFIDENTIAL INFORMATION

FOOTER—PAGE 2

143D ◆ (cont.)

7. Highlight Footer on the menu line and strike Enter.
8. At the *Enter footer* prompt, key the current date and strike Enter.
9. Highlight Margins on the menu line and strike Enter.
10. Highlight Left and strike Enter.
11. Key **15** (changes the left margin from the current setting to 15) and strike Enter.
12. Highlight Margins on the menu line and strike Enter.
13. Highlight Top and strike Enter.
14. Key **24** (changes top margin from current setting to 24) and strike Enter.
15. Move cursor to Quit on the menu line and strike Enter (displays Print Menu).
16. Move cursor to Go and strike Enter (executes the Print command).
17. When printing stops, move cursor to Page and strike Enter.
18. Move cursor to Quit and strike Enter.
19. Save worksheet as 143D.
20. Remove paper from printer and verify that header, footer, and margins printed correctly.

8. Strike Enter (accepts current settings for all other margins and sizes).
9. Press **Alt**, **P**, **P** (selects the Print option from the Print Menu).
10. Strike Enter (accepts present settings in dialog box and prints the ss).
11. Save worksheet as 143D.
12. Remove paper from printer and verify that header, footer, and margins printed correctly.

8. ~ File Menu and select Print option.
9. ~ appropriate options in Printer dialog box and then strike Return.
10. Save worksheet as 143D.
11. Remove paper from printer and verify that header, footer, and margins printed correctly.

Document 7

**Message from
JESSICA SAMPSON**

*Key the listing of homes
that will be in this year's
PARADE OF HOMES.
Use Parade of Homes for
the main heading and
June 7-21, 19--, as the
secondary heading.*

JS
5/14

Location	Builder	Price
3885 Wimbledon Lane	Brock *Construction*	$133,000
3892 Glencliffe Lane	Murphy Homes, Inc.	95,000
115 Fernbrook Lane	J & P Construction	215,000
803 Ashmore Drive	*Berry & Sons Construction*	149,000
5574 Blue Hills Road	Homes by Makely	99,000
4348 Mossridge Drive	Valleyview Home Builders	105,000
3872 Glencliffe Lane	*Dalton & James Realty*	91,000
120 Fernbrook Lane	Your Home Builders	175,000

Document 8

**Message from
JESSICA SAMPSON**

*Key the attached informa-
tion in announcement
form on a full sheet of
paper. You decide on the
layout; you've done a very
nice job with previous
announcements. The eight
builders are listed with
some of the other docu-
ments I've given to be
keyed. Make sure to list
them in alphabetical
order.*

JS
5/15

19-- *Parade of Homes*) Bold
June 7-21
Monday - Friday 5 p.m. to 9 p.m.
Saturday & Sunday 10 a.m. to 6 p.m.
Featuring homes built by
(List the eight homebuilders in alphabetical order)
Sponsored by *Ritter Realty Company* — Bold

Document 9

**Message from
JESSICA SAMPSON**

*Please send the attached
letter to:*

Mr. and Mrs. Paul Taylor
1320 Lori Lane #3
Ogden, UT 84404-4396

JS
5/14

Dear Mr. and Mrs. Taylor

¶ Rebecca Smithson, personnel manager of Tyson
Production Company, informed me that you have
accepted a position with them and will be moving
to Houston the first part of July. I know you will
enjoy living in this area.

¶ A copy of the "Movers' Guide" published by our real
estate company is enclosed. It is designed to give
helpful hints on making the move as painlessly
as possible. We hope you will find it useful as
you organize for the move to Texas.

¶ If we can be of assistance to you in locating a place
to rent or a house to purchase, please call our office.

Sincerely

APPLICATION ACTIVITY

Retrieve *Student's Template* file T139B1 and make the changes indicated below.

1. Insert a column between Columns A and B; make it 7 spaces wide.

2. Move the Hourly Rate column to the newly created Column B.

3. Insert a column between FRI and TOTAL HOURS; make it 4 spaces wide.

4. Key **SAT** as a column heading in the newly created Column H.

5. Copy the TUE hours of each employee into Column H.

6. In I6 compute total hours worked for Bates by using:
   Lotus   **@SUM(C6.H6)**
   Works   **=SUM(C6:H6)**

7. Compute each employee's wages by copying the formula that computed Bates's hours.

8. Format Column B as money with 2 decimal places; make Columns C through G 4 spaces wide; make Column I 5 spaces wide.

9. Right-align the column headings in Columns B through I.

10. Save worksheet as 143C—do not clear screen.

MARGINS, HEADERS, AND FOOTERS

Read the information at the right and then complete the steps below and on p. 284 for your ss software.

When printing worksheets, you have used default settings for left and top margins and did not print headers or footers on the worksheet. Resetting margins can make a worksheet more attractive. Headers and/or footers (see illustrations at top of p. 284) can make a worksheet more informative.

LOTUS

Place a header and footer and reset top and left margins on ss file 143C.

1. Key **/**, **P**, **P** (accesses Printer from the Print Menu).
2. With Range highlighted, strike Enter (selects range from Print Menu).
3. Establish the range of cells (A1.J16) to be printed.
   a. Move cell pointer to A1.
   b. Key period (.) (anchors A1 as beginning cell in the range).
   c. Move cell pointer to A16 and then to J16 (highlights cells to be printed).
   d. Strike Enter.
4. Move cursor to Options on menu line and strike Enter.
5. Highlight Header; strike Enter (selects Header option).
6. At the *Enter header* prompt, key your name and strike Enter.

WORKS DOS

Place a header and footer and reset top and left margins on ss file 143C.

1. Press **Alt**, **P**, **H** (selects Headers and Footers from the Print Menu).
2. In the Header line in the dialog box, key your name and use ↓ to move to the Footer line.
3. In the Footer line, key the current date and strike Enter.
4. Press **Alt**, **P**, **M** (selects Page Setup and Margins from the Print Menu).
5. At the Top margin line, key **2"** (sets the top margin 2" from top edge of paper).
6. Use ↓ to move to Left margin line; key **1.5"** (sets LM at 1.5").
7. Use ↓ to move to Header margin and key **1"** (places header 1" from top edge). This setting must be less than Top Margin setting.

WORKS MAC

Place a header and footer and reset top and left margins on ss file 143C.

1. Since you want to print an entire worksheet, make sure no more than one worksheet cell is highlighted. (If more than one cell is highlighted, only the highlighted cells will print.)
2. ~ File Menu and select Page Setup option.
3. Key your name at the insertion mark in the Header box in the dialog box.
4. ~ near the left edge of the Footer box and key the current date.
5. ~ the Left Margin box and change setting from 1 to 1.5.
6. ~ the Top Margin box and change setting from 1 to 2.
7. Strike Return (selects preset settings for all other options).

(continued on next page)

(continued on next page)

(continued on next page)

Document 10

**Message from
JESSICA SAMPSON**

*Please send the attached
letter to:*

Mr. Charles L. Atkins
1241 Warren Drive
Denver, CO 80221-7463

*JS
5/15*

Document 11

**Message from
JESSICA SAMPSON**

*Please key the attached
PARADE OF HOMES
schedule for Roxanne
Davis.*

*JS
5/16*

Dear Mr. Atkins

Evidently you would fit in very nicely with the "Ritter Realty Team." Your resume looks very impressive, and your references all speak very highly of you.

As you know from speaking with John Morgan about two weeks ago at the convention in Miami, we are looking for a person from outside the area who can bring in new ideas and who has been successful in promotion and sales. Your background shows a strength in both of these areas.

Would you be available to spend a day with us in Houston during the week of May 26-30 to discuss the position? I will call next week to determine your availability and to make arrangements for your visit.

_____

SCHEDULE FOR ROXANNE DAVIS)-Bold

June 5

[← Client	Phone	Time
Mr. and Mrs. Dave Johnson	555-4877	10 a.m.
Dr. and Mrs. Reed Kurth	555-8125	
Ms. Patricia Hansen	555-1143	1 p.m.
Mr. and Mrs. Scott Jones	555-1935	
Dr. Faye Snell	555-7680	4 p.m.
Mr. and Mrs. Timothy Reedsberg	555-4676	
Mr. and Mrs. Karl Hallie	555-2908	7 p.m.
Mr. and Mrs. Gregory Haas	555-1298	

June 6

Client	Phone	Time
Mr. Jerry Sawyer	555-1095	10 a.m.
Mr. and Mrs. Jason Walton	555-6547	
Mr. Robert Todd	555-7231	1 p.m.
Miss Sandra Kurtz	555-3452	
Ms. Gretchen Kuehn	555-9876	
Mr. and Mrs. Barry Bauer	555-2349	4 p.m.
Dr. and Mrs. Ronald Baker	555-1520	7 p.m.
Miss Tami Seymour	555-4822	

MOVE AND COPY FEATURES

Read the information at the right about Move and Copy features. Complete the following steps for your ss software.

A range of cell entries may be moved or copied from one location to another. When the Move feature is used, the range of cell entries is erased from its original location and transferred to the new location. When the Copy feature is used, the range of cells remains in its original location and also appears in its new location. These two features allow you to redesign worksheets without rekeying information.

LOTUS

Copy A4 through A30 to another range beginning with cell A33.

1. Retrieve *Student's Template* file T128B.
2. Highlight A4 (the first cell in the range to be copied).
3. Key *I*, **C** (selects Copy from the Main Menu).
4. At the *Copy What?* prompt, highlight A4 through A30 (specifies the range of cells to be copied).
5. Strike Enter.
6. At the *To Where?* prompt, key **A33** (identifies A33 as the beginning cell in the range to which the information is to be copied).
7. Strike Enter (executes the Copy feature).
8. Go to A33 (use F5); use ↓ to verify that the range of cells has been copied.

Move the range of cells N3 through S30 to a range that begins at B32.

1. Go to N3 (the first cell in the range to be moved).
2. Key *I*, **M** (selects Move from the Main Menu).
3. At the *Move What?* prompt, highlight cells through N30; then ⟶ through S30 (highlights the range of cells to be moved).
4. Strike Enter.
5. At the *To Where?* prompt, key **B32** (identifies B32 as the upper-left cell of the receiving range).
6. Strike Enter (executes the Move feature and returns the cell pointer to N3). **Note:** The entries in N3 through S30 have been erased.
7. Go to A32 and verify that the range of cells has been moved to the right of the names in Column A. (Do not save the changes.)

WORKS DOS

Copy A4 through A30 to another range beginning with cell A33.

1. Retrieve *Student's Template* file T128B.
2. Highlight A4 (the first cell in the range to be copied).
3. Press **Alt, S, E** (selects Cells from the Select Menu).
4. Highlight A4 through A30 (highlights the range of cells to be copied).
5. Press **Alt, E, C** (selects Copy from the Edit Menu).
6. Go to A33 and strike Enter (executes the Copy command).
7. Use ↓ to verify that the range has been copied.

Move the range of cells N3 through S30 to a range that begins at B32.

1. Go to N3 (the first cell in the range to be moved).
2. Press **Alt, S, E** (selects Cells from the Select Menu).
3. Use ↓ to highlight cells through N30; then ⟶ through S30 (highlights the range of cells to be moved).
4. Press **Alt, E, M** (selects Move from the Edit Menu).
5. Go to B32 (the upper-left cell of the receiving range).
6. Strike Enter (executes the Move command).
7. Use ↓ to verify that the range has been moved. (Do not save the changes.)

WORKS MAC

Copy A4 through A30 to another range beginning with cell A33.

1. Retrieve *Student's Template* file T128B.
2. Highlight A4 through A30 (the range of cells to be copied).
3. ~ Edit Menu and select Copy.
4. Highlight A33 (highlights the upper-left cell in the receiving range).
5. ~ Edit Menu and select Paste (executes the Copy command).
6. Use ↓ to verify that the range has been copied.

Move the range of cells N3 through S30 to a range that begins at B32.

1. Highlight N3 through S30 (the range of cells to be moved).
2. ~ Edit Menu and select Move.
3. Key **B32** as the destination cell in the dialog box (moves the range of cells to a new range beginning at B32).
4. Scroll down to verify that the range has been moved. (Do not save the changes.)

Message from
JESSICA SAMPSON

Three more clients have accepted invitations to the private showing. Retrieve the document filed as **HOMESHOW**. *Use the information provided below to create letters to each of the three clients. Be sure to change the date of the letter to May 16.*

Mr. and Mrs. Mark O'Mara
1583 Nassau Bay Drive
Houston, TX 77058-2196

Ms. Kathy S. Ristow
1418 Rainwood Drive
Houston, TX 77079-3170

Mr. and Mrs. Juan Cruz
4573 Red Maple Drive
Houston, TX 77064-4407

Mark Grayson will show Mr. and Mrs. O'Mara and Ms. Ristow the homes on Saturday, June 6, at 7 p.m. Matthew Sparks will show Mr. and Mrs. Cruz the homes on Friday, June 5, at 1 p.m.

JS
5/16

Document 13

Message from
JESSICA SAMPSON

Key the information at the right as a table. Use **SALES REPORT** *for the main heading and May 4 - 10 as the secondary heading.*

JS
5/16

```
NAME
ADDRESS
CITY, STATE, ZIP

Dear NAME

We are pleased to have you take part in our private showing
of the homes that will be in this year's Parade of Homes.
The eight homes you will see combine quality construction,
professional decorating, and exclusive landscaping to make
this year's show the best ever.

I have made arrangements with (AGENT'S NAME) to show you the
homes.  Please meet (HIM/HER) at our office at (TIME) on
(FRIDAY/SATURDAY), June (5/6).  It will take approximately
two hours to visit the homes.

I am looking forward to hearing your comments about the homes
after the showing.  If you have any questions before the
showing, please call me.

Sincerely
```

Jessica A. Sampson

```
Ms. Jessica A. Sampson
Branch Manager

xx

c (NAME OF AGENT)
```

Agent	Property	Price
Mary Carlson	3725 Gulf Street	$249,900
Yein Cheng	8210 Rosslyn Road	225,000
Roxanne Davis	5614 Monaco Road	185,400
Mark Grayson	310 Berryhill Court	149,500
John Morgan	2690 Spring Creek	129,800
Matthew Sparks	218 San Felipe Street	115,600
Mark Grayson	929 Whitney Street	110,200
Matthew Sparks	832 Axilda Street	99,500
Roxanne Davis	710 Rainwood Drive	89,900
John Morgan	2836 Yarberry Street	88,300
Mark Grayson	8219 Queen Street	79,300
Yein Cheng	3955 Hoyte Drive	69,500

WHAT IF
QUESTIONS

Read the information at the right about *What If* questions. Then complete the following steps.

An advantage of ss software is its ability to show the effects on all cells of a change in one cell. For example, in the worksheet just completed (142E2), you determined the next quarter quota for each salesperson if the company were to increase present quotas by 1.05 (or 105%). By changing the 1.05 in Cell A3 to other numbers representing other possible increases—say, 95% or 115%—the effect of the change on the quotas could be seen.

For example, WHAT IF the increase were 1.1 (or 110%). The answer can be determined quickly:

1. In worksheet 142E2, highlight A3 (the cell that has the value to be changed).
2. Key 1.1, and strike Enter/Return.
3. Read the numbers in Column C (these values were recalculated to reflect the change from 1.05 to 1.1).
4. In A3, experiment with other WHAT IF'S: Change 1.1 to 2; change 2 to .5; change .5 to 1.25.
5. Save the worksheet with the last change as 142F.

LESSON 143   USE MOVE AND COPY FEATURES

143A ◆
CONDITIONING
PRACTICE

each line twice

alphabet	1	Zachary bought two exquisite paintings of Alaska just before he moved.
figures	2	On March 29 they learned the 7, 1, and 5; on March 30 the 4, 6, and 8.
keypad	3	456 789 123 506 45208-1678 41018-2759 40517-3628 45176-2893 45231-1745
speed	4	The man in the wheelchair was down at the dock with my neighbor's dog.

gwam 1' | 1 | 2 | 3 | 4 | 5 | 6 | 7 | 8 | 9 | 10 | 11 | 12 | 13 | 14 |

Document 14

Message from JESSICA SAMPSON

Changes have been made to the PARADE OF HOMES table that you prepared. These changes are shown on the attached sheet. Check to see if these changes will make revisions necessary to any of the other documents created for the Parade of Homes.

JS 5/17

Document 15

Message from JESSICA SAMPSON

Send the attached letter with the changes shown to:

Ms. Katelin Andalusia
461 Brantwood Avenue
Green Bay, WI 54303-6624

JS 5/17

Document 16

Message from JESSICA SAMPSON

Mr. Jerry Sawyer has cancelled his appointment on June 6 with Roxanne Davis. I've scheduled Mr. and Mrs. Clayton Barns in place of Mr. Sawyer. Please revise Roxanne's schedule with this change and print a new copy for her. Also, send the form letter to Mr. and Mrs. Barns confirming their appointment. Their address is 929 Spring Creek Lane, Houston, Texas 77017-2600; their telephone number is 555-1955.

JS 5/17

PARADE OF HOMES

June 7-21, 19--

Location	Builder	Price
3885 Wimbledon Lane	Brock Construction	139,500 $133,000
3892 Glencliffe Lane	Murphy Homes, Inc.	95,000
114 Fernbrook Lane	J & P Construction	215,000
803 Ashmore Drive	Berry & Sons Construction	149,000
5574 Blue Hills Road	Homes by Makely	99,000
4348 Mossridge Drive	Valleyview Home Builders	108,000
3872 Glencliffe Lane	Dalton & James Realty	91,000
3/120 Fernbrook Lane	Your Home Builders	175,000

▲ RITTER
REALTY ▲ COMPANY
410 BRADLEY STREET ■ **HOUSTON, TX** ▲ **77009-3658** ■ **713-555-2758**

May 15, 19--

Mr. Charles L. Atkins   *Katelin Andalusia*
1241 Warren Drive
Denver, CO 80221-7463

Dear ~~Mr. Atkins~~

Evidently you would fit in very nicely with the "Ritter Realty Team." Your resume looks very impressive, and your references all speak very highly of you.

Mark Grayson
As you know from speaking with ~~John Morgan about two weeks ago at the convention in Miami~~, we are looking for a person from outside the area who can bring in new ideas and who has been successful in promotion and sales. Your background shows a strength in both of these areas.

Would you be available to spend a day with us in Houston during the week of ~~May 26-30~~ to discuss the position? I will call next week to determine your availability and to make arrangements for your visit.   *(June 2-6)*

Sincerely

Jessica A. Sampson
Ms. Jessica A. Sampson
Branch Manager

xx

Note: If formulas in all cells are not to be changed, key **/, R, F, T** (selects Text option from Range Format). To reverse the action so that values are displayed, repeat Step 2, substituting a different selection for Text from the Format Menu.

3. Strike any arrow key.
4. If needed, lengthen the cells to display all of each formula.
   Note: To reverse the action so values are displayed, repeat Steps 2 to 4 to turn off Show Formula feature.

Note: To reverse the action so values are displayed, select Show Values from the Options Menu.

142E ◆
APPLICATION ACTIVITIES

Activity 1

Key the worksheet at right; then follow directions to complete the worksheet, which includes absolute cell addressing.

1. Format Column A to 25 or more spaces with entries right aligned.
2. Format Column B as money with 2 decimal places; center the heading.
3. Format Column C as Percent with 0 decimal places; center the heading.
4. In B5, compute Gross Profit (sales – cost of candy).
5. In B7, compute Net Profit (gross profit – other expenses).
6. In C3 to C7, compute % of sales by dividing each number in Column B by the number in B3 (sales). **Reminder:** B3 is to be entered into the formula as an absolute cell address.
7. Display the formulas in the cells.
8. Save worksheet as 142E1.

	A	B	C
1	INCOME STATEMENT	APRIL	% OF SALES
2			
3	CANDY BAR SALES:	985.65	
4	COST OF CANDY BAR SOLD:	433.5	
5	GROSS PROFIT ON SALES:		
6	OTHER EXPENSES:	77.33	
7	NET PROFIT:		

Activity 2

Key the worksheet at right then follow the directions to complete the worksheet.

1. Format Column A to 16 spaces with left alignment of all entries; Columns B and C as money (no cents) with centered headings.
2. In C9, use the formula B9*$A$1 to compute the first salesperson's next quarter quota (Quota This Quarter x 1.05). Copy the formula to compute other salespersons' next quarter quotas.
3. Save worksheet as 142E2.

	A	B	C
1	DETERMINATION OF SALES QUOTA		
2			
3	1.05--COMPANY GOAL		
4			
5		QUOTA	QUOTA
6		THIS	NEXT
7	SALESPERSON	QUARTER	QUARTER
8			
9	JUAN AVIA	75000	
10	MARY ABELSEN	72000	
11	THOMAS WILLIT	67000	
12	UN CHIN	63000	
13	HENRY QUINEZ	55000	
14	SUZANNE EDDY	47500	
15	MARTY MERRY	43000	

Improve Letter/Memo Formatting Skills

Learning Outcomes: After completing this unit, you will be able to

1. Format letters/memos with improved skill.
2. Use more extensive word processing capabilities.

LESSON 97 — LETTERS

97A ◆
CONDITIONING PRACTICE

each line twice SS; then three 1' timed writings on line 4; find *gwam;* clear screen

alphabet	1	Jackie Wadman's next goal is to qualify for the event's bronze trophy.
figures	2	There were 12,087, 9,365, and 8,401 fans at the last three home games.
fig/sym	3	Jane practiced keying *, /, and _ on Monday; %, $, and # on Wednesday.
speed	4	Lay the clamshell at the end of the rug on the big shelf at the right.

gwam 1' | 1 | 2 | 3 | 4 | 5 | 6 | 7 | 8 | 9 | 10 | 11 | 12 | 13 | 14 |

97B ◆

REVIEW LETTER FORMATTING

File name: L97B

Letter 1

Review the formatting guides for letters on p. 116 and the personal-business letter model on p. 118. Format and key in block style with open punctuation the letter shown at the right. The letter is from **Richard B. Lyons**. Supply an appropriate closing.

words

3716 Rangely Drive | Raleigh, NC 27609-4115 | October 14, 19-- | Mr. Robert C.   15
Johnson | Wayler Insurance Company | 206 Polk Street | Raleigh, NC 27604-   28
4120 | Dear Mr. Johnson | Subject: INFORMATION ON CAREER OPPORTUNITIES   40

Please send information about career opportunities available with Wayler   55
Insurance Company in the administrative services area. As part of a class   70
assignment, I will be giving an oral report on a company for which I would   85
be interested in working. Wayler Insurance is an impressive company, and   99
I would like to do the report on career opportunities with your firm.   114

The report needs to address job titles, job requirements, educational require-   129
ments, salary, and opportunities for advancement. Any information that you   144
are able to provide on these areas will be greatly appreciated.   157

Letter 2

Format in block style with open punctuation the letter shown at the right. Use the following information for the closing lines:

Sincerely yours | Robert C. Johnson | Customer Relations Director | xx | Enclosure

October 20, 19-- | Mr. Richard B. Lyons | 3716 Rangely Drive | Raleigh, NC   14
27609-4115 | Dear Mr. Lyons   19

Wayler Insurance Company is always interested in potential employees. We   34
hope that you will consider us once you have graduated.   45

As you will see from reading the information that is enclosed, we have   59
different levels of administrative support positions in our company. Job ti-   75
tles, job requirements, educational requirements, and starting salaries are   90
included for each level. Our company philosophy is to reward loyal employees;   106
therefore, we like to promote from within when qualified employees are avail-   121
able. We also reimburse employees for additional job-related schooling   135
completed during their employment.   142

If you need further information or would like one of our administrative sup-   157
port supervisors to talk with your class, please call us.   (words in body: 149)   169

In worksheet 142B, Column C, compute each homeroom's percent of total sales by dividing the homeroom's sales by the total sales.

1. Highlight C4.

2. Key + (Lotus users) or = (Works users) **B4/$B$10** (divides B4 by B10). The $ makes B10 an absolute cell address when copied to other cells in Column C.

3. Strike Enter/Return and then copy C4 to C5 through C8.

4. Strike Enter/Return.

5. Highlight each cell in Column C and note that $B$10 is used in the formula in each row.

Compare RELATIVE and ABSOLUTE CELL ADDRESSING.

1. Highlight D4.

2. Use **B4/B10** (divides B4 by B10). In this formula, B10 is a relative cell address since $ signs were not keyed before the column and row references.

3. Strike Enter/Return; copy D4 to D5 through D8.

4. Strike Enter/Return. Notice that ERR appears in D5 through D7. ERR (error) resulted because the formula was adjusted automatically in each of the cells to which it was copied. For example, in D5 it wrote + or =B5/B11; in D6 it wrote + or =B6/B12; and in D7 it wrote + or =B7/B13. Thus, the software adjusted the formula downward by one cell each time it was copied to the next row in Column D.

Correct the results in D5 to D8 so that they agree with the results in C5 to C8.

1. Edit the formula in D5 so that Cell B10 is an absolute cell address: $B$10. (Works MAC users can edit the formula by placing the pointer to the right of the 0 and then selecting Absolute Cell Ref from the Edit Menu.)

2. Copy the formula in D5 to D6 through D8 and use ↓ to highlight each cell (shows that $B$10 was used in all rows in Column D).

3. Save the worksheet as 142C.

142D ◆

DISPLAY FORMULAS IN CELLS

Read the information at the right about displaying formulas and then complete the steps for your ss software.

Oftentimes it is easier to understand how a worksheet is constructed, to detect errors, and to follow references throughout the worksheet by displaying formulas in the cells rather than the formula values. Formulas in cells can be displayed by means of the Show Formula or Text feature. If needed, the worksheet can be printed with the formulas displayed in the cells.

Retrieve ss file 142C. After completing the following steps, save the worksheet as 142D.

LOTUS

1. Key **/**, **W**, **G**, **F**, **T** (selects Text from Worksheet Global Format).
2. If needed, lengthen the cells to display all of each formula.

(continued on next page)

WORKS DOS

1. Press **Alt**, **S**, **A** (selects All from the Select Menu).
2. Press **Alt**, **O**, **F** (selects Show Formulas from Options Menu).

(continued on next page)

WORKS MAC

1. Select Show Formulas from Options Menu.
2. If needed, lengthen the cells to display all of each formula.

(continued on next page)

MODIFIED BLOCK FORMAT

File name: L97C

1. Read the information at the right and study the model letter on p. 177 illustrating modified block format (blocked paragraphs) with mixed punctuation.
2. Key the model letter on p. 177; use spell check and proofread the document.
3. Reformat the letter; address it to:

**Mr. Karl M. Bedford
Berwick Drilling Co.
1088 Windsor Avenue
Waco, TX 76708-9316**

4. Indent the subject line and ¶s and change BLOCKED to INDENTED in the subject line.
5. For the first two lines, substitute the following:

This letter is arranged in modified block format with centered subject line and indented paragraphs. Another difference . . . *(continue lines)*.

Modified Block Letter Format

"Modified Block" simply means that the block format has been *modified;* that is, the date and the closing lines (complimentary close, writer's name, and writer's job title or department) start at the horizontal center of the paper instead of the left margin. Modified block format may have either blocked (p. 177) or indented (see model below) paragraphs.

Open and Mixed Punctuation

A letter in modified block format may be keyed with either open or mixed punctuation. In *open punctuation*, no punctuation follows the salutation or the complimentary close. In *mixed punctuation*, a colon follows the salutation and a comma follows the complimentary close.

```
D  ■ ■          DOCUMENT PROCESSING SPECIALISTS
■  P             6652 Remington Street
   S             New Haven, CT 06517-1498
                 (203) 266-8215


                                    April 16, 19--


         Mr. Karl M. Bedford
         Berwick Drilling Co.
         1088 Windsor Avenue
         Waco, TX 76708-9316

         Dear Mr. Bedford:

                 MODIFIED BLOCK LETTER FORMAT/INDENTED PARAGRAPHS

                 This letter is arranged in modified block format with inden-
         ted subject line and paragraphs.  Another difference between this
         letter format and the block format is that the dateline and the
         closing lines (complimentary close, keyed name of the originator,
         and his or her title) begin at the horizontal center point.

                 Mixed punctuation (a colon after the salutation and a comma
         after the complimentary close) is used in this letter.  If an
         enclosure is mentioned in the body of the letter, the word Enclo-
         sure is keyed a double space below the reference initials, flush
         with the left margin.  Copy notations are placed a double space
         below the enclosure notation or below the reference initials if no
         enclosure has been indicated.

                 A copy of the block format letter is enclosed so that you can
         compare the different formats.  As you can see, either format
         presents an attractive appearance.

                                    Sincerely yours,

                                    Jeffrey R. McKinley

                                    Jeffrey R. McKinley
                                    Word Processing Consultant

         ph

         Enclosure

         c William L. Gray
```

APPEARANCE OF LETTERS

1. Read the information at the right.
2. Retrieve the letters keyed for 97B.
3. Use the view/print preview feature; insert/delete blank line spaces as needed to enhance the appearance of the letters.
4. Preview the document again and make any additional needed adjustments.

Note: Your teacher may want you to print a copy of the document both before and after the changes are made so you can see the effect of the changes.

By using the document view/print preview feature of your software, you can determine if the top margin is approximately equal to the bottom margin of a formatted letter. If these margins do not appear about equal, blank lines (hard returns) can be inserted or deleted above the date to make the margins approximately equal. Doing so will enhance the appearance of the letter. It is better to have one or two fewer blank lines at the top than at the bottom.

WordPerfect Users:
WordPerfect's center page feature, used to center tables vertically (see p. 154), also can be used for equal top and bottom margins on letters. This automatic feature must be turned on before any part of the letter is keyed; or, after the letter has been keyed, the operator may use Home, Home, ↑ to place center page command at the beginning of the document.

142A ◆ CONDITIONING PRACTICE

each line twice

alphabet	1	Major plans for the next job will be finalized very quickly in August.
figures	2	On January 20, 1990, I moved from 2468 Bay Street to 1357 Lake Street.
keypad	3	107.86 109.35 146.90 256.30 293.68 303.99 469.35 786.03 862.93 1036.69
speed	4	Pamela's neighbor is apt to dismantle the small cubicle in the chapel.

gwam 1' | 1 | 2 | 3 | 4 | 5 | 6 | 7 | 8 | 9 | 10 | 11 | 12 | 13 | 14 |

142B ◆ PREPARE TO LEARN

Use the information at the right to prepare a worksheet. In B10, use the SUM function to find the Total Sales. Do not calculate the Percent of Sales at this time. Save the worksheet as 142B.

	A	B	C
1	Homeroom	Candy Bar	Percent of
2	Number	Sales	Total Sales
3			
4	101	357.25	
5	102	418.75	
6	104	298.5	
7	110	356.25	
8	111	298.5	
9			
10	TOTAL SALES	1729.25	

142C ◆ ABSOLUTE CELL ADDRESS

Read the information at the right about absolute cell addresses and then complete the steps (next page).

You have learned that ss software copies a formula across a row or down a column and automatically adjusts the formula placed in the new cells to reflect its new address and the address of other cells used in the formula. When the software copies formulas in this manner, it is using *relative cell addressing*. That is, the copy of the cell is related to its new address. Sometimes you will not want to change a formula to reflect its new address when copied across a row or column. In these instances, you want the software to use *absolute cell addressing*. Absolute cell addressing is done by keying a $ sign before the column and/or row reference in the cell address that is not to change. For example: If you want to divide all the numbers in Column B by a number that is in B10, you would make B10 an absolute cell address by keying a $ before the B and a $ before the 10 ($B$10).

DOCUMENT PROCESSING SPECIALISTS
6652 Remington Street
New Haven, CT 06517-1498
(203) 266-8215

		words in parts	total words
Dateline	April 16, 19-- QS 2" TM (Line 13)	3	3
Letter address	Miss Linda S. LaValley	8	8
	Vermillion Paper Products	13	13
	5067 Blackstone Lane	17	17
	Hartford, CT 06108-4913 DS	22	22
Salutation	Dear Miss LaValley: DS	26	26
Subject line	MODIFIED BLOCK LETTER FORMAT/BLOCKED PARAGRAPHS DS	10	35

Body of letter	This letter is arranged in modified block format with blocked	22	48
	paragraphs. The only difference between this letter format and	35	60
	the block format is that the dateline and the closing lines (com-	48	74
	plimentary close, keyed name of the originator, and his or her	61	86
	title) begin at the horizontal center point. DS	70	95
	Mixed punctuation (a colon after the salutation and a comma after	83	109
	the complimentary close) is used in this letter. If an enclosure	96	122
	is mentioned in the body of the letter, the word Enclosure is	109	134
	keyed a double space below the reference initials, flush with the	122	147
	left margin. Copy notations are placed a double space below the	135	160
	enclosure notation or below the reference initials if no enclosure	148	174
	has been indicated. DS	152	178
	A copy of the block format letter is enclosed so that you can	165	190
	compare the different formats. As you can see, either format	177	203
	presents an attractive appearance. DS	184	210

		words in parts	total words
Complimentary close	Sincerely yours, QS	3	213
	Jeffrey R. McKinley		
Keyed name	Jeffrey R. McKinley	7	217
Official title	Word Processing Consultant DS	13	222
Reference initials	ph DS	13	223
Enclosure notation	Enclosure DS	15	225
Copy notation	c William L. Gray DS	19	228

APPLICATION ACTIVITIES

Activity 1

Key the worksheet at the right and then follow the directions below to complete the worksheet.

1. Add a Column E: BONUS.
2. In the bonus column, compare the sum of the three month's sales to $17,500. If the sum is equal to or higher than $17,500, print 1500 in Column E to show that the employee is to receive a bonus of $1,500. If the total sales are less than $17,500, print 0 in Column E to show no bonus is to be paid. In E5, use this formula to make the comparison.
   Lotus:
   @IF(@SUM(B3.D3)<17500,0,1500)
   Works:
   =IF(SUM(B3:D3)<17500,0,1500)
3. Copy E5 to each remaining row in Column E to make the same comparison.
4. Format the worksheet appropriately and then save the worksheet as 141C1.

	A	B	C	D
1	PEOPLE	JAN	FEB	MAR
2				
3	JOHN	5431	6098	3982
4	MARY	6321	5542	7892
5	PEDRO	4521	8324	6790
6	MARIA	5576	6678	8842

Activity 2

Key the worksheet at the right. Follow directions below and on p. 278 to complete the worksheet.

1. In Column F, calculate each student's average score. (In F6, use the average function to compute the score for Abel/ Row 6 and then copy the formula to other rows.)
2. In Column G compare each student's average score to a score of 80. If it is less than 80, print the value of F6 in Column G; if it is 80 or more print 0. (In G6, use one of the formulas below and then copy it to other rows.)
   Lotus   **@IF(F6<80,F6,0)**
   Works   =IF(F6<80,F6,0)
3. In Column H, compare each average score to a score of 70. If it is less than 70, print the value in Cell F6; if it is 70 or more, print 0. Key and then copy one of the following formulas.
   Lotus   **@IF(F6<70,F6,0)**
   Works   =IF(F6<70,F6,0)
4. Format all columns to a width of 6.
5. Center all labels.
6. Format test scores and comparisons as Fixed, no decimal places.
7. Save the worksheet as 141C2.

	A	B	C	D	E	F	G	H
1	BUSINESS MATH GRADE BOOK							
2								
3		TEST	TEST	TEST	TEST		NEEDS	NEEDS
4	NAME	1	2	3	4	AVG	NOTE	TUTOR
5								
6	ABEL	78	85	72	78			
7	BOGGS	64	66	71	73			
8	CARR	78	82	76	75			
9	FRYZ	90	93	88	86			
10	GOOD	95	82	86	92			
11	MILLS	71	75	73	76			
12	POPE	62	71	73	66			
13	SIA	75	76	81	71			
14	TODD	66	65	50	61			
15	WILLS	72	64	75	70			
16	ZEON	81	74	65	60			

98A ◆
CONDITIONING PRACTICE
each line twice SS

alphabet	1	Quen said subzero weather may crack six big joints in the paved floor.
figures	2	Sid delivered 9,821 subcompact; 6,704 midsize; and 3,953 luxury autos.
fig/sym	3	At 2:45 p.m., Teams #9 & #7 (Court 3-5) and #6 & #10 (Court 1-8) play.
speed	4	The neighbor burns wood and a small bit of coal to make a giant flame.

gwam 1' | 1 | 2 | 3 | 4 | 5 | 6 | 7 | 8 | 9 | 10 | 11 | 12 | 13 | 14 |

98B ◆
LEARN INDENT FEATURE

Hanging Indent. Hanging indent is a formatting feature that positions the first line of text at the left margin and indents the remaining lines a specific number of spaces to the right (usually the first tab stop).

WORDPERFECT
1. Depress **F4**.
2. Depress **Shift Tab**.
3. Key the paragraph.
4. Return twice.
5. Repeat steps 1-4 for each paragraph to be formatted with a hanging indent.

WORKS DOS
1. Depress **Ctrl H**.
2. Key each paragraph to be formatted with a hanging indent.
3. Return twice.
4. Depress **Ctrl G** to turn off the hanging indent feature after all hanging indent paragraphs are keyed.

WORKS MAC
1. Move the left margin set to 0.5". The paragraph indent should remain at zero.
2. Key all paragraphs to be formatted with a hanging indent.
3. Return twice.
4. Move the left margin back to zero.

File Name: PASCUAL

1. Study the specific commands for the hanging indent feature for the software you are using.
2. Format and key the text at the right as a modified block letter with mixed punctuation. (WordPerfect Users: Use the center page feature.*) Use today's date and address the letter to:

   Mrs. Wanda Pascual
   Richland Manufacturing
   531 Fountain Drive
   Panama City, FL 32401-1294

   The letter is from **Troy G. McDaniels, Vice President**. Supply an appropriate salutation and complimentary close.
3. After keying the letter, use the view/print preview to check the appearance.

*1. **Shift F8**
2. **2**—Page
3. **1**—Center Page
4. **Yes**
5. Enter
6. Enter

Here is a brief description of the four programs that I indicated may be of interest to your company managers. Each workshop runs for two days for about 15 hours of instruction.

Leadership Development for Executives. Workshop designed to enhance skills in the areas of oral and written communication, managing conflict, delegation, time management, listening, and coaching.

Employee Motivation. Workshop on motivating subordinates. Focuses on how to motivate today's diverse employee work force through adapting individual leadership styles and creating the RIGHT environment.

Profits, Profits, and Profits. Increasing company profits by raising employee productivity, lowering employee turnover, and reducing employee absenteeism through positive employee morale is explained in this workshop.

Solutions Through Teamwork. Using the Quality Circles Team approach to solving company problems is the emphasis of this workshop. How to organize and implement quality circles will be outlined.

If you have specific dates when you would like the workshops offered, let me know as soon as possible so that we can coordinate the dates with the workshop presenters.

LOTUS

Compare the contents of A1 and B1 to determine if their sum is less than 75. If true, print *Help* in C1; if false, print *No Help* in C1.

1. In A1 key **25**; in B1 key **35**.
2. Highlight C1 (cell address where result of comparison will appear).
3. Key **@IF(A1+B1<75,"Help","No Help")**. A1+B1 identify the two cells and the operation involved in the comparison; < is the logical operator since you are determining if the sum of A1+B1 is less than 75; Help is the information that is to be printed in C1 if the sum of A1+B1 is less than 75; No Help is to be printed in C1 if the sum of A1+B1 is equal to or greater than 75. **Note:** When a label is to be printed as the result of a comparison, it must be enclosed within quotation marks. If the result to be printed is a formula or value, the quotation marks need not be used. If you want to right-align the printed label, insert the necessary number of spaces between the first " and the first letter in the label. For example, if you want to right-align *No Help* in a column that is 9 spaces wide, key two blank spaces after the " and before the N ("   No Help).
4. Strike Enter (executes the command and prints the results in C1).

Compare the difference in contents of A3 and B3 to the contents of C3. If the difference is equal to C3, print *Equal* in C4. If not equal, print *Not Equal* in C4:

1. In A3 key **679805**; in B3 **354098**; in C3 **350507**.
2. Highlight C4 and key **@IF(A1-B3=C3,"Equal","Not Equal")**.
3. Strike Enter.

Compare the sum of A5 through D5 to see if it is less than 150. If it is, print 150- as a label in E5; if not, print 149+ as a label in E5.

1. In A5, key **11**; **22** in B5; **33** in C5; **44** in D5.
2. Highlight E5 and key **@IF(@ SUM (A5.D5)<150,"150-", "149+")**.
3. Strike Enter and clear this worksheet.

WORKS DOS AND WORKS MAC

Compare the contents of A1 and B1 to determine if their sum is less than 75. If true, print 0 in C1; if false, print 75 in C1.

1. In A1, key **25**; in B1 key **35**.
2. Highlight C3 (cell where result of comparison will appear).
3. Key **=IF(A1+B1<75,0,75)**. A1+B1 identifies the two cells and the operation involved in the comparison; < is the logical operator since you are determining if the sum of A1+B1 is less than 75. The value 0 is to be printed in C1 if the sum of A1+B1 is less than 75. The number 75 is to be printed in C1 if the sum of A1+B1 is equal to or greater than 75.
4. Strike Enter/Return (executes the command and prints the results in C1).

In D3, compare the difference in contents of A3 and B3 to the contents of C3. If the difference is equal to C3, print value of C3 in D3. If not equal, print 0 in D3.

1. In A3, key **679805**; in B3, **354098**; in C3, **350507**.
2. Highlight D3.
3. Key **=IF(A3-B3=C3,C3,0)**.
4. Strike Enter/Return.

Compare the sum of A5+B5+C5+D5 to see if it is less than 150. If it is, print 0 in E5; if not, print 150 in E5.

1. In A5, key **11**; **22** in B5; **33** in C5; **44** in D5.
2. Highlight E5 and key **=IF(SUM(A5:D5)<150,0,150)**.
3. Strike Enter/Return and clear this worksheet.

98C ◆

BUSINESS LETTERS

Letter 1

File name: LYONS

Format the letter at the right in block style with open punctuation. Send the letter to:

Mr. Richard B. Lyons
3716 Rangely Drive
Raleigh, NC 27609-4115

Use current date and supply an appropriate salutation.

Letter 2

File name: SYKES

Format the letter at the right in modified block style with indented paragraphs and mixed punctuation. Use current date. Leave 1" between columns of the table.

Learning cue: To place a table within the body of a letter, follow these guidelines.

1. DS above and below the table; SS the body of the table.
2. Clear all tabs.
3. Determine and set the tab stop for each column of the table. (The table must be centered within the margins of the letter.)

Letter 3

File name: MISTLE

Reformat Letter 2 using block style with open punctuation and send the letter to:

Miss Michelle L. Mistle
2840 Ardwick Drive
Rockville, MD 20852-4127

Change the certificate number to **B-2995** and the value of the certificate to **$2,646.16**.

Letter 1   opening lines 19

Robert Johnson, our director of customer relations, indicated that you are   34
interested in career opportunities with Wayler Insurance Company in the   48
administrative support services division. He asked me to provide you with   63
additional information.   69

As word processing supervisor, I have the opportunity to interview and test   84
many applicants. We are looking for applicants with excellent communi-   98
cation and keyboarding skills. Both are extremely important skills for indi- 113
viduals to possess who wish to be an asset to our organization. Any course you 129
take to enhance these skills will increase your marketability.   142

If you would like to visit our word processing center before giving your re- 157
port, please let me know. You can call me at 555-7291.   (149) 169

Sincerely yours | Mrs. Mary A. Worthington | Word Processing Supervisor | 183
xx | c Robert C. Johnson   187

Letter 2

Mr. Cody G. Sykes | 625 Pacific Avenue | Rockville, MD 20853-3107 | Dear   14
Mr. Sykes: 19

How quickly time passes! It seems like only yesterday that you renewed   33
your 24-month certificate of deposit (B-2987) with our bank. On **March 15** it 49
will again mature.   53

For your convenience we processed the certificate so that it would be re-   67
newed automatically for the same time period at the current market rate. If   83
we do not hear from you prior to the maturity date, your certificate will be 98
renewed at 4.58 percent for the next two years. The value of your certificate 114
as of **March 15** will be **$1,323.08**.   121

Should you wish to have the certificate renewed for a longer period of   135
time at a higher interest rate, we can also do that. The time periods and cur- 151
rent interest rates are as follows: 158

36-month certificate	4.67 percent	165
48-month certificate	4.84 percent	172
60-month certificate	5.09 percent	178

Call or stop in if you decide to go with a longer period for your certificate. 194
We appreciate your patronage and look forward to assisting with your bank-   209
ing needs in the future.   (193) 214

Sincerely, | Mrs. Eiko R. Kimura | Investments | xx   223

LESSON 99 — LETTERS

99A ◆

CONDITIONING PRACTICE

each line twice SS

alphabet 1 This weekly journal gives exact sizes of old boat and plane equipment.

figures 2 I know the ZIP Code plus 4 for 49-13th Street is listed as 92057-1683.

fig/sym 3 The 72" x 96" tablecloth will cost $84.63 less discounts of 10% & 15%.

speed 4 The soggy field by the city dog kennels was good for a big tug of war.

gwam 1' | 1 | 2 | 3 | 4 | 5 | 6 | 7 | 8 | 9 | 10 | 11 | 12 | 13 | 14 |

SET MARGINS AND KEY HEADERS AND FOOTERS

Spreadsheet software permits you to set top and bottom and right and left margins that are different from the default settings. Headers and/or footers can be used to make worksheets easier to read and understand. The headers/footers do not appear on the worksheet until it is printed.

Lotus Key **/**, **P**, **P**, **O**; make choices from the Header, Footer, and Margin options on the Options Menu; select Quit option and continue with commands needed to print the worksheet.

Works DOS *Headers and Footers:* Press **Alt**, **P**, **H** and then key header/footer.

Margins: Press **Alt**, **P**, **M** and then key in desired settings.

Works MAC ~ File Menu and select Page Setup option; ~ desired choices and key header/footer and desired settings; strike Return.

L ESSON 141 USE LOGICAL FUNCTIONS

141A ◆ CONDITIONING PRACTICE

each line twice;
then 30" timings
on selected lines;
exit wp; access ss

alphabet 1 Evelyn was just shocked by the extremely crazy sequence of happenings.

figures 2 James drove 487 miles on May 19 and the remaining 356 miles on May 20.

keypad 3 .06 .09 .03 1.06 1.03 1.60 1.09 4.90 5.60 6.93 14.30 26.90 33.69 93.60

speed 4 My buddy may go with me when I visit the firms with the antique autos.

gwam 1' | 1 | 2 | 3 | 4 | 5 | 6 | 7 | 8 | 9 | 10 | 11 | 12 | 13 | 14 |

141B ◆

IF FUNCTION

Read the information about the IF function at the right and then complete the steps listed on p. 276 for your ss software.

A powerful feature of ss software is its ability to compare the relationship between the contents of two cells and then to take action based on the result of that comparison. The IF function, the name for this feature, contains three elements. The first element is the comparison between the contents of two cells (referred to as the comparison). The second element is the action that is to be taken if the result of the comparison is true. The third element is the action that is to be taken if the result of the comparison is false. Logical operators are used to make the comparison between the two cells. Logical operators include the following:

= Equal
< Less than
> Greater than
<= Less than or equal to
>= Greater than or equal to
<> Not equal

For example, if 50 is entered in Cell A1 and 75 is entered in Cell B1, the IF function could be used in Cell C1 to make comparisons such as:

a. Is A1 equal (=) to B1?
b. Is A1 less than (<) B1?
c. Is B1 greater than or equal to (>=) A1?
d. Is B1 not equal (<>) to A1?

In any of these comparisons, the IF function will make the comparison and then print information you designate in C1. You will designate the information to be printed if the comparison is true and different information if the comparison is false. For example, in "a" above you could designate that *100* be printed if the comparison is true (the two numbers are equal) and that *000* be printed if the comparison is false (the two numbers are not equal).

LEARN WORD PROCESSING FEATURES

1. Study the specific commands below for the search to find feature for your software.
2. Retrieve the file named SYKES.
3. Use the search command to find the underlined word at the right to answer the question.
4. Study the specific commands below for the search to replace feature for your software.
5. Retrieve the file named PASCUAL.
6. Use the search to replace command to:
   a. Replace *workshop* with **seminar**.
   b. Replace *15* with **16**.
   c. Replace *RIGHT* with **right**.

1. On what date does the certificate <u>mature</u>?
2. At what <u>percent</u> will the certificate be renewed?
3. What are the longer time periods for which the <u>certificate</u> can be renewed?

Search to Find. Search to find is a feature that locates specified text (a word or phrase) in a document.

Search to Replace. Search to replace is a feature that locates and replaces specified text in a document.

WORDPERFECT

Search to Find
1. Move the cursor to the location where you will start the search. (Strike **Home**, **Home**, ↑ to start from the beginning of the document.)
2. Depress **F2**.
3. At the → *Srch:* prompt, key the text you want to find.
4. Depress **F2**.
5. To search for additional occurrences of the text, depress **F2** twice. When no more occurrences of the word are found, **Not Found** briefly appears in the lower left corner of the screen.

Search to Replace
1. Move the cursor to the location where you will start the search. (Strike **Home**, **Home**, ↑ to start from the beginning of the document.)
2. Depress **Alt F2**.
3. At the *w/Confirm?* prompt, key **Y**(es). (If you key **N**(o), every occurrence of the text will be changed throughout the document.)
4. At the → *Srch:* prompt, key the text you want to find and depress **F2**.
5. At the *Replace with:* prompt, key the replacement text and depress **F2**.
6. The cursor will move to the first occurrence of the *Srch* word. At the *Confirm? No (Yes)* prompt, key **Y** if you want the text replaced, key **N** if you do not want it replaced.

WORKS DOS

Search to Find
1. Move the cursor to the location where you will start the search. (Depress **Ctrl Home** to start from the beginning of the document.)
2. Depress **Alt**, **Select**, **Search** (**Alt**, **S**, **S**).
3. On the *Search for* line, key the text you want to find.
4. Return.
5. To search for additional occurrences of the text, depress **F7**. When no more occurrences of the word are found, *No match found* will appear in the dialog box.
6. Strike Return to display the input screen.*
*Note: Striking Return when a word is highlighted in search mode will delete it. Use arrow keys to move the cursor away from highlighted word.

Search to Replace
1. Move the cursor to the location where you will start the search. (Depress **Ctrl Home** to start from the beginning of the document.)
2. Depress **Alt**, **Select**, **Replace** (**Alt**, **S**, **R**).
3. On the *Search for* line, key the text you want to find.
4. Strike Tab to move down to the *Replace with:* line and key the replacement text.
5. Strike Return.
6. Each time the word appears in the text, indicate whether you want the text replaced by keying **Y** or **N**.
7. When no more occurrences of the word are found, *No more occurrences* will appear in the dialog box. Strike Return to return to input screen.

WORKS MAC

Search to Find
1. Depress ⌘ **F**.
2. Key the text you want to find.
3. Strike Return.
4. Continue to strike Return to find additional occurrences of the word. When all occurrences of the word have been found, a dialog box will appear indicating *All occurrences of "word" have been found*.
5. Strike Return to return to the input screen.

Search to Replace
1. Depress ⌘ **R**.
2. Key the text you want to replace.
3. ~ *Replace With* box and key the replacement text. If there is already text in the box, ~ → over the text and then key the replacement word.
4. If you want all occurrences of the word replaced, ~ the *Replace All* box. If you want to select which occurrences of the word to replace, ~ the *Find Next* box. Each time the word is found the computer will stop. When you want the word replaced, you will ~ the *Replace* box and then ~ the *Find Next* box. When you don't want an occurrence of the word replaced, ~ the *Find Next* box.
5. When the dialog box appears indicating *All occurrences of "word" have been found*, strike Return to get back to the input screen.

UNIT 31

LESSONS 141-145

Enhance Spreadsheet Skills

Learning Outcomes: After completing this unit, you will be able to

1. Use the IF function to make a comparison.
2. Use an absolute cell address when copying formulas and displaying formulas.
3. Change values to answer *What If* questions.
4. Set top and left margins and key headers and footers.

SPREADSHEET FEATURE AND COMMAND GUIDE

DISPLAY FORMULAS IN CELLS
IF FUNCTION
MOVE AND COPY FEATURES
SET MARGINS AND KEY HEADERS AND FOOTERS

The spreadsheet features and commands used in this unit are explained below and on p. 275. Preview the topics presented in the unit by skimming this guide. As you work in Unit 31 and following units, refer to this guide. Also, use Appendix G (pp. 449-452) to recall software commands.

DISPLAY FORMULAS IN CELLS

Displaying formulas in cells, rather than their results, may help the user understand worksheet construction, detect errors, and follow references throughout the worksheet. If desired, formulas, rather than results, may be displayed on printed worksheets.

Lotus **Key /, W, G, F, T** (displays all formulas in cells). If all need not be displayed, key **/, R, F, T**.

Works DOS Select all cells by pressing **Alt, S, A**; then press **Alt, O, F** (to reverse the action, repeat the Alt, O, F command to turn off Show Formulas).

Works MAC Select Show Formulas from Options Menu (to reverse the action select Show Values from the Options Menu).

IF FUNCTION

The IF function compares contents of two cells. Conditions that contain *logical operators* provide the basis for comparison. Logical operators include the following:

= (value of two cells are *equal*)
< (value of one cell is *less than* the other)
> (value of one cell *greater than* the other)
<= (value of one cell is *less than or equal* to the other)
>= (value of one cell is *greater than or equal to* the other)
<> (values are unequal).

A comparison involves three elements: Comparison itself (one cell with another). Action to follow if comparison is true. Action to follow if comparison is false.

Lotus **@IF** (comparison, result-if-true, result-if-false).
Works **=IF** (comparison, value-if-true, value-if-false).

MOVE AND COPY FEATURES

When the Move feature is used, the range of cell entries is erased from its original location and transferred to the new location. When the Copy feature is used, the range of cells remains in its original location and appears in its new location.

Lotus **Key /, C** (for Copy) or **M** (for Move); specify range to be copied or moved; specify upper-left cell of the receiving range; strike Enter.

Works DOS Press **Alt, S, E**; specify the range to be copied; press **Alt, E, C** (for Copy) or **M** (for Move). Highlight upper-left cell in the receiving range; strike Enter.

Works MAC **COPY:** Highlight the range of cells to be copied; ~ Edit Menu and select Copy; highlight the upper-left cell in the range that is to receive the copy; ~ Edit Menu and select Paste.
MOVE: Highlight the range of cells that is to be moved; ~ Edit Menu and select Move; key address of receiving cell in dialog box.

99C ◆

MODIFIED BLOCK LETTERS

Document 1
File name: CLINE1
modified block format, blocked paragraphs; open punctuation

words

November 15, 19-- | Mr. Joshua D. Cline, President | Chadwick Insurance 14
Company | 3209 Roosevelt Way, NE | Seattle, WA 98105-6385 | Dear Mr. Cline | 28
Subject: Bellevue Branch Office 34

The renovation of the building we leased for the new branch office in 48
Bellevue is scheduled to be completed by December 1. This schedule should 63
give us ample time to have the branch operational by the target date of 78
December 15. 81

Erika Tudor from the Seattle home office has been promoted to branch 94
manager and will be in Bellevue by the first of December. Jason Reeves has 110
agreed to transfer from the Tacoma branch to be Erika's assistant. I am 124
confident they will do an exceptional job. 133

A complete roster of the Bellevue office personnel is enclosed. Two of 147
the agents are transferring from Seattle. The others are new and will have 163
completed our trainee program by December 10. 172

I will keep you informed on the progress of the Bellevue branch; I am sure 187
that it will be an excellent addition to our company. (163) 198

Sincerely | Parker S. Hawthorne | District Supervisor | xx | Enclosure 210/231

opening lines 19

Document 2
File name: WALSTROM
modified block format, indented paragraphs; mixed punctuation; use current date; send the letter to:
**Mr. Morris Young
904 Beatrice Street
Titusville, FL 32780-8192**
Supply a salutation.

Walstrom Industries has informed us that you have accepted a position in 33
their accounting department and soon will be moving to Rockville. Con- 47
gratulations and best wishes. 53

Our bank has designed a packet of information to help new citizens in the 68
community become acquainted with the local area. The packet includes a 83
map of the city, housing and rental guides, and a brochure that highlights 98
upcoming cultural and civic events. This material will provide you with 112
information that will make relocating a little easier. 123

Once you arrive in Rockville, we would appreciate having an opportunity to 138
discuss ways that the First National Bank of Rockville can accommodate 152
your banking needs. 156

Sincerely, | Ms. Marge L. Bowman | Customer Service | xx | Enclosures 168

Document 3
File name: CLINE2
Retrieve CLINE1. Replace the third paragraph with the paragraph at the right.

Ms. Tudor has finished hiring the rest of her staff. Courtney Edinburg and Forrest Hewitt will transfer from the Seattle office; the other two agents, Phillip Guerrero and Chiek Kanesko, will complete the trainee program in time to join the staff on January 2. The receptionist/secretary position has been filled by Dyan Silverhill.

139-140B ♦ (cont.)

6. Create and enter a formula (total hours times hourly rate); copy it as needed to compute wages for each employee. Format these values as dollars and cents.
7. Add **Menlo** in the proper row to maintain alphabetic order and record 8 hours for each day from Wednesday through Friday. Use $4.50 an hour as the pay rate and have the worksheet compute Menlo's total hours and wages.
8. Save as 139B1.

Activity 2

Retrieve *Student's Template* file T139B2 and complete the worksheet according to the following directions.

1. Format column widths and headings appropriately.
2. Format $ values with no decimals; percents to 2 decimal places.
3. Calculate the 2.5% salary increase (present salary x .025); new salary (present salary + 2.5% raise + merit raise); and % of increase (new salary – present salary) / present salary for each employee.
4. Calculate column totals and averages in cells not X'd out.
5. Draw lines as desired.
6. Save 139B2.

Activity 3

Complete the form letter (wp activity) as directed below.

1. Retrieve file T139B3 from *Student's Template*. Create three letters (block format, open punctuation) in one file named 139B3. Use the information on the business cards at the right to create a letter for each individual. Be sure to include the appropriate speaker's topic (above each card) at the proper place in each letter.
2. Use spell check; proofread for errors in meaning, grammar, etc. Check format from the screen or print preview.
3. Save the file as 139B3.

Activity 4

Create a worksheet as directed below.

1. Key the information at the right.
2. Add the following two-line column headings: Column F—OVERTIME RATE; Column G—GROSS PAY; Column H—NET PAY.
3. Set column widths so there will be at least two spaces between columns.
4. Right-align column headings of B through H; center Column A heading.
5. Format money columns with $ and 2 decimal places.
6. Format other number columns as Fixed with 1 decimal place.
7. In Column F, create and enter a formula to compute each employee's overtime rate, which is equal to regular rate x 1.5.
8. In Column G, create and enter a formula to find each employee's gross pay: (regular hours x regular rate) + (overtime rate x overtime hours).
9. In Column H, create and enter a formula to find each employee's net pay: gross pay – deductions.
10. For Susan Tofflin, insert 4 overtime hours.
11. Delete Gaston from this payroll journal.
12. Insert a column after A—column heading is EMPLOYEE NUMBER and the numbers beginning with first employee are 111, 112, 115, 120, 126, and 135 (format with no decimals).
13. Draw a line to separate the title from column headings.
14. Save worksheet as 139B.

"Pluralizing the Curriculum"

Helen T. Wilde, Ph. D.
Executive Director
(914) 555-2285

Eastern Economic Association
**98 HIGHVIEW AVENUE
NEW ROCHELLE, NY 10801-5315**

"Tolerating Differences"

Mrs. Emma T. Zappalo

LANDMARK DEVELOPERS
**103 VINE STREET
SHAMOKIN, PA 17872-5533**
Telephone: (717) 555-9462   Telecopier: (717) 555-3916

"Culture Does Begin at Home"

SCIENTIFIC RESEARCH, INC.

David F. Moore
Sales Manager
(301)-555-9278

500 Gorusch Ave.
Baltimore, MD
21218-3549

		HOURS	REGULAR RATE	OVERTIME HOURS	DEDUCTIONS
1	PAYROLL JOURNAL				
2					
3			REGULAR	OVERTIME	
4	EMPLOYEE	HOURS	RATE	HOURS	DEDUCTIONS
5					
6	Harriet Demonti	40	6.5	5	63.45
7	Sylvester Everett	40	7.5	2	67.87
8	Fredricka Gaston	36	8.25		45
9	Maryanne Gigliotti	40	6.5	6	57.85
10	Susan Tofflin	40	7.25		34.1
11	Beatrice Robertson	40	6.75	4	71.12
12	William Tellison	32	7.35		35.64

100A ◆
CONDITIONING PRACTICE
each line twice SS

alphabet 1 Maxine and Peggy requested that a dozen wives join the breakfast club.

figures 2 I answered 4,978; Sidney answered 5,102; the correct answer was 5,360.

fig/sym 3 Both courses (#23-981 & #45-760) meet every Tuesday night at 6:30 p.m.

speed 4 The ensign is to make a turn to the right when the signal is in sight.

gwam 1' | 1 | 2 | 3 | 4 | 5 | 6 | 7 | 8 | 9 | 10 | 11 | 12 | 13 | 14 |

100B ◆
LEARN MACRO FEATURE

File name: L100B

Macros. The macro feature of a software package allows the operator to save (record) keystrokes and retrieve (playback) them at a later time. For example, if a company name is used often in correspondence, the operator could create and use a macro instead of keying the company name each time it appeared in a document.

WORDPERFECT

1. Depress **Ctrl F10** to begin defining the macro.
2. When *Define macro:* appears on the screen, depress **Alt** and key any single letter. (For this exercise, depress **Alt V**. If *ALTV.WPM Already Exists:* appears, depress **1** R(eplace), **Y**(es).)
3. When *Description:* appears, strike Enter to create the macro without a description. (A brief description of the macro could be keyed at this point.)
4. Key the text or keystrokes you want to record as the macro. For this exercise, key **Vermillion Floral & Greenhouse**.
5. Depress **Ctrl F10** to end macro definition.

WORKS DOS

1. Depress **Alt /** to begin defining the macro.
2. Highlight **Record Macro** and strike Return. (The word RECORD appears in the lower right corner of the screen.)
3. When *Playback Key:* appears on the screen, depress **Alt V**, Return. If this key has a macro and *Record anyway?* appears, strike Return. (The new macro will be recorded over the old macro.)
4. Key the text you want recorded as the macro. (For this exercise, key **Vermillion Floral & Greenhouse**.)
5. Depress **Alt /**.
6. Highlight **End Recording** and strike Return. (RECORD will disappear after you End Recording.)

WORKS MAC

1. From the Macro Menu select **Macros On** if it is not checked.
2. From the Macro Menu select **Start Recording**.
3. In the *Key* box, key a single letter to be used to retrieve the macro. (For this exercise, strike **V**.) These keys cannot be used for macros: E, I, N, U.
4. To define a macro without a description, strike Return. To create a macro with a description, depress the Tab key; key a description of the macro; strike Return. If *Key is already in use* appears in the dialog box, ~ **Record** to replace old macro with the new macro.
5. Key the characters you want saved for the macro. (For this exercise, record **Vermillion Floral & Greenhouse**.)
6. From the Macro Menu select **Stop Recording**. When the dialog box appears, either ~ **Stop** or strike Return.

Activity 1
1. Following the steps outlined above for your software, define a macro for Vermillion Floral & Greenhouse.
2. Clear the input screen and key the text at the right, depressing **Alt V** (MAC users depress **Option V**) each time Vermillion Floral & Greenhouse appears in the text.

Activity 2
Search to replace Vermillion Floral & Greenhouse with Moorcroft Floral & Gift.

Vermillion Floral & Greenhouse sells fresh cut bouquets.

Vermillion Floral & Greenhouse delivers balloon bouquets.

Vermillion Floral & Greenhouse sells green plants.

Vermillion Floral & Greenhouse delivers fruit baskets.

Vermillion Floral & Greenhouse has silk and dry arrangements.

Vermillion Floral & Greenhouse has beautiful wedding flowers.

Vermillion Floral & Greenhouse has flowers for all occasions.

Vermillion Floral & Greenhouse is your full flower center.

Activity 2

Prepare a worksheet. Complete the following steps in what seems to you the most efficient manner.

1. Right-align all labels in the worksheet.
2. Format all values as money with no decimals.
3. Change all column widths to 6 spaces.
4. Change Column A width to 10.
5. Key the information at the right.
6. Create, enter, and copy formulas to find totals, averages, minimums, and maximums as needed.
7. Save as 138D2.

	A	B	C	D	E	F	G	H
1	UTILITY COST STUDY FOR 19--							
2								
3	MONTH	GAS	ELECT	WATER	SWGE	PHONE	C-TV	TOT
4								
5	JANUARY	115	120		72	45	17	
6	FEBRUARY	114	127	82		42	17	
7	MARCH	134	105			47	17	
8	APRIL	97	113		76	38	19	
9	MAY	77	109	83		35	19	
10	JUNE	56	102			42	19	
11	JULY	44	260		81	49	19	
12	AUGUST	34	230	76		44	19	
13	SEPTEMBER	36	255			41	19	
14	OCTOBER	44	154		76	53	24	
15	NOVEMBER	57	138	85		48	24	
16	DECEMBER	118	105			44	24	
17								
18	TOTAL							
19	AVERAGE							
20	MINIMUM							
21	MAXIMUM							

LESSONS 139-140 APPLY SPREADSHEET AND WORD PROCESSING SKILLS

139-140A ◆
CONDITIONING PRACTICE

each line twice

alphabet 1 Kay may quit publicizing the major events before the end of next week.

figures 2 Of the 12,874 votes cast, Kern received 6,305 and Bahr received 6,569.

keypad 3 645 978 312 808 1,123 4,456 7,789 4,714 5,825 6,936 1,040 2,050 13,060

speed 4 The visit by the six sorority girls may be a problem for their mentor.

gwam 1' | 1 | 2 | 3 | 4 | 5 | 6 | 7 | 8 | 9 | 10 | 11 | 12 | 13 | 14 |

139-140B ◆

APPLICATION ACTIVITIES

Activity 1

Retrieve *Student's Template* file T139B1 and complete the worksheet according to the following directions.

1. If needed, change Columns A and I to 9 spaces; B through F, 4 spaces; G and H, 8 spaces.
2. Right-align all labels.

3. Use the SUM function to compute total hours for each employee.
4. Format hourly rate as dollars and cents.
5. Add a column at the right; title it NET PAY; make it 8 spaces wide, and format as dollars and cents.

(continued on next page)

100C ◆
USE MACROS FOR LETTERS

File name: L100C

1. Standard paragraphs can be recorded as macros and retrieved to create a letter. Define a macro for each paragraph at right. Use the letter key indicated to save and retrieve each paragraph. WordPerfect (Define macro) and Works DOS (Playback key): Alt A, Alt B, Alt C, etc. Works MAC (Key box): A, B, C, etc.

   When *name of department* appears in a paragraph you retrieve for a letter, you will need to replace it with the specific name of the department.

2. Create Letters 1, 2, and 3 (below) using the macros indicated. Use block format, mixed punctuation. Use today's date and supply a salutation.

Letter 1
Mr. Joshua T. Heintz
424 Bluff Drive
Davenport, IA 52802-6112
Paragraphs: A, C, F, J
Department: Information Processing Center

Letter 2
Ms. Lea S. Fong
725 East Street
Davenport, IA 52803-2141
Paragraphs: A, D, H, J
Department: Accounting Department

Letter 3
Mr. Dennis M. Dupree
838 Glen Place
Davenport, IA 52804-7834
Paragraphs: A, B, F, J
Department: Sales Department

A Welcome to Midwestern Office Products! We are pleased that you have chosen to become part of our organization, and we are looking forward to your assistance in helping us achieve our goals and objectives in the years ahead.

B You will enjoy working with Thomas Chaney. He has been with the company for 12 years and is highly regarded by his colleagues. Since he was promoted to sales manager five years ago, company sales have grown tremendously. The new sales strategies that he implemented have been very successful.

C If you enjoy working with the latest technology, I am certain that you will enjoy being part of Olivia Reinhold's staff. Our Information Processing Center was recently featured in a national office technology magazine and is the envy of many organizations, due to the efforts of Ms. Reinhold and her talented staff.

D You will enjoy working with Rhonda Little; she is outstanding. She is one of those rare individuals who possesses people skills as well as technical expertise. She has completely computerized the Accounting Department since being appointed accounting supervisor.

F I am confident that your association with us will be rewarding. I am looking forward to visiting with you in person at the next meeting of the (name of department)

G Your association with us will be rewarding. I am looking forward to meeting you the next time I visit the (name of department)

H I am confident that your work in the (name of department) will be rewarding. I am looking forward to meeting you soon.

J Sincerely,

Sara C. Koontz
President

xx

Delete the following files from your disk (refer to 66D, p. 129, if necessary):

L64B	L78B	L84B
L65B	L81C	L84C
SABIN	L82C	L85D
L77B	L83C	L86B
L77C	L83D	L87B

option from Global Menu).

3. Move cursor to highlight Center (selects the Center option).
4. Strike Enter.
5. Key these headings in the cells designated:

A1: **TOYS**   B1: **CARS**
C1: **BATS**   D1: **OARS**
E1: **TOPS**

Change all columns to 12 spaces:

1. Key /, **W**, **G**, **C**.
2. Strike → 6 times.
3. Strike Enter.

Change all values to percents with 2 decimal places.

1. Key /, **W**, **G**, **F**.
2. Key **P** (selects the Percent format).
3. Key **2** (specifies 2 decimal places).
4. Strike Enter.
5. Clear the screen.

5. Key these headings in the cells designated:

A1: **TOYS**   B1: **CARS**
C1: **BATS**   D1: **OARS**
E1: **TOPS**

Change all columns to 12 spaces.

1. Press **Alt**, **S**, **A**.
2. Press **Alt**, **T**, **W**.
3. Key **12**.
4. Strike Enter.

Change all numbers to percents with 2 decimal places.

1. Press **Alt**, **S**, **A**.
2. Press **Alt**, **T**, **P** (selects the Percent format from Format Menu).
3. Strike Enter.
4. Clear the screen.

Center all labels.

1. ~ A1 and drag through E1.
2. ~ Format Menu and select Set Cell Attributes.
3. ~ Center in Align listing in dialog box.
4. Strike Return.

Change all columns to 12 spaces.

1. On Select Menu choose All Cells.
2. ~ Format Menu and select Column Width.
3. Key **12**.
4. Strike Return.

Change all numbers to percents with 2 decimal places.

1. On Select Menu, choose All Cells.
2. ~ Format Menu and select Set Cell Attributes.
3. ~ Percent in dialog box and strike Return.
4. Clear the screen.

138D ◆

APPLICATION ACTIVITIES

Activity 1
Prepare a worksheet.
(**Lotus users:** Change Label-Prefix default so all labels are centered.)
1. Change all column widths to 5.
2. Format numbers to Fixed with one decimal place.
3. Key information given at the right.
4. Use SUM, AVG, MIN, and MAX functions to create the formulas needed; enter the formulas into appropriate cells; copy them as needed.
5. Delete row pertaining to Room B113.
6. Add row for Room B115 and key **66**, **75**, **45**, **33**, **67**, **89**, and **76** for sales from MON through SUN.
7. Copy formulas as needed to include Room B115 in all calculations.
8. Save worksheet as 138D1.

	A	B	C	D	E	F	G	H	I	J	K	L
1	CANDY BAR SALES BY HOMEROOM											
2												
3	ROOM	MON	TUE	WED	THU	FRI	SAT	SUN	TOT	AVG	MIN	MAX
4												
5	A101	23	45	32	66	66	72	23				
6	A102	45	65	82	45	45	56	33				
7	A103	45	23	10	75	75	63	77				
8	A104	34	23	11	34	34	45	23				
9	B111	23	35	46	53	53	49	66				
10	B112	22	33	55	88	88	43	23				
11	B113	24	57	80	76	76	32	54				
12	B114	23	56	80	55	55	65	29				
13	C201	78	67	56	43	43	33	60				
14	C202	35	65	73	59	92	47	59				
15	C203	44	56	76	48	98	32	45				
16												
17	TOT											
18	AVG											
19	MIN											
20	MAX											

Master Keyboarding Skills

Learning Outcomes: After completing this unit, you will be able to

1. Demonstrate improved response patterns and tabulating skill.
2. Key rough-draft copy at a higher percentage of transfer.
3. Key straight-copy paragraphs at higher speed and with greater control.

LESSON 101 · KEYBOARDING SKILLS

SM: Defaults; LS: SS

101A ◆ 6'
CONDITIONING PRACTICE

each line twice SS; two 1' writings on line 4

alphabet	1	Four giddy children were amazed by the quick, lively jumps of the fox.
figures	2	This new edition boasts 1,380 photographs, 926 charts, and 475 graphs.
fig/sym	3	Check #1657 and $48.90, dated May 23, is made out to McNeil & O'Leary.
speed	4	He may hand me the clay and then go to the shelf for the die and form.

gwam 1' | 1 | 2 | 3 | 4 | 5 | 6 | 7 | 8 | 9 | 10 | 11 | 12 | 13 | 14 |

101B ◆ 12'

IMPROVE TABULATING

1. Clear existing tabs.
2. Set tabs at 1.6", 4.8", and 6.2".
3. Key the table.
4. Take two 1' writings; find *gwam* on each.

			words
Apworth & Jakob Corporation	$10,285.60	30 days	10
K. L. Hightower & Co.	4,396.57	30 days	18
Jamison Brothers, Inc.	3,401.93	30 days	26
C. B. Wilkenson & Sons	5,187.46	30 days	34
Arps & Liggett Corporation	2,046.72	60 days	42
Drexler Brothers Company	3,958.20	60 days	51
J. Wellington, Ltd.	6,047.95	60 days	58
Zoeller, Ruiz & Poe, Inc.	1,459.28	60 days	67

101C ◆ 15'

RESPONSE PATTERNS

1. Key the lines as shown.
2. Key a 1' writing on each of lines 10-12; find *gwam* on each.
3. Key another 1' writing on each of the 2 slowest lines.

letter response	1	in we on be no at up as my ad you are him was oil get ink few pin date
	2	no card I in case I on base I in fact I join in I be aware I after him I saw him get
	3	You based my case on a gas tax rebate; no tax rebate was ever awarded.
word response	4	with they them than when also such form then wish paid name held right
	5	to keep I for them I when she I and paid I may form I the city I big town I own land
	6	When he signs the form, title to all the lake land may go to the city.
combination response	7	if no do we is up to be it the are and you for him she ink aid oil pan
	8	for him I and you I the oil I pay tax I may get I am safe I all data I he ate a plum
	9	In case she signs the deed, the city may test the case with the state.
letter	10	Ada set up a few database cards only after a union started a tax case.
word	11	Their tutor may go with them when they go to the city for the bicycle.
combination	12	Pamela is to wear the pink gown to the union social at the civic hall.

gwam 1' | 1 | 2 | 3 | 4 | 5 | 6 | 7 | 8 | 9 | 10 | 11 | 12 | 13 | 14 |

PREPARE TO LEARN

Using the information at the right, prepare a worksheet.

	A	B	C	D	E
1					
2	87	47	47	68	88
3	82	366	86	78	32
4	52	26	55	36	12
5	24	43	72	52	62
6	25	48	47	94	54

138C ◆

FORMAT WORKSHEETS

Read the information about formatting worksheets at the right. Complete the steps listed for your software.

In many of the worksheets you have prepared, some columns are wider than others. Some headings are centered while others are aligned at the left or right. Some of the numbers are in Fixed format, while others are in Currency or Percent format. You, of course, formatted each column/row according to the type of data to be entered. When all columns/rows will contain the same type of data, naturally, all column widths and label and value formats can be the same. In those instances, the Global or Select All features may be used to set the format for all columns/rows at once.

LOTUS

Use the worksheet created in 138B and change all columns to 6 spaces.

1. Key **/**, **W**, **G** (selects the Global option from the Worksheet Menu).
2. Key **C** (selects the Column-Width option from the Global Menu).
3. Strike ← 3 times (changes width to 6).
4. Strike Enter.

Format all numbers as Currency with 0 decimal places.

1. Key **/**, **W**, **G**.
2. Key **F** (selects the Format option from the Global Menu).
3. Key **C**.
4. Key **0** (specifies 0 decimal places).
5. Strike Enter.

Center all labels by using Label-Prefix.

1. Key **/**, **W**, **G**.
2. Key **L** (selects the Label-Prefix

WORKS DOS

Use the worksheet created in 138B and change all columns to 6 spaces.

1. Press **Alt**, **S**, **A** (selects the All option from Select Menu).
2. Press **Alt**, **T**, **W** (selects the Column-Width option from Format Menu).
3. Key **6** (changes width to 6).
4. Strike Enter.

Format all numbers as Currency with 0 decimal places.

1. Press **Alt**, **S**, **A**.
2. Press **Alt**, **T**, **U** (selects the Currency option from Format Menu).
3. Key **0** (specifies 0 decimal places).
4. Strike Enter.

Center all labels.

1. Press **Alt**, **S**, **A**.
2. Press **Alt**, **F**, **S** (selects the Style option from Format Menu).
3. Key **C** (specifies center format).
4. Strike Enter.

WORKS MAC

Use the worksheet created in 138B and change all columns to 6 spaces.

1. ~ Select Menu and choose All Cells.
2. ~ Format Menu and select Column Width.
3. Key **6** (changes width to 6).
4. Strike Return.

Format all numbers as Dollars with 0 decimal places.

1. On Select Menu, choose All Cells.
2. ~ Format Menu and select Set Cell Attributes.
3. ~ Dollar in dialog box and key **0** (changes decimal places to 0).
4. Strike Return.
5. Key these headings in the cells designated:

A1: **TOYS** B1: **CARS**
C1: **BATS** D1: **OARS**
E1: **TOPS**

(continued on next page)

(continued on next page)

(continued on next page)

IMPROVE/ CHECK SKILLS

1. Key two 1' writings on each ¶; find *gwam* on each.
2. Key two 2' writings on ¶s 1-3 combined; find *gwam*.
3. Key a 3' writing on ¶s 1-3 combined; find *gwam*.
4. Key another 3' writing; find *gwam* and count errors.

gwam	¼'	½'	¾'	1'
20	5	10	15	20
24	6	12	18	24
28	7	14	21	28
32	8	16	24	32
36	9	18	27	36
40	10	20	30	40
44	11	22	33	44
48	12	24	36	48
52	13	26	39	52
56	14	28	42	56

all letters used | A | 1.5 si | 5.7 awl | 80% hfw

	gwam 2'	3'
A word processing system is an excellent tool young people can	6	4
use to develop their writing skills. When young people use such a	13	9
system to prepare papers for school or other purposes, the final copy	20	13
produced is likely to reflect their finest efforts because of the	27	18
amazing ease with which draft copies can be altered time after time.	33	22
Two basic functions of word processing systems that make it quite	40	27
easy to change writing are called insert and delete. These functions	47	31
permit the operator to add or take out a single space or character or	54	36
an entire word, sentence, paragraph, or document within a short period	61	41
of time with a great deal of ease.	64	43
When large amounts of material are moved from one place to	70	47
another, copied to another place, or deleted from the document, the	77	51
word processor often just marks the beginning and ending of the text	84	56
to be moved, copied, or deleted. To do this, the person operating the	91	61
system may use a special function key to mark the material at the	98	65
proper points.	99	66

gwam 2' | 1 | 2 | 3 | 4 | 5 | 6 | 7 |
3' | 1 | 2 | 3 | 4 | 5 |

LESSON 102   KEYBOARDING SKILLS

SM: Defaults; LS: SS

CONDITIONING PRACTICE

each line twice SS; two 1' writings on line 4

alphabet 1 The six boys quickly removed juicy chunks from a sizzling pot of stew.

figures 2 They washed 59 cars, 28 vans, 47 campers, and 30 bikes on November 16.

fig/sym 3 The 164 copies (priced at $8.75 each) may be shipped on June 29 or 30.

speed 4 Dodi may make a fuchsia gown for the civic social to be held downtown.

gwam 1' | 1 | 2 | 3 | 4 | 5 | 6 | 7 | 8 | 9 | 10 | 11 | 12 | 13 | 14 |

IMPROVE/ CHECK SKILLS

1. Key 1', 2', and 3' writings on 101D above as directed there. (Record 3' *gwam* for later use.)

1' Goal: 3 *gwam* increase
2' Goal: 2 *gwam* increase
3' Goal: 1 *gwam* increase

2. Key 101B, page 184, again to build speed on statistical copy.

APPLICATION ACTIVITIES

Activity 1

Retrieve ss file 137B and make these changes.

1. Draw a line from A5 through H5.
2. Draw a line from A9 through H9.
3. Save worksheet as 137D1.

Activity 2

Retrieve *Student's Template* file T137D2 and make the following changes.

1. Add **Greene** in Row 7 with sales of **1367** and salary of **410**.
2. Copy the formula for computing commission to applicable cells.
3. Copy formula for computing total to all applicable cells.

4. Insert a **Bonus** column as E; enter **125** for all salespersons.
5. Revise formula for finding total so that bonus is included; copy new formula to other cells as needed.
6. Delete **Helski** from worksheet.
7. Make space to key **APRIL PAY SCHEDULE** as a title in A1.

8. Center all column headings; format numbers as money with 2 decimal places.
9. Change column width so each column is about 2 spaces wider than its longest entry.
10. Draw a line to separate title from column headings.
11. Save worksheet as 137D2.

WRITE-TO-LEARN WORKSHOP

Access wp software and compose a description of a worksheet you would prepare for one of the following tasks:

1. To complete a problem in one of the courses you are taking.
2. To prepare and maintain a personal or family budget.
3. To keep financial records for a school club.
4. A task that you select.

Use the terms at the right to help organize your composition. Try to include some of the terms in your writing.

Spreadsheet	Labels	Values
Worksheet	Cells	Rows
Columns	Save	File
Default	Align	Help
Retrieve	Name	Cursor
Feature	Format	Copy
Formulas	Edit	Print
Range	Percent	Currency
Average	Sum	Minimum
Maximum	Insert	Delete

LESSON 138   GLOBAL CHANGES

138A ◆ CONDITIONING PRACTICE

each line twice

alphabet 1 The fabulous zoology complex will be located quite near Bjerke Avenue.

figures 2 Of the 830 surveyed, only 256 knew the importance of December 7, 1941.

keypad 3 .6 0.6 9.9 0.3 9.6 10.6 10.9 14.85 19.03 26.39 63.60 54.66 59.32 67.39

speed 4 The heir to the endowment may work on the problems with the six firms.

gwam 1' | 1 | 2 | 3 | 4 | 5 | 6 | 7 | 8 | 9 | 10 | 11 | 12 | 13 | 14 |

102C ♦ 15'

IMPROVE TECHNIQUE

1. Key the drill twice SS; DS between 2-line sets.
2. Key a 1' writing on each of lines 8, 10, and 12; find *gwam* on each writing.
3. Key another 1' writing on the slowest line.

Service keys

Space Bar

1 Ken may be in town next week to see his aunt and uncle for a few days.
2 Jody is to sign the form to pay the men for the work they did for him.

Shift keys

3 Jan works for Paulsen & Sons in Boston; Max, for Appel Corp. in Salem.
4 Mark Wolterman, president of Sparks Electric, lives near Jasmine Lane.

underline & Caps Lock

5 Members of ISBE sailed for London in August on the Queen Elizabeth II.
6 THE SUM OF ALL FEARS by Tom Clancy was reviewed in The New York Times.

Response patterns

letter response

7 act on | set in | was no | are you | act upon | car tags | milk ads | you were exact
8 Kim saw him serve a plump, sweet plum dessert on a terrace at my cafe.

word response

9 pen name | lay down | map work | big risk | may fish | hand down | such good goals
10 The girls cut and curl their hair when they visit their rich neighbor.

combination response

11 six ads | own age | tie pin | got him | bus tax | air bag | oak base may join them
12 The six ads we did for the nylon gowns were paid for by the big union.

gwam 1' | 1 | 2 | 3 | 4 | 5 | 6 | 7 | 8 | 9 | 10 | 11 | 12 | 13 | 14 |

102D ♦ 12'

ROUGH DRAFT

1. Key a 1' writing on each ¶; find *gwam*.
2. Key a 2' writing on ¶s 1-2 combined; find *gwam*.
3. Key a 3' writing on ¶s 1-2 combined; find *gwam*.
4. Compare 3' *gwam* with that attained in 102B, page 185.
5. Key another 3' writing on the slower kind of copy.

Goal: 80% transfer

all letters used | A | 1.5 si | 5.7 awl | 80% hfw

gwam 1' 2' 3'

To move up to the next level ~~rung~~ of word processing power, 10 5 3

you must demonstrate certain abilities. First, you must 22 11 7

~~now~~ show that you can ~~type~~ key with good tecnique, a modest 32 16 11

level of speed, and a limit on erors. Next, you must prop- 44 22 15

erly apply the basic ~~guides~~ rules of language use. Finally, you 56 28 19

must arrange basic documents properly. 64 32 21

If you ~~think~~ believe you have all ready learned enough, think 11 37 25

of the future. Many ~~of the~~ jobs, now today require a higher de- 21 42 28

gree of keying skill than you have acquired ~~up to now~~ so far. Recog- 33 48 32

nize, ~~too~~ also that other styles of letters and reports and 45 54 36

more complex tabels are in common use. ~~Consequently,~~ As a result 55 59 40

would you not bennefit from another ~~term~~ semester of training? 67 65 43

2. Key **/, W**.
3. Key **D** (selects Delete from the Worksheet Menu).
4. Key **R** (specifies that a row is to be deleted).
5. Strike Enter (accepts the default range of deleting one row).
6. Save worksheet as 137B.

2. Press **Alt, E, D** (selects Delete from Edit Menu).
3. Strike Enter (accepts the default range of deleting one row).
4. Save worksheet as 137B.

137C ◆

DRAW LINES

Retrieve T137B from your *Student's Template*. Read the information at the right; then complete the steps to draw lines using your ss software.

A worksheet is easier to read when horizontal lines are drawn to separate the parts. For example, a line of equal signs or hyphens is often used to separate worksheet titles and subtitles from the worksheet entries. Lines can be drawn by (1) filling the spaces in the cell where the line is to begin and copying the contents of that cell to others; (2) keying enough characters in the first cell so they extend across the desired number of columns (use an edit feature to add or delete spaces as needed to have them end evenly); (3) using a draw feature if the software has it.

Do the following to the file retrieved.

1. In A4, key **129450**.
2. In G4, key **395845**.
3. In A6, key **Sandy**.
4. In G6, key **Thomas**.

LOTUS

Method 1: Use the copy command to draw a line of = from A5 through G5.

1. Highlight A5 (the beginning cell in the line).
2. Key **\=**; strike Enter (fills the first cell with = .
3. Use the copy command (**/, C**) to copy A5 to B5 through G5.

Method 2: Use the beginning cell to draw a line of = from A7 through G7.

1. In A7, key = repeatedly until its length approximates the length of the line desired; strike Enter.
2. Use the Edit feature (F2) to shorten or lengthen the line so the last character is in G7.
3. Clear screen.

WORKS DOS

Method 1: Use the copy command to draw a line of = from A5 through G5.

1. Highlight A5 (the beginning cell in the line).
2. Key **"** and then **=** ten times; strike Enter (fills the first cell with =).
3. Press **Alt, S, E** (selects Cells from Select Menu).
4. Extend highlight to Column G (establishes range for the line).
5. Press **Alt, E, R** (selects the Fill Right command).
6. Use ↓.

Method 2: Use the beginning cell to draw a line of = from A7 through G7.

1. In A7 key **"** and then **=** repeatedly until its length approximates the length of the line desired; strike Enter.
2. Use the Edit feature (**F2**) to shorten or lengthen the line so the last character is in G7.
3. Clear screen.

WORKS MAC

Use the Draw feature to draw horizontal lines from A5 through G5 and A7 to the end of the entry in G7.

1. ~ Edit and select Draw On.
2. ~ Line Tool (+) in Tools palette .
3. ~ the line thickness that you want (choose one of the 5 thicknesses from the next-to-last box of the palette).
4. Move pointer to where the line is to begin (Cell A5) and ~; draw the line by dragging to where the line is to end (Cell G5); then release.
5. Repeat Steps 2 to 4 to draw a line from the beginning of the name in A7 to the end of the name in G7.
6. ~ Edit Menu and select Draw Off.
7. Clear screen.

UNIT 21

LESSONS 103-106

Improve Report Formatting Skills

Learning Outcomes: After completing this unit, you will be able to

1. Format reports more skillfully.
2. Use more extensive word processing capabilities.

LESSON 103 — REPORTS

103A ◆
CONDITIONING PRACTICE

each line twice SS; then three 1' timed writings on line 4; find *gwam*

alphabet 1 Maxim just now realized his favorite racquet broke from rough playing.

figures 2 Flight 108 leaves at 8:45 p.m., while Flight 2496 leaves at 10:37 p.m.

fig/sym 3 My Policy #49-3816 for $75,000 will mature 20 (twenty) years from now.

speed 4 They are to fix the problem with the right signal so it works at dusk.

gwam 1' | 1 | 2 | 3 | 4 | 5 | 6 | 7 | 8 | 9 | 10 | 11 | 12 | 13 | 14 |

103B ◆
LEARN NUMBERING FEATURE

Automatic Page Numbering. The automatic page numbering feature of your software will number document pages consecutively. Page numbers can be placed in a variety of locations on the page. The feature also provides for omitting the page number on the first page. Even after the numbering feature is activated, page numbers will not appear on the input screen but will appear on the printed document and the view/preview screen.

To have the automatic page numbering feature place page numbers in the upper right corner with no page number appearing on the first page, move the cursor to the beginning of the document.

In Works, the page numbering feature is part of the header/footer feature. A header is a line of text printed consistently in the top margin of each page of a multi-page document. A footer is a line of text printed in the bottom margin.

WORDPERFECT

Shift F8.
2—Page.
6—Page Numbering.
4—Page Number Position.
3—for Top Right location.
Return.
8—Suppress (this page only).
4—Suppress Page Numbering.
Y.
F7.

WORKS DOS

Alt, P, H.
Alt U (Activates Use header & footer paragraphs).
Alt N (no header on 1st page).
Return.
Delete the text on the footer line (**F**).
Move cursor to the header line (**H**).
Tab, Tab.
Alt, E, P.
P.
Return.
Depress ↓ twice.
Key document.

WORKS MAC

~ **File** and drag to *Page Setup*.
In the *Header Box* key **&, R &, P.**
Doing so instructs the computer to place a page number on each page at the right margin.
~ OK.
To prevent a page number from printing on the first page, ~ **Format** and drag to *Title Page*.

137A ◆
**CONDITIONING
PRACTICE**

each line twice

alphabet	1	Dr. Joswiak gave both of us excellent marks on the final physics quiz.
figures	2	Homes were built at 1683 Kari Road, 2705 Truax Drive, and 49 Oak Lane.
keypad	3	654 987 321 405 98105-6385 80219-6482 71601-4011 02115-7301 48209-2431
speed	4	When I visit the man in the wheelchair, I may go downtown to the firm.

gwam 1' | 1 | 2 | 3 | 4 | 5 | 6 | 7 | 8 | 9 | 10 | 11 | 12 | 13 | 14 |

137B ◆
**INSERT/DELETE
COLUMNS AND
ROWS**

Retrieve T137B from the
Student's Template. Read
the information at the right;
then complete the steps for
your ss software.

Just as rows or columns are added or deleted from tables when wp software is used, rows and columns may be added to and deleted from a worksheet. When ss software inserts or deletes columns or rows, it moves existing rows and columns and automatically adjusts the cell contents (including any formulas) to the new cell addresses. Thus the cell contents continue to refer to the same data.

LOTUS

Add two columns of telephone extensions that begin with the figure 3 between Columns A and B.

1. Position cell pointer on any row in Column B (where the new columns are to appear).
2. Key **/**, **W**.
3. Key **I** (selects Insert from the Worksheet Menu).
4. Key **C** (specifies that a column is to be added).
5. Move cell pointer one column to the right—or key the range (2) at the prompt (specifies that range to be added is 2 columns).
6. Strike Enter.
7. Key the following numbers into the new columns.

B1: **344**   B2: **354**   B3: **356**   B4: **321**
C1: **312**   C2: **396**   C3: **358**   C4: **311**

Delete the third row (A3 to E3) of telephone extensions.

1. Position the pointer on any column in Row 3 (the row to be deleted).

WORKS DOS

Add two columns of telephone extensions that begin with the figure 3 between Columns A and B,

1. Position cell pointer on any row in Column B (where a new column is to appear).
2. Press **Alt**, **E**, **I** (selects Insert from Edit Menu).
3. Key **C** (specifies that a column is to be added).
4. Strike Enter (adds one column).
5. Position cell pointer on any row in Column C (where another new column is to appear).
6. Repeat Steps 2 and 3 above.
7. Strike Enter.
8. Key the following numbers into the new columns.

B1: **344**   B2: **354**   B3: **356**   B4: **321**
C1: **312**   C2: **396**   C3: **358**   C4: **311**

Delete the third row (A3 to E3) of telephone extensions.

1. Position the pointer on any column in Row 3 (the row to be deleted).

WORKS MAC

Add two columns of telephone extensions that begin with the figure 3 between Columns A and B.

1. ~ B in the column head border (where a new column is to appear).
2. ~ the Edit Menu and select Insert (adds a column).
3. Repeat Steps 1 and 2 to add a second column.
4. Key the following numbers into the new columns.

B1: **344**   B2: **354**   B3: **356**   B4: **321**
C1: **312**   C2: **396**   C3: **358**   C4: **311**

Delete the third row (A3 to E3) of telephone extensions.

1. ~ 3 in the row border (the row to be deleted).
2. ~ the Edit Menu and select Cut (deletes the row).
3. Save worksheet as 137B.

(continued on next page)   (continued on next page)

103C ◆
UNBOUND REPORT

File name: L103C

Formatting Task

1. Review the formatting guides for unbound reports on p. 139 and the formatting guides for long quotations on p. 143.

2. Format the text as an unbound report. Prepare a title page (use your name, school, and date) and, from the information given below, a reference list on a separate page. Correct errors as you key.

3. When you finish, use spell check and proofread your copy to detect any additional keying errors you may have made.

References

Reiss, Levi, and Edwin G. Dolan. Using Computers: Managing Change. Cincinnati: South-Western Publishing Co., 1989.

Winsor, William M. "Electronic Publishing: The Next Great Office Revolution." The Secretary, June/July 1987, 29-30.

THE CHANGING OFFICE

An individual returning to an office job after a 25-year leave of absence would have a difficult time coping with the changes that have taken place during that time. Changing technology would best describe the challenges facing today's office worker. Two "buzzwords" which are currently being used in the office are electronic desktop publishing and electronic mail.

Electronic Desktop Publishing

Desktop publishing is the process of integrating text and graphics by utilizing computer software to produce professional-looking documents without using professional services. According to Winsor (1987, 29):

Desktop publishing has a bright future. . . . Desktop publishing enables people and businesses to develop their own brochures, newsletters, and other documents at a fraction of the cost and time expended sending the work out to a professional graphics studio.

Since today's firms are more concerned than ever about creating the proper image, it is expected that a greater number of firms will turn to desktop publishing to enhance their images.

Electronic Mail

The second "buzzword" being used extensively in the modern office is electronic mail (E-mail). E-mail is the sending, storing, and delivering of written messages electronically. Reiss and Dolan (1989, 529) identify two categories of electronic mail services:

1. In-house electronic mail. (E-mail which is run on a firm's computer system.)

2. Commercial electronic mail. (E-mail which is supplied by organizations such as General Electric Information Services and MCI Communication.)

Summary

Desktop publishing and electronic mail are but 2 of the changes which are shaping the future of information processing. Each year new technology enhances the ability of office personnel to produce quality information in less time.

column word counts: 4, 15, 25, 37, 49, 61, 72, 76, 88, 98, 109, 122, 130, 141, 153, 164, 175, 183, 194, 206, 220, 226, 238, 250, 262, 273, 279, 290, 295, 301, 318, 324, 327, 339, 351, 364, 374

APPLICATION ACTIVITIES

Activity 1

Prepare a worksheet.

1. Enter the information given at the right; use the default width for Column A and a width of 5 for all other columns.

2. In H9, use SUM function to compute the total score for the first student and then copy it to find other students' total scores.

3. In I9, use the formula (below) to compute the final score (the total score less the lowest score) for the first student. The range for the MIN function is Cells B9 through G9.
   Formula:
   Lotus +H9−@MIN(B9.G9)
   Works =H9−MIN(B9:G9)

4. Copy I9 formula to appropriate cells to find other students' scores.

5. In B20, use AVG or AVERAGE function to find the average score on Quiz 1. The range for the average is B9 through B18.

6. Copy B20 to appropriate cells to find the average score on each quiz.

7. In B21 and B22, use MAX and MIN functions, respectively, to identify and enter the maximum and minimum scores on Quiz 1. The range for both is B9 through B18.

8. Copy B21 and B22 to appropriate cells to find the maximum and minimum scores for each quiz, the total score, and the final score.

9. Save worksheet as 136D1.

Activity 2

Prepare a worksheet.

1. Enter the information given at the right; you decide the column widths.

2. Use the SUM, AVG (or AVERAGE), MAX, or MIN functions to calculate the total, average, maximum, and minimum attendance for each group, each date, and all groups on all dates.

3. Save the worksheet as 136D2.

	A	B	C	D	E	F	G	H	I
1	NAME OF STUDENT								
2									
3	ALGEBRA III GRADE BOOK								
4	MRS. ALVERSON								
5								TOTAL	FINAL
6	STUDENT	QUIZ 1	QUIZ 2	QUIZ 3	QUIZ 4	QUIZ 5	QUIZ 6	SCORE	SCORE
7	SCORE								
8									
9	J ADAMS	89	91	95	95	88	97		
10	T BELL	66	72	73	66	78	62		
11	C CARNEY	75	78	76	72	79	80		
12	F DARR	88	91	93	88	97	89		
13	S EAVEY	76	78	73	75	74	79		
14	P JUAN	88	91	82	85	87	91		
15	L MENEZ	64	72	68	76	72	74		
16	S SITO	96	92	91	89	95	90		
17	R TRUMP	72	74	73	78	75	78		
18	S VELEZ	53	72	68	70	71	65		
19									
20	AVG SCORE								
21	MAX SCORE								
22	MIN SCORE								

	A	B	C	D	E	F	G	H	I
1	MAY CONCERT ATTENDANCE								
2									
3	EVENT	MAY 1	MAY 5	MAY 11	MAY 23	TOTAL	AVG	MAX	MIN
4									
5	FREEBIES	9012	8765	7609	10003				
6	GREATS	10134	9451	12098	6953				
7	HANDOS	13578	12934	17032	12569				
8	MILLITT	5312	4129	6329	2587				
9	REEDS	4312	6581	5736	4982				
10									
11	TOTAL								
12	AVG								
13	MAX								
14	MIN								

104A ◆
CONDITIONING PRACTICE

each line twice

alphabet 1 Jeb, Dom, and I favor analyzing the weekly exchange prices frequently.

figures 2 I hope to bus 67 players, 140 band members, 23 teachers, and 598 fans.

fig/sym 3 The agreement (#19-723) must state that Payment #48 is $506; not $312.

speed 4 Diane and she may visit the ancient city chapel when they are with us.

gwam 1' | 1 | 2 | 3 | 4 | 5 | 6 | 7 | 8 | 9 | 10 | 11 | 12 | 13 | 14 |

104B ◆

UNBOUND AND LEFTBOUND REPORTS

File name: L104B1
Formatting Task 1

1. Format the text at the right as an unbound report. Prepare a title page (use your name, school, and date) and a reference page.
2. When you finish, use spell check and proofread your copy to detect any additional keying errors you may have made.

words

LISTENING ——————> 2

One of the most ~critical~ important skills that an individual 12

~acquires~ possesses is the skill of communicating. Studdies indicate 24

that a person spends 70-80 percent of ~his/her~ their time communicat- 36

ing. ~Nipon and West (1989, 28) give the following~ A break down for the average individual of the time 55

spent communicating: includes (Bell, 1987, 8): 60

SS {
Writing 9% 62
Reading 16% 64
Speaking 30% 67
listening 45% 70
}

~almost half~

Since ~most~ of the time spent communicating is spent listen- 83

ing, it is important to overcome any barriers that obstruct 95

our ability to listen and to learn new ways to improve our 107

listening ability. 111

Barriers to Listening 119

Anything that interferes with our ability to listen ~can~ is 130

be classified as a barrier to listening. Barriers that 141

obstruct our ability to listen can be divided into two basic 153

categories-external and internal barriers. 162

Internal Barriers. Internal barriers are those ~barriers~ that 178

deal with the mental or psychologcal aspects of listening. 190

The perception of the importance of the message, the emo- 202

tional state, and the tuning in and out of the speaker by 213

the listener are ~a few~ examples of internal barriers. 224

4. Range E1 through E5: In G4, key **@COUNT(E1.E5)**; strike Enter.

Use *@MIN* to identify the minimum value in a range of cells.

1. Range A1 through F1: In H1, key **@MIN(A1.F1)**; strike ↓ (function identifies smallest value in Cells A1 through F1).
2. Range A1 through F5: In H2, key **@MIN(A1.F5)**; strike ↓.
3. Range A3 through F4: In H3, key **@MIN(A3.F4)**; strike ↓.
4. Range F1 through F5: In H4, key **@MIN(F1.F5)**; strike Enter.

Use *@MAX* to identify the maximum value in a range of cells.

1. Range A1 through F1: In I1, key **@MAX(A1.F1)**; strike ↓ (function identifies largest value in Cells A1 through F1).
2. Range A2 through F2: In I2, key **@MAX(A2.F2)**; strike ↓.
3. Range E1 through E5: In I3, key **@MAX(E1.E5)**; strike ↓.
4. Range B1 through B5: In I4, key **@MAX(B1.B5)**; strike Enter.

Use *@SUM* to add the values in a range of cells.

1. Range A1 through A5: In A6, key **@SUM(A1.A5)**; strike → (function adds values in Cells A1 through A5).
2. Range A1 through F1: In B6, key **@SUM(A1.F1)**; strike →.
3. Range A2 through F3: In C6, key **@SUM(A2.F3)**; strike →.
4. Range F1 through F5: In D6, key **@SUM(F1.F5)**; strike →.

Use *@AVG* to average the values in a range of cells.

1. Range E1 through E5: In E6, key **@AVG(E1.E5)**; strike → (function averages values in Cells E1 through E5).
2. Range A1 through F1: In F6, key **@AVG(A1.F1)**; strike Enter.
3. Range A5 through F5: In G5, key **@AVG(A5.F5)**; strike →.
4. Range A1 through F5: In G6, key **@AVG(A1.F5)**; strike Enter.
5. Save worksheet as 136C.

2. Range A1 through F5: In H2, key **=MIN(A1:F5)**; strike ↓.
3. Range A3 through F4: In H3, key **=MIN(A3:F4)**; strike ↓.
4. Range F1 through F5: In H4, key **=MIN(F1:F5)**; strike Enter/Return.

Use *=MAX* to identify the maximum value in a range of cells.

1. Range A1 through F1: In I1 key **=MAX(A1:F1)**; strike ↓ (function identifies largest value in Cells A1 through F1).
2. Range A2 through F2: In I2, key **=MAX(A2:F2)**; strike ↓.
3. Range E1 through E5: In I3, key **=MAX(E1:E5)**; strike ↓.
4. Range B1 through B5: In I4, key **=MAX(B1:B5)**; strike Enter/Return.

Use *=SUM* to add the values in a range of cells.

1. Range A1 through A5: In A6, key **=SUM(A1:A5)**; strike → (function adds values in Cells A1 through A5).
2. Range A1 through F1: In B6, key **=SUM(A1:F1)**; strike →.
3. Range A2 through F3: In C6, key **=SUM(A2:F3)**; strike →.
4. Range F1 through F5: In D6, key **=SUM(F1:F5)**; strike →.

Continue in the appropriate Works column below.

WORKS DOS

Use *=AVG* to average values in a range of cells.

1. Range E1 through E5: In E6, key **=AVG(E1:E5)**; strike → (function averages values in Cells E1 through E5).
2. Range A1 through F1: In F6, key **=AVG(A1:F1)**; strike Enter.
3. Range A5 through F5: In G5, key **=AVG(A5:F5)**; strike →.
4. Range A1 through F5: In G6, key **=AVG(A1:F5)**; strike Enter.
5. Save worksheet as 136C.

WORKS MAC

Use *=AVERAGE* to average values in a range of cells.

1. Range E1 through E5: In E6, key **=AVERAGE(E1:E5)**; strike → (function averages values in Cells E1 through E5).
2. Range A1 through F1: In F6, key **=AVERAGE(A1:F1)**; strike Return.
3. Range A5 through F5: In G5, key **=AVERAGE(A5:F5)**; strike →.
4. Range A1 through F5: In G6, key **=AVERAGE(A1:F5)**; strike Return.

The mouse can also be used to enter functions (formulas) and should be used when it is more efficient than keying. Use the mouse to enter the SUM function to add Cells A1 through A6.

1. ~ A7; key **=SUM(**.
2. ~ A1 and drag down through A5.
3. Key **)** and ~ Enter box.

Use the mouse to create parts of the MIN function to find the minimum score in Cells B1 through B6.

1. ~ B7; key **=MIN(**.
2. ~ B1 and drag through B5.
3. Key **)** and ~ Enter box.
4. Save worksheet as 136C.

<u>External Barriers</u> ^{lc} External barriers are barriers other

than those that deal ^{with} the mental and psychological make up of

the listener that tend to[#]keep the listener from devoting ^{full} at-

tention to what is being said. Telephone interruptions,

^{uninvited} visitors, noise, and the physical environment are examples

of external barriers.

<u>Ways to Improve Listening</u> _DS_
Barriers to listening can be overcome. ^{lc} However, it

does take a conscientious effort on the part of the

listener. A <del>good</del> ^{stet} listener will try to maintain eye contact

^{with the speaker} and work to avoid tuning the speaker out. Removing as many

external distractins^o as possible is another means for

improving listening.

Listening is also improved by directing attention to

the message rather than <del>on</del> ^{to} the speaker^{'s appearance and mannerisms}. Focusing on the

main points being made by the speaker and taking notes, if

appropriate, are ways of directing attention to the message_. ^(Rader and Kurth, 1988, 417-419)

Nixon, Judy C., and Judy ^{F.} West. "Listning^e--The New Com-
^{ss} petency." <u>The Balance Sheet</u>, January/February 1989_{, 27-29.}

Rader, M. H. and Linda A. Kurth. <u>Business</u>
<u>Communication for the Computer Age</u>. South-
Western Publishing Company, Cincinnati, 1988.

Formatting Task 2

File name: L104B2

1. Read the information about leftbound reports.
2. Reformat the report in file L104B1 as a leftbound report.
3. Bold all headings in the report.
4. Change the first sentence of the report as follows:
   Communicating is one of the most important skills that an individual can possess.
5. Change the final sentence of the report to read:
   In order to direct attention to the message, focus on the speaker's main points and take notes, if appropriate.

Leftbound Reports

Many academic and business reports are bound at the left margin. A leftbound report has a left margin of 1.5", allowing 0.5" for binding the report and 1" for the right margin. All other spacing specifications are the same as the unbound report.

136A ◆ CONDITIONING PRACTICE

each line twice;
then 30" timings
on selected lines;
exit wp; access ss

alphabet 1 Wayne Mazzilli very quickly expressed his own feelings on the subject.

figures 2 The call numbers for the last two books are HD52.7.L86 and SG40.9.L13.

fig/sym 3 Invoice #694 was billed to credit card #C17305 for $805.23 on 8/02/94.

speed 4 If they are too busy with work, the visitor may be a problem for them.

gwam 1' | 1 | 2 | 3 | 4 | 5 | 6 | 7 | 8 | 9 | 10 | 11 | 12 | 13 | 14 |

136B ◆ CREATE A WORKSHEET

Use the information at the right to create a worksheet for use in 136C.

	A	B	C	D	E	F
1	95	88	87	94	99	92
2	74	78	79	68	76	74
3	82	76	86	78	69	83
4	62	72	65	76	72	78
5	85	82	88	90	81	86

136C ◆ STATISTICAL FORMULAS

Read the information at the right about functions. Then complete the steps listed for your ss software. **Note:** The @ is the shift of the 2 key.

Spreadsheet software has built-in equations, called *functions*, that speed up many processes relating to mathematical, statistical, logical, and financial calculations. Operators save time by using the function instead of writing and keying a complex formula. In this lesson, you will learn to use functions for counting, adding, and determining minimum, maximum, and average values.

LOTUS

Use @COUNT to count the number of values in a range of cells.

1. Range A1 through F1: In G1, key **@COUNT(A1.F1)**; strike ↓ (function counts the number of values in Cells A1 to F1).
2. Range A2 through F5: In G2, key **@COUNT(A2.F5)**; strike ↓ .
3. Range C2 through D5: In G3, key **@COUNT(C2.D5)**; strike↓.

WORKS DOS AND WORKS MAC

Use = COUNT to count the number of values in a range of cells.

1. Range A1 through F1: In G1, key **=COUNT(A1:F1)**; strike ↓ (function counts the number of values in Cells A1 to F1).
2. Range A2 through F5: In G2, key **=COUNT(A2:F5)**; strike ↓ .
3. Range C2 through D5: In G3, key **=COUNT(C2:D5)**; strike ↓ .
4. Range E1 through E5: In G4, key **=COUNT(E1:E5)**; strike Enter/Return.

Use = MIN to identify the minimum value in a range of cells.
1. In H1, key **=MIN(A1:F1)**; strike ↓ (function identifies smallest values in Cells A1 to F1).

(continued on next page)

(continued on next page)

LESSON 105 REPORTS

105A ◆ CONDITIONING PRACTICE

each line twice

alphabet 1 Max will authorize me to get quality products from major bike vendors.

figures 2 Each computer desk (42" wide x 36" long x 27" high) will cost $158.90.

fig/sym 3 Mary served 138 donuts, 279 danish, 60 cupcakes, and 45 elephant ears.

speed 4 They are proficient for the quantity and rigor of work they are to do.

gwam 1' | 1 | 2 | 3 | 4 | 5 | 6 | 7 | 8 | 9 | 10 | 11 | 12 | 13 | 14 |

105B ◆ UNBOUND REPORT

File name: L105B

1. Format and key the text on student organizations as an unbound report. Prepare a title page (use your name, school, and date) and a reference page.
2. When you finish, use spell check before proofreading your copy to detect any additional errors you may have made.

words

STUDENT ORGANIZATIONS 4

Student organizations play a vital role in the 14 educational process of students. Students who 23 participate in such organizations are given op- 32 portunities to test the concepts they were taught 42 in the formal classroom environment. Two such 52 organizations that are widely recognized in the 61 business education field are Future Business 70 Leaders of America and Business Professionals 80 of America (formerly called Office Education 89 Association). 92

Future Business Leaders 101

Future Business Leaders of America is a vo- 109 cational association that helps students bridge 119 the gap between the classroom and the business 128 world. Two of the major goals outlined in the 138 Future Business Leaders of America Handbook 155 (1985, 5) are as follows: 160

1. Develop competent, aggressive business 169 leadership. 171
2. Create more interest in and understand- 180 ing of American business enterprise. 187

Business leadership. Students have the oppor- 200 tunity to develop leadership skills by serving 209 as officers, attending conferences, working with 219 businessmen and businesswomen in the com- 227 munity, and participating in competitive events 237 sponsored by the organization. The organiza- 246 tion's strong emphasis on community service 254 provides another avenue for the development 263 of leadership skills. 268

Business enterprise. A greater understanding 281 of business enterprise is gained by students as 290 they participate in chapter projects dealing with 300 this important subject. These projects give stu- 310 dents experiences in learning more about the 319 operation of business enterprise in America. 328

Business Professionals of America 342

Business Professionals of America is another 351 vocational business and office education pro- 359 gram for students interested in developing per- 369 sonal, leadership, and office skills. According 378 to Goodman (1987, 11), the executive director 388 of the organization for 1987-88, the goal of the 397 organization has been to promote leadership 406 and professionalism among students in order 415 to prepare them for satisfying and successful 424 careers in the business world. 431

The two goals, developing business leadership 440 and understanding business enterprise, empha- 449 sized by FBLA are also emphasized by Business 458 Professionals of America. They, too, have pro- 467 grams designed to provide students with the op- 476 portunity to develop their leadership skills and 486 to foster a greater understanding of the role of 496 the entrepreneur in the free enterprise system. 506

REFERENCES 508

Future Business Leaders of America Handbook. 526 Reston, Virginia: FBLA-PBL, Incorporated, 534 1985. 536

Goodman, Dorothy M. "A New Image for Our 544 Organization," 1987-88 Chapter Handbook, 557 Columbus, Ohio: Office Education Associa- 565 tion, 1987. 567

UNIT 30

LESSONS 136-140

Extend Worksheet Skills

Learning Outcomes: After completing this unit, you will be able to

1. Use functions (built-in equations) to solve problems.
2. Insert and delete columns and rows and draw lines.
3. Use global commands to format values and labels and change column widths.

SPREADSHEET FEATURE AND COMMAND GUIDE

DRAW LINES
FORMAT AN ENTIRE
    WORKSHEET
INSERT AND DELETE
    COLUMNS
STATISTICAL FORMULAS

The ss features and commands explained below are presented in this unit. Use this guide to preview what you will learn in the unit. As you work—even in later units—use this guide as a reference. Appendix G, Application Software Commands, can also be used to look up features and commands quickly.

DRAW LINES

A line of equal signs or hyphens or a solid line is often used to separate parts of a worksheet. Lines can be drawn by: (1) filling the spaces in the cell where the line is to begin and then copying the contents of that cell to others; (2) keying enough characters in the first cell so they extend across the desired number of columns (use Edit feature to add or delete spaces as needed to have them end evenly); (3) using the Draw feature if the software has one.

Lotus	\ =, and then copy.
Works DOS	Fill first cell of line with = and then use Fill Right.
Works MAC	~ Window Menu and select Draw On; ~ Line Tool on Tools palette; draw line; ~ Window Menu and select Draw Off.

FORMAT AN ENTIRE WORKSHEET

To format all column widths, values, and labels in a worksheet in the same style, use the Global, All, or All Cells feature before selecting the format feature.

Lotus	/, **W**, **G**, select desired options.
Works DOS	**Alt**, **S**, **A**, select desired options.
Works MAC	~ Select; choose All Cells; select desired options.

INSERT AND DELETE COLUMNS

When ss software inserts or deletes columns or rows, it moves existing columns and rows and automatically adjusts the cell contents (including any formulas) to the new cell addresses so that the cell contents continue to refer to the same data.

Lotus	/, **W**, select **I** or **D.**
Works DOS	**Alt**, **E**, select **D** or **I.**
Works MAC	~ Row # or Column letter in border; ~ Edit; select Cut or Insert.

STATISTICAL FORMULAS

Spreadsheet software has built-in equations, called *functions*, that speed up processes for counting (COUNT), adding (SUM), and computing minimum (MIN), maximum (MAX), and average (AVG—Lotus and Works DOS; AVERAGE—Works MAC) values.

Lotus	@function (cell address.cell address).
Works DOS **Works MAC**	=function (cell and address:cell address).

106A ◆
CONDITIONING
PRACTICE
each line twice

alphabet 1 I would be very amazed if he objects to the back exercising equipment.

figures 2 Table A on page 3 lists 2,068 births in 1991 and 3,754 births in 1992.

fig/sym 3 A 17% discount off the marked price ($26,930.00) amounts to $4,578.10.

speed 4 If all the girls go to the formal social, she may pay for their gowns.

gwam 1' | 1 | 2 | 3 | 4 | 5 | 6 | 7 | 8 | 9 | 10 | 11 | 12 | 13 | 14 |

106B ◆

UNBOUND
REPORT

File name: L106B

Formatting Task

1. Format and key the text at the right as an unbound report. Prepare a title page (use your name, school, and date) and a reference page (information below).
2. When you finish, use spell check before proofreading your copy to detect any additional errors you may have made.

References

Anrig, Greg, Jr. "Making the Most of 1988's Low Tax Rate." Money, February 1988, 56-57.

Rachman, David J., and Michael H. Mescon. Business Today. New York: Random House, 1987.

words

TAXES   1

Americans are taxed in order to raise revenues to finance governmental   15
activities. Taxation has never been popular. Much time and energy have   30
been devoted by the legislature trying to devise a system that requires   44
everyone to pay his/her fair share. Taxes are generally based on the bene-   59
fits received and/or on the ability to pay. Two of the most common revenue   74
raising taxes are the personal income tax and the sales tax.   87

Personal Income Tax   95

The personal income tax is the tax individuals are required to pay on   109
their earnings. Employers deduct this tax from employees' paychecks.   123
When employees file their income tax returns, they will either receive a   137
refund for any excess which has been paid or they will have to pay the bal- 152
ance due.   154

Personal income taxes have been the Federal Government's largest single   169
source of revenue and a major source of state revenues as well. On the   183
federal level, the personal income tax is a graduated tax, which means   198
the more you make, the higher the percentage of your income you pay in   213
taxes (Rachman and Mescon, 1987, 529).   220

With the Tax Reform Act of 1986, the highest tax an individual paid was   235
33 percent. The amount an individual pays changes with each tax reform.   249
In the past, the top tax rate has been as high as 70 percent (Anrig, 1988, 56). 266

Sales Taxes   270

The sales tax is another tax with which most people are familiar. It is a 285
tax that is added to the retail price of goods and services. Two examples of 301
this type of tax are as follows: 308

1. General sales tax. The general sales tax is a tax levied by most states 326
on goods and services. The amount of tax and the specific goods and ser-   340
vices that are taxed vary by state.   348

2. Excise tax (selective sales tax). The excise tax is a state tax levied 369
against specific items. Examples of items with an excise tax include to-   384
bacco, alcoholic beverages, and gasoline.   392

While the income tax is a tax based on the individual's ability to pay, the 407
general sales tax and the excise tax are based on benefits received. For   422
example, taxes collected on gasoline are used for highways. Individuals   437
purchasing gasoline are those who benefit from the construction and   451
maintenance of highways.   455

DRILL AND PRACTICE

1. Key each line twice SS (once slowly, then faster).
2. Key a 1' writing on each line.
3. Rekey slower lines for speed.

alphabet	1	The judge observed as the expert workers quickly froze the boned meat.
figures	2	I ordered 36 desks, 49 chairs, 15 tables, 80 lamps, and 72 disk trays.
fig/sym	3	Guy Moss's order (#30-967) is for 42 almanacs, 15 atlases, and 8 maps.
Shift keys	4	Jay Sparks is going to Parsons College, but Max Roper has chosen Yale.
Space Bar	5	Any of them who object to my plan can say so at the next town meeting.
long reaches	6	Brig sang three hymns on my TV show and received many musical praises.
speed	7	Vivian may go to the ancient island city by the lake to work for them.

gwam 1' | 1 | 2 | 3 | 4 | 5 | 6 | 7 | 8 | 9 | 10 | 11 | 12 | 13 | 14 |

IMPROVE/ CHECK SKILL

1. Key two 1' writings on each ¶; find gwam.
2. Key two 3' writings on ¶s 1-3 combined; find gwam and count errors.
3. Key a 5' writing on ¶s 1-3 combined; find gwam and count errors.

all letters used | A | 1.5 si | 5.7 awl | 80% hfw

gwam 3' | 5'

Firms that plan to operate at a profit must employ people who are willing to work as a team to achieve goals. Various management styles have been used in the past to achieve company goals. These range from an autocratic style where decisions are made by one person to a democratic style where decisions are made by a group of employees. The team method of decision making has become more accepted by many firms.

One of the more democratic forms of management that is becoming quite popular is the quality circles concept. Employees are invited to participate as part of a team to make decisions and deal with the problems related to their jobs. The idea behind quality circles is to have the workers who are most familiar with the job make all of the decisions directly related to it rather than those who are further removed.

Research shows that employees who feel they are a valuable part of a company team are more satisfied with their jobs. The end result of job satisfaction is a higher level of achievement. Of course, a higher achievement level means more profit for a firm and more benefits to the worker. Because of the recent success of quality circles, more firms are using this approach to help maximize employee output.

| gwam 3' | | 1 | | 2 | | 3 | | 4 | | 5 | |
| gwam 5' | | 1 | | | 2 | | | 3 | | |

REFORMAT REPORT

File name: L106C1

1. Retrieve L105B and format it as a leftbound report; make the changes indicated at the right.
2. Move the paragraph about <u>Business enterprise</u> before the paragraph about <u>Business leadership</u>.

Student organizations play a ~~vital~~ *important* role in the ~~educational process~~ of students. Students who participate in such organizations are given opportunities to test the concepts they ~~were~~ *are* taught in the formal classroom environment. Two such organizations that are widely recognized in the business education field are Future Business Leaders of America *(FBLA)* and Business Professionals of America *(BPA)* ~~(formerly call Office Education Association)~~.

<u>Future Business Leaders</u>

Future Business Leaders of America is a vocational association that helps students bridge the gap between the classroom and the business world. Two of the major goals outlined in the ~~Future Business Leaders of America~~ *FBLA* Handbook (1985, 5) are as follows:

1. Develop compentent, aggressive business leadership.
2. Create more interest in and understanding of American business enterprise.

File name: L106C2

Retrieve L106B and format it as a leftbound report; make the changes marked at the right.

Delete the following files from your disk (refer to 66D, p. 129, if necessary):

Ritter Realty	MISTLE
L97B	CLINE1
L97C	WALSTROM
PASCUAL	CLINE2
LYONS	L100B
SYKES	L100C

Americans are taxed in order to raise revenues to finance governmental activities. Taxation has never been popular. ~~Much time and energy have been devoted by~~ *has spent a considerable amount of time* the legislature trying to devise a system that requires everyone to pay his/her fair share. Taxes are generally based on ~~the benefits received and/or on~~ the ability to pay *and on the benefits received*. ~~Two of the~~ most commmon revenue raising taxes ~~are~~ the personal income tax and the sales tax *are the two*.

DRILL AND PRACTICE

1. Key each line twice SS (once slowly, then faster).
2. Key a 1' writing on each line.
3. Rekey slower lines for speed.

alphabet	1	Jan analyzed her quest for perfection by examining a few vital skills.
figures	2	They sold 14 clips, 93 rings, 50 watches, 168 clocks, and 72 tie pins.
fig/sym	3	After May 5, Al's new address will be 478 Pax Avenue (ZIP 92106-1593).
Shift keys	4	We have visited Alabama, Kansas, Colorado, Maine, Florida, and Hawaii.
Space Bar	5	Both men may go to the city to work on the audit of the big soap firm.
double letters	6	A tall fellow in the pool hall stuffed his jeans into his muddy boots.
speed	7	The ivory box with the shamrock and iris is by the door of the chapel.

gwam 1' | 1 | 2 | 3 | 4 | 5 | 6 | 7 | 8 | 9 | 10 | 11 | 12 | 13 | 14 |

IMPROVE/ CHECK SKILL

1. Key two 1' writings on each ¶; find *gwam*.
2. Key two 3' writings on ¶s 1-3 combined; find *gwam* and count errors.
3. Key a 5' writing on ¶s 1-3 combined; find *gwam* and count errors.

all letters used | A | 1.5 si | 5.7 awl | 80% hfw

gwam 3' 5'

The computer is an amazing machine. It is amazing because of the   4 2 38
many things it does, the speed at which it does its operations, and the   9 6 42
degree of accuracy it maintains. In short, the computer is one of man- 14 8 44
kind's most important inventions and a resource that seems to be every- 19 11 47
where and do everything.   20 12 48

Computers are used by students in many classes. They are used by 25 15 51
people who work in health, law, farming, and athletics to record, keep, 30 18 54
and process data. Rock stars use them to run concerts and to write music. 35 21 57
Computers run and work on assembly lines and are used to design many con- 40 24 60
sumer goods.   40 24 61

Computers have changed extensively in the short period they have 45 27 63
existed. Early ones had to be kept in special areas and run by trained 50 30 66
personnel. Today, young children use them to learn or for play. The 54 33 69
jumbo, slow computers of yesteryear have given way to the small, quick 59 35 71
computers in use today.   61 36 72

gwam 3' | 1 | 2 | 3 | 4 | 5 |
gwam 5' | 1 | 2 | 3 |

Master Keyboarding Skills

Learning Outcomes: After completing this unit, you will be able to

1. Demonstrate improved response patterns and tabulating skill.
2. Key straight-copy paragraphs at higher speed and with more control.
3. Demonstrate improved transfer of straight-copy speed to rough draft.

LESSON 107 — KEYBOARDING SKILLS

SM: Defaults; LS: SS

107A ◆ 6'
CONDITIONING PRACTICE

each line twice SS; two 1' writings on line 4

alphabet	1	After a wild jump ball, the guards very quickly executed a zone press.
figures	2	The invoice covered 115 sofas, 270 desks, 476 chairs, and 1,398 lamps.
fig/sym	3	Order the #284, #365, and #1790 cartons (untaped) from O'Brien & Sons.
speed	4	A big firm kept half of the men busy with their work down by the lake.

gwam 1' | 1 | 2 | 3 | 4 | 5 | 6 | 7 | 8 | 9 | 10 | 11 | 12 | 13 | 14 |

107B ◆ 12'

IMPROVE TABULATING

1. Clear existing tabs.
2. Set tabs at 1.0", 2.7", and 5.3". If default left margin is 1", use it for the first column, instead of setting a tab at that position.
3. Key the mailing list.
4. Take two 1' writings; find *gwam* on each.

			words
Cynthia Bixby	1834 W. Southern Ave.	Mesa, AZ 85202-4867	11
James Epson	802 Crawley Road	Odessa, FL 33556-9512	21
Juan Gomez	1908 Association Drive	Reston, VA 22091-1591	32
Janet Markham	1049 Sunny Vale Lane	Madison, WI 53713-3358	44
Zoe Sparks	901 Fifth Avenue	Dayton, KY 41074-0258	54
Lance Wolfe	3173 Murphy Drive	Memphis, TN 38106-1001	64

107C ◆ 15'

RESPONSE PATTERNS

1. Key the drill as shown.
2. Key a 1' writing on each of lines 10-12; find *gwam* on each.
3. Key another 1' writing on the 2 slowest lines.

letter response
1 onion weave union beads pupil defer holly erase imply serve jolly gate
2 in my bag | at ease | be at my | bad debt | grade on my test | you better beware
3 In my opinion, my award was based on my grade average on my art tests.

word response
4 giant field right rocks focus amend blend cycle ivory snake their girl
5 fix it | paid for it | go to work | go with them | sign the title | their island
6 The haughty girls did pay for their own gowns for the sorority social.

combination response
7 bush best corn acre idle join paid pull hair milk torn draw rush knoll
8 for joy | may jump | did face | the best | with tact | good wage | pay him to join
9 Were they paid to join a craft union in the big oil firm as you imply?

letter 10 Gregg saw you set up a data card on my mill gas pump as you are aware.
combination 11 Only a few of the girls were at the edge of the lake when we saw them.
word 12 I paid the man by the dock for the six bushels of corn and the turkey.

gwam 1' | 1 | 2 | 3 | 4 | 5 | 6 | 7 | 8 | 9 | 10 | 11 | 12 | 13 | 14 |

135A ◆ CONDITIONING PRACTICE
each line twice

alphabet 1 Gladyce bought two dozen quarts of jam and five extra jars of pickles.

figures 2 The team batting average went from .389 on June 16 to .405 on June 27.

keypad 3 11-987456-123 22-654789-321 33-564897-123 44-206375-918 55-291463-780

speed 4 When they fix the chair by the door, they may also work on the mantle.

gwam 1' | 1 | 2 | 3 | 4 | 5 | 6 | 7 | 8 | 9 | 10 | 11 | 12 | 13 | 14 |

135B ◆ APPLICATION ACTIVITIES

Activity 1
Retrieve T135B1 from your template disk and make the following changes.
1. In G3, key **TOTAL** as column head.
2. In G5, write a formula to add the total registrations for accounting.
3. Copy this formula to appropriate rows in Column G.
4. In A18, key **TOTAL** at right edge of cell.
5. Copy the formula in B18 to C18 through G18.
6. Format Column A to 26 spaces; G to 7; all others to 6.
7. Correct spelling of entries in A10, A15, and A16.
8. Format values without commas and decimal places.
9. Center all column headings.
10. Print the worksheet and save it as 135B1.

Activity 2
Use wp software and complete the following steps to prepare a report.
1. Retrieve T135B2 from your template.
2. Set top and side margins for unbound report format.
3. Set line spacing for DS.
4. Key the main heading in bold, ALL CAPS; side and paragraph headings in bold, underlined.
5. Format the long quotation and enumerated items SS, indented 0.5" from LM.
6. Move paragraph headings and paragraphs so they appear in this order in the report: Skills, Interests, Values.
7. Use Widow/Orphan Protection.
8. Number the second page.
9. Check spelling; then proofread and check format on screen.
10. View and then print the report when it is correct.
11. Save the report as 135B2.

Activity 3
Complete these steps to create a worksheet.
1. Key the information below as a worksheet.
2. Add a column; use a two-line heading TOTAL HITS.
3. In this column, calculate the total hits for each player.
4. Add a TOTAL row and calculate the number of singles, doubles, triples, home runs, and total hits for all players.
5. Format the column headings attractively.
6. Print the worksheet and save it as 135B3.

	A	B	C	D	E
1	STATISTICS OF THE TOP FIVE HITTERS				
2					
3					HOME
4	PLAYER	SINGLES	DOUBLES	TRIPLES	RUNS
5					
6	LU CHE SUN	53	5	9	1
7	AL SANCHEZ	41	11	2	12
8	BILL MYERS	17	19	0	19
9	HECTOR RUIZ	25	5	8	3
10	LEE HORAN	22	6	2	8

IMPROVE/ CHECK SKILLS

1. Key two 1' writings on each ¶; find *gwam* on each.
2. Key two 2' writings on ¶s 1-3 combined; find *gwam* on each.
3. Key a 3' writing on ¶s 1-3 combined; find *gwam*.
4. Key another 3' writing; find *gwam* and count errors.

gwam	¼	½	¾	1'
20	5	10	15	20
24	6	12	18	24
28	7	14	21	28
32	8	16	24	32
36	9	18	27	36
40	10	20	30	40
44	11	22	33	44
48	12	24	36	48
52	13	26	39	52
56	14	28	42	56

all letters used | A | 1.5 si | 5.7 awl | 80% hfw

gwam 2' | 3'

Knowing that there are sixty seconds in every minute and sixty min- 7 | 4
utes in each hour, we should be able to schedule our activities into the 14 | 9
available time without difficulty. Why, then, do so many people end up 21 | 14
rushing around in a frenzy, trying to meet deadlines? The answer is in 28 | 19
the psychological nature of time. When we are enjoying ourselves, time 36 | 24
seems to fly away; but time spent on tedious jobs seems endless. 42 | 28

Do you ever "goof off" for an hour or more with a television pro- 48 | 32
gram or a visit on the telephone and discover later that you haven't ac- 56 | 37
tually enjoyed your leisure? Each nagging little vision of homework or 63 | 42
chores to be completed always seems to result in taking the edge off your 70 | 47
pleasure. And you still have to complete whatever you postponed--prob- 77 | 52
ably in a hurry. 79 | 53

If you fit the situation above, don't waste valuable time feeling 86 | 57
guilty; for you have lots of company. What you should feel is cheated-- 93 | 62
out of leisure that you didn't enjoy and study time that didn't produce 100 | 67
results. Check with your companions who always seem ready for a good 107 | 71
time but are also ready for unexpected quizzes. The secret is in the 114 | 76
budgeting of your time. 116 | 78

gwam 2' | 1 | 2 | 3 | 4 | 5 | 6 | 7 |
3' | 1 | 2 | 3 | 4 | 5 |

LESSON 108   KEYBOARDING SKILLS

SM: Defaults; LS: SS

CONDITIONING PRACTICE

each line twice SS; two 1' writings on line 4

alphabet 1 Fine cooks brought piquant flavor to exotic foods with zesty marjoram.

figures 2 I reviewed 50 magazines, 127 books, 189 pamphlets, and 364 newspapers.

fig/sym 3 Items marked * (as PC-478* and WP-360*) were reduced 15% May 26, 1991.

speed 4 The panel may then work with problems of the eight downtown firms.

gwam 1' | 1 | 2 | 3 | 4 | 5 | 6 | 7 | 8 | 9 | 10 | 11 | 12 | 13 | 14 |

IMPROVE/ CHECK SKILL

1. Key 1', 2', and 3' writings on 107D above as directed there. Record 3' *gwam* for future reference.

1' Goal: 3 *gwam* increase
2' Goal: 2 *gwam* increase
3' Goal: 1 *gwam* increase

2. Key 107B, page 194, again to build statistical keying speed.

134C ♦ (cont.)

8. Strike Enter (accepts the range to be printed).
9. Key **A** (selects Align and sets the internal line counter to 0).
10. Key **G** (for Go—tells the printer to begin printing).
11. When printing stops, key **P** (for Page—tells the printer to advance to the top of the next page). This step is omitted when a network printer is used.
12. Key **Q** (for Quit—this command exits the Print Menu and returns software to the Ready mode).
13. Clear the worksheet screen.

	A	B	C	D
1	FINANCIAL HIGHLIGHTS			
2				
3	=IN MILLIONS EXCEPT PER SHARE AMOUNTS=			
4				
5		1994	1993	Change
6				
7	Operating Revenue	$6514.00	$6559.00	-0.7%
8	Operating Expenses	$6688.00	$7060.00	-5.3%
9				
10	Operating Loss	($174.00)	($501.00)	
11	Net Loss	($3.05)	($454.00)	-99.3%
12	Loss Per Common Share	($7.62)	($10.89)	-30.0%
13	Stockholder's Equity	$1318.00	$1434.00	-8.1%
14	Shares of Common Stock	$46.60	$45.50	2.4%
15	Book Value Per Common Share	$28.26	$31.50	-10.3%

134D ♦
CANCEL PRINTING

Read the information at the right about canceling printing once it has begun.

If you must stop printing a worksheet after printing has begun, the cancel printing command will stop the printer shortly after the command is executed.

LOTUS

To stop printing after it has begun, use Ctrl Break.

WORKS DOS

Press Esc at any time to cancel printing.

WORKS MAC

Follow the instructions in the dialog box displayed while printing is in progress (Press ⌘ and .).

134E ♦
APPLICATION ACTIVITY

Complete the steps below to prepare a worksheet.

1. Format Column A for 20 spaces; B for 7; C for 6; D for 7; E for 8; and F for 7.
2. Key the information at the right.
3. Add the number of plane models owned and leased and print the results in Column F.
4. In D13, calculate the total number of airplanes owned; in E13, the number leased.
5. In F13, calculate the total number of planes owned and leased.
6. Format Column G width to 6 spaces.
7. In Column G, enter TOTAL SEATS as a two-line heading.
8. In Column G, calculate the total number of seats per model and for all planes. Print the worksheet.
9. Print the worksheet.
10. Save the worksheet as 134E.

	A	B	C	D	E	F
1	ROYAL AIRLINES FLEET					
2						
3			MEAN			
4	PLANE MODEL	SEATS	AGE	OWNED	LEASED	TOTAL
5						
6	Morris F-36	55	6.5	5	2	
7	Baker B11	65	11.7	19	6	
8	Aircraft 1000-23	115	3.4	26	0	
9	Harrison Jet 5000X2L	121	9.7	14	8	
10	Harrison Jet 6000X3L	135	7.5	12	4	
11	Airstream 50X2000	175	8.9	23	10	

RESPONSE PATTERNS

1. Key the lines once as shown.
2. Key a 1' writing on each of lines 2, 4, 6, 8, and 10; find *gwam* on each.
3. Practice the 3 slowest lines.

balanced hand
1 if he but own held firm sign visit girls profit height entitle visible
2 The men may visit the ancient town by the lake when he signs the form.

double letter
3 all too off zoo good food door hall keep small issue sorry allow shall
4 All seem to meet my new speed goal; few will keep within three errors.

combination response
5 six you the joy for are also best such only form wear work union title
6 Only six of them serve on the wage panel for the oil union in my town.

adjacent key
7 as buy saw top try pod fort post ruin owes coin dare glass opens moist
8 We are going to post top scores at the regional meet and at the state.

long reach
9 my sun ice mug sum gym sect nice curb bran must cent under bring curve
10 Myra served a number of guests a mug of iced punch after the gym meet.

gwam 1' | 1 | 2 | 3 | 4 | 5 | 6 | 7 | 8 | 9 | 10 | 11 | 12 | 13 | 14 |

SKILL TRANSFER: ROUGH DRAFT

1. Key a 1' writing on each ¶; find *gwam*.
2. Key a 2' writing on ¶s 1-2 combined; find *gwam*.
3. Key a 3' writing on ¶s 1-2 combined; find *gwam*.
4. Compare the 3' *gwam* with that attained in 108B, p. 195.
5. If you did not transfer 90% of straight-copy *gwam* to rough draft, key another 3' writing on the ¶s at the right.

all letters used | A | 1.5 si | 5.7 awl | 80% hfw

	gwam 1'	2'	3'
Your basic keying skills will continue to grow develop during	11	5	4
the processing of leters, memos, and reports. It is a good fine	23	12	8
idea, however, to return from time to time to straight	34	17	11
copy materials for special skill-building drills. Even if	46	23	15
keying typing speed does not transfer at a high level to document	58	29	19
production processing, the production skill will be severely limited	67	34	22
unless your keying skill is high. Work on both as often	79	39	26
as possible you can.	81	41	27
Another way to improve build production speed skill is to give	10	46	30
special attention emphasis to quickening speeding up the spacing between docu-	21	51	34
ments parts so that more of your the time is spent in keying	33	57	38
copy. Make this a major top goal in the days ahead. How you	44	63	42
spend your utilized the time between completing finishing one document and	55	68	45
starting another is of utmost importance, also. Realize	66	74	49
this now and attempt to reduce decrease the time you spend use between	78	79	53
one problem and the next.	83	82	55

APPLICATION ACTIVITY

Complete the steps below to prepare a worksheet.

1. Change Column A width to 27; Column B to 11; Column C to 12; and Column D to 8.
2. Key the information at the right.
3. Center all column headings.
4. In B10, enter a formula using B7-B8 to find the Operating Loss for 1994.
5. Copy the B10 formula to C10 to find the Operating Loss for 1993.
6. In D7, enter a formula using (B7-C7)/C7 to find percent of change in operating revenue.
7. Find the percent change on other rows by copying the D7 formula to other rows in Column D as needed.
8. Format appropriate cells in Columns B and C as money with 2 decimal places.
9. Format appropriate cells in Column D as Percent with 1 decimal place.
10. Save the worksheet as 134B.

	A	B	C	D
1	FINANCIAL HIGHLIGHTS			
2				
3	=IN MILLIONS EXCEPT PER SHARE AMOUNTS=			
4				
5		1994	1993	Change
6				
7	Operating Revenue	6514	6559	
8	Operating Expenses	6688	7060	
9				
10	Operating Loss			
11	Net Loss	-3.05	-454	
12	Loss Per Common Share	-7.62	-10.89	
13	Stockholder's Equity	1318	1434	
14	Shares of Common Stock	46.6	45.5	
15	Book Value Per Common Share	28.26	31.5	

LEARN PRINTING WORKSHEETS

Read the information about printing at the right. Complete the steps listed for your software.

Spreadsheet software prints worksheets within default left, right, top, and bottom margins. If you do not change the defaults but the worksheet exceeds these settings for a single page, the remaining columns or rows will be printed on another page.

LOTUS

1. Retrieve file 134B, if it is not displayed, and prepare the printer for printing.
2. Key **/**, **P** (selects Print option).
3. Key **P** (selects printer for the output and displays a Print Settings dialog box).
4. Key **R** (enables you to specify the range of cells that is to be printed).
5. Highlight A1 (marks A1 as first cell in the range to be printed).
6. Key **.** (anchors A1).
7. Highlight through D15 (the last cell in the range to be printed).

WORKS DOS

1. Retrieve 134B, if it is not displayed, and prepare the printer for printing.
2. Press **Alt**, **P** (selects the Print Menu).
3. Key **P** (selects Print from the Print Menu).
4. Strike Enter (accepts 1, the default, as the number of copies to be printed).
5. Close this file.

WORKS MAC

1. Retrieve 134B, if it is not displayed, and prepare the printer for printing.
2. ~ File Menu and select Print.
3. Check printing information in the dialog box and make needed changes.
4. ~ Print box.
5. Close this file.

(continued on next page)

UNIT 23

LESSONS 109-112

Improve Table Formatting Skills

Learning Outcomes: After completing this unit, you will be able to

1. Format tables with greater skill.
2. Use more extensive word processing capabilities.

LESSON 109 — TABLES

109A ◆ CONDITIONING PRACTICE

each line twice SS; then three 1' timed writings on line 4; find *gwam*

alphabet 1 Viki will begin to expedite the zone office's major quarterly reports.

figures 2 The team averages 28,915 fans per game in a stadium that seats 34,760.

fig/sym 3 Catalog item #9087 will cost Anessi & Co. $432.65 (less 10% for cash).

speed 4 The toxic gas odor in the air did make the girls sick when they slept.

gwam 1' | 1 | 2 | 3 | 4 | 5 | 6 | 7 | 8 | 9 | 10 | 11 | 12 | 13 | 14 |

109B ◆
SIMPLE TABLES

File name: L109B

Table 1

1. Review the guides for vertical and horizontal centering given for your software on pp. 153 and 154.
2. Format and key the text at the right. Leave 1.5" between columns.

		words
COMMONLY MISSPELLED WORDS		5
absence	arrangements	9
academic	audit	12
access	authorized	16
already	benefits	19
alternative	calendar	24
appreciate	commission	28

Table 2

Format and key the text at the right as a table. Center vertically and horizontally; leave 1" between columns.

			words
OTHER COMMONLY MISSPELLED WORDS			6
addition	fiscal	maintenance	12
approximately	foreign	material	18
especially	implementation	means	25
expenditures	industrial	maximum	31
facilities	initial	minimum	36
faculty	limited	mortgage	41

APPLY COPYING FORMULAS

Use the same spreadsheet as 133F to do the following:

1. Write a formula that will add A1, A2, A3, and A4; print the result in A5.
   Ans: 1968

2. Copy A5 to B5 through E5.

3. Check the answer in E5—the correct answer is approximately 449733.

4. Save the worksheet as 133G.

133H ◆

APPLICATION ACTIVITY

Use the information at the right to prepare a worksheet and then make the changes indicated below.

1. In B12, enter a formula to add the sales in Column B; copy this formula to Columns C through G.
2. In G5, enter a formula to add cells in Row 5; copy this formula to G6 through G10.
3. Format all values as Currency/Dollars with no decimal places.
4. Change all column widths to 11 except Column A; use default width in A.
5. Center all column headings (labels).
6. Save the worksheet as 133H.

	A	B	C	D	E	F	G
1	SALES REPORT						
2							
3	MONTH	JOHN	MARY	LUIZ	PEDRO	SARA	TOTAL
4							
5	JANUARY	5567	6623	7359	4986	6902	
6	FEBRUARY	2457	7654	3569	2093	6432	
7	MARCH	6930	3096	5792	4607	7908	
8	APRIL	4783	6212	4390	5934	5402	
9	MAY	5042	5092	4500	9453	5321	
10	JUNE	5430	6098	5781	5009	6023	
11							
12	TOTAL						

LESSON 134   PRINT WORKSHEETS

134A ◆
CONDITIONING PRACTICE

each line twice

alphabet 1 James very quickly placed the two extra megaphones behind the freezer.

figures 2 The 120 computers were purchased in 1987; the 34 typewriters, in 1965.

keypad 3 00-713964-528 10-589467-23 20-471659-38 30-574892-16 40-962531-17 85231

speed 4 When we do the work for him, we may also fix their neighbor's bicycle.

gwam 1' | 1 | 2 | 3 | 4 | 5 | 6 | 7 | 8 | 9 | 10 | 11 | 12 | 13 | 14 |

109B ♦ (cont.)

Table 3
Format and key the information at the right as a table. Center vertically and horizontally; leave 1" between columns; block column headings.

	SPRI^GNTIME TOURS		3
Tour	^Dates — DS	Cost	9
Niagara by Night	*April 4-10*	$799	16
Washington D.C.	*April 5-12*	629	22
William Penn Again	*April 7-12*	*699*	29
Baseball Fever	*April 15-22*	359	35
Holland Tulip Festival	*May 4-8*	859	42

109C ♦

LEARN FONT SIZE FEATURE

File name: L109C

Print (Font) Size. Most word processing software packages have features that allow the size of print to be changed. The software as well as the printer you use and the fonts installed with the printer will determine the degree of changes that can be made to the size of the print.

WORDPERFECT

Ctrl F8.
1—Size.
6—Vry Large.
Turn on bold.

WORKS DOS

Alt, T.
Font & Style.
Alt S.
Select larger print size by using ↓ and ↑ .
Return.
Turn on bold.

WORKS MAC

Format.
Size (18 point).
Turn on bold.

words

1. Use the instructions shown above to change the print size for your software.
2. Triple-space (TS) copy; center text vertically and each line horizontally.

DRUGS: FACTS OR FICTION	5
January 23, 19--	8
3:30 p.m.	10
High School Gymnasium	15
Sponsored by:	18
McNamara Drug Treatment Center	24

LESSON 110   TABLES

110A ♦
CONDITIONING PRACTICE
each line twice

alphabet 1 Jim wants both freshmen guards to execute the zone press very quickly.

figures 2 They won the last three games by scores of 135-117; 102-94; and 80-76.

fig/sym 3 Ed called (505) 257-5980 before 1:15 p.m. and 413-6766 after 4:15 p.m.

speed 4 Pamela may name an official tutor to work for the widow and eight men.

gwam 1' | 1 | 2 | 3 | 4 | 5 | 6 | 7 | 8 | 9 | 10 | 11 | 12 | 13 | 14 |

133E ◆

APPLY EDIT FUNCTION

Using the same worksheet as 133D, edit formulas in the cells designated at the right. Check worksheet answers against the printed answers. Edit the formula again, after reviewing parts of 133D, if answers do not match. Be sure each item is correct before going to the next item.

1. Edit formula in D1 so that A1+B4 is divided by B2.

   Ans: .676

2. Edit formula in D2 so that A4 and B4 are added and then multiplied by B3.

   Ans: 63635

3. Edit formula in D3 so that B3, B4, A1, A4 are added and then multiplied by .5.

   Ans: 800

4. Edit formula in D4 so that B2 is used in place of A4.

   Ans: 379964

5. Leave worksheet on the screen.

133F ◆

COPY FORMULAS

Read the information at the right about copying formulas and then complete the steps listed below for your ss software. (The Copy feature is presented in 131B, p. 246.)

The Copy feature may be used to copy formulas. When formulas are copied from a cell to one or more other cells, the copy is not exact. Rather, ss software considers the cell addresses used in the formula to be "relative" and, therefore, automatically changes cell addresses in the formula to reflect the new locations.

LOTUS

Use the same worksheet as 133E and write a formula in E1 that adds the contents of A1, B1, C1, and D1 (Ans: approximately 1112); then copy that formula to cells E2 through E4.

1. Highlight E1 and key /, **C** (the *Copy what?* prompt appears).
2. Strike Enter (*To where?* prompt displays).
3. Highlight E2 (the first cell of the range being copied to) and key **.** (anchors E2).
4. Highlight E4 (the last cell in the range) and strike Enter.
5. Highlight E2 (Ans: 65913) and look at the Control Panel: Notice that cell addresses in the formula were changed to A2+B2+C2+D2 so they would be relative to E2.
6. Highlight E3 (Ans: approximately 1648) and then E4 (Ans: 381051), noting that each formula was made relative to E3 or E4.
7. Leave worksheet on the screen.

WORKS DOS

Use the worksheet on the screen and write a formula in E1 that adds the contents of A1, B1, C1, and D1 (Ans: approximately 1112); then copy that formula to cells E2 through E4.

1. Highlight E1 and press **Alt, S, E** (chooses Cells from the Select Menu).
2. Extend highlight to E4 (selects E2—E4 as the range of cells receiving the copy).
3. Press **Alt, E, F** (selects Fill Down from the Edit Menu).
4. Highlight E2 (Ans: 65913) and look at the Control Panel: Notice that cell addresses in the formula were changed to A2+B2+C2+D2 so they would be relative to E2.
5. Highlight E3 (Ans: approximately 1648) and then E4 (Ans: 381051), noting that each formula was made relative to E3 or E4.
6. Leave worksheet on the screen.

WORKS MAC

Use the worksheet on the screen and write a formula in E1 that adds the contents of A1, B1, C1, and D1 (Ans: approximately 1112); then copy that formula to cells E2 through E4.

1. ~ E1, drag down to E4, and strike Return (selects E2 to E4 as the range of cells receiving the copy).
2. ~ Edit Menu and select Fill Down.
3. ~ E2 (Ans: 65913) and look at the Entry Bar: Notice that cell addresses in the formula were changed to A2+B2+C2+D2 so they would be relative to E2.
4. ~ E3 (Ans: approximately 1648) and then E4 (Ans: 381051), noting that each formula was made relative to E3 or E4.
5. Leave worksheet on the screen.

110B ◆
FORMAT TABLES

File name: L110B
DS all lines; format the tables given at the right; block column headings; correct errors.

Table 1
Table With Main and Column Headings
CS: 1"

Table 2
Table With Main and Column Headings and Source Note
CS: 1.5"

Table 3
Table With Main, Secondary, and Column Headings and Total Line
CS: 1"

Table 4
Revision of Table 2
Include the 1990-1993 World Series Champions:
1990—Cincinnati (NL)
1991—Minnesota (AL)
1992—Toronto (AL)
1993—Toronto (AL)

Table 5
Revision of Table 3
Update the table to include donations from two additional companies:
Sabin's Graphics, Inc. $800
Carling's Real Estate $400

EXECUTIVE OFFICERS

Position	Name	
		4
Position	Name	9
Chief Executive Officer	Donald Espinosa	17
Chairperson of the Board	Alice Gomory	25
Chief Financial Officer	Gregg Foster	32
Senior Vice President	Michael McCoskey	40
Vice President	Mary Whitney	45
Treasurer	Nancy Schneider	50

1983-1989 WORLD SERIES CHAMPIONS

Team	Year	
		7
Team	Year	10
Baltimore (AL)	1983	14
Detroit (AL)	1984	18
Kansas City (AL)	1985	22
New York (NL)	1986	26
Minnesota (AL)	1987	30
Los Angeles (NL)	1988	34
Oakland (AL)	1989	38
		41

Source: World Almanac.   48

UNITED WAY

(July Donations)

Company	Amount	
		2
		6
Company	Amount	11
Gunderson Construction Company	$1,500	19
Lakeview Data Products	1,500	25
Wilkerson Automotive	1,000	30
First National Bank	500	40
Bates Photography	400	48
Krause Associates	250	56
Anderson's Home Furnishings	200	64
Total	$7,050	66
Lakeview Marina	500	
Your Travel Network	900	
The Clock Shop	300	

LEARN EDIT FUNCTION

Read the information about editing at the right and then complete the steps listed below for your software.

Spreadsheet software has an Edit feature that allows you to change information already in a cell. Edit is accessed by pressing a function key after the cell to be edited has been highlighted. Once the function key is depressed, the current cell contents appear in the Control Panel or Entry Bar. The cell contents are edited by moving the cursor. The Insert, Typeover, Delete, and Backspace features can be used in the same manner as they are used in word processing.

LOTUS

In C1, use Edit to change the formula so that B1 is subtracted from A1.

1. Highlight C1 and strike **F2** (accesses Edit feature).
2. Use ← to position cursor at the + between the cells; use Typeover to change + to − and strike Enter (recalculates answer using edited formula).
3. Check result in C1 (-200).

In C2, edit the formula so that A4 and B4 are added.

1. Highlight C2 and strike **F2**.
2. Strike Esc (erases existing formula).
3. Key **+A4+B4** (enters revised formula) and strike Enter.
4. Check result in C2 (979) .

In C3, edit the formula so that B1 is added to A4/B30.

1. Highlight C3 and strike **F2**.
2. Key **+B1** (adds B1 to existing formula) and strike Enter .
3. Check result in C3 (770.707).

In C4, edit the formula so that A3 and B4 are added and then multiplied times 3.

1. Highlight C4 and strike **F2**.
2. Strike Home key (moves cursor under first character).
3. Use → to position cursor at A and key **(**.
4. Use → to position cursor at * and then change * to **+** .
5. Use → to position cursor one space to the right of the 4 in B4 and insert **)**.
6. Key ***3** (multiplies the sum of A3+B4 by 3) and strike Enter.
7. Check result in C4 (108).
8. Leave worksheet on the screen.

WORKS DOS

In C1, use Edit to change the formula so B1 is subtracted from A1.

1. Highlight C1 and strike **F2** (accesses Edit feature).
2. Use ← to position cursor at the + between the cell addresses; use Typeover to change the + to − and strike Enter (recalculates result using edited formula).
3. Check result in C1 (-200).

In C2, edit the formula so that A4 and B4 are added.

1. Highlight C2 and strike **F2**.
2. Use Backspace key repeatedly to erase all but the = sign in the existing formula.
3. Key **=A4+B4** (enters revised formula) and strike Enter.
4. Check result in C2 (979).

In C3, edit the formula so that B1 is added to A4/B30.

1. Highlight C3 and strike **F2**.
2. Key **+B1** (adds B1 to existing formula) and strike Enter.
3. Check result in C3 (770.707).

In C4, edit the formula so that A3 and B4 are added and then multiplied times 3.

1. Highlight C4 and strike **F2**.
2. Strike Home key (moves cursor under first character).
3. Use → to position cursor at A and key **(**.
4. Use → to position cursor at * and then change * to **+**.
5. Use → to position cursor one space to the right of the 4 in B4 and insert **)**.
6. Key ***3** (multiplies the sum of A3+B4 by 3) and strike Enter.
7. Check result in C4 (108).
8. Leave worksheet on the screen.

WORKS MAC

In C1, use Edit to change the formula so that B1 is subtracted from A1.

1. ~ C1, ~ Entry Bar and drag across +, key − (changes + to − in the formula).
2. ~ Enter Box (recalculates result using edited formula).
3. Check result in C1 (-200).

In C2, edit the formula so that A4 and B4 are added.

1. ~ C1, ~ Entry Bar and drag across entire formula.
2. ~ Edit Menu and select Cut.
3. Key **=A4+B4**.
4. ~ Enter Box (recalculates answer using edited formula).
5. Check result in C2 (979).

In C3, edit the formula so that B1 is added to A4/B3.

1. ~ C3, ~ Entry Bar.
2. Key **+B1** (adds B1 to existing formula) and ~ Enter Box or strike Return.
3. Check result in C3 (770.707).

In C4, edit the formula so that A3 and B4 are added and then multiplied times 3.

1. ~ C4, ~ Entry Bar and drag across entire formula except for the = sign.
2. ~ Edit Menu and select Cut.
3. ~ Enter Box or strike Return.
4. Key **(A3+B4)*3**.
5. Check result in C4 (108).
6. Leave worksheet on the screen.

111-112A
CONDITIONING
PRACTICE
each line twice

alphabet 1 Mary's parents will quickly join Geoff to criticize both taxi drivers.
figures 2 Bad weather canceled 35 flights with 2,460 passengers on June 7, 1989.
fig/sym 3 Parsit & Brown received Model #239-089/A with Serial #465-17-49 today.
speed 4 Dirk may hand the girls eight shamrocks when they are at their formal.

gwam 1' | 1 | 2 | 3 | 4 | 5 | 6 | 7 | 8 | 9 | 10 | 11 | 12 | 13 | 14 |

111-112B ◆
FORMAT TABLES

Table 1
Three-Column Table With Blocked Column Headings and Total Line
CS: 1"; DS table
File name: SALES

words

MARCH SALES

Sales Manager	Territory	Sales	
			2
			14
Diane Aldredge	Connecticut	$204,500	21
Marcia Kelly	Maine	135,200	27
Ruth Peterson	Massachusetts	125,000	34
Rebecca Johnston	New Hampshire	135,800	42
Orlando Martinez	New York	172,900	48
Jonathan Akervik	Rhode Island	88,200	56
Roger McDonald	Vermont	115,200	64
Total Sales		$976,800	69

Table 2
Three-Column Table With Blocked Column Headings and Notation
CS: 1"; DS table
File name: BALLET1

HAMBURG SCHOOL OF BALLET ITINERARY
19-- Summer Tour*

Sponsor	City	Date	
			7
			11
			17
Boston Ballet	Boston	June 4	24
Ballet Academy of Miami	Miami	June 11	32
Dallas Ballet Academy	Dallas	June 18	39
Ruth Page Foundation	Chicago	June 25	47
Northwest Ballet	Minneapolis	July 1	54
Colorado Ballet Center	Denver	July 8	61
Dancers' Stage Company	San Francisco	July 15	70
Pacific Northwest Ballet	Seattle	July 22	79

82

*Leave for Boston on June 1; return to Hamburg on July 27. 94

2. Key **+A1+B1** and strike Enter (enters the formula and performs the desired calculation).
3. Check C1—the result (1312) is recorded in C1 and the formula appears on the first line of the Control Panel.

Subtract B2 from A2 (use the – key) and print the result in C2.

1. Highlight C2.
2. Key **+A2-B2** and strike Enter.
3. Check C2—the result (413) is a negative number (shown in parentheses).

Divide A4 by B3 (use the / key) and print the result in C3.

1. Highlight C3.
2. Key **+A4/B3** and strike Enter.
3. Check C3 for result (14.707).

Multiply A3 by B4 (use the * key) and print the result in C4.

1. Highlight C4.
2. Key **+A3*B4** and strike Enter.
3. Check C4 for result (299).
4. Leave worksheet on the screen.

---

3. Check C1—the result (1312) is recorded in C1 and the formula appears on the first line of the Entry Bar.

Subtract B2 from A2 (use the – key) and print the result in C2.

1. Highlight C2.
2. Key **=A2-B2** and strike Enter.
3. Check C2—the result (413) is a negative number (shown with a minus sign).

Divide A4 by B3 (use the / key) and print the result in C3.

1. Highlight C3.
2. Key **=A4/B3** and strike Enter.
3. Check C3 for result (14.707).

Multiply A3 by B4 (use the * key) and print the result in C4.

1. Highlight C4.
2. Key **=A3*B4** and strike Enter.
3. Check C4 for result (299).
4. Leave worksheet on the screen.

---

3. ~ C1—the result (1312) is recorded in C1 and the formula appears on the Entry Bar.

Subtract B2 from A2 (use the – key) and print the result in C2.

1. ~ C2.
2. Key **=A2-B2** and strike Return.
3. ~ C2—the result (413) is a negative number (shown with a minus sign).

Divide A4 by B3 (use the / key) and print the result in C3.

1. ~ C3.
2. Key **=A4/B3** and strike Enter.
3. Check C3 for result (14.707).

Multiply A3 by B4 (use the * key) and print the result in C4.

1. ~ C4.
2. Key **=A3*B4** and strike Enter.
3. Check C4 for result (299).
4. Leave worksheet on the screen.

APPLY WRITING FORMULAS

Use the worksheet created in 133B. Write and enter formulas to do the calculations shown at the right. Check the answer on your worksheet against the answer printed here. If it is not the same, review the appropriate section of 133B; then recalculate. Be sure No. 1 is correct before doing No. 2, and so on.

1. In D1, add A1 to B4; divide the result by B3.

   Formula: (A1+B4)/B3
   Ans: 8.907

2. In D2, subtract A2 from B2; multiply the result by B3.

   Formula: (B2-A2)*B3
   Ans: 26845

3. In D3, multiply A4 times A3; divide the result by B4.

   Formula: A4*A3/B4
   Ans: 540.347

4. In D4, multiply A2 by A4; add B1 to the results.

   Formula: A2*A4+B1
   Ans: 424264

5. Leave worksheet on the screen.

words

Table 3
Table With Centered Column Headings
CS: 0.5"; DS table
File name: SCHEDULE
You may need to change side margins to 0.5" for table to fit on page.

> **Learning cue:** To center column headings shorter than column entries, follow these steps.
> 1. Determine placement of columns in usual way.
> 2. From column starting point, space forward once for each two strokes in longest entry. From this point, backspace once for each 2 strokes in column heading.
> 3. Key and underline column heading.

19-- SPRING RECRUITMENT *Schedule*			7
Martin Bartlett			10
University	Date	Area of Specialization	27
San Diego *State* University	March 3	Marketing	36
Arizona State University	March 10	Management Information	47
University of Colorado	March 10	Management Information	58
University of Kentucky	March 24	*Management*	67
Tennessee State *University*	March 31	Accounting	76
Florida A & M	April 7	Marketing	83
Duke University	April 14	Accounting	90

Table 4
Table With Centered Column Headings
CS: 1"; DS table
File name: PARKS1

Table 5
Retrieve Table 2 (BALLET1) and make the following changes.
1. Center column headings.
2. Change *Minneapolis* to **St. Paul**.
3. Add: **Oregon Ballet Troupe, Portland, July 27** to the tour.
4. Change the return date to **August 3**.
File name: BALLET2

Table 6
Reformat Table 4 (PARKS1).
Alphabetize the table by name of national park.*
CS: 1.5"
File name: PARKS2

*(WordPerfect Sort feature, see 86B, p. 162.)

National Parks			3
(Established 1872-1917)			8
National Park	*State*	*Year*	18
Yellowstone	*Wyoming*	*1872*	23
Sequoia	*California*	*1890*	28
Yosemite	*California*	*1890*	33
Mount Rainier	*Washington*	*1899*	39
Crater Lake	*Oregon*	*1902*	44
Wind Cave	*South Dakota*	*1903*	49
Mesa Verde	*Colorado*	*1906*	54
Glacier	*Montana*	*1910*	58
Rocky Mountain	*Colorado*	*1915*	64
Hawaii Volcanoes	*Hawaii*	*1916*	70
Lassen Volcanic	*California*	*1916*	76
Mount McKinley	*Alaska*	*1917*	82
			85
Source: Encyclopedia Americana.			96

133A ◆ CONDITIONING PRACTICE
each line twice

alphabet 1 Maxine was amazed frequently by the project check arriving so quickly.

figures 2 The combined population of the same 23 towns in 1989 was only 146,750.

keypad 3 482-3711 472-3600 817-561-3640 213-871-5069 206-791-4583 312-471-8659

speed 4 With their profit they may pay for an emblem of the shantytown chapel.

gwam 1' | 1 | 2 | 3 | 4 | 5 | 6 | 7 | 8 | 9 | 10 | 11 | 12 | 13 | 14 |

133B ◆ WRITE FORMULAS

Read the information at the right about writing formulas and then complete the steps listed for your software.

The ss software can add, subtract, multiply, and divide numeric data that have been entered into cells. The software performs the calculations by following the order of operations contained in formulas entered at the cell address where the results of the calculation are to appear. When interpreting formulas the software performs multiplication and division, in the order that they occur, before performing addition and subtraction, in the order that they occur. Operations inside parentheses are performed before those outside.

Access your ss software and enter the following values in the cells designated:

A1: 556   B1: 756

A2: 443   B2: 856

A3: 13   B3: 65

A4: 956   B4: 23

LOTUS

Formula Characteristics
a. Cannot contain blank spaces.
b. Must begin with a figure or one of these symbols: . + - (@ # $.
c. Must begin with a + sign if the formula begins with a cell address.
d. Viewed by highlighting the cell that contains the formula and reading the first line of the control panel.

Add the numbers (use the + key) in A1 and B1 and print the result in C1.

1. Highlight C1 (the cell address that is to contain the answer).

WORKS DOS

Formula Characteristics
a. Cannot contain blank spaces.
b. Must begin with equal sign (=).
c. Viewed by highlighting the cell that contains the formula and reading the formula in the entry line.

Add the numbers (use the + key) in A1 and B1 and print the result in C1.

1. Highlight C1 (the cell address that is to contain the answer).
2. Key **=A1+B1** and strike Enter (enters the formula and performs the desired calculation).

WORKS MAC

Formula Characteristics
a. Cannot contain blank spaces.
b. Must begin with equal sign (=).
c. Viewed by highlighting the cell that contains the formula and reading the formula in the entry line.

Add the numbers (use the + key) in A1 and B1 and print the result in C1.

1. ~ C1 (the cell address that is to contain the answer).
2. Key **=A1+B1** and strike Return (enters the formula and performs the desired calculation).

(continued on next page)   (continued on next page)   (continued on next page)

WORDPERFECT TABLE FEATURE

File name: PRESIDEN

1. To create the table, depress **Alt F7**, **2**—Tables, **1**—Create.
2. At the *Number of columns* prompt enter the number of columns (**3**) and return.
3. At the *Number of rows* prompt enter the number of rows (**13**) and return. (You are now in the table editor.)
4. Depress **F7** to exit the table editor. (The status line shows that the cursor is now in Cell A1.)
5. Key **President**, depress Tab.

6. Key **Term**, depress Tab.
7. Key **Party**, depress Tab. (The cursor is now in Cell A2.)
8. Key all information for the table. Use the Tab key to move from cell to cell. If you accidentally use the return key to go to the next line, strike the Backspace key to delete the hard return.
9. Use ↓ to move the cursor outside the table; return once and key the source note.

10. To center the column headings, place the cursor in Cell A1. Depress **Alt F7** to activate the table editor. Turn on block (**Alt F4**) and strike the End key.
11. Depress **2**—Format, **1**—Cells, **3**—Justify, and **2**—Center.
12. To center the Column 2 entries, place the cursor in Cell B2. Turn on block. Depress Home, ↓ .
13. Depress **2**—Format, **2**—Column, **3**—Justify, and **2**—Center.

14. To center the table *horizontally*, depress **6**—Options, **3**—Position of Table, **3**—Center, **F7**.
15. Exit the table editor (**F7**).
16. To key the table headings, strike **PgUp** to move the cursor above the table. Return two times. Strike **PgUp** and then center and key the table headings.
17. To center the table *vertically*, depress **PgUp**, **Shift F8**, **2**—Page, **1**—Center Page, Yes, **F7**.
18. Print the table.

Table 1

1. Study the commands for formatting text using the WordPerfect table formatting feature.
2. Use the feature to format the text at the right as a lined table.

Table 2

Update Table 1 to include **William Clinton**, **1993-19--**, **Democrat**.

Hint: Place the cursor within the table; activate the table edit mode (**Alt F7**). Insert another row as follows:

1—Size
2—Rows
Key **14**
Return
F7
Key new information

Delete the following files from your disk (refer to 66D, p. 129, if necessary):

L103C	L106B
L104B1	L106C1
L104B2	L106C2
L105B	

PRESIDENTS OF THE UNITED STATES

1923-1992

President	Term	Party
Calvin Coolidge	1923-1929	Republican
Herbert Hoover	1929-1933	Republican
Franklin Roosevelt	1933-1945	Democrat
Harry Truman	1945-1953	Democrat
Dwight Eisenhower	1953-1961	Republican
John Kennedy	1961-1963	Democrat
Lyndon Johnson	1963-1969	Democrat
Richard Nixon	1969-1974	Republican
Gerald Ford	1974-1977	Republican
Jimmy Carter	1977-1981	Democrat
Ronald Reagan	1981-1989	Republican
George Bush	1989-1992	Republican

Source: Collier's Encyclopedia.

4. Use ⇢ repeatedly until numbers appear in Column D (the column width is widened by one space each time the ⇢ key is used). Instead of using the ⇠ (to shorten the column width) or the ⇢ keys, the column width can be changed by keying the desired number when the column width number is displayed after the Set-Width feature is selected.

5 Strike⇢ two more times so that 2 spaces are left between columns C and D and then strike Enter.

the values entered in Column D require 13 spaces, and 2 spaces were added to leave room between Columns C and D.
4. Strike Enter (selects OK).

were added to leave room between Column C and D).
4. ~ OK.

Alternate Method

You can make columns wider or narrower by ~ the column border (a column divider bar will appear) and dragging to the desired location.

1. Point and drag the column divider bar to the left of D in the border line about 5 spaces to the left (makes Column C narrower).
2. Point and drag the column divider bar to the right of B about 6 spaces to the right (makes Column B wider).

132D ◆

APPLY CHANGING COLUMN WIDTHS

Use the worksheet created in 132C to make the following column width changes:

Change width of Column A to 8, B to 13, C to 25, and D to 20.

132E ◆

APPLICATION ACTIVITY

Prepare the worksheet at the right and then make the changes listed below:
1. Column A—format as Fixed with 0 decimal places and width of 8 spaces.
2. Column B—format as Fixed with 3 decimal places and width of 8 spaces.
3. Column C—format as Currency (Dollar for Works MAC users) with 2 decimal places and width of 11.
4. Column D—format as Percent with 4 decimal places and width of 11 spaces.
5. Save the worksheet as 132E.

	A	B	C	D
1	FORMATTING NUMBERS			
2				
3	FIXED	FIXED	CURRENCY	PERCENT
4	12.34	90.9	45.1	1
5	2.345	8.989	56.2	0.1
6	3456	0.7878	67.3	0.01
7	4567	676.7	7.874	0.001
8	5678	0.5656	89.5	0.0001
9	67.89	0.4545	9.06	121
10	789	3.343	21238	0.2
11	890.1	23.23	23.05	2.2
12	9012	0.1212	34.97	12.22

UNIT 24

Master Keyboarding Skills

Learning Outcomes: After completing this unit, you will be able to

1. Key straight-copy paragraphs with higher speed and greater control.
2. Demonstrate improved skill transfer to rough-draft copy.
3. Demonstrate improved skill transfer to script copy.

LESSONS 113-114

LESSON 113 — KEYBOARDING SKILLS

SM: Defaults; LS: SS

113A ◆ 6'
CONDITIONING PRACTICE

each line twice SS; two
1' writings on line 4

alphabet 1 Patti may quit cutting flax when jet black clouds cover the azure sky.
figures 2 Her order 3927 is for 10 hostas, 5 ferns, 8 yews, and 64 ajuga plants.
fig/sym 3 Roy paid Invoice #7349 (dated 6/25/94) for $581.02 on July 7 less 10%.
speed 4 The firm may spend the profit for land to make a big lake by the city.

gwam 1' | 1 | 2 | 3 | 4 | 5 | 6 | 7 | 8 | 9 | 10 | 11 | 12 | 13 | 14 |

113B ◆ 14'
RESPONSE PATTERNS

1. Key each pair of lines 3 times.
2. Two 1' writings on line 7 and on line 8; find *gwam*.

letter
response
1 sad you set nip rag pun are mill cast jink tear hill gaff jolly barter
2 gear pump were monk cave mink fast jump state plump trade holly exceed

word
response
3 then sham they mend auto when maps than soaps their small fight island
4 make visit cycle ivory forms handy turns bossy firms buddy slams right

combination
response
5 she was | they were | auto gear | make fast | when were | they cast | make a trade
6 if she was | a big jump | of the case | if they are | make a cast | fix the pump

word
combination
7 Rob may go with me to the big island to visit the boss of a soap firm.
8 Dee may cycle up to the mill to fix a gear on a small gas pump for me.

gwam 1' | 1 | 2 | 3 | 4 | 5 | 6 | 7 | 8 | 9 | 10 | 11 | 12 | 13 | 14 |

113C ◆ 13'
IMPROVE SPEED

1. Key two 1' writings on ¶1 (easy copy); find *gwam*.
2. Key two 1' writings on ¶ 2 (average copy); find *gwam*.
3. Key two more 1' writings on the slower ¶; try to equal or exceed best *gwam* in Steps 1 and 2.
4. Repeat Steps 1-3.

¶1   Do you think it is all right to cheat as long as you do not get caught? Some people do. They think that what they get away with does not concern anyone except themselves. If you cheat to move ahead, you deny someone else the right to the prize, and that is wrong.

¶2   Some of the major rules by which we live have been devised to protect us from one another; that is, to prevent one person or group from taking unfair advantage of another person or group. Equally important tenets are intended to keep us from being unfair to ourselves.

Percent Format

Format the values in C1 through C5 as percents with one decimal place:

1. Highlight C1.
2. Key **/**, **R**, **F**, **P** (selects Percent format from the Format option).
3. Key **1** (specifies one decimal place) and strike Enter.
4. Highlight C5 and strike Enter.

Percent Format

Format the data in D1 through D5 as percents with 4 decimal places:

1. Highlight D1; key **/**, **R**, **F**, **P**; key **4**, strike Enter; and highlight D1.
2. Strike Enter (some cell entries are a line of ******** because the format selected exceeds the preset column width. Leave the worksheet as is and proceed to 132C to learn how to change the * signs to figures).

Percent Format

Format the values in C1 through C5 as percents with one decimal place:

1. Highlight C1.
2. Press **Alt**, **S**, **C**.
3. Press **Alt**, **T**, **P** (selects Percent from the Format Menu).
4. Key **1** (selects decimal place).
5. Strike Enter (accepts the default decimal place setting and changes values to percent format with 1 decimal place) and strike any arrow key.

Percent Format

Format the data in D1 through D5 as percents with 4 decimal places:

1. Highlight C1; press **Alt**, **S**, **C**; press **Alt**, **T**, **P**; key **4**.
2. Strike Enter (some cell entries are a line of ########## because the format selected exceeds the preset column width. Leave the worksheet as is and proceed to 132C to learn how to change the # signs to figures).

Percent Format

Format the values in C1 through C5 as percents with one decimal place.

1. ~ C1 and drag to C5.
2. ~ Format Menu and select Set Cell Attributes.
3. ~ Percent in dialog box.
4. Key **1** (sets decimal places to 1).
5. ~ OK (formats numbers as percents).

Percent Format

Format the data in D1 through D5 as percents with 5 decimal places:

1. ~ D1 and drag to D5.
2. ~ Format menu and select Set Cell Attributes.
3. ~ Percent in dialog box.
4. Key **5** (sets decimal places to 5).
5. ~ OK (formats values as percents—some cell entries are a line of ########## because the format selected exceeds the preset column width. Leave the worksheet as is and proceed to 132C to learn how to change the # signs to figures).

CHANGE COLUMN WIDTHS

Read the information at the right about changing column widths and then complete the steps for your software.

The default column widths are as follows: Lotus, 9 characters; Works DOS, 10 characters; and Works MAC, 12 figures (the number of letters you can put in the Works MAC default column-width setting varies since letters have different widths). Often, wider worksheet columns are needed. In which case, column widths must be changed.

LOTUS

1. Highlight a cell in any row in Column D (the column that is to be widened).
2. Key **/**, **W**, **C** (selects Column option from the Worksheet Menu).
3. Key **S** (selects Set-Width feature from the Column option and displays the default width, 9).

(continued on next page)

WORKS DOS

1. Highlight a cell in any row in Column D (the column that is to be widened).
2. Press **Alt**, **T**, **W** (selects Column Width option from the Format Menu).
3. Key **15** (changes the column width to 15): 15 was chosen because the format selected and

(continued on next page)

WORKS MAC

1. ~ any cell in Column D (the column that is to be widened).
2. ~ Format Menu and select Column Width.
3. Key **15** (changes the column-width to 15); 15 was chosen because the format selected and the values entered in Column D require 13 spaces, and 2 spaces

(continued on next page)

IMPROVE/ CHECK SKILL

1. Take a 1' writing on ¶1; find *gwam*.
2. Add 2-4 *gwam* to the rate attained in Step 1, and note quarter-minute checkpoints in the table below.
3. Take two 1' guided writings on ¶1 to increase speed.
4. Practice ¶s 2 and 3 in the same way.
5. Take a 3' writing on ¶s 1-3 combined; find *gwam* and count errors.
6. Repeat Step 5.

gwam	1/4'	1/2'	3/4'	1'
20	5	10	15	20
24	6	12	18	24
28	7	14	21	28
32	8	16	24	32
36	9	18	27	36
40	10	20	30	40
44	11	22	33	44
48	12	24	36	48
52	13	26	39	52
56	14	28	42	56

all letters used | A | 1.5 si | 5.7 awl | 80% hfw

gwam 3' | 5'

For many people in the early part of the century, staying in the — 4 | 3

same job with a single company or institution for their entire produc- — 9 | 5

tive lives was not too uncommon. Now it is thought that many fledgling — 14 | 8

workers will switch jobs several times in their working lifetimes. — 18 | 11

The pace of change in the national job arena today requires that — 23 | 14

all people prepare themselves to move upward or outward in the same com- — 27 | 16

pany or from firm to firm. Such moves demand widened experience and — 32 | 19

education. Often the moves result in better pay and benefits. — 36 | 22

So do not envision your diploma or your initial job as the end of — 40 | 24

anything. Recognize that they are merely milestones in the ongoing — 45 | 27

process of preparing for a richer, more responsible life. Living is a — 50 | 30

process of becoming rather than a state of being. — 53 | 32

LESSON 114 — KEYBOARDING SKILLS

SM: Defaults; LS: SS

114A ♦ 6'
CONDITIONING PRACTICE

each line twice SS; two 1' writings on line 4

alphabet 1 Jevon may quickly fix two bikes for a dizzy girl with tawny pink hair.

figures 2 Flight 147, with 90 passengers, left Gate 56 at 2:38 p.m. for Chicago.

fig/sym 3 Of 280 people tested, 15% scored 94 or better; 26%, 87-93; 47% 80-86.

speed 4 Nancy may go with them to the city to bid for the antique ivory forks.

gwam 1' | 1 | 2 | 3 | 4 | 5 | 6 | 7 | 8 | 9 | 10 | 11 | 12 | 13 | 14 |

114B ♦ 17'
MASTER TECHNIQUE: SERVICE KEYS

each set of lines twice (once slowly, once faster); repeat

Space Bar (quick down-and-in thumb motion)

1 an am by pen buy aim boy plan buoy from fury clan duty clam they clean

2 The man and his son swam by an old buoy on their way to a lazy lagoon.

Shifting with symbols (finger reaches to shift keys and symbols)

3 Apt. #40 I for $726 I Epson & Sparks I a 30% discount I by August 1 I Order 25#.

4 May & Co. sold a 60# bag of grass seed ($5.95/lb.) to a man from Kent.

Underline and Caps Lock (quiet hands and arms)

5 change ain't to am not I main should be major I use Works DOS or Works MAC

6 Did your CPA send your income tax return to the IRS by RPS or by USPS?

Currency. The Currency format option puts a $ before each value and a comma after the thousands and millions places in applicable cell entries. In addition, it uses the number of decimal places selected by the software user and displays negative numbers in parentheses. (For users of Works MAC, this format is called *Dollar* format.)

General. The General format option is the default value display; it does not display commas in large values; it displays only decimals that are entered.

Percent. The Percent format option displays the percent equivalent of a value. A percent symbol (%) is written after the value and the number of decimal places to be displayed can be specified by the user.

On a clear worksheet screen, key the following values into the cells designated:

A1: 1	B1: 2	C1: 3	D1: 400
A2: 5	B2: 6	C2: .7	D2: 800
A3: 9	B3: 10	C3: 1.1	D3: 1310
A4: 13	B4: 14	C4: .15	D4: 1600
A5: 17	B5: 18	C5: 1.9	D5: 2000

LOTUS

Fixed Format

Format the values in A1 through A5 in Fixed format with 3 decimal places.

1. Highlight A1 (the first cell in the range to be formatted).
2. Key **/**, **R**, **F**, **F** (selects Range from Main Menu, selects Format option and Fixed format).
3. Key **3** (changes default decimal setting of 2 places to 3).
4. Strike Enter.
5. Highlight A5 (the last cell in the range) and strike Enter (changes values to desired format).

Currency Format

Format the data in B1 through B5 in Currency format (2 decimal places).

1. Highlight B1.
2. Key **/**, **R**, **F**, **C** (selects Currency format from the Format option).
3. Strike Enter (accepts the default decimal setting).
4. Highlight B5 and strike Enter.

WORKS DOS

Fixed Format

Format the values in A1 through A5 in Fixed format with 3 decimal places:

1. Highlight A1 (the first cell in the range to be formatted).
2. Press **Alt**, **S**, **C** (selects Column from the Select Menu).
3. Press **Alt**, **T**, **X** (selects Fixed from the Format Menu).
4. Key **3** (selects 3 decimal places in the dialog box).
5. Strike Enter (changes numbers to fixed format with 3 decimal places) and strike any arrow key.

Currency Format

Format the data in B1 through B5 in Currency format (2 decimal places).

1. Highlight B1.
2. Press **Alt**, **S**, **C**.
3. Press **Alt**, **T**, **U** (selects Currency from the Format Menu).
4. Strike Enter (accepts the default decimal place setting and changes numbers to Currency format) and strike any arrow key.

WORKS MAC

Fixed Format

Format the values in A1 through A5 in Fixed format with 3 decimal places.

1. ~ A1 and drag to A5 (selects the range of cells to be formatted).
2. ~ Format Menu and select Set Cell Attributes.
3. ~ Fixed in dialog box.
4. Key **3** (sets decimal places to 3 in the Decimal Places box).
5. ~ OK (changes numbers to fixed format).

Dollar Format

Format the data in B1 through B5 in Dollar format with 2 decimal places.

1. ~ B1 and drag to B5.
2. ~ Format Menu and select Set Cell Attributes.
3. ~ Dollar in dialog box.
4. ~ OK (accepts the default decimal place setting and changes numbers to currency format).

(continued on next page)　　　(continued on next page)　　　(continued on next page)

IMPROVE/ CHECK SKILL

1. Key a 1' unguided and two 1' guided writings on each ¶. (Record your best *gwam* for later use.)
2. Key two 2' writings on ¶s 1-3 combined; find *gwam* on each writing.
3. Key a 3' writing on ¶s 1-3 combined; find *gwam* and count errors.
4. Repeat Step 3. Record your rate for use in 114D below.

gwam	¼'	½'	¾'	1'
20	5	10	15	20
24	6	12	18	24
28	7	14	21	28
32	8	16	24	32
36	9	18	27	36
40	10	20	30	40
44	11	22	33	44
48	12	24	36	48
52	13	26	39	52
56	14	28	42	56

all letters used | A | 1.5 si | 5.7 awl | 80% hfw

	gwam 2'	3'
A job description is a formal statement of the duties performed by	7	4
a worker. It may include both quality and quantity factors. The job	14	9
description is used to select new workers and place them in jobs that	21	14
best fit their abilities. A brief summary of the job description may	28	18
be given to people who show interest in working for a company.	34	23
A performance appraisal form is a formal method of assessing the	40	27
performance of workers. It defines each level of excellence a person	47	32
may reach. It then lists in major groups the duties workers in a job	54	36
class perform. The supervisor rates the person on each duty, using a	61	41
scale of one to five, with a rating of three representing the standard.	68	46
A job description and an appraisal form may have a section on work	75	50
habits: attitude on the job, working well with others, proper use of	82	55
time, skill in writing and speaking, and initiative. When a job is done	89	60
equally well by two workers, the one who shows better work habits and	96	64
attitudes will usually get the prized promotion or pay increase.	103	69

gwam 2' | 1 | 2 | 3 | 4 | 5 | 6 | 7
3' | 1 | 2 | 3 | 4 | 5

ROUGH DRAFT AND SCRIPT

1. Key a 1' writing on each ¶; find *gwam* on each.
2. Divide each *gwam* by your best 1' *gwam* on 114C above to find % of transfer.
3. Key two more 1' writings on each of the slower ¶s to improve transfer.
   Goals: 80% on ¶1
   90% on ¶2
4. Key a 2' writing on each ¶.

	gwam 1'	2'
Whether you must ~~have to~~ earn money or not, make part time or	11	5
summer work a part of your career plan. A carefully chosen	22	11
work experience can offer ~~many chances~~ opportunities to meet workers in	34	17
your career field and to observe firsthand ~~directly~~ many of the activi-	46	23
ties and features of the jobs related to that field. You can	59	29
make such work a valuable career learning experience.	69	35
Do not expect your first position to be near the top of	11	40
your chosen career ladder. Although you may not be required	23	46
to begin at the very bottom rung, realize that you have to	35	52
demonstrate your capability of performing at a higher level	47	58
before you will be placed there. To advance in your chosen	59	64
career, you must gain related experience of increasing value.	71	70

APPLICATION ACTIVITY

Retrieve worksheet T128B on the *Student's Template* and make these changes:

1. Erase these columns: TOT QUIZ SCORE, AVG QUIZ SCORE, and WD QUIZ SCORE.

2. Erase these columns: PAP AVG SCORE and WD PAP SCORE.

3. Copy J30 to K30 and L30.

4. At K6 enter a cell full of **x**'s; then copy K6 to K7 through K29.

5. At L6 enter a cell full of **o**'s; then copy L6 to L7 through L29.

6. At M6 enter a cell full of **x**'s; then copy M6 to M7 through M29.

7. At A3 enter a cell full of -'s; then copy A3 to B3 through M3.

8. At A5 enter a cell full of .'s; then copy A5 to B3 through M3.

9. Erase contents of K4 through M4.

10. Erase range of cells beginning with K27 through M28.

11. Save the worksheet as 131H.

L ESSON 132   WORKSHEET FORMAT CHANGES

132A ◆
CONDITIONING
PRACTICE
each line twice

alphabet 1 A jazz player acquired six or seven big weekend dates from his agents.

figures 2 Jan's 67 stores in 19 states gave discounts of 20, 35, and 48 percent.

keypad 3 511-74-582 456-12-7928 582-04-0631 610-48-2753 693-21-4578 704-19-3682

speed 4 Six girls may visit the city to see the giant robot make an auto body.

gwam 1' | 1 | 2 | 3 | 4 | 5 | 6 | 7 | 8 | 9 | 10 | 11 | 12 | 13 | 14 |

132B ◆

MAKE RANGE CHANGES

Read the information at the right about various changes that can be made to a range of cells and then complete the steps for your ss software.

The Range feature can be used to format labels or values in a range of cells. For example, a range of cells containing labels can be highlighted and then centered over the column width or aligned at the left or right edge of the column.

Also, a range of cells containing values can be identified (highlighted or keyed) and then formatted in different ways. Some of the more common formats for values are Fixed, Currency, General, and Percent.

Fixed. The Fixed format displays the number of decimal places specified by the software user. Negative numbers are displayed with a minus sign (–).

(continued on next page)

Educational Products, Inc.

Learning Outcomes: As you complete this unit, you will

1. Apply your knowledge of document formatting.
2. Demonstrate your abilities to prepare documents from script and rough-draft copy.
3. Practice following general directions to complete a variety of tasks.
4. Apply many of the word processing features learned.

EDUCATIONAL PRODUCTS, INC.

A Word Processing Simulation

Before you begin processing documents, read the following information carefully. Make notes of any standard procedures that you think will save you time as you produce the documents.

Suggested work plan (daily)

Conditioning practice . . . .   5'
Simulation . . . .   45'

You have accepted part-time employment at Educational Products, Inc. (EPI), as a document processing trainee. EPI, located at 3929 Braddock Road, Fort Meyers, FL 33912-8357, manufactures and sells educational software. Your supervisor, Ms. Annette O'Toole, supervises document processing, trains personnel, and schedules and coordinates the workloads of document processing specialists and trainees.

During your orientation period, you were told to format all company letters in block style with mixed punctuation. The originator's business title is to be keyed on the line below the originator's keyed name in the closing lines. Use simplified memo format for memorandums.

Processing instructions from Ms. O'Toole will be attached to each document assigned to you. For some documents, specific instructions are not given; you will be expected to make appropriate decisions on the basis of your knowledge and experience. Since EPI has based its word processing

manual on your textbook, you can also use this book as a reference to assist you in making formatting decisions.

Special guides for jobs requiring unusual specifications are provided in "Excerpts from EPI's Document Processing Procedures Manual." Review these guides before you begin your work.

Excerpts from EPI's Document Processing Procedures Manual

Leaders. Leaders are a series of periods and spaces (. . .) that are keyed between two items in tabular material to make reading easier. They "lead the reader's eye" from one columnar item to another. They are primarily used when the distance between certain items in two columns is so great that matching columnar items is difficult.

Leaders are made by alternating the period (.) and a space. The lines of leaders should be aligned in vertical rows and should end at the same point at the right.

To align leaders, key all periods on either the odd or the even numbers on the status or ruler line guided by their position in the first line of leaders. Begin the first line of leaders on the second space after the first item in the column and end the leaders 2 or 3 spaces to the left of the beginning of the next column.

Agenda. An agenda is one example of a business document that makes use of leaders. Educational Products, Inc., uses the unjustified format for agendas: All items in Column 2 are left aligned (left tab). The margins used for the agenda: top, 2"; sides 1"; and bottom, 1". The heading as well as the body of the agenda are double-spaced. Study carefully the agenda shown below.

```
                   AGENDA
               Marketing  Meeting
                February 12, 19—

1.  Call to Order . . . . . . . . .     Sarah  McLaughlin

2.  Minutes of Last Meeting . . .    Greg  White

3.  Special Reports

         Southern Region Sales . . .    Troy  Coffax

         Eastern Region Sales  . . .    Sally  Marshall
```

Second-page headings for correspondence. The heading for a multipage letter or memorandum begins 1" from the top of a page. Key the heading SS in block format at the left margin. Include the name of the addressee, the page number, and the date. DS between the heading and the body.

```
Mr. William Thomson
Page 2
February 18, 19--

It is our plan to have a comprehensive elementary math program
completed within the next two years.  Updates on the program will
```

Second-Page Heading

APPLY COPYING
TO A RANGE

Erase the worksheet. Key each set of characters in the cells shown in the chart below so that the entire cell is filled with the specific character. Copy the cell containing each set to the range of cells indicated in the right column. (Lotus users can key the characters into each cell rapidly by keying **\x, \%, \s, \p, \?,** and **\),** respectively, and should use both copying methods given in 131D.)

Cell	Key Character	Copy to
A3:	xxxxxxxxx	B3 through G3
A6:	%%%%%%%%	B6 through H6
A9:	ssssssss	A10 through A50
D8:	pppppppp	D9 through D20
E9:	????????	E11 through E15
G9:	))))))))	G13 through M13

ERASE A RANGE
OF CELLS

Read the information at the right about erasing the contents of a range of cells and then complete the steps listed for your software.

In previous lessons you erased or cleared the contents of an individual cell or an entire worksheet. Spreadsheet software also allows you to erase or clear the contents of a range of cells while leaving its formatting. Simply specify the range to be erased and select the Erase or Clear command.

LOTUS

1. Highlight E9 (the first cell of the range that is to be erased).
2. Key **/, R, E** (selects the Range option from the Main Menu and the Erase command).
3. Highlight through E15 (the last cell in the range that is to be erased).
4. Strike Enter (erases the range of cells).

WORKS DOS

1. Highlight E9 (the first cell of the range that is to be cleared).
2. Press **Alt, S, E** (selects the Cells option from the Select Menu).
3. Highlight through E15 (the last cell in the range that is to be cleared).
4. Press **Alt, E, E** (selects Clear from the Edit Menu).
5. Strike any arrow key (clears the range of cells).

WORKS MAC

1. ~ E9 (the first cell of the range that is to be cleared).
2. Drag across through E15 (the last cell in the range to be erased).
3. ~ Edit Menu and select Clear (clears the range of cells).
4. ~ anywhere on screen.

APPLY ERASING A
RANGE

Using the spreadsheet created in 131E, erase the following cell ranges:

A3 through G3; A6 through C50; D6 through H6; B6 through M19

The worksheet screen should be clear.

115-119A
CONDITIONING
PRACTICE

each line twice SS; then three 1' writings on line 4; find *gwam*

alphabet 1   Becky poured the liquid wax from the old jug into a dozen glass vials.

figures 2   I had 489 points, 160 rebounds, 57 assists, and 36 steals in 24 games.

fig/sym 3   The computers will cost $34,679 (less discounts of 20%, 15%, and 18%).

speed 4   The rich widow and the maid may make the usual visit to the city dock.

gwam 1' | 1 | 2 | 3 | 4 | 5 | 6 | 7 | 8 | 9 | 10 | 11 | 12 | 13 | 14 |

115-119B ◆

SIMULATION

Document 1

Processing Instructions from Annette O'Toole

Retrieve the table saved as PRICELST and make the changes shown on the attached copy.

NEW PRODUCT PRICE LIST

February 25, 19--

Number	Software	Price
B929	Basic Spreadsheets	$139
E246	Computer Geography	~~269~~ *259*
E786	Computerized Reading	189
E561	Creative *Business* Letters	125
B821	Data Controller	~~329~~ *309*
E320	English Enhancement	219
B689	Financial Advisor	99
E758	Keyboarding Composition Skills	155
E615	Language Arts Skills	139
B731	Quick Key WP	75
E641	Spelling Mastery	139
B658	Telephone Directory	119
B839	The Art Gallery	249
~~B658~~	~~Telephone Directory~~	~~119~~
B794	Your Time Manager	69
B952	*Tax Assistant*	*129*
B586	*Graphics Designer*	*165*

COPY TO RANGE OF CELLS

Read the information about copying the contents of one cell to a range of cells and then complete the steps listed for your ss software.

The contents of one cell may be copied to many other cells, as illustrated below. Copying is done by specifying the range of cells to which the information is to be copied and then giving the copy command.

LOTUS

1. On a clear worksheet screen, enter **10010** in A1.
2. With the cell pointer in A1 (the cell that is to be copied), strike **/**, **C** (*Copy what? A1* appears) and strike Enter (*To where? A1* appears).
3. Key **B1.E1** (indicates the beginning and ending cells in the range to which A1 is to be copied) and strike Enter (copies A1 to B1 through E1).

Alternate Method (arrow keys specify the range of cells). In A3, key **20020**.

1. Key **/**, **C**, Enter to mark A3 to be copied.
2. At the *To where? A3* prompt, move the cell pointer to B3 (the starting cell of the range being copied to) and key **.** (indicates B3 as the anchor cell).
3. Move cell pointer to F3 (identifies the last cell in the receiving range). Cells B3 through F3 should be highlighted.
4. Strike Enter (copies A3 to B3 through F3).

	A	B	C	D
1				
2	→	Copy Cell A1 to a range of cells (B3 through D3)		
3	1234	1234	1234	1234
4				
5	5678			
6	5678			
7	5678			
8	5678	Copy Cell A5 to a range of cells (A6 through A11)		
9	5678			
10	5678			
11	5678			

WORKS DOS

1. On a clear worksheet screen, enter **10010** in A1.
2. With A1 highlighted, press **Alt, S, E** (selects A1 as the cell you want to copy).
3. Strike → repeatedly to highlight B1 through E1 (selects B1 through E1 as the range into which the copy will be placed).
4. Press **Alt, E, R** (selects Fill Right from Edit Menu).
5. Use the arrow key to move cell pointer (completes copying).

WORKS MAC

1. If needed, clear the worksheet screen (alternate method to clear when save is not needed—choose All Cells from the Select Menu and then choose Clear from the Edit Menu).
2. Key **10010** in A1.
3. ~ A1 (the cell that is to be copied).
4. Drag across B1 to E1 (selects B1 through E1 as the range into which the copy will be placed).
5. ~ Edit Menu and select Fill Right (places copy of A1 in B1 through E1).
6. ~ anywhere on screen.

Processing Instructions from Annette O'Toole

Retrieve the letter saved as SALESREP and make the changes shown on the attached copy. The added postscript should be placed a double space below the Attachment notation.

Ms. McLaughlin would like the revised letter sent to the three new sales reps whose cards are attached.

Note: The merge feature is presented in Appendix F, pp. 446-447.

February ~~1~~ 25, 19—

<Sales Representative>
<Address>
<City>, <State> <ZIP>

Dear <Name>:

Subject: New Product Sales Information

~~Nine~~ *Sixteen* new/revised software programs have been released by our Product Development Division since you received the first quarter price list. Attached is a listing of those products, the purchase order numbers, and the prices. The second quarter price list will be mailed to you before April 1.

Our Shipping Department has been instructed to send copies of these software packages along with the promotional materials that have been developed. You should receive them within the next ten days. Any questions you may have about these programs should be directed to our support specialists at (813) 555-6601.

If there are additional materials that will assist you in your sales efforts, please let us know.

Sincerely,

Sarah R. McLaughlin
Director of Marketing

xx

Attachment

Congratulations on your new position with Educational Products, Inc. I am looking forward to working with you.

I EPI ◆ **EDUCATIONAL PRODUCTS, INC.**

▲ 3929 Braddock Road, Fort Meyers, FL 33912-8357

Miss Janice B. Brown
Representative

(813) 555-6600

Home address:
310 Rossville Avenue
Chattanooga, TN 37408-8340

EPI ◆ **EDUCATIONAL PRODUCTS, I**

29 Braddock Road, Fort Meyers, FL 33912-

Mrs. Maureen C. McCarver
Representative

(813) 555-6600

Home address:
849 Rockridge Drive
Columbia, SC 29203-7401

I EPI ◆ **EDUCATIONAL PRODUCTS, INC.**

▲ 3929 Braddock Road, Fort Meyers, FL 33912-8357

Mr. Felipe R. Hernandez
Representative

(813) 555-6600

Home address:
2230 Atlantic Road
Miami, FL 33149-1745

LEARN COPYING ONE CELL

Read the information at the right about copying the contents of one cell to another cell and then complete the steps listed for your ss software.

The copy command allows the contents of one cell to be copied into another cell. This feature eliminates the need to enter the same cell contents more than once.

LOTUS

1. In A1 (the cell contents to be copied) key **398** and strike Enter.
2. Key *I*, **C** (selects the Copy option from the Main Menu—the prompt, *Copy what? A1* appears).
3. Strike Enter (accepts A1 as the default cell and another prompt, *To where? A1* appears to the right of the *Copy what?* prompt).
4. Key **B1** (the receiving or target cell) *or* move the cell pointer to B1 and strike Enter (either action replaces the default cell, A1, with the name of the target cell, B1, the cell to which the information is to be copied) and strike Enter (copies contents of A1 to B1).

WORKS DOS

1. In A1 (the cell contents to be copied) key **398** and strike Enter.
2. If needed, highlight A1 and press **Alt, S, E** (selects A1 as the cell to be copied).
3. Strike → once to extend highlight to B1 (selects B1 as the receiving or target cell).
4. Press **Alt, E, R** (selects Fill Right from Edit Menu).
5. Move cell pointer to another cell (completes the copy command).
6. Repeat Steps 2 through 5 and use Fill Down to copy A1 to A2.

Alternate Method for use when copying to a cell not adjacent to the default cell:

1. Highlight A1.
2. Press **Alt, E, C** (selects Copy from the Edit Menu).
3. Highlight **C1** (the receiving or target cell) and strike Enter (copies contents of A1 to C1).

WORKS MAC

1. In A1 key **398.**
2. ~ A1 (the cell contents to be copied).
3. Drag across B1 (selects B1 as the receiving or target cell).
4. ~ Edit Menu and select Fill Right (copies A1 to B1).
5. ~ anywhere on screen.

Alternate Method for use when copying to a cell not adjacent to the default cell:

1. Highlight A1.
2. ~ A1.
3. ~ Edit Menu and select Copy.
4. ~ B5 (selects B5 as the receiving or target cell).
5. ~ Edit Menu and select Paste (copies A1 contents to B5).

APPLY COPYING ONE CELL

1. Enter the following values and labels in the cells designated:

   A1: Tom   C1: **65**   B2: Sue   D2: **101**

2. Copy the contents of selected cells as follows:

   A1 to B1; C1 to D1; B2 to B5; D2 to D7

Document 5

Processing Instructions from Annette O'Toole

Mr. Griffin Caswell, Director of Product Development, would like the attached material formatted as a two-page letter to Mr. Henry Boswell, President. *Date the letter* February 28 *and use* New Software Developments *for the subject line.*

Document 6

Processing Instructions from Annette O'Toole

Mr. Caswell would like his Boswell letter (Document 5) reformatted as a simplified memo to the Product Development Staff. *Use the same date and subject line.*

The information from the educational survey you had ~~conducted~~ Jay Hancock of Research Associates conduct for us has been most helpful in planning for the future. The responses from 350 elementary school teachers support our belief that teachers are eager for additional computer-aided instructional materials.

Over 40 percent of the respondents indicated that they are currently using some type of instructional materials requiring the computer. A very high percentage (93%) ~~of the respondents~~ believed that future curricular revisions will require the use of computers in their classrooms.

Math was the subject area the survey respondents most frequently listed ~~as the course~~ in which they would like to see additional software materials developed. Many of the respondents indicated that they would like to have an individualized ~~math~~ program for students with math difficulties.

Currently two computer programs for individualized math instruction are being pilot tested by our department, ~~which~~ These programs appear to meet the elementary teachers' requirements. Mark Sanderson's individualized computer program, "Back to Math Basics," has great sales potential. With a few modifications the software could serve a wide market. ¶ Instructional objectives, periodic self-checks, and post tests are all enhanced by computer graphics that should be very appealing to elementary students. Jennifer Shields has worked with Mark to develop a more advanced math package that can be used after completing the "Back to Math Basics" program. ¶It is our plan to have a ~~complete~~ comprehensive elementary math ~~individualized~~ program completed within the next two years. ~~I will provide periodic~~ updates on the progress will be provided periodically ~~of these two individualized math programs.~~

EDIT CELL CONTENTS

Use the Edit feature to change information already in a cell. To use Edit, highlight the cell to be edited and then strike a function key or ~ the mouse pointer on the Entry Bar to display the cell contents on the Control Panel or Entry Bar. Change the cell contents by moving the cursor (mouse or cursor move keys such as ←, →, Home, and/ or End). Insert, Delete, and Backspace features can be used in the same manner as they are used in word processing to insert, replace, or delete characters.

Lotus F2, make changes, Enter.
Works DOS F2, make changes, Enter.
Works MAC ~ Entry Bar, make changes, Return.

ERASE A RANGE OF CELLS

The erasing feature clears or deletes the contents of a range of cells while leaving its formatting. A range of cells must be specified before the command to erase is used.

Lotus /, R, E; highlight cells to be erased; Enter.
Works DOS Alt, S, E; highlight cells to be erased; Alt, E, E.
Works MAC ~ first cell in range to be erased and drag to last cell in range; ~ Edit and select Clear.

FORMAT A RANGE OF LABELS AND VALUES

Format a range of labels or values by using the Range feature in connection with formatting commands. For example, a range of cells containing labels (text) can be selected and then centered over a column or aligned at the left or right edge of the column. Also, a range of cells containing values (numbers) can be identified (highlighted or keyed) and then formatted in different ways, such as Fixed, Currency, General, or Percent.

Lotus Highlight first cell in range; /, R, F; select format; Enter; highlight last cell in range; Enter.
Works DOS Highlight first cell in range; Alt, S; select option; C, Alt, T; select format; Enter.
Works MAC Highlight the range; ~ Format and select Set Cell Attributes; select options in dialog box; Return.

PRINT WORKSHEETS

The default left, right, top, and bottom margins may be used when a worksheet is printed. If you do not change the defaults and your worksheet exceeds the default settings for one page, the remaining columns or rows will be printed on other pages.

Lotus /, P, P, R; highlight range; Enter; A, G (to print); P, Q (when printing has stopped).
Works DOS Alt, P, P; Enter.
Works MAC ~ File Menu and select Print; select options; ~ OK.

WRITE FORMULAS

Spreadsheet software adds, subtracts, multiplies, and divides values put in the cells. First, enter a formula in the cell where the results of the calculation are to appear. Then, the software interprets the formula, following this order of operations: calculations inside parentheses are done before those outside parentheses. Multiplication and division are performed, in the order that they occur in the formula, before addition and subtraction, which also are done in the order of occurrence.

Lotus +; key formula with no blank spaces.
Works DOS and Works Mac =; key formula with no blank spaces.

L ESSON 131   RANGES IN WORKSHEETS

131A ◆ CONDITIONING PRACTICE

each line twice;
then 30" timings
on selected lines;
exit wp; access ss

alphabet 1 This bright jacket has an amazing weave and is of exceptional quality.

figures 2 Flight 679 will leave on Runway 28 at 10:45 p.m. with 13 crew members.

keypad 3 100 941 804 972 60435-9203 80443-7011 10038-7103 94104-2486 97267-1498

speed 4 Iris held half the land for the endowment for the ancient city chapel.

gwam 1' | 1 | 2 | 3 | 4 | 5 | 6 | 7 | 8 | 9 | 10 | 11 | 12 | 13 | 14 |

Document 7

Processing Instructions from Annette O'Toole

Process the attached letter for Mr. Colfax's signature.
Date: February 28.
Address:
Ms. Regina R. Chan
EPI Sales Representative
310 Rushmore Drive, NW
Knoxville, TN 37923-7492

Dear Ms. Chan:

Your proposal that EPI sponsor a software institute for business education teachers prior to the tennessee vocational conference is excellent. When teachers preview our software programs, they are much more receptive if they have received instruction during the preview from one of our specialists. This conference would be a perfect place to provide such instruction.

On March 17 I will be meeting with president Boswell to discuss the merits of your proposal. Prior to the meeting, I will need a detailed budget outlining the anticipated expenditures for the institute.

Sincerely,

Troy S. Colfax
Regional Vice President

Document 8

Processing Instructions from Annette O'Toole

Prepare the attached table in final form for Mr. Colfax.

SOUTHERN REGION

19--/19-- Sales Comparison

State	Previous Year	Current Year	% Change
Alabama	$ 258,960	$ 275,980	+ 6.6
Florida	429,395	525,650	+22.4
Georgia	499,800	406,310	- 18.7
Kentucky	265,290	275,390	+ 3.8
Mississippi	320,180	338,250	+ 5.6
North Carolina	340,395	334,970	- 1.6
South Carolina	288,345	325,390	+ 12.8
Tennessee	250,200	265,300	+ 6.0
Virginia	205,320	267,490	+30.3
Totals	$ 2,857,885	$3,014,730	+5.5

Work With Basic Worksheets

Learning Outcomes: After completing this unit, you will be able to

1. Copy a cell; copy to and erase a range of cells.
2. Format values, edit cell contents, and change column width.
3. Write and copy formulas and print a worksheet.

SPREADSHEET FEATURE AND COMMAND GUIDE

CHANGE COLUMN WIDTHS
COPY ONE CELL
COPY TO A RANGE OF CELLS
EDIT CELL CONTENTS
ERASE A RANGE OF CELLS
FORMAT A RANGE OF LABELS AND VALUES
PRINT WORKSHEETS
WRITE FORMULAS

The spreadsheet features and commands are explained below and on p. 245. The feature and command guide at the beginning of each unit can be used to preview the unit topics. Also, this guide is an easy-to-use reference for reviewing features and commands while working in this unit or another unit. Appendix G, a listing of frequently used software application commands, can also be used as a reference.

CHANGE COLUMN WIDTHS

The width of a column must be changed when the default width (9 spaces for Lotus, 10 spaces for Works DOS, and 12 spaces for Works MAC) is not appropriate.

Lotus Put cursor in desired column; **/**, **W**, **C**, **S**, key number of spaces desired; Enter.

Works DOS Put cursor in desired column; **Alt**, **T**, **W**, key number of spaces desired; Enter.

Works MAC ~ a cell in desired column; ~ Format and select Column Width; key number of spaces desired; ~ OK.

COPY ONE CELL

A copy command used to copy the contents of one (default) cell to another (receiving or target) cell. This feature eliminates the need to enter the same cell contents more than once.

Lotus **/**, **C**; specify cell to be copied; specify receiving cell; Enter.

Works DOS **Adjacent cell**—**Alt**, **S**, **E**; extend or move cursor to receiving cell; **Alt**, **E**, select Fill Down or Fill Right.
Nonadjacent cell— highlight cell to be copied; **Alt**, **E**, **C**; highlight receiving cell; Enter.

Works MAC **Adjacent cell**— ~ cell to be copied; drag to receiving cell; ~ Edit; select Fill Down or Fill Right.
Nonadjacent cell— ~ cell to be copied; ~ Edit and select Copy; ~ receiving cell; ~ Edit and select Paste.

COPY TO A RANGE OF CELLS

A copy command is used to copy the contents of one cell to many other cells.

First, specify the range of cells receiving the copy; then give the copy command.

Lotus **/**, **C**, specify cell to be copied; specify receiving range of cells; Enter.

Works DOS **Adjacent cells**—**Alt**, **S**, **E**, extend highlight to receiving cells; **Alt**, **E**; select Fill Down or Fill Right.
Nonadjacent cells—**Alt**, **S**, **E**; highlight upper-left cell in receiving range; Enter; then use Fill Down or Fill Right as needed.

Works MAC **Adjacent cells**— ~ cell to be copied; drag to receiving cells; ~ Edit and select Fill Down or Fill Right.
Nonadjacent cells— ~ cell to be copied; ~ Edit and select Copy; ~ upper-left cell in the receiving range; ~ Edit and select Paste; use Fill Down or Fill Right as needed.

Document 9

Processing Instructions from Annette O'Toole

Retrieve the document saved as SALESRPT. Make the changes made by Mr. Colfax on the rough-draft copy. After the changes have been made, be sure to include a page number on the second and third pages.

SOUTHERN REGION SALES REPORT
Educational Products, Inc.

The Southern Region of EPI increased overall sales by 5.5 percent last year with total sales amounting to $3,014,730; This increase was 1.5% higher then forecast for the year.

Sales by States

The figures for each state in the region are outlined below. The figures are presented for total dollar sales and for percentange of increase or decrease for the state for the year.

Total dollar sales. Florida replaced Georgia as the state generating the highest total dollar sales with sales of $525,650. Georgia ($406,310) was the only other state with total sales in excess of $400,000. The remaining seven states generated sales between $265,300 to $338,250. A complete breakdown by state in the region is shown below:

State	19-- Sales	% Change
Alabama		
Florida		
Georgia		
Kentucky		
Mississippi		
North Carolina		
South Carolina		
Tennessee		
Virginia		

Use information from the last two columns of Southern Region Sales Comparison Table.

Percentage increase/decrease. As you can see from the above table, Virginia had the greatest percentage of total sales increase with 30.3 percent; Florida was second with a 22.4 percent increase. Both states increase is do to the addition of a sales representative. A knew rep was added to Floridas sales force in March and to Virginia's in July.

Two states decreased in sales this year--Georgia by 18.7 percent and North Carolina by 1.6 percent. The

130A ◆ CONDITIONING PRACTICE

each line twice SS

alphabet 1 He was extremely helpful in moving the jazz band quickly to the stage.

figures 2 For more information on our rates, phone 615-889-2743, Extension 5077.

fig/sym 3 He bought 50 shares of BB&Q at $36.95 ($1,847.50) with 12% commission.

speed 4 If the firms do the tax audit, we may make the signs for their social.

gwam 1' | 1 | 2 | 3 | 4 | 5 | 6 | 7 | 8 | 9 | 10 | 11 | 12 | 13 | 14 |

130B ◆ APPLICATION ACTIVITIES

Activity 1

Use the information given below to create a worksheet. You decide the format and save it as 130B1.

	A	B	C	D
1	EMPLOYEE TUITION REIMBURSEMENT REPORT			
2				
3	AS OF QUARTER ENDED MAY 31, 19--			
4				
5		FIRST	SECOND	ALL PREV
6	NAME	QUARTER	QUARTER	QUARTERS
7				
8	E Wilson	430	860	5655
9	J Baker	325		1870
10	S Bajwa	890	445	4286
11	F Danoff	1115	575	8760
12	D Foseco	145	290	870
13	C Genti		450	450
14	C Kern	925	470	10270
15	D Mason		1010	1010
16	C Seger	840		15780
17	S Yoko	750	750	2250
18	C Leven	1400	1400	8400

Activity 2

Use the information given below to format a worksheet. Save it as 130B2.

	A	B	C	D	E
1	OFFICE SUPPLIES				
2					
3	INVENTORY VALUE				
4					
5	ITEM	APRIL	MAY	JUNE	JULY
6					
7	Ink Pads	75	80	83	88
8	Tape	125	135	103	115
9	Pens	356	378	395	295
10	Trays	1025	1120	997	1045
11	Openers	45	47	48	35
12	Staplers	675	780	690	741
13	Scissors	555	579	556	603

Activity 3

Preview the spreadsheet glossary on pages 224 and 225. Read and study the definitions of 15 terms that are unfamiliar to you. Compose a sentence for each term that reveals—or at least suggests—its meaning. Proofread and correct all errors. Save the file (130B3).

significant decrease in Georgia can be attributed to ~~having~~ a depleted sales force. terminated employment two sales representatives ~~quit~~ during the year without giving prior notice. These unexpected terminations not only created a problem in their districts but also in the districts of the representatives ~~that tried to~~ who ~ed for them cover while replacements were being hired and trained. Comments and Projections

¶S Overall, the past year was a vary [e] successful one. Our goal for this year is to increase total sales by 10 percent, with no state falling below a 7.5 percent gain.

The new products showcased at the January board meeting along with the improvements made to existing product lines should have a significant impact on sales during the next year. The addition of much-needed sales representatives in Tennessee, Florida, and South Carolina will also create a positive impact on the total sales picture.

Steps are being taken to establish a new policy for distribution of sales commissions. This step is being taken to prevent future occurrences of the problems such as those ~~we~~ experienced in Georgia. The combination of all these factors should make it quite easy for the Southern region to achieve and exceed the 10 percent projected increase.

Document 10

Processing Instructions from Annette O'Toole

Ms. Lopez would like the attached agenda keyed as soon as possible.

AGENDA
PRODUCT DEVELOPEMENT EVALUATION COMMITTEE MEETING
2:30 p.m., March 15

1. Introductory Comments. . . . . Lynda Lopez
2. Presentation of "Back to Math Basics". . . . . Mark Sanderson
3. Special Reports
   - Production Cost Projections . . . . . . Susan St. Claire
   - Market Projections . . . . Dave Masters
   - Cost/Price Structure Projections . . . . . . Jason Hibbard
4. Discussion of Proposal . . . . Committee Members
5. Summary of Discussion: Pros and Cons... Griffin Caswell
6. Call for Vote . . . . Lynda Lopez
7. Adjournment

words

heading 4

Activity 3
Retrieve wp file T129B3 from the *Student's Template* and process this report in un-bound format. Correct all marked and unmarked errors. Use **REPORT OF OPEN HOUSE** for the title.

The annual Open House of Boutiques International in the   15

New Orleans ~~office~~ *complex* was held on July 15, 19--. During the   27

hours of 9 a.m. and noon, 126 people toured our *facilities* ~~company;~~ dur-   40

ing the hours of 1 p.m. and 4 p.m., 237 ~~more~~ *additional* people took the   53

tour. Note should be *taken* made of the *big* increase *during* ~~in~~ the afternoon   67

hours. At the 2 p.m. and 2:30 p.m. tours, the meeting room   79

was unable to accommodate the number of people present *and* we   91

were forced to asked some people to wait for the *next* ~~following~~ tour.   103

The tour of the mail room went smoothly; and the expla-   114

nation of our order processing system was a highlight of the   126

tour thanks in great measure to the interesting presentation   139

given by Maria Rodrigues, *one of our machine operators.*   150

The tour through warehouse B *en route to the shipping department* was not a success. The   168

noise of the equipment prevented any explanation of the op-   179

erations. Further, the *continuous* stream of people through the   192

warehouse tended to disrupt *operations* work.   200

The refreshments served in the employee's dining room   211

were welcomed by all visitors. The group *immediately* ~~just~~ before and   224

after the noon hour, however, disrupted operations. *of the kitchen personnel*   240

The following recommendations are made *to improve future tours of this nature*   256

DS

1. Backup accommodations should be provided for the over-   267

SS
flow during the afternoon hours.   273

3
2. The refreshments at the close of the tour should be   297

served in a location other than the employee's dining room.   309

2. The tour through Warehouse B should be eliminated.   285

Document 11

Processing Instructions from Annette O'Toole

Key the attached material as a memorandum for Lynda V. Lopez, Committee Chair. Make all the changes marked on the copy. Be sure to include an enclosure notation. Date the memo February 28.

Product Development Evaluation Committee Members

MARCH 15 COMMITTEE MEETING

The next meeting of the Product development Evaluation Commitee will be held wednesday, march fifteenth, at 2:30 P.M. in the conference room. Mark Sanderson will be demonstrating the computer math program, Back to the Basics, which he recently developed. Because of the time lines of the product, mr. Caswell has requested Susan St. Clair and Dave Masters to present information at our meeting on production costs and sales. Jason Hibbard will present an estimate of the cost/price structure for the software package. Mr. Caswell and I agree that we should move as quickly as possible to assure that this program is on the makret before something appears from another company. A copy of Mr. Caswells letter to president Boswell which provides additional background information is attached.

Documents 12 and 13

Processing Instructions from Annette O'Toole

Errors appear in Mr. Colfax' table (Document 8). Make the changes outlined on the attached copy and on the report (Document 9).

SOUTHERN REGION

19--/19-- Sales Comparison

State	Previous Year	Current Year	% Change
Alabama	$ 258,960	$ 275,980	+ 6.6
Florida	429,395	525,650	+22.4
Georgia	499,800	406,310	-18.7
Kentucky	265,290	275,390	+ 3.8
Mississippi	320,180	338,250	+ 5.6
North Carolina	340,395	334,970	- 1.6
South Carolina	288,345	325,390	+12.8
Tennessee	250,200	265,300	+ 6.0
Virginia	205,320	267,490	+30.3
Totals	$2,857,885	$3,014,730	+ 5.5

LESSON 129 APPLY SPREADSHEET AND WORD PROCESSING ESSENTIALS

129A ◆ CONDITIONING PRACTICE
each line twice

alphabet 1	Jack or Megan will buy the exquisite bracelet made of topaz in Denver.
figures 2	Their office buildings are at 2581 State, 7349 Dorbe, and 608 Sherman.
fig/sym 3	Kent & Sons donated $3,500 (Check #478) to the United Way on 12/16/91.
speed 4	They may both make the goals if they keep busy in their own cornfield.

gwam 1' | 1 | 2 | 3 | 4 | 5 | 6 | 7 | 8 | 9 | 10 | 11 | 12 | 13 | 14 |

129B ◆

APPLICATION ACTIVITIES

Activity 1
Create, name (129B1), and save the following worksheet. Left-align the titles, center the headings, and right-align the values.

Activity 2
Create, name (129B2), and save the following worksheet. Left-align the titles, center the headings, and right-align the values.

	A	B	C
1	STUDENT NAME		
2			
3	CELLULAR TELEPHONES		
4			
5		REGULAR	SALE
6	MODEL	PRICE	PRICE
7			
8	P-911	1699	888
9	P-9110	1999	999
10	P-9111	1549	825
11	CP-243	1749	925
12	CP-343	1224	749
13	XTZ-14	1924	975
14	XTZ-34	1399	649
15	XTZ-2A	1599	848
16	ST-457	1799	949

	A	B	C
1	STUDENT NAME		
2			
3	TUITION INCOME		
4			
5		THIS	LAST
6	DEPT	YEAR	YEAR
7			
8	ACCTG	96948	89543
9	AD MGT	25548	24697
10	BTE	14750	15324
11	CIS	124654	122379
12	ENGLISH	44563	43543
13	FINANCE	35980	33988
14	HISTORY	112274	110934
15	MGT	95613	97683
16	MRKTG	78564	77639
17	SP MGT	7693	7651
18	SOCIOLOGY	23459	22495

Processing Instructions from Annette O'Toole

*Two new software programs have been added and one price change made since the **New Product Price List** was last updated. Make the changes shown at the right. The rest of the information remains the same as Document 1.*

NEW PRODUCT PRICE LIST

March 10
~~February 25~~, 19--

Number	Software	Price
E 325	*Basic Composition*	*$225*
B929	Basic Spreadsheets	$139
E246	Computer Geography	2~~5~~9 / 6
E786	Computerized Reading	189
E 787	*Computerized Reading (Advanced)*	*225*
E561	Creative Business Letters	125

Document 15

Processing Instructions from Annette O'Toole

Attached is the February sales report. Prepare the report in final form for Mr. Colfax.

Notes: Works users key the information as a four-column table; disregard the lines. WordPerfect users follow the instructions on p. 215 to complete the table with lines.

MONTHLY SALES REPORT *(Bold)*

Month of *February*

Sales Representative	Territory	Sales for Month	Total Sales for Year
Adams, Becky	South Carolina	$ 18,760	$ 34,810
Brown, Janice	Tennessee	5,195	5,195
Chan, Regina	Tennessee	21,240	39,490
Rodriguez, Mario	Florida	12,560	22,380
Vanberg, Shawn	Georgia	13,500	27,980
Russell, Karin	Alabama	12,345	23,120
Jones, Lisa	North Carolina	15,895	33,125
Hernandez, Felipe	Florida	6,870	6,870
Nelson, Nancy	Virginia	18,755	34,900
Conrad, Greg	Kentucky	21,179	37,500
Vue, Cha	Mississippi	12,790	23,410
Spencer, Briget	North Carolina	16,050	36,185
McCarver, Maureen	South Carolina	7,385	7,385
Ryan, Shari	Alabama	15,380	25,790
Okenek, Jarom	Georgia	14,760	31,850
Lange, Diane	Mississippi	13,780	27,650
Cloud, Lee	Florida	10,980	21,860
Newton, Steve	Florida	15,760	29,485
Thomas, Jan	Georgia	15,675	27,390
Total Sales		268,859	496,375

NAME/SAVE WORKSHEET FILES

Read the information at the right. Then complete the steps listed for your software to name and save the worksheet from 128F that is on your screen.

To save a worksheet so that it can be retrieved later, the software requires that you name the worksheet and give the computer instructions to copy it from the computer's temporary memory to a disk where you want it to be stored.

LOTUS

1. Key **/**, **F**, **D** (selects Directory from the File option in the Main Menu so, if needed, you can change the directory selection to the disk drive that houses your data disk).
2. Key **B** (the directory where the worksheet likely should be saved—may be another drive/letter).
3. Strike Enter (changes default drive).
4. Key **/**, **F**, **S** (selects Save from the File option).
5. Strike Esc key (removes the listed file name).
6. Key **128G** (this names the file 128G.WK1). Lotus automatically adds the .WK1 file extension. Lotus allows the use of a combination of up to 8 characters (without spacing and punctuation) in a file name.
7. Strike Enter (*Wait* will appear in upper right of screen while the file is being saved; when *Ready* is indicated, the file is saved even though a copy of it remains on the monitor).
8. Key **/**, **Q**, **Y** (quits the software).

WORKS DOS

1. Press **Alt**, **F**, **S** (displays a dialog box that lets you name and save a file to a specific directory).
2. Verify that the directory named in the "directory line" is the directory (drive) to which you want the ss saved. If not, press **Alt I** (moves highlight to Directories) and use the menu pointer to highlight the directory you want. Strike Enter (executes the command and returns you to the Save File As line in the dialog box where you will name the file).
3. Save first time: Key **128G** (this names the file 128G.WKS). Works automatically adds the .WKS extension to the file name. Works allows the use of up to 8 characters (without spacing and punctuation) to name a file (do not use * ? / ., ; [ ] + = \ : | < > in a file name). Save previously named file: To save a copy of a file, use the Save As option from the File Menu and give the copy a different name.
4. Strike Enter (executes the command). **Note:** To make a copy of a file, use a different file name in the Save As dialog box. Works will save the copy under that file name.
5. Press **Alt**, **F**, **X** (exits the software).

WORKS MAC

1. Select the Save option from the File Menu (opens the Save As dialog box when the worksheet is untitled; when the worksheet is titled, the worksheet will be saved without the dialog box being displayed).
2. Verify that the directory named above the file listing is the directory (drive) to which you want the ss saved. If not, ~ the proper drive button to display the Desktop, and ~~ the desired directory name in the Desktop listing to change to the desired directory.
3. Key **128G** and ~ the Save box (enters the name of the file and saves the file to the desired directory). Works MAC allows the use of up to 32 characters in a file name. To make a copy of a file, use the Save As option and key a different file name in the dialog box and Works will save the copy under that file name, leaving the original file and name.
4. Close all files; ~ Quit from the File Menu; and, if appropriate, turn off your MAC.

WordPerfect Table Feature (for Completing Document 15)

1. **Alt F7**, **2**—Tables, **1**—Create.
2. At the *Number of columns* prompt, key the number of columns (**4**) and return.
3. At the *Number of rows* prompt, key the number of rows (**21**) and return. (You are now in the table editor.)
4. Strike **F7** to exit the table editor. (The status line shows that the cursor is now in Cell A1 [first column, first row]).
5. Key **Sales**, strike Return.
6. Key **Representative**, depress Tab.
7. Return, key **Territory**, Tab.
8. Key **Sales**, strike Return, key **for Month**, Tab.
9. Key **Total Sales**, strike Return, key **for Year**, Tab. (The cursor is now in Cell A2 [first column, second row]).

10. Key all the information for the table except the Totals line at the bottom. Use the Tab key to move from cell to cell. If you accidentally use the Return key to go to the next line, use the Backspace key to delete the hard return. Some of the names are too long for the cells and will split into two lines. These will be adjusted later.
11. Place the cursor in Cell A1. Depress **Alt F7** to activate the table editor. Turn on block and strike the End key.
12. Depress **2**—Format, **1**—Cells, **3**—Justify, and **2**—Center.
13. Place the cursor in Cell C2. Turn on block. Strike → to include Cell D2 in the block. Then depress **Home**, ↓ .

14. Depress **2**—Format, **2**—Column, **3**—Justify, and **3**—Right.
15. Place the cursor in Cell B21. Depress **3**—Lines, **1**—Left, **1**—None to remove the left line.
16. Move the cursor to C21 (second column, last row). Depress **5**—Math, **4+**. The column total will be calculated automatically.
17. Move the cursor to D21 and calculate the column total.
18. If totals do not agree with text, verify numbers in each column and recalculate totals after correcting all errors.
19. Move the cursor to Cell D21. Hold the **Ctrl** key while you strike the ← key three times. Do the same thing in Cell C21.

20. Move the cursor to A9. Hold **Ctrl** while you depress the → until the name is all on one line.
21. To center the table *horizontally*, depress **6**—Options, **3**—Position of Table, **3**—Center, **F7**.
22. Exit table editor (**F7**). Move the cursor to Cell B21 and key **Total Sales**.
23. Delete the decimal point and zeros in Cells C21 and D21.
24. Depress **PgUp** to move the cursor above the table. Return two times, depress **PgUp**, and then center and key the table headings.
25. Depress **PgUp**, **Shift F8**, **2**—Page, **1**—Center Page, Yes, **F7**.
26. Print the table.

Document 16

A new sales rep has been hired for Mississippi. Ms. McLaughlin would like you to send the form letter (Document 2) to the new rep. Date the letter March 15 *and make any necessary changes. Attach a copy of the* **New Product Price List** *that was revised on March 10.*

▌EPI ♦ EDUCATIONAL PRODUCTS, INC.

▲ 3929 Braddock Road, Fort Meyers, FL 33912-8357

Ms. Carolee West
Representative

Home address:
516 Eldorado Avenue
(813) 555-6600   Biloxi, MS 39532-4360

Document 17

Here are the sales figures for the month of March. Prepare a **Monthly Sales Report** *like Document 15 using these sales figures. You will need to compute the* **Total Sales for Year** *by using information in the February report.*

March Sales Figures

Adams	$20,176	Vue	15,980
Brown	9,185	Spencer	15,300
Chan	19,180	McCarver	15,820
Rodriguez	13,980	Ryan	16,200
Vanberg	15,800	Okenek	12,380
Russell	11,325	Lange	10,800
Jones	16,531	Cloud	12,670
Hernandez	10,880	Newton	16,210
Nelson	19,210	Thomas	20,500
Conrad	26,580	~~West~~	5,900

128E ◆ (cont.)

to instruct the computer to left-align the label).

7. Check your screen: The label in A3 should be aligned at the right; A5 should be centered; and A7 should begin at the left edge.

8. Key **Year** (centers the label in A5).
9. Highlight A7 and key **Year** (the software automatically left aligns the label).
10. Check your screen. The label in A3 should be right-aligned; A5 should be centered; and A7 should begin at the left edge of the column.

in the Align listing in the dialog box and then ~ OK box (selects center as the format for the cell entry).

6. Key **Year** and move the cursor to A7 (enters and centers label in A5).
7. In A7, key **Year** and strike Return (the software automatically chooses left alignment unless you specify right or center alignment).
8. Check your screen: The label in A3 should be right-aligned; A5 should be centered; and A7 should begin at the left edge of the column.

128F ◆

APPLICATION ACTIVITY

Beginning with a clear screen, use the information at the right and the following directions to create a worksheet.

1. Center the headings in Columns A and B.
2. Right-align the months of the year that serve as column headings.
3. Left-align MONTHLY EXPENSES in Column C.
4. When you are done, leave the worksheet on the screen and go to 128G.

	A	B	C	D	E
1	Student Name				
2					
3	BUDGET AND EXPENSES				
4					
5			MONTHLY EXPENSES		
6	ITEM	BUDGET	JAN	FEB	MAR
7					
8	RENT	400	400	400	410
9	ELECTRIC	44	46	43	42
10	OIL	110	115	90	72
11	WATER	20		60	
12	SEWAGE		22		67
13	TELEPHONE	35	32	38	45
14	CABLE TV	20	20	20	20
15	AUTO LOAN	425	425	425	425
16	INSURANCE	80	120		95
17	FOOD	315	305	302	325
18	CLOTHING	75	60	90	55
19	LEISURE	75	55	80	60
20	PERSONAL	90	90	85	100
21	AUTO EX	80	80	95	110
22	SAVINGS	185	185	185	185

UNIT 26

LESSONS 120-122

Prepare for Assessment

Learning Outcomes: As you complete this unit, you will

1. Reinforce letter/memo processing skills.
2. Reinforce report processing skills.
3. Reinforce table processing skills.
4. Reinforce word processing skills.

LESSON 120 — PREPARE FOR ASSESSMENT: LETTERS/MEMOS

120A ◆ CONDITIONING PRACTICE

each line twice SS; then three 1' writings on line 4; find *gwam*; clear screen

alphabet	1	Just before moving back to Venezuela, they acquired a few exotic pets.
figures	2	The main office was located at 4623 Oxford Drive from 1970 until 1985.
fig/sym	3	You can save 25% ($376.98) by purchasing the 20 desks before March 15.
speed	4	Their neighbor on the island did the handiwork for them at the shanty.

gwam 1' | 1 | 2 | 3 | 4 | 5 | 6 | 7 | 8 | 9 | 10 | 11 | 12 | 13 | 14 |

120B ◆ LETTERS/MEMOS

For Documents 1-3 use today's date and supply a salutation and complimentary closing. The letters are from **KayAnn Nelson, Director**.

Document 1

File name: CRUZ1

Format the text as a modified block letter, mixed punctuation.

Address the letter to:

**Mr. Raul De La Cruz
Hemett Regal Maui
425 Kihei Road
Wailea, HI 96753-9711**

MAKE TIME FOR FUN IN THE SUN is the subject line. Create a macro for Sails for Rent. See 100B, p. 182.

Document 2

File name: FILIPPI

Format the text as a modified block letter, mixed punctuation.

Address the letter to:

**Ms. Anita Filippini
Director of Services
Hemett Regal Maui
425 Kihei Road
Wailea, HI 96753-9711**

BRINGING YOUR GUESTS BACK! is the subject line.

words

opening lines 27

Sails for Rent invites you to get wet again--before you leave the 40
Islands! Go sailing! Join a snorkeling safari! Go windsurfing! Meet sea 55
creatures in deep water on a scuba adventure--or enjoy any of the 68
other great water activities we offer! There is still time to make 82
reservations for the water adventure--or adventures of your choice! 96

You likely noticed that members of the **Sails for Rent** staff are 109
well-qualified. Our instructors are the best in the field of water 122
recreation. Their goal is to help you have an excellent sea adventure-- 137
no matter what activity you select. 144

A certificate for a 10 percent discount is enclosed. Use it for fun in 159
the sun with any **Sails for Rent** activity on any island. 170

closing lines 178

---

opening lines 31

"I love this place! Best vacation I've ever had; I'll be back next 44
year!" Is this the comment you hear from your departing guests? **Sails** 59
for Rent can help make this happen. 66

Sails for Rent can bring great recreational activities to your magnifi- 80
cent Maui facilities--and more guests who return! When you establish 94
Sails for Rent recreational activities at your hotel, you expand the 108
Hawaiian experiences of your guests. Your guests, for example, can 122
learn to windsurf right on the beach without getting wet. Scuba and 136
snorkeling safaris to Molokini Island usually bring big adventures. Call 150
or write for more information on establishing a link with **Sails for** 164
Rent. Make a commitment to increase the number of guests who 176
return again and again. 181

Sails for Rent wants to help. You and selected members of your staff 195
can sample our services. Just call (555) 166-1234 and get ready for 209
the aquatic time of your life! 216

closing lines 223

128D ◆

CLEAR SCREEN

Read the information at the right and then complete the steps listed for your software to display a blank worksheet screen.

Whenever a worksheet is no longer wanted on a screen, the Worksheet Erase or Close feature can be used to clear the worksheet screen so another worksheet can be started. Since this command removes the worksheet from the computer's temporary memory, be sure to save the worksheet before using Worksheet Erase or Close if the worksheet will be needed later. (When it doubt, save it!)

LOTUS

1. If needed, strike Esc repeatedly to get to the Ready mode.
2. Key **/**, **W**, **E** (selects the Erase option from the Worksheet Menu), **Y** (selects option to erase).
3. Check your screen: Is it clear? If not, repeat the steps above.

WORKS DOS

1. Press **Alt**, **F**, **C** (selects the Close option from the File Menu).
2. If changes were made to the worksheet, a dialog box appears and you are to key **N** (closes without saving) or **Y** (if save is wanted).
3. Key **N** (selects Create New File option). If the dialog box does not appear, key **N** (selects Create New File) and then key **S** (selects spreadsheet as the application program and opens a new file).
4. Check your screen: Is the worksheet area blank? If not, repeat the steps above.

WORKS MAC

1. ~ File Menu and select Close or ~ Close box.
2. ~ No (closes without saving; if save is wanted, ~ Yes).
3. ~~ the ss icon in the Open File dialog box.
4. Check your screen: Is the worksheet area blank? If not, repeat the steps above.

128E ◆

ALIGN LABELS

Read the information at the right, create a new file, and then complete the steps listed for your software to align labels in a cell.

Labels will begin at the left edge of a cell unless you instruct the software to do otherwise. (Numbers [values] will align at the right edge by default.) To center or right-align labels, select the cell you want to format and use the following commands.

LOTUS

1. Highlight A3.
2. Key **"Year** (the " instructs the software to right-align the label).
3. Highlight A5. (Locate the ^ key on your keyboard and decide which finger should make this reach.)
4. Key **^Year** (the ^ instructs the software to center the label).
5. Highlight A7.
6. Key **Year** (the software automatically inserts an ' before the label

WORKS DOS

1. Highlight A3.
2. Press **Alt**, **T**, **S** (selects the Style option from the Format Menu).
3. Key **R** (selects Right Alignment from the Alignment Menu) and strike Enter.
4. Key **Year** (right-aligns the label in A3).
5. Highlight A5.
6. Press **Alt**, **T**, **S**.
7. Key **C** (selects Center from the Alignment Menu) and strike Enter.

WORKS MAC

1. Highlight A3 and select Set Cell Attributes from the Format Menu.
2. ~ button beside Right in the Align listing in the dialog box; then ~ OK box (selects right alignment as the format for the cell entry).
3. Key **Year** (enters and right-aligns the label in A3).
4. Highlight A5 and select Set Cell Attributes option from the Format Menu.
5. ~ the button beside Center.

(continued on next page)   (continued on next page)   (continued on next page)

words

Document 3
File: CRUZ2
Retrieve Document 1; make these changes. Underline <u>still</u> in ¶1 and <u>well-qualified</u> in ¶2. Include **Call us today at 166-1234.** as the last sentence of the last ¶.

Document 4
File name: SEMINARS
Format the text at the right as a simplified memo.

Documents 5
File name: FILIPPI2
Retrieve Document 2 (FILIPPI). Use the search to replace feature to change *Sails for Rent* to **SFR** every time it occurs.

November 4, 19--	3
All Employees	6
PROFESSIONAL DEVELOPMENT SEMINARS	13

The company is implementing a new program for professional development this year. Every employee will be given one day off to attend one of the company-sponsored professional development seminars. | 27 42 53

Tentative topics for this year's seminars are the value of leadership, improving oral communication skills, integrated software applications, and stress management. Indicate your preference for each of the seminars on the attached form by placing #1 by your first choice, #2 by your second choice, and so forth. | 67 82 97 111 116

We will try to accommodate everyone's first or second choice. The more popular programs will be offered twice during the year in an effort to control the number of participants at each seminar. | 130 145 155

Sophia Ramirez, Personnel	160
xx	161
Enclosure	162

LESSON 121   PREPARE FOR ASSESSMENT: REPORTS

121A ◆ CONDITIONING PRACTICE
each line twice

alphabet	1	Everyone except Jake was amazed by how quickly the fight was finished.
figures	2	The editor made changes on pages 40, 63, 71, 82, and 95 of the script.
fig/sym	3	Their assets ($153,450) were greater than their liabilities ($96,782).
speed	4	The maid paid the men for the work they did on the shanty by the lake.

gwam 1' | 1 | 2 | 3 | 4 | 5 | 6 | 7 | 8 | 9 | 10 | 11 | 12 | 13 | 14 |

121B ◆
PREPARE FOR ASSESSMENT: REPORTS

File name: WORKRPT1
Formatting task
Document 1
Unbound Report

1. Format the text at the right as an unbound report. Prepare a title page (use your name, school, and date) and a reference page.
2. Use spell check and proofread your copy to detect any additional keying errors you may have made.

words

QS   WORK--TODAY AND YESTERDAY   5

Even though some people question the existence of the   16
american work ethic, most americans still believe it exists   28
in the (U.S.) today. Included as part of this work ethic is   42
the belief that   45

DS   1. Workers ~~should~~ take pride in their work and do   55
their jobs well.   59

2. Employees ~~should~~ have feelings of commitment and   69
loyalty to their profession, their company, and their   80
DS   work group.   83

3. People should acquire wealth through honest labor   93
and retain it through thrift and wise investments.   109

(Cherrington, 1980, 20).

7. Strike **F5** (selects Go To feature).
8. Key **C9** then strike Enter (moves cell pointer to C9).
9. Press **End**,↓ (moves to filled cell at next intersection of blank or filled cell); press **End**,↓ once more to see how it moves to next intersection of filled and blank cell.
10. Strike **F5** and key **E13** (moves cell pointer to E13).
11. Press **End**,↓ (moves to filled cell at next intersection of blank or filled cell).
12. Press **End**,← (moves left to filled cell at next intersection of blank or filled cell).
13. Press **End**,→ (moves right to filled cell at next intersection of blank or filled cell).
14. Strike **Home** (moves cell pointer to A1).
15. Practice the rapid cursor commands of your choice to increase your proficiency in moving around a worksheet.
16. Leave this worksheet on the screen and go to 128D.

7. Strike **F5** and then key **C9** and strike Enter (uses the Go To feature to move to C9).
8. Press **Ctrl**↓ (moves to filled cell at next intersection of blank or filled cell); press **End**,↓ once more to see how it moves to next intersection of filled and blank cell.
9. Strike **F5**, key **E13**, and strike Enter (moves cell pointer to E13).
10. Press **Ctrl**↓ (moves to filled cell at next intersection of blank or filled cell).
11. Press **Ctrl**← (moves left to filled cell at next intersection of blank or filled cell).
12. Press **Ctrl**→ (moves right to filled cell at next intersection of blank or filled cell).
13. Press **Ctrl Home** to move cell pointer to A1.
14. Practice the rapid cursor commands of your choice to increase your proficiency in moving around a worksheet.
15. Leave this worksheet on the screen and go to 128D.

4. Select Last Cell option from the Select Menu (displays and makes active the last cell in the worksheet).
5. Select Go To option from the Select Menu, key **K30** in the dialog box, and ~ OK box (displays the window with K30 but does not make it the active cell).
6. Select Find Cell option from the Select menu, key **B4** in the dialog box, and ~ Find Next box (displays and makes active B4).
7. Use Go To option to move to M33.
8. Select Use Show Active Cell option from the Select Menu to display the highlighted or active cell (B4 should be displayed and highlighted).
9. Move the mouse pointer to the left scroll arrow and ~ a few times (each ~ scrolls the worksheet one position to expose another column of the worksheet).
10. With the pointer on the horizontal scroll arrow, ~ and hold the mouse button for a second or two (additional columns of the worksheet are displayed while the mouse button is held).
11. Move the pointer to the right scroll arrow and depress and hold the mouse button until Column A appears.
12. Move the pointer to the vertical scroll arrows and practice the same operations to move vertically within a worksheet.
13. Practice these rapid movement commands to increase your proficiency in moving around a worksheet.
14. Leave this worksheet on the screen and go to 128D.

121B ◆ (cont.)

Reference Page
Use the following information to prepare a reference page.

Cherrington, David J. The Work Ethic. New York: AMACOM Division of the American Management Association, 1980.

Manning, George, and Kent Curtis. Morale: Quality of Work Life. Cincinnati: South-Western Publishing Co., 1988.

Title Page
Prepare a title page for the report using your name, school, and current date.

Document 2
Leftbound Report
File name: WORKRPT2

Retrieve Document 1 and reformat it as a leftbound report. Make these changes:

1. Bold all headings.
2. Use the move feature to move enumeration #1 to make it #3. Number 2 will become #1 and #3 will become #2.
3. Change the second sentence under Job Satisfaction to read: **The emphasis following the depression which was placed on income and job security has been replaced by an emphasis on job satisfaction.**

Regard less of change (or lack of it) in the American — 119
Work Ethic over the years, work and how it is viewed have — 131
changed. Because of technology, jobs are less physical and — 143
more mental than ever before. Worker expectations of jobs — 155
has also changed. Jobs are no longer viewed as simply a — 166
means of putting food on the table. Such things as job — 177
satisfaction and employee morale are now extremely important — 190
to employees as well as employers. — 197

Job Satisfaction — 204

Today's employees are more concerned than workers of — 215

the past about job satisfaction. The emphasis following the — 224

depression which was placed on income and job security has — 239

been replaced by an emphasis on job satisfaction. This — 250

switch is directly related to a more affluent society with — 262

many well-paying jobs available. As a result, workers can now be more — 278

selective in choosing jobs that offer personal fulfillment. — 291

Employee Morale — 297

With research indicating a direct relationship between — 308

job performance and employee morale, employers are continually evaluating — 323

ways in which employee morale can be increased. Manning and Curtis — 336

(1988, 71) believe morale energizes people and brings out — 348

the best in their job performance. They define morale as a — 360

person's attitude toward a work experience. The job itself, — 381

the work group, management practices, and economic rewards — 393

are included as part of this work experience. —

references and title page 467

L ESSON 122 — PREPARE FOR ASSESSMENT: TABLES

122A ◆ CONDITIONING PRACTICE

each line twice

alphabet	1	Umezaki, the exchange student from Japan, plays racquetball very well.
figures	2	He was born on May 25, 1987, at 4:30 a.m. and weighed just over 6 lbs.
fig/sym	3	The shipping expenses ($29.76) were not included on Invoice #A184-350.
speed	4	The widow of the tax auditor of the firm did handiwork for the chapel.

gwam 1' | 1 | 2 | 3 | 4 | 5 | 6 | 7 | 8 | 9 | 10 | 11 | 12 | 13 | 14 |

122B ◆

PREPARE FOR ASSESSMENT: TABLES

File name: L122B

Make a list of the problems at the right. Prepare for the assessment of table processing by formatting and keying the problems on your list.

page 198, 109B, Table 3
page 200, 111-112B, Table 2
page 201, 111-112B, Table 3
page 201, 111-112B, Table 4

cell pointer from one location to another rapidly. Frequently used commands are given in the chart below.

RAPID MOVEMENT COMMANDS

Movement	Lotus	Works DOS	Works MAC
Left one screen	Shift Tab or Ctrl ←	Ctrl Page Up	~ ← scroll arrow
Right one screen	Tab or Ctrl →	Ctrl Page Down	~ → scroll arrow
Up one screen	Page Up	Page Up	~ ↑ scroll arrow
Down one screen	Page Down	Page Down	~ ↓ scroll arrow
Lower right cell	End, Home	Ctrl End	End *
Upper left cell	Home	Ctrl Home	Home *
To intersection of blank and nonblank cell	End ↓, End ↑, End → , or End ←	Ctrl ↓, Ctrl ↑, Ctrl → , or Ctrl ←	
To specific cell	F5 and enter cell	F5 and enter cell	Choose Find Cell or Go To Cell option from Select Menu
Scroll	Hold down ←, →, ↑ or ↓	Hold down ←, →, ↑ or ↓	~scroll arrow that points in desired direction

*Standard keyboards on Macintosh Classic and Macintosh LC do not have Home or End keys.

LOTUS

1. If needed, strike **Home** to go to A1 (beginning of worksheet).
2. Use **Page Down** to go to A21 (next screen down).
3. Use **Page Up** to go to A1 (next screen up).
4. Press **Ctrl →** to go to H1 (next screen right).
5. Press **Ctrl ←** to go to A1 (next screen left).
6. Press **End**, **Home** to go to ending cell in worksheet.

(continued on next page)

WORKS DOS

1. Strike **Ctrl Home** to go to A1 (beginning of worksheet).
2. Use **Page Down** to go to top of next screen.
3. Use **Page Up** to go to A1 (next screen up).
4. Press **Ctrl Page Down** to go to H1 (next screen right).
5. Press **Ctrl Page Up** to go to A1 (next screen left).
6. Press **Ctrl End** to go to ending cell in worksheet.

(continued on next page)

WORKS MAC

1. ~ J28 (highlights and makes J28 the active cell).
2. If you have an End key, strike **End** (displays but does not highlight last cell entry). If you do not have an End key, use scroll arrows to locate cell S29, the last cell in this worksheet.
3. If you have a Home key, strike **Home** (displays but does not highlight the first cell). If you do not, use scroll arrows to locate cell A1.

(continued on next page)

Assess Document Processing Skills

Learning Outcomes: As you complete this unit, you will

1. Evaluate letter/memo processing skills.
2. Evaluate report processing skills.
3. Evaluate table processing skills.
4. Evaluate word processing skills.

LESSON 123 ASSESS LETTER/MEMO FORMATTING

123A ◆
CONDITIONING PRACTICE

each line twice SS;
then three 1' writings
on line 4; find *gwam*

alphabet	1	Three dozen packages of equipment were expected to arrive before July.
figures	2	Chapter 20, pages 253-264, of the 1987 edition contains grammar rules.
fig/sym	3	The deductible was changed to $250 on your policy (Q194-837) on May 6.
speed	4	The six haughty men did the work on the bus for the neurotic neighbor.

gwam 1' | 1 | 2 | 3 | 4 | 5 | 6 | 7 | 8 | 9 | 10 | 11 | 12 | 13 | 14 |

123B ◆
LETTERS/MEMOS

File name: TEST1
Document 1
Letter
Format and key the material at the right in modified block format, mixed punctuation.

words

October 13, 19--|Ms. Natasha J. Bartlett, President|Banking Institute Corpo- 17
rate Office|628 Nicolet Avenue, N|Chicago, IL 60631-6485|Dear Ms. 30
Bartlett: 39

Attached is a tentative listing of the seminars we plan to offer through the 54
Banking Institute next year. If you would like any of the titles changed be- 69
fore we start promoting the seminars in November, please let me know by 84
October 23. 86

In addition to distributing materials at this year's two remaining seminars, 102
we will be processing a mailing to current members and advertising in two 116
banking publications. Any other suggestions you may have for promoting 131
next year's seminars would be appreciated. Our goal for this coming year is 146
a 20 percent increase in attendance. 154

Sincerely yours,|Ryan S. Woodward|Institute Director|xx|Attachment 170/195

Document 2
Simplified Memorandum
Format and key the copy at the right as a simplified memorandum. Date the memo **July 7, 19--**. Send the memo to **Nichole A. Russell, Marketing Manager**. Use **SECOND QUARTER SALES REPORT** for the subject line.

Here are the sales figures for the second quarter. Overall they represent a 31
7.3 percent increase over the previous quarter and a 3.8 percent increase 46
over the second quarter sales of a year ago. 55

Annette North has given notice that she is resigning effective August 12 to 70
return to school to work on an advanced degree. I believe we should discuss 86
the feasibility of combining her territory with that of Douglas Sheridan. He 101
has indicated a concern about the lack of growth potential in his area. I be- 117
lieve this would be a solution to his concern. He has done a fine job with his 133
current territory, and I agree that there is not much potential for growth. 148

I'll bring additional information about the two territories for discussion at 164
our July 20 meeting. 168

James R. Woodward, District Manager|xx|Enclosure 178

RETRIEVE WORKSHEET FILES

Read the information at the right and then complete the steps listed for your ss software to retrieve a worksheet.

Worksheets are often saved on a disk so that they can be retrieved at a later time to be revised, updated, and/or printed. To retrieve a worksheet file, you must move to the appropriate directory and instruct the computer to search the disk drive for the file. Once the worksheet is found, the computer loads a copy of it into temporary memory and displays the worksheet on the monitor.

LOTUS

Access the disk drive containing the *Student's Template*.

1. Insert *Student'sTemplate* in proper drive (usually Drive B).
2. If needed, change your default directory to the disk drive that houses the template disk by keying **/, F, D** (selects File option from Main Menu and Directory from submenu). Then, key **b** (changes the default directory [usually A] to the directory housing your data disk [usually B]).

Retrieve a worksheet file:

1. Key **/** (displays Main Menu when ss software is in Ready mode).
2. Key **F, R** (selects File from Main Menu and Retrieve from the submenu and displays a list of worksheet file names). The file name extension .WK1 is automatically added by Lotus, and it becomes a part of each file name.
3. Highlight worksheet file T128B.WK1 by moving the menu pointer to that file and strike Enter (selects the highlighted file and displays it on your monitor).
4. Leave T128B.WK1 on the screen and proceed to 128C.

WORKS DOS

Access the disk drive containing the *Student's Template*.

1. Insert *Student's Template* in proper drive (usually B).
2. If needed, change your default directory (usually A) to the disk drive that houses the data disk by pressing **Alt, F, O** (selects Open New File option from File Menu) and **Alt I**. Highlight the directory that houses your data disk (usually B); strike Enter.

Retrieve the worksheet file:

1. Press **Alt F** (selects the File option that displays a list of files on the data disk).
2. Highlight ss file T128B.WKS by moving the menu pointer to that file and strike Enter (selects and displays the desired file on the monitor). The file name extension .WKS is automatically added by Works and becomes a part of each ss file name.
3. Leave T128B.WKS on the screen and proceed to 128C.

WORKS MAC

1. ~ File Menu and select the Open option (displays a dialog box with files listed on the current disk). If the current disk does not contain the file you want, insert the desired disk into the disk drive.
2. Move mouse pointer to T128B and ~~ (selects and displays that file on the monitor).
3. Leave T128B on the screen and proceed to 128C.

RAPID MOVEMENT COMMANDS

Read the information at the right about moving rapidly in a worksheet. Practice rapid movement commands by completing steps listed on p. 236 for your software.

You can move much faster in a worksheet by using rapid movement commands rather than using arrow keys to move cell by cell. Specific keys or combinations of keys can be used, a mouse pointer can be used, and/or menu options can be selected to move the

(continued on next page)

Document 3
Letter

Format and key the material at the right in block style with open punctuation. Insert the following information for the numbers in parentheses: (1) **May** (2) **Houston** (3) **managing human resources** (4) **November 13** (5) **Milwaukee** (6) **Marc Plaza**

Document 4
Letter

Use the letter created for Document 3. Send the letter to:

Ms. Renae A. Santiago
Suwannee National Bank
5507 Ranchero Road
Tallahassee, FL 32304-9340

Use the following information for the blanks: (1) **June** (2) **Pittsburgh** (3) **customer advertising** (4) **October 1** (5) **Houston** (6) **Hyatt Regency**

words

November 15, 19-- | Mr. Lewis G. Mackenzie | Human Resources Manager | 13
Bank of Nottingham | 1295 Kensington Avenue | Detroit, MI 48230-5286 | Dear   27
Mr. Mackenzie   30

The seminar you presented last (1) in (2) for the Banking Institute on   45
 (3) was very well received. Several Institute members have requested   63
that the seminar be offered again this coming year.   74

The seminar is scheduled for (4) in (5) at the (6) . Are you available   92
on this date to present the seminar? The honorarium for conducting the   107
seminar has been increased to $1,800. Of course, all your expenses would   122
be paid by the Institute.   127

Please let me know by December 1 whether you will be able to work with us   142
on next year's seminar.   147

Sincerely | Ryan S. Woodward | Institute Director|xx   160

closing lines 187/**210**

LESSON 124   ASSESS REPORT FORMATTING

124A ◆
CONDITIONING
PRACTICE

each line twice

alphabet 1   Vicky Lopez is extremely qualified for a management job with our firm.
figures 2   Crowds of 49,872 and 51,360 saw the games between the Giants and Mets.
fig/sym 3   The invoice (96A103) which is for $2,745 should be paid before June 8.
speed 4   She is apt to yell when they cut down the iris by the giant cornfield.

gwam 1' | 1 | 2 | 3 | 4 | 5 | 6 | 7 | 8 | 9 | 10 | 11 | 12 | 13 | 14 |

124B ◆

ASSESS REPORTS

Document 1
Unbound Report

File name: REPORT1

1. Format the text at the right as an unbound report. Prepare a title page (use your name, school, and date) and a reference page.
2. Use spell check and proofread your copy to detect any additional keying errors you may have made.

words

The President of the United States   7

The highest elected office in the United States is that   18
of President. The President who is elected by the *lc* citizens   30
of the United States represents "all the people." The Presi-   43
dent plays a ^major role in determining the course of direction for   56
the United States under a democratic form of government.   68

4. Highlight a topic you want to learn about, strike Enter, read, and then strike **F8** when finished.
5. Select other topics as desired and when finished, strike Esc as many times as needed to return to your worksheet.
6. Leave the worksheet on the screen.

3. Read the information (use **Page Down** as needed); strike Esc (return to the worksheet).
4. Access the Help Index (*Works 2.0*) or the Table of Contents (*Works 3.0*) and select other topics.
5. Leave the worksheet on the screen.

3. Browse through the Help Index or select commands from the menu to become more proficient with Help.
4. When done, ~ Close box in Help window to return to the worksheet.
5. Leave worksheet on the screen.

127D ◆

APPLICATION ACTIVITY

1. Add to your worksheet by keying the information in the cells at the right.
2. When done, check the format of your worksheet from Rows 10 through 21. Columns A and D should be blank; Columns B and E should have numbers and names; Column C should have numbers.
3. Exit the ss software (see below).

	A	B	C	D	E
10			45		
11		345			21
12			43		
13		Tom			Bill
14			89		
15		657			54
16			66		
17		Sue			Ann
18			53		
19		426			23
20			98		
21		Ted			Nell

LOTUS

Key **/**, **Q**, select **N** (not saving), **Y.**

WORKS DOS

Press **Alt F**, **X**, **N** (not saving).

WORKS MAC

Close file, ~ No (not saving).

L ESSON 128   RETRIEVE, SAVE, AND NAME WORKSHEETS

128A ◆
CONDITIONING PRACTICE
each line twice SS

alphabet 1 Jake will buy a very good quality zinc from the experts at the stores.
figures 2 The license plate numbers for her cars are 247951, 836067, and 443086.
fig/sym 3 Leah just renewed Policies #23-4598-623 (auto) and #35-9107-44 (home).
speed 4 My field hand saw the small dirigible signal the men in the cornfield.

gwam 1' | 1 | 2 | 3 | 4 | 5 | 6 | 7 | 8 | 9 | 10 | 11 | 12 | 13 | 14 |

words

<u>Term in Office</u>   73

    Since the ^*enactment* of the twenty-second amendment to the Con-   86

stitution, the President can serve only two terms. Prior to   98

~~the~~ this amendment the president could serve as long as the   109

people ~~would~~ elect^*ed* him to the office. Franklin # Roosevelt was   121

the last P(er)sident to serve more than two terms.   131

DS
<u>Qualifications</u>   136

    The qualifications required for running for the execu-   147

tive office of the United States are out lined in the Con-   158

stitution (article II ^ section 1 ^ paragraph 5). The person   170

must be 35 ^*years of age*, a natural-born citizen of the United States, and   185

a resident of the United States for ~~the past~~ 14 years.   194

DS
<u>Responsibilities</u>   200

    Also outlined in the Constitution (article II, sections   211

2 and 3) are the responsibilities of the executive office.   223

The (outlined) responsibilities are, however, quite general   235

and are often open for interpretation. The Constitution   246

states that the President is the Commander in C~~c~~hief of the   258

armed forces. The person holding the office is ~~also~~   268

responsible for making treaties, appointing ambassadors ^ and   280

appointing judges to the Supreme Court. Additional respon-   292

sibilities of the President include giving Ｔhe State of the   304

Union Address, rec(ie)ving foreign dignitaries, enforcing the   316

laws, and protecting the rights of ^*t*he citizens of the   327

United States.   330

    The role of the President has ^*remained* ~~been~~ about the same as   341

when the Constitution was written. (However, Davis ^ states *(1987, 4)*   354

that the responsibilities to fulfill) that role have in-   366

creased.   368

1. Load your software (refer to "Access Spreadsheet Software" in command guide on p. 226 for review).
2. In A1 key a title, **Identification Numbers.**
3. Look at A1 (note that an entry wider than the column extends into the next column when the cell to the right is empty).
4. Highlight A4 and begin keying the information shown at the right in the designated cells (enter the information by moving left to right, row by row).
5. When finished, check your worksheet. You should have a 5-column worksheet with names in Row 4, nothing in Row 5, and values in Rows 6-8. If not, study your worksheet to find where you made an error.
6. Leave this worksheet on the screen and go to 127C.

	A	B	C	D	E
1	Identification Numbers				
2					
3					
4	Mary	Henry	Pablo	Susan	Arnold
5					
6	135790	673592	439021	901278	569021
7	102938	547612	102938	601925	514620
8	687910	432987	657843	775599	347810

127C ◆

HELP FEATURE

Read the information at the right and then complete the steps listed for your software to use the Help feature.

Spreadsheet software provides an on-line Help feature. You can use it while working on a worksheet to get information about your software. Help explains various ss commands, skills, and procedures.

LOTUS

To get help related to a command (Save command is used in this example):

1. Key **/**, **F** and then highlight the Save option.
2. Strike **F1** (displays Help's information about Save).
3. Read the first screen and then use the **Page Down** key as needed to read other screens.
4. Strike Esc (displays the Save option where you would normally continue). Since this worksheet is not to be saved, strike Esc as needed to return to the worksheet.

To use Help to get information about a topic (About Help is used in this example):

1. Strike **F1** (accesses Help).
2. If needed, use the cursor key to highlight the topic About Help and then strike Enter (displays information about the Help feature).
3. Read the information (use **Page Down** as needed); then strike **F8** when done (displays Help Index).

WORKS DOS

To get help related to a command (Save command is used in this example):

1. Press **Alt**, **F**, **S** (selects Save).
2. Strike **F1** (displays Help's information about Save).
3. Read the first screen and then use the **Page Down** key as needed to read other screens.
4. Strike Esc (displays the dialog box where you would normally continue). Since this worksheet is not to be saved, strike Esc again to return to the worksheet.

To use Help to get information about a topic (Closing a File is used in this example):

1. *Works 2.0*: Press **Alt**, **H**, **H** (selects Help Index from the Help Menu).
   Works 3.0: Press **Alt**, **H**, **T** (selects Table of Contents from the Help Menu).
2. Use cursor key to highlight the desired topic (Closing a File) and strike Enter (displays information about the topic).

WORKS MAC

To get help related to a command (Save command is used in this example):

1. ~ Window Menu and select Help (accesses the Help Menu).
2. Use the mouse pointer (a question mark when Help is accessed) to select Save from the File Menu. (Clicking on a specific operation such as Save while in Help takes you directly to the information in the Help Index).
3. Read the screen; scroll down to read the remaining information about Save.
4. ~ Close box in the Help window to return to the worksheet.

To use Help to get information about a topic:

1. ~ Window Menu and select Help (accesses the Help Menu).
2. Scroll up and down through the Help Index to find a feature you want and then read Help's information about that topic.

(continued on next page)   (continued on next page)   (continued on next page)

124B ◆ (cont.)

Reference Page & Title Page
Key a reference page using the information given at the right. Prepare a title page for the report using your name, school, and current date.

Document 2
Leftbound Report
File name: REPORT2
Retrieve REPORT1 and make the following changes before saving it as REPORT2.
1. Change it to a leftbound report.
2. Bold all headings.
3. Place the *Qualifications* paragraph before the *Term in Office* paragraph.

~no new~   ~(1986, 14-15)~

¶   Koenig^ suggests that today's President has the respon-   381

sibility of dealing with:^ℓ   386

. . . survival problems in which the very future of the hu-   398
man race, is at stake; the threat of nuclear weapons tech-   409
nology; the persistence of war abroad; the remorseless   420
growth of population, production, and pollution, and their   432
endangering of the environment; grave unemployment and in-   444
flation; blighted cities and pervasive poverty and crime;   455
excessive violations of civil rights and liberties; grossly   467
inadequate provisions of health services, mass transit, edu-   479
cation and the care of the elderly.   486

As can be seen in^ ~the~ *Koenig's* description of the presidential   499

responsibilities ~outlined by Koenig,~ the President of the   506
United States has ^*a job with* many important^ *and varied* responsibilities.   519

Davis, James W. <u>The American President: A New Perspective</u>.   542
New York: Harper & Row Publishers, 1987.   550

Koenig, Louis W. <u>Chief Executive</u>. 5th ed. San Diego: 562
Harcourt Brace Jovanovich, Inc., 1986.   569

LESSON 125   ASSESS TABLE FORMATTING

125A ◆
CONDITIONING
PRACTICE
each line twice

alphabet	1	Gavin expects the banker to formalize quite a few details before July.
figures	2	Jay hit .359 with 86 singles, 20 doubles, 7 triples, and 14 home runs.
fig/sym	3	Our 1993-1994 service & supply budget was $16,780, an increase of 25%.
speed	4	The eight girls and the auditor may burn down the shanty by city hall.

gwam 1' | 1 | 2 | 3 | 4 | 5 | 6 | 7 | 8 | 9 | 10 | 11 | 12 | 13 | 14 |

125B ◆

ASSESS TABLES

File name: TEST3
Table 1
center column headings; CS: 1"; DS table

words

MARCH AND APRIL TRAVEL EXPENSES			
<u>Employee</u>	<u>March</u>	<u>April</u>	6
			14
Candice Block	$ 291.56	$ 358.92	20
Gavin Brownell	438.15	375.10	26
Kathy Courtland	391.87	408.91	32
Rebecca Krivano	654.20	692.16	39
Cherly McIntyre	612.89	541.23	45
Troy Torres	638.90	321.79	50
Craig Underwood	<u>719.88</u>	<u>429.07</u>	60
Total Expenses	$3,747.45	$3,127.18	67

LOTUS

1. Strike **/** (displays Main Menu on Control Panel).
2. Key **Q** (selects the Quit option).
3. Key **Y** (selects the option to quit without saving).
4. Key **Y** (executes the Quit command—select **N** to return to the worksheet if you do not wish to quit).

WORKS DOS

1. Press **Alt F** (displays the File Menu).
2. Key **X** (selects the Exit Works option).
3. Key **N** (selects the option to exit without saving).

WORKS MAC

1. ~ File Menu and select Close.
2. ~ No in dialog box (selects the option to close without saving).

126G ♦

APPLICATION ACTIVITY

If you quit the spreadsheet program as directed in 126F, access (reenter) it now. Then enter the values given at the right in the cells designated, and exit the software.

	A	B	C	D	E
1	554433				435465
2		665544		192038	
3			776655		
4		313131		235690	
5	283746				685472

LESSON 127   WORKSHEETS WITH VALUES AND LABELS

127A ♦
CONDITIONING PRACTICE
each line twice

alphabet 1 Chad thought Pamela's long joke about the next quiz wasn't very funny.

figures 2 Bill is to read pages 271-305 for history and pages 69-84 for English.

fig/sym 3 Mary bought 30 (15%), David bought 78 (39%), and Lynn bought 92 (46%).

speed 4 The busy maid is to rush the cocoa to the eight men on the dorm panel.

gwam 1' | 1 | 2 | 3 | 4 | 5 | 6 | 7 | 8 | 9 | 10 | 11 | 12 | 13 | 14 |

127B ♦

ENTER LABELS

Read the information at the right about labels and values and then complete Steps 1-5 at the top of the next page.

Labels are letters, words, or figures that are entered on a worksheet. Labels cannot be used in worksheet calculations; they are generally used as titles, column headings, or used to identify cell entries in order to make the worksheet more easily understood. The numbers used in calculations are known as values.

words

Table 2
block column headings; CS: 1";
DS table

STATE OFFICERS   3

[Name	[Position	[Phone
Laura Wesphal	President	836-4978	17
Josh Rubinstein	Vice President	739-2075	25
Maria Fernandez	Membership Director	684-7825	34
Chris Chan	Secretary	836-2091	40
Mark Strasman	Treasurer	235-6511	47
Brett DeWitz	Past President	412-4010	54
Jacqueline McLain	President Elect	633-7189	63

(Name/Position/Phone = 10)

Table 3
center column headings; CS:
0.5"; DS table

19-- BANKING INSTITUTE SCHEDULE   6

Seminar	Date	Location
Game Plans for Loan Originators	January 15	Boston	27
Creative Financing	March 16	Chicago	35
Symposium for Branch Managers	April 20	Portland	44
Todays Automated Banking	June 10	Atlanta	53
Accounting Update in Banking	August 15	Tuscon	62
Customer Advertising	October 1	Houston	70
Managing Human Resources	November 13	Milwaukee	79

(Seminar/Date/Location = 17)

Table 4
center column headings; CS:
0.5"; DS table
Use **SPECIAL RESORT
ACTIVITIES** for the main
heading and **May-September**
for the subheading.

Activity	Date(s)	Coordinator
Festival of the Stars	May 15-17	J. Dennis Phelps	29
Mesa Ski Exhibit	May 29	Scott Snell	36
Hot Air Balloon Day	June 15	Marsha Schneider	45
American Jazz Festival	June 28	Carlos Santiago	55
Wildlife Art Exhibit	July 15	Rhea Bosworth	63
Mesa Bicycle Classic	July 29	Sydna Mincher	72
Little Big-Top Circus	August 8	Cha Xang	80
Hang Gliding Contest	August 20	Scott Snell	89
Mesa Golf Classic	September 3-4	Carmen Pascual	98

(Activity/Date(s)/Coordinator = 19)

MOVE CELL POINTER

Read the information at the right and then complete the steps listed for your ss software.

Spreadsheet software requires the user to move a cell pointer around the worksheet. The cell pointer can be moved from cell to cell by the use of a mouse or the four arrow keys: ↑, ↓, ←, and →. If the arrow keys on the numeric keypad are used to move the cell pointer, the number lock (NUM LOCK) key must be in the off position. On many keyboards, a NUM LOCK light above the NUM LOCK key indicates whether NUM LOCK is on or off. Also, many ss software packages indicate that NUM LOCK is on by displaying NL or NUM LOCK on the worksheet screen.

LOTUS

With Num Lock key off, create a 3-column worksheet by using arrow keys to move from cell to cell as figures are entered.

1. Strike **Home** to highlight A1 if A1 is not highlighted.
2. Use ↓ to highlight A6.
3. Use → to highlight B6.
4. In B6, key **254978** (shows 254978 in the Entry Line but not the cell; it will appear in B6 when an arrow key is struck).
5. Use → to highlight C6; key **759021** (enters 254978 in B6 and 759021 in Entry Line).
6. Highlight D6; key **903612**.
7. Highlight D7; key **529681**.
8. Highlight C7; key **401544**.
9. Highlight B7; key **809954**.
10. Strike any arrow key or Enter (enters 809954 in B7).
11. Leave data on the screen and go to 126F.

WORKS DOS

Use arrow keys to move from cell to cell to create a 3-column worksheet. Be sure the Num Lock key is off.

1. Press **Ctrl Home** to highlight A1 if A1 is not highlighted.
2. Use ↓ to highlight A6.
3. Use → to highlight B6.
4. In B6, key **254978** (enters data in the Formula Bar and B6).
5. Use → to highlight C6; key **759021**.
6. Highlight D6; key **903612**.
7. Highlight D7; key **529681**.
8. Highlight C7; key **401544**.
9. Highlight B7; key **809954**.
10. Strike any arrow key or Enter (enters 809954 in B7).
11. Leave data on the screen and go to 126F.

WORKS MAC

Use the mouse to move from cell to cell to create a 3-column worksheet.

1. ~ B6 (highlights and makes B6 the active cell).
2. In B6, key **254978** (shows data in the Entry Bar).
3. Use arrow key to highlight C6; key **759021**.
4. Highlight D6; key **903612**.
5. Highlight D7; key **529681**.
6. Highlight C7; key **401544**.
7. Highlight B7; key **809954**.
8. Strike any arrow key or Return (enters 809954 in B7).
9. ~ the Enter Box to enter **123456** in B8, **234567** in C8, and **345678** in D8 (instead of using the arrow keys).
10. Leave data on the screen and go to 126F.

EXIT SPREADSHEET

Read the information at the right about quitting spreadsheet software and then complete the steps listed for your software on p. 232.

When quitting (exiting) the ss software at the end of a work session or entering a different software package, select the Quit, Close, or Exit option. Quitting the software returns the user to the computer's operating system or to an option for selecting another software package.

PART 3

Spreadsheet Applications

Absolute Cell Address   A cell address that does not change when copied to another location. In a formula, the cell marked with an absolute address contains dollar signs (*see* Relative Cell Address).

Alignment   The position of a label in a cell. Labels can be aligned with the left or right edge of a cell or centered in the cell.

Anchor Cell   The beginning cell in a range of highlighted cells.

Arrow Keys   Keys (up, down, left, and right) used to move a pointer or cursor (*see* Cursor Control Keys).

Bar Chart   A chart (graph) that uses a vertical bar to represent a spreadsheet number.

Border   The horizontal bar at the top of a worksheet that contains the column letters and the vertical bar at the left of a worksheet that contains the row numbers.

Cell   The basic unit of a worksheet in which data are stored. The intersection of a column and row forms a cell, and each cell is referenced by an address.

Cell Address   The location of a specific cell derived from the intersection of a column and row. For example, the cell at the intersection of Column C and Row 5 has a cell address of C5.

Cell Entry   A number (or value), label, or formula entered into a cell.

Cell Pointer   A reverse-video bar, sometimes referred to as a cursor, that is as wide as the worksheet column it is referencing.

Chart   (*see* Bar Chart and Pie Chart)

Clear   To erase a previously specified setting, range, or value.

Column   A vertical block of cells in a worksheet.

Current Cell   The current location of the cell pointer.

Cursor   Display screen's special character that is used to indicate where the next character will be keyed.

Cursor Control Keys   The arrow keys used to move the cursor up, down, left, and right (*see* Arrow Keys).

Data Disk   The disk used to store worksheet and graphic files.

Data Range   The range of values used to create a chart.

Default   A predetermined setting the software uses unless different instructions are given by the operator.

Default Disk Drive   The disk drive accessed automatically by the computer when a file-oriented command is given.

Edit   To change the input data.

Footer   A line of text that appears at the bottom of every page of a document.

Formula   An arrangement of numbers and/or cell addresses and arithmetic operations used to manipulate data.

Function Key   One of the F1-F12 keys that allows special functions to be completed with minimal keystrokes.

Functions   Formulas or processes built into a software package that serve as shortcuts.

Global   A spreadsheet command that allows changes to affect an entire worksheet.

Graphics   The system used to display graphs, such as bar charts and pie charts.

Header   A line of text that appears at the top of each page of a document.

Help   The software's on-line reference manual. To get Help about the current procedure, strike the Help key.

126D ◆ (cont.)

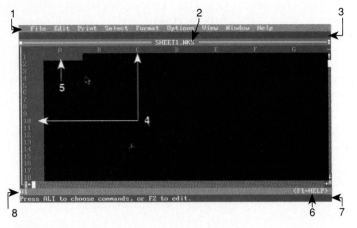

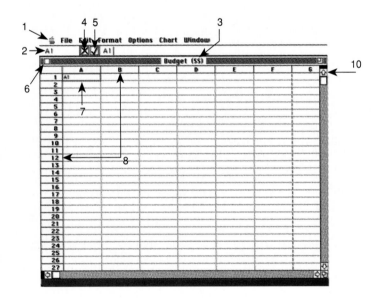

Note: *Works 3.0* has a Toolbar between the Menu Bar and the Title Bar. The Toolbar is for mouse users who want to use it for commands and tasks that occur frequently.

WORKS DOS (see illustration at left)

1. **Menu Bar**—displays the menu choices that can be selected; commands appear as pull-down menus when a choice is made.
2. **Title Bar**—displays the file name.
3. **Entry Line**—displays the data being entered in a cell.
4. **Border**—identifies worksheet columns and rows. Columns run vertically and are identified by letters (A, B, C, etc.); rows run horizontally and are identified by numbers (1, 2, etc.).
5. **Cell Pointer**—rectangular highlight that identifies the active cell.
6. **Help Reminder**—displays the command for the Help feature.
7. **Message Line**—tells what action to take or displays a brief description of the highlighted command.
8. **Status Line**—gives address of active (highlighted) cell.

WORKS MAC (see illustration at left)

1. **Menu Bar**—displays menu choices that can be selected; commands appear as pull-down menus when a choice is made.
2. **Entry Bar**—displays active cell address, cancel and enter boxes, and contents of active cell.
3. **Title Bar**—displays the file name and is used to reposition the window.
4. **Cancel Box**—cancels an entry before it is entered into a cell (displays in the Entry Bar only when data is being keyed into a cell).
5. **Enter Box**—enters data into a cell (displays in the Entry Bar only when data is being keyed into a cell).
6. **Close Box**—closes a file (when clicked).
7. **Active Cell**—the cell highlighted with the rectangular border and listed at the left of the Entry Bar.
8. **Border**—identifies worksheet columns and rows. Columns run vertically and are identified by letters (A, B, C, etc.); rows run horizontally and are identified by numbers (1, 2, etc.).
9. **Page Break Indicator** (not shown)—indicates the end of page depth (when running vertically) or width (when running horizontally).
10. **Scroll Arrow**—brings worksheet contents into view from any direction when you click on a directional arrow.

Glossary, continued

Home   The upper-left cell position in a worksheet.

Integration   The process of combining several software applications. For example, software often combines spreadsheet, charting, and database applications.

Keyboard   Hardware used to input characters, commands, and functions to the microcomputer. Most keyboards have a typewriter keyboard, function keys, and numeric keypad.

Label   A worksheet entry that begins with a letter or label-prefix character.

Label-Prefix Character   A character used to indicate a cell label. A label-prefix character must be used with label entries that begin with numbers and with some symbols.

Legend   A charting feature that labels sets of data to make a chart easier to understand.

Menu   A list of commands from which the software user makes selections.

Menu Pointer   The highlight used to select an item from a menu.

Move Command   A command that moves the contents of a cell or range from one part of a worksheet to another.

Numeric Keypad   Section of the keyboard that contains numeric keys (in 10-key arrangement) and editing keys. To use the numeric keys to enter numbers, the Num Lock key switch must be turned on.

Numeric Lock Key   Key used to switch the numeric keypad between numeric entry and editing.

Order of Operations   The order in which arithmetic operations in a formula are carried out. Multiplication and division are done first, in the order that they occur. Addition and subtraction are done next, in the order that they occur. Operations inside parentheses are performed before those outside.

Operating System   A computer's program that permits a user to control the computer's resources. Examples: MS-DOS, PC DOS, Macintosh OS.

Pie Chart   A chart that displays worksheet data in a circle of pie-shaped wedges (or slices). Pie charts are frequently used when the data represent parts of a whole.

Pointer   (*see* Cell Pointer)

Program   Set of instructions that tells a computer how to perform tasks. Lotus 1-2-3 and Microsoft Works are programs.

Prompt   Any message displayed when a command is being used; usually requests information from user.

Range   Rectangular or square area of a worksheet consisting of two or more cells.

Relative Cell Address   A cell reference that adjusts to its new location when copied (*see* Absolute Cell Address).

Row   A horizontal block of cells in a worksheet.

Spreadsheet   Computer software program that can be used to manipulate data arranged in rows and columns on a worksheet.

Value   A number or the result of a formula or function. Values can be used in computations.

Window   The portion of a worksheet that is displayed on the monitor.

Worksheet   The electronic representation of a spreadsheet. A worksheet is divided into columns and rows and is used to enter and manipulate spreadsheet entries. Charts are based on cell entries in the worksheet.

X-axis   The horizontal (left-to-right) axis on a bar chart.

Y-axis   The vertical (up-and-down) axis on a bar chart.

LOTUS

1. Access the disk drive and/or directory which houses Lotus.
2. At operating systems prompt, key **123**.
3. Strike Enter (this loads Lotus into temporary memory and displays a blank worksheet screen).
4. Leave the worksheet screen blank and go to 126D.

WORKS DOS

1. Access the disk drive and/or directory which houses Works.
2. At operating systems prompt, key **Works** (this loads Works into temporary memory).
3. *Works 2.0*: Press **Alt**, **F**, **N** (selects Create **New** File from the **File** Menu); then key **S** (selects New Spreadsheet from the dialog box and displays a worksheet screen).

   Works 3.0: Key **N**, **S**, and strike Enter (selects Create a New File from the Quick Start Menu and Spreadsheet from the Create New File Menu).
4. Leave the worksheet screen blank and go to 126D.

WORKS MAC

1. Open the disk drive on which Works is stored.
2. ~~ the Microsoft Works icon (this loads Works into temporary memory).
3. ~~ the Spreadsheet icon (loads ss software into temporary memory and displays a blank worksheet screen).
4. Leave the worksheet screen blank and go to 126D.

126D ◆

WORKSHEET SCREEN

Read the information at the right describing a worksheet screen. Then read the list for your ss software (Works on p. 230) as you study your blank worksheet screen.

A worksheet screen is a grid of rows and columns. The worksheet is made up of many cells (a cell is the intersection point of a row and column and is the part of the worksheet where information is stored). The worksheet screen reveals menus, the location of cells, and other indicators to show the highlighted (active) cell, rows, columns, formulas, status, errors, and/or date and time.

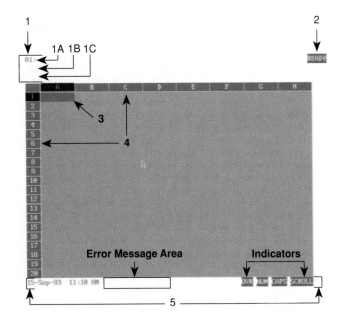

LOTUS (see illustration at left)

1. **Control Panel**—shows top 3 lines of worksheet screen.
1A. **First Line**—displays cell address, format, and contents.
1B. **Second Line**—displays the current entry when you enter or edit data, displays the Main Menu (a list of commands) when you press /.
1C. **Third Line**—displays submenu commands or a description of the highlighted command when the Main Menu is displayed; gives information about the highlighted command when the menu is displayed.
2. **Mode Indicator**—gives status information about the ss software.
3. **Cell Pointer**—identifies the active cell.
4. **Border**—identifies worksheet columns and rows. Columns run vertically and are identified by letters (A, B, C, etc.); rows run horizontally and are identified by numbers (1, 2, etc.).
5. **Status Line**—displays date and time, error messages, and status indicators (CAPS, NUM, CALC, etc.).

Get Started With Spreadsheets

Learning Outcomes: After completing this unit, you will be able to

1. Access and exit spreadsheet (ss) software.
2. Read a worksheet screen, use menus, submenus, dialog boxes, and Help.
3. Retrieve, move within, change, name, and save a worksheet.
4. Enter and format column labels, values, and/or titles.

SPREADSHEET FEATURE AND COMMAND GUIDE

ACCESS SPREADSHEET SOFTWARE
ALIGN LABELS
CLEAR WORKSHEET SCREEN
HELP FEATURE
QUIT SPREADSHEET SOFTWARE
RETRIEVE A WORKSHEET FILE
SAVE AND NAME A WORKSHEET

The spreadsheet (ss) features and commands are listed alphabetically at the left and explained below and on p. 227. The feature and command guide at the beginning of each unit can be used to preview unit topics. It is also an easy-to-find reference for reviewing features and commands while you work. Appendix G (pages 449-452), a listing of frequently used software application commands, can also be used as a reference.

ACCESS SPREADSHEET SOFTWARE

Spreadsheet software such as Lotus 1-2-3 is accessed from the operating system prompt by keying characters that identify the software. Integrated software packages such as Microsoft Works are loaded into temporary memory from the operating system and then the ss application is selected from a dialog box.

Lotus	Key **123**; Enter.
Works DOS 2	Key **Works**; **Alt**, **F**, **N**, **S**.
Works DOS 3	Key **Works**; **N**, **S**, Enter.
Works MAC	~~ (double-click) disk icon where Works is filed; ~~ Works icon; ~~ ss icon.

ALIGN LABELS

Labels will begin at the left edge of a cell unless you instruct the software to do otherwise. To center or right align labels, select the cell you want to format and use the following commands.

Lotus	Key a ^ before the label to center; a " to right align the label.

Works DOS	Press **Alt**, **T**, **S**; select desired format (**R** for right, **C** for center); Enter.
Works MAC	Select Set Cell Attributes from Format Menu, ~ circle beside Right or Center; ~ Okay box.

CLEAR A WORKSHEET SCREEN

Whenever a worksheet is no longer wanted on a screen, the Worksheet Erase or Close feature can be used to clear the screen so another worksheet can be started. Since this command removes the worksheet from the computer's temporary memory, be sure to save the worksheet before Worksheet Erase or Close is used if the worksheet will be needed later.

Lotus	/, **W**, **E**; select **N** or **Y**.
Works DOS	**Alt**, **F**, **C**; Enter; select **Y** or **N**.
Works MAC	Select Close from File Menu (or ~ Close box); ~ Yes or No; ~~ ss icon in dialog box.

HELP FEATURE

Spreadsheet (ss) software provides an on-line Help feature that can be used while you are working on a worksheet. The Help feature provides information about the software program and explains various ss commands, skills, and procedures you may need to learn or review to complete a specific task.

Lotus	Strike **F1** for help on the command being used, or **F1** and select desired topic.
Works DOS	Strike **F1** for help on command being used, or **Alt**, **H**, **H** (Works 2.0); **Alt**, **H**, **T** (Works 3.0), and proceed as directed.
Works MAC	Select Help from the Window Menu; proceed as directed.

When using ss software, the user must plan the worksheet layout. Numbers and words must be entered on a worksheet and verified for accuracy; mathematical operations must be written and entered; the worksheet must be arranged (formatted) so that it will be easy to read and understand; and the worksheet information may then be graphed, printed, and/or saved.

A spreadsheet lets you create formulas to calculate simple numbers such as a total or average—and complex numbers, as you'll see later. In this example, formulas are used to calculate the averages and the high and low scores. Using titles and headings for the columns and using rows and lines to separate parts of the worksheet make a worksheet easier to read.

AC104 Gradebook				
Student	Avg	Test 1	Test 2	Test 3
Lu Chi	88.7	88	93	85
Tom Keno	79	85	80	72
Juan Perez	81	74	83	86
Sally Roper	86.3	92	83	84
Class Average	83.8	84.8	84.75	81.8
High Score		92	93	86
Low Score		74	80	72

	A	B	C	D	E
1	AC104 Gradebook				
2					
3					
4	Student	Avg	Test 1	Test 2	Test 3
5					
6	Lu Chi	=Average(C6:E6)	88	93	85
7	Tom Keno	=Average(C7:E7)	85	80	72
8	Juan Perez	=Average(C8:E8)	74	83	86
9	Sally Roper	=Average(C9:E9)	92	83	84
10					
11	Class Average	=Average(C11:E11)	=Average(C6:C9)	=Average(D6:D9)	=Average(E6:E9)
12	High Score		=Max(C6:C9)	=Max(D6:D9)	=Max(E6:E9)
13	Low Score		=Min(C6:C9)	=Min(D6:D9)	=Min(E6:E9)
14					

This illustration shows the formulas that have been entered so that the spread-sheet software will automatically calculate each student's average score and the average, high, and low score for the class.

If a worksheet value needs to be changed, the spreadsheet automatically recalculates all appropriate formulas. In this example, if a test score is changed, the spreadsheet recalculates the formula and changes the average, high, and low scores as needed.

126C ◆

ACCESS SPREADSHEET

Read the information at the right about entering spread-sheet software. Then complete the steps listed for your software on p. 229.

Lotus 1-2-3 spreadsheet is accessed directly from the operating system prompt by keying characters that identify that program. Works software is accessed from the operating system prompt by keying characters that identify Works; the software is then accessed from the screen that shows all of Works' applications.

QUIT SPREADSHEET SOFTWARE

When work on a worksheet has been completed, you need to exit the ss software by selecting the Quit option. When you quit Lotus, you are returned to the operating system. When you quit the Works ss, you are returned to a window that lets you select other software packages.

Lotus /, **Q**, select **N** or **Y**, **Y**.
Works DOS **Alt**, **F**, **X**, select **Y** or **N**.
Works MAC Select Close from the File Menu; ~ Yes or No.

RETRIEVE A WORKSHEET FILE

Worksheets are often saved on a disk so that they can be retrieved later and revised, updated, and/or printed. To retrieve a worksheet file, you must instruct the computer to search the disk drive on which the file to be retrieved is saved. Once the worksheet is found, the computer loads a copy of it into temporary memory and displays the worksheet on the monitor.

Lotus /, **F**, **R**, select disk drive from which file is to be retrieved; select or key desired file name.
Works DOS **Alt**, **F**, **O**, select disk drive from which file is to be retrieved, **Alt F**; select desired file name.
Works MAC Select Open from the File Menu; select disk drive from which file is to be retrieved, highlight desired file name, ~ Open.

SAVE AND NAME A WORKSHEET

To save a worksheet so that it can be retrieved later, name the worksheet and instruct the computer to copy it from temporary memory to a disk where you want it to be filed.

Lotus /, **F**, **S**, Esc as needed to name disk drive to which the file will be saved; key file name, Enter.
Works DOS **Alt**, **F**, **S**; key file name in dialog box, Enter.
Works MAC Select Save from the File Menu; select disk drive to which it is to be saved; key file name in dialog box, ~ Save.

L ESSON 126   GET STARTED WITH SPREADSHEETS

126A ◆
CONDITIONING PRACTICE

each line twice; then 30" timings on selected lines; exit word processor and access spreadsheet

alphabet 1 That expensive black racquet is just the wrong size for many children.

figures 2 Linda has 72 blue, 68 yellow, 49 red, 30 green, and 15 orange marbles.

fig/sym 3 Norman was born 7/10/42, Mary was born 9/3/46, and I was born 5/15/48.

speed 4 The ensign works with the official to right the problem with the dock.

gwam 1' | 1 | 2 | 3 | 4 | 5 | 6 | 7 | 8 | 9 | 10 | 11 | 12 | 13 | 14 |

126B ◆

LEARN SPREAD-SHEET SOFTWARE

Read the material at the right and then study the worksheet illustrations on p. 228.

With ss software you can create worksheets (like the one on p. 228) that calculate numbers: you can add, subtract, divide, and multiply two or more numbers, or you can use formulas to calculate answers to complicated problems. When the numbers are changed, the ss software automatically recalculates all related "answers," which saves the operator time. Most ss packages generate graphs or charts so the worksheet information can be viewed graphically.

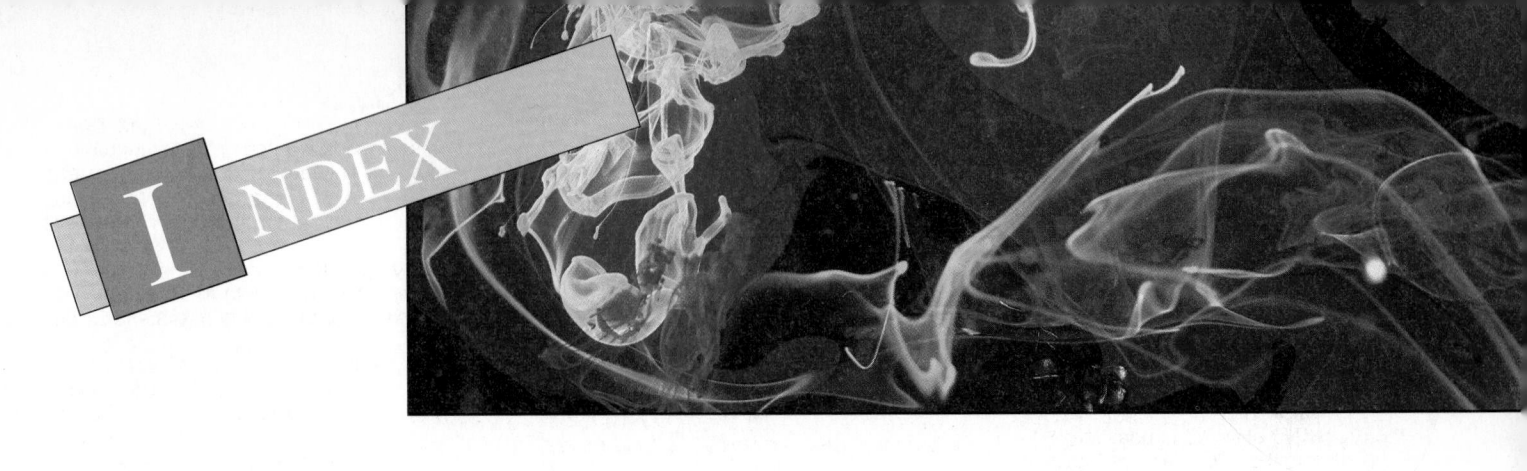

INDEX

Executive Editor: Karen Schmohe
Marketing Manager: Al Roane
Coordinating Editor: Susan Richardson
Production Manager: Deborah Luebbe
Senior Production Editor: Alan Biondi
Production Editors: Timothy Bailey, Yvonne Stearns
Photo Editor: Fred M. Middendorf
Development: Penworthy
Internal Design: Barbara Libby
Cover Design: Graphica
Art Production: Miller-Meyers and Associates, Inc.

HARDWARE/SOFTWARE CREDITS

IBM® is a registered trademark of International Business Machines Corporation.
Macintosh® is a trademark of Macintosh Laboratory, Inc., and is used by Apple Computer, Inc., with its express permission. References to Mac also refer to this note.
Microsoft® Works is a registered trademark of Microsoft Corporation. References to Works also refer to this note.
MS-DOS® is a registered trademark of Microsoft Corporation. References to ÎOS also refer to this note.
WordPerfect® is a registered trademark of WordPerfect Corporation.
Lotus® is a registered trademark of Lotus Development Corporation.
1-2-3® is a registered trademark of Lotus Development Corporation.

PHOTO CREDITS

Photographer (Unit Openers/Internals): Mimi Ostendorf-Smith
Unit Opener photos are award winners in the Kodak 1993 Impact Through Applied Photography Competition.

p. 4: Photo courtesy of Apple Computer, Inc.
p. 6: Photo courtesy of Epson America, Inc.
pp. ii, 1, 9, 113, 224, 309, 371, 426, and Index 1: ©Phillip A. Harrington